Interpersonal Practice
in Social Work
PROCESSES AND PROCEDURES

Charles D. Garvin/Brett A. Seabury

School of Social Work/University of Michigan

Prentice-Hall, Inc., Englewood Cliffs, New Jersey 07632

Library of Congress Cataloging in Publication Data

Garvin, Charles D.
  Interpersonal practice in social work.

  Bibliography: p.
  Includes index.
  1. Social case work. .2. Interpersonal relations.
I. Seabury, Brett A.,   II. Title.
HV43.G33   1984   361.3'2   83-17648
ISBN 0-13-475095-0

DEDICATED TO
the memory of Dorothy Robinson
and Lee Kroman whose lifelong
commitments to services to people
served to inspire us

Cover design: Lundgren Graphics, Ltd.
Manufacturing buyer: John Hall

Printed in the United States of America

10 9 8 7 6 5 4

ISBN 0-13-475095-0

Prentice-Hall International, Inc., *London*
Prentice-Hall of Australia Pty. Limited, *Sydney*
Editora Prentice-Hall do Brasil, Ltda., *Rio de Janeiro*
Prentice-Hall Canada Inc., *Toronto*
Prentice-Hall of India Private Limited, *New Delhi*
Prentice-Hall of Japan, Inc., *Tokyo*
Prentice-Hall of Southeast Asia Pte. Ltd., *Singapore*
Whitehall Books Limited, *Wellington, New Zealand*

Contents

Preface

We have written this book to describe the ways social workers, and other professionals with similar purposes, help people to cope with problems in their social functioning. Social functioning, as we shall describe in more detail later, encompasses all the ways that we respond to the demands of our social environment—an environment that includes family, peers, organizations, communities, as well as the entire society.

Social workers help through one-to-one, family, or group transactions. Workers also help people by intervening in aspects of their social environment. Such assistance may deal with current problems, or with the likelihood that problems will emerge in the future because of the individual's vulnerability to social stesses.

This volume has been written for both practitioners and students in the human services. The former may find it a handy reference as well as a way of "catching up" with new developments in the field. In our thinking, the types of students likely to use this book are advanced undergraduates in human service programs and graduate students beginning their study of interpersonal helping processes. The parts of this book that describe differential work approaches with individuals, families, and groups can also serve as the bases for more advanced study of those topics.

Our approach is a generic one in that it stresses common elements in work with individuals, families, and groups. These elements include the value and ethical considerations that underlie interpersonal helping; an emphasis on enhancing individual-environmental transactions through such practice; a problem-solving, goal oriented, contractually based set of procedures; and ways of examining and resolving problems of people that focus on both individual and environmental factors. In addition, we believe that a common pool of knowledge from the behavioral and social sciences as well as social work practice experience forms the basis of all interpersonal helping methods and that all practice should employ procedures that have been or can be tested for effectiveness. The consequences of the use of social work procedures should also be continually monitored by the worker.

We also are convinced that people can be helped by individual, family, or peer-group approaches; yet one or another may be the preferred one for a particular client with a particular problem, in a particular situation, when offered by a particular practitioner. Workers, therefore, should adapt their ways of helping to the needs of service recipients and not the reverse. Workers who specialize in one approach should refer clients to others when clients' needs require this. It is for this reason that the training of workers should begin with a broad base such as that provided by this book.

While there is a common foundation of values, knowledge, and even method that lies beneath various forms of interpersonal practice, there also are differences. These have to do with the size as well as function of one-to-one, family, and group systems. A comprehensive discussion of such differences is well beyond the scope of this volume. We, nevertheless, discuss the major work approaches with individuals, families, and groups with which workers should be familiar. We also, throughout this book, have varied our examples so as to illustrate individual, family, and group approaches even when these are similar. This discussion of differences should establish a base from which the reader can either pursue the study of similarities and differences among approaches or a deeper study of a single one.

We are convinced that this examination of differences, as well as similarities among individual, family, and group approaches, serves several additional functions. First, attention to differences should induce the reader, as it did for us, to examine more closely what is "generic" and what is "specific" in interpersonal practice. On numerous occasions in writing this book, we were forced to examine whether the principles and procedures we discussed did apply to individual, family, and group services or whether they only applied to one or two of these. Second, as we recognized differences, we directed our efforts to examining them in detail. Our book, therefore, reaches a high operational level, as well as one of specificity for work with families and groups, as well as individuals.

Another objective we have sought to attain in this text is to give the reader a set of *principles* to guide practice as well as *specific practice procedures* and guidelines based on these principles. We have included many case examples of worker activities to present an even clearer idea of how to enact these ways of helping.

There are a number of different theories about human behavior that we believe point to effective ways of helping people cope with problems. These include modern ego psychology, behaviorism, cognitive psychology, small group theory, family sociology, organizational sociology, and ideas about systems. We have drawn upon all of these in our thinking about social work intervention. In this sense, we see ourselves as eclectic, and we are more interested in identifying effective ways of helping than in presenting a unified approach. There are contradictions and paradoxes among current ideas about human behavior and ways of changing it, and we are sure these are reflected in our book. While adherence to one theoretical system may be useful to many workers, as a way of organizing their thinking, this has not been possible for us. We do, however, believe that any procedure should be subjected to research and evaluation before it becomes firmly established in the profession's repertoire.

We are convinced, furthermore, that much can be learned by systematic attention to what has been called "practice wisdom." Many of the ideas about helping that we describe come from our own experience as well as from that of our colleagues and students. Thus we have great respect for the value of social work experience and research, yet we believe that this must be integrated with knowledge from the social and behavioral sciences as well as from biology, medicine, and such allied professions as law, education, and public health.

To present this material, we have organized our book into four sections. The first section presents background information on the profession of social work and the place of interpersonal practice within it. The ethics, values, and knowledge base of this practice are also described. The second chapter in this section presents the assumptions upon which our model of practice rests and defines the major concepts we shall use throughout the book.

The next two sections of the book relate to the sequence of events in the helping process, with Section II devoted to beginning and Section III to middle- and ending-phases. In Section II, in addition to chapters on the effects of how clients have been contacted and how a sound beginning is attained, several chapters are devoted to skills that are important to *all* stages. These are facilitative communication, contracting, and evaluation. We present in detail ways of assessing individuals, groups, families, and organizations.

Section III offers a broad view of the ways that workers help people to change themselves and their situations. Each chapter relates change concepts to specific processes, namely to those directed respectively at individuals, families, and groups.

Workers must be prepared to vary the practice approach depending upon the sex, ethnicity, and age of clients; and in the last section, we show how this is done. While we have stressed common elements in practice throughout the book, we wish to remind the reader that the characteristics and status of the client make a great deal of difference in the kinds of services we should offer.

Acknowledgments

Both of us, as authors, wish to acknowledge that we have developed many of our ideas through discussions with social work students. In such circumstances it is hard to recall how much of the result is a consequence of our input as compared to theirs. Thus, we could not have written this book without this type of interaction. We have also benefitted from the inputs of our colleagues in the many challenging discussions we have had with them. A note of thanks goes to the reviewers—Ron Toseland, the School of Social Welfare, the State University of New York at Albany; Charlene Urwin, the Social Work Program, North Texas State University; Jon Conte, the School of Social Service Administration, the University of Chicago; Charles Cowger, the School of Social Work, the University of Illinois; Gil Spielberg, San Diego State University; and Paul Leuenberger, the School of Social Work, the University of Illinois. Each reviewed an early draft of the manuscript, and for the time they devoted to this task, but more importantly for their many helpful comments, suggestions, and criticism, we are deeply appreciative. Finally, we would like to acknowledge the efforts of the staff at Prentice-Hall, particularly Susan Taylor and Andrew Roney; their presence took much of the 'sting' out of the process of turning the completed manuscript into a bound book.

I (CG) wish to acknowledge the benefits I have received from my many discussions with Rosemary Sarri, Sallie Churchill, Harvey Bertcher, Beth Reed, Joyce Beckett, Alfreda Iglehart, Nathalie Drews, Kathleen Faller, Chuck Wolfson, and Ann Hartman. Beth has been particularly helpful in deepening my understanding of gender issues and Joyce and Alfreda of ethnic ones. Rosemary reminds me always of what the environment does both for and against people. I also wish to acknowledge that my wife Janet and my children David, Amy, and Tony have had to put up with a great deal while I was writing.

I (BAS) would like to acknowledge four different reference groups that have helped to raise my consciousness and have contributed to the development of ideas that I have presented in this text. Such a text would not have been possible without the continuous exchange and interaction with hundreds of social work students here at Michigan and earlier at Maryland. My interaction with students has been and continues to be the most significant source of feedback and most direct check on my ideas about interpersonal practice. I also want to acknowledge the positive influence of mentors from my doctoral-work days at Columbia. Professors Carel Germain and Carol Meyer have supported and influenced my ideological perspective to social work practice. I also want to thank a number of colleagues and close friends with whom I taught at Maryland in the early seventies—Ruth Young, Donald Fandetti, Doris Polston, Jeff Moss, Stephen Lescht, and Pallassana Balgopal. Their ideas and the supportive social network that they offered has shaped many of the exercises that are presented in this text. Finally, I want to recognize the influence of colleagues here at Michigan (Ann Hartman, Sallie Churchill, Harvey Bertcher, Frank Maple, Al Connor, and Madison Foster) with whom I have had the pleasure of team teaching and interacting in the development of our basic, introductory methods courses. My greatest debt of appreciation goes to Charles, the senior author of this text who knows more about different models of social work practice than any other academician. His knowledge of the subject matter as well as his patience about "deadlines" have earned him a place next to Job.

Charles Garvin/Brett Seabury

one

Interpersonal Practice in Social Work

NATURE AND SCOPE

The purpose of this chapter is to help the reader relate the content of this book to the purposes, domains, and definitions of social work practice. This analysis is necessary because social work now encompasses a vast array of activities in countless settings. The size of the social work enterprise alone creates many controversies as to what social workers should know and what they should seek to accomplish. In addition to this source of complexity is the fact that social work is affected by political processes and has political consequences.

The political—and in a broader sense, social—system affects social work in several ways: first, social work has a commitment to serve populations that themselves are centers of controversy such as persons who are in poverty, who experience racism and sexism, or who—like prison inmates— have been labeled "deviant" by the society; second, the social welfare enterprise consumes a significant proportion of the resources of any developed country—in the United States, for example, in fiscal year 1975, total welfare

expenditures were 20 percent of the gross national product, and in Canada and Western Europe the expenditures for many welfare categories were larger than those in the United States.[1]

The types of persons served by social work and the budgetary issues involved in this are part of a larger series of social and political questions having to do with the type of economy and society we wish to have. The reader should remember, therefore, as we portray various practice issues in this and succeeding chapters that these are not petty arguments among social workers but relate to these and many other societal concerns.

Taking these matters into consideration, we will clarify several issues in this chapter. One is how social work defines itself as a profession and how this definition relates to the social functions of the profession. Another is how such definitions and functions manifest themselves in the various fields of social work practice as these respond to different kinds of social problems. A third concern, since most of social work practice takes place in social agencies (private practice is probably the major exception to this), is how practice is affected by social agency sponsorship.

After we have presented this information on what social work is, how it is defined, and where it is practiced, we will describe how social work practice—particularly with individuals, families, and small groups—is guided by three types of information. The first is information about human behavior and its social setting; the second is information about the ethics and values of the profession; the third is information about the range of actions that are compatible with social work knowledge, values, and training, the so-called "action repertoire" of the social work profession.

Finally, since this book is primarily oriented to the knowledge required by social workers who are engaging in interpersonal practice with and on behalf of individuals, families, and small groups, we will discuss the rationale for the training of these workers. This grows out of the recent history of social work practice, the kinds of tasks that practitioners are now asked to perform, and the knowledge that is now available to guide social work interventions.

Social Work Defined

A number of definitions of social work practice have become widely accepted.[2] These have the following ideas in common:

1. The focus of social work practice is upon the way in which the individual seeks to meet needs in the environment and the way in which the environment responds to the needs of the individual.[3]
2. The role of social workers in responding to this relationship between individuals and environments may be fulfilled in several ways:
   a. By reducing or resolving problems that grow out of dysfunctional individual-environmental interactions

   b. By preventing the emergence of dysfunctional individual-environmental interactions
   c. By strengthening the potential of people to lead creative and satisfying lives in their environments.
3. The improvement of conditions or resolution of problems related to individual-environmental transactions can be brought about in several ways, such as
   a. By enhancing the problem-solving and developmental capacities of people
   b. By helping people cope with their environments and develop their creative potential through improving the quality of their associations with the groups of people with whom they are most intimately involved (e.g., their families, friends, neighbors, and fellow workers)
   c. By promoting the responsive, effective, and humane operation of systems that provide people with resources and services.[4]
   d. By linking people with systems that provide them with resources, services, and opportunities.[5]

As can be seen, a theme that pervades this and all definitions of social work practice is that it focuses upon the interactions between individuals and their environments. The ultimate measure of the success of social work activity is the well-being of individuals, but this well-being is a result of the way individuals both draw from and contribute to the relevant aspects of their environments. These environments range from the most immediate such as friends and family, to larger entities such as the workplace and the community, and finally to the largest systems such as the state or the country.

In working to create individual-environment interactions that are of optimum benefit to the individuals affected by them, at times the worker's emphasis will be on changing the behavior of the individual, at times on changing some aspect of the environment, and frequently on changing both.

Also, the decision as to whether the individual seeks to change his or her own environment or the worker does so is based on the unique character of the situation and is negotiated between the social worker and the individual concerned. The requirement placed on the social worker, however, is to consider individuals and environments as always in interaction and to take measures commensurate with this view.

Interpersonal Practice

Since this book is about interpersonal practice, it is important to locate this level of practice within all of social work practice. Interpersonal practitioners concern themselves with transactions between people and environments with respect to specific individuals, families, or groups who either seek such help or to whom it is offered and by whom, it is hoped, it is eventually accepted. The primary activity of interpersonal practitioners is with such individuals and their immediate environments—their families, schools, workplaces, and peer groups. On occasion, interpersonal workers will help people, usually referred to as clients, to seek changes in larger entities (e.g., schools, welfare departments, hospitals) that affect them. This occurs, more often than not, when the worker facilitates the work of a group of clients, because it is hard for only one person to accomplish such changes unless allied with peers or with a worker to influence social institutions.

Other social work practitioners engage in efforts to create the "responsive, effective, and humane operation of the systems" that we referred to earlier. When such systems are communities, we refer to the workers as community organizers; when they are welfare organizations to deliver services, we refer to workers not directly working with clients as administrators; and when the

organizations establish or seek to establish programs or services, we refer to the workers as social planners. This last segment includes departments of government as well as special interest groups. Research-oriented workers are also trained to provide new knowledge about services and to evaluate them.

A point of view that we share with Harriet Bartlett, who has written widely on the professional role of social workers,[6] is that workers should make the services of the profession available to people, whether or not those services are offered by the immediate worker. Thus, an interpersonal practitioner working as a school social worker may initially help a child to complete classroom assignments and at the same time help the teacher to pace these assignments so as to consider better the needs of the child. The policies of the entire school system, however, may not be conducive to the needs of the class of children represented by this child (e.g., handicapped children or minority children). In this case, the interpersonal worker may act to change these policies. It is more likely, however, that the worker will seek the help of (1) administrators of the social work program, (2) a researcher, who will study the effects of the policies, (3) a planner within the central office of the school system, or (4) even planners within the state board of education who can generate new and better programs. The tasks of the interpersonal practice worker are to be aware of these kinds of solutions to the problem and to develop linkages to other social work professionals, thus enlisting the full range of social work activities to achieve them.

The idea that the interpersonal practitioner should view himself or herself as a conduit to the full services of the profession of social work is closely related to Schwartz's idea that the mission of the social worker is to convert "private troubles" into "public issues," that is, to see the relationship of the problems brought by individuals and families to social agencies to social conditions and social policies present in the society.[7] This relationship should be brought to the attention of all relevant social workers such as community organizers, administrators, policy planners, and researchers, whose social work commitment will require them to seek necessary changes within their purview.

Use of Ecological Concepts

While we discuss in more detail in later chapters the theories and knowledge that social workers utilize, it is important to note here that many social workers have come to believe that the historic mission of social work to enhance the transactions between individuals and their environments can best be fulfilled by using concepts from ecology. Ecology was originally a biological conception of the relationships between organisms and their environments and now has been broadened into one of humans and their social relations as well. As Germain and Gitterman, who have contributed to this development in social work, state,

> The ecological perspective provides an adaptive, evolutionary view of human beings in constant interchange with all elements of their environment. Human beings change their physical and social environments and are changed by them through processes of continuous, reciprocal adaptation. When it goes well, reciprocal adaptation supports the growth and development of people and elaborates the life-supporting qualities of the environment. When reciprocal adaptation falters, however, physical and social environments may be polluted.[8]

Unlike such texts as that of Germain and Gitterman, we have not sought to create a book committed totally to what they term "ecology as a practice metaphor." We are supportive of the development of ecological ideas in social work because they are so compatible with its mission, but we do not believe they are, as yet, comprehensive and detailed enough to convey all the information we wish to present, although this may occur eventually. We do, however, seek to imbue all of our discussion about social work practice with the idea that the activities of the worker must relate to individuals and environments in interaction. We anticipate a time when ecological concepts will be sufficiently developed to encompass many of the important practice ideas because the use of the large number of conceptual systems drawn upon by social workers is confusing and is close to being the bane of the profession. Nevertheless, we have chosen to mix our metaphors, so to speak, rather than to oversimplify this complex field. This topic will be elaborated upon in the chapters that follow.

Current Practice Dilemmas

The variety of conceptual systems drawn upon by social workers is not the only source of confusion about the domain of social work. The person who enters this profession must be prepared to live with a good deal of ambiguity about its purposes and boundaries. Reasons for this state of affairs include the following:

1. *Nonexclusive Domain*. The activities of social workers are also engaged in by nonsocial workers who sometimes are not trained in any human service profession. Thus, advice regarding personal problems, for example, will be offered by psychiatrists, teachers, nurses, and psychologists as well as by family and friends. The profession currently faces a civil service "declassification" in which it is asserted that many social work tasks can be carried out by untrained persons. This had led to a current flurry of activ-

ity on the part of social workers to define the types of skills they employ. Other professionals (e.g., public health nurses, community psychologists) also state that they focus on individual-environmental transactions.

2. *Status of Clientele*. Many of the activities of social workers are criticized by influential people as undesirable. An example of this is the help offered to an unemployed person who some argue does not "deserve" help. The concept of "deserving" and "undeserving" has long been the source of controversy in our society and our profession. In any case, social services are often used by persons who are poor, powerless, or stigmatized in other ways. There are arguments, also, as to whether social services should be offered to such groups of persons as criminals or those refusing them such as some abusive parents or spouses.

3. *Priorities for Services*. Limits on social resources have led to discussions as to what the priorities for social services should be, since all needs cannot be equally met. Thus, for example, mental health, social service, and school social workers may be involved in a struggle to divide scarce resources.

4. *Problems of Measurement*. The phenomena with which social workers deal are often hard to measure. Examples are subjective feelings of well-being, self-concept, a good "fit" between individual capacities and environmental opportunities, or "growth" in an emotional and psychological sense. Social workers also deal with the well-being of families and groups, and this is more complex to measure than that of individuals.

5. *Value Considerations*. Social workers, as well as all other citizens, will have different points of view about all the issues just raised based upon their personal values. These values grow out of how people are socialized, what their social class positions are,

what their ethical and religious training has been, and with what groups in society they identify. Social work is not a value-free profession; rather, *every* social work activity relates to a large number of value positions.

These issues make it impossible for us to produce an extensive presentation of the purposes and limits of social work practice without incorporating inconsistencies and contradictions. This is in the nature of social work practice today, a practice that is interwoven with issues about the nature of humans, their societies, and the most desirable states for each. The skills of the social worker should include an ability to identify contradictions and clarify them for others. Workers should seek consensus on solutions, when this is possible, and reasonably articulate and defend differences of opinion when consensus is not possible. It is to this task that we hope our work makes a contribution rather than to the idea that we now possess a set of completely clear and unchanging definitions of the nature and extent of social work activity.

The Scope of Practice

The ideas that we have just outlined regarding the focus of social work upon the interactions between people and their environments have often been referred to by social workers as a focus upon *social functioning;* we shall use that term to refer to such interactions. We may then declare that the major purpose of social work is to prevent or resolve problems in social functioning. Obviously, such problems result from how well people respond to their environment and how well the environment provides the opportunities people require.

If we define practice in this way, we require concepts and theories related to this definition. Role concepts, for example, have been used extensively because they relate both to how persons act as well as to the requirements of their situations. Aspects of role include the expectations others hold for the role, the resources they provide for its enactment, the rewards and punishments they offer the role performer, or the way in which they perceive his or her behaviors.[9] We shall discuss role theory later in this chapter when we present the knowledge base of interpersonal practice.

Fields of Service

The emergence of fields is largely a result of how agency services developed in response to social needs or problems. They led to social work specializations as knowledge became too extensive for any one person to encompass. There are many problems for clients related to the existence of fields of service because clients can be "lost" among agencies specializing in different client problems or clients can be confused when they deal with several workers, each concerned with different "segments" of the person.

Examples of fields that developed out of the historical emergence of agency services are the following: one set of agencies devel-oped to place children (child welfare); another to help with the special consequences of illness (medical social work); others to help students with problems that interfere with learning (school social work); and still others to provide money and material resources (welfare departments as well as charity organization societies, the latter the forerunner of many family agencies).

In the early phases of the development of such agencies, there was no strong consensus that staff members should be drawn from a single profession such as social work. The original title of the conference attended by such people was the National Conference of Charities and Corrections, and the title was not changed to the National Conference of Social Work until 1917 (it was changed again in 1950 to the National Conference on Social Welfare).

One of the central ideas, however, that contributed to the eventual identification with each other of social work staff offering interpersonal services in each of these types of agencies was their common interest in social functioning, albeit with the social functioning of persons with reference to different roles. Table 1-1 summarizes the major fields in which interpersonal practice in social work occurs.

Table 1-1

1. *Family Welfare*. The focus is upon family roles such as parent, child, and grandparent. Relevant agencies are usually referred to as family agencies, although some focus on only some roles such as youth and the aged. Other agencies that are also classified under this heading deal only with certain types of role problems such as those that seek to prevent family violence.

2. *Child Welfare*. The focus is upon either strengthening family roles or helping the child to reestablish such roles in substitute families created under adoptive, foster care, or institutional arrangement. An important category of child welfare services is protec-

tive services, and these are brought into play when the danger of current family patterns to the child is immediate and severe. Another specialized category of services, usually linked to the field of child welfare, is school social work. In that field, the emphasis is upon how the student role may be affected by other roles such as those within the family. Relevant agencies are usually referred to as child welfare, although these are increasingly combined with family agencies into family and children's agencies.

3. *Criminal Justice*. The focus is upon helping persons who have been in deviant roles to relinquish these in favor of socially acceptable ones. This often involves enhancing the client's performance as spouse, employee, and citizen. Relevant agencies include prisons, training schools, and courts.

4. *Physical Health Care*. The focus is upon how persons can best fulfill the requirements of their other roles as well as the patient role while entering or leaving the patient role. Relevant agencies include hospitals and rehabilitation programs.

5. *Mental Health Care*. The focus is upon how persons who require or, without help, will require psychiatric or other forms of mental health care, or who have entered the role of mental patient, can enhance their social functioning as spouse, employee, or citizen. Relevant agencies include hospitals, community mental health programs, and clinics. We also classify agencies that help people with developmental disabilities (e.g., retardation) here.

6. *Leisure Time and Youth Services*. The focus is upon helping persons to fulfill all roles better through enhancing their creative potential and ability to work cooperatively with others. Youth services are often emphasized in such agencies as community centers and "Y's," and these services focus upon the developmental needs of persons in that role. Relevant agencies include settlement houses and community centers.

7. *Income Maintenance, Job Training, and Employee Assistance in Industry*. Because relevant agencies focus on resource and provider and employment roles, we have grouped them together. The last-named category, industry, is one of the newest fields of practice for social workers. Agencies include welfare departments, personnel training and placement programs, and employee assistance departments in businesses and industries.

8. *Substance Abuse*. A number of agencies focus entirely on helping people who are abusers of alcohol and drugs. Most of the fields of service already discussed also help many substance abusers, but these clients will also be referred to specialized agencies. Relevant agencies are alcohol and drug treatment programs.

9. *Private Practice*. Social workers in increasing numbers have entered private practice, often in addition to their agency practice. In 1967, it was estimated that between 3,000 and 4,000 were engaged in this. In 1975, the estimate was between 10,000 and 20,000.[10] Private practitioners operate independently or in partnership with other social workers. The people who seek help from such workers usually must be affluent enough to pay fees. They are typically "couples with marital problems and families with interpersonal difficulties"[11] and thus are the kinds of people also seen in family and mental health agencies.

In view of our position, to be expanded on later, in which we regard social work's primary responsibility to be to work with the oppressed, the powerless, and the poor, we will not emphasize issues in private practice in this book. Nevertheless, this practice is recognized by the National Association of Social Workers (NASW) as a legitimate field for interpersonal practice, although that organization has also stated that "practice in socially sponsored organizational structures must remain the primary avenue for the implementation of the goals of the profession."[12]

In all these fields, the social work purpose is to improve social functioning, that is, to help people to interact in more functional ways with their situations and to change aspects of themselves and their situations that will enhance such interactions. For example, in a family agency a worker helped family members to fulfill their family roles better and helped the family to become a well-functioning one. In a criminal justice setting, a worker helped a client to develop behaviors that were more adaptive and also helped the client to change her workplace so it would better meet her needs. In a rehabilitation setting, the worker helped a handicapped person to develop new skills and also helped the client to make community institutions more aware of the need to be accessible to the handicapped.

A Problem Focus

Our model has in common with most social work models the idea that the purpose of social work practice is to enhance social functioning through the prevention or amelioration of *problems* in social functioning. This differs from some models that seek to enhance growth, as such, or that seek to attain specified conditions such as "maturity" or "autonomy." We do not disagree with the value of maturity and autonomy, but we be-

lieve that these terms in themselves are too broad to guide practice or to lead to the generation of useful practice guidelines.

In interpersonal practice, we mean by problem some aspect of the person-environment interaction that does not or is not likely to satisfy the wants of the individual. We have chosen to use the word *wants* for reasons similar to those cited by Reid.[13] The more usual expression is needs rather than wants, yet the former is a term around which there are many conceptual problems. One is that *needs* often are presumed to be what *others* think the person requires. Another is the question of how genuine or necessary the need is. Thus, one might say that another needs "support" or "love" or "limits" without any well-thought-through evidence for the existence or legitimacy of the need. Stating that an individual *wants* to be more affectionate to a spouse, or *wants* more money from a welfare department, or *wants* to communicate more effectively with an employer is less subject to conceptual confusion than is the statement that the person "needs" these things.

The issue of the existence or legitimacy of a want can then be faced in its own right—namely, whether a person's wants can be demonstrated to, in fact, be his or her needs. The husband, for example, who wants to be more affectionate can investigate whether he experiences a deep-felt desire (need) to express and receive such affection or whether this is, for example, an effort to relive some past relationship or to secure some trade-off other than affection. Thus, wants can be reflected on by the individual concerned who can subsequently decide whether to continue to seek their fulfillment or not.

In a more precise sense, Reid defines a want "as a cognitive affective event consisting of an idea that something is desirable and a feeling of tension associated with not having it."[14] A want can also be expressed in negative terms when the individual wishes to get rid of something that is undesirable.

Obviously, we have many wants, and these motivate most of our actions: we want food so we eat, we want sleep and so we rest, and so forth. As Reid states, however, the wants that bring people to social workers tend to be persistent, occupy a good deal of the individual's attention, and are relatively intense.[15]

A problem focus related to unsatisfied wants in individual-environmental transactions has several advantages over other conceptions of the focus of practice. A concentration upon helping individuals to realize such wants gives a clear definition to clients, workers, and relevant others of the purpose and goals of the helping process. Tasks of the client and of the worker can be clearly delineated and justified as to whether they relate to solving such problems or not. The length of time during which service will be offered will be related to this purpose. And, finally, the effectiveness of the service and the validity of the outcome can be examined more easily when the purpose is so explicit.

We advocate that problems should be stated as specifically as possible so as to have the effects on practice that we have just noted. We realize, however, that many clients have difficulty being precise and that workers cannot be precise, in many situations, either, until they learn a great deal about the client's situation. For many complex problems, therefore, precision is something that is pursued during the helping process instead of being realized in advance of it. We will have a great deal more to say on this subject in our chapters dealing with assessment, contracting, and evaluation.

Service Priorities

An issue that has confronted social workers as long as there has been an awareness of the range of problems with which they can help is whether, with limited resources, some problems have a higher priority for service than others. We believe that an answer to this question must take two points into consideration:

1. The degree to which other resources are available for solution to the problem than those provided by the social service systems
2. The degree to which the problem relates to the central purpose of social work to help with problems in the interactions of persons and their environments

We believe that these two points lead to the conclusion that the problems of certain groups in the society are the priority ones for social work practice. These are the problems of people who are poor, oppressed, or physically or emotionally handicapped. Included are members of such ethnic minority groups as blacks, Chicanos, native Americans, and Asian Americans, as members of all these groups have been the targets of racist practices. Since, as we described earlier, social work has a preventive function, the situation of persons who are likely to become poor or otherwise handicapped also deserve such service priorities.

We believe that social work has an historic commitment to these kinds of groups as affluent persons or persons in powerful positions have access to many resources to resolve interpersonal difficulties and to enhance personal development. This does not mean that we should withhold social work services from such groups but rather that they deserve a lower priority when scarce social work resources are an issue. This is consistent, for example, with the NASW stance cited earlier that recognizes the legitimacy of private practice but asserts the primacy of social services in welfare organization settings.

Another reason for our position, drawn from the central purpose of social work, is that members of the groups with priorities for services are likely to be the ones with the most dysfunctional transactions between themselves and their environments. This is not to deny the hypothesis that members of all groups suffer from the effects of injustice and inequality but, rather, to assert that the major place for social work to fulfill its tasks is with those with the fewest resources to deal with injustice and inequality. Since, as we have stated, most of the types of services we discuss in this book take place in social welfare agencies, we now turn to a closer examination of such settings. To be considered are the types of agencies and their specific effects on interpersonal practice.

The Agency Context of Practice

As we have indicated, with the exception of private practice, social work activities take place under the auspices of agencies. These agencies have been created either by government or by private citizens to offer services in the various fields we have outlined. The agencies established by government include departments of welfare and community mental health, state institutions for the mentally ill, and schools. Those maintained by private boards (often with government assistance) include many family agencies, child guidance clinics, and community centers.

In some agencies, the staff is primarily recruited from the field of social work. An example is a nongovernmental family and children's service. In other agencies, another profession is the one that either supplies most of the staff or has the most influence in determining agency practices and policies. These are referred to as *host settings* and include schools, hospitals, prisons, and psychiatric clinics in which the more numerous or dominant professionals may be educators, doctors, custodial personnel, or psychiatrists.

In primary settings, social work values and objectives are not usually the sources of conflict in the agency. Disagreements are most likely to arise between administrative actions to maintain the agency, referred to by sociologists as bureaucratic requirements, and the actions taken to accomplish social work professional purposes.[16] For example, in one agency the workers believed that they should be available evenings to interview parents who worked in the day. The agency decided to remain closed at night because of cost factors.

In host settings, conflicts arise in addition to those between bureaucratic and professional concerns because of disagreements between social workers and other professionals as to their respective goals and roles. These conflicts become even sharper when one of the other professions occupies the central policy making position in the agency. One example of this was a psychiatrist in a hospital who saw social work activities as restricted to history taking and work with relatives; another example is a school principal who saw social work activities as confined to reducing the student's noncompliance with school rules. Increasingly, social workers are taught how to build professional teams as one way of coping with these types of situations.[17]

How Agencies Affect Practice

As we indicated, the agency is not simply a physical setting for social work practice; rather, it strongly influences, if not determines, what such practice will be like. In Chapters 7 and 13 we will discuss how the worker, to serve clients better, can assess and change agency conditions. At this point, we have introduced the topic to indicate that an understanding of the agency is essential for any comprehension of social work practice today.

The way in which we view how agencies

affect social work practice is drawn from concepts of the agency as a *social system*, a concept we shall use throughout this book. A social system is an identifiable unit of two or more persons who interact in such way that change in one or more such persons initiates change in other persons, and this change, in turn, produces change in the persons with whom the interaction began.[18] The interactions affect the whole unit as well as its parts. The unit, furthermore, has a "structure," which is the relationship among the people in it at a specified time. The clients who may be served by the agency, as any "input" into a social system, go through phases of entering the system and leaving the system. The agency's effects may be analyzed in terms of stages of the client's career in the agency that in systems terms can be referred to as "input," "throughput," and "output." We shall expand on such systems concepts in the next chapter.

Effects on the Entering Stage.   The agency will determine who may "enter" the agency system through proclaiming recruitment policies and intake rules. The agency can also determine which aspects of the client or the environment or both will become targets for change. For example, the policy of a department of social work in a school system was that clients must be students in the school, that they must be referred by their teachers, and that classroom behaviors are the targets.

Effects on the Change Stage.   Agency rules indicate which persons in the agency are authorized to interact with the client, what social work approaches are approved by the agency, and what resources will be made available for the utilization of these approaches. In the example of a school social work department just cited, the policies of the department required all students who are

referred to a social worker to also be interviewed by the school psychologist for possible psychological testing; the agency descriptions of social work practice described the social worker's approaches as "problem solving," "referral," and "support." The social workers were provided with such resources as psychiatric consultation but they are not allocated any funds for the equipment used in child therapy situations.

Effects on the Termination Stage.   The agency, in its policies, has statements regarding the goals and purposes of its services. Clients should terminate their use of agency services when they have attained such goals. Thus, in the example of a school social work program, social work services are discontinued when a student functions in school in the specific ways sought through the referral to such services. It is also possible that the school staff will determine that such services are not effective for a child or the child and child's family may refuse to continue with the services. Some agencies limit services to a specified time period or number of social work sessions, whether or not the goals of service have been reached, as a way of allocating resources.

Agency Structure and Environment.   In addition to policies and procedures that have specific effects on entering, change, and ending stages, agencies also have relationships among their subsystems that constitute the agency's *structure*. These relationships include how communications take place (e.g., staff meetings, memoranda); how power is allocated; who interacts most with whom; who is expected to do what; and who hires, assigns tasks to, and fires staff. All these aspects of structure can have an effect on all transactions between clients and social workers. The agency also establishes a physical environment consisting of its buildings, its rooms, its furniture, and its decor. The way in which workers can identify these structural and agency environment factors and take them into consideration is explained in Chapter 5.

Agency Functions

The functions of social welfare agencies that employ social workers are not identical to the functions of the social work profession. The ways in which professions evolve in society are seldom in full correspondence with the ways in which the institutions that employ their members evolve, and this is one of the factors contributing to the professional-bureaucratic conflicts mentioned earlier.

To help the reader to understand agency functions as they relate to professional purposes, we present a categorization of such functions. This use of categories does not imply that an agency fulfills only one function. Rather, an agency may seek to fulfill functions singly or in any combination. Some combinations, however, may be confusing or contradictory.

Our categories were derived from the work of Vinter,[19] who described agencies as fulfilling socialization or resocialization functions. Hasenfeld provided a description of these agency functions when he wrote in reference to group services,

> In socialization agencies such as the public school, the youth serving agency, and the community center, the purpose of group services will be to supplement and complement other socialization methods. Clients will be perceived as "normal" and as motivated to change. However, group work may also perform a control function in such organizations to serve clients judged to be failing or lagging in their socialization process. In resocialization agencies such as the child guidance clinic, welfare department, and mental hospital, the purpose of group work and other techniques is to achieve major behavioral

changes in clients who are defined as deviants.[20]

In using the categories of socialization and resocialization, we find it useful to subdivide them one step farther.[21] Thus, under the heading of socialization we identified the two functions of *anomie reduction* and *role attainment*.

Anomie reduction is the function of helping persons to determine their socialization goals. The word "anomie," as Hartman states, refers to "a state of societal demoralization, of normlessness, created by the disjunction of goals, and norms for reaching these goals."[22] We believe that people have difficulty in determining socialization goals because of such societal conditions. Examples of agencies fulfilling anomie reduction functions are helping women decide how to determine their goals in view of changing sex roles and helping "gay" people determine their goals in view of the changing societal values regarding homosexuality.

Role attainment is the function of helping people to pursue socialization goals. This may involve helping them to secure resources as well as to overcome barriers to socialization. Examples of role attainment functions are helping students succeed in school and older persons prepare for retirement.

For resocialization, we identified the two functions of *social control* and *alternative role attainment*. Social control represents the mandate for an organization to control antisocial behavior. Examples of social welfare organizations fulfilling this function are prisons, as they limit illegal behavior of inmates, and mental hospitals, as they limit the behavior of patients that is a danger to themselves or others. Many complex issues enter into how social work fulfills its purposes under social control conditions that go beyond the scope of this book.

Alternative role attainment is the function of helping persons to change their behaviors from deviant to socially acceptable role performances. It differs from role attainment in that there are many barriers to leaving the deviant role that the agency must help the client overcome. Alternative role attainment occurs when the client desires to participate in this process; if the client does not, the appropriate category is social control. Many prisons and mental hospitals fulfill both social control and alternative role attainment functions and which one is operative depends on the readiness of the client to relinquish a deviant role.

As we stated earlier, some agencies seek to fulfill only one function. Thus, one outpatient psychiatric clinic that employed social workers, psychologists, and psychiatrists limited its intake to voluntary clients who, nevertheless, performed very poorly in family or occupational roles. Persons seeking help with normal socialization tasks and who were functioning more adequately were referred to other agencies. This agency, therefore, fulfilled only an alternative role attainment function.

In contrast, a counseling service in a university that employed social workers, psychologists, and personnel from the counseling and guidance field sought to help students to cope with separation from their families, a normal socialization task, as well as students who experienced serious stress because of academic deficits or problematic personal life-styles. The stressed students required help with problems that were more severe due to conflicts within their current roles, thus making this an alternative role attainment issue. This agency, therefore, sought to accomplish role attainment as well as alternative role attainment functions. As is often the case, the agency, in trying to fulfill two functions, encountered problems because people who saw themselves as "normal" feared that association with the agency subjected them to a stigma because of its service to more dysfunctional students.

It is important for workers to understand how agencies view their functions. This will affect all of the agency conditions we described earlier such as how clients are recruited, what techniques are preferred, and what goals are sought. In addition, the agency structure and the roles of staff will be affected by such functions. A problem in organizational design, one beyond the scope of this book but still of concern to interpersonal practitioners, is how to create agencies that have procedures and structures that are appropriate to their functions. In Chapter 15, we shall describe further how workers take agency function into consideration in planning service.

Thus far in this chapter, we have analyzed the purposes of social work, the social problems to which social work addresses itself, and the agency contexts of practice. The next section of this chapter discusses interpersonal practice in terms of its knowledge base, values, skills, and roles.

The Bases of Interpersonal Practice

Social work professional practice, as does that of any other profession, consists of (1) a body of *knowledge*, (2) a set of *values*, and (3) a series of *actions* that are related to the knowledge and values. These actions are referred to as the interventive repertoire of the profession. Later in this book, we shall discuss values, knowledge, and actions that workers utilize in specific circumstances. Our purpose here is to provide a general introduction to these three facets of professional social work practice.

Social Work Knowledge

Knowledge for interpersonal practice originates outside the profession as well as inside it. Knowledge that social workers draw upon from outside the profession includes that from the social and biological sciences as well as that from such other professions as education, psychiatry, public health, and law. When social workers use information created by others, it has to be redefined and tested for applicability to social work tasks.

For example, social workers may use such psychiatric concepts as the unconscious, the defenses, and the ego, but they seek to understand how these phenomena are affected by environmental inputs and the way individuals cope with these. Social workers use behavioral concepts (e.g., reinforcement) but consider such social work values as the self-determination of the client when using reinforcement procedures.

Analogously social workers have borrowed the ideas relevant to advocating for clients from law, teaching clients skills from education, and identifying at-risk populations from public health. All these have been modified, however, when utilized for social work purposes.

Social workers will, of course, predominantly use knowledge developed within the profession of social work. This includes the results of research conducted by social workers, the accumulated and shared experiences of practitioners, and the workers' learning from their own experiences. Some fine lines can be drawn to create a definition of whether something is "social work knowledge" or "knowledge from outside social work." Many social workers have become competent social scientists, and many social scientists have interacted closely with social workers and share values and perspectives with them. In reality, therefore, there is a continuum from knowledge applicable to the social work situations but obtained by social scientists in laboratories to knowledge generated by social workers possibly from examination of social work practice experiences. We do not want to place some precious and unique quality on the second type although we argue that any knowledge, however obtained and by whatever investigator, must ultimately be applied and evaluated in relevant social work settings by professionally trained social workers before its usefulness for professional practice is proclaimed.

Knowledge required for professional practice includes two types: propositional knowledge and procedural knowledge.[23] Propositional knowledge, as described by Siporin, "consists of factual, descriptive and theoretical propositions or information bits.[24] The propositional knowledge utilized by interpersonal practitioners includes information about the causes of dysfunctional behaviors, the factors in interpersonal situations that contribute to such behaviors, and comprehensive theories about such behaviors.

For a long time most of the knowledge used by social workers from either theory or research was of the propositional type. Social workers could cite a great deal of information from psychoanalytic or role theory, for example, but did not use tested procedures and theories about how to change behavior or situations. The "how to" knowledge of social workers tended to be what was termed "practice wisdom" passed on from teachers, supervisors, and co-workers.

The "how to" knowledge, referred to as procedural knowledge, is defined by Scheffler as "a skill, a trained capacity, a competence, or a technique."[25] Only in the last few years have social workers given sustained attention to defining procedural knowledge in specific ways so that it can be reported to others, tested for effectiveness, and incorporated in practice theories and models.

A few examples of these two types of knowledge will make this distinction clearer:

Propositional Knowledge

1. Adolescents experience more ambivalence with regard to authority than do younger children.
2. Frustration frequently leads to aggression.
3. Cohesive groups are more likely than those that are not cohesive to control the behavior of their members.
4. Reinforcement that follows voluntary behavior is likely to lead to an increase in the occurrence of that behavior.

Procedural Knowledge

1. The worker helps the adolescents to feel less ambivalent toward authority by supporting adolescents' efforts to set limits for themselves.
2. Workers, when they perceive the client's aggression as related to specific sources of frustration, should help the client to direct the aggression constructively toward the sources of frustration. The goal should be to identify ways for the client to reduce his or her frustration by acting to satisfy his or her needs.
3. The worker can increase cohesiveness of client groups by reinforcing members for attendance and by helping the group to plan gratifying activities. The worker should point out to the group that the resulting potential to control member behavior should be utilized to facilitate the attainment of members' goals.
4. Group workers with groups of socially inadequate members should help the group to identify and subsequently reinforce social skills.

A large quantity of procedural knowledge has been developed by social workers who draw much of their propositional knowledge from the social sciences. Most social work writers include in the major theories about human behavior that social workers utilize psychoanalytic theory, behavior theory, role theory, and organizational theory. We believe that we can be most helpful to the reader if we describe the kinds of psychological and social phenomena that interpersonal workers seek to understand and then indicate the theories that supply this understanding.

The knowledge the practitioner must have includes information about the structure of systems, the way in which they change, and the nature and causes of the "behavior" of the system. For example, individuals can be described in terms of such structures as their physiology, personality, and behavioral repertoires. Individuals change, as a result of such processes as maturation, problem-solving activities, and decisions regarding personal goals. The "causes" of individual behavior may include ego strengths, the conscience or superego, the psychological drives of the individual, and the effects of environmental contingencies on the individual. (These concepts of systems and change are elaborated upon in the next chapter.)

Similarly institutions, such as schools in which the individual may be enrolled, have structures such as the location of power in the system and the subgroupings into which the system is divided. Institutions change as a result of the development of institutional goals, movement through stages of institutional development, and the inputs to the institution from the environment. The causes of institutional behavior (e.g., types of instruction in a school, school policies) include the technologies to which the institution is committed (e.g., the "open classroom") and the decisional rules accepted by the institution (e.g., majority rule, executive prerogatives).

As can be seen from this brief discussion, the practitioner must have knowledge about the behavior and characteristics of individuals and their relevant systems. This knowledge includes information about such individuals and social systems as separate entities as well as how the individuals and systems interact with each other and affect one another. Thus, for example, the worker seeks to understand the personality of the individuals as well as how personality is affected by immediate social situations, by the institutions in which the individual participates, and by the larger society (e.g., culture, social policy, societal crises, the economy).

Because interpersonal practitioners in social work seek to enhance the functioning of individuals, families, and small groups, they are most likely to utilize theories that relate to the behavior of these entities. They will, therefore, seek to understand how individuals, families, and small groups are affected by interactions among each other as well as with aspects of larger social systems. From a systemic point of view, every level of social organization has an effect on every other level (e.g., the "society" has an effect upon institutions, and vice versa). The study of interactions among larger social systems, however, while relevant to interpersonal practice is of less central concern to it. We shall, as a consequence, describe in detail the theories most utilized for interpersonal practice. Further discussion of these theories will be presented at appropriate points throughout this book.

Theories Regarding Individual Behavior

Since the 1930s, at least, social workers heavily drew upon psychoanalytic theory and concepts. A major shift toward an ego psychological orientation has taken place in the last few decades. Ego psychology is an outgrowth of psychoanalytic theory but one that is more germane to the purposes of social work practice. Compton and Galaway provide a succinct statement of the basic premise of psychoanalytic theory as follows:

> Psychoanalytic theory conceives of the human being as a dynamic energy system consisting of basic drives and instincts which in interaction with the environment serve to organize and develop the personality through a series of developmental stages. Individuals from birth are pushed by these largely unconscious and irrational drives toward satisfaction of desires which are largely unconscious and irrational. Because of the operation of an unconscious defense system and the structure of the mind, people go through life largely unaware of these irrational forces that have tremendous effect on their behavior and on the way they relate to others.[26]

Ego psychology, in contrast, focuses on understanding the aspect of personality known as the ego. Ego functions represent the way in which individuals cope with both the environment and internal states to attain their objectives. These functions, therefore, represent the rational, problem-solving, aspects of personality. Ego psychologists have argued that such rational operations are much stronger than was acknowledged by the earlier psychoanalysts who emphasized the role of unconscious instinctual drives.

Some social workers became dissatisfied with a sole reliance on ego psychological concepts because these concepts are often difficult to operationalize and their usefulness in practice has not been fully supported by research findings. One approach these workers turned to was that of social learning theory, primarily its behaviorism aspect. This theory presents behavior as arising directly from the individual's transactions with the environment. Workers analyze such processes in terms of gratification (positive reinforcement) as well as pain (punishment) that are supplied by the environment. Stated simply, they view human action as determined by its consequences.

The environment is also the source of "stimuli" to which the individual responds and that elicit behaviors in predictable ways. Through the process known as conditioning, stimuli may substitute for each other in their capacity to elicit responses. Somewhat different processes are seen as emerging when the individual's behavior is voluntary as compared with involuntary or reflexive. Among the most important responses social workers must deal with in the reflexive category are fear and anxiety.

Behaviorists have extended the scope of their attention to an examination of thought processes and problem solving. The phrase "cognitive behavior theory" is now used to refer to the modification of thought processes in therapy. Behaviorally oriented workers have used behavioral concepts to develop techniques to enhance the client's self-esteem, rational thought, and ability to analyze his or her behavior.

Both behaviorism and ego psychology provide ways of analyzing individual-environmental interactions, but they do not contribute sufficiently to an understanding of some of the complex aspects of these interactions. For this reason, many social workers use *role* and *systems* theory because these theories focus on the ways in which behavior results from individual-social transactions.

Role theory describes how behavior stems from the positions that individuals occupy in the systems of which they are part and the expectations held for occupants of such positions. These positions can be formally recognized in the social structure such as parent, employer, or teacher. They can also emerge through social interactions and be idiosyncratic to these such as the positions of "fool" or "scapegoat."

Variables considered in role theory include the way an individual views the expectations he or she must meet because of occupying a position, the expectations others have for position occupants, the kinds of ambiguity or conflict that can arise among sets of positions, and the ways people act when positional behaviors are approved or disapproved. People often move from one position to another in a planned sequence that constitutes a "career." Thus, a person who desires to become a doctor will move through positions of college student, medical student, intern, and resident. The organization of these steps and the forces that affect individual progression are important extensions of role theory and constitute the topic of *socialization*.

Role theory also contributes to *deviance theory* because deviant positions such as the lawbreaker or mentally ill person can be examined in terms of social roles. The relationship of individual deviance to social policy can also be analyzed by asking how society recognizes deviant roles and makes it possible for persons to fulfill them. Society also often makes it difficult for deviant persons to move into other roles.

The difficult task of conceptualizing individuals, environments, and transactions between the two has caused social workers to seek concepts and theories that approach this problem. Increasingly, they have turned to *systems theory* and to an *ecological* perspective. As it is currently developed, systems theory has some clear limitations. In reference to this, Compton and Galaway state:

> Systems theory is not in itself a body of knowledge, nor does it contain any prescriptions as to actions that a social worker might take. Rather, systems theory presents us with tools of analysis that may accommodate knowledge from many sciences. It is a way of thinking—a way of viewing and organizing data. Because it is a way of thinking that requires the abandonment of the linear approach to causation and the substitution of an understanding of the reciprocal relationships

among all parts of the field (transactional approach) and an interactive focus, in which the effects of one system on another are dealt with, systems theory requires considerable study for any real understanding.[27]

The most important systems idea is that systems of various sizes and functions form a complex whole in which each part has effects upon other parts as well as upon the whole. A system is made up of smaller systems that bear the same relationship to it as it bears to even larger ones. The behavior of any system must be understood in terms of interactions incorporated within it as well as outside of the system. Because of the importance of systems concepts to our model of practice, much of the next chapter is devoted to explaining them.

Social workers also make extensive use of *communication* theories to understand and modify individual behavior. Some of the approaches to communication are systems oriented as they view communications in systems terms such as constituting inputs, throughputs, and feedback. Because of the central role played by communications in social work helping, we devote a full chapter to this (see Chapter 3).

Theories Regarding Small-Group Behavior

A number of different theories regarding the small group exist.[28] A summary of or comparison among them is well beyond the scope of this chapter. Social workers draw extensively from small-group theories to understand group forces in such practice relevant groups as client groups, peer groups, and family groups.

These group forces include the ways the group develops over time, the pressures that members experience regarding their behavior through such phenomena as group norms, the attraction the group holds for members, and the ways in which the group responds to conflict. Small-group theories describe the patterned behavior among members, known as group structures, as well as group processes such as problem-solving, scapegoating, and responses to deviance.

Another theory of a social psychological nature relevant to understanding small-group processes as well as those of other systems is *attribution theory*, which seeks to explain the social and psychological inputs into how people understand the causes of events.[29] Theories of *social influence*, that is, how persons control the behavior of others, are also useful in social work.[30] An important concept in the social psychology of influence is social power.

The family, also a small group, has devoted to it a large body of social science literature. Because of the obvious fact that all clients are products of families and social workers often work with whole families, this literature is of great importance in interpersonal practice.[31] Knowledge about families that is essential to social work practice is (1) the nature of changes in families over time as children are born, age, and eventually leave; (2) the ways that family interactions maintain family patterns; (3) the kinds of processes that occur between the nuclear and extended family; and (4) how individual behaviors are related to family conditions. These concepts are amplified in Chapter 7 where we discuss family and group assessment.

Theories Regarding Organizational and Community Behavior

As we have indicated, interpersonal practitioners must seek to understand the impact of larger systems upon clients. These include the service agency itself as well as other agencies in the community. Another level that must be understood is the community in which the client resides (i.e., the neighborhood) as well as communities with which the client identifies (e.g., ethnic and religious communities). At times, these complex systems will be targets of change because of the negative impact they have upon specific clients.

The interpersonal practitioner, therefore, should have a knowledge of the fundamentals of organizational analysis as these apply to social welfare organizations.[32] Important organizational concepts are organizational goals, structure, decision making, and the client "career" in the organization. This literature also includes ideas for organizational designs that support social work professional goals. Interpersonal practitioners can influence, at times, the ways in which their agencies are organized and should have ideas on how administrative and supervisory structures, governance procedures, personnel practices, and policies regarding clients can be attained that facilitate good interpersonal practice.

Workers must also seek to understand community factors.[33] A highly relevant community concept for interpersonal practice is *community networks*.[34] Social workers are becoming more knowledgeable about the relationships between the ability of the individual to cope with stress and the existence of a network of friends, relatives, and community institutions that provide support and other resources. This is not only an issue when the individual has already been dysfunctional but also for preventing this from occurring. Social workers, therefore, must know not only how to assess the nature of networks but also how to build such networks when they are deficient.

In addition, interpersonal practitioners must know how to assess an array of community factors to avoid serious errors in understanding and responding to clients. Among the most important of these are ethnic condi-tions that relate to communication patterns, economic and social opportunities, family and social structures, and behavioral norms.[35] For example, workers can be ineffective or even harmful if they do not understand the client's speech, ignore the client's lack of economic opportunities, violate the community's behavioral norms, or do not understand the roles of family members as derived from cultural norms.

Social Work Values

As we have just described, social workers derive practice principles from propositional and procedural knowledge. In addition, workers must relate practice principles to sets of beliefs that stem from social work philosophy, ethics, and values. While writers may relate philosophy, ethics, and values to each other and sometimes even derive one from the other, for analytic purposes these can be seen as separate. Social work philosophy is the broadest category and incorporates and justifies social work ethics and values. The word "philosophy," itself, refers to views about what constitutes knowledge, reality, human nature, and what is desirable, beautiful, and good. As Siporin states,

> A philosophy is a set of beliefs and attitudes, ideals, aspirations and goals, values, and norms, ethical precepts or principles. It enables us to understand and give meaning to existence and reality, to ourselves and our world, to our history and development.[36]

Insofar as these dimensions are relevant to social work activities, one can speak of social work philosophy.

Values constitute conceptions of what is desirable and undesirable, whereas ethics constitute statements of what behaviors should or should not be engaged in because they are consistent or inconsistent with either a set of values or a philosophical premise or both. Social work professional ethics, as those of any profession, are beliefs about what social workers should and should not do in their professional roles and are derived from philosophical and value beliefs of social workers. Later in this section we shall discuss the Code of Ethics of the National Association of Social Workers.

Statements about social work philosophy and values refer to the positions of the persons who make them, as no one philosophical system has a complete consensus among social work professionals except at a highly abstract level. There is general support that social work philosophy in Western societies is based on Judeo-Christian ethics. It is also generally agreed, that social work philosophy incorporates a humanistic view—humanism is a set of beliefs that declares human welfare to be related to a recognition of the worth of each individual.[37]

More specifically, social workers are likely to agree on a number of values derived from humanistic and other comparable philosophical systems. These include the following:

1. *Self-determination:* the responsibility of the social worker to respect the right of clients to determine their own goals and means of achieving them

2. *Caring:* the responsibility of the social worker to act with concern for the welfare of others and to help clients to enlarge their capacity to care for others[38]

3. *Social responsibility:* the responsibility of social workers to act to enhance the ways in which society promotes the general welfare and to help clients to develop their capacity for similar concerns

Two skills must be attained by practitioners in relationship to values such as these just outlined: how to recognize the value components of social work situations and how to make decisions in situations where values conflict.

Recognizing Value Issues

It can be difficult for beginning, as well as experienced, social workers to recognize the value, knowledge, and factual components of social work situations. The importance of making these distinctions is severalfold: knowledge can be tested and facts can be checked but values are matters of personal belief. Thus, workers will ascertain the validity of knowledge, and the truthfulness of statements about fact, but clarify their relevant value positions. Social workers can also help themselves and others to identify the consequences of acting on the basis of specified values. Value judgments can then be made about these consequences also.

These issues can be illuminated through the example of Mrs. J who consulted a social worker about the problems she was having, as a single parent, with her son, David, who was age 16. David wanted to leave school, and yet he had no specific plans as to what he would do afterward regarding education or employment.

There are a number of kinds of knowledge that a social worker will use in this situation, such as information about adolescent development, the problems of a mother and son in the absence of a father, the peer pressures that adolescents experience, and the ways in which adolescents are affected by contemporary society. The worker will also have knowledge about the effects of social work procedures that may be utilized on a one-to-one basis, in family sessions, and in group sessions with members of this family.

The social worker will also be concerned about factual issues in this situation. These include in what specific manner the son indicated he wanted to leave school and under what circumstances he stated this. How the mother responded to her son is also a relevant fact.

Value issues include the worker's, mother's, and son's beliefs about school attendance and education as desirable in themselves. Beliefs that school completion enables one to "succeed" in life or to have higher self-esteem are knowledge issues in that they can be tested empirically. Another value issue is the worker's belief that it is or is not appropriate to discuss the son with his mother in the son's absence. The consequences of doing so, however, can be observed and value judgments can be formed regarding those consequences.

It is our conviction, therefore, that workers must carefully separate knowledge, factual, and value issues. Each of these has different implications for intervention in social work situations. Confusion arises when values are treated as tested facts or when theories are applied to situations based on facts that have not been adequately established.

Resolving Value Conflicts

The problem of relating values to knowledge and practice does not lie primarily in implementing values. Social workers are aware of self-determination or professional honesty or other values and, we are convinced, make strong efforts to act in ways that are consistent with these. The difficulty arises when conformity with one value contradicts conformity with another. For example, it may be consistent with self-determination to accept an alcoholic's refusal of help and consistent with respect for the value of life to reach out aggressively to such a person with offers of service. It may be consistent with "caring" to work with some clients, yet, when resources are scarce, consistent with "social responsibility" to allocate one's time to others with higher priorities for service.

We have not discovered any system that we can support to reduce value conflicts on the basis of a comprehensive, universally acceptable philosophical system, set of value principles, or logical structure. Workers must, however, resolve value conflicts as these arise in almost all professional situations. One approach they utilize is to derive a personal value hierarchy in which some values take precedence over others. Thus, some workers will allocate the highest priority to respect for life and may expand this term to mean not only physical existence but the achievement of one's maximum potential.

Another approach is to weigh the consequences of acting in accord with one value as opposed to another. Thus in one situation, that of a potential suicide, a worker may place respect for life ahead of self-determination and continue to reach out to the individual; in another situation, that of counseling a school dropout, a worker may respect the youth's self-determination and cease service even though the youth may not achieve his or her life potential without such help.

In any case, we believe that workers must clarify their value positions for clients and relevant others and help the clients to clarify and protect their positions. This should be done so that the client is alerted to the worker's biases in offering services. Under some circumstances, clients should transfer to workers whose positions are nearer to their own. This is often required when lifestyles are at stake such as gay versus straight, new family forms versus traditional ones, or an orientation toward one religion as opposed to another or none at all.

Value Issues

Workers are more likely to recognize value issues in their work if they utilize the following typology of components of a social intervention.[39]

1. *The choice of goals to which the change effort is directed.* What clients choose to accomplish as a result of social work helping will not only be determined by what is possible but by what they or their workers or both see as desirable, "worth" the effort, or even a "social obligation" to achieve. (A worker who values education highly may inappropriately urge a client to go to college.)

2. *The definition of the target of the change.* Again, there is a combination of empirical and value issues associated with this dimension. These relate not only to the outcomes that may be achieved by seeking to change one's self or others but also whose obligation it is to change. (A client may appropriately seek change in his workplace while a "psychologically minded" worker focuses only on client behavior.)

3. *The choice of means used to implement the intervention.* One of the most hotly debated action issues, from a moral perspective, is the relationship of ends to means. Even if one asserts that the means determine the ends, and that immoral means create immoral ends, the relationship of means to ends is too complex and varied for this to be more than an untestable assertion. This places the worker in the position of assessing, and helping others to assess, the ethics and values behind the selection of means. The specific kinds of questions that frequently arise are how a choice of means may affect others as well as one's self. This kind of question is most relevant when the means the client uses to achieve his or her goals prevents others from reaching theirs. A major consideration is whether or not any form of force or coercion is justified as part of a social work process. (A father was "taught" by one worker to use rewards to obtain his child's compliance. Another worker criticized this as "bribery".)

4. *The assessment of the consequences of the intervention.* Ethical issues are posed by how and when the outcomes of the social work process are to be measured. Even accepting the fact that the requirement to evaluate outcomes is an ethical one, there are value as well as empirical issues as to what should be evaluated. (A behaviorist may assert that a worker should evaluate the attainment of outcomes that were agreed to in advance while existentially oriented workers may often argue that a subjective view such as the feeling of well-being of the client is of equal importance.) Many workers assert that the "unanticipated consequences" (that is, "side effects") of the intervention should be identified and assessed. Approaches must be found to anticipate what the consequences may be so they can be studied—consequences of this sort may involve the client's self-esteem and affects as well as the well-being of persons affected by the client's new behavior.

Professional Ethics

The National Association of Social Workers has sought to codify the beliefs of the profession regarding ethical behaviors. This ethical code serves as a guideline for professional behavior and is also utilized, through processes established by the NASW, to censure social workers who are found to have engaged in unethical behavior. As the code was employed, limitations in it were identified and it has been amended. The version we describe here was passed by the 1979 delegate assembly of the association.

The first section of the code deals with the social worker's conduct and comportment. It details the worker's responsibility to maintain competence, to give the highest priority to service, to have integrity, and to remain committed to scholarly inquiry. The second section refers to ethical responsibility to clients. This includes placing client's interests first, respecting client self-determination, maintaining confidentiality, and ensuring that any fees charged are fairly determined.

The third section refers to ethical responsibilities to colleagues such as maintaining respect and fairness. Workers should also maintain appropriate relationships with clients of colleagues. The fourth section considers professional responsibilities toward employers and employing organizations, such as working to improve policies, to eliminate discrimination, and to use resources appropriately.

The fifth section describes responsibilities to the profession, which include upholding its mission and practices, making its services available, and adding to its knowledge base. The last section notes the worker's responsibility to promote the general welfare of the society through the elimination of discrimination against any person or group and the expansion of opportunity. This section also requires the worker to seek to maintain a culturally diverse society, policy and legislation that improve social conditions, and the informed participation of the public in all matters that affect it.

Throughout its various revisions, the Code of Ethics has been made more specific and more related to contemporary issues. Undoubtedly as revisions continue to be made and as they are tested through application to actual situations and cases, the profession of social work will evolve an even more comprehensive Code of Ethics that will leave even less confusion in the minds of workers and the members of the public as to the social worker's ethical stance. This should add to

the ability of the profession to monitor the behavior of its members and to earn the respect of its beneficiaries.

Social Work Action Repertoire

As we have stated, social work practice consists of actions that are utilized in a manner consistent with social work values. The use of actions is also determined by reference to a body of knowledge. The rest of this book elaborates on this action repertoire; however, we introduce this topic here with a general discussion of actions employed by social workers. Because of the fact that the word "intervention" is also commonly used to mean the actions of workers, we shall use these terms interchangeably.

One issue is whether social workers' professional actions are different from those employed by members of other human service professions. We cannot assert that social workers exclusively possess any techniques. The distinguishing features of social work are its focus on individual-environmental transaction and the purposes that we have also described in regard to these—not how social workers carry out their purposes. This is not to deny the fact that social workers have pioneered in the development of a number of procedures such as those of family treatment, group work, individual problem solving, advocacy, and brokerage—all of these to be discussed in detail later.

Another issue is that of specialization among social work practitioners. For most of its history, social workers defined themselves in terms of one of the following methods: casework, group work, community organization, social welfare administration, or social policy analysis and implementation. This kind of division would be appropriate if the ways of solving problems of individuals and systems corresponded with such a definition of methods.

Unfortunately, correspondence of problems and methods, is not the case. Serious questions have been raised in recent years regarding the effectiveness of many social work methods. One of the conclusions that social workers have reached as to ways of increasing effectiveness is that methods must be adapted to the needs of clients instead of offering the client only the method in which the worker has been trained.

This more generic approach has led to several alternative ways of defining specialization in social work. One that has had considerable influence in social work education is the separation of training for practice with individuals, families, and groups (usually referred to as direct practice, clinical practice, interpersonal practice, or micro practice) from that with communities and organizations (usually referred to as indirect practice, macro practice, or social policy and administration).

We regret this bifurcation of social work into direct and indirect practice because it detracts from the focus of all social work upon both individuals and environments and their interaction, although we recognize that some specialization along these lines is necessary. Concepts described earlier, such as those from systems theory, have become popular because they avoid such dichotomies. This has led to still other solutions to the problem of specialization. One is to promote specialization by field of service. Thus, for example, a social worker in the correctional field should become expert at both direct work with clients in that field as well as influencing policy issues affecting such clients. Another solution is the promotion of teamwork in which workers are trained in the identification of desirable procedures and take responsibility to make the full services of the profession available to clients. The utilization of this approach requires agencies to develop service teams with a wide range of expertise.

Because of our conviction that individual, family, and group approaches must be integrated with each other and be expeditiously used, we support the movement to offer training that combines the teaching of these approaches, and we have developed this book with that type of training in mind. At the very least, the interpersonal practitioner should recognize when individual, family, or group approaches are appropriate and desirable and secure them for clients; increasingly, we believe, almost all interpersonal practitioners will be skillful in all these. A few, because of strong preferences, will specialize in less than the full range but will utilize a team approach so that clients receive the services they need.

We also believe that effective service to clients will require many interpersonal workers to intervene in community and agency processes and, therefore, have included material on these in this book. Some division of labor is inevitable between the micro and macro aspects of service; however, the dividing line must be a shifting one as circumstances require, as models of practice evolve, and as the needs of the client are assessed. In all cases, the openness of lines of communication among workers with different tasks related to common problems must be maintained.

Beyond the general issues relating to the division of labor among social workers, it may be helpful to call attention to the foci of the chapters of this book devoted to practice details. This also broadly indicates the components of a practice skill repertoire. All workers should have skills required for different time phases of work. These phases are divided into the following:

1. Initial engagement with clients (Chapter 5)
2. Assessment (Chapters 6 and 7)
3. Planning and preparation (Chapter 9)
4. Implementation (Chapters 11, 12, and 13)
5. Evaluation of the change and termination (Chapters 10 and 14)

Because many different skills may be used to accomplish the tasks of each one of these phases—some that are used with all action systems (i.e., individual, family, group) and some that differ—chapters in Part Three of this book separately discuss interventions with each system.

The skills that are called for to implement change plans can also be categorized by whether they apply to individuals, to environmental systems affecting individuals, or to the interactions between the two. These skills can be clustered, and these clusters can constitute different worker roles. Thus, in facilitating changes in individuals, workers fulfill roles as enablers of change, as teachers, as behavior modifiers, or as promoters of insight and awareness of feelings. Workers who locate systems to meet the needs of clients function as *brokers;* workers who argue the client's cause in relationship to organizational policies and processes function as *advocates;* workers who help clients negotiate with other individuals and systems, so that the needs of both may be met, function as *mediators*. These roles are discussed further in Chapter 13.

When they offer "indirect" services, social workers engage in many activities such as social action, social planning, and locality development. While any comprehensive treatment of these is beyond the scope of this book, it should be emphasized that there are times when interpersonal practitioners engage in such activities or, at the very least, support them when they are carried out by others in ways that benefit clients.

Summary

In this chapter, we have sought to describe the current status of interpersonal practice in social work. To accomplish this, we have presented and discussed a definition of social work. This definition emphasizes the functions of the profession as preventing or resolving dysfunctional individual-environmental transactions and as strengthening the potential of people to lead creative lives in their environments. We clarified the role of the interpersonal practitioner in social work as accomplishing this function through interactions with individuals, families, and groups.

We subsequently described the scope of interpersonal practice in terms of fields of practice and the types of agencies that employ such practitioners. We introduced our model of practice as one that employs the concept of social functioning, is problem focused, and gives priority to people who are oppressed in modern society.

Our model also recognizes that, since most interpersonal practice occurs in agency settings, the implications of this must be fully understood, and this topic was also elaborated upon. For this analysis, we presented a typology of agency functions in terms of the socialization or resocialization of clients.

In the final portion of the chapter, we discussed professional service as based upon knowledge, values, and an action repertoire. We elaborated upon each of these dimensions as they have been developed for interpersonal practice.

As we have stated, the purpose of this chapter was to introduce the reader to the range of roles and actions of social workers in interpersonal practice. These also constitute the subject matter of the rest of this book. Before we present the specifics of worker actions, however, we shall present more details of the components of our model of practice.

NOTES

1. Ida C. Merriam, "Financing Social Welfare: Expenditures," *Encyclopedia of Social Work*, Vol. I (New York: National Association of Social Workers, 1977), p. 456.

2. The major sources of such definitions are the Commission on Social Work Practice, National Association of Social Workers, "Working Definition of Social Work Practice," *Social Work*, Vol. 3 (April 1958), pp. 5–8, and Werner W. Boehm, "The Nature of Social Work," *Social Work*, Vol. 3 (April 1958), pp. 10–19.

3. Most definitions use the phrase "individuals and groups." We prefer to place the emphasis here on the person and then refer, as we do in point 3(b), to the fact that the quality of intimate associations of the person (e.g., in families or groups) is essential to his or her well-being and, consequently, will determine when the practitioner seeks to help individuals, families, or groups or all of these.

4. Adapted from the West Virginia Undergraduate Curriculum Development Project cited in Beulah Roberts Compton and Burt Galaway, *Social Work Processes*, rev. ed. (Homewood, Ill.: The Dorsey Press, 1979), p. 6.

5. Ibid.

6. See, for example, her book, *The Common Base of Social Work Practice* (New York: National Association of Social Workers, 1970).

7. William Schwartz, "Private Troubles and Public Issues: One Social Work Job or Two," in *Social Welfare Forum, 1969* (New York: Columbia University Press, 1969), pp. 22–43.

8. Carel B. Germain and Alex Gitterman, *The Life Model of Social Work Practice* (New York: Columbia University Press, 1980), p. 5.

9. For a comprehensive discussion of role concepts, see Bruce Biddle and Edwin Thomas, eds., *Role Theory: Concepts and Research* (New York: John Wiley, 1966).

10. Estelle Gabriel, "Private Practice in Social Work," *Encyclopedia of Social Work*, Vol. II (New York: National Association of Social Workers, 1977), p. 1056.

11. Ibid., p. 1055.

12. Ibid., p. 1058.

13. William J. Reid, *The Task-Centered System* (New York: Columbia University Press, 1978), pp. 25–32.

14. Ibid., p. 26.

15. Ibid., p. 27.

16. For a discussion of this issue in relationship to social work settings, see A. D. Green, "The Professional Worker in the Bureaucracy," *Social Service Review*, Vol. 40 (March 1966), pp. 74–83.

17. See chapter entitled "The Nature of Teamwork" in Compton and Galaway, *Social Work Processes*, pp. 451–478.

18. This definition was adapted from Amitai Etzioni, *The Active Society: A Theory of Societal and Political Processes* (New York: The Free Press, 1968), p. 65.

19. Robert D. Vinter, "Analysis of Treatment Organizations," *Social Work*, Vol. 8 (1963), pp. 3–15.

20. Yeheskel Hasenfeld, "Organizational Factors in Service to Groups," in Paul Glasser, Rosemary Sarri, and Robert Vinter, eds., *Individual Change Through Small Groups* (New York: The Free Press, 1974), p. 308.

21. Charles Garvin, *Contemporary Group Work* (Englewood Cliffs, N.J.: Prentice-Hall, 1981), pp. 47–55.

22. Ann Hartman, "Anomie and Social Casework," *Social Casework*, 50 (1969), p. 132.

23. This discussion of knowledge draws heavily upon Max Siporin, *Introduction to Social Work Practice* (New York: Macmillan, 1975), pp. 364–367.

24. Ibid., p. 364.

25. Israel Scheffler, *Conditions of Knowledge* (Glenview, Ill.; Scott, Foresman, 1965), p. 92, quoted in ibid.

26. Compton and Galaway. *Social Work Processes*, p. 90.

27. Ibid., p. 77.

28. See, for example, R. B. Cattell, D. R. Saunders, and G. F. Stice, "The Dimensions of Syntality in Small Groups," *Human Relations* , Vol. 6 (1953), pp. 331–356 (syntality theory); J. W. Thibaut and H. H. Kelley, *The Social Psychology of Groups* (New York: John Wiley, 1959 (exchange theory); R. F. Bales, *Interaction Process Analysis: A Method for the Study of Small Groups* (Reading, Mass.: Addison-Wesley, 1950) (systems theory); and Dorwin Cartwright and Alvin Zander, *Group Dynamics: Research and Theory*, 3rd ed. (New York: Harper & Row, 1968) (group dynamics theory).

29. Sharon S. Brehm, *The Application of Social Psychology to Clinical Practice* (New York: John Wiley, 1976), pp. 177–198.

30. Dorwin Cartwright, "Influence, Leadership, Control," in J. G. March, ed., *Handbook of Organizations* (Chicago: Rand McNally, 1965), pp. 1–47.

31. Norman W. Bell and Ezra F. Vogel, *A Modern Introduction to the Family*, rev. ed. (New York: The Free Press, 1968).

32. Yeheskel Hasenfeld and Richard English, *Human Service Organizations* (Ann Arbor: University of Michigan Press, 1974).

33. For a broad introduction to community study, see Roland Warren, *The Community in America* (Chicago: Rand McNally, 1963).

34. Jeremy Boisservain and Mitchell J. Clyde, *Network Analysis: Studies in Human Interaction* (Paris: Mouton, 1973.)

35. Wynetta Devore and Elfriede G. Schlesinger, *Ethnic-Sensitive Social Work Practice* (St. Louis: C. V. Mosby, 1981).

36. Siporin, *Introduction to Social Work Practice*, p. 62.

37. See Elizabeth L. Salomon, "Humanistic Values and Social Casework," *Social Casework*, Vol. 24 (1967), pp. 26–32.

38. Siporin has an excellent and thorough discussion of the concept of caring in his *Introduction to Social Work Practice*, pp. 70–71.

39. Herbert C. Kelman and Donald P. Warwick, "The Ethics of Social Intervention: Goals, Means, and Consequences," in Gordon Bermant, Herbert C. Kelman, and Donald P. Warwick, eds., *The Ethics of Social Intervention* (Washington, D.C.: Hemisphere, 1978), p. 4.

two

Basic Assumptions and Concepts

In this chapter we shall present the rationale, major assumptions, and basic theoretical concepts that underlie the model of practice that is presented in this text. This should help the reader to understand the criteria that have been used for the selection of concepts and prescriptions. This discussion highlights our biases about practice, theoretical orientation, and, therefore, both the strengths and "blind spots" of our model.

Rationale

As discussed in Chapter 1, this text is designed to be generic in that it presents the common elements of social work practice with individuals, families, and small groups. However, to compose a text exclusively with generic concepts would leave out knowledge that a practitioner must also have to work with individuals, families, and small groups. Therefore, we include specific knowledge

that we also consider to be crucial to interpersonal practice. Our own experiences in practice and education have taught us that a beginning practitioner needs both types of knowledge to be effective with different-sized client systems.

Our theoretical approach to interpersonal practice is eclectic. We do not concentrate upon any one theory or ideology. Although both authors are strongly committed to eclectic practice, each brings different practice experiences, educational backgrounds, and theoretical interests to the text. This blend has created an expanded eclectic model, and we value the richness this creates.

Although this text is eclectic, we do not survey all theory used in practice either. Although comparative theory texts have been written,[1] we have no intention of including all practice theory in this text. We do draw from various practice "theories" (e.g., task centered, ego psychological, systems, behavioral), and we seek to bring together knowledge from all behavioral and social sciences.

The rationale behind our choice of concepts and prescriptions from various theories has been shaped by four general considerations: applicability, practice potency, empirically demonstrable efficacy, and generality. *Applicability* means that concepts, prescriptions, and organizing variables should be readily operational in social work practice with individuals, families, and small groups. Our descriptions of concepts should clearly fit the work of practice and be understandable to beginning practitioners. High-level abstractions may be briefly discussed at points, but the focus of the text is on clear, operational conceptualizations.

Practice potency means that principles and prescriptions should make a difference in practice and significantly shape and influence what a practitioner can accomplish in work with individuals, families, and small groups. For example, a biochemical theory of human emotion may have empirical validity, yet a social worker cannot use this knowledge to intervene directly into the chemical structure of individuals to influence their emotions (although a psychiatrist may be able to); therefore, not all theories of human behavior can have practice potency for social workers. Successful practitioners also operate with many uncodified, untested principles that significantly shape their practice, and this "practice wisdom" is important to a model of interpersonal practice.

We would like to be able to write a text that is exclusively based on our third criterion: *empirically demonstrable efficacy*. Social workers would be uniquely sought after as change agents if all their technologies were empirically researched for effectiveness. There is, however, not enough empirically validated, prescriptive knowledge in social

work to create a comprehensive guide to interpersonal practice. Such a text has been attempted,[2] but it falls prey to major deficiencies beyond the author's control. At this stage of knowledge development, an empirically validated model of practice must inevitably contain large gaps. An empirical model can leave such gaps to be filled in as research and knowledge accumulate; however, a practitioner cannot limit clients to such a constraint. Practitioners must use both what is known as well as "uncertainty," and interventions cannot be withheld until light overcomes all darkness.

Good practitioners will use empirically validated principles and practice wisdom that have been learned from colleagues and their own experience. At other times, practitioners may be required to "muddle through." We strongly believe it is important for a text to contain empirically validated knowledge, but if it is to be useful to practitioners of the 1980s, it must also incorporate other forms of knowledge as well. The latter, however, must be systematically examined so that the empirical base of practice can be expanded and so that change taking place case by case can be monitored.

Finally, our conceptualizations should have enough generality to fit a variety of practice settings and a wide range of clients with various social problems. Conceptualizations that are efficacious to a unique client, setting, or problem and are not generalizable to other practice situations are not emphasized. For example, the interventions of a medical social worker with a postoperative patient who has just undergone open heart surgery have been carefully detailed,[3] yet the specific knowledge of such procedures may not be particularly useful to practitioners in other settings with clients facing other kinds of problems. Our attempts to present conceptualizations that have generality have inevitably produced some breadth at the expense of depth.

Underlying Assumptions

Although we are trying to be broad and eclectic in our approach to interpersonal practice, there are ideological biases and assumptions that underlie our model of practice. As we discussed in Chapter 1, the general purpose of social work practice is to improve social functioning, and thus our general approach to practice is from a social problem perspective. Social problems are not viewed as special disease entities or syndromes that individuals succumb to, but instead social problems are seen as the inevitable social disruptions that all individuals experience and face at various stages of life. There is nothing abnormal or unique about social problems. They are the likely consequence of living in a rapidly changing, complex society, and no one (except the deceased) can be assured of immunity. In our model the primary task of the worker and client is to work together to resolve or cope with problems of living, or both.

The framework for change in our model is goal oriented. Unlike some models of change that focus on historical antecedents to problems to uncover and neutralize them, our approach assumes that change is accomplished through a rationally planned, goal-oriented process. For heuristic reasons our problem-solving model, as stated in Chapter 1, is organized around five phases that unfold in practice. Service begins with an (1) engagement phase and is then followed by (2) assessment, (3) planning and preparation, (4) implementation, finally ending with a (5) termination and evaluation phase. While these are presented sequentially, we recognize

that these phases often occur simultaneously; a back-and-forth movement can also occur.

Viewing interpersonal practice as a sequence of phases is deliberately designed to emphasize the changes that take place over time in the service process. There are some fundamental differences in how worker and client will interact and what their responsibilities are to each other in the beginning phase as compared with successive later phases. We clearly acknowledge that social work practice is not a lockstep sequence of unique phases, and as we have just stated, there are many similarities and overlaps from phase to phase (evaluation begins during assessment but becomes more predominant at termination).

Our incorporation of phases into our model is designed to help students and beginning practitioners recognize what is essential and salient about the service process as it unfolds. Most other models of interpersonal practice have also been organized into a phasic structure (study–diagnosis–treatment[4]; beginnings–middles–endings[5]; intake–diagnosis–planning; group composition and formation–group development–evaluation–termination[6]). Unfortunately there has not been enough research conducted on the question of phases[7] to suggest an empirically sound way of dividing the service process. Even though we do not have strong research support for a five-phase model, we still believe that a phasic construction is essential to any practice model. Writers who state that practice cannot be so conceptualized are giving up prematurely in the face of complexity.

Although we do not present rigid prescriptions regarding time limits for service, our model is clearly not open ended, extended, or long-term. Studies of practice have consistently demonstrated that most clients who enter service do not stay very long.

Clients do not expect service to take a long time[8]: about half are gone by the sixth interview,[9] and only about one-third remain in service by the tenth interview.[10] In fact, long-term services should be selectively offered as few clients (about 1½ percent who start) make it to the fiftieth inverview.[11]

In the face of empirical evidence that clients do not stay around very long, a number of social work fields are developing time-limited service, even in areas in which service was traditionally considered to last several years. For example, child welfare services are being restructured into three- or six-month planning and intervention episodes in which children are expected to be returned home or an alternative, permanent plan (such as adoption) instituted.[12] Community mental health services are also being reorganized along brief, time-limited service held to 10 or 20 sessions.

We conceptualize a service sequence as taking place within a three-month or shorter time frame. We are not rigidly committed to a set time limit for service as are some models of practice (1 session,[13] 1 weekend,[14] or 12 prescribed visits[15]), but we want to emphasize that most clients will remain briefly in service. Therefore, because service must be designed to be delivered in the shortest time possible, worker and client have neither the luxury of exploring *everything* in detail nor can they "get around to issues in due time" but instead must move expeditiously to produce an optimal impact.

This model has a "contract orientation" in which client participation and acceptance of service are important values. We believe that there is enough research evidence to conclude that service is significantly facilitated when clients know what they are getting into and when they agree with it. What is more, we firmly believe that it is unethical to coerce or "trick" clients into

service or into changing parts of their lives without their knowledge or consent.

Consistent with our contract orientation is our commitment to evaluation and accountability. We believe that a worker has a responsibility to develop or employ, or both, procedures to evaluate the overall effectiveness of service as well as the efficacy of particular actions and interventions. These evaluation procedures are important because the worker is accountable to client, agency, and profession—to the client to demonstrate the effect service has had on the target problems, to the agency to help determine how scarce resources are being utilized and with what effect, and to the profession to generate, validate, or challenge its knowledge base. Contracting and evaluation are such important concepts in our model that an entire chapter is devoted to each. (See Chapters 8 and 10.)

A final bias in our model is the importance of action[16] as a primary dimension of interpersonal practice. The worker actively intervenes and actively facilitates the client's participation in the problem-solving process. The worker is not only active but so is the client. "Doing" and "acting" are essential to the client's sense of mastery and competence.[17] Furthermore, in studies of discontinuance, poor and oppressed clients are turned off by service that primarily emphasizes "talking," "reflecting," and "understanding."[18] Clients from lower socioeconomic groups expect, want, and seek action-oriented solutions to their problems, *not* an elaborate, detailed understanding of the cause and consequences of their present troubles.[19] We are not against a worker being reflective or nondirective, at times, with clients, but our approach firmly emphasizes that the worker and client should actively engage in problem-solving actions.

Such an action-oriented stand may be

criticized by devotees of nondirective prac-tice as "impulsive," "bullying," or "moving too fast." We are aware of the danger of act-ing prematurely and accept it as a potential problem of an action-oriented model. We are, however, much more concerned about the inaction and resultant frustration that many clients experience in reflective, nondirective practice. The needs and prob-lems of oppressed clients are so great that a service model cannot afford to frustrate fur-ther these clients and thus contribute to their dropping out of service.

Metaphors

We shall use the term "metaphor"[20] to de-scribe the highly abstract, often implicit, organizing frameworks that practitioners use in attempting to understand and change their practice world. A metaphor is a general per-spective or world view that helps individuals to organize the complexity of the world around them. Even though metaphors are highly abstract and far from the world of ex-perience, they are important because they shape how a practitioner will experience the practice world. (For example, they direct a practitioner to focus on some events and to exclude others.) There are many metaphors that can be extrapolated from social work practice, but we have chosen to focus on three—*moral, disease,* and *nature*—because these are evident in contemporary practice and often clash and conflict with each other.

Before we describe each metaphor and relate it to social work practice, we take note of several qualifiers. Unlike a theory that by definition is supposed to be testable or open to validation, a metaphor cannot be directly validated. The strength of a metaphor does not arise from its "scientific correctness" or empirical validity but instead from its utility and comprehensiveness. Metaphors are use-ful ways of broadly organizing the complexity of the world around us, and although individ-uals may believe strongly in one metaphor as compared with another, it is senseless to ar-gue that one metaphor is "better" or "more accurate" than another. Each of the meta-phors that we shall describe has utility for so-cial work practice, and each continues to help practitioners understand the human condi-tion. Although our model of practice clearly reflects a bias toward the nature metaphor, the other two metaphors must be understood because of their impacts.

It is beyond the scope of this chapter to give a detailed explanation of the origins of each metaphor.[21] The reason for discussing metaphors is to alert students to some of the inherent conflicts in practice that emerge when different practitioners or agencies ap-proach a situation from divergent metaphor-ical bases. In some agencies there is a mix-ture of metaphorical orientations that can be confusing and sometimes overwhelming to students who want to know "what's the right way to do it!"

Moral Metaphor

The moral metaphor is historically the oldest metaphor of the three we shall discuss. The central issue of the moral metaphor is good versus evil. The behaviors and condi-tions of people can be understood and cate-gorized as bad, immoral, and evil or right-eous, moral, and good. Many theories of human behavior are an extension of this met-aphorical orientation. For example, in the Puritan work ethic, wealth and hard work are next to godliness and poverty and lack of ef-fort are the work of the devil.[22] The eugenics movement at the turn of the century[23] sug-gested a rationale for sorting out superior races (good) from inferior races (bad). Nineteenth-century social work practice was influenced by this metaphor. Clients of that day were sorted into "worthy" and "unworthy" categories,[24] and the forerunner to the modern-day practitioner was the morally superior "friendly visitor" whose job it was to visit the poor and lift their spirits through "moral suasion."[25] Service delivery systems of the day were designed to limit or control "pauperism" through registration, restriction, and limited, in-kind aid.[26]

The interventions that evolved from the moral metaphor were death, punishment, control, and isolation. Death and punishment were justifiable reactions to immorality and evil. Control and isolation were necessary to keep evil and immorality from spreading and influencing the rest of society. Witches were burned or drowned, thieves had their hands severed, debtors were imprisoned, infidels were banned or excommunicated from the community, and the poor, sick, and homeless were crowded into slums or workhouses to die of neglect or to be sold at public auction to the highest bidder.

The moral metaphor, however, is not something only of the past but continues to influence society and social workers today. The not-so-moral majority's condemnation of homosexuality and women's rights, the growing support to reinstitute capital punishment, the Reaganomics attack on social welfare programs that "don't serve the truly needy," and the fundamentalist belief that the spirit of Jesus Christ can heal all are examples of the way in which the moral metaphor continues to exert influence on society today.

This metaphor also exerts influence on social workers. Alcoholism and drug addiction were viewed by some social workers as irresponsible behaviors (reflecting some weakness in the client's personality), and, therefore, remedial efforts must involve strong measures of control and "penance"

such as those that occur at Alcoholics Anonymous meetings. Some workers are morally outraged at the behavior of parents who abuse their children and may be overly zealous in moving toward termination of parental rights as a solution to child abuse. Some support strong limits, controls, and even punishment for institutionalized juvenile offenders who are prone to violent behavior.

The moral metaphor will always be with us because it is an inevitable consequence of any social system. The stability of social systems depends in part on normative structures, and whenever there are norms, there are bound to be norm breakers who must be addressed somehow by the social system. Many areas of social work practice can be conceptualized as focusing on norm breakers.

Disease Metaphor

The disease metaphor has a shorter history than does the moral metaphor and in many ways arose as a reaction to the latter. The early adherents to the disease metaphor were viewed as revolutionaries—for example, Phillipe Pinel, Benjamin Rush, and Dorothea Dix all wanted to unchain the "mentally ill" and treat rather than punish them.[27]

The central issue of the disease metaphor is health versus disease. From this orientation, various human conditions are seen as manifestations of disease entities or disease processes. As with the moral metaphor, these disease processes were undesirable and required eradication; however, unlike the moral metaphor, the victim or host was not responsible or culpable. The culprit was not the victim but some precipitating, noxious agent.

Understanding the human condition from a disease orientation required practitioners to search the host's past for the causes of the present disorder and to understand how the disease emerged and progressed (etiology). This led to categorizing the disease into a diagnosis that differentiated it from other disease entities and finally to prescribing some form of treatment to neutralize or eliminate the causes of the disorder. The development and scientific validation of germ theory strongly enhanced the power of the disease metaphor as did later developments such as the discovery of antibiotics and tranquilizers.

In addition to influencing biologically oriented practitioners (such as doctors), the disease metaphor also influenced psychology and sociology. The nineteenth-century works of Emil Kraeplin, J. M. Charcot, and Pierre Janet enhanced the development of psychopathological categories as a way of understanding various "psychological diseases."[28] The metaphor even influenced sociology, and terms such as "social disease" or "social pathology" emerged. Even racism and poverty have been described as social diseases that can grow like cancers and destroy the entire body (society).[29]

The primary intervention that flowed from the disease metaphor was treatment. Treatment or therapy was expected to eradicate or neutralize the noxious, causative agents and to promote the health of the host. Unfortunately, not all technologies developed from this metaphor have left the host so untouched, and some even seem to possess the punitive character of the moral metaphor. For example, in one application of the moral metaphor, exorcism was developed to eliminate the evil spirits that possessed a witch, but it also eliminated the host through burning at the stake, ritual drowning, or driving a stake through the heart. Many of the interventions of the disease metaphor were likewise brutal, such as leeching, blood letting, and lobotomies. Even with the development of modern technologies, the

"cure" may have disastrous side effects for the host. For example, prolonged use of certain tranquilizers may lead to serious brain damage (e.g., tardive diskinesia), and cancer patients face severe side effects from both radiation and chemotherapy.

Social work practice has been strongly influenced by the disease metaphor because of the profession's close association with medicine and psychiatry during this century. Modes of practice has been developed both in casework (the psychosocial study, diagnosis, treatment model[30]) and group work (e.g., the remedial model[31]) that relate this metaphor to practice. Today social workers in a number of practice settings (to please third-party vendors and insurance companies) must use diagnostic labels (such as those outlined in DSM-III[32]) to describe their clients and client conditions.

The problems with using labels as outlined in DSM-III is that such diagnostic systems attempt to categorize almost every conceivable form of human behavior into some "disease" category. Even though we recognize the thrust of DSM-III to be multifaceted and environmental, is it reasonable to consider all forms of the human condition as potential, diagnostic entities? For example, patients who choose not to follow their doctor's recommendation or advice are diagnosed as V15-81, "Noncompliant with Medical Treatment." The DSM-III, however, does not have a category for patients who follow their doctors' recommendations, and, therefore, one must assume that such patients are paradoxically "healthy"!

Another problem with the disease metaphor is the narrowing effect it has on the definition of problems. Troubles to be treated are seen as lying within individuals or parts of individuals (such as personality dynamics), and thus social causes, consequences, or related conditions tend to be ignored and not addressed. Social casework has been repeatedly criticized for ignoring the social environment,[33] and many technologies that developed are open to criticism as conservative and even repressive as they do not address the social conditions of clients.[34]

Nature Metaphor

The nature metaphor has experienced increased interest over the past decade though it has been around as long as the disease metaphor. Today traditional medicine is criticized by advocates of "holistic medicine." Focusing on disease is no longer adequate in medical practice, and doctors must have knowledge of nutrition, physical activity, exercise, work and home environments, and stress in order to understand their patients' troubles.

The central issue of the nature metaphor is growth versus decay. From this metaphor various aspects of the human condition can be understood as manifestations of growth, decay, or combinations of the two. Growth and decay are the inevitable consequences of two fundamental processes in the universe—one ontogenetic and the other ecological. The ontogenetic process is the inevitable journey that living organisms take from creation, development, maturation, to death. But this journey does not unfold in a vacuum, and the ontogenetic process is significantly influenced and determined by environmental (ecological) factors. The processes of creation that include growing, thriving, and finally dying are significantly shaped by the quality and quantity of environmental resources and opportunities. For example, poor nutrition, poor sanitation, or inadequate health care during pregnancy, infancy, and early childhood can dramatically influence physical size and intellectual capacity during adulthood, or even whether the individual will have an adulthood!

In contrast to the moral and disease metaphors, there is no implicitly desirable side to the contrasting aspects of the nature metaphor. Growth and decay are neither desirable nor undesirable but inevitable. Organisms and their ecosystems cannot escape either condition, and the optimal (desirable) state is a "balance" or "match" between organism and ecosystems. Although it may seem that decay is undesirable, it is absolutely essential to growth both ontogenetically and ecologically. Our bodies continuously build, break down, and rebuild our cellular structures, and the fertilizers and nutrients of nature, so necessary to growth of organisms, are only made possible through the decay and breakdown of previous organisms. Decaying organisms and their by-products are the food for future generations.

The interventions that flow from the nature metaphor involve matching, balancing, fitting, and "tinkering." Intervention cannot create the ontogenetic and ecological forces, although ontogeny can be tinkered with through genetic engineering, and ecology can be disrupted through such changes as uncontrolled pollution or elimination of part of a food chain (such as draining wetlands). Interventions can attempt to improve the delicate balance between ontogeny and ecology. These can be directed at the interface between the ontogenetic state of the organism and the ecological factors that surround and shape it.

Although the life model of Germain and Gitterman[35] (so named to contrast it to a disease model) is clearly an extension of the nature metaphor into social work practice, many earlier models of practice seem to fit this metaphor also. For example, crisis theory and crisis intervention[36] conceive of a crisis as a normal, expectable event that happens to all systems that have the potential for growth as well as decline. Opportunity theory [37] presented delinquency not as some form of psychopathology or evil behavior but, rather, as a career to which youths were attracted when there were few opportunities for success in their social environment. In fact, the "social functioning" perspective discussed in Chapter 1 is clearly consonant with the nature metaphor because "social functioning" involves both the individual and the social context.

The major value and attractiveness of the nature metaphor as an orientation for social work practice is the breadth of possible interventions that flow from it. Interventions can be directed at individuals with regard to their ontogenetic development (a young expectant parent may be helped to learn parenting skills); at significant parts of the environment (a worker may advocate against a school procedure that does not allow a pregnant student to continue in regular classes); at the transaction between individual and environment (a worker mediates to improve the relationship between the young, expectant parent and her own parents); or at all three at once or in various combinations. Unlike the moral and disease orientations, to improve the "match" or "balance" between individuals and their environments, a worker does not have to focus on individual change or adjustment. Balance can be achieved by changing environmental forces as well as by influencing basic transactions between individual and environment. In some cases improvements may be achieved by moving individuals out of deleterious environmental situations into more growth-enhancing environments.

Although the nature metaphor is an attractive orientation for social workers, it is not without its limitations and deficiencies. The nature metaphor introduces tremendous complexity into the understanding of the human condition. Not only must a practitioner understand the basic developmental stages of organisms and social systems, but the practitioner must also understand the ecological cycles and forces that impinge on the organism as well as the various transactions that occur between organism and environment. The sheer number of variables that account for "optimal balance" are staggering, and at present, such an optimal state may be difficult to define empirically (in much the same way that "health" is an elusive condition of the disease metaphor). For example, many factors (both internal and environmental) produce stress on organisms as they develop. Some stresses are necessary to growth while clearly others are debilitating. With too little stress, an organism may be understimulated, whereas with too much stress, an organism may be overwhelmed. The optimal balance is further complicated because each individual at different ontogenetic stages and within his or her own individual range has different capacities to respond and handle stress.

One way around the complexity issue is not to focus on optimal social functioning. This may be an ideal and cannot be empirically defined. Instead it may be more useful and empirically more demonstrable to focus on examples of social dysfunction, that is, situations in which there clearly is a *non*optimal balance between individual and environment, and to address these social problems of living in order to restore a better balance or fit. This is in line with the purpose of this text, which describes common social problems and presents basic prescriptions designed to restore more optimal balance. At times, also, our state of knowledge or ability to deal with complexity may still force us to utilize the disease metaphor, and some contradictions in this text are reflections of this dilemma.

What value is it for practitioners to try to understand how metaphors shape social work practice? Many conflicts that arise in practice between practitioners are not just technological (a matter of what works best) but instead represent fundamental clashes in metaphorical orientation. It is not *un*common during a case conference for several professionals working with the same individual client to have conflicts about "what's wrong?" or "what's best for the client?" or "what's the best way to help?" These are the day-to-day practice decisions, but these decisions often create conflict among professionals. Because the moral, disease, and nature metaphors presently exist in social work practice (as well as in most human services), all three of these orientations are represented in the perspectives or viewpoints of workers or professionals. For example, how can three professionals be expected to agree with each other when one sees the client's behavior as irresponsible, requiring sanctions and limits, the second sees the same client's behavior as psychopathological, requiring psychotherapy, and the third sees the same client's behavior as a dysfunctional response to a stressful, nonneed-meeting environment?

Metaphors do not necessarily have to work against each other in the practice world. For example, medical social work sometimes blends the strengths of both the disease and nature metaphors. A medical social worker may be working with patients who are recovering from a particular disease. The onset, treatment, and recovery may be fairly predictable events, yet the worker may attempt to connect the patient with new resources (a nursing home) or mobilize support from the patient's intimate environment (encourage family involvement) so that recovery is facilitated and the patient reenters the social environment outside the hospital. The worker may have to take into account specific aspects of the disease and the prescribed medical regimen and attempt to balance these with elements of the posthospital situation such as the patient's home environment, resources, and ethnic factors, all of which may complicate recovery. The optimal recovery in this case requires the use of both metaphors.

In summary, we remind the reader of several points. Metaphors are implicit and not easily recognized although they fundamentally influence how social workers view clients and interventions. Practitioners rarely question their own metaphorical orientation although they question that of others when it differs from their own. Metaphorical orientations may be very hard to change, so that practice decisions that involve a conflict of metaphors may be difficult to resolve rationally. Instead, such conflicts in decision making are often resolved politically or institutionally, that is, by the most powerful individuals in a given situation. Therefore, the disease metaphor can be expected to prevail in medical and psychiatric settings, the moral metaphor in correctional or court-appointed services, and the nature metaphor in organizations serving oppressed ethnic groups.

"System" and Change

In this section of the chapter we discuss two concepts: system and change. The presentation will be the most abstract part of this text and may not be immediately useful to beginning practitioners. However, it has importance as a way of relating our model to other theories in the behavioral and social sciences.

Systems concepts have appeared in social work literature for the past three decades. Both the general systems theories of von Bertalanffy and Miller and the social systems theories of Parsons and Merton have had an influence on social work's knowledge base. The pioneering literature of Hearn[38] and Lutz[39] during the 1950s was influenced by general system theory (GST), and the works of Cloward and Stein[40] reflected the influence of social systems theory.

One problem of any general discussion of "systems theories" is that there are almost as many "systems theories" as there are authors writing on the subject.[41] For example, Ervin Laszlo's writings[42] focus on philosophical issues; Ludwig van Bertalanffy[43] looks mostly at biological and psychological systems. Walter Buckley's works[44] concern sociological and social psychological issues. Katz and Kahn[45] have applied systems concepts to organizations, Kenneth Boulding[46] to economics; James Miller[47] has presented a "grand theory of systems." To muddy the waters even further, social work literature is also replete with various ideas regarding the uses of systems theory. Systems theories have been applied to casework,[48] to group work,[49] to family work,[50] as well as to generic practice models.[51] It is beyond the scope of this chapter (in fact, maybe any single text) to sort out all these different versions, variations, and applications of systems theory, except to reiterate that systems concepts are firmly entrenched in social and behavioral sciences as well as in social work literature.

In this chapter we shall introduce our own use of selected systems ideas as organizing concepts. We shall try to be clear on how we are applying them in our model as well as on the values and problems this entails. We want to emphasize that we are not trying to write a "systems" text[52] or review all system concepts.[53]

Definition and Properties of "Systems"

Ludwig von Bertalanffy has presented a concise definition of system: "sets of elements standing in interactions."[54] This definition contains three basic parts that can be found in most definitions of "system." First is the notion of wholeness or entativity (i.e., sets, complexes, wholes). A system is an entity that has a boundary or properties that distinguish it from other entities in the universe. Second is the notion that elements, units, components, and structures comprise the totality of the system. Thus, a system is an identifiable entity that is composed of similarly identifiable, smaller units or parts. And third, the parts or elements within the system may be interacting, transacting, interdependent, or interrelated. The parts of a system are connected by ongoing, exchange processes, and these internal processes are stronger, more significant, and more obvious than are transactions with units outside the boundary of the system.

Systems can be dichotomized into *theoretical* and *empirical* systems. Theoretical systems are the abstract model or theories that are in the mind of the scientist.[55] Theoretical systems are constructed to explain empirical systems, and most theoretical systems are designed to be clearly representative of the empirical systems they are trying to understand. (If only the elements are presented in relation to each other, this is often referred to as a model.) Although theoretical systems attempt to mirror empirical systems, they are unique and have an existence separate from the empirical world. For example, the "great ideas," knowledge, or theories of a civilization can be identified and studied separately from the world they sought to explain.

Empirical systems represent the systems of the world of experience that we perceive through our senses (or extensions of our senses). There are three general kinds of empirical systems: mechanical, organic, and process.[56]

Many consider science to be the most knowledgeable about mechanical systems such as cars, computers, or watches and natural mechanical systems such as solar systems or chemical reactions. Because mechanical systems may have fewer components and forces than social systems, we can precisely predict, design, and calculate the processes and structures of these empirical systems.

We know less about organic systems such as cells, organs, or bacteria than we do about mechanical systems. The fact that organic systems grow, regenerate, and have "life" makes them much more complex than mechanical systems; however, we are discovering much more about organic systems, and many of the basic processes and structures are being better understood (the explosion of knowledge in genetics).

We know least about human psychological and social systems, which are the most changeable and complex of all empirical systems. These include individual personality, the family, formed groups, organizations, societies, and cultures. The disciplines that study such systems (psychology, sociology, economics, and political science) have produced few (if any) lawful principles. Prediction is probabilistic at best, and, in most cases, the knowledge of basic processes and structures is extremely tentative.

We know least about such systems, yet they are the ones that most directly concern the social work practitioner. Engineers work with great certainty on machines; physicians work with some certainty on the human body; yet social workers must work with great *un*certainty with people and their problems. Another important reason for this is that humans, unlike the components of other systems, can also picture the system and seek to inflict their will upon it.

One of the most thorny issues that arises in "system thinking" is the boundary issue. For theoretical systems, boundary problems can be easily resolved. Theoreticians simply *define* the boundary where they want it to be in the model they develop. We shall be doing this later in this chapter when we define some of the basic system constructs of our model. The boundary issue, however, is much more complicated when we move to empirical systems.

How are the boundaries of empirical systems in the real world determined? Some system theorists have suggested that there are a series of hierarchical levels for various empirical systems.[57] The universe can be conceptualized as an interlocking set of larger and larger systems so that each system is a part or unit of a larger system (e.g., particles, atoms, molecules, cells, organs, persons, groups, societies).[58] In fact, these hierarchical levels are infinite and our expanding universe may be just a subatomic particle in another vast universe, and, conversely, our small, subatomic particles may represent vast solar systems of other universes.[59]

But these designations of empirical systems are not adequate for the social work practitioner for two reasons. These proposed levels are an oversimplification of the various empirical systems in the universe. Many empirical systems exist that are a mix or combination of different levels such as a pilot operating a jet or a medical expert a dialysis machine. Although these hierarchically organized, empirical systems seem distinct and seem to represent clearly identifiable referents, on closer scrutiny they are gross generalizations and are not clearly operational. For instance, what is the boundary of a family system? Is a family system represented by the members of a household? What about a nonblood-related boarder or a young adult who is away at college? Are these members part of or excluded from the family? What about the extended family living nearby whose members have daily contact with the household unit? Social workers have long grappled with the question of what constitutes a family system, and depending on one's perspective in a given case, the family system may have various referents. In an extreme example, Ross Speck and Carolyn Attneave[60] conceptualize family as a tribal network of 50 to 250 members.

The dilemma that arises in operationalizing the various empirical systems that social work practitioners work with is related to a theoretical problem. One clear-cut theoretical way of operationalizing a boundary around a given system is to *close* that system.[61] In a closed system, there is no exchange across the boundary. Therefore, the elements within the boundary are clear because there can be no interaction among elements except those within the boundary.

Theoretically this makes sense, but pragmatically it is impossible. The social work practitioner cannot close empirical systems; in fact, the living systems with which practitioners work are all open and cannot be closed.

Besides the pragmatic impossibility of closing an open system, there is also the problem that in an open system, interaction and exchange occur across the boundary, and therefore, it may not be clear which elements are on either side of the boundary. For instance, an open system may have three primary elements (A, B, and C) that interact

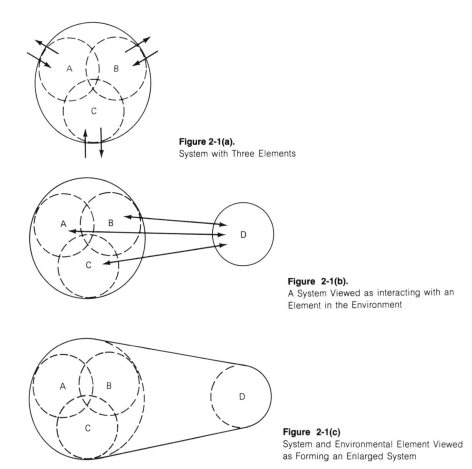

Figure 2-1(a).
System with Three Elements

Figure 2-1(b).
A System Viewed as interacting with an Element in the Environment

Figure 2-1(c)
System and Environmental Element Viewed as Forming an Enlarged System

with each other and with the system's environment. Now suppose that this open system interacts fairly regularly with an element (D) in the environment. It is theoretically possible to redefine this open system as having four elements (A, B, C, and D) instead of three (A, B, C). (See Figure 2-1.)

This dilemma of fixing a boundary around an empirical system can be clarified further if the example given is operationalized. Let the open system (A, B, C) be a nuclear family consisting of father (A), mother (B), and child (C), who live in a two-bedroom apartment. (D) is the mother's (B) widowed mother who lives around the block and both (D) and (B) have daily contact with each other. As Leichter's study[62] demonstrates, if this were a Jewish-American family, it could be devastating for the social worker to overlook or ignore the widowed mother (D).

James Miller attempts to resolve the boundary issue in an open system by asserting that elements or units within the boundary will be more interrelated with each other, than with elements or units in the environment of the system.[63] In other words, the boundary of an open system acts as a semipermeable barrier that may permit exchange with the environment, but this exchange with the environment is more difficult for elements in the system than the exchanges these elements can carry on with each other. This explanation is logical from a research perspective that establishes values for elements and measures how various elements covary. However, from a practitioner's perspective, such an explanation is not operational because a practitioner ordinarily does not employ these levels of analysis. Furthermore, some empirical systems seem to isolate internal elements that are apparently within their boundaries and also interact with external elements in their environments. For example, a state mental hospital may seem to "ignore" its back wards while at the same time worry about a beautification project on its grounds to impress the surrounding community and the legislative committee responsible for appropriations.

This issue of boundary is used a little differently in Siporin's concept of "situation."[64] Siporin discusses the difference between "situation" and "environment":

> A social situation should be distinguished from a social environment. The social environment is a network of overlapping social systems and social situations, including ecological systems, cultures, and institutions. This network influences the individual from outside of the self, and where there is an internalization of these influences, from within the self. A social situation is an impinging segment of the social environment. It is a segment that has meaning for the individual and that is uniquely perceived and interpreted by him, in which he has one or more status roles and identities, is a group member, and a role performer.[65]

The empirical system that is the unit of attention for Siporin is the individual in his or her situation as distinguished from the individual in his or her environment. Siporin's conceptualization of this empirical unit may encompass a wide range of heterogeneous elements of the universe, but these elements are all given significance by their relationship to the individual. Such a conceptualization is flexible, but unless it is carefully and clearly specified in each individual case, the risk of ambiguity and diffusion of the boundary of the social situation is great.

There is considerable discussion of this boundary issue in social work practice as it relates to the client, case, or unit of attention.[66] Rather than resolving this issue, these discussions only highlight the significance of the boundary dilemma in social work practice. Some authors[67] assert that a systems approach solves the boundary issue by offering an organized view of the multitude of variables that make up a case or unit of attention. Unfortunately, a systems approach only heightens the boundary dilemma and does little to solve it. Because a systems approach is holistic, a great many variables are identified for consideration in any case situation.[68] In fact, a systems approach has no way of specifying the domain of all possible variables:

> The general problem of specifying the environment of a given system is far from trivial. To specify completely an environment one needs to know all the factors that affect or are affected by a system; this problem is in general as difficult as the complete specification of the system itself. As in any scientific activity, one includes in the universe of system and environment all those objects which he feels are the most important, describes the interrelationships as thoroughly as possible and pays close attention to those attributes of most interest, neglecting those attributes which do not play essential roles. One "gets away" with this method of idealization rather well in physics and chemistry: massless strings, frictionless air, perfect gases, etc., are commonplace assumptions and simplify greatly the description and analysis of mechanical and thermodynamical universes. Biologists, sociologists, economists, psychologists, and other scientists interested in animate systems and their behavior are not so fortunate. In these fields it is no mean task to pick out the essential variables from the nonessential; that is, specification of the universe and subsequent dichotomization into system and environment is in itself, apart from analysis of interrelationships, a problem of fundamental complexity.[69]

For the purposes of this text, the clearest way to resolve boundary dilemmas is to recognize the imprecision that exists in establishing the boundaries of empirical systems yet also the necessity of clearly specifying these boundaries.[70] Boundaries of theoretical and empirical systems may be determined arbitrarily by any rationale. Whatever the rationale, both the boundary and rationale must be clearly specified. Once a boundary is established, and as other conditions develop, it may be useful or necessary to reestablish the boundaries of the given empirical system. The new boundaries, as with the old, must also be clearly specified. The idea of boundary specification will be referred to throughout our text so that ambiguity around boundary decisions can be minimized.

Basic Concepts: Client, Worker, Target, and Action Systems

Although we have suggested that the ideal unit of attention for social workers is the person-in-situation configuration,[71] such a broad conception is useful for assessment but impractical for intervention. As a practitioner attempts to understand a client and his or her problems, a systems perspective uncovers numerous variables; however, when it comes to intervention, the practitioner requires concepts to partialize, focus, and delimit the complexity of an individual's situation. Four systems concepts—client system, worker system, target system, and action system—are just such partializing concepts. Although there may be many variables and processes that are on-going in a client's life, the concepts of client, target, worker, and action systems help to specify those people and interactions that are essential to change efforts.

The Client System

The client system is a term that derives from planned change literature[72] and has also become common in social work literature as well.[73] The client system has been variously defined as the beneficiary of service or the individual or group asking for help or engaging the services of the helper.[74] There are weaknesses with both these definitions. The client system may not be the only "beneficiary" of service, and in some cases, even "unwilling targets" may benefit from change efforts. Furthermore, just because you ask for help does not mean that you will receive it. As we shall discuss in our clienthood chapter (Chapter 4), becoming a client is much more than just initiating or asking for help.

As we shall analyze in more detail later, clienthood does not occur until there is a contract or working agreement established between client and worker.[75] The client system is defined by this contractual process. In some cases, the client system is the person or persons who request(s) help, whereas in other situations, a number of contacts with many different individuals may transpire before the identity of the client system emerges. For example, a wife may come to an initial interview and express concerns about her marriage. In the next session the husband might be seen alone, and finally, in a third session both husband and wife might agree to pursue marital counseling with the worker and the couple becomes the client system.

In interpersonal practice the most common client systems are individuals, couples (marital pairs, parent-child dyads), families (parents and children, several generations of a family), or some small groups. (In many cases, we consider the group members, the client system, and the group to be the action system.) Although "client system" is more bulky in usage than is "client," it does reflect the variable size of the unit that contracts with the worker, and we want to emphasize that interpersonal practice is much more than individual casework and involves work with many different-sized client systems.

The Worker System

The worker system consists of the social worker and the employing agency. The worker system is larger than the individual social worker who contracts with the client system. Individual workers are influenced by their employing agency's policies, procedures, and resources, by their fellow workers and supervisors, and by professional ethics and standards of practice. Figure 2-2 represents the components of this system.

A large body of literature in social work points to some of the consequences of these influences on the worker. Organizational routines and procedures may reinforce insensitive, bureaucratic, and detached responses in workers.[76] Sometimes the organizational role that is defined for the client is so dehumanizing and degrading that it is almost absurd to call such organizations "human services."[77] Some writers have pointed out that the role created for clients in our welfare system can at times be characterized by dependency, insecurity, humiliation, intimida-

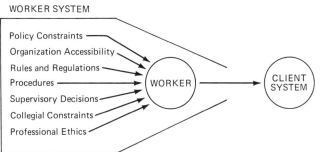

Figure 2-2.
The Worker System

tion, colonialism, and totalitarian control.[78] The role conflicts that workers experience in agencies may seriously affect their performance and may contribute to alienation, anxiety, and "burnout."[79] The influence of the profession both through its code of ethics and standards of practice may act on individual workers to make them less willing to engage in or help clients engage in social change.[80] Although this literature is discouraging and does point out how much change-effort social workers must direct toward their own organizations, it shows the "reality" of interpersonal practice and the network of forces that acts on it.

Our view of the worker system as a complex network of forces has been challenged by those who suggest that "autonomous" practice is possible.[81] Even in private practice, which is held up as a prime example of autonomous practice, the individual worker is not autonomous and is influenced by many forces. A private practitioner must meet licensing and registration requirements as well as those of insurance carriers or third-party vendors, must maintain a referral network, must collaborate with other professionals, and must secure case supervision or consultation. Even if "autonomous" practice were possible, we strongly believe that it is undesirable because a social worker is an integral part of both an agency and professional context that holds the individual practitioner accountable for practice decisions and behavior. Along with this comes the responsibility of individual workers to address and to change the dysfunctions in the worker system.

We have rejected the term "change agent system"[82] from our model because it is both bulky and nonspecific. Social workers are a particular kind of change agent. A social worker cannot agree with helping clients to engage in violent actions (help a client "run

over" his or her oppressive slum lord) nor can a social worker engage in sexual intercourse with clients no matter how intense the clients' needs are to express their sexuality.

In some social work literature, the term "therapist" is used as a substitute for the term "worker." This is an unfortunate trend because "therapist" is a much narrower conception than is the more generic and traditional term of "worker." Social workers may engage in therapy or counseling with clients, but they also may be advocates, brokers, mediators, and evaluators. Our view of the worker system includes the notion that a social worker may engage in many roles when serving clients, and these roles are all given sanction and meaning by the organizational and professional context of social work practice.

The Target System

Target systems are those individuals or groups of individuals that the client and worker system seek to change or influence in order to achieve the client's goals. Although the term "target" has repugnant, militaristic connotations, the concept *target system* has achieved common usage in social work literature.[83] In some cases the target system will be identical to the client system as when a husband and wife contract with a worker to solve their marital problems. In other case situations, the target system is separate from the client system. In an advocacy situation the target system may be a particular decision maker in an organization that withholds resources from a client system. In some cases, the target system may be a part of the worker system when client and worker attempt to change some aspect of the worker's agency that stands in the way of the client's goals.

When target and client systems do not overlap and do represent separate individuals, a question arises as to the ethics or responsibilities the worker has to the individual(s) who are identified as the target system. In some practice situations, the separate target system will be in agreement (issue consensus) with the goals the client and worker systems are pursuing; and the worker and client will have no problems contracting or interacting with it. However, target systems are not always in agreement with such goals. Sometimes they are apathetic about changes sought or more concerned about other issues. Sometimes the target system may be adamantly opposed to the change.[84] What are the worker's responsibilities to a target system that is in disagreement with the client system's goals or change objectives? Can a worker attempt to change someone against his or her will? Does a worker have to be open and relate honestly to the target? Can a worker and client secretly collude to make plans to change or manipulate a target system in ways it may not wish to change.

The NASW Code of Ethics[85] spells out the ethical responsibilities a worker has to the employing organization and to other colleagues and professionals; but the code is also clear that the worker's primary responsibility is to clients. It is ethical as well as reasonable for the worker and client to develop "secret" or "confidential" plans that are not disclosed to the target system. The ethical position of confidentiality and privileged communication between worker and client supports this. A worker may see an adolescent client who wishes to change the parents' position on an issue. Even if the parents (target system) request information about what is going on with their son or daughter, the worker is not obligated to disclose this information without the son's or daughter's consent.

In an advocacy situation, the target system is often more powerful than the client system in that the target system controls resources or can sanction the client in some other way. Obviously, when a target system such as a decision maker in some organization is against the client's and worker's goals, it would be imprudent for the worker and client to be candid about strategies. One way a client and worker have of neutralizing some of the target system's power is the lever of surprise, leaving the target system unprepared to defend itself. It, therefore, is ethical and tactically desirable for the client and worker systems not to be open and honest when planning to influence an unwilling, more powerful, target system. Surprise and stealth are ethically acceptable, but as we have stated before, violent tactics are clearly not ethical and cannot be used as a social work tactic to influence an unwilling target system.[86]

The Action System

The action system involves the notion of social situation. The action system includes all the significant individuals involved in the change effort. It includes the client system, the target system, the worker system, and all other individuals the worker and client may enlist for particular actions, tasks, or objectives to be accomplished.

The action system conception is important to our model because it reinforces a view of social work as "boundary work."[87] The action system in psychotherapy is usually the individual client and therapist interacting in a 50-minute office interview. The action systems in social work are much more complex—especially in working with oppressed clients. Besides the client and worker, the action system is likely to involve decision makers from formal organizations (judges, employers, landlords, probation officers, housing inspectors), other helping professionals (teachers, nurses, psychiatrists, psychologists, etc.), indigenous healers (spiritualists, *curanderos*, palmists, root doctors, chiropractors), self-help groups (Alcoholics Anonymous, Parents Anonymous, etc.), religious and community leaders (ministers, rabbis, priests, tribal councils, bartenders), and relatives and family members of the client system.

Because action systems in social work practice can be so complex, a social worker must not only have skills in relating and contracting with clients, but the worker must also have skills in coordinating, collaborating, monitoring, negotiating, and advocating with other individuals in the action system.[88] An example is the responsibility of a worker in a mental health clinic (see Figure 2-3, The Action System). Consider the amount of effort that is involved in coordinating and collaborating with the various individuals involved in the life of this 15-year-old youth (client system) who is on parole and is placed in a foster home.

In concluding this discussion, we wish to emphasize that each system (client, worker, target, action) must be carefully defined as service progresses. Such delineation is important because these systems constantly change as service unfolds. In the beginning of service, there is no a priori way to be certain what is the "best" or "right" client, target, or action system for a given case. The empirical referents for each of these systems will probably change (and usually do) as the case unfolds.

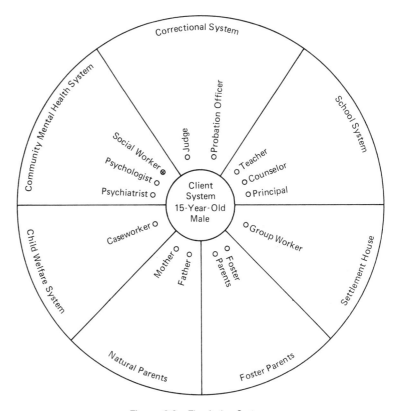

Figure 2-3. The Action System

Change

In this final section of the chapter we present a general, fairly abstract discussion of the concept of "change." We present some general change approaches that are used in social work practice as interpersonal practitioners help clients to solve their social problems.

"Change" as a continuous, natural phenomenon can be conceptualized from a number of perspectives.[89] Some notions of change are dialectical (competing, conflicting forces are synthesized to create innovation); others are evolutionary (incremental, additive shifts in basic structures); and still others are cyclical (there is no such thing as progress—change reflects back-and-forth fluctuations and perturbations in a repetitious cycle).

General theories of change are not as useful to social workers as are particular change principles because social workers are not just "observers" of change. We do not sit on the sidelines and reflect on the human condition; instead we are in the middle of things deliberately trying to influence, shape, and divert the human currents in the society.

Agology[90] is the study of "changers" (people who are in the business of trying to change various parts of the universe) and their change principles. Many fields and professions fall under agology. An engineer trying to design a particular machine, or a surgeon replacing a defective organ, or a social worker trying to influence an administrator all have in common the intention of changing things. The significance of agology is that it focuses on change that is purposive and planned by human beings. Occasionally, a social worker may benefit from an unintended consequence of some action, but for the most part the actions of a social worker are deliberately designed and carried out with a desirable outcome in mind.

Not all change that social workers engage in should be seen as "making something happen" or "creating something new." In some practice situations a social worker may struggle to *maintain* or consolidate changes that have already taken place or to *prevent*, halt, or slow down changes that have begun to occur. For example, a social worker may help a husband, who during past unemployment became violent and abusive to his family, to join a men's support group when faced with a layoff notice.

What then are some of the basic agological principles that social workers employ? A social worker cannot employ any or all agological principles. For example, a basic change mechanism of the moral metaphor is exorcism, driving the evil spirit out of the host. Interpersonal practitioners will not knowingly employ such change technologies!

There are a number of ways of conceptualizing change for social work practice. Concepts of change can be organized around what a social worker is trying to change. When a social worker employs change strategies with individuals as target systems, there are many possible elements that can be altered in this target system. Change strategies may be aimed at behavior, attitudes, expectations, perceptions, aspirations, expressions of affect, skills, decisions, knowledge, or personal metaphors, to name only some. When a social worker employs change technologies with groups or families as target systems, there are also many possible units that can be changed. Social workers employ change strategies to influence the environments of individuals, families, and small groups. There are, in fact, so many different things that a social worker may try to change that any attempt to produce a comprehensive list would be overwhelming and of dubious value.

Change can also be approached not by the object but by *how* change principles are supposed to work, that is, what process or mechanism is involved in the change strategy. There are five basic change principles that social workers employ regularly in practice: social influence, tension increase, tension reduction, informing, and doing. These five agological principles cut across many practice theories and models and are presented here as generalizations about how social workers attempt to change client and target systems.

Social Influence

Even though many social workers view some forms of influence negatively (manipulation, use of authority), many techniques and strategies that social workers employ fall into this category.[91] Social influence concerns the subtle forces that individuals exert on each other whenever they interact. These forces are usually intended to shape another's decisions or actions.

Interpersonal practitioners engage in many kinds of "influence" processes. Persuasion, advice, setting limits, and manipulation are clear examples of influence. In practice a worker may attempt to *persuade* an intake worker to accept a client who does not quite meet all eligibility requirements for service, or that same worker might *advise* clients on how to present themselves during intake so that service will not be denied. Social influence also operates when social workers place individuals in formed groups or work with the family of the individual to produce changes in the individual. Change of organization and community conditions are other examples of this process.

Using formed groups or social networks as influence structures to change individuals may be the most effective way that social workers have of employing influence processes.[92] Research on small groups has demonstrated that group pressures influence individual member's behavior, attitudes, and decisions.[93] The point of this discussion is that social influence is a change mechanism that is available to interpersonal practitioners. It should not be looked down on as "undesirable" but, instead, should be understood and employed effectively.

Tension Increase

It may seem contradictory that social workers employ change mechanisms that deliberately increase the stress that clients and target systems may experience, yet tension increase is a common mechanism. When social workers deliberately use tension increase strategies, they are not doing this out of some sadistic need, nor is tension increase the ultimate aim. Such strategies are purposively employed to produce changes in the client and the target systems that relate to service goals. Tension increase is simply a means to these goals. In fact, tension-increase strategies are viewed as temporary and transient and are employed with the expectation that the tension will be resolved constructively.

When a worker *confronts* a client about his or her behavior or *interprets* a sensitive issue for the client, tensions will be generated. When a worker encourages individual clients to risk themselves in a group or helps a family to focus on a sensitive, secretive issue, tensions will rise. In some practice situations, the worker may employ some reality testing with clients to help the clients to recognize the seriousness of issues. Tension increase strategies may be used to secure someone's attention or even to motivate someone to begin making changes. For example, a worker may threaten or embarrass a decision maker into responding more favorably to a client's request. Even the most unlikely techniques of silence or exploration can generate a great deal of tension in interviews with client and target systems.

The point is that conflict and tension are common in practice and should not necessarily be avoided. They are a "fact of life" in the troubled lives of clients, and the worker cannot expect to help by avoiding conflict. Sometimes the worker and client may be in conflict (for example, in protective service situations), and social workers must not be afraid to generate as well as handle the conflicts and tensions.[94] Interviews with individuals, families, and small groups are not simply pleasant conversations, and the "work" that worker and clients do together may be highly charged emotionally.

Tension Reduction

Tension reduction strategies often go hand in hand with or closely follow tension increase strategies. Tension reduction strategies are deliberately and consciously employed to reduce or decrease the tensions or conflicts that a client or target system may be experiencing. Such strategies are employed when the tension is overwhelming and prevents clients from completing or accomplishing their normal routines. Tensions that are dysfunctional are reduced so that the clients can return to their tasks of living.

We can offer many examples of tension reduction. Social workers themselves may be *supportive* of clients through (1) *reassuring* or *encouraging* or *focusing on strengths,* (2) mobilizing a group or family to be supportive and nurturant of a client, (3) using *logical discussion* or *universalization* to assuage an immobilized client's guilt or anxiety, or (4) encouraging *emotional ventilation* to help release underlying affect. The recognition that a sensitive, trusting, empathic relationship between worker and client is a powerful healing phenomenon has been emphasized for decades as a significant aspect of helping.[95]

Because tension reduction strategies are such a prominent part of the technology of interpersonal practice, social workers have been stereotypically viewed as bleeding hearts or do-gooders. This sometimes misleads entering students who must discover that social work practice is more than just support and nurturance.

Informing

Informing is a "feedback" process. As we shall discuss in more detail in Chapter 3, feedback has a number of theoretical and technical meanings. Informing thus means giving client and target systems information that will increase their awareness or understanding of themselves and their situation, or both. There are two general kinds of informing that workers employ: workers may give information to client and target systems that relate directly to their individual attributes. Brown has termed this kind of informing "ascriptive feedback":

> "Ascription" is the act of attributing or imputing a characteristic to someone. . . . The characteristic ascribed may be any one that the social worker perceives in the client (or target system) and communicates to him. It may refer to physical, psychological, or social attributes of an individual or a group including their relationships. It may have a socially positive or negative meaning and it may refer to past, present or future. The only criterion is that the statement clearly inputs something to the client (or target system) with whom the worker is interacting.[96]

When workers *suggest* to clients that they look upset or angry or confused, they are using ascriptive feedback. When workers *interpret* what clients may have been feeling in some past experience ("that must have been terrifying"), they are employing ascriptive feedback. Many techniques that a worker uses such as *interpretation, clarification,* or *insight promotion* are designed to increase the client's awareness of some aspect (or attribute) of themselves. Workers may help clients join consciousness-raising or self-help groups to increase their awareness of the commonality of their problems. A worker may show family members a videotaped sequence of their interactions to help them understand a problematic communication. A worker may encourage other members of a group to give feedback to an individual about how others perceive his or her behavior, problem, or participation.

The second kind of informing that workers employ concerns feedback about aspects of the client's or target's environment: how others react to the client, the consequences of the target's behavior on others, and so forth. There are many practice technologies that provide clients and targets with feedback about their environment. During an interview a worker may state his or her feeling that relates to what is transpiring. Thus, a worker stated that she was feeling sad about what the client was discussing. A worker may present evidence to an administrator (target system) that a decision to change some aspect of a procedure will have severely negative consequences for some agency clientele. In a group experience, a worker helped a member state her feelings about another member's behavior.

Informing is a common agological principle used by practitioners, and it is central to a number of practice models. There is some controversy in the field about this principle and its importance to change. Some practitioners argue that informing and awareness are fundamental to personal change and must occur if significant change in client and target systems is to occur. Whether understanding and awareness precedes behavior change, or accompanies it, or even follows it it not important to us.[97] All three possibilities are real, and the important point is that in-

forming is a major strategy and one that practitioners regularly employ.

Doing

Doing is the final principle of our agological framework. The basic agological mechanism that underlies "doing" is that, through engaging in actions or participating in activities, client and target systems change.

There are many "doing" technologies that a practitioner may employ. A worker may engage a client in a role-play simulation so that the client can practice a behavior. The worker can play a significant other in the client's life and the client can rehearse a way of interacting. During a marital interview, a worker may help a couple to complete a structured exercise that requires changes in the couple's problematic mode of communication. Workers often assign homework tasks that clients are expected to complete between sessions. One client was expected to complete an application and another to go to a job interview. Workers may plan an activity or game for a treatment group to help individual members deal with problematic behaviors. Another worker engaged a group of children in a cooperative rather than competitive activity (drawing a group mural) so that competitive behaviors in the group were reduced. A third worker suggested to an administrator that a new procedure be used on a trial basis before final approval or rejection as a way of changing organizational behavior.

The importance of "doing" as a change principle is that it allows the client or target system to practice a piece of behavior and, in some cases, to modify it. "Doing" also can have a rippling effect on other areas of the client's life. Once a client acts on desired changes, other forms of inertia are affected and may melt away. "Doing," therefore, may increase an individual's sense of confidence, self-esteem, and empowerment and thus help him or her to pursue other changes.

Summary

This chapter has presented some of the major dimensions of our model of practice, dimensions that throughout this book we will utilize and expand upon. These include the ideas that practice occurs in phases and is primarily of a short-term nature. We indicated that the goals, and means to achieve goals, of social work practice are thought about through one or more of three "metaphors": moral, disease, and nature. While we lean toward the use of the nature metaphor, we recognize the necessity of incorporating the disease metaphor despite the paradoxes and contradictions that this may sometimes produce. We also pointed out that an understanding of all three metaphors will help the worker to clarify some of the communication problems and other conflicts that arise not only in conferences with members of other professions but also in interactions among social workers.

We proceeded to discuss the concept of systems because of its emergence as one of the most important notions in social work to-day as well as its centrality to our own model. We recognized the limitations of systems concepts and, therefore have repeatedly stated that we do not consider this to be a "systems" text but rather an eclectic one that makes extensive but not exclusive use of systems concepts. We discussed the concept of boundaries and developed this idea further in a definition of client, action, worker, and target systems.

The final section of the chapter presented our idea of change, inasmuch as this book is basically one about the change efforts of interpersonal practitioners. We indicated that the changes brought about by social workers can be classified as occurring through social influence, tension increase, tension reduction, informing, and doing. These processes were described at a higher level of abstraction than can be immediately employed in practice. The rest of this book is devoted to a detailed explication of these terms so that they can be effectively employed by workers. The next chapter initiates this task by describing the beginning phases of work as client systems are created, worker systems are defined, and the boundaries of the problem are identified.

NOTES

1. See, for example, Francis J. Turner, ed., *Social Work Treatment: Interlocking Theoretical Approaches* (New York: The Free Press, 1974); Robert Roberts and Robert Nee, eds., *Theories of Social Casework* (Chicago: University of Chicago Press, 1970); and Robert Roberts and Helen Northen, eds., *Theories of Social Work with Groups* (New York: Columbia University Press, 1976).

2. Joel Fisher, *Effective Casework Practice: An Eclectic Approach* (New York: McGraw-Hill, 1978).

3. C. R. Beagle, "Social Service Supports Cardiac Patients," *Hospitals,* 48 (1974), pp. 135–136: 140–141.

4. Florence Hollis, *Casework: A Psychosocial Therapy* (New York: Random House, 1964).

5. Ruth E. Smalley, *Theory for Social Work Practice* (New York: Columbia University Press, 1967).

6. Paul Glasser, Rosemary Sarri, and Robert Vinter, *Individual Change Through Small Groups* (New York: The Free Press, 1974).

7. Group work literature has been more cognizant of the issue of phases than of casework and family treatment. See, for example, James K. Whittaker, "Models of Group Development: Implications for Social Group Work Practice," *Social Service Review,* September 1970, pp. 308–322, and Robert Bales and Fred Strodbeck, "Phases of Group Problem Solving," in Dorwin Cartwright and Alvin Zander, eds., *Group Dynamics: Research and Theory* (New York: Harper & Row, 1968), pp. 389–398.

8. For an excellent review and discussion of client expectations of service, see Anthony Maluccio, *Learning from Clients: Interpersonal Helping as Viewed by Clients and Social Workers* (New York: The Free Press, 1979).

9. Sol L. Garfield, *Psychotherapy: An Eclectic Approach* (New York: John Wiley, 1980), pp. 43–52, and Sol L. Garfield, "Research on Client Variables in Psychotherapy," in Sol L. Garfield and A. E. Bergin, eds., *Handbook of Psychotherapy and Behavior Change: An Empirical Analysis*, 2nd ed. (New York: John Wiley, 1978), pp. 195–197.

10. Ibid.

11. Ibid.

12. Theodore J. Stein, *Social Work Practice in Child Welfare* (Englewood Cliffs, N.J.: Prentice-Hall, 1981).

13. Bernard L. Bloom, "Focused Single-Session Therapy: Initial Development and Evaluation," in Simon H. Budman, ed., *Forms of Brief Therapy* (New York: Guilford Press, 1981), pp. 167–216.

14. R. MacGregor, A. M. Ritchie, A. C. Serrano, and F. P. Schuster, *Multiple Impact Therapy with Families* (New York: McGraw-Hill, 1964).

15. James Mann, *Time Limited Psychotherapy* (Cambridge, Mass.: Harvard University Press, 1973).

16. Anthony N. Maluccio, "Action as a Tool in Casework Practice," *Social Casework*, Vol. 55 (January 1975), pp. 30–35, and William J. Reid, *The Task-Centered System* (New York: Columbia University Press, 1978).

17. Anthony N. Maluccio, "Promoting Competence Through Life Experiences," in Carel Germain, ed., *Social Work Practice: People and Environments* (New York: Columbia University Press, 1979), pp. 282–302.

18. Betty Overall and H. Aronson, "Expectations of Psychotherapy in Patients of Lower Socioeconomic Class," *American Journal of Orthopsychiatry*, Vol. 33 (April 1963), pp. 421–430; H. Aronson and Betty Overall, "Treatment Expectations of Patients in Two Social Classes," *Social Work*, Vol. 11 (January 1966), pp. 35–41; Phyllis R. Silverman, "The Client Who Drops Out: A Study of Spoiled Helping Relationships," unpublished doctoral dissertation, Brandeis University, 1969; Phyllis R. Silverman, "A Reexamination of the Intake Procedure," *Social Casework*, Vol. 51 (December 1970), pp. 625–634; and John E. Mayer and Noel Timms, "Clash in Perspective Between Worker and Client," *Social Casework*, Vol. 50 (January 1969), pp. 32–40.

19. Ibid.

20. The term "metaphor" is gaining popularity in clinical practice to describe the healing power that certain kinds of symbolic communications have in therapeutic practice: see, for example, Sheldon Kopp, *Guru: Metaphors from a Psychotherapist* (Palo Alto, Calif.: Science and Behavior Books, 1971); Jay Haley, *Uncommon Therapy: The Psychiatric Techniques of Milton Erickson* (New York: W. W. Norton, 1973); and Paul Watzlawick, *The Language of Change: Elements of Therapeutic Communication* (New York: Basic Books, 1978). In this text, the term "metaphor" is used in a slightly different (though related) manner, and the meaning employed here is philosophical and psycholinguistic. See Max Black, *Models and Metaphors: Studies in Language and Philosophy* (Ithaca, N.Y.: Cornell University Press, 1962).

21. Such a discussion can be found in Carel Germain, "Casework and Science; An Historical Encounter," in Robert Roberts and Robert Nee, eds., *Theories of Social Casework* (Chicago: University of Chicago Press, 1970), and Walter L. Miller, "Casework and the Medical Metaphor," *Social Work*, Vol. 25 (July 1980), pp. 281–285.

22. For a discussion of these issues, see Blanche D. Coll, *Perspectives in Public Welfare: A History* (Washington, D. C.: Government Printing Office, 1969), and Samuel Mencher, *Poor Law to Poverty Program* (Pittsburgh: University of Pittsburgh Press, 1967).

23. Ibid.

24. Ibid.

25. Roy Lubove, *The Professional Altruist* (New York: Atheneum, 1960).

26. Coll, *Perspectives*.

27. Robert W. White, *The Abnormal Personality* (New York: The Ronald Press, 1956), pp. 7–24.

28. Ibid.

29. *Report of the National Advisory Commission on Civil Disorders* (New York: Bantam Books, 1968).

30. Hollis, *Casework*.

31. Glasser, Sarri, and Vinter, *Individual Change Through Small Groups*.

32. *Diagnostic and Statistical Manual of Mental Disorders*, 3rd ed. (Washington, D.C.: American Psychiatric Association, 1980).

33. Richard Grinnell, "Environmental Modification: Casework's Concern or Casework's Neglect?"*Social Service Review*, Vol. 47 (June 1973), pp. 208–220.

34. Germain, "Casework."

35. Carel Germain and Alex Gitterman, *The Life Model of Social Work Practice* (New York: Columbia University Press, 1980).

36. Naomi Golan, *Treatment in Crisis Situations* (New York: The Free Press, 1978), and Howard Parad, ed., *Crisis Intervention: Selected Readings* (New York: Family Service Associations of America, 1965).

37. Richard Cloward and Lloyd Ohlin, *Delinquency and Opportunity* (Glencoe, Ill.: The Free Press, 1960).

38. Gordon Hearn, *Theory Building in Social Work* (Toronto: University of Toronto Press, 1958).

39. Werner Lutz, *Concepts and Principles Underlying Social Work Practice*, *Social Work Practice in Medical and Rehabilitation Settings*, Monograph 3 (New York: NASW, 1958).

40. Herman D. Stein and Richard A. Cloward, *Social Perspectives on Behavior* (New York: The Free Press, 1958).

41. Irma Stein, *Systems Theory, Science, and Social Work* (Metuchen, N.J.: Scarecrow Press, 1974), pp. 1–27.

42. Ervin Laszlo, *The Systems View of the World* (New York: George Braziller, 1972), and Ervin Laszlo, *The Relevance of General Systems Theory* (New York: George Braziller, 1972).

43. Ludwig von Bertalanffy, *General Systems Theory: Foundations, Development, Applications* (New York: George Braziller, 1968), and Ludwig von Bertalanffy, *Robots, Men, and Minds: Psychology in the Modern World* (New York: George Braziller, 1967).

44. Walter Buckley, ed., *Modern Systems Research for the Behavioral Scientist* (Chicago: Aldine, 1968), and Walter Buckley, *Sociology and Modern Systems Theory* (Englewood Cliffs, N.J.: Prentice-Hall, 1967).

45. D. Katz and R. L. Kahn, *The Social Psychology of Organizations* (New York: John Wiley, 1966).

46. Kenneth Boulding, "Economics and General Systems," in Ervin Laszlo, ed., *The Relevance of General Systems Theory* (New York: George Braziller, 1972), pp. 77–92.

47. James Miller, "Living Systems: Basic Concepts, Structure and Process: Cross Level Hypotheses," *Behavioral Science*, Vol. 10 (1965), pp. 193–237, 337–379, 380–411, and James Miller, "The Nature of Living Systems," *Behavioral Science*, Vol. 16 (1971), pp. 277–301.

48. Ann Hartman, "To Think About the Unthinkable," *Social Casework*, Vol. 51 (October 1971), pp. 467–474; Gordon Hearn, ed., *The General Systems Approach: Contributions Toward an Holistic Conception of Social Work* (New York: Council on Social Work Education, 1969); Sister Mary Paul Janchill, "Systems Concepts in Casework Theory and Practice,"*Social Casework*, Vol. 50 (February 1969), pp. 71–82; and Irma Stein, *Systems Theory, Science and Social Work* (Metuchen, N.J.: Scarecrow Press, 1974).

49. Gordon Hearn, "The General Systems Approach to the Understanding of Groups," *Health Education Monographs*, No. 14, New York: Society of Public Health Educators, 1962.

50. Ann Hartman, "Diagramatic Assessment of Family Relationships,"*Social Casework*, Vol. 59 (October 1978), pp. 465–476.

51. Howard Goldstein, *Social Work Practice: A Unitary Approach* (Columbia: University of South Carolina Press, 1973), and Allen Pincus and Anne Minahan, *Social Work Practice: Model and Method* (Itasca, Ill.: F. E. Peacock, 1973).

52. See, for example, Goldstein, *Social Work Practice*.

53. See O. R. Young, "A Survey of General Systems Theory," *General Systems*, Vol. 9 (1964), pp. 61–80, and A. D. Hall and R. E. Fagan, "The Definition of a System," in *Modern Systems Research for the Behavioral Scientist*, pp. 81–92.

54. von Bertalanffy, *General Systems Theory*.

55. Robert Dubin, *Theory Building* (New York: The Free Press, 1969), p. 9.

56. Buckley, *Sociology*, pp. 8–41.

57. Arthur Koestler and J. R. Smythies, eds., *Beyond Reductionism: New Perspectives in the Life Sciences* (New York: Macmillan, 1970).

58. Miller, "The Nature of Living Systems," pp. 285.

59. This perspective was expressed by Carl Sagan in his television series *Cosmos*.

60. Ross Speck and Carolyn Attneave, *Family Networks* (New York: Pantheon, 1973).

61. Dubin, *Theory Building*, 127–128.

62. Hope Leichter and William Mitchell, *Kinship and Casework* (New York: Russell Sage Foundation, 1967).

63. Miller, "The Nature of Living Systems,' pp. 295–296.

64. Max Siporin, "Situational Assessment and Intervention,"*Social Casework*, Vol. 53 (February 1972), pp. 92–109.

65. Ibid., p. 94.

66. Scott Briar and Henry Miller, *Problems and Issues in Social Casework* (New York: Columbia University Press, 1971), pp. 106–118; Carel Germain, "Social Study: Past and Future,"*Social Casework*, Vol. 49 (July 1968), pp. 406–409; Goldstein, *Social Work Practice*, pp. 105–119, and Carol Meyer, *Social Work Practice: A Response to the Urban Crisis* (New York: The Free Press, 1970), pp. 115–137.

67. Germain, "Social Study," pp. 407–409; Goldstein, *Social Work Practice*, pp. 118–119; and Meyer, *Social Work Practice*, p. 124.

68. Goldstein, *Social Work Practice*, pp. 105–119; Meyer, *Social Work Practice*, pp. 129–137; Lynn Hoffman and Lorence Long, "A Systems Dilemma," *Family Process*, Vol. 8 (September 1969), pp. 211–234; and Ben Orcutt, "Casework Intervention and the Problems of the Poor," *Social Casework*, Vol. 54 (February 1973), pp. 85–95.

69. Hall and Fagan, "The Definition of a System," p. 84.

70. Ibid., pp. 83–84, and Miller, "The Nature of Living Systems," p. 285.

71. Person-in-situation configuration has been stressed in early casework literature. See Gordon Hamilton, *Theory and Practice of Social Casework*, 2nd ed. (New York: Columbia University Press, 1951).

72. Ronald Lippitt, Jeanne Westley, and Bruce Westley, *The Dynamics of Planned Change: A Comparative Study of Principles and Techniques* (New York: Harcourt, 1958).

73. Pincus and Minahan, *Social Work Practice*, and Goldstein, *Social Work Practice*.

74. Lippitt, et al., *The Dynamics of Planned Change*, p. 12, and Pincus and Minahan, *Social Work Practice*, p. 56.

75. We are in agreement with Pincus and Minahan, ibid., here.

76. Andrew Billingsley, "Bureaucratic and Professional Orientation Patterns in Social Casework, *Social Service Review*, Vol. 38 (December 1964), pp. 400–407, and Peter Blau, "Orientations Towards Clients in Public Welfare Agency," *Administrative Science Quarterly*, Vol. 5 (1960), pp. 342–346.

77. Irving Goffman, *Asylums: Essays on the Social Situation of Mental Patients and Other Inmates* (Garden City, N.Y.: Doubleday, 1961); Alfred Stanton and Morris Schwartz, *The Mental Hospital: A Study of Institutional Participation in Psychiatric Illness and Treatment* (New York: Basic Books, 1954); Eliot Studt, "Fields of Social Work Practice: Organizing Our Resources for More Effective Practice, *Social Work*, Vol. 10 (October 1965), pp. 156–165; and David Wineman, "Captors, Captives, and Social Workers in a Civil Society," unpublished position paper at Wayne State University, School of Social Work, February 26, 1968.

78. Scott Briar, "Welfare from Below: Recipients' View of the Public Welfare System," *California Law Review*, Vol. 54 (1966), pp. 370–385; Martin Eisman, "Social Work's New Role in the Welfare Class Revolution," *Social Work*, Vol. 14 (April 1969), p. 81; Betty Mandel, "Welfare and Totalitarianism," *Social Work*, Vol. 16 (January 1971), pp. 17–26; and Henry Miller, "Social Work in the Black Ghetto: The New Colonialism, *Social Work*, Vol. 14 (July 1969), pp. 65–76.

79. Michael Aiken and Jerald Hage, "Organizational Alienation: A Comparative Analysis," *American Sociological Review*, Vol. 31 (August 1966), pp. 497–507; A. D. Green, "The Professional Social Worker in the Bureaucracy,"*Social Service Review*, Vol. 40 (March 1966), pp. 71–83; and Harry Wasserman, "The Professional Social Worker in a Bureaucracy," *Social Work*, Vol. 16 (January 1971), pp. 89–95.

80. Irwin Epstein, "Social Workers and Social Action: Attitudes Towards Social Action," *Social Work*, Vol. 13 (April 1968), pp. 101–108.

81. Laura Epstein, "Is Autonomous Practice Possible?" *Social Work*, Vol. 18 (March 1973), pp. 5–12; Virginia Franks, *The Autonomous Social Worker* (Madison: University of Wisconsin School of Social Work, 1967).

82. Pincus and Minahan, *Social Work Practice*, pp. 54–56.

83. Ibid., pp. 58–61.

84. Herman Resnick and Rino Patti, "Changing the Organization from Within," *Social Work*, Vol. 17 (July 1972), pp. 48–57.

85. NASW Code of Ethics.

86. Harry Specht, "Disruptive Tactics," *Social Work*, Vol. 14 (April 1969), pp. 5–15.

87. Gordon Hearn, "General Systems Theory and Social Work, in Francis Turner, ed., *Social Work Treatment* (New York: The Free Press, 1974), pp. 364–366.

88. William Reid and Laura Epstein, *Task-Centered Casework* (New York: Columbia University Press, 1972), p. 141; Brett A. Seabury, "Boundary Work: The Casemanager's Role," paper presented at the NASW Clinical Practice Conference, Washington D.C., November 21, 1982.

89. Kenneth Boulding, *A Primer on Social Dynamics: History as Dialectics and Development* (New York: The Free Press, 1970).

90. Harold Lewis, "Agology, Animation, Conscientization: Implications for Social Work Education in the U.S.A.," *Journal of Education for Social Work*, Vol. 9 (Fall 1973), pp. 31–38.

91. Nina Toren, "The Structure of Social Casework and Behavioral Change," *Journal of Social Policy*, Vol. 3 (1973), pp. 341–352, and Hiasura Rubenstein and Mary Bloch, *Things That Matter: Influences on Helping Relationships* (New York: Macmillan, 1982).

92. Toren, "The Structure of Social Casework."

93. Dorwin Cartwright and Alvin Zander, eds., *Group Dynamics: Research and Theory* (New York: Harper & Row, 1968), and Ken Heap, *Group Theory for Social Workers: An Introduction* (Oxford: Pergamon Press, 1977), pp. 43–76.

94. Brett A. Seabury, "Negotiating Sound Contracts with Clients," *Public Welfare*, Vol. 37 (Spring 1979), pp. 33–38.

95. Felix Biestek, *The Casework Relationship* (Chicago: Loyola University Press, 1957); Helen Harris Perlman, *Relationship: the Heart of Helping People* (Chicago: University of Chicago Press, 1979); and J. Fischer, *Effective Casework Practice* (New York: McGraw-Hill, 1977), pp. 189–219.

96. Robert A. Brown, "Feedback in Family Interviewing," *Social Work*, Vol. 18 (September 1973), p. 53 (parentheses added).

97. Robert D. Carter and Richard B. Stuart, "Behavior Modification Theory and Practice: A Reply," *Social Work*, Vol. 15 (January 1970), pp. 37–50.

three
Communication

Human communication is complex and ubiquitous, and practitioners should understand this in order to initiate relationships with clients and intervene with them successfully. Some of the problems that clients also have are often caused or exacerbated by communication problems. All social work interventions require considerable skill in communication processes to facilitate change. Knowledge of communication processes is also useful for the worker in collaborative and adversarial relationships with colleagues, resources, people, and social agencies.

This chapter will present concepts about human communication that can help the interpersonal practitioner understand the complex communication processes that emerge in practice. Basic assumptions and concepts will be presented and operationalized through a discussion of communication problems. This chapter also describes communication strategies designed to resolve such problems. The communication issues that arise in multiperson systems (families and small groups) will also be considered.

Assumptions About Communication

Central to Life

Communication processes play a central role in the survival of organisms. From a general systems perspective, open systems engage in two fundamental exchange processes with their environments: one concerns information and the other concerns matter and energy.[1] For human systems to develop and survive, they must exchange various forms of matter and energy with the environment (e.g., air, food, water, warmth). Growth and survival are also dependent on receiving and releasing various forms of information. Some information processes are internal to human systems such as the discomfort that warns of physical disability or the flush of emotion that accompanies a fantasy or memory. Some information processes involve external exchange processes between human systems and their environment. In our modern complex society, an individual often has to process several external messages simultaneously. For example, a person driving a car responds to a red light by braking the car while continuing to argue with a passenger about the folly of increasing military spending.

Human biological functioning and development require information processing. The brain and nervous system must constantly instruct, monitor, and react to various bodily functions through a variety of chemical and electrical signal systems. The development of life forms themselves would not be possible without the unfolding of information stored in genetic codes. But human beings are not only biological systems; they are also social-psychological systems. Why are solitary confinement and the silent treatment perceived as severe forms of punishments? Why is bonding so important to infant development and social support so essential to the terminally ill? Communication processes are as critical to our social psychological well-being as to our biological well-being.

Learned and Innate

Human communication is both learned and innate.[2] Language behavior, as well as the nonverbal behaviors that accompany speech (such as gesture,[3] posture,[4] and spatial behavior[5]), is culturally determined. For example, a black youth raised in an urban ghetto will learn to speak black English, with its derived Africanisms,[6] as well as how to move (e.g., profile, jiving, 'shucking')[7] when making utterances. To a white youth raised in the suburbs, the black youth's utterances and behaviors may appear strange, and vice versa.

On the other hand, the physical apparatuses of human communication are biologically determined. Vocal cords can produce only a limited range of sounds, volume, pitch, timbre, and so on, and ears and eyes can only discriminate a narrow range of sounds and sights. Not only has form evolved but so has function.[8] For example, facial expressions such as surprise, fear, anger, happiness, sadness, and disgust have universal configurations that are common to all human beings expressing these affects.[9] Ethologists also argue that many communicative behaviors in humans have evolved from fight-flight patterns evident in animals.[10]

In spite of the commonality and universality of some communicational patterns, the diversity that is created by cultural factors is what makes human communication so rich and complex. Because social workers interact with clients from many different ethnic and subcultural backgrounds, it is important for practitioners to recognize how cultural factors influence human communication. It is even more critical that practitioners avoid an ethnocentric perspective that views differences in communication patterns from the worker as "abnormal" or "dysfunctional." There is no ideal, modal, or normal communication pattern in practice, and the social worker should learn to adapt and respond to the array of patterns that multiethnic practice may bring.

Verbal and Nonverbal—A Multichannel Process

Although words and language are important, human communication does not refer to words only.[11] Birdwhistell[12] estimates that only about one-third of the meaning of human communication is carried by words, and Mehrabian[13] estimates the verbal impact at about 7 percent. Many researchers of human communication agree that to focus only on the words of an encounter is to miss most of it.[14] Human communication is much more than just "exchanging words," and social workers should be attuned to more than language.

Because there is a tendency to reduce

human communication to words, there is a concomitant tendency to reduce communication to speech and hearing as though it were essentially an aural-auditory exchange. The aural-auditory channel carries a great variety of information. Not only are words transmitted through this channel, but so too are variations in volume, pitch, timbre, rate of speech, rhythm, and enunciation.[15]

The aural-auditory channel is not the only channel that humans use to communicate. There is also a kinesthetic-visual channel, an odor-producing olefactory channel, a gustatory channel, and a contact-tactual channel. In fact audition may not be as important a sense to the human organism as sight and touch. Audition stores only about half the information that is received.[16] Neurologically the eyes account for about two-thirds of all electrical inputs that enter the brain,[17] and most of an individual's environment seems to be experienced through the eyes and skin[18]—not the ears. Human communication is not a simple one-channel process but is a highly complex multichannel affair that involves all senses simultaneously.

A multichannel perspective of human communication should have an impact on how a social worker assesses and intervenes with various clients. Empathetic understanding not only emerges from *listening* carefully to what and how the client vocalizes but also by *observing, smelling,* and sometimes *feeling* (tactually) the client. By observing the clothes, grooming, posture, gestures, facial expression, a worker can gather a great deal of information that a client presents. Odors are usually ignored by individuals in our culture as it is a taboo to pay attention to (or worse to bring attention to them), yet smells are an important element of human exchange. From the cosmetic odors of deodorants and perfumes to the body odors of sweat, disease, and incontinence come a wide range of signals. What social worker has not been impressed by the range of odors that crash in on the senses when making home visits—the smells of food and seasoning from cooking, the smell of rotting garbage and filth, or the stench of urine in a dark hallway.

Touch, too, is an important communication channel. Watching a marital couple or a parent and child interacting tactually is an important source of information about these relationships. Social workers intervene tactually when they use touch to comfort or reassure, to share expressions of joy with a hug, or even to contain and subdue an aggressive child until control is regained.

Because human communication is nonverbal as well as verbal and involves all sense channels, it is continuous. While verbal communication is emergent, discontinuous, and arbitrary, nonverbal communication is analogic and continuous.[19] Human communication involves much more than words; thus, one cannot stop communicating by halting speech. "Although an individual can stop talking, he cannot stop communicating through body idiom; he must say either the right or wrong thing."[20] Only by leaving the presence of another can one stop communicating; and even the act of leaving communicates.

Importance of Context

Human communication cannot be understood without an understanding of the context (both physical and sociocultural— in which the encounter occurs.[21] Research has shown that the physical space that surrounds an encounter has a major impact on that encounter.[22] Some spatial arrangements and distances tend to promote interaction (sociopetal), and some tend to discourage interaction (sociofugal).[23] Aesthetics and architectural design,[24] temperature,[25] and lighting[26] also affect human interaction.

Much of the social meaning of an encounter depends on the setting—where and between whom the communication occurs. It is not enough to be able to recognize all the various verbal and nonverbal signals that are sent between interactants to understand what is happening. One must also recognize that the role relationship of the interactants (worker-client, doctor-patient) and the setting of the encounter (home or office visit) have important consequences for the communication process. "The recognition that communicational behavior can be congruent in one setting and incongruent in another should serve as a warning against any theory of meaning which suggests that particles carry meaning in and of themselves.[27] The act of drinking from a water fountain may seem like a mundane, trivial act, yet it served as a powerful climax to the film *Autobiography of Miss Jane Pittman* because of the social context of this act (a violent, segregated South).

Transactional Exchange

Human communication is a circular, transactional process in which feedback principles are important. Each interactant in the communication process is simultaneously both a sender and a receiver of messages, constantly adapting to the flow of information.[28] A crucial aspect of communication is the"perception of perception"—the recognition that each participant is perceived by the other.[29] Communication begins between two people when a feedback loop beteen them has been established.

A simple example illustrates the importance of feedback in human communication:

While on a first date, a young man places his arm around his date. On the surface this appears as a simple example of tactual commu-

nication when the young man initiates intimacy. This simple gesture, however, involves a whole network of messages sent back and forth tactually between the couple. Not only is the young man's gesture an overture, but it is also a reception of how that overture is received. Whether his date stiffens, pulls away, relaxes, or cuddles will be sensed by his arm, and the sense he gathers will in turn determine how closely, stiffly, firmly he holds her or whether he lets her go.

The whole process is a series of moves and countermoves that lead from one change to another. As this example illustrates, "without the participants being necessarily aware of it, human beings are constantly engaged in adjustments to the presence and activities of other human beings.[30]

A Functional Perspective

To understand human communication and its importance in practice, social workers should approach it from both a "functional" and a "transactional" perspective. A functional perspective addresses such questions as

- Why does an individual communicate?
- What purposes does the communication serve for the individual?

There are numerous answers to these questions, and these can be summarized in four general ways. Human communication functions to *inform, deceive, express,* and *influence,* and although all these functions are interrelated, it is useful to view them separately. Each has implications for social work practice, and all have received considerable attention in social science as well as in practice literature.

Informing

The most apparent function of human communication is that of informing. Human beings engage in communication to inform, share information, and convey knowledge. This function of human communication has been aptly described as the "transfer of meaning."[31] Although informing is an important function of human communication, it has been overemphasized. For example, there are numerous institutes, symposia, lectures, workshops, and self-help books that bombard the public with the promise of improving one's ability to write and speak more clearly, honestly, and assertively. In many of these events, there is a naïve assumption that interpersonal problems can be reduced to communicational problems. This is an overly simplistic conception because to inform someone with clarity and precision may produce more conflict than to do the same ambiguously or vaguely.

The informing function of human communication is related primarily to language usage. Individuals who have mastery of a language have a wide range of symbols that can be used to convey subtleties of experience. Bilingual and multilingual individuals have an enlarged capacity to inform others through multiple symbol systems (languages).

The implications for practice are important. If one does not understand another's language, the capacity to inform and understand the experiences of another are severely limited. To cope with this reality in multiethnic communities, some agencies have organized their workers into bilingual teams of workers (e.g., Chinese American, Hispanic American) so that services can reach the diverse, ethnic groups within their area.[32]

Workers inform clients with regard to many different topics: how to receive services, perform tasks in a competent manner, behave more assertively, and communicate more effectively.

Deceiving

Closely related to the informing function is that of deceiving. The line between informing and deceiving may be so slight that in practice the two often accompany each other. With some forms of deceit the speaker is not aware of the deception. For example, individuals with organic brain syndrome may make up information about their experiences and not realize that this distorts their communications. In other kinds of deception, speakers are aware of their deceit and have deliberate control of the distortions of their messages.

A common form of deception in human communication is that of *hyperbole*. With hyperbole the individual enhances the message by exaggerating or spicing up the events presented. This form of "harmless deceit" is designed to make the message more exciting, humorous, or profound and may actually help to maintain the listener's attention. Rather than actually changing the main events being conveyed, this tends to emphasize the content.

Another form of deception is that of understatement. This is more misleading than hyperbole because the speaker deliberately leaves out parts of the experience so that an incomplete picture is conveyed. The listener then draws imperfect conclusions from the data. This form of deception is employed when the speaker wants to influence the listener to reach a particular decision. Some communicators (such as politicians) are so successful with this form of deception that they are able to turn the most unpleasant experience into a success. For example, President Reagan and his aides emphasize the "cost-cutting benefits" of budget cuts rather than the devastation that these cuts may have on the people who depend on such programs. Social workers who advocate for clients may resort to this kind of deception by emphasizing clients' strengths and achievements rather than their weaknesses.

The most blatant form of deception is the lie. The lie is deliberately designed to alter most or all of the experience conveyed in the message. The simplest lie is a denial; more elaborate lies may involve lengthy statements. This form of deception is often employed when a person tries to avoid responsibility for some action or experience. The original experience may be too painful or the conseqences too hard to bear. For example, parents who abuse their children frequently deny their abusive behavior. In fact, it is senseless for social workers to attempt to get parents to "confess"—especially in the beginning of service. A more productive approach is to work on problems that the parents acknowledge.

On the surface, deceit appears to be an undesirable form of human communication, and a skilled worker, whenever possible, should labor to eliminate this kind of communication. Hidden agendas, family secrets, and gross lying can be detrimental to human relations; however, it is overly simplistic and idealistic to assume that all forms of deception are dysfunctional. Some forms of deceitful communication serve desirable and even admirable social purposes.[33] For example, party platforms are deliberately written to be ambiguous so that as large a consensus as possible can be mobilized.

Deception is not always negative. Deceit may or may not be socially desirable, and that depends on the situation in which deception occurs. In fact, one way of viewing deceit is to realize that it may represent one of humankind's highest intellectual capacities. A person's ability to use symbols either to inform or deceive demonstrates the power that individuals can exert on the environment. This point can be illustrated by comparing human communication with some forms of animal communication. When a honey bee returns to the hive after discovering an area with flowers, the bee engages in a communicative dance that tells the other bees the location of the flowers.[34] It never occurs to the bee to send the hive on a "wild goose chase" by deliberately doing the wrong movements in the communicative dance.

Two practical issues related to social work practice are relevant here: one relates to those situations in which the worker uses deceit; the other is the worker's approach to the deceitful communications of others.

Using deceit in the way we have defined it, workers will use exaggeration or understatement with clients to draw attention to particular content:

Example

A worker in a family session strongly praised a thoughtful comment of a child who had been labeled by all other family members as inconsiderate. This began the change process with reference to the role of that child in the family.

A more complex use of deceit is involved in the use of what has come to be called *paradoxical communication*. In such acts, the worker suggests a behavior that is either ambiguously or differently stated from the presumed intent of the worker. The potency of such acts have, in fact, been thoroughly demonstrated.[35] This technique must be planned so that it does not appear to be either a naïve use of so-called "negative psychology" or a careless and even hostile act:

Example

A worker suggested to a husband who refused to do any household chores that he should continue in this pattern since it allowed his wife to take care of him. The husband began to perform these activities, possibly because he did not find such caring appropriate or because of a negative reaction to the worker.

We shall discuss this technique again in a later chapter when we consider changes in family conditions.

It is also likely that the worker will seek to change deceitful communication patterns occurring in client or action systems. When clients deceive workers, workers sometimes make the point that they accept the clients' statements as the truth insofar as the clients understand it. If clients choose to deceive workers, this can only hinder the clients' problem solving. When clients deceive one another, as in family and group situations, this can be subtly confronted through asking the individual concerned to reconsider a position or more directly confronted through a clear statement of disbelief.

Social workers should be aware of forms of deceit and should understand the purposes that deceit serves in a given interaction. In some situations deception should be questioned; in others it should be left unchallenged.

Influencing

Besides informing and, its antithesis, deceiving, another function of human communication is influence. This aspect is emphasized in two bodies of literature and research. (1) The early research of Gregory Bateson, Don Jackson, and Jay Haley on double-bind communication (the basis of paradoxical communication) and the function of metacommunication in family relationships[36] has generated a large therapeutic literature.[37] It emphasizes control and influence in human interaction. (2) At about the same time, Eric Berne developed transactional analysis as a way of understanding the "games people play" with each other when interacting.[38] Both these bodies of literature conceptualize human communication as an influence process in which actors jockey for control in a relationship or attempt to shape the thoughts and actions of others. The danger of these perspectives is that they overdramatize the influence function of human communication and portray human beings as manipulative game players who communicate to maximize personal gain or reduce social threat.

It is beyond our purpose to review all the concepts in these two bodies of literature, but selected ones are important and deserve mention. Human communication can be used by interactants to define their relationship as either egalitarian or hierarchical.[39] A "symmetrical" relationship is one between equals, such as friends and peers, whereas "complementary" relationships include ones in which an interactant has power over another such as parent over a child or teacher over a student.[40]

Individuals may move in and out of these positions as interaction progresses. For example, the worker-client relationship may be complementary with the worker up (in a power position) and the client down (in a dependent position), yet this is certainly not always the case. At some times the worker and client will have parity in decision making, and both will be expected to participate as equals (symmetry). At other times a client may be one up on the worker, as when the client refuses to follow through on a given plan.

There is nothing inherently good or bad about complementary or symmetrical relationships. Both commonly appear in human interaction. What is important about these concepts is that they are useful in identifying interpersonal problems that arise as relationships develop. Some clients may feel uncomfortable in a symmetrical relationship with their worker. Such clients may feel most comfortable when the worker's authority and decision making prevails in service. When a worker attempts to contract with a client and asks what the client wants, this may touch off a struggle as the client tries to avoid the position of either being up on or in parity with the worker. In other situations, clients may be so threatened or angered by the worker's institutional authority that they may push unrealistically for symmetry or even attempt to be one up on the worker. This latter situation is common with adolescents who often enter service with a chip on their shoulder and a strong need to control the relationship.

These kinds of power and control issues arise in practice with individuals, families, and small groups, and it is important for social workers to be able to recognize them when they arise and to be flexible in their own approach to clients. Social work students sometimes find it easier to be symmetrical with clients and much harder to handle authority and be "one up" on clients even when that is appropriate. On the other hand, some senior practitioners may be so accustomed to being "one up" that they have trouble moving into symmetry with clients or students.

Workers who seek to use communications to increase their influence can do so by referring to their expertise, by being directive, by using rewards, and by reasoning logically, to name a few techniques. A decrease in influence can be secured by refusing to offer advice or direction, by pointing out the worker's limitations or the client's strengths, and by directly discussing the unequal relationship and how it might be altered.

Expressing

Besides the influence and informative functions of human communication, people communicate for expressive purposes. Hu- man communication can be a creative, sharing experience in which two human beings express their feelings to each other. The differences between expressive and informative communication are significant and may even be produced by different sides of the brain.[41] The left side seems to be the logical, digital, linguistic processor, while the right side seems to be the creative, analogic, emotional processor. How different these kinds of communication processes are can be illustrated by a common practice example.

A worker in assessing a family may *talk* with the parents about what is going on in the family (left side, informative), while that same worker may ask the child in the family to *draw a picture* of the family and describe feelings about what is going on in the picture (right side, expressive). The worker will obtain a composite of the family through two separate sources of information processing. It may be that it is easier to communicate with the left side of the adult's brain through language and the right side of the child's brain through art; however, the worker should realize that different kinds of information and communication processes are involved in this situation.

Unfortunately some practitioners do not recognize the vast differences between expressive and informative communication. As a result, clients are sometimes asked to "verbalize feelings" rather than to "express feelings." Asking someone to verbalize feelings is comparable to asking someone to make love over the telephone. The medium of expression is severely limiting; little of the experience is conveyed, and the results are unsatisfactory to both parties.

Social work practitioners are expected to be sensitive to expressive communication, and the use of empathy training programs in social work education reflects a commitment to these skills. Research on affective communication suggests that the major signal systems for affect are the face, tone of voice, and body posture and gesture.[42] Clearly affect is communicated through nonverbal channels. When people are angry, they do not have to say they are angry. Their furrowed brows and clenched teeth, loud tone of voice, squared shoulders, and clenched fists communicate this expressive state more accurately (and quickly) than what is verbalized.

A great deal of research has been conducted over the past century on affective communication.[43] The facial muscles that move when a particular affect is aroused are the same for all human beings; however (1) the evoking stimuli (events, memories, fantasies) linked with an affect, (2) the display rules for showing the emotion, and (3) the behavioral consequences are all markedly influenced by social learning and vary within and between cultures.[44] For example, the stimulus of a funeral may elicit different emotions in different cultures (e.g., sadness in one culture and joy in another). Once an emotion is evoked, various display rules come into play to manage the expression of that emotion. The felt emotion may be intensified, deintensified, neutralized, masked with one expression, or be quickly followed by another that qualifies the first.[45]

There are six basic emotions that people from various cultures recognize: surprise, fear, anger, happiness, disgust, and sadness.[46] Even though these feelings are universal, they are constantly modified when they are displayed. People do not naturally let their feelings out. Small children do, but adults have been socialized to know what is an appropriate expression of affect in a given situation.

There are four basic display rules that operate when individuals experience emotions: cultural, vocational, personal, and situational.[47] Cultural display rules are conventions about emotional expressions that are followed by all nondeviant members of a given social class, subculture, or culture.[48] For example, in American society there are prohibitions against men showing fear or sadness in public and against women showing anger in public. Even when men and women feel these emotions, they must learn to control them. Obviously these display rules reflect the "macho" image that is associated with masculinity and the nonassertive image that is associated with femininity in our culture.

Cultural display rules are important in social work practice, particularly when the worker and client are from different subcultures. To be empathetic and sensitive to the client's affective experiences, a worker should be aware of cultural display rules that may shape the client's expression of feeling. For example, a white social worker who encourages a native American client from some tribes to express feelings may be pushing against a strong cultural display rule that prohibits such expression. The psychiatric term "flat affect" may have less to do in some people with individual psychopathology than with their ethnicity.

Vocational display rules refer to conventions that are characteristically associated with a person's vocational role. Various professions and occupations require that individuals manage their affective expressions. Novices often have not developed the "composure" or "bedside manner" that goes with the new position, and beginning social workers sometimes find these demands difficult to meet. For example, social work practitioners are expected to show moderate amounts of interest and concern for their clients whether they feel that way or not. Too much or too little interest is not appropriate. Workers are expected to keep their own feelings under control except when "self-sharing" has some tactical value to the worker-client relationship. Workers are expected to remain fairly neutral to the client's expression of feeling—workers do not counterattack when they are provoked by a hostile client.

The issue with vocational display rules is that sometimes these rules violate the cultural display rules of clients so that what is expected of the worker is in conflict with what is expected in the client's cultural context. For example, Spiegal points out how Irish-American patients view the "benevolent neutrality" of the psychiatrist:

> In the perceptions of the Irish-American patient, such an attitude is hypocritical. It smacks of the benevolence of the upper classes toward the "deserving poor." It signifies merely that one's real feelings remain undeclared behind a mask of condescension. Hiding one's feelings is a familiar affair, and according to his experience, is inevitably followed by brutal frankness when it is least expected. So this "neutrality" is merely a matter of waiting for the ax to fall.[49]

Personal display rules refer to the norms regarding affective expression that are the product of family life.[50] Children in some families are taught never to express anger at people in authority, while in other families children are taught to control tears (stiff upper lip). In some families, there are strong rules against expression of any affect. Personal display rules may be variations of cultural display rules, or in some cases, they may be in contradiction to cultural display rules. For example, the record, *Free to Be You and Me,* included a song titled, "It's All Right to Cry," which suggested that parents encourage sons to cry when sad in spite of cultural prohibitions to the contrary.

The implications of personal display rules for social work practice are numerous. Workers who serve individuals and families must become aware of personal display rules and how they affect the client's expression of emotion in an interview. In some families, there may be a great deal of conflict around personal display rules. For example, an histrionically inclined individual will generate a great deal of conflict in an emotionally controlled family. For some individuals, personal display rules may make certain kinds of human interaction almost impossible. For example, individuals with personal display rules that lead to the suppression of a particular emotion will find it almost impossible to express this emotion to another person. Thus these individuals may seem "deaf" to some expressions of affect much to the consternation of individuals in their environment. For other individuals, personal display rules may conflict with the demands of vocational display rules, and therefore they will find some occupations difficult to perform. For example, an individual who has been taught to mask feelings of sadness may not act appropriately as a mortician.

Situational display rules refer to conventions that center on the context or need of the moment. For example, when defendants are sentenced by a judge in court, they are expected to look "remorseful" even if they feel like laughing at a light sentence. The situational display rule in an interpersonal practice context is usually that the expression of all feelings is sanctioned, expected, and encouraged. Psychological literature usually affirms that many psychological, interpersonal, even physical problems may be exacerbated or even caused by the suppression of emotions. Whether in individual, group, or family sessions, workers should create a climate in which clients can express their feelings. This can be done both by stating that feelings can be expressed and by the worker expressing his or her feelings.

The dilemma with these situational rules

are that they may contradict a client's cultural and personal display rules. How a worker manages these contradictions is a complex issue. The worker should openly discuss what the implications for the therapeutic relationship are when a male client cries (or is even encouraged to cry) in front of a female worker or when an individual in a family session is encouraged to express feelings honestly and there can be serious consequences after the session when the family returns home.

From this discussion we can see that human communication serves many functions in human encounters. We do not simply communicate to inform others, as human communication also involves deceit, expression, and control. Thus, human communication is intricately involved in most of the problems clients bring to social workers.

A Transactional Perspective

In our opinion, an essential way of conceptualizing human communication is from a transactional perspective. The most commonly conceptualized model for this perspective is sender-receiver exchange[51] (see Figure 3-1).

In a simple dyadic exchange, one person (the sender) transmits a thought or an idea to another person (receiver). The idea is encoded into a set of signals such as words, facial movements, and hand gestures. These signals are sent out and received by the other person through sense receptors such as eyes and ears, and they are then decoded and finally understood by the brain. Unlike computer-to-computer communication in which there is a high degree of accuracy between sender and receiver, in human communication, it is unlikely that the idea sent will completely resemble the idea finally received. The process of encoding–transmitting–receiving–decoding will inevitably change the information sent. Because message distortion is inevitable, human communication is a continuous loop of exchanges and counterexchanges with individuals trying to obtain feedback about what was intended and how it was received. This model of communication is important for social workers because it outlines the various points at which human communication problems can arise in practice. The next sections of this chapter discuss the common communication problems that arise in encoding, transmitting, receiving, and decoding messages as

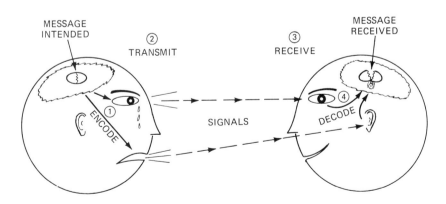

Figure 3-1 Sender/Receiver Exchange

well as those problems that arise in feedback and the context of the communication.

Encoding problems concern the abilities and capacities of the sender to select signals that the receiver will be able to understand. A sender has a wide range of signals from which to choose to communicate with a receiver, and the sender must select that array of signals (words, gestures, facial expressions) that will best convey the message. Unfortunately, what is best for the sender may not always be best for the receiver. For example, a psychiatric patient used a private language system that was known only to himself. This "word salad" was incomprehensible to others. Family members may develop special ways of communicating messages within the family. The worker who enters this family system will have to learn what these special signals mean. In other situations senders may possess a limited set of signals that they can call upon to transmit messages. For example, young children are pressed to use language to express themselves, and patients with neurological problems such as aphasia or severe retardation may have limited encoding capacities.

A common encoding problem is that of *referent confusion*. Because signs such as language carry no meaning but instead are assigned meaning by their users,[52] a particular sign (word) may have more than one referent in the real world, and a particular referent may have more than one sign or designation in a given signal system (language).[53] For example, referent confusion occurred when a nun in a Catholic school asked her class to bring in their Missals the next day, and two children responded by bringing in their model rocket ships. The second kind of referent confusion can be exemplified by looking at any common object that is used by different groups of people. For example, an automobile might be referred to as a "hog," "car," "wheels," "machine," or "bomb."

There are many implications of referent confusion in social work practice. New workers who enter their first job in a drug clinic or drug program are often overwhelmed by the jargon of the drug culture. Workers who run groups composed of people from specific subcultures must have a mastery of their jargon or run the risk of being largely excluded from what is being said.

Other examples of referent confusion involve the use of particular words that may have sensitive, multiple meanings. If a white, suburban, middle-class social worker refers to someone as a "punk" (i.e., a troublemaker or wiseacre), and the worker is talking to a black, inner-city youth who interprets "punk" as a homosexual, there will be obvious confusion in such an exchange. Another example involves the use of the expression "mad." For some patients in a mental health center, "mad" may mean "crazy," and being asked if they are mad is the same as being asked if they are insane.

Another encoding problem is that of the ambiguous message. With an ambiguous message, the sender deliberately encodes the message in such a way that it has little meaning or many possible meanings for the receiver. The weather forecaster's sign off expression to viewers of "Have a happy!" is a harmless example of an ambiguous message.

Ambiguous messages can occur in many areas of social work practice, as we saw in our earlier discussion of paradoxical communication. Another example is a worker who, to avoid the client's reaction to being rejected from benefits, deliberately makes it unclear what decision "the agency" has made, why the decision was made, and who took part in the decision-making process. Some policy formulations offer another example of ambiguous messages when they incorporate general rules that cover a broad range of situations. The result may then be the opposite of what was intended. For example, some of the policies that workers follow may actually contribute to divorce and separation.

Ambiguous messages can also be used for constructive purposes. For example, in a first group session, a social worker might be deliberately vague about the purpose of the group to encourage the group to struggle to establish its own purpose.

Transmission Problems

Transmission concerns the manner in which the encoded information is organized into cues: some signals may be understated and others overstated. Some senders speak so softly with slight gestures and neutral affect that it is almost impossible for receivers to pick up the signals that are being sent. Other senders may speak so loudly and gesture so dramatically that the receiver is distracted or even intimidated by the volume of cues. For example, a common communication problem in small groups, especially in early sessions, is that some members may speak so softly (both verbally and nonverbally) that other members cannot perceive or understand what is communicated.

Other transmission problems concern the rate at which signals are sent. Some senders speak rapidly so that receivers cannot follow or keep up with all the information presented, while in the opposite situation, the sender may speak so slowly that the receiver becomes impatient. This commonly happens with stutterers when they try to send a message and listeners fill in the words that the stutterers struggle to express.

Problems of rate of transmission concern the amount of "redundancy" that is built into

a transmission. In the statistical theory of communication, "information" is conceptualized as signals that are unexpected, uncertain, and not predictable, while "redundancy" constitutes signals that repeat or are predictable and expected.[54] The English language is about half information and half redundancy.[55] This means that about half the signals that an English speaker sends are repetitious and either repeat or reinforce other signals that carry information. Communication that is redundant bores receivers; communication that is highly efficient and packs much information is potentially confusing and misunderstood.[56] It is important for the sender to build enough redundancy into the message, by repeating important information, that this critical information can be received. Thus, some repetition is often necessary.

Senders usually increase the redundancy of their message when they perceive that they are not understood, when they try to convey a complex subject matter, or when the context is noisy (one with many distractions or disruptions). Nevertheless, most workers have had the experience of trying to look interested and involved when a client retells an incident for the third or fourth time, although this may mean that the client does not believe he or she has been heard.

It is possible for an individual to send information via one channel that is contradicted by information sent through another channel. A common example of this form of double message is sarcasm. The verbal statement that is expressed is contradicted by vocal qualities, facial expressions, or gestures that supposedly demonstrate that the words should be disqualified or accepted as meaning the opposite. Another common example of two-channel contradiction occurs when someone enters a conversation that is already in progress between others and states: "I don't mean to interrupt, but . . ." and then proceeds to interrupt the conversation. The "I don't mean to but" expression is a harmless social amenity in which there is a contradiction between words and actions; however, this construction can be used in interaction to disguise a heavy payoff—"I don't mean to sound critical, but that is the most foolish idea I have ever heard!" or "I don't want you to think I dislike you, but I never want to see you again!!"

There are many examples of double message communication in social work practice. Group leaders may verbally state that they would like group members to feel free and open to express themselves; yet the first person to risk himself or herself is attacked or severely criticized by the leader or the leader condones an attack by other group members. A private practitioner may express deep concern and commitment to an individual client, yet only see that client during rigidly scheduled office interviews and not accept the client's phone calls "after hours." Social agencies may initiate "minority recruitment drives" yet talk about "maintaining standards."

The examples of double message communication are endless, and it is the consequences of such miscommunications that should concern social work practitioners. The risks of being misled, confused, and having false hopes generated are serious consequences of double message communication that should be avoided in the communication process between worker and client. It is also important for the social worker to be able to recognize the consequences of double messages within the client system (i.e., family, couple, group) when these relate to the problems and issues an individual is trying to resolve. For example, parents in a family should be helped to give up such communication (referred to as a "double bind") with their child so that the child will have a clearer understanding of what is expected.[57]

Receiving Problems

Receiving concerns perception, that is, the way in which various signals are perceived by the receiver. Unlike a tape recorder that records all sound available to the microphone without discrimination, human perception is not reactive but proactive and selective.[58] The human brain through its receptors—the eyes, ears, nose, mouth, and skin—is constantly bombarded with stimuli; yet little of this is received. Most goes right by us because we selectively pay attention to only part of our experiential life space. Unfortunately the receiver may not notice or may even ignore important bits of a complex message. This process of selection may significantly alter for the receiver what the sender intended to communicate. If the receiver misses the disqualifying cues of a sarcastic message, the wrong half of the double message may be received and the opposite meaning of what was intended will have been conveyed.

Selective attention is present in all human encounters, but it can become a severe communication problem. In work with families or couples, often the complaint emerges that one or another of the family members "tunes out" messages from other family members. In fact, some clients are such poor listeners that they are unable to repeat even short statements that are communicated to them by significant others. In groups, some members seem to pay such poor attention to the discussion that they ask a question about a topic that was discussed earlier in the session.

This kind of "tuning out" can be explained from a so-called "neurolinguistic" perspective.[59] Individuals seem to develop preferred modes for perceiving and experiencing their environment. These habits of perception can become so strong that individuals will rely almost exclusively on one or another channel of perception. Some individuals appear to be "visual," some "auditory," and others "kinesthetic." Problems arise when two individuals with strong yet different styles try to interact.

What happens when a visual person tries to communicate with a kinesthetic one? Because the signals are exchanged through different perceptual modes, much information is lost in the back-and-forth exchange. The visual person may describe (and view) the experience as "dazzling, bright, and enlightening," while the kinesthetic person may describe (and sense) the same experience as "moving, touching, or exhausting." Although they may be discussing the same event, it will be presented and experienced in different languages. The language may be so different that the other person may not even pick up what is being discussed because it differs dramatically from his or her way of perceiving.

"Tuning out" may also result when an individual "daydreams," thus focusing on an internal communication process (fantasy) to the exclusion of the outside world. What student has not sat in class daydreaming about weekend plans and missing the pearls of wisdom put forth by the professor! Daydreaming can also be a normal, expanded state of consciousness and can be useful to an individual as a preparatory or even a problem-solving process.[60] This form of selective attention becomes problematic when daydreaming takes precedence over other forms of communication and the individual no longer attends to external signals that demand a response.

In practice, preoccupation with "internal communication" can manifest itself as a severe communication problem in a number of ways. When a psychotic patient engages in auditory or visual hallucinations, it is difficult to communicate with this patient. Similarly an individual responding with acute grief to the death of a loved one may be so preoccupied with the image of the deceased that person-to-person communication is severely limited. Social workers who work with severely disturbed youngsters realize how short the attention span of these youngsters can be. These workers also experience the tremendous emotional effort it requires to break into an autistic child's world even to gain attention for a few fleeting moments.

Another common receiving problem is overload. People have a finite capacity for processing information.[61] When one individual attempts to handle all significant information, and the second individual sends more information than can be processed, an overload situation exists. During overload, the individual who is unable to manage all the information that is presented will become much less efficient at handling any information.[62]

The significance of overload in social work practice can manifest itself in the communications between worker and client. For example, some workers may ask a client a three- or four-part question and then become impatient when the client is confused, silent, or unable to respond. For example, "How long have you known your wife?—How would you characterize your relationship with your wife?—and What connection does your present problem have with any previous problems in your marriage?"

Individuals have different capacities to respond to the information flow in their surroundings, and part of this variance is related to cultural experiences. Some cultures are "polychronic"; others are "monochronic." In a polychronic culture, an individual will schedule time so that many events will be handled simultaneously, whereas persons in a monochronic culture tend to do one thing at a time.[63] Americans tend to be monochronic, although some complex roles like motherhood demand a polychronic orientation. To a person who organizes time monochronically, a polychronic person's life seems chaotic and overwhelming; whereas a polychronic person might see a monochronic person's life as inefficient and dull. The important point in this discussion is that when individuals with different information-receiving capacities interact, what is the normal pace or exchange for one individual may be overwhelming or tedious to an individual with a different capacity. Because the worker's responsibility is to facilitate the client's expression in the interview, it is important that social workers have some sense of their own information sending and receiving capacities. They should seek to expand their capacity through training, as well as through a careful examination of their own communication behaviors.

Decoding Problems

Decoding like encoding is a transformation process in which the signals are transformed back into information that the receiver's brain can "understand." Many of the problems of encoding are decoding problems as well. If referents for the message are ambiguous or if the receiver does not have the common code to understand the signals being sent (is illiterate in that particular language), decoding will be problematic. For example, *si no hablas Espanol, entonces no vas a entender lo que te quiero decir*. But even when these problems are minimized, the decoding process is limited by the phenomenon of "selective interpretation."

Selective interpretation is an extension of the process of selective attention. Not only does selective attention distort incoming messages but so does selective interpretation. There is no such thing as immaculate perception. The world cannot be perceived as it really is. Human perception is a mental reflection of reality and, thus, not a perfect representation of it. Mental constructs of reality are based on learning (experience) as well as on structural components of the brain.[64] What this means is that people reconstruct messages and signals into what they have experienced or have been structured to perceive. Sometimes the previous programming is so strong, as in the case of prejudice, that major distortions of the present event or message will occur during perception. For example, the "halo effect" may allow one individual's behavior to be overlooked, while bigotry may require another individual, who perpetrates the same act, to be severely punished.

The consequence of selective interpretation for the communication experiences between worker and client is significant. What the worker hopes to communicate will only partially resemble what the client receives. Distortion is not only a problem for the transactions between worker and client, but it is also the basis of many problems that clients bring into the service process. For example, family members may be in conflict because they attribute intentions that are not present to messages from other family members.

Both client and worker continuously distort each other's messages during decoding. This problem is magnified when the interactants have had very different life experiences. As one writer states,

> Like everyone else, the psychiatrist is apt to interpret some conduct as improper merely because he is not familiar with the involvement idiom and the involvement rulings of the culture or group from which the patient comes. It is possible to observe, for example, a male lower-middle-class, middle-aged, Jewish refugee psychiatrist make confident detailed judgments about the symptomatic significance of the affective tone of a female, lower-class adolescent, Negro patient—an interesting achievement, since there are not many engagements in which both of these persons could find the immediate presence or

conduct of the other a natural, easeful thing.[65]

Because inferences represent the subjective, evaluative impressions of the speaker and facts and observations represent more accurately the subject being discussed, in recording case material the worker should be clear to separate factual, observational descriptions (the female was crying and had cut her wrists) from diagnostic impressions and evaluations (the female is depressed and suicidal). Both are important aspects of recording and should not be confused or omitted. A case record that gives demographic background on a client, such as "Mrs. R is a young, attractive woman who has been married for a short time," presents no factual information. How old is Mrs. R? What are her physical characteristics? How long has she been married? This confusion is common in case records, and it is no surprise that some workers find that their first contact with a transferred client is not consistent with the picture in the record. Because the image conveyed was based on the last worker's inferences, it contains more of the last worker's subjective impressions than it does hard data about the client.

It is also important in interviews with clients and others to collect both kinds of information. The informants' subjective reactions and impressions of the event are as much hard data about events as any other they can give. For example, in an advocacy situation, before a worker challenges an injustice the client experiences, the worker should document the grievance.

Feedback Problems

Feedback processes are central to human communication because they increase the accuracy of messages and they help to maintain and regulate the communicational flow between interactants. One-way communication or feedbackless communication loops are prone to error and distortion because the sender cannot monitor how the intended message was received. An example of this kind of one-way communication is the one you are experiencing right now—reading a written text. Even with editing and outside reviews, readers' reactions, confusion, and misunderstanding are lost to the authors as information that would help them change, improve, and revise the written text. In a mass communication situation, the audience rarely has a chance to give the sender feedback, and therefore the inevitable distortions in the message will not be checked, clarified, and corrected.

The opportunity for corrective feedback is greatest in face-to-face communication in which interactants can, all at once, be senders, receivers, and monitors of messages. But even in face-to-face communication, feedback problems can emerge. Sometimes individuals do not monitor the impact of the information they send to someone else.

In some families or formed groups, individuals may be oblivious to the reactions and comments of other members—especially when that feedback is not what they want to hear.

In some situations, individuals may behave unilaterally and rarely check things out with other members. When family members do not check with each other, many kinds of misunderstandings can emerge. Role problems often appear in this kind of situation. Some members may behave in contradiction to what is expected by other family members because they do not know what is expected of them. Other members may behave consistently with what they think is expected of them but never check out this role conception to see if it is consonant with family expectations. A common marital problem involves a wife who performs a behavior (e.g., packing her husband's lunch) because she thinks that he wants it that way, yet the husband is irritated by this particular behavior and wishes his wife would stop. Neither person has taken the time to clarify the situation through corrective feedback.

The regulative function of feedback is also important to human communication. In research on human communication, there is a category of behaviors called "regulators."[66] Regulator activities serve to

> maintain and regulate the back-and-forth nature of speaking and listening between two or more interactants. They tell the speaker to continue, repeat, elaborate, hurry up, become more interesting, less salacious, give the other a chance to talk, etc. They can tell the listener to pay special attention, to wait just a minute more, to talk, etc.[67]

Regulator activity seems to be performed for the most part without awareness, is involuntary, and represents highly overlearned habits. Regulators are learned patterns of behavior that are culture dependent and vary with role, setting, ethnicity, and social class.[68]

Examples of regulator behavior include the head nod, eye contact, the pacing of speaking and listening, the distance maintained between interactants, and the postural shifts that occur during a conversation. Regulators have been conceptualized as the rhythmic patterns that interactants must maintain to communicate. Researchers have discovered highly organized patterns of rhythmic activity related to both cultural and biological determinants.[69]

Human communication can be viewed as an elaborate dance in which the two interactions are intertwined in a series of moves and countermoves. Because these elaborate rhythmic patterns are culture dependent, people from different cultures who try to communicate in a common language experience as much strain as two dancers who try to dance together while doing different dances. Interactants from different backgrounds maintain different patterns of eye contact,[70] stand at different distances apart,[71] and maintain different levels of hand and body motion while conversing.[72]

It is important for the worker to have some knowledge of the major regulators and to use them consciously to put the client at ease. Workers should be flexible in response to the client's use of space, amount of eye contact, and patterns of responding and listening in an interaction. The rhythmic flow of arm and postural shifts is probably beyond the capacity of a worker to adjust to in each encounter; however, one researcher has suggested that if one truly wants to learn how to converse with an individual from another culture, then one must learn the dances of that culture.[73]

To understand the importance of regulators in social work practice, the following discussion will focus on the regulators just mentioned. The first is *space*. When two individuals enter a conversation, they move back and forth spatially until they feel comfortable in the exchange. How close two individuals will stand in a conversation depends on many variables (e.g., status relationship, sex, age, height, body orientation, mood).[74] The cultural background of interactants also significantly influences the spatial arrangement of the conversation.[75] For example, black Americans stand farther apart in a conversation than do white Americans,[76] Mexicans and Greeks stand closer together than do North Americans,[77] and Middle Eastern Arabs stand close enough in conversation to smell each other's breath.[78] In some cross-cultural conversations, the variability of comfortable distance may be so great that interactants are unable to find a comfortable distance in which to interact. For example, a black American in a conversation with a Middle Eastern Arab might find the Arab's attempts to get close very provocative, rude, or sexually inviting, whereas the Arab might find the black American's attempt to move away to a comfortable distance some kind of flight from or reluctance to engage in the conversation. Because the chances are great in social work practice that a worker will find himself or herself in cross-cultural interviews, interviewing space should be responsive to the client's comfort, not the worker's.

Eye contact and the *direction of gaze* during communication have been studied by researchers.[79] The amount of eye contact maintained by interactants is related to the mood of the interactants. A hard stare in our culture is associated with anger or a threat, and avoidance of eye contact is associated with sadness or shyness.[80] Eye contact is also a significant regulator and is used by a listener in a conversation to indicate to the speaker that "I'm still listening." For example, if one is listening to another person in a conversation and suddenly begins to look in another direction away from the speaker, the speaker will usually pause or try to find out if the listener is paying attention to something else. If the listener avoids all eye contact and gazes elsewhere, the speaker will usually stop talking altogether and will become irritated by the listener's apparent inattentiveness.

The problem that arises with eye contact as a regulator occurs when interactants come from different subcultural contexts in which the quantity and pattern of eye contact during a conversation is significantly different for each interactant. A person from a subcultural context that requires continuous, intense eye contact will find it difficult to engage in a conversation with a person from a subcultural context in which minimal, fleeting eye con-

tact is all that is necessary to maintain the conversational flow. The first interactant may feel that the second individual is not paying attention or is withdrawing from the conversation, whereas the second interactant may find the first individual's continuous state a source of intrusion, an act of threat, or a sexual invitation. The dilemma with this regulator incompatibility is that it does not directly affect the meanings of the words in the exchange, but it does produce discomfort in the conversation, and the source of this discomfort is usually out of awareness of both interactants.

This incompatibility becomes significant for social work practice when client and worker are of different racial backgrounds. There is some evidence that black Americans have different rules for eye contact than do white Americans, and the rhythmic pattern of eye contact is dissynchronous between black and white Americans.[81] This type of regulator incompatibility can become a source of discomfort in transracial encounters. More importantly, however, white social workers must be cautious about making inferences about black clients' moods or attentiveness based solely on what black clients do with their eyes.

Speak-listen patterns refer to the on-off flow of speech between interactants. A variety of possible speak-listen patterns can develop in a conversation. In some situations only one person speaks at a time and all others listen: _____ _____ _____ . In this pattern there is a clear junction between speaking episodes. The norm is "everyone must wait for his or her turn," and these are elaborate nonverbal cues that interactants must employ to move into the speaker position. The opposite of this pattern is a situation in which everyone speaks and listens at once:

——————   All interactants in this situation are simultaneously both speakers and listeners.

There are other combinations and variations of these patterns; however, these two descriptions are illustrative of problems that are encountered when interactions come from subcultural contexts that reinforce different patterns. For example, if an individual member who is used to pattern ————— ——— is placed in a group with pattern ————, that individual member will rarely get a chance to speak and may become an isolate. In the reverse situation, the individual member may be in continuous conflict with other group members for being "rude," "too aggressive," and not waiting for his or her turn to speak.

Because regulator behavior is significantly culture dependent, it is likely that tension will arise in transactions in which individuals are from different backgrounds (e.g., a white, Jewish, middle-class worker visiting a poor, black family), and the attitudinal barriers that exist in a cross-racial interview may not be the only source of tension in establishing a relationship. The worker may have to pay as much attention to regulator incompatibilities as to racist attitudes and suspicions to reduce destructive tensions in the worker-client relationship.[82]

Contextual Problems

Human communication does not occur in a vacuum. Much of the meaning of a communicational experience is dependent on the context in which interaction occurs. To exchange information successfully, both sender and receiver should work on building an "exchange context." There are two major ways in which a successful exchange context is established: attention to physical context and to social context.

The physical context of human communication is important because it can facilitate, distract, or hinder information exchange. Seating or standing arrangements that facilitate interaction (sociopetal) are right angular or face to face.[83] People who want to interact freely at a table either sit across from each other or sit on either side of the corner of the table.[84] It is more difficult for individuals to interact with each other when they sit side-by-side (on a couch or bench) or lengthwise across a long table. These sociofugal arrangements tend to inhibit interaction, and when given a choice, individuals will either avoid or move from these arrangements when they want to converse with someone else. Sociofugal arrangements are functional, though, in situations in which interaction is expected to be minimal (in a public auditorium).

The implications of these arrangements are that the interview spaces that workers use in practice should be carefully planned. Workers may unwittingly arrange their office space in a way that inhibits client interaction. For example, some workers have arranged their offices so that interviews are conducted across the top of a large desk.[85] This configuration places a barrier between worker and client and forces them to interact over a large distance (at least six feet). On the other hand, some workers have arranged such an intimate interview space (large pillows in a circle on the floor) that some clients may be threatened by this arrangement. Adolescents in a group may enjoy an unstructured, informal seating arrangement, yet the adolescents' parents would probably be uncomfortable with this arrangement.

Flexibility is important, and the worker should try to provide an interview context in which the client has a choice about seating.

Chairs in the interviewing areas should be movable so that clients are comfortable in the interview. Workers on home visits should ascertain in what room the interview should take place and where the client wants the worker to sit. Territorial invasion[86] of a client's special chair during a home visit will be as disrupting to the client as it would be to the worker in an office interview for the client to sit in the worker's chair.

Besides planning the seating configurations of the interview space, a worker should also be concerned about privacy. Privacy is a subjective notion that varies greatly from person to person. Some individuals can gain "privacy" by going inside and daydreaming or meditating to the exclusion of all activity around them. Other individuals may require isolation from others in their own private space before a sense of privacy is achieved. And to some individuals privacy is equated with a log cabin in the woods 50 miles from any other human being.

In social work practice, privacy is operationalized in many ways, too. Some agencies have secure, soundproof interviewing rooms with strict prohibitions against interruptions of interviews. Others have open cubicles with no doors or may even hold interviews in the waiting room. Obviously each setting will convey a different experience of privacy for the client and worker.

The point of this discussion is that the physical context does have an impact on the communication process between worker and client and should not be ignored. It is true that some aspects of the physical context are impossible to change (e.g., the size of the room, placement of doors); however, much of the physical context can be changed or controlled by the worker. Chairs can be rearranged, children and neighbors asked to leave the room, television sets turned off, fellow workers told not to interrupt, and secre-

taries informed to hold all calls. Of these, the first three should be accomplished with the client's agreement, but the last two can be unilaterally decided by the worker.

What is meant by social context? Human beings are not computers. Two compatible computers can be connected, and they are immediately ready to exchange information; however, in human communication this is not the case. Surrounding all human communication experiences is a series of expectations, rituals, and habitual behaviors that interactants engage in to enter or terminate an encounter.[87] These entrance and exit rituals give interactants a chance to size each other up. These rituals also help to establish a routine for the interactants so that each feels some comfort and security in the exchange. Although these behaviors do not bear directly on the subject matter of the communicational experience, they are significant parts of the process because, if not properly performed, they interfere with an interactant's entry into and exit from an encounter and create enough discomfort so that individuals do not want to continue or return.

There are numerous examples of the way in which the ritual order affects communicational experiences. Certain social amenities are expected when individuals enter and leave an encounter—for example, greetings, recognition, handshake, kiss, introduction. Even when an individual engages the services of a formal organization, there is a ritual order that may be complex and demanding. For example, entrance into a service agency may require certain entrances, lines, reception areas, forms to be filled out, and tests and evaluations to be completed.

Because the habitual behaviors associated with the ritual order are learned and are mostly out of awareness, considerable confusion and discomfort can result when the ritual order of one interactant does not mesh with the ritual order of the other interactant. Incongruities are likely to occur when worker and client are from different backgrounds. A worker from a subculture in which food is always politely rejected refused a cup of coffee and piece of cake from a client who came from a subcultural experience in which the sharing of food is a significant ritual that must precede business. The result of the ensuing interview was unsatisfactory. The client was uncooperative and withholding during the interview in the same way that the worker was when the worker refused food and drink at the inception of the interview.

Throughout our discussion of communication issues, we have combined theory, concepts, and practical applications. To reinforce the discussion of practical application, we shall summarize and conceptualize in a slightly different manner than heretofore some of the major ways workers can respond to communication problems. We have identified three types of solutions to communication problems: feedback, anchoring, and tuning.

Feedback is the basis for many techniques utilized by social workers. Clarification of an issue is often a feedback process in which the client hears the worker's perspective on a given matter. Perception checking and asking another interactant to repeat what was communicated are other examples of feedback processes. Feedback techniques are employed whenever clarity is lacking or there is a chance that the information content of a message will be misunderstood. Feedback is useful in resolving referent confusion, ambiguous messages, double messages, and selective interpretation. When there is gross loss, addition, or distortion between information sent and received, feedback techniques will highlight these discrepancies so that they may be corrected.

Anchoring has a technical meaning for researchers who wish to establish the reliability of judgment,[88] but it also is a useful concept in all communication. Anchoring refers to grounding an idea or concept, usually through an example or illustration.

If one's supervisor complains that "many clients called while you were out" on an extended lunch hour, anchoring such a complaint involves determining what number or range of numbers constitutes "many." Anchoring can occur during communication as well as after. Many people give examples and illustrations of their subject matter during a conversation. Anchoring is an effective way of reducing selective interpretation, referent confusion, and inference-observation confusion.

Tuning is a complex strategy because it is designed to tackle the most difficult problems (ritual order incongruence, overload, and regulator incompatibility). Technicially, tuning refers to the process of adjusting frequencies to a desired pitch, and metaphorically, this is what is involved in human communication. Tuning involves the adjustments made by interactants in their modes, expectancies, and style of interaction so that a mutually understood pattern of communication can develop and information can be comfortably exchanged. Some individuals have a wide and flexible range to their communication modes (former New York Mayor LaGuardia's political success has been related to his abilities to use Italian, English, and Yiddish as well as appropriate gestures), while others have a narrow, restricted range. For interactants to remain tolerably comfortable in a transaction, there must be some overlap or commonality in their modes. When demographic differences between interactants are great, the potential overlap of communication modes is much smaller and prone to disharmony. For example, for some beginning social work students, the field experience, with its demands on skill development and the expansion of the student's capacities to relate to various, different client populations can be stressful for this person as well as for others.

It is essential that social work practitioners continuously expand and create greater flexibility in their modes of communication. This occurs through education about different client groups and their values and modes of behavior; and it also comes through experience in interacting with various clients. For example, "cultural shock" and subsequent readjustment of Peace Corps volunteers, anthropologists, and immigrants, upon entering a new culture, is an example of tuning. Another way in which social work practitioners can expand their communication modes is to work with indigenous workers or collaborate with other social workers who have been raised in or have the experience of subcultural contexts that differ from the worker's. It is also possible to do "tuning" by recognizing one's limitations and referring those clients who are outside one's range to another worker who can interact within the client's range. We shall discuss this topic further in Chapter 15 when we describe ethnic factors that affect practice.

SUMMARY

The chapter began with a description of the function of communication in human existence and how communicative behavior is determined. We emphasized that communication is both verbal and nonverbal and, thus, takes place through many channels. Communication occurs in a context, and it is impossible to understand the effects of communications without taking the situation into account.

After this introductory material, we presented a functional perspective on communications that views the purpose of communication as to inform, deceive, express, and influence. We discussed each of these in turn and pointed out their impacts on social work practice. Then we described a transactional perspective that takes into account four communications processes occurring between people: encoding, transmitting, receiving, and decoding. Again, we indicated the implications of these for practice.

From a systems perspective, an aspect of communications that has extensive implications for behavior is feedback. We, therefore, singled out this topic for a more extensive discussion. Some of the behavioral aspects that we considered were behavioral correction and regulation. Important regulators are space, eye contact, and speak-listen patterns.

We concluded the chapter with a summary of some of the major solutions to communications problems that had been illustrated in the preceding sections. These included the corrective use of feedback, anchoring, and tuning.

NOTES

1. James Miller, "The Nature of Living Systems," *Behavioral Sciences*, Vol. 16 (1971), p. 292.

2. Jurgen Ruesch and Weldon Kees, *Nonverbal Communication: Notes on the Visual Perception of Human Relations* (Berkeley: University of California Press, 1970), pp. 15–25.

3. D. Efron, *Gesture and Environment* (New York: King's Crown Press, 1941); F. C. Hayes, "Should We Have a Dictionary of Gestures?" *Southern Folklore Quarterly*, Vol. 4 (1940), pp. 239–245; and Weston LaBarre, "The Cultural Basis of Emotions and Gestures," *Journal of Personality*, Vol. 16 (1947), pp. 49–68.

4. Ray L. Birdwhistell, *Kinesics and Context: Essays on Body Motion Communication* (Philadelphia: University of Pennsylvania Press, 1970), and Albert Scheflen, *How Behavior Means* (Garden City, N.Y.: Doubleday, 1974).

5. Edward T. Hall, *The Hidden Dimension* (Garden City, N.Y.: Doubleday, 1969).

6. J. L. Dillard, *Black English* (New York: Random House, 1972).

7. Edith Folb, "Rappin' in the Black Vernacular," *Human Behavior*, Vol. 2 (August 1973), pp. 16–20.

8. Paul Ekman, ed., *Darwin and Facial Expression: A Century of Research in Review* (New York: Academic Press, 1973).

9. Paul Ekman, Wallace Friesen, and Phoebe Ellsworth, *Emotion in the Human Face* (Elmsford, N.Y.: Pergamon Press, 1972).

10. Robert Ardrey, *African Genesis* (New York: Atheneum, 1961), and Konrad Lorenz, *On Aggression* (New York: Harcourt Brace, 1966).

11. Ruesch and Kees, *Nonverbal Communication*, p. 4.

12. Birdwhistell, *Kinesics and Context*, pp. 157–158.

13. Albert Mehrabian, "Communication Without Words," in Joseph DeVito, ed., *Communication: Concepts and Process* (Englewood Cliffs, N.J.: Prentice-Hall, 1971), p. 107.

14. Birdwhistell, *Kinesics and Context*, p. 50; Scheflen, *How Behavior Means*.

15. Mark L. Knapp, *Nonverbal Communication in Human Interaction* (New York: Holt, Rinehart and Winston, 1972).

16. Ralph Nichols and Leonard Stevens, *Are You Listening* (New York: McGraw-Hill, 1957, and Otto Lerbinger, *Designs for Persuasive Communication* (Englewood Cliffs, N.J.: Prentice-Hall, 1972), pp. 130–140.

17. R. W. Gerard, "Units and Concepts in Biology," in Walter Buckley, ed., *Modern Systems Research for the Behavioral Scientist* (Chicago: Aldine, 1968), p. 51.

18. Ashley Montague, *Touching: The Human Significance of the Skin* (New York: Columbia University Press, 1971).

19. Ruesch and Kees, *Nonverbal Communication*, p. 193.

20. Erving Goffman, *Behavior in Public Places* (New York: The Free Press, 1963), p. 35.

21. Scheflen, *How Behavior Means*.

22. Hall, *The Hidden Dimension*; Knapp, *Nonverbal Communication in Human Interaction*, pp. 25–62; and Robert Sommer, *Personal Space: The Behavioral Bases of Design* (Englewood Cliffs, N.J.: Spectrum, 1969).

23. Humphry Osmond, "Function as the Basis of Psychiatric Ward Design," *Mental Hospitals*, April 1957, pp. 23–29.

24. Hall, *The Hidden Dimension*, and Sommer, *Personal Space*.

25. W. Griffith, "Environmental Effect of Interpersonal Affective Behavior: Ambient Effective Temperature and Attraction," *Journal of Personality and Social Psychology*, Vol. 15 (1970), pp. 240–244.

26. John Arehart-Treichel, "The Good Healthy Shining Light," *Human Behavior*, Vol. 4 (January 1975), pp. 16–22.

27. Birdwhistell, *Kinesics and Contexts*, p. 179.

28. Goffman, *Behavior in Public Places*, pp. 16–17.

29. Ruesch and Kees, *Nonverbal Communication*, p. 82.

30. Birdwhistell, *Kinesics and Concepts*, p. 48.

31. Don Fabun, *Communications: The Transfer of Meaning* (Beverly Hills, Calif.: Glencoe Press, 1970).

32. Sherida Bush, "A Family-Help Program That Really Works," *Psychology Today*, May 1977, pp. 48–50, 84–88.

33. Charlotte O. Kursh, "The Benefits of Poor Communication," *The Psychoanalytic Review*, Vol. 58 (Summer 1971), pp. 189–208.

34. Edward O. Wilson, "Animal Communication," *Scientific American*, Vol. 227 (September 1973), pp. 53–54.

35. See Peggy Papp, "Paradoxes," in Salvador Minuchin and H. Charles Fishman, eds., *Family Therapy Techniques* (Cambridge, Mass.: Harvard University Press, 1981), pp. 244–261.

36. Don Jackson, ed., *Communication, Family, and Marriage* (Palo Alto, Calif.: Science and Behavior Books, 1967).

37. See, for example, Virginia Satir, *Conjoint Family Therapy* (Palo Alto, Calif.: Science and Behavior Books, 1967); Jay Haley, *Strategies of Psychotherapy* (New York: Grune & Stratton, 1963); Jay Haley, *Changing Families: A Family Therapy Reader* (New York: Grune & Stratton, 1971); Jay Haley, *Problem-Solving Therapy: New Strategies for Effective Family Therapy* (San Francisco: Jossey-Bass, 1976); Paul Watzlawick, J. H. Beavin, and Don Jackson, *Pragmatics of Human Communication* (New York: W. W. Norton, 1967); Paul Watzlawick, *How Real Is Real?* (New York: Random House, 1976); and Paul Watzlawick, John Weakland, and R. Fisch, *Change: Principles of Problem Formation and Problem Resolution* (New York: W. W. Norton, 1974).

38. Eric Berne, *Games People Play* (New York: Grove Press, 1964).

39. Judith Nelsen, *Communication Theory and Social Work Practice* (Chicago: University of Chicago Press, 1980).

40. Ibid.

41. Robert E. Ornstein, ed., *The Nature of Human Consciousness* (New York: Viking Press, 1973).

42. Knapp, *Nonverbal Communication in Human Interaction*, pp. 158–164.

43. Ekman, *Darwin and Facial Expression*, and Carrol Izard, *The Face of Emotion* (New York: Appleton-Century-Crofts, 1971).

44. Ekman, Friesen, and Ellsworth, *Emotion in the Human Face*, and Paul Ekman and Wallace Friesen, "The Repertoire of Nonverbal Behavior: Categories, Origins, Usage, and Coding," *Semiotics*, Vol. 1 (1969), pp. 73–76.

45. Paul Ekman and Wallace Friesen, *Unmasking the Face* (Englewood Cliffs, N.J.: Prentice-Hall, 1975), pp. 140–143.

46. Ibid.

47. Ibid., pp. 114–128.

48. Ibid.

49. John Spiegal, "Some Cultural Aspects of Transference and Countertransference," in Frank Reissman, ed., *Mental Health of the Poor* (New York: The Free Press, 1964), pp. 303–320.

50. Ekman and Friesen, *Unmasking the Face*, pp. 114–128.

51. Wilbur Schramm, "How Communication Works," in *Communication: Concepts and Process*, pp. 12–21.

52. Cholin Cherry, *On Human Communication* (Boston: M.I.T. Press, 1966), p. 69.

53. For a detailed discussion of these issues, see William Haney, *Communication and Organizational Behavior* (Homewood, Ill.: Richard D. Irwin, 1967), pp. 245–282.

54. Cherry, *On Human Communication*, pp. 117–123.

55. Schramm, "How Communication Works," p. 15.

56. Ibid.

57. Don Jackson, ed., *Therapy, Communication and Change* (Palo Alto, Calif.: Science and Behavior Books, 1968).

58. Cherry, *On Human Communication*, pp. 258–304.

59. Richard Bandler and John Grinder, *The Structure of Magic* (Palo Alto, Calif.: Science and Behavior Books, 1975).

60. R. Desoille, "The Waking Dream in Psychotherapy: An Essay on the Regulatory Function of the Collective Unconscious," *Le Réve Éveille en Psychothérapie* (Paris: Universitaire, 1945).

61. George A. Miller, "The Magical Number Seven, Plus or Minus Two: Some Limits on Our Capacity to Process Information," *Psychological Review*, Vol. 63 (1956), pp. 81–97.

62. Ibid.

63. Edward T. Hall, *The Silent Language* (Garden City, N.Y.: Doubleday, 1959). pp. 138–139.

64. Bandler and Grinder, *The Structure of Magic*.

65. Goffman, *Behavior in Public Places*, p. 233.

66. Ekman and Friesen, "The Repertoire of Nonverbal Behavior," pp. 82–84.

67. Ibid., p. 82.

68. Ibid.

69. Paul Byers and Happie Byers, "Nonverbal Communication and the Education of Children," in Courtney Cazden, ed., *Functions of Language in the Classroom* (New York: Teachers College Press, 1972); W. S. Condon and W. D. Ogston, "A Segmentation of Behavior," *Journal of Psychiatric Research,* Vol. 5 (1967), pp. 221–235; and Adam Kendon, "Some Functions of Gaze Direction in Social Interaction," *Acta Psychologica,* Vol. 26 (1967), pp. 22–63.

70. Byers and Byers, "Nonverbal Communication and the Education of Children," and O. M. Watson and T. D. Graves, "Quantitative Research on Proxemic Behavior," *American Anthropologist,* Vol. 68 (1966), pp. 971–985.

71. Albert Mehrabian, *Nonverbal Behavior* (Chicago: Aldine, 1972), pp. 6–7, 20–21.

72. Efron, *Gesture and Environment;* Scheflen, *How Behavior Means,* pp. 97–106.

73. Personal Communication with Paul Byers.

74. Sommer, *Personal Space,* and Hall, *The Hidden Dimension.*

75. Hall, *The Hidden Dimension,* pp. 131–164.

76. J. C. Baxter, "Interpersonal Spacing in Natural Settings," *Sociometry,* Vol. 33 (1970), pp. 444–456, and F. N. Willis, "Initial Speaking Distance as a Function of the Speaker's Relationship," *Psychonomic Science,* Vol. 5 (1966), pp. 221–222.

77. K. B. Little, "Cultural Variations in Social Schemata," *Journal of Personality and Social Psychology,* Vol. 10 (1968), pp. 1–7, and Baxter, "Interpersonal Spacing in Natural Settings," pp. 444–456.

78. Hall, *The Hidden Dimension,* pp. 159–160.

79. Mehrabian, "Communication Without Words," pp. 21–24, and Knapp, *Nonverbal Communication in Human Interaction,* pp. 129–135.

80. Ekman and Friesen, *Unmasking the Face.*

81. Byers and Byers, "Nonverbal Communication in the Education of Children."

82. For a discussion of attitudinal problems in transracial communication, see Arthur L. Smith, *Transracial Communication* (Englewood Cliffs, N.J.: Prentice-Hall, 1973).

83. Osmond, "Function as the Basis of Psychiatric Word Design."

84. Sommer, *Personal Space.*

85. Brett A. Seabury, "Arrangements of Physical Space in Social Work Settings," *Social Work,* Vol. 16 (October 1971), pp. 43–49.

86. Erving Goffman, *Relations in Public: Microstudies of the Public Order* (New York: Basic Books, 1971), pp. 49–58.

87. Goffman, *Relations in Public,* pp. 62–94, and Berne, *Games People Play,* pp. 35–40.

88. Ben Orcutt, "A Study of Anchoring Effects in Clinical Judgments," *Social Service Review,* Vol. 38 (December 1964), pp. 408–417.

four
Becoming a Client

This chapter describes how individuals in the society become the recipients of social work services. The term "client" is customarily used to refer to such recipients and is defined as the person or persons who come for help to a social agency and who expect to benefit directly from it; who determine, usually after some exploration and negotiation, that this was an appropriate move; and who enter into an agreement—referred to as a contract— with the social worker with regard to the terms of such service.

In this chapter we discuss some of the details of how persons become clients. A number of possibilities exists related to the reasons for seeking service, the kind of motivation present, and whether the person comes individually or with others; we shall present the implications of these alternatives. Since the social worker will also have contact with others on behalf of clients, we shall also discuss the nature of these additional contacts and the kinds of obligations they create.

Definition of a Client

Although the word "client" is widely used, some controversy attaches to it. Those, like us, who defend it do so because it is analogous to the terminology of other professions. Lawyers, doctors, engineers, and architects all refer to those whom they serve as clients. Opponents of the term "client" insist that the social work relationship is different. Clients in many other professions are manipulated in some way (e.g., a surgical operation), are given a product (a building), or are represented before a third party (a law court). In social work, in contrast, the major task of the worker is to facilitate the work of clients on their own behalf. Some opponents of the term "client" also believe that the status and power differences between professionals and clients in other professions should not be present in social work relationships. An alternative term, however, has not gained acceptance, although terms such as service user or service recipient have been suggested.[1]

A notable exception to the use of the word "client" in social work is the use of the word "member" in group work. Many group workers prefer this term because the vehicle of service is the group, and if any entity is the "client," for them it is the entire group. There are models of group work, however, in which the individual member is viewed as the client.

The question that arises in regard to group work with unrelated individuals is whether the client is the group or the individual members. The answer depends on what the worker's practice model is as well as on what the member's expectations are. Some practice theorists describe the group as client and direct the worker to help the group establish optimal group conditions to achieve group goals. Other theorists view the members as clients, help them to choose individual goals, and move to create group conditions that facilitate the attainment of individual goals. Of course, group members may have ideas on this that are at variance with the worker's.

While social work relationships are not identical with those in other professions, we still choose to use the word "client" in this book because of its wide acceptance. We believe the use of this term has not prevented a recognition of the special aspects of the social work client role including those noted by the critics of the term.

When social work was equated primarily with work with one person at a time, the word "client" was understood to mean a single individual. With an increase in work with groups and whole families, the term has been extended to include more than one person as when several people seek help for themselves as a family, a group, or even an organization.[2] To avoid some confusion, the phrase "client system" was introduced in Chapter 2, and we shall employ "client" and "client system" interchangeably.

An example of a family as a client was one that sought out a social worker to improve communications among all family members. While they assumed this would benefit each of them individually, they had reached consensus among themselves that they all wished to change their family system with the help of a social worker.

Pathways to Clienthood

Voluntary Clients

Some clients voluntarily seek out the services of a social worker or social agency. These are frequently people whom the community considers to be "normal" and whose problems may well occur in the course of socialization into such life phases as adolescence, parenthood, or retirement. They may, for example, seek help in making crucial decisions relevant to their role transition. Another group of persons seeking help on a voluntary basis are those who experience an event beyond their control, such as a natural disaster. Still another category of voluntary clients is comprised of those who perform a service for the society, such as adopting or fostering children. The role of foster parents, however, is somewhat ambiguous as such people may be seen as having staff functions.

Other voluntary clients are those who wish to improve their social skills or who wish to resolve identity or relationship concerns. These clients often come from social or educational backgrounds that are supportive of psychologically oriented services—they are usually the more affluent members of the community. Such potential clients are unlikely to seek services from public agencies because they associate these with poor or otherwise stigmatized groups. They may, however, seek private, possibly sectarian (on either a religious or ethnic basis) agencies or private practitioners.

Voluntary clients usually hear about services from publicity disseminated by the agency or are told about services by other professionals (e.g., school personnel, physicians, employers). Agencies will often distribute news releases about such services as parent education, support groups for single parents, preparation for retirement activities, and programs to facilitate career planning. In the terms that we presented in Chapter 1, these services largely fulfill anomie reduction and socialization functions.

Nonvoluntary Clients

There is a category of client that falls between the voluntary and involuntary client—one that we call nonvoluntary.[3] If they do not accept services, these clients do not face legal or other serious social sanctions, but they are pressured to do so. Examples are people who others see as having problems such as a wife who views her husband as causing their marital stress, a teacher who assesses a student as having emotional problems that interfere with learning, and an employer who believes that an employee's personality causes job-related difficulties.

In these types of nonvoluntary situations, while clients are not legally required to accept services, they may suffer unpleasant consequences if they refuse: the wife may leave her husband, the teacher may not promote the student, and the employer may fire the employee. We believe that a large proportion of social work clients are nonvoluntary and that this fact must be dealt with if the client is to benefit from services. How this can be done is described in Chapter 5

when we discuss the process of engagement between the client and worker. In nonvoluntary referrals, the purpose may still be one of socialization in which an individual resists to some degree expectations for socialization into such roles as spouse, employee, or student.

Involuntary Clients

The third type of client is the involuntary one who is either legally required to utilize services or subjected to some unpleasant social sanction for refusing services. Examples are people who have been placed on probation or parole and are required to see a social worker as a condition of their liberty and people who are committed to mental hospitals and other institutions. Protective service situations in which one member of a family has abused another may also fall in this category. In this latter situation, the protective service agency must investigate certain categories of abuse such as child abuse and may institute court proceedings against a family member.

In a sense, there is no such thing as an involuntary client as we defined a client as a person or persons who accept a contract for social work services. In addition, as we discussed earlier, a major value in social work practice is self-determination. The value, however, that social workers place on individual life and growth induce them to encourage and even pressure many involuntary persons to accept services. In any case, the fact that the referral for social work services has been made despite the individual's preferences has profound implications for how the worker will initiate contact. These implications will also be explored later.

Involuntary clients are usually served by agencies who view one of their purposes as social control. They draw, as we indicated earlier, their sanction for such services from legislation or other procedures established by the society.

The Entry Process

Whether individuals enter the agency on a voluntary, nonvoluntary, or involuntary basis, the worker must consider their feelings about this entry as well as their perceptions of it and the events leading up to it. We turn now to a consideration of these phenomena and the worker's responses to them.

Feelings About Clienthood

People are likely to approach a social agency with mixed feelings, even those who do so voluntarily.[4] Positive feelings will derive from the idea that the agency may be of help, that it will create new opportunities, that the staff will be enjoyable to interact with, and that burdens may be shared. Negative feelings are likely to be present because the service may be seen as doing no good or even harm to a person, because others may be critical of this move, and because there may be additional and unexpected consequences. The client may incur obligations, other persons may be affected, and a process once started may be hard to stop. Clients may have heard stories about incompetent staff or they may even have had experience with such people.

In relation to the issue of stigma, the client may be viewed by friends or relatives as crazy; the latter may believe that only inadequate, poor, or other undesirable types of people use social services. There are, in any case, psychological costs when one asks another, particularly a professional, for help. One often feels that this places the helper in a superior position because the helper learns the ways in which the client is vulnerable.

There are approaches to dealing with these concerns, however, that we shall discuss later.

Perceptions of Agencies

As implied by our discussion of the stigma that can attend receiving social welfare services, the way in which the agency is perceived by the applicant will have an impact on the approach to services. There are both subjective and objective components to the client's views. The subjective ones will relate to the client's unique history—whether the client has received social work services before, what outcome was produced, what other ways the client has sought help, and how strongly the client now feels that help is necessary.

In addition, the agency will affect the perceptions of applicants by virtue of the services it has previously provided, whether or not these reflect its current practices. Former clients will speak about their agency experiences in the community, and these stories will be repeated and sometimes magnified. The agency will also have contemporary effects based on its location and its physical appearance. Some agencies are housed in storefronts, some in converted churches, some in impressive buildings, and some in old, rundown structures. All people will not be affected in the same way: an affluent person may be uncomfortable in the rundown structure while a poor person may be uncomfortable in an extremely elegant one. We speak here of extremes—few, if any, persons will wish to remain in a setting that does not communicate respect for clients through adequate maintenance and furnishings.

Applicants will be affected by how they are greeted when they enter the building. Some receptionists are courteous and respectful; others are insulting. Confidentiality may or may not be observed by what is asked in the waiting room and how it is asked. The waiting area may be pleasant and comfortable or stark and in disrepair. Bruno Bettleheim describes in detail how the room in the Orthogenic School (a treatment center for severely dysfunctional children, adolescents, and young adults) where persons are first seen was furnished and decorated.[5] Each object was carefully chosen to communicate something about the institution or to promote interactions that helped staff and applicants to become acquainted.

Events Leading to Clienthood

The individual's way of experiencing the agency will also be affected by the events leading up to the application. A crisis in the life of the client constitutes one type of event. A crisis is a sudden occurrence that is experienced as overwhelming. The magnitude of the stress in a crisis is so great that the client's customary ways of coping are not adequate for the situation.[6] Examples of events that create crises for some people are the death of a family member, termination from employment, an offer of a new job, severe financial reverses, or serious illness. According to crisis theory, the individual, in a relatively short time, establishes some way of responding to the event that may either reduce stress or add to it. Individuals who experience a crisis are often very receptive to help from a professional and may even feel desperate for it.

It may seem from this discussion that an application during a crisis indicates that the client is a voluntary one. It is also possible that the circumstances leading up to an involuntary referral (e.g., an arrest or psychiatric commitment) may be the crisis events.

Because of the likelihood that some resolution of the crisis will take place within several weeks of the event—and motivation for help will then drop—it is important that persons in crisis receive an appointment soon after calling. For this reason, many agencies that previously maintained waiting lists abandoned this practice. People who called for an appointment were either seen immediately, if staff were available, or were referred to other resources.

Many clients, however, are not in a crisis when they apply for social work services. This, then, raises the issue of why the client has appeared in a social agency at this time, since some event must have occurred, situation altered, or perceptions and feelings about a situation changed *at this time* to cause this encounter. In systems terms, something must have shifted in the equilibrium within the individual or between the individual and other individuals and objects in the environment. The worker will seek to understand the nature of these events because these events can, and usually do, have profound effects on subsequent work with the client. For example, the client's motivation to accept help and the aspects of himself or herself and the environment the client selects for change are products of this history.

The client's motivation to involve himself or herself in social work services will be a function of the client's perceptions about his or her life situation. If the client perceives this situation as having so seriously deteriorated that change is hopeless, motivation will be low. The client must either believe that a previous situation can be restored or that a tolerable substitute can be found.[7] An example of this is an applicant for service who was divorced from her husband. She wished to either explore the possibility of a reconciliation with him or to learn ways of rebuilding her social life. Since she believed that one of these two outcomes was possible, her motivation for becoming a client was high. An-other woman, however, whose husband had died believed that she would never reestablish that kind of relationship and that she was doomed to a lonely existence; her mo-tivation, consequently, for service, was low. This does not preclude working with the poorly motivated client, but it indicates that steps must be taken to heighten motivation in those who lack it, for example, by supplying reinforcement for coming to the agency.

The client's motivation will also be re-lated to his or her feelings about the event or situation that led to seeking service. The feel-ings to assess are the degree of discomfort the client experiences and the degree of hope the client has that change will occur. There is probably, at least in theory, an optimum bal-ance of the two. Weak feelings of hope or of discomfort may preclude an investment in being helped, whereas strong feelings may overwhelm the person and limit his or her energy for work. In the latter case, the worker—with proper ethical regard for the rights of the client—may seek to reduce the amount of external stress to alleviate the overwhelming nature of events. Examples are locating housing, providing emergency fi-nancial assistance, securing medical atten-tion, or assigning a homemaker to a family whose routines have been severely disrupted.

The immediate events or situational changes that lead to seeking services will have effects on what the client seek to mod-ify, namely, the targets of change. Some cli-ents seek to change their environments, some themselves, and some both. The client is likely to select some aspect of the environ-ment when the environment has recently undergone some change, whether or not this will substantially reduce the problem. Thus, a youth who came to an agency, after being expelled from school, immediately sought help with selecting a new school rather than with looking at his behavior that led to this expulsion.

The worker should also recognize his or her own subjective reactions to the factors that brought the client to the agency. If the client has experienced a loss, the worker may experience sorrow; if the client has been abused, the worker may feel anger. These feelings, in themselves, may facilitate client-worker engagement if they create empathy in the worker. On the other hand, these feel-ings may incapacitate the worker, particu-larly if they remind the worker of his or her own unresolved issues. One worker's sorrow prevented him from recognizing the full ar-ray of client feelings and the client's ways of coping with them. Another worker's anger, prevented her from identifying the client's contribution to the events that had occurred.

Parallel to the client's attribution of causes of the problem to immediately ante-cedent events, the worker may also make similar attributions. This may prevent the worker from correctly assessing other aspects of clients and their situations. An adolescent client, for example, charged her stepfather with sexual abuse. The worker's first re-sponse was to discuss only the stepfather's behavior as the relevant data in the situation. However, the worker soon recognized that this was a central but limited perspective and subsequently explored the larger situation, particularly the roles of the girl's mother, bi-ological father, siblings, and friends to decide on appropriate professional goals and tasks. This did not preclude immediate action to safeguard the client.

The nature of the antecedent events will determine with whom the worker intervenes as well as the initial nature of interventions. The persons involved in precipitating events will often be interviewed by the worker or at least described by the client to the worker. They may also be potential clients themselves or become part of a multiperson client system. In the example just cited of the adolescent who accused her stepfather of abuse, the worker held interviews with the mother, stepfather, biological father, and siblings. Ultimately all of them were seen together in family treatment sessions.

In the face of events such as those just described, people actually make contact with agencies in a variety of ways. Some hear about a service that relates to their needs through newspapers, radio and television announcements, and other communications of the mass media. Others are approached through the outreach efforts of agencies.

At one time, agencies assumed that people who needed their services would either know of these or be referred by those who did. This was not true of many people who most needed services because they were the poorest, the least educated, and the newest to the community. In the 1960s, when concern for such people was high in the United States and many other nations, agencies considered new ways to reach out. This included engaging in door-to-door contacts, placing staff as speakers in churches, schools, and other indigenous institutions; and having staff approach people living in at-risk situations by reason of exposure to poor housing, health hazards, economic hardships, and similar stresses.

The issue of access to social agencies is a crucial one for members of many ethnic groups. Some of the most necessary services are not available in many Asian-American, Hispanic, native American, and black communities. Even when these services are located there, they are likely to be staffed by people who do not come from the ethnic

groups in the community. The agencies may appear strange to such potential clients because of language, norms, procedures, and even decor. Example of this are a hospital program for elderly people that did not serve the familiar foods, speak the language, or understand the family situations of the Chinese Americans in its neighborhood and an alcohol treatment program that did not understand the history and meaning of alcohol consumption to the native Americans in its locale. When members of these groups were referred to the programs, they tried to avoid following through on the referrals because of the information that had been disseminated about the agencies.

This raises the topic of referrals. Potential clients are referred by social workers, ministers, teachers, lawyers, and members of almost any group that serves people. Several tasks are essential for anyone to fulfill who seeks to make such a referral. First, the referring agent must have sufficient knowledge of the needs and requirements of individuals to know that these needs will be met by the referred agency. Second, that agent must know enough about the agency to know that it can and will meet these needs.

Third, the individual (or family or group) to be referred must be prepared for the referral. This includes giving information about the reason for the referral and what may be expected from the agency. The feelings that the person(s) has about the referral must also be handled, including fears about acceptance in the new agency and rejection from the referring agency. Fourth, the agency to which the person has been referred should also be prepared. Ideally, then, that person can ask for a specific staff members with the assurance that he or she is expected. In some cases the referring worker will accompany the person to the agency, will meet with him or her until the referral is established, and will advocate on his or her behalf if services are not appropriately offered.

In this chapter, we have used the word "client" to refer both to the person who has entered into a contract with the worker as well as the one who potentially will do so. Many writers usefully distinguish between these two sets of persons, and we now discuss this issue using the word "applicant" to denote a potential client.[8]

The Worker's Tasks with Applicants

When the individual comes to a social agency, he or she has not necessarily made any commitment to solve problems with the help of the agency. In fact, as we have seen, this move may have been made on a nonvoluntary or involuntary basis. Until this commitment is made, and is reciprocated by the worker and the agency, it is appropriate to speak only of the individual as an applicant. The only obligation on the part of the applicant is to explore whether or not the service is of potential use and whether he or she wishes to use it.

Constraints are placed on the worker also because of the individual's applicant status. The worker has an obligation to present the relevant aspects of the agency's service in a manner that the applicant can understand. Agencies have often prepared written materials for this purpose, but some also have audio or audiovisual presentations that illustrate agency services. Some will even invite applicants to view actual agency services such as group meetings—with the permission of the other individuals involved.

The worker should identify clearly for the applicant the information that will be required for both the applicant and the agency to make a decision as to whether the service is appropriate. An extensive inquiry into the applicant's history or the elicitation of any data that are not relevant for this purpose is unethical and intrusive.

The worker also has no right to begin any process of change of the applicant or the applicant's situation until the applicant becomes a client. This is not to deny the dictum that help begins with the first interview, and a discussion of the move from applicant to client status can have beneficial consequences for applicants whether or not they become clients. They can feel understood; they may gain an awareness of aspects of their situation of which they were unaware; and a decision to seek or not to seek service or to seek it elsewhere can represent a greater degree of clarity than they had prior to such an exploration.

The applicant is likely to have many feelings about that status. If the problem causes the applicant a great deal of discomfort, he or she is likely to feel impotent and, consequently, irritated with the application (intake) process. Some agencies also have separate intake and service workers so that the period between application and "actual" help may be long and may entail relating to two or more staff members.

The applicant, also, may have doubts about whether the choice to come was correct or whether his or her energy could have been employed in a more productive way. This feeling will be even more intense if, as is likely, the applicant has had to miss work or school, or hire a baby sitter, or arrange for travel to attend the session. This is not to imply that the feelings of applicants will be all negative. There may also be an expectation of help and relief from pain—a comfort in knowing that a burden will be shared.

The worker throughout the helping process, as we shall discuss later, must communicate to the applicant-client that his or her ideas and feelings are perceived and understood. This serves the dual function of reassuring the applicant of the understanding of the worker and of providing the worker with feedback on the accuracy of the worker's own perceptions and attributions regarding what they mean. This process begins with the first interview when the worker reflects an understanding of what it may mean for the applicant to ask for help.

In this application process, the worker helps the applicant to express his or her reasons for coming, and the response is usually in the form of a general statement of the problem. The following are a few examples:

- I'm failing in school.
- My wife and I argue all the time.
- I've just lost my job.
- I don't have any friends.

The worker's next task as the applicant provides such answers is to ask about the range of concerns and/or problems the applicant may have. Sometimes applicants will dwell upon what is later identified as a lesser problem because of fears as to the worker's reaction to more severe problems. This is a complex issue for the worker to confront because some applicants will be best able to tackle more severe problems after they either test out the worker's competence or experience some success with minor ones. Other applicants require only some encouragement or mild confrontation ("That can't really be why you're here") to reveal their "real" reasons for coming to the agency. The worker may have to assess some aspects of the client's situation to make this decision.

A central value in our system of practice is that the problem to be worked on should be chosen by the applicant or client. This does not restrain the worker from suggesting that the applicant or client work on other problems, but the worker should respect the applicant's right to make the final choice. Some workers will utilize a problem inventory to help in this process. Such an inventory includes questions about how the applicant is functioning in various roles such as employee, parent, spouse, or friend. Even this type of procedure should be engaged in only with the permission of the applicant. In practice, since the ways in which workers can influence clients are extensive, how problems are chosen is seldom as simple as this. This leads to some contradictions and paradoxes related to this principle, particularly in the case of involuntary referrals.

One typical issue arises when the applicant has been referred for one problem yet wishes to work on another or refuses to work on any at all. An illustration of this is a child referred to a school social worker for failure on numerous occasions to follow the teacher's instructions. The child refuses to acknowledge this as a problem. The worker ultimately contracts with the child to help her cope with times when the teacher seeks to control her behavior, and consequently she becomes upset.

This example raises another important point as to whether some problem statements are unacceptable to the worker. Some workers only consider statements that place the responsibility for the problem upon the applicant. We find this an unnecessary barrier to service. If a husband, for example, states that his wife is the problem, the worker can accept this and respond, "Let's then discuss what you can do about it." This type of response focuses on the applicant's behavior while accepting his or her definition of the problem. Another complex issue involves *reframing*, a term which describes the worker's attempt to redefine a problem as a means of making it more amenable to change.

Workers should also remember that the word "problem" is aversive to some applicants. Synonyms such as "concerns" can be used as substitutes. Based on these considerations, we have prepared the following lists of worker and applicant tasks undertaken during the application process:

1. The worker should inquire of the applicant how he or she arrived at this agency.
   a. Was this a voluntary, nonvoluntary, or involuntary process?
   b. Was this a result of a crisis or a new force brought to bear on an ongoing situation?
2. The worker should explain to the applicant the nature of the agency and its policies insofar as they may be relevant to the applicant.
3. The worker should identify and reflect an understanding of the applicant's feelings about coming to the agency. If these feelings are angry ones or in other ways reflect resistance, the worker should indicate an acceptance of these feelings and should not proceed to the next phase until the applicant is ready to do so.
4. The worker should elicit the applicant's view of the problems that have led to coming to the agency. Other problem areas should be explored with the permission of the applicant. Some ranking of problems should be attempted.
5. The worker should explain, at least in general terms, what will happen at the next stage if the applicant becomes a client. While this will be discussed later in the book in more detail, it consists of greater specifications of the problem, assessment of the client and his or her situation relevant to the problem, and selection of a plan for beginning to work on a solution to the problem.
6. The worker should explore any values or other worker characteristics that will influence the offer of service (for example, race, religious, and gender differences).
7. The worker should discuss whether the action system will be the individual, family, or a group of unrelated individuals.
8. The worker should determine on the basis of the foregoing whether the applicant should,

in fact, become a client. If this is not agreed upon, a referral process to another resource may be required. The feelings of the applicant about not becoming a client should be elicited and responded to.

Similarly the applicant has a series of tasks:

1. The applicant should present reasons or experiences relevant to coming to the agency.
2. The applicant should seek to understand services and policies of the agency.
3. The applicant should explore his or her feelings about being an applicant.
4. The applicant should present problems that he or she will work on if he or she becomes a client.
5. The applicant should explore worker characteristics that may affect the choice to become a client, work on one problem rather than another, or work in one way rather than another.
6. The applicant should participate in decisions as to steps to be taken in the first stage of clienthood, including a definition of the action system.
7. The applicant who does not become a client should explore other alternatives for problem solving and embark on one of them—including coping on one's own without professional help.

The following is an example of an effort to accomplish these tasks.

Example

Mrs. W, age 69, had recently been hospitalized for a heart problem, but her medical condition has now been stabilized. Because she is a widow and lives alone, her doctor referred her to the hospital social worker to consider whether this living plan will still be feasible for her. She made the appointment but questioned at the beginning of the interview why she should see a social worker. The worker indicated that one of the functions of medical social service is to help persons to make plans that are required by their health needs. The worker asked Mrs. W if she was willing to discuss this further to see if Mrs. W could use such services. Mrs. W asked what this would involve. The worker indicated that they could go over the doctor's recommendations to see if Mrs. W needed any help in planning how to follow them, such as those regarding climbing stairs, lifting, or doing heavy work. Mrs. W said she could see this discussion might be helpful.

The worker asked Mrs. W if she had some concerns about talking to a social worker. Mrs. W said that she had a friend who was also a widow and who had fallen and broken her hip. She was now in "one of those homes for old people," and Mrs. W said that a social worker and the friend's son had "put her there." Mrs. W thought that once you became involved with a social worker, the worker might find some way to force you to do things you didn't really want to.

The worker replied that she couldn't answer for what another worker had done as she didn't know anything about the situation. She was aware of Mrs. W's concerns about losing her freedom, however. She could promise Mrs. W that she would help her *only* to think through what she wanted to do in her situation. Mrs. W was fully capable of making her own decisions, and the worker said she would respect that. The referral from the doctor said that Mrs. W might wish some help in deciding whether she wanted to try to keep up her large family home by herself or to make another arrangement. This, the worker reiterated, was completely up to Mrs. W.

We can identify, in this example, many of the characteristics of applicant situations just described. Mrs. W did follow through on her obligation as applicant to find out if the service could be of use by asking for the purpose of a medical social service department. The worker observed the principles we have referred to in that she gave a simple explanation of the service relevant to Mrs. W's needs. The worker did not ask many questions but sought permission to explore Mrs. W's functioning as it was affected by her health. The worker was also careful to explain that her questions would be relevant to Mrs. W's situation. The worker exhibited empathy with regard to Mrs. W's fears of losing her freedom and sought to reassure her this would not be infringed upon by the worker.

Tasks with Nonclients

The ethical responsibilities of the social worker cover all professional encounters, although issues arise with people who are not clients that differ from those with clients. When the individual is an applicant, the principles of confidentiality, self-determination, and respect for persons apply to the same degree they would if the person were a client. In addition, the worker has the responsibility to help the person to secure the best possible service. This means that the worker must not attempt to push his or her own service if it appears that another agency's services are more appropriate. The worker must also consider whether even another worker in the same agency should be utilized. This requires considerable self-awareness on the part of the worker, as well as courage, as the worker must admit fallibility on his or her part as well as the agency's.

"Significant Others" in the Client's Life

We believe that everyone who "enters" the agency must be regarded as a potential client and given the same rights as an applicant. Thus, for example, if an interview is arranged with a family member, the worker must maintain a dual focus. On the one hand, the worker interviews the family member on behalf of the client and focuses on the needs of the client. On the other hand, the family member also has needs, and these should at least be acknowledged to prevent the family member from becoming an "object" manipulated for the benefit of the client. In addition, the family member may wish to utilize the agency's services, or that of some other resource, to attain his or her own goals, and, as with any applicant, the social worker has a responsibility to help that person to contact the appropriate facility.

The example of the family member seen on behalf of the client constitutes a single-person type of "action system" that does not coincide with the "client system." Types of multiperson action systems are groups of unrelated members, families, committees, community groups, and staff groups in organizations. The ethical principles for a family member apply to any single-person action system. Additional issues are raised when the worker interacts with a multiperson action system on behalf of an individual client.

Two different situations are possible when one works with a multiperson action system: one occurs when all members of the system have the same position with regard to the worker. This is true when doing group work and all members have joined the group for personal enhancement. The ethical principle under these circumstances is that the worker may engage in actions that will benefit some members but not others but should not do anything that helps some but harms others.

In the second type of situation, some members of the system are clients but not others. This occurs, for example, when a worker has accepted a nuclear family (two parents and their children) as clients but invites members of the extended family (e.g., grandparents or aunts and uncles) to attend a session when interactions with them will be helpful to that nuclear family. All persons present assume that the people for whose benefit the session was arranged are these in the nuclear family. The members of the extended family may find value in the session,

but the session has not been planned with this in mind.

The worker has the following ethical obligations in this second type of situation:

1. To indicate to those who are not clients any risks they may incur by participating in the session
2. To help such persons to become clients, if they so wish, although the workers may reach the conclusion that they should be referred to another worker

The risks referred to in (1) should be taken seriously. Harm may befall persons in a confrontation with clients such as withdrawal of financial support or other resources in the possession of the client or a termination of the relationship with the client. In addition, nonclients may be provided with information that is painful for them to hear. Unpleasant results of this magnitude, if the risks of incurring them are clearly presented, do not present as much of a moral problem for workers as do more severe ones, as when a client may inflict physical harm on others or greater pain than is required to attain justifiable objectives. We believe under no circumstances should workers facilitate the inflicting of physical harm or the imposition of greater costs on nonclients than a situation warrants, and workers should seek to prevent these outcomes.

Others Selected as Target Systems

Ethical issues also surround the ends, and means utilized to achieve ends, with regard to target systems. The following are examples in which target systems were utilized. In the first, a youth is asked to plan how he will make a request of his teacher; the teacher is the target system. Another is a group that plans to petition the agency to change rules regarding group fund raising;

the agency is the target system. A third is work with a client to help the client compose a letter in opposition to proposed welfare legislation; the legislature is the target system.

When target systems are involved, the worker incurs ethical obligations by virtue of participating in a process that has effects on people even though they are not clients. This is not to deny the fact that the primary responsibility rests with the client to decide to take the action. The worker, nevertheless, has the obligation to avoid participation in events that harm or deceive others. (A further discussion of selection of target systems is presented in Chapter 9.)

This raises the question of the client's right to survive and to attain more power in situations where the client is relatively powerless. A client, for example, in a union dispute, is not required to inform management of union strategy or to forbear from demands that will cost the employer money. It is commonly understood in these situations that such strategies are legitimate. Actions affecting primary relationships, however, such as those with family members and friends, should be governed by a strict set of moral principles, and the worker should also be bound by this.

Defining the Client in a Multiperson Client System

As we have noted, several persons can jointly constitute a client system in which the contract represents a consensus between members of the system and the worker; the goals of service are expressed in terms of the "group" rather than the individuals; and attainment of goals is measured in "group" rather than individual terms. Such client systems are found in family treatment, some approaches to group work, and work with "nat-ural" groupings such as people assigned to cottages in residential treatment centers.

One issue in practice is whether the worker and the people who receive service have the same view as to who is the client. The worker, for ideological or theoretical reasons, may view the "group" as client and may seek changes in it that are not expressly agreed upon by the service recipients. The concept of "group as client" is a fairly abstract one, and one that even workers may find it hard to utilize. Some even insist that the individual is always the "client."

An example of this kind of problem is Haley's belief that when a family presents one of its members as the identified patient (i.e., the family member whose behavior has led to seeking service), the worker should accept this problem definition.[9] Haley, however, thinks of changes in terms of family interactional sequences and hierarchies. An explicit discussion of the rationale for a family perspective is regarded as dysfunctional by some workers because of the countermoves that such an explanation might evoke in the family. In Haley's approach, it is unclear as to who the client is, as issues of definiton of clienthood are not extensively dealt with by that author. In our approach, however, we argue that the definition of the client system must be clarified with the applicant.

Since few families, or other natural groups, come for service with a presentation of their problems in systemic terms, the worker who thinks in this way has an obligation to explain this perspective and to secure informed consent to the implications of this view. If the family or other group is provoked into taking measures to protect the way in which it has been functioning as a system, this is their right. We believe that people have the right to define their difficulties in either individual or group terms. The worker who has an intellectual or ideological commitment to a perspective that is different from the client's also has a right to pursue this; as we have stated, the worker, then, has a responsibility to inform applicants of this perspective and to help them to consider seeking help elsewhere when perspectives clash. Although there is some evidence that supports family perspectives as being more effective than individual ones under specified circumstances, one cannot make an across-the-board claim of the superiority of family approaches under all circumstances.[10] Whenever research suggests this kind of uncertainty of outcomes, we believe that emphasis should be placed on client preferences. This is a complex issue, however, and we shall discuss it much more thoroughly later (see Chapter 12).

In some practice models *both* the individual and the group are considered "clients," and contracts are made with both regarding goals and means of achieving them.[11] In one of these models, the worker functions as the mediator between systems and seeks to help each system to negotiate with the other so that, through a recognition of their interdependence, they may attain desired objectives.[12]

It is also possible for changes in the definition of the client system to occur with the same persons over time. Thus, one might start out by working with an entire family as the client and ultimately shift to working with individual family members as clients, or the opposite might also occur. The same can happen in work with groups of unrelated persons. The important issue in the concept of the client is not that the use of the concept directs the worker as to who is the client but rather that it forces the worker to be explicit

as to whom he or she is working with and on whose behalf the worker's activities are conducted.

Agency Conditions and Definitions of Client

Presumably the social agency primarily exists to serve clients; without the presence of people who need the services of the agency, it would disband and its resources would be reallocated. Despite this fact, other agency purposes exist because of the objectives of people who are not clients. Workers may seek particular experiences: researchers, data; board members, the prestige that comes from membership; and legislators, the political support of those who favor programs and policies. Thus, despite the best of intentions, if clients are powerless to affect agency practices, their needs can be subverted to those of other groups. A number of organizational conditions affect the client's position, and consequently, how client needs, in comparison with those of other groups, are met.

One of these is whether the clients, staff, and agency policymakers come from similar ethnic, social class, and cultural backgrounds. When they do, client needs may be respected because of the linkages among these groups. One must consider all the variables that affect social distance, as similarity on one dimension does not mean similarity on another. For example, earlier in this century services were established for Eastern European Jews by German and other Western European Jews who had emigrated to the United States much earlier. These service providers recognized a social obligation to clients, yet viewed the newcomers as inferiors "who must be Americanized in spite of themselves."[13] This led to pressure on clients to relinquish their cultural patterns, a process that must have taken its toll in low self-esteem and cultural impoverishment.

In recent years there has been pressure on agencies to invite representatives of client groups to join agency policymaking bodies. When this is done, the way in which it is done, who is chosen, and who has ultimate power will also affect how clients are seen in the agency. The concept of clients as indigenous workers has been proclaimed as a way of changing the status of the client, but this, too, has been an idea surrounded by controversy as to the influence and role of such staff.

A radical idea regarding the position of clients was espoused by Bertha Reynolds almost 40 years ago. [14] She recognized the limitations on client autonomy posed by the powerless role of clients in most agencies. As an alternative, she developed the idea of social workers as employees of an organization controlled by clients and implemented this through the United Seamen's Services of the National Maritime Union. She believed that when social services are established in this way, clients would not be stigmatized, would trust the service, and would ultimately benefit more than from services under other auspices.

We suggest, therefore, that workers examine carefully how clients compare with other groups related to the agency, the implications of similarities and differences, the positions that clients or people from the same social groups as clients hold in the agency, and whether in the agency the client means constituent, creator, or partner on the one hand or inferior, pawn, or necessary nuisance on the other. The results of this examination will include working for agency-changes that will reduce discrepancies between agency and client perspectives on problems.

Summary

The chapter began with a discussion of the term "client" and its meaning in social work. We justified our use of the term, although we recognized some of the controversies related to power and interactional issues implied by its usage. We also noted that, in social work, the client may be an individual, family, or group, and we analyzed some of the implications of this fact.

The use of the word "client" also raises issues as to the terms to be employed for other people with whom social workers interact. We join with other writers in applying the concepts of worker, action, and target systems to designate others.

The major portion of the chapter was devoted to describing the implications for subsequent processes and tasks of how people become clients. An important distinction is whether the individual chooses independently to seek help (voluntary client), is pressured to come (nonvoluntary client), or faces serious consequences for not coming (involuntary client). Another distinction is whether the event precipitating coming to the social worker is a severe, recent, and debilitating one or a chronic one. In the case of the chronic event, the worker will inquire as to how the decision to seek help at this time was reached. The answers to these and other questions will affect the client's motivation for working on his or her problems as well as what the client wishes to change to resolve such problems.

Until the individual has determined that he or she has come to the right place for help and wishes to accept such services, and until the worker has reached the same conclusion, the individual is not properly a client. The word "applicant" has been used for people engaging in this process, and we, therefore, discussed the role of applicant and the process that occurs in moving from the applicant to client role.

We subsequently discussed the workers' responsibilities to other people with whom they interact on behalf of clients. These include members of the "action system" who are not clients, namely, family members and peers. Another category is those people who are targets of change with whom the client but not the worker interacts, such as teachers and employers. This section of the chapter also described some of the issues that arise when the client system consists of several people as in family treatment. The chapter concluded with a consideration of the effect upon all clients of the relationship of the status of clients as a group to the status of other groups in the agency such as staff and board.

In the next chapter we shall consider another phase in the process of becoming a client. This phase, engagement, is one in which the problem is further specified, goals identified, and a preliminary contract agreed upon.

NOTES

1. See such usage in Jeffrey Galper, *Social Work Practice: A Radical Perspective* (Englewood Cliffs, N.J.: Prentice-Hall, 1980), pp. 128–151.

2. Allen Pincus and Anne Minahan, *Social Work Practice: Model and Method* (Itasca, Ill.: F. E. Peacock, 1973), pp. 53–68.

3. For an earlier discussion of this concept, see Charles Garvin and Paul Glasser, "The Bases of Social Treatment," in Paul Glasser, Rosemary Sarri, and Robert Vinter, eds., *Individual Change Through Small Groups* (New York: The Free Press, 1974), p. 488.

4. See David Landy, "Problems of the Person Seeking Help in Our Culture," in *The Social Welfare Forum 1960,*(New York: Columbia University Press, 1960), pp. 127–145.

5. Bruno Bettelheim, *A Home for the Heart* (New York: Knopf, 1974), pp. 91–173.

6. For an extensive discussion of crisis theory, see Naomi Golan, *Treatment in Crisis Situations* (New York: The Free Press, 1978).

7. This conclusion is related to the finding that the client's hope (as well as the worker's) is an important predictor of outcomes. See E. Stotland, *The Psychology of Hope* (San Francisco: Jossey-Bass, 1969).

8. For a discussion of the concept of applicant, see Helen H. Perlman, "Intake and Some Role Considerations," *Social Casework*, Vol. 41 (1960), pp. 171–177.

9. Jay Haley, *Problem Solving Therapy* (New York: Harper & Row, 1976), pp. 9–15.

10. Alan S. Gurman and David P. Kniskern, "Research on Marital and Family Therapy: Progress, Perspective, and Prospect," in Allen E. Bergin, and Sol L. Garfield, eds., *Handbook of Psychotherapy and Behavior Change: An Empirical Analysis*, 2nd ed. (New York: John Wiley, 1978), pp. 817–902.

11. See, for example, the chapter "Working with the Group as Client," in Lawrence Shulman, ed., *The Skills of Helping: Individuals and Groups* (Itasca, Ill.: F. E. Peacock, 1979), pp. 232–262.

12. Ibid., pp. 10–12.

13. Irving Howe, *World of our Fathers* (New York: Simon & Schuster, 1976), p. 230.

14. Bertha C. Reynolds, *Social Work and Social Living* (New York: Citadel, 1951).

five
Engagement

In the last chapter, we described some of the events that lead people to enter a social agency for service either as willing or unwilling applicants and subsequently move toward becoming clients. In this chapter, we consider the subsequent transactions between workers and clients that lead, for some individuals and workers, to joint efforts to solve client problems and, for others, to a decision to pursue change through some other means.

The process of becoming a client may be viewed as occurring at two stages. At the first stage, the one considered in the previous chapter, the individual moves from applicant to client status as he or she decides that the agency is the right place to bring the problem, a problem often stated in fairly general terms. The client views this decision as appropriate because the methods used by this worker in this agency promise to be useful for solving the client's problems, although the nature of such methods may be understood only in general terms by the client. During

this stage, other terms of service are agreed upon such as time and length of sessions, fees for service, and other obligations on the part of both workers and clients.

At this point, which is usually reached in one or two sessions, another stage, which we call engagement, begins (although in short-term work, this can happen concurrently) during which the problem is specified in greater detail; goals regarding changes in the client, the environment, or both are established as ways of solving the problem; and the part of the contract that incorporates these goals as well as means for attaining them is negotiated. Such goals, and means for attaining them, have been selected on the basis of the worker's and client's assessment of the client and the client's situation. The time that it takes to accomplish the task of this second stage varies considerably based on the complexity of the client's problem, the client's motivation, and even whether the client has presented the problem he or she "really" wants to work on, or whether a period of redefining the problem is required. Thus, for some clients this stage may require a few sessions while for others it may last for months.

During this stage, also, the relationship among clients and between clients and workers must develop to the point that it will sustain the problem-solving work. In this chapter, consequently, we shall discuss the factors that promote the client's commitment to this relationship, the kinds of relationship factors that are conducive to problem solving, and the procedures that are utilized to clarify the roles of people who comprise the worker and client systems. There are similarities and differences in how this occurs in individual, family, and group contexts that will also be considered in this chapter. Some of the problems that occur to prevent the attainment of these conditions for problem-solving work will also be discussed and solutions suggested.

In this chapter, we shall also discuss those aspects of engagement incorporated in problem specification and relationship development. Assessment, planning, and the full details of contracting and monitoring change will be discussed in subsequent chapters. Prior, however, to beginning this discussion of engagement, we describe some research findings that are highly relevant to the issues posed in this chapter, namely, research on continuance and discontinuance of client-worker relationships.

Continuance and Discontinuance

As we have indicated, the overall objective of this phase is to build a foundation that ensures that the client and worker will work together to attain the client's goals. If this interaction terminates prior to goal attainment, that will obviously limit the usefulness of the social work process. The reader should also recognize that the social work service should terminate when goals are attained, as a delayed termination can actually undo goal attainment and the client can regress in order to justify remaining in the relationship.[1] It is also possible that the service is inadequate or inappropriate, and this is another reason to end it.

We believe, also, that much remains to be understood about the planning of termination. What is known will be discussed in greater depth in Chapter 14. At this point, however, it should be clear that the client must be helped to remain until goals are attained or until it is evident that this social work encounter is not the appropriate way of achieving them. Research into the causes of termination prior to goal attainment can help us to understand some of the issues that the worker and client must resolve in order to build a foundation for their work together— issues that constitute the subject matter of this chapter.

Much of the research on continuance and discontinuance seeks to compare people who continue with an interpersonal helping process with those who do not. An early social work study bearing upon the issue of continuance was that of Ripple and her colleagues.[2] In looking at client outcomes, the investigators divided the clients into two groups: those who had "external" and those who had "psychological" problems. Factors associated with the discontinuance of the individuals in the former group were that the responses of their social workers were discouraging or their environmental conditions were restrictive and unmodifiable. Clients in this category, those who had low motivation and capacity, continued to seek service if they received encouragement from the very beginning of the intake process.[3]

For clients with psychological problems, the factors of motivation and capacity were crucial for continuance in casework, at least casework of the traditional variety; yet such persons also must have experienced support from other persons in their lives. Limitations in regard to motivation, capacity, and such support were overcome and clients continued to make use of service when supplied with strong encouragement by workers. These variables were very potent as they enabled the researchers to predict accurately continuance and discontinuance for 93 percent of the clients with external problems and 86 percent of the clients with psychological problems.

Encouragement from workers was crucial with both groups of clients. It is interesting to note that the investigators defined discouragement as "a bland, seemingly uninvolved eliciting and appraisal of the client's situation, in which the worker appeared neutral in affect, left the client's discomfort untouched, and offered no basis for hope that the situation could be improved."[4] The other kind of discouragement was the placement of the client on a waiting list, often for an indefinite period.

Garfield has reviewed a number of studies of discontinuance in psychotherapy that are also relevant to social work services. He concludes, from a representative group of studies, that "a majority of clinics have lost one-half of their therapy clients before the eighth interview."[5] The median length of treatment was 3 to 12 interviews, but there was a clustering around 6 sessions.

A number of variables have been identified that discriminate between continuers and discontinuers in psychotherapy. One of these is social class: more middle-class than lower-class clients remain in psychotherapy. Other variables related to social class also produce the same kinds of findings.

For example, education also has been found to be associated with continuance. Race, a variable that is hard to separate from social class, is also predictive of continuance in that black clients are more likely than white clients to terminate early from psychotherapy. This finding should, however, be viewed in the light of another finding that black clients remain in treatment longer when matched with a therapist in regard to both race and social class.[6]

Another issue that complicates our understanding of the effects of social class is the reactions of the worker to the client's social class. Workers often seek to avoid lower-class clients because they predict that such clients are not amenable to therapy: predictions of this sort are undoubtedly turned into reality, actually a self-fulfilling prophesy.

This is not to deny that lower-class clients have different expectations of therapy than do middle-class ones. Several research studies have shown that lower-class clients are likely to expect therapists to be active whereas middle-class clients do not have the same expectation. Lower-class clients are also more likely than middle-class ones to expect advice. Nevertheless, we suspect that there is a continuum of these variables among all clients and that therapist expectations about social class are strong determinants of how much clients are encouraged to continue.[7]

We also should note that age, sex, and psychiatric diagnosis are not associated with continuance. There may be prejudices among practitioners regarding the effect of these dimensions on dropout rates, but this is not supported by research findings.

This presentation of research findings is not meant to discourage the reader from serving groups that have high discontinuance rates but rather to seek ways of working with these clients—such as approaches that are action oriented rather than primarily verbal—so that they find social work a useful service. This conclusion is one that we shall consider throughout this chapter, because social workers' clients are likely to be the ones who tend to drop out of psychotherapy: they are often people who are poor, who have less education, who are members of oppressed ethnic minorities, and who, therefore, are not likely to be as oriented to investing their time in long-term, verbal, introspective procedures as are middle-class clients.

Somewhat different forces may well be in operation in relationship to continuance in groups because group members' reactions are directed at other group members as well as at the worker. Yalom, in his examination of data on group dropouts, cites nine reasons for such discontinuance. Some of these are related to "traits which the patient brings with him to the group, whereas others are related to problems arising within the group."[8] Those related to the former are categorized by Yalom as "external factors," "group deviancy," and "problems of intimacy."[9]

The category of "external factors" incorporates several dimensions. One is conditions, such as lack of transportation and scheduling conflicts. These factors may actually be rationalizations for discontinuing group membership or they may be costs that outweigh benefits but, in either case, they are frequently cited by dropouts. Another external issue is when events in the life of the group members are so disturbing that the individual cannot tolerate attention to anyone else's problems than his or her own. Under this circumstance, individual approaches are more appropriate than group ones.

"Group deviancy," as used by Yalom, refers to a situation in which a group member's behavior differs substantially from that of other members—for example, disruptive be-

havior or nonparticipation. Such people, according to Yalom, also may have "a lack of psychological sophistication, a lack of interpersonal sensitivity, and a lack of personal psychological insight manifested in part by the common utilization of denial."[10] These group members are often of a lower socioeconomic status and educational level than others.

The issue of group deviance is very much a product of the purpose of the group, and the characteristics of all of the members and this issue will be further considered in Chapter 12 when we discuss group composition. At this point, however, we should take note of the fact that the attributes of some individuals may be so extreme in regard to those of other members of a group that their dropping out of groups is assured. In addition, we see in Yalom's conclusions the same social-class-related expectations that are referred to in the individual treatment literature, expectations that grow out of a conception of treatment as primarily a cognitive and verbal process. It is hoped that social workers, with the mission of the social work profession in mind, will not limit themselves to sets of procedures that depend primarily on psychological-mindedness and sophistication.

The third variable emphasized by Yalom, "problems of intimacy," refers to two sets of individuals: those who are reluctant to share personal concerns in groups and those who shock other members with the rapidity with which they reveal themselves. The likelihood that the client will act in these ways will predict an early dropout from group psychotherapy, but, again, social work groups that utilize nonverbal program activities more than verbal interactions may not have this effect.

Still other factors may affect dropouts of either individual family members or the entire family from family treatment. Individuals may drop out if they are extensively scapegoated by the other family members or if they perceive the worker as biased against them. This is a highly complex issue, as we shall see later, as families usually enter treatment with one member labeled the "patient." Even more complex an issue is the discontinuance of the entire family if this is due to the refusal of influential members to come or the way such members influence others to drop out. Much research, therefore, remains to be done on discontinuance in family and marital treatment situations.

The information on discontinuance from individual, group, and family situations should provide a backdrop to the rest of the chapter in which we consider the role of the worker in engaging the client in problem-solving efforts. The worker should take from this review of research the ideas that the process of engagement must relate to the client's motivation and capacity, the client's expectations of the helping process as influenced by education and culture, and the kinds of supports required from the worker to create bonds between worker and client, in one-to-one, and among clients, in group situations.

At the time that the worker and client enter this engagement phase, by definition they will have agreed that *this* agency is the appropriate place for *this* person with *this* problem. The client should then be made aware, as we shall describe, of the tasks of the next phase and should have made an informed commitment to pursue them. The worker and client, together, should estimate—given the nature of the client and the problem—how much time it is likely to take to assess the client and his or her circumstances and to generate goals and a general plan for attaining them. The client should be asked to make a commitment to this time and this process. We call this commitment *the preliminary contract*.

In the process of clarifying the problem, engaging in an assessment, and determining goals, the worker and the client must also clarify their respective roles. This clarification process is the subject of the following discussion.

Orientation to the Client Role

There are several ways of clarifying roles that can be used singly or in some combination to help the applicant move into the role of client. This process, referred to as *role induction*, has been well researched. Findings from this research show that training of clients for the client role is associated with better outcomes.[11] Inducting the client is a cognitive process in which the worker and client together examine the expectations that clients and worker have of their respective roles. We shall now describe one approach to this process.

A Role Clarification Procedure

When worker and clients interact, four sets of role expectations must be clarified: (1) the client's and (2) the worker's expectations for the client's role and (3) the client's and (4) the worker's expectations for the worker's role. We discuss each of these in turn and then describe a specific procedure for clarifying such expectations.

The client's expectation for his or her role is a product of the client's previous experiences with helping processes, both professional and informal, as well as of the client's concept of what the social work process is. Some clients believe that their major responsibility is to indicate the problem and the social worker will prescribe a solution. Other clients think that they will carry out the prescribed solution, while still others assume that they can continue to play a passive role, while others take the required actions. Still other clients will either assume that they should play a cooperative role in problem-solving or that they will even do most of the "work" with minimal help and support from the worker.

The worker's expectation of the client's role will be a product of the worker's theoretical orientation as well as of the worker's assessment of the client's motivation and capacity. Most theoretical orientations to practice require that the clients participate in solving their problems and in implementing solutions. An exception is some behavioral procedures in which the worker prescribes a behavioral change activity that has been proven effective for the type of problem presented. Even in this case, the client is expected to cooperate by complying with the recommended procedure. Any theoretical orientation must take into consideration that clients, such as young children or severely retarded people, will not be as active in their own behalf as otherwise well-functioning adults who face situational difficulties.

Problems arise when the worker and client hold conflicting expectations for the role of the client. A very frequent type of conflict is when workers expect clients to participate actively and the clients expect the workers to solve their problems for them. The reverse pattern, as we have implied, is much less likely to occur, as in most cases the practitioner's objective is to encourage the clients' activity on their own behalf. The exception is the use of behavioral or other structured procedures that the client is expected to follow.

The worker's and the client's expectations of the role of the worker should fit with the expectations of the role of the client. Workers will have the self-expectation that they should act in a competent manner to assess the client's problems and to recommend ways of reducing or solving them. They will

also hold the self-expectation that they should be able to secure the participation and cooperation of the clients in their own behalf. Clients will also expect the worker to have these competencies.

A conflict may arise around the workers' self-expectations regarding securing client participation. Many clients will expect the worker to be much more active on their behalf than the workers will expect themselves to be. These contrasting expectations grow out of the fact that the worker's expectations are largely a product of worker professional training while client expectations are a result of the client's previous experience with authority and helping figures, often their parents, combined with whatever previous exposure they have had to professional helping.

A phenomenon that makes this issue of expectations more complex is that workers and clients may have role expectations that are recognized and avowed as well as role expectations that are unrecognized and unavowed.[12] These two sets may contradict one another. An example of this is a man who stated that he primarily wanted the worker to help him make a decision as to whether or not to ask his girlfriend to marry him. His avowed expectation, therefore, was to be fully active in his own behalf. On the other hand, this client had a mother who had frequently made decisions for him. He acted, with a female worker, as if he wanted her to tell him what to do in this situation even though this was not the role for her that he had stated. His unavowed expectation, therefore, was not to make his own decisions, and the worker pointed this out to him.

This issue of avowed and unavowed expectations is sometimes analyzed in terms of the psychoanalytic concept of *transference*, which refers to expectations of relationships that correspond to those instilled early in life primarily in reference to parents. These expectations continue to govern contemporary relationships in ways of which the person is unaware. This is only one of many possible bases of avowed and unavowed expectations regarding workers that may be in conflict. For this reason, we prefer to analyze role expectations in role rather than in psychoanalytic terms.

It is, of course, possible and even likely that workers will also hold avowed and unavowed expectations of clients that are contradictory. The reasons for this grow out of the same sources as conflicts in clients: the worker's previous experiences with clients as well as with other significant persons in the worker's life. (In psychoanalytic terms, this relates to countertransference.) One of the most important functions of the supervision of the worker is to help the worker to resolve such conflicting expectations of clients. The worker can also become aware of and resolve these through the procedure we now describe.

The role clarification process involves three steps: explicating various expectations, comparing and identifying discrepancies in expectations, and negotiating agreements on expectations.

1. *Explicating expectations.* In this step, clients are asked to state specifically (orally or in writing) what they expect or want of the worker and what they expect their own responsibilities in the service process to be.

When these two sets of expectations are fairly complete, the worker also states what he or she considers to be the worker's role responsibilities and the client's role responsibilities.

It is important that the clients state their expectations first, or at least independently, so that worker's expectations do not contaminate or shape the client's.

2. *Comparing and identifying discrepancies.* In this step, the worker's and client's expectations of the worker are compared and the worker's and client's expectations of the client are similarly examined. This will indicate any conflicts or ambiguity that exist between the two sets of expectations.

3. *Negotiations.* In this final step, workers and clients seek to come to terms with the discrepant or conflicting perspectives. This process should also reinforce the areas where no conflicts exist.

With some clients there will be a tendency to accept the worker's perspective on roles and to deny their own. To prevent such premature closure on discrepancies, that is, to keep clients from "selling out" in the face of worker authority, workers should tell clients that there can be legitimate differences and that they and the clients will attempt to reach agreement. The worker and client should see differences as constructive, as they can lead to a clarification of many distortions in relationships that prevent the client from interacting effectively with others.

When the client system is a family or group, this role clarification procedure can be repeated for each person, or all individuals can discuss role issues and reach a common perspective. The former process is utilized in therapy groups in which individual goals are established and in which each individual with the help of other group members works toward his or her goals. When there is more of an emphasis on the group as such, as in family treatment, the members also can work together to clarify their respective responsibilities.

This process may be seen as cumbersome, and we do not recommend it routinely. Workers should adapt it to their own purposes, either by utilizing only part of the process or by utilizing it fully with clients when role complementarity is a significant problem. Workers should also generate creative and interesting ways to pursue a role clarification process (use of diagrams, puppets used in pairs, placing the information on large sheets of newsprint).

Role Training

Another approach to role clarification is to provide role training. Yalom describes an interview procedure for group therapy clients that he found led to better outcomes than the outcomes for those clients not prepared in this way.[13] Yalom's approach included an explanation of what group therapy is, the results that can be expected from it, the reasons why it presumably works, and the difficulties that are encountered in initial sessions and that may tempt some clients to terminate prematurely.

Yalom reports on the effectiveness of his training procedure only for long-term group psychotherapy. We have proposed that analogous procedures for other forms of experience can and should be developed and tested.[14] The basic components of such procedures are a description of what is likely to occur in the individual, family, or group experience; what will be expected of clients; what the rationale for the particular approach is; and what the outcomes have been.

Procedures have been developed and tested for individual psychotherapy. Orne and Wender developed a role induction interview with four components: (1) a general exposition of psychotherapy, (2) the expected behavior of patient and therapist, (3) preparation for such phenomenon in therapy as resistance, and (4) expectation for improvement within four months of treatment.[15]

Another approach to role training for clients is to provide them with examples of client behaviors. This can include tape recording of interviews or group sessions, written descriptions, or even observation of sessions with the permission of the observed clients. A variant of this is to ask previous clients to share some of their experiences with new clients. This last approach has been utilized in such situations as preparation of adoptive parents, foster parents, and persons newly admitted to residential settings.

Undoubtedly these procedures are even more essential when class or other cultural differences produce expectations and perceptions of social work processes that are discrepant between worker and clients. Research findings bear out the value of role training with disadvantaged populations. Preparation of such clients, however, is only half the requirement for successful outcomes. Additional findings support the conclusion that training workers to work with lower-class clients is of equal importance.[16] Such worker preparation includes recognition of feelings and attitudes toward lower-class clients and understanding of the lifestyles, needs, and expectations of members of these groups.[17]

Systematic research on client preparation has been done more in relationship to psychotherapy than social work processes. Information, therefore, must be secured on the nature and consequences of such approaches in social work situations. Particularly important are systems of preparation for social work services that diverge from long-term psychotherapy such as short-term, structured, or reality-oriented problem-solving approaches. Effective ways of preparing nonvoluntary clients to accept services should also be developed and tested.

After role induction experiences have been used, the worker must begin the problem-solving process as well as create the kind of worker-client or worker-member-group relationship that will support this process. We now consider these topics.

The Initiation of Problem Solving:

Specifying the Problem

During the process of deciding to become a client, applicants define problems that they and their workers believe fall within the purview of the agency. When these problems are expressed in general terms, as is often the case, workers help clients to specify the problem in concrete terms, usually by asking the clients about the details of events related to the problem. Workers will typically ask about recent events as these are likely to be clear to the clients and clients may also be motivated to reveal them. The aspects of the problem to be specified are the performance discrepancy, the time dimension, the relevant people in the process, and the varying perceptions of significant individuals.

Performance Discrepancy. While the worker will make note of the specific way in which the client defines the problem, it is often helpful to rephrase the problem so as to infer the kinds of changes in the client or situation that may resolve it. One way of rephrasing the problem is in terms of a *performance discrepancy* of either the client or relevant others or both.[18] A *performance* is the specific way in which one or more individuals (such as a family) act, think, or feel in a specific situation. A *discrepancy* indicates that this performance is different from the desired performance.

If some or all of the behaviors involved in the performance are increased or decreased, the discrepancy is reduced. Examples of desired increases in behaviors are more communication between a husband and wife or parent and child, more homework by a child, or more social engagements attended by an isolated person. Examples of desired decreases in behaviors are fewer periods of depressed or anxious feelings, fewer occasions when a child is abused, or fewer obsessive thoughts.

To state a performance discrepancy, therefore, the worker and client must determine what the situation was in which the performance occurred, what the performance was, and what is a more desirable performance. Some examples of such statements are the following:

1. Mrs. J becomes very anxious when she leaves her house, so she stays in all of the time. She would like to feel calm enough when she leaves the house to shop, work, or attend social engagements.

In this example, Mrs. J's performance was her feelings of anxiety as well as her failure to leave the house. The discrepancy was between that and the desired performance of feeling calm and accomplishing a variety of tasks outside the house. The situation consisted of events relevant to when she wants to go out.

2. When Mr. S returns home after having worked late at the office, he and his wife have severe arguments about his behavior that end with their not speaking to each other for days. Mr. and Mrs. S want to resolve the issue of how to handle such situations without having severe arguments.

In this example, the performance of the couple was a severe argument followed by not talking for days. The situation was when Mr. S returned home after working late at the office. The discrepancy was between having severe arguments and having problem-solving discussions.

In addition to a formulation of the problem as a performance discrepancy, there are a number of other dimensions of the problem that the worker will clarify during this phase. It is hoped that the client will often provide this information as it is important that any interview with a client be as spontaneous as possible. Occasionally, however, the worker will raise appropriate questions, reflect client responses, and comment on client feelings.

Time Dimensions. How frequently has the problem occurred and when did the problem start? This dimension has relevance for understanding the client's motivation to solve the problem as well as for determining the systems that are involved in maintaining the problem.

Relevant People. Who else is involved in the problem situation as a participant in, as a victim of, or as a labeler of the problem? For example, a husband and wife had severe arguments in which the husband physically abused the wife. Several children in the family did poorly in school. The wife's mother, however, was the person who called the police. In this situation, the participants were the marital pair, the children, and the wife's mother. This inventory of persons has relevance for recommending the composition of the client system, hypothesizing the possible causes of the problem, and determining persons who may be included in action or target systems.

Process. In a specific situation in which the problem was present, how did a manifestation of the problem begin? Who did or said what to whom? What events occurred next and in what order? Who was involved at each stage and what were their roles? This information, in addition to having relevance for determining the ultimate client, action, and target systems, is also important for the assessment of the problem, particularly with reference to causal factors. Finally, the solution of the problem often lies in a change in the system in which it occurs; such a change does involve altering the process (that is, the sequence of events) of the situation. In family interviews, and other group situations, the worker should obtain the perceptions of all the family members on the sequence of events in the problem situation.

Varying Perceptions. Do all relevant persons see the problem in the same way? This question can be asked of the other persons, or of the client, or both. A similarity in perceptions helps to establish the reliability of the facts presented by the client. On the other hand, contrasting perceptions provide clues to the nature of the situation and the forces that may be maintaining the problem. For example, a mother stated that her child was compliant in school while a school psychologist observed the child acting toward the teacher in a provocative way. The social worker learned that the mother also acted in a provocative manner to other family members, a trait that she sought to deny in both herself and her daughter. The *conflicting descriptions* of the daughter's behavior were clues to this pattern.

Client Priorities

After the client has described one problem, other problems are usually identified. The worker should help the client who has multiple problems to order them in terms of importance and to choose one on which to begin. Some questions that help clients and workers to do this are:

1. Which problem is the most distressing to the client?
2. Which problem is most distressing to others?
3. Which problem can be most readily solved or, if solved, will reinforce the motivation and capacity of the client to solve other problems?
4. Which problem, if solved, will simultaneously reduce other problems?

5. Is there a logical order to take up problems such as when the solution to a problem requires solution to an antecedent problem?

Problem Specification in Family and Group Systems

When the worker interacts with a family as a client system, unique components to problem specification arise. One of these is whether to approach a definition of the problem in terms of individual or family conditions. This issue is also problematic because families who come for help often define one member as the "problem." This person is referred to in the family therapy literature as the "identified patient." Differences exist among family practitioners as to how to respond to this. Some accept an individual definition of the problem because rejecting this definition may lead to premature termination as the family's reality has been denied. Others quickly move the family to a statement of the problem in terms of the whole family.

We prefer, as in most matters, to operate flexibly in this regard. If the family strongly presents the problem as an individual one, we accept this. If the family, on the other hand, is likely to see the problem in family terms, we work from that perspective. We believe that there is a difference between a definition of the problem and an assessment of it. We can accept a statement of the problem as "Johnny does not go to school" and an assessment of it as Johnny remains at home to prevent his father and mother from fighting. We do not insist that the family must define this problem as, for example, having poor ways of resolving family conflicts—although some families are prepared to think in such terms.

An important dynamic in many families, in addition, is that different members may define the "problem" in different terms. When this occurs, it tells the worker a great deal about how the family functions and will ultimately be used by the worker to help the family reconcile their differences and to work toward common goals.

In group situations, the worker helps the members to help each other to specify their problems. The worker will often do this by modeling (as in a role play) how one member can help another. The worker will subsequently coach the members as to how they may ask each other questions that will lead to a specification of problems. As the members frequently have similar life situations, they can help each other to provide the details of problem situations. Their ability to empathize with each other because of their similarities will also lead to a natural reinforcement for sharing their "stories" with one another.

Categories of Problems

It is useful to have some idea of the types of problems in social functioning for which social workers customarily offer help. At this point, this will clarify for the reader another important dimension of the scope of social work service. Later, we shall elaborate on the idea that the direction to take in developing effective service procedures is to apply research findings and practice experience to the question; What procedures help which clients with *what kinds of problems* in what situations? This requires a classification of problems such as the one that follows. The effort to make practice more scientific depends on our ability to use our knowledge as much as the realities of human existence permit—and often, unfortunately, the realities will never permit such precision!

There are seven dimensions we use to classify the kinds of problems with which social workers help clients. We hope that eventually research findings relevant to each of these dimensions will be available. For now, however, this classification can be used to assemble relevant data.

1. *Level of social organization.* Problems may pertain to the most intimate of associations such as family and friends or to more remote systems such as large agencies and governments.
2. *Stage of development of the relevant system.* Problems may relate to entering a system, beginning phases of interaction, carrying out tasks after interaction has begun, or terminating interactions.
3. *System target.* The goals of the client may be attained by changes in the client, the system, or the pattern of transactions between the client and the system.
4. *Type of interaction sought.* When the focus is on an interaction between the client and others, the nature of the problem, and its solution, will vary depending on the type of interaction desired as an outcome. Thus the client may wish to attain a state of cooperation, competition, or exchange, of goods and services with other people.
5. *Type of output sought.* This item refers to what the client wants, if anything, from the environment. This includes tangible resources, a change in policy, an emotional response (such as affection), a change in attitude, or clear communications.
6. *Source of problem definition.* The reference here is to whether the problem is defined as such by the client, some aspect of the environment, or both. When the client and the environment agree on the problem, the client usually seeks help voluntarily and is often defined as "normal." When the environment defines the situation as problematic, the client is often an involuntary one and may be defined as "deviant."
7. *Type of role sanctions associated with change.* At times when the client has been labeled as deviant, this deviance has been maintained by inputs from social groups and institutions. A change, even when sought by the client, will usually expose the client to contrasting sanctions from different groups— some in the direction of deviance and others in the direction of nondeviance. The nature and existence of such pressures are components of the problem.

A few examples follow of the application of this classification to problems with which social workers help:

Example from the Family Welfare Field. A social worker worked with a family experiencing marital conflict. In this situation we classified the problem as follows:

- *Level of social organization.* Problem pertains to family interactions.
- *Stage of development of the relevant system.* This family system was at the stage of carrying out tasks that arose after the system had passed its formative period.
- *System target.* The family saw the problem as related to the pattern of transactions among members.
- *Type of interaction sought.* The family wished to develop a cooperative system for performing family tasks.
- *Type of output sought.* The family saw the problem as a lack of appropriate and sufficient emotions as well as communications.
- *Source of problem definition.* The family defined itself as having problems.
- *Type of role sanctions associated with change.* Part of the problem was associated with the actions of the husband's parents who expected him to be the "boss" of the family. The solution to the problem will entail some way of coping with this environmental source of stress.

Example From the Criminal Justice Field. A social worker sought to help an offender, whose prison term was almost over, to consider possibilities for employment.

- *Level of social organization.* Problem pertains to interactions between the client and places of employment.
- *Stage of development of the relevant system.* The relevant stage is one of entering the relevant system, the workplace.
- *System target.* The problem lay in both the behaviors of the client and of the targeted system. The client will have to develop work

related behaviors and the workplace will have to be willing to hire an ex-offender.

- *Type of interaction sought.* The type of interaction will be one of exchange in which the client will offer services in exchange for money.
- *Type of output sought.* The client wants financial resources from the workplace. He will require in-service training to handle a job.
- *Source of problem definition.* In this case, the client did not define unemployment as a problem. This was the definition supplied by the prison system. The client was not a voluntary one and was defined as deviant by the service system.
- *Type of role sanctions associated with change.* The client's peers urged him to secure resources illegally. Part of the solution to the problem will require that the client have some way of coping with this pressure.

This classification system is in a preliminary stage of development. As we stated, we hope that this will lead to efforts to link information about problem, person, and situation with the kinds of interventions that are most likely to create desired outcomes. We leave the topic of problem definition to consider how to create relationships that will sustain problem-solving efforts. Additionally, in group situations, this process includes building relationships between the worker and clients and among the clients themselves. We now describe the components of these relationships and how they may be developed.

The Initiation of Relationships

From the earliest efforts to conceptualize social work practice down to the present, this practice has been described as involving the creation and use of relationships between the worker and others. As Gordon Hamilton, one of the most influential persons in the evolution of casework practice theory, wrote,

Our most fundamental considerations lie in the concept of human relationships—their importance, their dynamics, their use in treatment. Casework, groupwork, and community organization are alike grounded in the art and science of relationships.[19]

While the relationships between workers and clients contain many subtle elements created out of the unique nature of each person, there are five common elements that are sought in social work helping relationships. These elements have been extensively researched and consist of the following:

1. Social workers seek to attain *accurate communication* of thoughts and feelings between themselves and their clients.
2. Social workers seek to achieve *full communication* of pertinent information between themselves and their clients.
3. Social workers seek to *communicate feelings of warmth and caring* to their clients.
4. Social workers seek to create worker and client *roles that complement each other* so that each facilitates the other's contribution to the purposes of the interaction.
5. Social workers seek to create a *trust* that they and their clients will honor commitments made to each other.

Each of these will now be elaborated upon.

Accurate Communication

For purposes of analysis, we divide accurate communication into transmission and correct reception of *thoughts* and *feelings*. By accurate we mean that the speaker perceives that the listener has correctly received the message. This requires that the listener provide information to the speaker as to what he or she has heard. This information is supplied if the listener precisely repeats the content or emotional expression back to the speaker. In most cases, however, social workers do not

engage in such repetition because such responses can be experienced as mimicry,
which has unpleasant connotations. Hearing
our own words repeated back to us may also
indicate that the listener has memorized our
comments rather than understood them.
People are more likely to think that they are
understood when listeners repeat what they
have heard in their own language yet still are
accurate. People also experience understanding when the response is appropriate, even if
it is not limited to a reflection of what was
heard. This issue is closely related to the
topic of feedback described earlier in Chapter 3.

A concept relevant to what we have just
been discussing is *empathy*, which is the act
of experiencing another person's responses as
if one were that other person. The phrase "as
if" is important because the concept of empathy relates to the act of experiencing something in a manner similar to another person
while still retaining a sense of who one is and
what one's separate responses may be. After
a worker experiences another person in an
empathic way, the worker may provide an
empathic response in which he or she communicates what was understood.

The literature on empathic responding
does not consistently make a clear distinction
between responses to another's thoughts and
feelings. Because these are two different
types of reactions, we refer to a communication regarding another's feelings as an
empathic response and another's thoughts as
a *reflective response*.

Particularly in the beginning of a social
work relationship, it is important for the
worker to provide empathic and reflective responses. The worker is not yet sufficiently familiar with the client to be sure that his or
her understanding of the communications of
the client are correct. In addition, the client
may not yet be sure that the worker is lis-

tening or that the worker correctly understands the client's communications. The
worker must also facilitate the client's exploration of his or her situation and beginning of
problem-solving efforts. Empathic and reflective responses are softer, subtler, and less
directive ways of reinforcing these client efforts than are direct questions.

Much research has been done on the relationship of empathic responses to therapeutic outcomes.[20] The initial research findings
supported Carl Rogers's hypothesis[21] that
the so-called *facilitative conditions* of empathy, genuineness, and unconditional positive
regard were necessary and sufficient conditions for desired therapeutic outcomes. As
more research was done, however, the findings became mixed. We agree, therefore,
with the following conclusion:

> Researchers of process and outcome of psy-
> chosocial interventions have accepted the
> wisdom of pursuing a more complex model.
> The importance of the "therapeutic relation-
> ship" is not dismissed but is included as one
> of a number of important factors to be
> considered.[22]

Since these responses are at least one important component of many helping processes,
all practitioners must understand them and
identify those situations when they are
required.

A complete empathic response has several components: one is a restatement in the
worker's own words of the feeling the person
experiences. In fact, empathy training programs have been devised,[23] and one of the
first tasks is to train the participant to recognize "feeling" words and their synonyms. A
second component of an empathic response
is a reference to the situation that elicited the
feeling. For example, if a client says, "I was
pissed off when I came home for dinner and
my wife was out," an empathic response is

"You were angry because your meal wasn't ready when you came home and because your wife wasn't there." The word angry is synonymous with "pissed off," and the situation was specified as the lack of a meal and the absence of the wife.

Work has also been done on rating levels of empathic responses. One such scale has five levels.[24] The first level, the poorest response, is assigned to worker responses that demonstrate little awareness of the client's feelings; the situational reference is also vague. The second level connotes a misunderstanding of the intensity of the feeling and the situational reference is not specific. The third level is deemed the minimum facilitative one. Obvious feelings are correctly identified, and at least some aspects of the situation are specified. Levels 4 and 5 are reserved for worker responses that refer partially or fully to client feelings that are "deep" or not clearly expressed. This occurs when the situation in which the feelings are embedded is a highly personal or painful one.

Many empathy training programs for volunteer and other "lay" helpers direct the trainees to restrict themselves to level 3 responses because of the risk of causing pain or confusion to the client through using the higher levels incorrectly or inappropriately. Levels 4 and 5 require advanced training in therapeutic communication. In the beginning stages of the social work process, it is wise to utilize level 3 responses so as not to prematurely direct the client into dealing with painful feelings. As Eisenberg and Delaney state:

> Additive responses offered too early in the process can have a disruptive influence on the counseling relationship. Such responses may go beyond where the client is at the present time and thus threaten or intimidate the client. At least the client will become

very self-conscious and monitor what he or she says. At worst, the client might become so threatened as to terminate.[25]

Reflective responses primarily have the effect of letting the client know that his or her thoughts are understood as well as helping the worker to check out whether this understanding is correct. The effect on clients is to induce them to reflect further on the situation or to reconsider their points of view. The worker should be clear that this is what is desired, as too frequent use of empathic and reflective responses can be unpleasant to clients. After a trusting relationship has been established, workers can directly ask clients to elaborate on a discussion, examine a feeling, or reconsider a point of view. Reflective and empathic types of responses can then be reserved for times when support is required or when the worker is unclear about his or her understanding of the client's ideas and feelings.

Full Communication

By full communication we refer to an interaction in which the worker and the client communicate *all* the thoughts and feelings they are aware of that will help them to attain their mutual purposes. Full communication incorporates two dimensions: *genuineness* and *self-disclosure*. Since our emphasis here is on worker responses that serve to build the helping relationship, we shall focus primarily on the *worker's* genuineness and self-disclosure.

These two terms are not synonomous, and we shall discuss them separately. Genuineness, according to Rogers, refers to a worker who is "a congruent, genuine, integrated person" and whose responses are consistent with the worker's self-awareness." The worker, in addition, may or may not choose to *disclose* personal material depending on the appropriateness of such disclosure.[26]

Genuineness is another of the facilitative conditions to which Rogers and many subsequent investigators have referred. Through the research and training programs devoted to it, genuineness, like empathy, has been carefully specified and scales to measure it devised. Schulman describes the dimensions of genuineness as correspondence, self-disclosure, and confrontation (although, as we have stated, we believe that self-disclosure should be considered as a separate but related variable).[27] We, therefore, in reference to genuineness, discuss the two scales, correspondence and confrontation.

Correspondence is the degree to which the worker's verbal and nonverbal actions match as well as the degree to which the worker communicates his or her feelings. Five levels of correspondence are identified by Schulman. The first is worker responses that are unrelated to what the worker is feeling and contradictions are clearly evident. The second level is a response in which correspondence between worker thoughts and feelings is present but the worker's presentation has a "canned" quality or is very bland.

The third level, the minimum facilitative one, is one in which verbal and nonverbal components are congruent but cues are missing that these may represent "deeper" reactions—they may actually be slightly artificial. Level 4, on the other hand, is not only fully congruent but also one in which "there is no evidence of false front, of defensiveness, or of professionalitis." Level 5, in addition, is a transaction in which the worker is "freely and deeply himself," is "nondefensively open," and is able to use the situation "for deeper exploration for himself and for the client."[28]

Confrontation is the act of calling the attention of clients to aspects of themselves and

their behavior that they deny. Confrontation is considered an aspect of worker genuineness in that the worker provides feedback to the client even though this may result in client anger or rejection. On the other hand, to perceive aspects of the client's behavior and not to share this perception is not genuine.

Five levels of confrontation are also identified by Schulman. Level 1 is the worker's nonresponse to inconsistencies in the client's behavior, while level 2 is the worker's vague or ambiguous reference to such behavior. In level 3, the minimum facilitative level, the worker makes reference to inconsistencies through questions but does not directly point them out. Level 4 is worker responses that directly address client inconsistencies. The fifth level differs from the previous one in that the worker's response to client inconsistencies is "understanding" yet "sharply tuned in."[29]

As we stated earlier, the worker's disclosure of aspects of himself or herself, such as worker feelings and experiences, are "genuine" responses but must be used with sensitivity and judgment so as to enhance and not inhibit client problem-solving. While social workers have shared aspects of their experiences with clients naturally, the counseling literature has frequently ignored this or warned against it.

Much of the opposition to worker self-disclosure stems from principles of psychoanalytic therapy. Freud, himself, warned against self-disclosure because he believed that it interfered with the client's self-exploration through the reinforcement of the client's curiosity about the therapist.[30] Specifically, Freud stated, "the doctor should be impenetrable to the patient and, like a mirror, reflect nothing but what is shown to him."[31]

On the other hand, the more humanistic therapies and encounter groups are frequently associated with a portrayal of the worker as a natural and equal participant in the therapeutic process.

Because of the controversy surrounding the issue of self-disclosure, this response has been the subject of a number of research efforts.[32] Weiner, who has reviewed this research as well as the therapeutic literature, has concluded that self-disclosure can be a useful worker response if careful judgment is exercised as to the nature of the therapeutic situation and the needs of the client. He discusses the use of self-disclosure, for example, in reference to a number of therapeutic strategies. When the strategy involves training the client, the worker's own experience with the training plan may help the client to follow the plan.

In what Weiner calls an "ego supportive" mode, a moderate amount of worker self-disclosure may help to confront client defenses. An example of this is a worker's statement that he or she would experience a stated feeling were he or she in a situation similar to the client's.[33] Weiner sees a use for self-disclosure in therapeutic modes where the major emphasis is on uncovering deep psychic phenomena. The purpose for such disclosure is to clarify the worker's reality if this will remove a barrier to the therapeutic relationship. Examples are explanations of external events in the worker's life that have interfered with treatment or expression of genuine feelings when the client has experienced a catastrophe.[34]

Weiner summarizes the major occasions for self-disclosure as follows:

1. Enhance reality testing by defining the therapist as a real person and by defining the real patient-therapist relationship.
2. Heighten self-esteem by conveying respect, thus facilitating identification with a respected person (the therapist).
3. Provide feedback about the impact of the client on others.
4. Promote identification with positive aspects of the worker, for example, his or her calmness, reasonableness, and interpersonal skills.
5. Sufficiently gratify the client's transference and object needs so as to establish and maintain a therapeutic alliance.
6. Resolve certain transference resistances.[35]

Weiner has developed a similar list of occasions when self-disclosure is very undesirable. Occasions include those when the therapist seeks to seduce a patient into a situation, including therapy, to which the patient is seriously opposed; those that primarily meet therapist needs; those that reinforce the patient's pathological patterns; and those that perpetuate the patient's dependence.[36]

In conclusion, we believe that in all therapeutic approaches there are some occasions for the worker to reveal personal experiences, attitudes, or feelings. Within some of the constraints described, there are times in most social work interactions for the worker to engage in such self-disclosure.

Feelings of Caring

The next dimension of the social work relationship we shall discuss is the communication of positive feelings from worker to client. This dimension is a subject of controversy as some workers view it as "overinvolvement;" they argue that workers who care "too much" for clients are unable to remain objective and seek to use clients to meet their own needs. We do not believe that caring for clients leads to these negative dimensions. Worker feelings that are harmful to clients do, of course, occur, but we believe that these do not stem from positive feelings toward the client but rather from feelings that workers have toward themselves and their own problems. In fact, caring for the client in the way we conceive is the opposite of using the client to meet one's own needs.

Evidence from a number of studies exists to support communication of the worker's caring feelings. Ripple and her colleagues, in a study of people who had good outcomes from casework service, found "the most important single variable was service and concern, not the skill in specific activities, but rather the amount of encouragement given the client during and immediately after the initial interview." Discouragement did not mean negative attitudes on the part of the worker but rather a "bland, seemingly uninvolved eliciting and appraisal of the client's situation, in which the worker appeared neutral in affect, left the client's discomfort untouched, and offered no basis for hope that the situation could be improved."[37]

The dimension of caring is also closely related to the third of Rogers's facilitative conditions, which has been called "unconditional positive regard" or "nonpossessive warmth." These terms connote the idea that the worker maintains a spirit of warm goodwill toward the client regardless of what the client says, values the client as a human being, treats the client as a person with dignity, and "expresses continuing willingness to help no matter what the behavior of the client and no matter whether he approves or disapproves the client's behavior." Finally, the worker takes interest in the client's concerns and pleasure in the client's achievements.[38]

Schulman has devised a scale for rating worker levels of warmth in addition to her empathy and genuineness scales. The scale is divided into two components: positive regard and respect. Level 1, the poorest one, applies to worker acts in which the worker does not show regard by criticism, disapproval, and even dislike. On this level, the worker communicates contempt for the cli-

ent by failing to elicit and respect the client's thoughts. Level 2 responses of the worker are those that fail to show regard through being mechanical or passive; the worker's responses may vary depending on how the client responds. Respect, at this level, is not shown or varies a good deal depending on what the client is talking about.

Level 3 responses, the minimum facilitative ones, show regard for the client in that workers communicate that the client's feelings and behavior matter to them. Respect is shown through the worker's appreciation of the client's feelings and experiences and the worker values the client's opinions and expressions. Level 4 responses, in addition, show a deeper commitment for the client's welfare and an expectation that the client will be able to progress rather than regress. Respect is shown through a high level of appreciation for the client's potential. The highest-level responses, level 5, are those that show totally unrestricted thoughtfulness, kindness, and consideration for the client, no matter what the client's beliefs may be, so that the client feels fully free to be himself or herself. This level of respect is demonstrated through the worker's full measure of appreciation and pleasure as the client develops and manifests his or her capacities. The worker recognizes the client as being of great importance to himself or herself as well as to others.[39]

In reviewing the levels of warmth, it appears that level 3 is considered the minimum facilitative one because it represents the type of response the client should receive from the first interview on. The higher-level responses are more likely to occur at later periods in the relationship as the worker bases his or her feelings on previously shared experiences with the client and expresses an appreciation for changes the client has attained.

Complementary Roles

This dimension of the social work relationship reflects the idea that in a functional interaction, each person facilitates the goal attainment of the other person. The role of the worker in this respect is to support the problem-solving of the client individually or as a member of a family or other group. The role of the client is to engage in the work of solving problems and to provide the kind of information to the worker that will permit the worker to be helpful. These roles facilitate rather than hinder each other. At times in the social work process, however, roles emerge that require a more specific reciprocal response from the other person so that a constructive relationship can continue, and we shall discuss some of these.

At all times in a multiperson system, the system has task requirements and social-emotional requirements. The task requirements, as we described them, relate to the phases of the problem-solving effort. The social-emotional requirements relate to the management of tensions that threaten the system. When one person attends to the task requirements, others can complement this by attending to the social-emotional requirements. Frequently, in the social work process, the client engages in the task activity, problem-solving. When this occurs, the worker often attends to social-emotional requirements by responding to client feelings so as to reduce tensions. The reverse can also occur. A client and a worker may be intensively engaged in a problem-solving activity as tensions mount. The client may then play a social-emotional role for example, by using humor to reduce this tension. At that time, the client and worker are fulfilling complementary roles.

Another type of complementarity occurs through raising and answering questions. If both the worker and the client see each other as only raising questions rather than seeking answers, conflict rather than complementarity occurs. There is no general rule for such issues. Rather, the worker and the client should recognize when they are functioning in a conflictual manner and should search for the kind of roles that complement one another and also accomplish the purposes of the interaction. Another simple example of complementarity involves one person in the role of speaker and the other in the role of listener. In some social work relationships, albeit not good ones, clients and workers can vie with each other to speak or even to remain silent.

Trust

The last component in our list of the types of relationships social workers seek to develop with clients is trust between both parties—a trust that each is what he or she is represented to be, each honors commitments made to the other, and each is honest in all encounters with the other. Trust, therefore, is closely related to the full communication dimension we have described, but it also touches upon additional issues.

One of these issues is the competence of the worker. The worker has represented himself or herself as being able to undertake the kind of helping activities the client requires. It would be naïve to assume that workers are ready for all exigencies. Workers will at times confront client problems for which they lack competence. The broader issue regarding worker competence is that workers should know the limts of their abilities and should seek consultation, bring in other workers, or even refer a client to others when they have reached such limits.

The client should be able to trust the worker's commitment to this principle. When asked, workers should answer questions honestly regarding their abilities. Some clients will use this issue to express hostility to workers (that is, to question their competence), but this type of client defense should be approached as such.

Another component of trust is confidentiality. The commitment the worker makes to all clients is that nothing will be revealed about the client without the client's knowledge. This implies that the type of records the worker and the agency accountability system keep should be information that is available to the client. Recent legal decisions have often required workers to make the client's case records available to that client. This poses problems to workers who use technical jargon to describe clients or who record conjectures regarding the meaning of client behavior. In some cases, the client's knowledge of this will not harm the client as much as some workers fear. In other cases, it is clear that workers will have to refrain from placing such material in records—a change that we also believe will not have the dire effects some practitioners predict. In fact, benefits may accrue in terms of a reduction in the number of labels attached to clients.

An issue that is more crucial than the client's *knowledge* of dissemination of information about them is their *consent* to this. The ethical rule we use is that nothing is revealed about the client without the client's consent. We accept the idea, however, that there can be exceptions to this rule—exceptions that are explained to the client in advance. Social workers do not promise to keep information confidential when this will endanger the lives of clients or others. In general, social workers do not commit themselves to keep their knowledge of illegal acts confidential but will report this to the appropriate authorities. The usual approach, however, is to help clients to take this responsibility themselves. This situation usually occurs when the offense is serious: social workers are not in the business of reporting minor traffic violations but will take the offense of a client who was a "hit and run" driver seriously by urging the client to report the event or ultimately by reporting it themselves.

Some clients such as young children, psychotics, and the severely retarded may not be capable of making decisions regarding confidentiality. The worker in such situations will secure releases from family members or others responsible for such clients or from people who represent the interests of the client.

The issue of confidentiality in addition to the worker's provision of information to others includes securing information. The client is always regarded as the primary source of information about himself or herself, and the worker should ask the client's permission to obtain information from others. The client has the right to have that information shared with him or her, and the informant is told when the client wishes to exercise this right.

Relationships in Group Situations

In group work, workers seek to develop among the members as well as with themselves the relationship dimensions we have just described. We will comment, therefore, on each relationship dimension as it applies to intermember relationships.

1. *Accurate Communication.* Workers will describe the processes of empathy and of reflective responses to members and will seek to model these. Workers can train members to make empathic responses through role plays, tapes, and reinforcement of these responses when they occur naturally. Workers will, at times, use such exercises as asking members to repeat the statement of the member who had previously spoken before making additional remarks. This has the ef-

fect of both providing feedback to the previous speaker and ensuring that members listen carefully to one another. When this is done in groups, it is after the group has identified inaccurate communication as a problem and has agreed to handle it in this way.

2. *Full Communication.* The issue of disclosure is a very important one in groups, as many persons express anxiety about sharing personal information in group situations. This issue, therefore, is invariably discussed with the group at the first meeting. Sometimes, exercises focused on this problem are used. For example, members are asked to think of an issue that they are reluctant to discuss in the group. They then are asked to imagine sharing this information as well as the reactions of other group members to this. The kinds of anticipated reactions (not the actual sensitive topic) are then discussed in the group. This usually has the effect of encouraging the members to take greater risks in sharing information about themselves.

With regard to full communication, we previously also discussed the importance of correspondence between verbal and nonverbal communications. Members are usually not confronted in early meetings about a lack of correspondence between these aspects of communication as this will often be too threatening. After early meetings, however, this represents an important kind of feedback in groups devoted to helping members resolve problems in interpersonal communication.

3. *Feelings of Caring.* Members will work on their problems in group situations when they ascertain that the other members care for them; otherwise they will be reluctant to give or take help from them. The worker, therefore, will reinforce expressions of caring among the members and will seek to resolve interactions that prevent this type of caring from emerging.

The following is an example of this:

SAM: (to Sarah) I felt the same way you did when my boss criticized me.
WORKER: (to Sarah) Did you notice the caring feelings Sam has toward you?

At times in groups, the members will express such caring for a member who, because of self-concept problems, will be unable to recognize or accept it. The member may even declare that the others are not honest in that expression. Helping the member to recognize this type of perceptual distortion can be invaluable in enhancing that member's relationships. Ultimately, expressions of caring among members in the group will be one of the most treasured aspects of the experience because it cannot be discounted, as it may be from the worker, on the basis of "that's his job!"

4. *Complementary Roles.* The role structure in groups is more complex than in one-to-one situations because of the number of individuals involved. Members will initially have to be helped to understand what the role of member is: namely, each individual has a responsibility for the welfare of the group and the other members in it. The role of the worker must also be understood as one who facilitates the way in which *members* take responsibility for the group. Beyond this, in ways that we discuss later in this text, the worker helps members to complement each other in the way they *share* leadership roles, task roles, and other group facilitation roles such as mediator, negotiator, spokesperson regarding norms, and provider of emotional support. A good distribution of roles helps each person to feel that he or she is important to the group. An exercise used

by workers to enhance this is for the group to list the roles needed and compare this with the roles that each member has fulfilled.

5. *Trust.* Of equal importance with these dimensions is trust. This aspect of relationships among members includes expectations that all will attend regularly, come on time, and maintain confidentiality. Trust presumes a desire to help rather than to harm one another and a commitment to be truthful in giving feedback.

Each of these dimensions of one-to-one relationships as well as group relationships takes time to develop. The worker, however, must understand the nature of relationships, help the clients to understand them, and, from the very beginning, find ways of facilitating the development of each dimension. The relationship dimension is important because, in addition to the fact that it provides support for problem solving, clients invariably seek help with problems in relationships. The learning that comes from working on relationships with the worker, and in groups, with other members, is a prototype for skills to be employed in life beyond the social work situation.

Relationships in Family Situations

The relationship that the worker seeks with family members, when the worker is interacting with an entire family (or with several but not all family members), differs from the one that the worker seeks in group and one-to-one helping situations. This difference is due to the fact that the family members have had long-standing relationships with each other well before the worker has entered the scene. In addition, the worker's target is usually the family, as a system, rather then the behavior of each family member singly. These relationship differences relate to the following propositions:

1. The family "problem" often lies in the kinds of relationships that exist among some or all family members. Thus, some members may be rejected or scapegoated by others or, in contrast, may be the ones most frequently approached for solutions to problems or for nurturance. Families frequently act so as to draw the worker into these patterns, particularly when the pattern is dysfunctional for the family. The worker, therefore, must be very aware of the kinds of relationship patterns the family seeks to establish with him or her.

2. Another kind of pattern families may seek to establish with the worker is for the worker to have closer relationships with some family members than with others. Again, this pattern may not be a desirable one for the family, and the worker must then avoid this. The worker, particularly in the beginning, seeks to establish relationships with *all* family members. These can be initiated by referring to each family member by name and interacting, however briefly, with each person. The worker must make extra efforts to initiate interactions with the members of the family who are most passive in the family session. The worker may also first seek to establish a relationship with family members (often the father) who can influence the family's decision to return for subsequent sessions.

3. The list of relationship dimensions with which we began this section of the chapter can be used to assess relationship patterns within the family that are either related to the presenting problems of the family or the family's strengths for problem-solving. The worker will use this knowledge to seek to change some family relationship patterns or to reinforce others. We do not deal with this

topic extensively here as it will be a major one when we consider family assessment later (see Chapter 7). A few illustrations, however, will help to clarify this point.

In reference to *accurate communication,* family members as well as those in any group often distort their communications to each other to maintain dysfunctional roles or power positions. In one family, the husband failed to express any empathy with his wife's anger about his neglect of family responsibilities because he did not wish to increase these responsibilities. In another family, a father did not reflect any understanding of his son's school difficulties, even though the son discussed these, because the father did not believe he had the skills to intervene on behalf of his son.

In regard to *full communication,* a wife did not tell her husband about some of the difficulties that were occurring in her life for fear that he would be angry with her for her presumed incompetence. The husband, in turn, did not describe some relationships he had with nonfamily members for fear his wife would be jealous of these. The *feelings of caring* dimension is a crucial one, also, with respect to family relationships as the family is one of the main institutions in society for receiving and offering caring. The worker, with one family, noticed that when a child approached the father, the father responded in a bland, mechanical, and uncaring manner. The worker subsequently learned that the father did not believe he was the biological father of this child and his unresponsiveness was an important dimension of his relationship with both the mother and the child.

Barriers to Engagement

Thus far in this chapter, we have asked the reader to assume that if the worker's agency is the appropriate place for the client, if the worker and client agree on the problems they will work on together, and if a relationship is skillfully built, a sufficient basis for problem-solving exists. Under some circumstances, however, these necessary ingredients are *not* sufficient for such engagement.

One such barrier stems from personal limitations of the client. These limitations may be of a temporary or of a permanent nature. One temporary situation is when the client is so overwhelmed by a crisis (for example, a recent death of a relative) that he or she cannot focus on a problem or respond to the worker's offer of a relationship. Under these circumstances, the worker will try to help the client deal with the immediate crisis. On other occasions, the worker may empathize with the client and offer to initiate the helping process at a later time. The client may also be temporarily overwhelmed by financial or other burdens. Again, the worker may seek to help with these or may postpone the initiation of service.

Other clients have a more permanent limitation on their ability to engage in a social work process. It is a fact of life, one difficult for new workers to accept, that social workers cannot help everyone. Some people cannot or will not enter into a helping relationship, or they seek to exploit inappropriately all such relationships. Other persons lack the mental capacity or contact with reality required to engage in such a relationship. The worker may decide to act on behalf of such persons by securing resources for them or by advocating for improvements in their environmental conditions. Mutual problem solving, however, is out of the question. The major caution in these cases, however, is that the worker should not abandon problem-solving efforts because it is difficult but *not* impossible to work with some people. Working with them in regard to their family or environmental systems is also a significant possibility.

A related issue is that posed by clients who by virtue of ethnic, social, or racial differences do not wish to engage themselves with a particular worker. While this issue can be explored and sometimes resolved without changing the assignment of the worker, clients' desires in this area should be respected. These clients may be correct in their assessment of the role models they need or the understanding they require. The difficulty is that workers with the appropriate background may not be available. Agencies and workers, however, should consider innovative approaches to this question such as the use of paraprofessionals and lay helpers. Another, at least partial answer, is to compose a group of members from the same culture and the worker becomes a facilitator of peer helping; the group members can supply each other with role models and high levels of understanding. The worker's skills often are best employed to create such a group.

Finally, barriers from the client's environment may act to prevent engagement. The client's family, for example, may seek to hinder the client's use of the agency. In this case, the worker should usually seek to recruit the family as a client or at least to have a series of interviews with the family members who pose this problem. In these interviews, with the permission of the client, the worker may be able to alleviate the concerns that exist. Again, however, these barriers may be so great as to prevent some people from becoming clients.

In come cases, interprofessional competition may serve as a barrier to service. A teacher-social worker conflict may cause the teacher to hinder a pupil from seeing the worker. This also can be an issue in residential treatment centers for children where conflicts between child care workers and social workers exist, each resenting the influence of the other. The worker must seek to develop the kind of team relationships that allow such conflicts to be resolved. In many cases, however, a resolution of interprofessional conflicts requires the presence of an outside facilitator who can promote open communication between the potential team members through reduction of fears and misunderstandings.

The Preliminary Contract

Our approach to practice incorporates the idea that the worker should interact with clients on the basis of a "contract." We discuss the reasons for this in detail in Chapter 8. Because the period of engagement concludes with a "preliminary contract," we introduce this concept now. A contract in social work is not a legal document and may, in fact, not be written down at all. It is a concept that connotes that the worker should seek to have as clear an agreement as possible with the client as to what they are doing together, why they are doing it, and what their mutual responsibilities are. The initial engagement phase incorporates the following types of agreement:

1. The social worker and the client agree as to what the problem(s) is (are) that they will seek to solve together. This may change later, but nevertheless, an agreement exists for the present.
2. The social worker and the client agree that they will continue to work together on these problems because this appears to be the appropriate agency and worker for this effort.
3. At least a minimum, if not maximum, amount of time for work together has been agreed upon. (For example, the client will meet with the worker at least three times or will attend at least three group meetings or family sessions.)
4. The client and worker agree that the next phase will include the gathering of information about the problem, the client, and the situation (referred to in this book as an assessment), and this will enable the client and worker to agree on short-and long-range goals

and means of achieving them. The client will cooperate in supplying the information required for the assessment and goal-setting process; the worker will be responsible for identifying the information that is required and will be able to justify the need to secure such information.

5. Additional requirements of the client and worker have also been identified and agreed upon. For the client, this may include fees and the time of appointments. For the worker, this also includes a commitment to the appointment time as well as any rules for further availability. Both parties agree to notify the other when appointments cannot be kept as well as with regard to any changes in the conditions specified in points 1 through 4.

Summary

In this chapter we have detailed the actions of workers as they engage the client in the social work process. We began the chapter with information about research on why some clients continue and others do not. This literature suggests that continuance will be dependent on an agreement as to what the purposes of the interaction are as well as on the emergence of a facilitative relationship.

For this reason we analyzed these two processes in detail. In regard to agreement on purpose, we saw this as agreement on amelioration or solution of problems. Such problems must, consequently, be specified in detail, and we described what is involved in such a specification. We analyzed the components of a facilitative relationship in social work as consisting of accurate communication, full communication, feelings of caring, complementary roles, and trust. While these dimensions must occur in all social work relationships, they have additional facets in multiperson client systems such as families and groups.

Many social work helping situations move easily through processes of problem specification and relationship development, but others do not. We discussed problematic engagement in terms of barriers and saw these barriers as developing out of cultural differences, client attributes, and situational impediments. In all cases, the initial engagement period ends when agreement has been reached between workers and clients that the worker, agency, and client are appropriately matched; that a focus for work (usually in terms of problems) has been established; that a commitment has been made to continue for a specified time; and that the obligations of the worker and client are understood.

The next chapter continues from this point and describes the kinds of information the client and worker will now seek about the client, his or her problem, and his or her situation in order to define goals and a way of working toward them. We shall describe the basic principles for securing such information and how this knowledge may be usefully organized as it pertains to individuals, families, groups, and the organizations with which they interact.

NOTES

1. For a discussion of this and similar issues, see William J. Reid and Ann W. Shyne, *Brief and Extended Casework* (New York: Columbia University Press, 1969), pp. 194–218.

2. Lilian Ripple, Ernestina Alexander, and Bernice W. Polemis, *Motivation, Capacity, and Opportunity: Studies in Casework Theory and Practice* (Chicago: School of Social Service Administration, 1964).

3. Ibid., pp. 198–199.

4. Ibid., p. 203.

5. Sol L. Garfield, "Research on Client Variables in Psychotherapy," in Sol. L. Garfield and Allen Bergin, eds., *Handbook of Psychotherapy and Behavior Change*, 2nd ed. (New York: John Wiley, 1978), p. 195.

6. Ibid., pp. 197–202.

7. Ibid., p. 206.

8. Irvin D. Yalom, *The Theory and Practice of Group Psychotherapy*, 2nd ed. (New York: Basic Books, 1975), p. 225.

9. Ibid.

10. Ibid., p. 227.

11. David E. Orlinsky and Kenneth I. Howard, "The Relation of Process to Outcome in Psychotherapy," in *Handbook of Psychotherapy and Behavior Change*, pp. 308–310.

12. Entire systems of social work treatment have been predicated upon the idea that clarifying and reconciling avowed and unavowed expectations is a significant force for personal growth and change; see Roy R. Grinker et al., *Psychiatric Social Work: A Transactional Casebook* (New York: Basic Books, 1961).

13. Yalom, *Group Psychotherapy*, pp. 290–298.

14. Charles Garvin, *Contemporary Group Work* (Englewood Cliffs, NJ: Prentice-Hall, 1981), p. 78.

15. M. T. Orne and P. H. Wender, "Anticipatory Socialization for Psychotherapy: Method and Rationale," *American Journal of Psychiatry*, Vol. 124 (1968), pp. 1202–1212.

16. Raymond P. Lorion, "Research on Psychotherapy and Behavior Change with the Disadvantaged: Past, Present, and Future Directions," in *Handbook of Psychotherapy and Behavior Change*, p. 917.

17. Ibid., p. 915.

18. For further discussion of the concept of performance discrepancy, see D. M. Gottman and S. R. Leiblum, *How to do Psychotherapy and How to Evaluate It.* (New York: Holt, Rinehart and Winston, 1974), pp. 25–27.

19. Gordon Hamilton, *Theory and Practice of Social Casework*, 2nd rev. ed. (New York: Columbia University Press, 1951), p. 27.

20. For a summary of this research, see Morris B. Parloff, Irene Elkin Waskow, and Barry E. Wolfe, "Research on Therapist Variables in Relation to Process and Outcome," in *Handbook of Psychotherapy and Behavior Change*, pp. 242–252.

21. Carl R. Rogers, "The Necessary and Sufficient Conditions of Therapeutic Personality Change," *Journal of Consulting Psychology*, Vol. 21 (1957), pp. 95–103.

22. Parloff, Waskow, and Wolfe, "Research on Therapist Variables," p. 251.

23. John Milnes and Harvey Bertcher, *Communicating Empathy* (San Diego: University Associates, 1980).

24. Eveline Schulman, *Intervention in Human Services*, 2nd ed. (St. Louis: C. V. Mosby, 1978), pp. 213–214.

25. Sheldon Eisenberg and Daniel J. Delaney, *The Counseling Process*, 2nd ed. (Chicago: Rand McNally, 1977), p. 95.

26. Rogers, "Necessary and Sufficient Conditions," p. 97.

27. This is consistent with Rogers's view as he stated that the therapist can "choose to express attitudes which are strong and persistent, or not to express them at this time if that seems highly inappropriate," in his *On Encounter Groups* (New York: Harper & Row, 1970), p. 53.

28. Schulman, *Intervention in Human Services*, p. 219.

29. Ibid., pp. 220–221.

30. Ibid.

31. Sigmund Freud, "Recommendations for Physicians on the Psychoanalytic Method of Treatment," in *Collected Papers of Sigmund Freud*, Vol. II (New York: Basic Books, 1959), pp. 323–333.

32. For a presentation of this research, see Myron F. Weiner, *Therapist Disclosure: The Use of Self in Psychotherapy* (Boston: Butterworths, 1978), pp. 35–45.

33. Ibid., p. 74.

34. Ibid., p. 75.

35. Ibid., p. 87.

36. Paraphrased from ibid., p. 102.

37. Ripple, Alexander, and Polemis, *Motivation, Capacity, and Opportunity*, pp. 199–203.

38. Schulman, *Intervention in the Human Services*.

39. Ibid., p. 231.

six

Assessing Individuals

This chapter will present issues that are germane to all assessment procedures as well as a framework for individual assessment. In the succeeding chapter the assessment of families, small groups, and organizations will be discussed. Assessment and intervention are both continuous processes, and successful intervention depends on good assessment.

Assessment processes are designed to help the worker understand the client system in interaction with its environment. This, however, does not require a comprehensive understanding of all aspects of the client system and its environment. A worker does not have sufficient time for that nor is it desirable to understand everything there is to know about other human beings and their situations. Therefore, our approach to assessment will be bounded by both ideological and pragmatic considerations.

Purposes of Assessments

Pragmatic considerations concern how much information is required to make a sound intervention plan. In earlier models of practice, workers were encouraged to collect massive amounts of information about their clients.[1] No piece of information was too trivial, and agency records resembled metropolitan telephone directories. Now, however, we instruct workers to be selective of the data they collect in the assessment process. Salience as related to the issue at hand should influence the data collection process.[2] Although some agencies continue to put their applicants through a long series of evaluation procedures (social histories, medical histories, psychological tests, psychiatric evaluations), this kind of comprehensive data collection is an unnecessary luxury in these times of shrinking resources. Extensive data collection procedures are also time consuming, and as we stated in Chapter 2, time is short when working with oppressed clients in the midst of crises.

Extensive evaluation procedures often seem more designed to meet the needs of professionals or agencies rather than the needs of clients. Such lengthy evaluations also rarely draw the client into the assessment process. At their worst, they may make the client a passive object rather than an active partner in a process to enhance both the client's and the worker's understanding of the client's problems. The worker during assessment should encourage, include, and value the client's participation in exploring his or her problems and life situation.

Assessment as a "Label"

Some models of practice emphasize an assessment phase early in the service process (Hollis's concept of study and diagnosis[3]). This assessment phase is often concluded when the worker reaches a professional judgment (a diagnostic impression) of the client's trouble. This diagnosis is intended to inform the treatment process that follows, and in certain ideal situations it does. Although mental health services, medical services, and services reimbursed through third-party payments such as Blue Cross and Blue Shield are required to report a diagnosis of the client, we are uncomfortable with such a labeling procedure. Diagnostic labels are inferences, conclusions, or judgments that professionals make about a client's behavior.

Sometimes these labels take on a life of their own, and agencies and professionals treat them as though they were fundamental "truths" about the client. When labels are treated in this manner, they are hard to change and may remain with a client for the rest of the client's organizational life—even though the client's behavior and attitudes may have dramatically changed. Another shortcoming of diagnostic labels is that they focus on individual behavior or states of being. Thus they pay little attention to interactive problems that clients may have with other individuals or organizations in the client's environment. With some insurance carriers, a worker may be required to diagnose each individual member of the family even though the worker is seeing and working on a systemic problem that involves the whole family.

Assessment as a Process

We conceptualize assessment as an ongoing activity that worker and client system engage in throughout the entire helping process. Although assessment is continuous, it varies in each phase of service. During engagement, assessment is designed to clarify the client's initial concern and determine whether the client has come to the correct agency. The client (actually an applicant at this point) is helped to understand the nature of services that are available and how these services may be useful in the client's present circumstances. If the client's problems do not seem to fit the agency's services or the client does not want to use the services that are offered, then the client is helped to locate another agency in which more appropriate service can be rendered.

During engagement, the critical decision concerns what service can be matched to the client's problem, and therefore, extensive data collection and assessment are undesirable. Screening is a more appropriate strategy and involves two basic decisions. The client should be able to identify a specific concern or problem that he or she wants to work on, and the client should agree to use the services of the agency to work on the identified problem. Once these decisions have been reached, the worker and client can begin to explore the client's identified problem in greater detail.

During this next phase of service (the subject of this chapter and the one that follows), the worker and client system collect the most information about the client's present circumstances. The worker will take an active role in exploring the client's identified problem and salient factors that may be associated with the target problem. This information is collected so that the worker and client can reach another set of important decisions in the helping process: goals for service and a plan of action to achieve these goals. Assessment during this phase will help the worker and client to decide what modalities might work best (individual, family, or group) and what other services should be mobilized in the helping process.

Even during the later, implementation phases, of service, assessment is important to evaluate and monitor the strategies employed and to plan and implement new strategies as the need arises. During termination, assessment is crucial because the worker and client evaluate the results of their efforts as well as of others who were involved in the action system. Assessment is also critical at termination to plan what should happen next for the client and to consider ways in which the client may structure his or her life so that changes made during service can be maintained and not reversed.

Data Collection

Data collection is central to assessment, and this section of the chapter presents the common practices used to collect data, typical sources of data, ethical issues in data collection, and special considerations that worker and client must be aware of in weighing the accuracy and reliability of data collected.

A psychiatrist employs a mental status examination (a series of systematic questions and exercises) to determine the psychopathology of patients. A psychologist may employ a variety of standardized and projective tests to understand the personality and emotional state of clients. A social worker, in contrast, relies heavily on the face-to-face interview to gather information about clients and their situations. Although social workers are increasingly using instruments that they, themselves, have devised, it is important for a social worker to have mastery of interviewing techniques; and although a worker is not expected to do mental status examinations or to administer and interpret psychological tests, a worker should be familiar with other professionals' data collection procedures so that the accuracy and reliability of information presented by other professionals can be weighed.

Methods

In practice there is no ideal or ultimate way of collecting data about the client. Each method of data collection has its limitations and biases. Psychological tests are culturally, racially, and often socioeconomically biased because many have been developed on white, middle-class individuals. The proverbs used in one section of the mental status examination can be culturally irrelevant to some patients. And in face-to-face interviews there is no certain way to assure that the respondent is telling the truth and not telling one lie after another.

Data collected by more than one method (and source) are more likely to offer a broader, less biased view of the client. When there are several methods and sources of data used in assessment, at least there is a chance that the biases of one method will counterbalance those of another.

Social workers engage in a number of data collection methods. Workers perform face-to-face interviews with various respondents to collect information. Besides direct contact, interviews may be conducted over the telephone, through an interpreter when language is a barrier, or even through letters when illiteracy is not a problem. A competent interviewer relies on open-ended questions[4] (questions that cannot be answered by a yes or no). For example, a closed-ended question such as, "Do you argue with your parents?" is better queried as; "How do you and your parents get along?" A closed-ended question does not give the respondent the range of options that open-ended questions provide.

Another basic interviewing strategy is to avoid using "why" questions. Although a worker may want to ask a "why" question to discover the explanation for some action of the client, "why" questions are often misperceived, and the client may react defensively and respond with an excuse for the action under discussion. Too many " why" questions in an interview may make the worker seem like an interrogator, not an interviewer. By simply substituting "how" for "why" in an interview, the worker can avoid making the client feel defensive. For example, a worker might say, "How did you end up in such an argument?" rather than the accusatory, "Why did you end up in such an argument?"

A successful, information gathering interview also balances both responsive and systematic questions.[5] Responsive questions are often empathic and follow up on the client's previous statement. One client discussed her demeaning experience in the agency, and the worker's responsive question was, "How did you react in such a frustrating situation?" Systematic questions on the other hand are designed to keep the client's focus on a particular line of inquiry without getting side-tracked by discussions of extraneous information. Another worker helped a client to keep her focus on a topic by saying, "Your reaction to school is important, but before we discuss that, let's finish exploring what happened in the argument with your husband."

Sources

A social worker should not only have skill in collecting verbal information but should also be a good observer. As we have already discussed in the chapter on communication, a great deal of information is exchanged outside the verbal channel. A perceptive worker is aware of visual, auditory, tactual, and even olefactory information that is conveyed. Observational methods of collecting information are applied particularly in home, school, or workplace visits as the worker collects data about the client system in its interactive environments.

Another common method that social workers use to collect assessment data is the questionnaire. Questionnaires exist in many forms, lengths, and styles. Some are designed to collect demographic and other identifying information about the client system. This kind of questionnaire is routinely required of most applicants who enter any complex organization; and in some organizations, this information is not even collected on a form but is asked by a clerk at a computer terminal. Such information as name, address, telephone number, age, sex, race, marital status, and number of children are examples of such data. Often these intake questionnaires also ask the applicant for the general reason for seeking help or entering the organization at this particular time.

A social worker may employ background questionnaires also to collect information about such areas of the client's life as medical history, family history, or employment history. We do not think that questionnaires should be routinely required of all clients. Questionnaires should be employed only when the information collected on the questionnaire is salient to the problem that the client and worker have identified or required for a legitimate organizational purpose such as describing the population served in order to anticipate needs for more services.

Obviously the most important source of

information is the client system itself. The client is central to the problems to be explored and understood and, therefore, is an essential source of information about it. As with all sources, the client is biased and information may be distorted. Because information from *any* source has some built-in distortion, it is the worker's responsibility to identify biases that may require correction as compared with those in which the client's perceptions, right or wrong, are all that matters.

Common distortions that clients bring to data are the tendencies to look either too much at external causes for their problems or at causes of their own doing.[6] Some clients may be most influenced by emotional factors associated with their problems, and others may be most affected by cognitive issues. The consequence of these common distortions is that data collected will be skewed in the direction of the client's bias. Therefore an individual client who focuses on external causes will have trouble considering internal factors, and vice versa.

Another important source of information about the problem is the "significant others" in the client's life who know the client and the particular problem situation. These may be relatives, close friends, neighbors, peers at work or school, supervisors or bosses, or anyone with knowledge about the client's problem. As does the client, each of these sources will bring biases, too, depending on how involved they may be in the client's problems. For example, a relative had negative feelings about a client, and information gathered from him blamed the client for the relative's trouble. Another common bias of significant others is a tendency to "gossip" and share a lot of hearsay information about which they do not have firsthand knowledge. A worker will have to sort out carefully information about which others have direct knowledge or experience from that which is hearsay or secondhand.

Issues in Use of Sources

The worker cannot simply approach significant others and collect information about the client's problem. Confidentiality requires that the client be consulted before others are contacted and grant permission for this. In most situations, the client should know who is to be contacted and the purpose of the contact, and a written release should be signed by the client authorizing the worker to contact the significant other.[7] The client has a right to control information that is collected about him or her as well as to control information that is released. Although it may seem that such a requirement is unnecessarily time consuming, we support these procedures because they show respect for the clients and ensure that they will be involved in decision making. Such protection of the client's right to confidentiality also allows the worker to check out the appropriateness of other sources before they are contacted.

Another source of data about the client's problem is other professionals who have had contact with the client. As with the other sources, there are biases in the information collected by professionals and agencies. Professionals tend to be specialists, and therefore, the information they collect often is focused in the area of their specialization. A doctor may have information on a client's physical health and know nothing about a client's social or job skills. This kind of narrow approach to the client can be misleading when trying to understand the client. In another example, a priest knew about an individual's attendance at mass, observances of church rituals, and the generous amount of his contributions, but little about the man's family and business affairs. (This example is from the film *The Godfather*.) Another common bias in data from other professionals is their tendency to focus on the client's weaknesses and to ignore strengths and capabilities. This bias is the inevitable consequence of such roles as "client" or "patient" in which weakness, defect, or incapacity are so often associated with these roles. The records from professionals and agencies make poor source materials for a balanced autobiography.

Issues of confidentiality are also involved in data collected from other professionals and from agency records. Some agencies require clients to sign a blanket release form at the beginning of service so that information can be released or sought from other professionals or agencies later. A blanket release does not protect the client's confidentiality. Each time a worker intends to seek or release information about the client, the client should be informed and a release obtained.

The issues presented in this section of this chapter point out that the worker cannot simply collect data from any source or accept the data at face value. When information has been collected from a variety of sources, the worker should be able to sort through this information and understand how accurate and reliable the information is. When information is inaccurate or the source very unreliable, the chances of jumping to false conclusions are great.[8]

Generally information can be categorized into two general types. Information can be factual and observational, or it can be inferential.[9] Factual and observational information is extentional and represents the world of experience, while inferences are intentional and represent the subjective world of the observer. Both kinds of information abound in professional records, and both have their place, but they must never be confused. Inferences are not facts but conclusions or subjective reactions of the individual presenting the information. Good inferences can be supported by evidence (facts or observation), and the worker should be able to see when data contain weak inferences and are missing hard facts.

To clarify these issues in data collection, an excerpt of case material is presented. The first few paragraphs of the material present observational and factual data, while the last paragraph presents the inferences that have been drawn from this situation. The major inferences have been italicized, and the analysis that follows points out those inferences that are poorly supported by the data from those that do seem to have some support.

Mrs. X is a 52-year-old widow. Since her husband's death two years ago, she has lived alone in a two-room apartment. Her two daughters are both married and live in another state. Mrs. X receives a small pension and survivor's benefits from Social Security. She lives in a section of town that is scheduled for urban renewal. The three-floor walk up that she occupies is located on a block that has over 50 percent abandoned buildings. Her building is in the process of being condemned and is scheduled to be torn down in three months.

When the social worker from the housing authority contacted Mrs. X to inform her of the condemnation procedures and also help her find other housing, Mrs. X stated that she would never leave her apartment and would kill anyone who tried to make her move. She showed the worker her revolver that she had purchased to protect herself from drug addicts that she claimed were breaking into her apartment and stealing her appliances.

Mrs. X's apartment was piled waist deep with 21 stacks of old newspapers. Roaches were visible in both rooms, and her kitchen sink and countertops were covered with dirty dishes. Four bags of trash and garbage were overflowing onto the kitchen floor. When the worker asked Mrs. X if she needed any help managing her apartment, she burst into tears and stated that she had saved every newspaper since her husband's death. She asked the worker if he had any hobbies or liked to collect things.

Mrs. X was dressed in a frayed cotton dress that had food stains and several holes in the front. The apartment smelled of urine, and there was soiled underwear strewn in the corner of the room. Mrs. X had not been to a doctor in over two years. Her eyesight is poor, and she has misplaced her glasses. She is not worried about her poor eyesight and assured the worker that she could shoot straight if attacked by addicts. She explained that she had been taught to shoot a pistol by her husband who trained in a paramilitary unit of the Ku Klux Klan. Mrs. X opened the closet door and showed the worker her husband's Nazi uniform. The worker noticed that the brass was shiny, the uniform pressed, and the leather straps highly polished.

Mrs. X stated that she felt the uniform would fit the worker and then called the worker by her husband's first name and asked the worker if he planned to spend the night. The worker explained that he would have to go now but would return to help Mrs. X with some of her problems. Mrs. X burst into tears and pleaded with the worker not to "leave again." The worker reassured Mrs. X that he would return and quickly left the apartment. On his way down the stairs, the worker was mugged by two assailants. His wallet and briefcase were stolen, and his nose was broken in two places.

Diagnostic Impressions and Recommendations

Mrs. X is a *middle-aged widow* who is *incapable of caring for herself*. She has *created numerous health hazards* in her apartment. Her *paranoid ideation, incontinence, and flat affect* are all manifestations of a *psychotic, involutional melancholia*. She is *depressed* and has an *unresolved grief reaction* from her husband's death. Mrs. X is in a *state of crisis* and is a *danger to the community*. She needs *immediate hospitalization at the State Hospital*.

The following inferences seem to have supporting data from what transpired in the interview with the relocation worker:

- "middle-aged"—Mrs. X is 52 years old.
- "created numerous health hazards"—This inference has some support because her poor eyesight and piles of old newspaper could represent a fire hazard. The garbage and dirty dishes may also attract vermin that could bring disease. The inference "created" might be challenged because it not only seems like blaming the victim but also ignores the reality of her environment. There may be no garbage or trash collection for her building, and she may not want to leave the apartment for long because of the risk that it might be ransacked.
- "depressed"—There is some evidence for this inference becasue she broke into tears at several points in the interview, but more information should be collected.
- "unresolved grief reaction"—There are several pieces of information that support this inference. She maintains her husband's uniform, continues to collect papers since his death, and confuses the worker's identity with her hope that he is her husband. She pleads with the worker not to leave again.
- "state of crisis"—She is living in a very stressful environment and is trying hard to survive when the worker appears to tell her that she must move. Such threats of relocation may be overwhelming to an elderly person who has lived a while in an area.

The following inferences do *not* seem to have much support and, instead, appear to represent the worker's subjective reactions and feelings about his experiences in this interview:

- "incapable of caring for herself"—This seems to be contradicted by the reality that she has lived for two years by herself and somehow managed to pay her bills, feed herself, and handle her pension and benefits, all accomplished in a rather hostile and inadequate environment.
- "paranoid ideation"—This inference seems contraindicated by the evidence that she lives in a very dangerous environment (the worker was mugged), and one would expect her to

feel threatened by a worker who tells her she will have to move.

- "incontinence"—Soiled underwear and the smell of urine do not prove incontinence. Her toilet facilities may be malfunctioning.
- "flat affect"—This inference is contradicted by her crying outbursts.
- "psychotic involutional melancholia"—The worker did not perform a mental status examination or do psychological testing. Much more investigation by other professionals is necessary before such a conclusion can be drawn.
- "danger to community"—The community is a danger to her well-being. The worker can attest to that.
- "immediate hospitalization at the State Hospital"—There are many other options that should be explored besides this drastic one. Unfortunately this recommendation seems to meet the needs of the worker to get Mrs. X removed from the building and does not really address some of the problems she may experience at the present.

This case example and analysis have pointed out how a worker can analyze data collected from other sources to determine how reliable the information that is being presented is. Social workers can learn from lawyers that not all information has the same reliability. Some evidence is "harder" that others.

Individual Assessment Framework

This section of the chapter presents the framework for our approach to individual assessment. In Chapter 1 we presented a problem typology that reflects the common kinds of social problems that clients bring into service. That problem framework was designed to be descriptive; and in this section we explain how social problems develop and manifest themselves in peoples' lives. The perspectives we shall discuss are described in greater detail in other sources.[10] We shall summarize the critical elements of these theoretical approaches and how such perspectives are operationalized for interpersonal practice.

To understand how social problems appear in an individual's life, the two dimensions previously discussed in the "nature metaphor" need further elaboration. Social problems are the product of two fundamental processes and can be conceptualized as the dislocations and necessary changes that these processes demand of individuals. Individuals are caught in the unfolding changes of development from conception to death; and they are also stressed by the continuous balances that must be established between themselves and their surrounding environments at each stage of this development. To understand the confluence of all these forces, the worker must have an understanding of the basic developmental issues that individuals experience and how these stages are significantly shaped by various ecological balances that must be maintained for the individual to grow and develop.

A Developmental Perspective

Because our model focuses on social problems and social functioning as the starting points for individual assessment, our developmental conception is socially and interactionally oriented. In the behavioral sciences, there are numerous developmental models that explain systematic changes in the growth of individuals. Freud's psychosexual model of developmental, Piaget's developmental model of childhood cognition, and Erikson's psychosocial model of human development are all examples of developmental conceptions of individual growth and change. All these conceptions have merit, but our focus here is on the stages of social development that individuals experience in their lifetimes.

Role transitions are a useful way of conceptualizing development because social workers are familiar with the "role" concept, and roles are salient for all individuals. In the same way that an individual cannot "not communicate," an individual cannot be roleless. Roles are an inherent part of an individual's social being, and even efforts to isolate oneself result in the adoption of yet other roles such as hermit or recluse.

Another advantage of the role concept is its obviousness and the ease with which individual roles can be identified. With some developmental models, the boundaries between different stages are blurred and difficult to differentiate; therefore, individuals may appear to be struggling with issues from different stages. It is difficult then for the worker to decide which stage the client may be attempting to achieve. Because role boundaries are much more differentiated, transitional struggles that the client is experiencing are much easier to identify.

Development can be conceptualized as a long time line drawn down a sheet of paper. On the top of the line is birth and on the bottom of the line is death. All along the life line, individuals are faced with transition after transition, from one role to another. Role transitions are a continuous process for individuals, and later life has as many transitions as does infancy and childhood.[11] Although role transitions may differ in different cultures, the reality of continuous transitions is present in all cultural contexts. In our complex, pluralistic, American culture, there are numerous roles that individuals may achieve or adopt. Many roles and the transitions that individuals must accomplish are fairly predictable, and most individuals can expect to move through these various role transitions.

(See Figure 6-1 for such roles and transitions in schematic form.)

In early childhood an individual must learn to become a son or daughter, often a brother or sister, a niece or nephew, a cousin, a grandchild, and so on. Family life brings numerous role possibilities. Family roles are not the only transitions that children must learn to handle, and a number of cultural and organizational roles will require mastery. A child must learn to make the transition to student (whether in nursery school or in kindergarten), to member of teams, to member of organizations such as the Scouts, to member of religious groups such as Catholic, Moslem, or Jew, and to citizen of the dominant culture in which he or she grows up. Childhood may be conceptualized as constant socialization for individuals to prepare them for membership in various social groupings. This socialization to various roles and membership in social organizations continues throughout life.[12]

During adolescence an individual will have to make transitions to different schools, clubs, first employment experience, various roles engaging the opposite sex (date, steady, and so forth), and a transition to adulthood also begins with changes in the expectation of old roles that need revision. For example, the old roles of daughter and son will need revision as biological maturity stimulates growth in size and sexuality.

In young adulthood an individual may make transitions to being independent and living away from home for the first time. This transition may occur by becoming a recruit in the military, a student away at college, or a leasee in one's own apartment. A young adult may experience his or her first career or employment roles and the roles associated with creating a family, such as spouse and new parent.

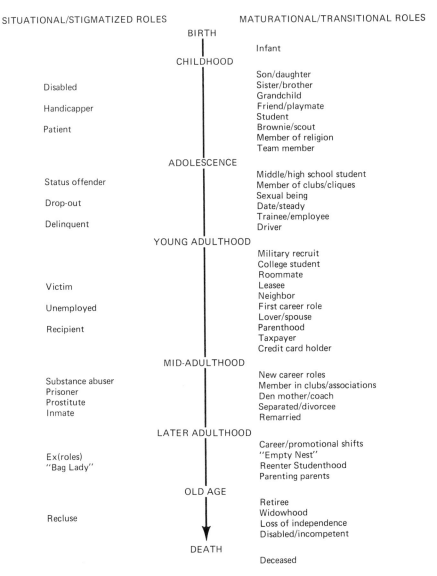

SITUATIONAL/STIGMATIZED ROLES   MATURATIONAL/TRANSITIONAL ROLES

BIRTH

Infant

CHILDHOOD

Disabled

Handicapper

Patient

Son/daughter
Sister/brother
Grandchild
Friend/playmate
Student
Brownie/scout
Member of religion
Team member

ADOLESCENCE

Status offender

Drop-out

Delinquent

Middle/high school student
Member of clubs/cliques
Sexual being
Date/steady
Trainee/employee
Driver

YOUNG ADULTHOOD

Victim

Unemployed

Recipient

Military recruit
College student
Roommate
Leasee
Neighbor
First career role
Lover/spouse
Parenthood
Taxpayer
Credit card holder

MID-ADULTHOOD

Substance abuser
Prisoner
Prostitute
Inmate

New career roles
Member in clubs/associations
Den mother/coach
Separated/divorcee
Remarried

LATER ADULTHOOD

Ex(roles)
"Bag Lady"

Career/promotional shifts
"Empty Nest"
Reenter Studenthood
Parenting parents

OLD AGE

Recluse

Retiree
Widowhood
Loss of independence
Disabled/incompetent

DEATH

Deceased

Figure 6-1. Roles and Transitions

During middle adulthood, individuals continue to face a number of role transitions through career shifts, changes in location, membership in clubs and associations, membership in organizations their children may be active in (den mother, coach), as well as some stressful transitions such as becoming separated, divorced, or remarried.

In later adulthood individuals will continue to make career transitions either through promotions to new positions within their professions or in totally new career adjustments. Individuals may have to handle the role reversal of "parenting" their aged parents at a time when their own children are "emptying the nest" and becoming independent. This is a time when many women seek to reenter the job market or return to school for more education on the way to a second career beyond motherhood.

During old age there are still many role transitions that an individual must handle: retirement, widowhood, loss of independence or greater dependence on adult children, and patient in medical facilities and nursing homes. In our own culture, these are fairly normative and expected role transitions that individuals will make in their lifetime. In Chapter 15 we shall discuss how the worker's intervention approaches must also vary for people in different stages of life.

All role transitions in an individual's life are stressful. Some transitions are potentially overwhelming and may create serious social dysfunctioning for the individual. Research has demonstrated that some role transitions are much more stressful than others.[13] For example, death of a child or spouse, divorce, and marriage are much more stressful transitions than are promotions or shifts in employment.

Besides these common transitions, there are also a number of role transitions that are situational or idiosyncratic. All individuals run the risk of becoming disabled or handicapped by accident or disease.[14] Some individuals may find themselves caught in negatively valued roles that society either stigmatizes or considers deviant.[15] For example, an individual may choose a gay lifestyle or be incarcerated in a prison or mental institution or find himself or herself on the roles of a welfare program during hard economic time. Such negatively valued roles are not only stressful as "transitional," but they are also made more stressful because of the stigma, embarrassment, and shame that individuals may feel in finding themselves in such roles.

Role transitions are related to social problems because these transitions are not always successfully accomplished by individuals. There are many reasons why an individual may fail to make a successful transition to another role. An individual may take on too many transitions at once or have so many role responsibilities that adding a stressful transition may overload the individual's capacities to cope with all role demands.[16] This kind of role overload is common in graduate students who may be enrolled full time in a graduate program, working part time to pay for their studies, and struggling to maintain some semblance of family responsibilities to spouse, children, relatives, and so on. Some role transitions are stressful enough without adding them to an already overloaded set of role demands.

Another reason that role transitions may be overwhelming for individuals is that the individual may not be properly prepared (sometimes even misprepared) for the role transition.[17] For some roles in society, there are few presocialization experiences to help an individual make the transition to the new role. In American society, parenthood is a role transition that has few presocialization experiences. In some ways the role is even idealized as a special, fulfilling experience, while the responsibility and hard work are underemphasized. Parenthood is not a role that can be easily discarded once it has been adopted, and for most individuals, it lasts the rest of their lives.

Another problem that individuals face with some role transitions is they do not have the skill or capacity to handle the responsibilities and expectations placed on them in the new role. Sometimes the skills can be acquired, and sometimes the individual lacks the basic capacity to handle the role success-fully. For example, in some practice situa-tions, a worker may help a neglectful mother to improve her parenting skills, while in an-other situation the worker might work to ter-minate parental rights when parents are un-willing and incapable of caring for their children.

Another source of difficulty with some role transitions is the confusion, ambiguity, or vagueness associated with the role. Some societal and organizational roles are unclearly perceived, or there is a great deal of confu-sion and disagreement about how individuals should behave when they occupy the role.[18] Our society has a difficult time, for example, deciding what to expect of disabled individu-als and how even to understand and accept some disabilities. Sometimes the disabled are infantilized and expected to stay in their homes and are not given a chance to partici-pate in the job market or act as a consumer in society.

"Handicappers" have had to struggle for a barrier-free society, the blind have had to push for special resources such as talking cal-culators, and the hearing disabled have had to struggle to have sign language institution-alized into television programming. Society is not sure whether individuals with various disabilities should be normalized or mainstreamed and allowed to compete with the rest of the citizenry, or whether they should be treated specially and segregated into smaller, homogeneous communities by themselves. This kind of expectation is stressful for the disabled individual because it ignores the reality that disabilities often only affect one area of functioning and the disabled may only need special attention to this area of their functioning.

To understand how the stress of role transitions contributes to the social disfunc-tioning of individuals, we return to the case of Mrs. X, the widow facing removal from her apartment. Mrs. X faces several stressful role transitions. She is a widow and has obviously not adjusted well to this role transition that was forced on her by the death of her hus-band. Because her children do not live nearby, her husband's death has isolated her from family supports. She is also facing an-other forced transition in that her apartment building is scheduled for demolition and she is being required to relocate. This threat may be the final blow in a series of realities that she has had to face in her attempts to con-tinue to live and survive in a deteriorating neighborhood.

The threat of removal should not be taken lightly by the worker. Such transitions for elderly individuals are extremely stressful and can result in various forms of social dys-functioning or even death.[19] Mrs. X also faces another stressful transition and that is the consequence of losing her status as an in-dependent adult. If the worker's recommen-dations are to prevail, Mrs. X will have to cope with the likelihood of being incarcer-ated in an institution and having to adjust not only to the demands and expectations of that role but also to giving up the special privi-leges of an independent person. On the sur-face her threats to shoot anyone who tries to make her move may seem extreme, yet when we account for the stress in all these transi-tions, it seems justifiable and even reasona-ble for her to react this way.

An Ecological Perspective

An individual must not only handle the stresses of life transitions but must also bal-ance a variety of individual factors with envi-ronmental realities. Stress not only emerges at transitional interfaces but also at the trans-actional interfaces between the individual and the surrounding environment. For an in-dividual, three critical exchanges must be balanced for the individual to grow and thrive. Individual needs must be balanced by environmental resources; individual wants and aspirations mut be balanced by environmental opportunities; and an individual's skills and capacities must be balanced by environmental demands and expectations.[20] These three fundamental transactions cannot be perfectly balanced in any situation because both the individual and the environment constantly change.

Individual	Transactions	Environment
Needs	————————	Resources
Aspirations	————————	Opportunities
Capacities	————————	Expectations

An individual's needs can be conceptualized as existing on several levels.[21] At the most basic level are the survival needs that must be immediately attended to in order to maintain basic biological functioning. A biological organism must obtain oxygen, water, food, and shelter and be able to expel waste in order to grow and develop. When the environment cannot provide these resources, the organism will die or be severely damaged. A social worker might be involved in improving these transactions for an individual client by helping a client link up with better housing or by providing the client with an emergency grant to pay for fuel oil or by helping a client to apply for food stamps or meals on wheels to improve nutritional intake.

An individual also has safety needs that somehow must be met by environmental resources. All of us have a need to be secure and protected from the various dangers and violence of the world around us. In some inner-city neighborhoods, the incidence of violence is so prevalent that it it hard to imagine how an individual can protect himself

or herself from muggings, larceny, and theft. Sometimes security is extolled by those who create the hazards, and sometimes the home itself is a place of violence and danger.

An individual has a need for belongingness and love in close, intimate relationships. Some relationships allow for sexual expression as well as for mutual caring and support. Life for individuals who are isolated from family and friends and who lack close human support systems is highly stressful, and social functioning may suffer severely. Social workers can be involved in improving these transactions by developing self-help groups for isolated clients or by encouraging clients to reengage significant others in their social context or by encouraging others in the client's environment to be more supportive when a client is passing through a particularly difficult transition.

Finally, an individual has a need to be respected and valued by others. Self-esteem is an important need of individuals, and when an individual's environment is belittling or continuously disqualifying, severe social disfunctioning may occur. When individuals begin to internalize and accept negative messages sent to them, they may withdraw from meaningful social contact and develop any number of negative traits or behaviors that fulfill the negative images sent to them by their environments. Social workers may be involved in improving these transactions by trying to change the client's internalized negative images as well as trying to move the client into more supportive environments or changing the sources of the negative messages.

In returning to the case of Mrs. X, she is experiencing a number of stressful transactions in the needs-resources dimension. Although she has a weapon that she uses as a resource to provide herself with security from her dangerous living situation, her present environment is clearly hostile, and some serious efforts must be made to remove the hazards present. It also seems clear that a woman of her age ought to have more careful monitoring of her physical well-being and she should have a medical checkup. Although she has been living on her own, it would also be useful to know how she does her shopping and bill paying, to assure that she cares for her basic needs adequately and that her income covers her basic living expenses. Her apparent social isolation should also be a concern to the worker, and some kind of reinvolvement with others (such as family, friends, support groups) in meaningful social interaction is indicated.

An individual's aspirations are determined by many factors such as values, life experiences, and present circumstances. The dominant American culture can be viewed as materialistic, competitive, hedonistic, and youth oriented. Within such a context it is understandable that individuals want to accumulate more things than their neighbors, want to spend their income on leisure and recreational activities, and want to be slim, attractive, and youthful by running, exercising, and eating properly. These dominant values will not necessarily appear in all individuals, and some clients may have aspirations that contradict the dominant culture. For example Hispanic and American Indian values tend not to promote materialism and competition, but instead promote cooperative relationships with others in the family, tribe, or community. Thus aspirations of minority clients will reflect different underlying values. These issues will be further discussed in Chapter 15.

The number of aspirations that an individual may have are almost unlimited. The distinction between need and want is significant for individuals. Aspirations and wants do not carry the same imperative that needs do

for the individual, yet a great deal of an individual's behavior and striving are tied to wants and not needs. Maslow's higher-level needs (self-actualization, knowledge, and aesthetics)[22] reflect the kinds of aspirations that motivate individuals to pursue all kinds of enterprises—sometimes at great expense.

No social worker *needs* to be in graduate school, and the power of aspirations to motivate individuals to achieve should never be underestimated. But aspirations do not just happen; they require the environment to provide the opportunity to be realized. The opportunity structures of individuals is never ideal. In the real world, opportunities are either blocked or underdeveloped by the "isms." Sexism, racism, classism, and ageism are just a few of the barriers that limit opportunity structures and keep individuals from achieving their aspirations. Social workers become involved in these dysfunctional transactions when they advocate for clients to open up blocked opportunity or when they work to develop opportunities that are not available in the client's environment.

Racism and sexism are common in the human services as well as societal institutions,[23] and the worker is ethically bound by the code of ethics to work to eliminate discrimination in the workplace. In the case of Mrs. X, we see a common occurrence in practice: from the record we know very little about Mrs. X's wants and aspirations. The only want we do know about is her adamant desire to remain in her present apartment, and the only reason this is reported is that it directly contradicts the worker's purpose in contacting Mrs. X. Regrettably, too much of practice focuses on what clients need at the expense of what clients want. Aspirations and wants are a powerful source of motivation that can be mobilized to help clients make significant changes in their lives.

The final ecological transaction that

workers should understand in a client's life is how well balanced the expectations of significant others are to the client's capacities and skills. All of us have basic capacities to perform various life tasks, and as our life unfolds, we constantly add to our skill repertoire. At different ages and with different experience, our capacities and skills may vary greatly, and therefore so must the expectations and demands that our environments place on us as individuals.

An individual's capacitiies exist in three basic areas of functioning: intellectual, emotional, and performance. Individuals have a capacity to think, solve problems, understand, make decisions and be rational. Individuals also have a capacity to be emotional and express their feelings. Some individuals are limited in their ability to express their feelings to others, some are easily overwhelmed by their feelings, and others are able to handle their emotions appropriately for the context in which they are being expressed. Individuals also have a capacity to perform or act appropriately with regard to what's expected of them in various roles. Whether it's tying a shoe, driving a car, or making love, an individual is constantly acting or behaving in relationship to others' expectations.

Many social workers have used concepts from ego psychology to identify client capacities. These concepts enable the worker to generate an ego assessment related to such ego functions as reality testing, perception, and logical reasoning. Such an assessment also includes the types of defenses—such as projection, denial, and reaction formation— utilized by the client. Workers who draw upon this framework do so in terms of how the ego functioning of the client facilitates or hinders the way the client copes with the environment. For example, in the case of Mrs. X, her collecting of newspapers, her mainte-nance of her husband's uniform, and her confusion of the worker with her deceased husband can be understood as poor reality testing and the operation of denial (defense mechanism) as a way of coping with the loss of her husband. As we shall see in Chapter 11 on individual change, social workers do use procedures drawn from ego psychology to help clients modify how they respond to environmental stresses.

If an individual is not pushed, coaxed, and encouraged to take advantage of skills and capacities, these personal resources will not develop and may actually atrophy from disuse. This kind of imbalance can be dramatically seen in mediocre classrooms that do not recognize or provide special learning opportunities for gifted or bright students. Students caught in such a mismatched environment may end up causing "trouble" simply to cope with boredom and the meaninglessness of the educational experience.

On the other hand, environments can place unrealistic demands on the capacities of individuals, which may push them into situations of constant failure that may seriously hurt their self-images. Expecting too much of an individual may be as harmful as expecting too little. Sometimes clients cannot handle the responsibilities that are given them, and they need help to improve their skills in order to meet others' expectations.

Some social workers have found it helpful to conceptualize individual-environmental transactions in terms of behavioral theory. In one of the paradigms generated by this theory, voluntary acts of the individual are seen as occurring in relationship to the following sequence: *antecedent-response-consequence* (or alternately as *stimulus-response-stimulus*). The antecedent—or initial stimulus—is the environmental occasion for the response. The resulting individual response occurs in reference to the individual's capacities and previous learning experiences. The final environmental response, when pleasurable, leads to an increased likelihood of the response reoccurring, when aversive, to the opposite. For example, in the case of Mrs. X, her hoarding of newspapers and maintenance of her husband's uniform can be interpreted as behaviors that are reinforced because these activities may serve to keep part of her husband present and thus mitigate some of the loneliness of her widowhood. Continuing to do things for "him" may be her way of continuing an important, pleasurable relationship. As we shall see in Chapter 11 on individual change, this theoretical approach also produces ways workers can intervene to help clients cope with their environments.

Sometimes individual environmental imbalances are internalized by individuals, and an individual will develop unrealistic expectations of his or her capacities. Individuals may believe that they do not have the capacity to pursue a venture, or they may be unnecessarily hard on themselves when their performance is less than perfect. These internalized kinds of imbalances may be as stressful and dysfunctional as those that occur between the individual and significant others in their environment.

Workers may be involved in a number of ways to improve imbalances in these transactions. A worker may help a client to increase or acquire the skills to meet the expectations of others (a neglectful client may attend a parenting group to improve parenting skills so that a court-ordered removal of her children can be rescinded), or a worker may try to renegotiate expectations with the other to remove unrealistic demands on the client (an anxious mother may be encouraged not to worry that her 3-year-old child is not yet reading). The worker may also be involved in

increasing the demands that others place on clients to help clients work up to capacity. For example, a worker might suggest to parents that they set firmer limits on a problematic child so that the child is clearer about expectations and will acquire a sense that the parents are sincere.

In the case of Mrs. X, we have a confused picture of her capacities even though the worker attempts to build a case that Mrs. X is incapable of caring for herself. She cries easily and confuses the worker with her husband, yet she has successfully managed to survive on her own since her husband's death; and if the worker had not entered her life space, there is no indication that she would not have continued to survive. Obviously she could use support and services to improve her living situation, but she should not be denied a chance to continue in an independent living situation.

Although this ecological assessment framework presents these three kinds of transactions as distinct exchanges, in real life these three are interdependent and closely interrelated. Recent attempts to build barrier-free structures and facilities has not only been a change in resources (handicappers can now use bathrooms away from home), but this restructuring of resources has also opened up the opportunity structure for handicappers so that many can return to school, seek employment outside sheltered workshops, or just use public facilities as nonhandicapped citizens do. This opening of opportunity may encourage handicappers to aspire toward new careers and to reach out and develop latent capacities that were dormant in an earlier, more restricted, opportunity structure. Furthermore, this growth in capacity and skill for the handicapped may help society to reevaluate its expectations of the disabled. This kind of rippling back and forth among these three transactions demonstrates their interdependence and the reality that change in one area may promote change in others. And in the long run, these changes will permit a greater chance for individuals to achieve their maximum potential.

Summary

This chapter has presented an assessment framework for the way individuals cope with the social problems they face in their lives. This framework consists of both a developmental and ecological perspective for the understanding of an individual's social functioning. Both dimensions are interdependent, and an individual can only be understood when both dimensions are accounted for in the assessment process. The value of this framework for interpersonal practice is that it supports both individual intervention as well as interventions aimed at the transactions in a person's life space. This framework also respects both the client's competencies and strengths as well as the troubles and stresses in individual social functioning.

To reinforce this perspective, we summarize its salient aspects in the following outline:

I. Developmental Issues
   A. Recent changes (past few months) in client's life
   B. Expected changes (next few months) in client's life
   C. Inventory of roles the client presently occupies
   D. Most recent roles acquired
       1. Preparation for transition
       2. Supports for transition
II. Ecological Issues
   A. Needs/resources
       1. Resources for survival needs
       2. Resources for security needs
       3. Resources for belongingness and love needs
       4. Resources for the need to be respected and valued
   B. Aspirations/opportunities
       1. Client's wants and desires
       2. Available opportunities
       3. Barriers to opportunities
   C. Capacities/expectations
       1. Intellectual, emotional, and behavioral repertoire
       2. Expectations and demands of significant others
       3. Client's expectations of self

NOTES

1. Carel Germain, "Social Study: Past and Future," *Social Casework*, Vol. 49 (July 1968), pp. 406–409.

2. Ibid.

3. Florence Hollis, *Casework: A Psychosocial Therapy* (New York: Random House, 1964), pp. 167–203.

4. For a more comprehensive discussion of interviewing techniques, see Alfred Benjamin, *The Helping Interview*, 2nd ed. (Boston: Houghton Mifflin, 1974), and Eveline D. Schulman, *Intervention in Human Services: A Guide to Skill and Knowledge*, 3rd ed. (St. Louis: C. V. Mosby, 1982).

5. William J. Reid and Laura Epstein, *Task-Centered Casework* (New York: Columbia University Press, 1972), pp. 121–138.

6. Edward E. Jones, *Attribution: Perceiving the Causes of Behavior* (Morristown, N.J.: General Learning Press, 1972).

7. Suanna Wilson, *Confidentiality in Social Work: Issues and Principles* (New York: The Free Press, 1978).

8. Sanford Berman, *Why Do We Jump to Conclusions?* (San Diego: International Communications Institute, 1962).

9. William V. Haney, "The Inference-Observation Confusion: The Uncritical Inference Test," in Mary S. Morain, ed., *Teaching General Semantics* (San Francisco: International Society for General Semantics, 1969), pp. 1–19, and Mona Campbell, "Extensional and Intentional Levels of Abstraction," in *Teaching General Semantics*, pp. 45–52.

10. Carel B. Germain, *Social Work Practice: People and Environments: An Ecological Perspective* (New York: Columbia University Press, 1979); Naomi Golan, *Passing Through Life Transitions: A Guide for Practitioners* (New York: The Free Press, 1981); and Leo Goldberger and Shlomo Breznitz, eds., *Handbook of Stress: Theoretical and Clinical Aspects* (New York: The Free Press, 1982).

11. Orville Brim and Stanton Wheeler, *Socialization After Childhood* (New York: John Wiley, 1966).

12. Ibid.

13. Barbara S. Dohrenwend, Lawrence Krasnoff, Alexander Askenasy, and Bruce Dohrenwend, "The Psychiatric Epidemiology Research Interview Life Events Scale," in *Handbook of Stress*, pp. 332–363.

14. Edwin Thomas, "Problems of Disability from the Perspective of Role Theory," in Edwin Thomas, ed., *Behavioral Science for Social Workers*, (New York: The Free Press, 1967), pp. 59–77.

15. H. Becker, ed., *The Other Side: Perspectives on Deviance* (New York: The Free Press, 1967).

16. For a discussion of various kinds of role problems, see Charles Atherton, Sandra Mitchell, and Edna Schein, "Locating Points for Intervention," *Social Casework,* Vol. 52 (March 1971), pp. 131–141; John Spiegel, *Transactions* (New York: Basic Books, 1974), pp. 112–139; and Edwin Thomas and Ronald Feldman, "Concepts of Role Theory," in *Behavioral Science for Social Workers*, pp. 27–50.

17. For a discussion of role problems in the family, see Bruce Biddle and Edwin Thomas, eds., *Role Theory: Concepts and Research* (New York: John Wiley, 1966); F. Ivan Nye, *Role Structure and Analysis of the Family* (Beverly Hills, Calif.: Sage Publications, 1976); and Spiegel, *Transactions*, pp. 143–186.

18. For a discussion of organizational roles and role problems, see D. Katz and R. Kahn, *The Social Psychology of Organizations* (New York: John Wiley, 1966), pp. 171–198, and H. Schein, "Organizational Socialization," in B. L. Hinton and H. J. Reitz, eds., *Groups and Organizations*, (Belmont, Calif.: Wadsworth, 1971), pp. 210–215.

19. Margaret Blenkner, *Serving the Aged: An Experiment in Social Work and Public Health Nursing* (New York: Community Service Society of New York, 1964).

20. This ecological framework is borrowed from Professor Jeff Moss, University of Maryland, School of Social Work and Community Planning. See also Lillian Ripple, *Motivation, Capacity, and Opportunity: Studies in Casework Theory and Practice* (Chicago: School of Social Service Administration, 1964).

21. Abraham Maslow, *Motivation and Personality* (New York: Harper & Brothers, 1954).

22. Ibid.

23. Louis Knowles and Kenneth Prewitt, *Institutional Racism in America* (Englewood Cliffs, N.J.: Prentice-Hall, 1969), and Brett A. Seabury and Madison Foster, "Racism and Sexism in Social Work Agencies: Casing Your Agency from Within," paper presented at the NASW Minority Affairs Conference, Los Angeles, June 1982.

seven

Assessing Groups, Families, and Organizations

Introduction

In our discussion of assessment, to this point, we have been concerned with the behavior of a single individual. Situational variables have primarily been introduced in terms of their impact on that individual. In many ways, individual assessment is artificial if it is not done simultaneously with an assessment of the individual's environment and the interaction between the individual and the environment. People live in constant interaction with others in small groups, such as family and peers, and in larger systems, such as places of employment and residence. Behavior is always a consequence of forces present in these groups and organizations.

An understanding, therefore, of individual behavior involves an assessment of both the individual and these other systems. The only question, therefore, is how extensive this broader assessment will be. When working with the individual as an action system, the worker may spend only a moderate effort on a complex assessment of family, peer

group, and organizational dynamics. On the other hand, when these entities become client and action systems, the worker will assess them in greater detail. (In this book, however, we do not consider worker roles with any multiperson *client* systems other than the peer group or family.)

Some workers argue that because of the strong impact of systems, particularly the family, relevant systems should always be assessed in detail and the worker should invariably seek to work directly with them as action systems. We are not doctrinaire on this topic and will remain neutral until more evidence is forthcoming to support such a position. There is insufficient evidence to support the superiority of working with family or peer groups for *all* clients, although this has been established for some limited categories.[1] Our position, nevertheless, is that family, group, and organizational factors should be identified in broad terms for all clients and pursued in detail for some. The greatest amount of detail should be sought when the impact of these systems is a strong force in producing the problem or is a major resource for change or both. In any case, such a detailed assessment will be required when the worker and client determine that larger systems will constitute action or target systems.

For many beginning workers, as well as for those whose training was oriented only to individual assessment, the idea of an assessment of a system is an unfamiliar concept. The question is often raised as to whether system characteristics are as real or as measurable as individual ones. Our answer is that system variables represent the interaction among persons and that these interactions can be as stable and measurable as the personality characteristics of an individual. What is even more important is that system characteristics can account for as much, if not more, of the behavior of individuals as their personalities. Changes in systems, therefore, can be sought as a means of resolving individual problems. In addition, changes in systems may be sought as ends in themselves: family members may wish to live in family situations, inmates of residential institutions in group situations, and community members in community situations that are more pleasant and functional than their current ones.

In assessing systems such as families, groups, and organizations, the worker should remember that these are also embedded in the larger society and that the influence of the society should be identified. Thus, the worker who "blames" the family for some family problem, to the exclusion of recognizing relevant societal factors, makes the same type of mistake as the worker who "blames the individual" without seeing family or group situational causes. The worker, therefore, should be able to see how such conditions as the energy crisis, the inflation-recession cycle, the deterioration of confidence in government, racism, changing sex roles, the likelihood of military conflict, and the depersonalization of the individual in urban communities affect individual, family, and small-group dynamics. This does not mean that social workers can "solve" individual problems with some rapid solution of these societal issues; rather individuals and groups may, in many cases, feel relieved to have some degree of responsibility for the stresses they experience appropriately removed from them. Some clients may also experience relief when they decide to direct their energies toward societal conditions and not simply toward an inward quest.

System Variables

In later sections of this chapter, we shall discuss the variables that workers seek to measure when they assess families, groups, and organizations. Our purpose here is to identify, in more general terms, the nature of variables intrinsic to any system.

Identification of Variables

1. *System goals and purposes.* All systems have reasons for existing as well as some things they seek to accomplish through their existence. Thus, families exist to fulfill the needs of members for intimacy and to socialize children; groups exist to help members improve their social skills or change social conditions. More specific goals also emerge in these systems.

The family may save money to buy a new car; the group may choose to increase the assertiveness levels of each of the members. These goals and purposes are important to identify because their absence can be demoralizing to the system and their presence can help the system to make decisions regarding courses of action.

2. *The culture of the system—its traditions, norms, rules, beliefs, and history.* Sys-

tems throughout their history evolve belief systems regarding what is true and desirable. These beliefs are embedded in traditions and ceremonies. In addition to helping the system determine actions, these beliefs create a sense of cohesiveness and belonging among members. At times, such phenomena support goal achievement, and at other times they impede it.

3. *The structure of the system.* Systems develop patterns in the relationships among participants. These patterns tend to persist over time or to change in predictable ways as the system develops. While structure is an entity with many facets, it is difficult to describe it except with reference to these facets, which consist of the following: who is attracted to whom or who rejects whom (sociometric structure); who talks to whom and about what (communications structure); who influences whom and how (power structure); how are tasks divided among participants (division of labor); and which participants are expected to assume which clusters of tasks (role structure). An important component of the role structure is the leadership structure. The role structure includes formal roles such as president or secretary and informal ones (identified through observation of the system) such as scapegoat or clown.

4. *The processes that occur in the system.* Process on a systemic level means changes in systemic conditions over time; these changes may be assessed either as they occur over long periods or as they occur from moment to moment as evidenced in the sequence of responses of system participants. There are several kinds of processes: one is problem solving and decision making; a second is the sequence of events in a system as it engages in a task (for example, a group playing baseball or a factory assembling an automobile); a third is the sequence of events related to the control of participant behavior; a fourth is a

sequence in which tensions arise and are dealt with. Another way to look at process is to examine a series of acts as they occur in a system and to analyze these acts, and their sequence, in terms of the kinds of processes just listed. Some processes are cyclical and repetitive; others may occur only once.

5. *The stage of development of the system.* Many writers see system development as one type of process. Because of the fact that development incorporates many elements, we prefer to consider it separately. The concept of system development is analogous to that of individual development in that systems proceed through phases that differ qualitatively from one another. Examples of such phases are those of system formation and system termination. The "middle phases" are quite different in different types of systems and will be described in detail later. An understanding of phases is important because it helps the worker to determine whether aspects of system performance are inevitable or are responses to abnormal and problematic circumstances.

6. *The resources available to the system.* All social systems are "open" in that they draw resources from the environment, distribute these resources within the system to accomplish the purposes of the system, and ultimately return a "product" to the environment. In social agencies, this product is usually a change in the client. Problems occur in social systems when the supply of resources is inadequate or when the distribution of resources within the system affects the quality or quantity of the product. Examples of this are a group of children that must operate without adequate program supplies, a family in which some children are favored in terms of the clothing or toys they receive compared with their siblings, or an agency that does not have money to employ sufficient staff. Obviously, even with structures and processes

conducive to goal attainment, a system will be stymied in its efforts without adequate resources.

7. *The interaction between and among systems*. In relationship to resources, as well as many other factors, a system must interact with other systems in the environment. Thus, a children's group facilitated by a group worker may interact with the agency, other agencies, the families of the children, and their schools. Systems often establish specialized roles for conducting such "business" with other systems. In "treatment" groups, for example, the worker usually negotiates with the agency on behalf of the members; in some other groups, members are elected to fulfill this function. In a family, a division of responsibility may take place in which one parent negotiates with the school while another registers complaints with business establishments.

8. *The boundaries of the system and how they are maintained*. Systems have boundaries in terms of a definition of who (and what) belongs within the system or outside of it. The system acts to define this boundary and to maintain it; one way that this is done is through selecting new members and discharging old ones. Groups, for example, will recruit additional members and will pressure members whom members regard as "deviant" to leave. An agency will "admit" clients and will terminate those who have attained their goals.

9. *System climate*. Finally, systems can be described in terms of the "feeling tone" that is prevalent at specified times and the quality of the relationships among the system's participants. Thus, a group may appear relaxed, the relationships among workers in an organization may be tense, and family members may be cheerfully occupied with accomplishing household tasks. While this variable may be harder to measure than some

of the others, it is usually recognized by participants and has an impact on the functioning of the system.

Measurement of System Variables

Later we will discuss in detail some of the specific instruments that can be used to assess groups, families, and organizations. The general nature of such approaches, however, will be indicated here. One, for example, is the use by the worker or other observers (sometimes even system members) of observational instruments. These can consist of records of who communicates, or associates, with whom and under what circumstances. Another approach is to ask the system participants to fill out questionnaires about their interactions with others, whom in the system they perceive as fulfilling certain roles, or whom they consider to be "members" of the system.

A third approach is to utilize existing records kept by the system. These might be attendance records, records of the disbursement of funds, budgets, or histories. In the case of agencies, and other organizations, more detailed records are kept such as data on clients, statistics on types and quantities of agency services and information on workers' job descriptions.

A fourth kind of data source is accounts of system activities through process records and tape recordings. The content in these can be analyzed and recorded so as to reveal information about system goals, culture, processes, and atmosphere. Still another kind of data is provided by diagrams that represent system variables. These are often created by workers, in conjunction with system members, to represent relationships within the system. The purpose of this kind of information is to enable workers and system participants to consider more easily complex information because it is in a visual form.

Examples are tables of organization of agencies and geneological charts of families.

Last, and often most important, is the worker's observation of what happens in the system as he or she interacts with it. Now that we have presented some of the general considerations regarding dimensions of systems to be assessed, we will provide specific details on assessment of families, groups, and organizations. An assessment of families and other groups will have many similarities but will differ because of the different histories, purposes, and functions of these two *small groups*. Organizational assessment differs from the other two because of the size, purpose, and complexity of large systems compared with small ones.

Family Assessment

A family assessment may be undertaken for several different reasons. The interpersonal practitioner will *always* assess the family conditions of clients even when other family members are not brought into the action system and even when the client is living alone. This family assessment is done because much of the variance in our behavior is determined by our interactions with our families, no matter how physically distant we may be from them. In addition, historical events in our family life continue to affect our emotions, attitudes, and behaviors through our recollections of them.

When the family is the client and action system, the worker's responsibility for a comprehensive family assessment is even greater, and the vast amount of data available to the worker about the family is commensurate with this task. An additional purpose is fulfilled through the assessment process when working with the entire family (or some subgroup of the family). Families usually en-

ter treatment with the idea that the problem is primarily that of one member of the family, the "identified patient." Examples of this are two families that sought help: one because a child was failing in school and the other because a parent had suffered a "nervous breakdown." As the worker with these families discussed other family circumstances, they both came to see family variables that defined and maintained the problems of the identified patient. The attention of the family or worker or both then shifted to these family circumstances. We shall now consider how system variables occur in families.

Family Goals

Family goals are important because they help to mobilize the energies of the family and to encourage cooperative activity among the members. The first aspect of family goal assessment is to determine what the family's goals are and whether they are shared and understood by all family members. Family goals may be short term (to take a vacation together) or long term (to secure education for all family members). They may be more concrete (buy a new refrigerator) or less so (the family wants to be respected by other families in the community).

The worker can ascertain family goals by asking family members what they hope to accomplish, how they would like things to be different, and how they plan on using their resources. These questions can be asked of individuals and subsequently of family members in the presence of each other. In families, therefore, it is possible to identify (1) individual goals for the family, (2) goals that represent a consensus among the family, and (3) family members' perceptions of what family goals are. These three types of goals may be similar to, or different from, each other, and this will have implications for family functioning. In one family, for example, one parent wanted the family to have the goal of buying a home; the family members each had goals that differed from this use of the family's resources; the other parent, in addition, told the worker that the members had all agreed to invest surplus family income in stocks and bonds.

The worker will assess how family goals affect other areas of family functioning. Thus, some family goals allow individuals to pursue their individual goals while others hinder this. Also, some family goals that are understood by all family members have been arrived at by consensus after a good deal of discussion while others have been imposed by one or more powerful family members.

Family Culture

One important component of the family culture is determined by the ethnic group to which the family belongs. Each ethnic culture prescribes family roles, values, and beliefs.[2] The worker, however, in assessing the impact of ethnicity on families must be aware of the fact that all families within an ethnic group are not alike and that a statement about ethnicity may reflect only ethnic families of a given social class level or geographical location. Even then, the statement may refer to a significant proportion of such families, and the family in question may be an exception. An awareness of such cultural values—for example, those found in many Chinese families on family solidarity and loyalty, or in many Appalachian families on maintaining independence from social agencies—will help the worker to understand such families. This topic is discussed more extensively in Chapter 15.

In addition to ethnic, social class, and religious factors, each family will develop its own unique culture. The worker can learn about this by asking family members what they consider important. This kind of information will often be forthcoming as the parents describe their own "families of origin," the kinds of values their parents sought to instill in them, ceremonies they experienced in their families, and what was rewarded and punished. If workers ask the family to review its history from the courtship of the parents to the present, many of the family's cultural dimensions will be revealed.

Family Structure

Minuchin has contributed a great deal to our understanding of family structure and its relationship to family functioning. He explains that the family's structure is maintained by "universal rules" such as those related to its power hierarchy. Structure is also maintained by idiosyncratic factors such as mutual expectations among family members developed after many years of living together.[3]

An important concept in Minuchin's structural approach is that of family subsystems developed to carry out the functions of the family. Boundaries exist around each subsystem and can be either rigid or flexible. Thus, in one family, an older child may occasionally join the parental subsystem and provide care to younger siblings. In another family, a more rigid one, the older child may be forbidden to join the parental subsystem in this way.

Minuchin asserts that the nature of subsystems and boundary arrangements in the family is a major determinant of family functioning. He analyzes subsystems by diagramming the family through the use of the following symbols: a clear boundary (- - - -); a diffuse boundary ($\cdots$); a rigid boundary (————); and conflict (————//————). Additional symbols are used to denote affiliation (/), overinvolve-

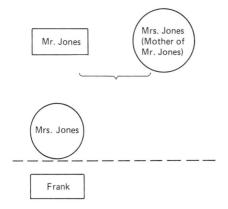

Figure 7-1. The Jones Family

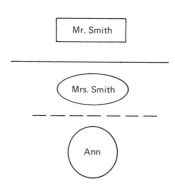

Figure 7-2. The Smith Family

ment (≡≡≡), coalition ([   ]), and detouring (→).[4] A clear boundary is one in which subgroups function flexibly, yet with a definite indication of their existence. A diffuse boundary is one in which some family members are overinvolved with each other, whereas a rigid boundary is one in which some members have little or no interaction with others. Detouring exists when two members of a family communicate with each other through a third family member.

A family structure that is often related to family problems is a subgroup that cuts across generational lines. Figure 7-1 presents an overview of one such family. Another structure that can be problematic is one in which a rigid boundary separates a parent from interactions with the other parent or the children or both (see Figure 7-2).

The worker ascertains the nature of family structures through observation of family interaction as well as through information supplied by the family members. The worker who wishes to be more rigorous about this aspect of assessment can secure counts of the frequency with which members interact with one another, engage in tasks together, or seek each other out for advice or instructions.

Family Process

In families, it is vital to assess processes that include a sequence of events that maintains the family's problem. Haley gives an example of this as it occurs in a "three-generation conflict":

1. Grandmother takes care of grandchild while protesting that mother is irresponsible and does not care for the child properly. In this way grandmother is siding with the child against the mother in a coalition across generation lines.

2. Mother withdraws, letting grandmother care for the child.

3. The child misbehaves or expresses symptomatic behavior.

4. Grandmother protests that she should not have to take care of the child and discipline him. She has raised her children and mother should take care of her own child.

5. Mother begins to take care of her own child.

6. Grandmother protests that mother does not know how to take care of the child properly and is being irresponsible. She takes over the care of the grandchild to save the child from mother.

7. Mother withdraws, letting grandmother care for the child.

8. The child misbehaves or expresses symptomatic behavior.

At a certain point, grandmother protests that mother should take care of her own child, and the cycle continues, forever and ever.[5]

The objective of the worker is to alter such processes, a topic that we will consider in Chapter 12. The first step is to identify the process. One way this is done is through what Minuchin calls "tracking." In this procedure, the worker "follows the content of the family's communications and behavior and encourages them to continue."[6] While tracking, the worker observes the order of events as they occur in the session. Another procedure is to secure a chronology of events, usually beginning with the problematic situation. This chronology can often be elicited by the phrase "And what happened then?"

Workers will also assess short-term processes in the family that are dysfunctional and should be changed. One such process relates to family problem solving. The worker can devise problem-solving and decision-making tasks to assess the family's decision-making process. A family may be asked, for example, to plan a short trip while the worker observes the process, sometimes through a one-way window, so that the worker's influence on the process is minimized. The worker notes whether the family uses a rational process of problem solving (for example, gathering information, evaluating it, and then applying it as the basis for a decision). The worker notes whether some members influence the decision more than others, remove themselves from the deliberations, or disrupt them.

Family Development

Families pass through a number of stages and must accomplish tasks appropriate to these stages. These incorporate the life phases of the children and include, therefore, the early period of marriage before children arrive; the periods when the children are infants, school age, and adolescent; the period when the children become young adults who should be ready to leave; the period of the "empty nest" after children are gone; and, finally, the period of retirement.

The worker will identify which stage the family is in and whether, and how well, the family is accomplishing necessary tasks. For example, one task of a family with school-age children is the training and education of the children. At the same time, the parents must succeed at their occupational careers so as to secure adequate resources for the family. The tasks of a family whose children are leaving include redefining the relationships between the spouses and preparing for eventual retirement.

The worker assesses the adequacy of the family's task accomplishment by first identifying the appropriate tasks. After this, the worker inquires as to whether and how members accomplish these tasks. Meyer has developed a comprehensive chart of the family's phases and the kinds of problems that are likely to develop at each one. This helps the worker to relate family problems to family developmental tasks.[7]

Family Resources

The family is the major vehicle people use for securing and allocating resources among individuals. In many families, the income of several or all family members is combined and is used to satisfy the family's material wants. Public assistance agencies consider the family's needs as a unit when determining the amount of assistance. The family, through its decisional processes, determines who gets what—whether parent or child obtains a new coat, whether some or all go on vacation, who sleeps in what room (alone or with others). The amount of resources and their allocation will be associated

with peace or tension in the family and ultimately the health and well-being of all family
members.

The worker, therefore, will be attentive
to these resource questions. They may determine whether the worker focuses on material
or social-psychological questions and whether or not the family's problem should be
defined as allocation of resources. Workers,
for example, have helped families to budget
their resources and to adhere to that budget.
The assessment of resources also includes
how the family members interact with relatives around money. This includes whether
the family gives or receives money from
other family members and whether the nuclear family is more or less affluent than other
parts of the extended family.

Data on these questions are usually not
difficult to secure. One problem, however, is
the idea held by the worker or by the family
that this information should be confidential,
even more so than facts about sexuality or
lawbreaking. This becomes a major issue
when the family's economic picture affects
the kinds of service the agency supplies due
to its fee structures or the determination of
eligibility for services.

Interaction with Other Systems

Family conditions are also a consequence
of the way in which the family interacts with
other systems including community institutions, peers of members, places of employment, and the extended family. Two instruments are frequently used to assess these
interactions. The *ecomap* presents the relationship of the family to other contemporary
systems; the *genogram* emphasizes interactions with the extended family and has the
additional virtue of portraying aspects of the
family's history that may still affect contemporary beliefs and behaviors.[8]

The ecomap is created by placing the

names of members of the household or nuclear family in a circle in the center of a large
sheet of paper. A series of circles placed
around the nuclear family is labeled to represent all the institutions and persons that play
a significant role in the life of the family or
household. Lines are drawn between the
family/household circle and the other circles.
Different colors or types of lines are chosen
to indicate strong, weak, and stressful associations. Arrows are placed on the lines to indicate the flow of energy and resources.

Figure 7-3 is an ecomap of the interactions between the Appel family and its environment. The family was referred to an
agency because of the school problems of the
11-year-old son, Al. The diagram of the Appel family shows that Al's main source of
stress is with the school, as he has strong in-
vestments in both peers and recreational programs. The ecomap also shows that the father
is seriously stressed by both friends and his
place of work. An older son, Bob, who no
longer lives with his parents, also appears to
have work and financial stresses, and Karen,
with whom Bob lives, receives unemployment compensation. While the mother has
satisfying work and friendship interactions,
we suspect that Al's problems may be associated with how she, as well as the whole family, copes with the father's and Bob's situations. The ecomap has the advantage of
suggesting these types of explanations. It can
also be used as an instrument for vividly recording changes in the family's environmental interactions as these occur over time.

The genogram, in contrast, focuses on
the extended family as a system and its relationship to historical antecedents. In form,
the genogram looks roughly like a family
tree. It, too, is created with the client so that
the client's perceptions and reflections can
be observed. Figure 7-4 is a genogram of the
Emerson family. It portrays three genera-

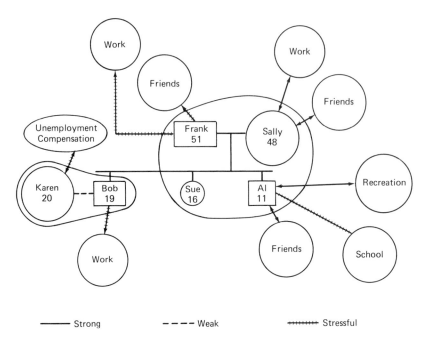

Strong ———— Weak – – – – Stressful ++++++

Figure 7-3. Ecomap of the Appel Family

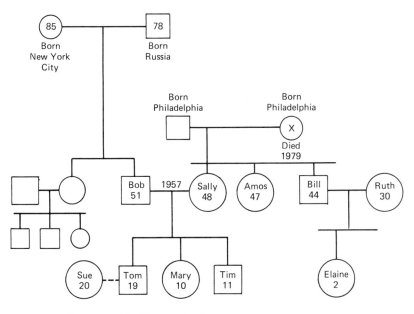

Figure 7-4. Genogram of the Emerson Family

tions in the family, although, depending on the issues the worker and family wish to explore, more generations may be identified. The convention observed in such charts is to identify males with squares and females with circles. Names and ages are placed inside the lines, and other pertinent data (dates of death, geographical location, significant facts) are placed below.

To develop the genogram, the worker secures important facts and events and places them on the chart; the worker and family choose aspects of the chart to explore in more detail as this can serve to illuminate the forces pertinent to the family's problems. These facts include demographic information such as date of birth, physical location, religion, ethnicity, and occupation. In addition, other data that the client considers important will be included such as economic status, health, and behavioral characteristics. Traumatic events in the extended family will be elicited such as the causes of death, imprisonment, mental illness, and other catastrophes.

The worker will inquire into issues that are significant to the family and that may center on some members of the family. These might be strongly held beliefs or highly sensitive topics that still affect family behavior and that may be sources of conflict. Examples of these topics are alcoholism, abortion, out-of-wedlock pregnancies, elopements, and family fights. Finally the worker will inquire about the flow of resources and interactions in the family by asking about who gives money to whom, who visits or calls whom and how often, and where the family (or some part of it) gathers for special occasions.

The genogram can be used to provide assessment information such as the following:

1. What behavioral patterns have occurred in the family that have persisted through several generations?

2. What are the sources of mutual reinforcement of values in the family as well as sources of value conflict?

3. What resources exist that are or could be of help to the family subsystem incorporating the client system?

4. What are the kinds of issues related to the family's beliefs and common experiences that function either to limit the family's problem solving and decision making or to enhance it?

Many other implications will occur to the worker and client system as they create and examine the genogram. Beyond its help in understanding the client system's problem and functioning, the genogram is often retained and treasured by the family as a testament to its continuity through time and its historical ability to survive obstacles.

Family Boundaries

The issue of boundaries between it and the environment is as important to a family as to any other system. For example, how soon is the new spouse of a family member "accepted" by other family members? How is the divorced spouse of another family member regarded by the family? What "rituals" must a child go through to be regarded as a full-fledged participant in family affairs? Is a boarder to be treated as other family members are? Is a live-in lover part of the family?

The answer to questions such as these will have implications for the family's problems and how it handles them. The worker can assess boundary issues by asking questions such as the following:

1. How do you define family membership?

2. How have new family members (for example, spouses) been treated?

3. Describe how the family has treated persons who have left the family (as through divorce). Are some persons who were in the family now considered out of the family? Describe the circumstances surrounding this.

Family Climate

Because of their intense involvement with each other, the emotional reactions of one family member affect others, and all are influenced by the emotional climate that prevails. If this climate is a happy and animated one, family members who experience situational problems are likely to feel nurtured and replenished by interaction with the family; on the other hand, if the climate is depressed or tense, the person with the same type of problem is likely to feel isolated and frustrated in the company of other family members.

Workers can assess this variable by observing affects in the family, and they can ask questions to obtain the family member's perceptions of their climate. Such questions are whether the family experiences itself as *generally* happy or unhappy, tense or relaxed, full of energy or lacking in energy. A caution, however, that should be observed is that some severely dysfunctional families will deny their emotional state and declare a much more optimistic view of the family than they really believe to be the case.

Other Family Conditions

Family theorists note additional variables that do not seem to be incorporated in the foregoing listing.[9] One is family *resonance* that Minuchin defines as the family's "sensitivity to the individual members' actions." Minuchin explains that "Families fall somewhere on the range between enmeshment, or such extreme sensitivity to individual members' inputs that the threshold for the activation of counterdeviation mechanisms is inappropriately low, and disengagement, or such extremely low sensitivity to individual members' inputs that the threshold for the activation of counterdeviation mechanisms is inappropriately high."[10]

The degree of resonance can be assessed by observing the family members' reactions to each other. In one family, even a sneeze elicited an immediate offer of a handkerchief from all other family members—a highly resonant situation. In another family, a child's injury was ignored by all family members—a situation very low in resonance.

Another variable that is vital to family approaches is the way in which the identified patient's "symptoms" serve to maintain the family's patterns. Family theorists search for this connection as a way of reducing the problem behaviors of the individual while, at the same time, supporting the emergence of a more functional family. The assessment of this phenomenon is closely related to the way in which the family process is studied: the worker examines the events in the family occurring prior to and subsequent to the problem behavior of the identified patient (I. P.) This will often uncover a repetitious cycle of family events.[11] In one family, the problem behavior was that the adolescent boy in the family struck his mother. The sequence of events was as follows:

1. The boy asked mother for car (expresses closeness to mother).
2. Mother refused (expresses distance from son).
3. Boy cursed mother (boy now expresses distance from mother).
4. Mother slapped son.
5. *Son struck mother* (identified problem behavior of I. P.).
6. Mother approached stepfather to complain about son (expresses closeness to stepfather).
7. Stepfather provided support for mother's position (stepfather expresses closeness to mother).
8. Stepfather got drunk (withdraws from mother).
9. Mother turned to son for support (expresses closeness to son).

10. Son responded to closeness by making a request of mother, thus repeating the cycle.

The reader should note that our indication of a "beginning" of the cycle is arbitrary. Since it is a cycle, we can begin a description of events at any point.

This type of analysis of the sequence of events in which the "symptoms" are included has several uses. It indicates the process that the worker will have to modify (or help the family to modify) to achieve the changes sought by the family. It also helps the worker to identify other problems that have not been stated by the family such as the stepfather's drinking behavior and the way in which the mother "uses" her son. All families have sequences to maintain the system's equilibrium. The problem is when they incorporate behavior that is deemed undesirable by the family or others.

Now that we have described some of the details of family assessment using the system variables we identified, we will consider how to use these variables to assess group conditions. As we will see, there are similarities, as well as differences, in the assessment of families and small groups.

Group Assessment

In this discussion of group assessment, we will focus on groups that constitute action systems for the attainment of the goals of their members. The worker, however, may have occasions to assess other groups that affect the behavior of individual clients such as their peer groups, institutional living groups, and community groups. This material can also have relevance for these situations.

An issue related to group assessment is whether or not to consider the group as a client system. In some approaches to group

work, the worker does view the group as the "client" and works to create a democratic and well-functioning group; the assumption is that such a group will enhance the growth and coping capacities of its members. In other approaches to group work, the individual member is the client and the worker helps members to create those group conditions that are conducive to the attainment of individual goals.

In the former circumstance, when the group is considered the client, the worker's assessment will focus on group conditions associated with its smooth and democratic functioning. In the latter circumstance, when members are considered clients, the worker's focus is upon group conditions that enhance or hinder individual goal attainment. The discussion of group assessment that we present incorporates variables from which the worker can select those that pertain to either approach to practice.

Group Goals

One of the major processes that occurs during the group formation stage is the determination of group purposes and goals.[12] We view group purposes as consisting of general statements of why the group was formed or continues to exist, such as to help individuals acquire social skills or to help unwed mothers decide whether or not to place their children for adoption. Goals consist of specific changes the members seek in themselves or others to accomplish group and individual purposes.

When workers assess group purposes or goals, they seek several kinds of information. The first is whether or not there is a group consensus. This can be ascertained by asking members individually (possibly through a questionnaire) what they believe the group's purposes and goals are; the group members also can be asked this question at a group session to see how this relates to the distribution of individual responses and how members respond in the presence of others. Many problems in group functioning, such as the ability to agree on group tasks and activities, are related to either a dissensus on goals or to members' incorrect perceptions of what others think. Members may even struggle to agree on purposes and goals, and the worker seeks to assess their progress in reaching agreement.

A second issue is whether members have "private" ideas about group purposes and goals that are not shared with the other members. Thus, a member of a "therapy" group may have the sexual seduction of another member as a goal. This may lead to behavior that is antithetical to group purposes. The worker can ascertain such hidden goals by identifying behavior of members that is contrary to stated individual and group objectives. Members may also express hidden agendas in individual sessions with the worker (although there are differences among workers in their attitudes toward individual sessions with members).

A third consideration is how much specificity workers seek in goal statements. In two groups, for example, both of which had the purpose of enhancing the member's social skills, one had a consensus that the goal was for the members to "make new friends," while the other had such goals as "the members will learn effective ways to initiate conversations" and "the members will learn constructive ways of coping with interpersonal conflict." In the former group, because the group's goal was abstract, the members argued about group tasks because these could not easily be deduced from the goals. When goals are more concrete, members are more likely, if there is disagreement, to argue about the goals themselves.

The group members' ethnic, religious, or other culture background will strongly influence the group's culture. Thus, groups sometimes begin meetings with prayer or song, conduct business in a sedate and orderly manner, or choose some activities over others because these actions are part of their cultural heritage. The worker is well advised to learn about the traditions of the natural groups existing within the community before seeking to facilitate groups in that environment.

Groups will also develop traditions that are unique to themselves. These can include ceremonies, rules, and ways of viewing events. The existence of such traditions is important to the group as it helps members to feel closer to the group. Workers who begin to work with groups after their formation should learn about their traditions as quickly as possible. Observing such traditions will help the workers to enter the group system; at the very least, the worker will avoid the rejection that comes from unknowingly violating rules and traditions.

Elsewhere we have referred to what we termed "shared attribution" defined as "understanding of events that are held by all or most of the group members and developed out of group processes."[13] These understandings form part of the traditions of the group. They are important because groups are very potent in defining reality for members.[14] In social work groups, these shared attributions may be contrary to social work values, for example, a sexist or racist belief, superstition, or an inappropriate blame for a problem. They may also be constructive, for example, having members learn to value self-awareness and rationality in problem solving.

The worker can assess the nature of the group culture by asking the members the reasons for their behavior. Similarities among members' beliefs, perceptions, and explanations of behavior suggest the existence of group cultural factors rather than individual ones.

Group norms are very powerful determinants of group events and member behaviors. Some norms are stated as group rules, for example, coming on time, maintaining confidentiality, and informing a group about out-of-group intimacies between members. Other norms are covert, for example, implicit rules against members confronting or questioning each other. The worker will seek to clarify the existence of norms by taking note of consistencies in behavior among members and questioning them about the bases for these.

Group Structure

The group's structure represents the pattern that exists in the interactions among members. This is a complex totality that is more easily analyzed in terms of the following components:

1. *Communications Structure.* This involves who talks to whom and about what. The worker will study the communications structure to see whether some members are isolated from interactions and thus are not influenced by or do not influence others in the group. In contrast, the worker will also seek to identify members who communicate much more frequently than others and who, therefore, have the effect of either dominating group decisions or hindering effective group problem solving.

The worker can assess the communications structure in several ways. One is to record when a member speaks and when the worker speaks, as follows: M M M W M W M M. This provides an indication of whether members are communicating more with the worker than with each other. Another approach is to record to whom members speak on a chart such as that shown in Figure 7-5. Simple schemes also exist to assess what members say to one another. One, developed by Rose, employs the following content categories[15]: suggestion/opinion-giving response, questions, responses to questions, self-suggestion responses, negative affect, positive affect, and information giving. Rose employs observers in therapy groups to code each remark in terms of who said it, to whom it was directed, and its category. The worker and the member can utilize these data either to support communication behavior or to determine the basis for a change in it.

2. *Sociometric Structure.* This represents who chooses to associate or not to associate with whom. When charted, this information indicates who the isolated individuals

	John	Frank	Bill	Sam
John	X	11		
Frank	1	X		
Bill		111	X	
Sam				X

Figure 7-5.

Communication Structure: Boy's Treatment Group

in the group may be and who participates in which subgroup. The identification of subgroups is also important as subgroups often differ from one another on behavior and values related to the group's objectives. Thus, in one group of delinquent adolescent boys, one subgroup tended to support the treatment objectives of the agency while another tended to oppose them.

Workers will sometimes use sociometric questionnaires to identify subgroups. These consist of a few questions as to which other members of the group one would most like to associate with in specified activities. Some instruments also ask who one would least like to affiliate with, but this is a threatening question in social work groups. In fact, in many groups, the use of any sociometric questionnaire is a problem because of the anxiety it creates related to fears of rejection. Under these circumstances, the worker will assess the sociometric structure through observing who sits close to, enters or leaves with, or volunteers to work with whom. The sociometric structure is usually diagrammed in the way shown in Figure 7-6.

3. *Power Structure.* This represents who has the most influence on group decisions and processes and how that influence is used. The power structure of a group includes the nature of the worker's influence as well as

that of the members. It can be appropriate if it furthers the purposes for which the group was formed as when workers or members influence others to be more rational or effective in their actions. Undesirable uses of power are an influence on members to increase their deviance, an intimidation of members, and a destructive challenge to the worker's role.

The worker should assess the sources of power, which includes possession of expert knowledge, control over resources, ability to inflict discomfort, being a source of identification, and the rights one has through position in the group.[16] This assessment helps the worker to increase the constructive uses of power in the group as well as to decrease the destructive ones. In addition, the worker may wish to increase the influence that some members have on the group and decrease that of others so that all the members may experience themselves as having an appropriate share in the control of group events.

4. *Role Structure.* Group roles consist of the way in which members and workers carry out the responsibilities of their positions in the group. In the broadest sense, this structure includes the roles of worker and member, and the worker should assess how the members view the worker's role as well as their own.[17] Groups also develop other roles

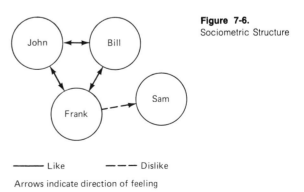

Figure 7-6.
Sociometric Structure

——— Like — — — Dislike

Arrows indicate direction of feeling

related to tasks and activities. In some groups, this is represented in formal positions such as president and secretary; roles are created through activities such as pitcher and catcher in baseball; other roles grow out of interactions and may be constructive as those of members who function as mediators or tension reducers or destructive as those of members who function as scapegoats.

Workers assess the role structure to determine whether the group has created the roles it requires, whether roles exist that are destructive to the group, and whether individuals possess the skills for the roles they enact. This assessment includes an appraisal of both formal and informal roles. The latter can be identified by asking whether someone in the group is considered to be the group mediator, clown, negotiator, expert, scapegoat, and so forth. The latter inquiry is often conducted through the use of questionnaires or individual interviews so as to avoid creating roles rather than identifying them.

One aspect of the role structure is the leadership pattern in the group. Many definitions of leadership are available. We use the distinction made by Bales between task and social-emotional leadership roles.[18] Task leadership consists of acts that lead to the accomplishment of group purposes; social-emotional leadership consists of acts that reduce tensions and increase attraction and support among group members. While all members may behave in these ways, some do so much more than others and are, therefore, defined as leaders. Bales, in his work, has utilized observational instruments in which these acts are specifically defined.

Group Process

Group processes are changes in group conditions. Elsewhere, we have classified group processes as those related to (1) changes in task conditions, (2) changes in

social-emotional conditions, and (3) changes in either task or social-emotional conditions.[19]

One process related to either task or social-emotional conditions is that of *role differentiation*. This process occurs as new positions are created in the group and members are socialized to occupy them. Examples are the election of a group chairperson, the training of group members in their membership responsibilities, and the reinforcement of member roles that further the purposes of the group.

The other process that relates to either task or social-emotional conditions is that of *role integration*. This process consists of communications among members as they seek to facilitate each other's role performances. This also includes the feedback provided to members on their role performances. Thus, when members help each other to understand why they chose their roles and why they enact them as they do, this process is occurring. As Yalom states, "If the powerful curative factor of interpersonal learning is to be set into motion, the group must recognize, examine, and understand process. It must examine itself, it must transcend pure experience and apply itself to the integration of that experience."[20]

A process related only to task conditions is that of *goal determination*. It occurs as members determine the desired group objectives. This process occurs as members define long-range goals (for example, become more assertive as a result of group participation or create conditions in the environment supportive of assertive behavior). It may also occur around short-term goals (for example, take a trip, invite a speaker, or learn the differences between assertive and nonassertive behaviors).

Another process related to task conditions is *goal pursuit*. It includes all actions to attain group goals. These actions may be chosen as part of a rational process as in *problem solving*. At other times, the actions are known to all or most members as they play a game or produce a play. The process may unfold in a creative manner such as in brainstorming, role playing, and producing a work of art.

The worker will assess the processes of goal pursuit by seeking answers to the following types of questions:

1. Do the activities of the group further the purposes of the group?
2. If the group's activities require rational processes, do these occur in an orderly fashion proceeding through phases of collecting information, evaluating information, and making decisions on the basis of such an evaluation?
3. Are members free to produce creative and innovative responses?
4. Are there more effective or efficient ways to attain goals than the ones employed?

Mills views social-emotional processes as occurring on three levels: the behavioral, the emotional, and the normative.[21] The behavioral processes relate to the use of influence to control member behavior and to reduce deviance. The emotional processes relate to changes in the amount of and nature of attraction among group members: normative processes relate to the development of norms that govern behavior and of sanctions related to behavior. In many therapeutic groups, the members are helped to examine these social-emotional processes to understand the emotional bases of their social interactions and to change those that inhibit satisfying social interactions.

Group Development

Hartford conceptualizes group phases as follows:[22]

I. Pregroup Phases
   A. Private pregroup phase
   B. Public pregroup phase
   C. Convening phase
II. Group Formation Phase
III. Integration, Disintegration, and Conflict, Reintegration, or Reorganization Synthesis Phase
IV. Group Functioning and Maintenance Phase
V. Termination Phase
   A. Pretermination phase
   B. Termination
   C. Posttermination phase

This represents an idealized view of group development—group members at a given time may experience events that typify several phases. Also, all groups do not experience every phase; groups can terminate during any phase and still may have accomplished the purposes for which they were formed. Groups under some circumstances may return to a level of functioning typical of an earlier phase. An example of this event was an established group that, when new members were added, reconsidered its purposes, thus repeating formation events.

An understanding of phases of group development is important for two reasons. First, it helps the worker to anticipate group events and plan ways to be helpful in regard to them. Second, the worker is less likely to be apprehensive about events when they are understood to be inevitable components of the group's growth. For this reason, we now discuss Hartford's model in greater detail.

The processes characteristic of the group formation phase are the determination of group purposes and the development of relationships among members. The group also makes decisions about the kinds of formal and informal structures to adopt. As these issues are resolved, members cope with conflicts between their attraction to the group, stemming from the benefits they might receive, and fears that they either will receive no benefits or be harmed by the group experience.

The next phase of the group, phase III, is marked by efforts to determine and initiate group activities that will result in the attainment of group purposes. This inevitably leads to the development of more complex group structures and of a group culture incorporating norms and rules. As these changes occur, conflicts inevitably arise in the group among factions holding different perspectives on these matters. These conflicts often are experienced as struggles related to the leadership of the group. As groups cope with and surmount these difficulties, they achieve a higher level of group cohesiveness. Some groups, however, fail to cope with these difficulties and either terminate or return to issues of formation.

The fourth phase represents a well-functioning group in which an integration of member efforts to support group functioning has been achieved. In addition, members have attained sufficient security with one another to allow for a necessary degree of individuality and independence. If additional periods of conflict occur, as is likely in long-term groups, the group has the stability and resources to respond well to them and to recover with a higher level of integration.

Groups finally enter a termination phase in which members should reduce the ties that bind them to other members, resolve the feelings of loss of the group, and plan for alternative ways of meeting needs. Hartford recognizes that there will be a post-termination phase in which members continue to work on these issues independently although they may still seek to maintain contact with some other group members (or all, as in the case of group reunions).

An assessment of groups must incorporate an analysis of the phase of development of the group. As we have shown, some of the major variables associated with group phases are consensus on group purpose and task, complexity of structure, movement toward the attainment of group purposes, and definition of group rules and norms. These can be identified in most cases by observation of group events. The degree of cohesiveness in the group, defined as the forces that retain members in the group, can be assessed by asking members to complete questionnaires in which they indicate how attracted they are to other members, the group as a whole, the goal of the group, the activities of the group, and the status of group member.

Group Resources

Groups, like all other social systems, require resources to survive. Successful groups have achieved success because of the resources they were able to attain. The kinds of resources required by social work groups include an adequate meeting room, equipment for the group activities (comfortable chairs, play space, games, storage space), space for additional activities (a gym for adolescents or children), materials required for the social work technology (rewards in a behavioral modification program), and appropriately trained staff and consultants. An assessment of a group's resources, consequently, will depend on the purposes of the group and the human and physical inputs required to attain those purposes.

Extragroup Transactions

Groups sponsored by social agencies and their members do not function in a vacuum but transact with other groups in the agency, with the agency itself, with institutions outside of the agency, and with the families of members. These transactions occur in unplanned ways as well as through activities promoted by the social worker. In some agencies, there are even formal structures for dealing with extragroup transactions such as councils made up of representatives of each group.

The worker will have many opportunities to assess these transactions. They will be described without much prompting by members as they discuss their problems and how these problems are affected by their families and social institutions; the worker may also devise questionnaires to find out how members interact with others. When the target of the worker's activity is the group's transactions with other systems, these transactions should be assessed. One example of this occurred in a group of husbands who had abused their wives. After the men began to take responsibility for their behavior, a joint meeting was set up with the wives. The worker established goals for this meeting with the men, such as their presentation of their concerns, while at the same time asked for their willingness to listen to their wives' grievances. The meeting was tape recorded, with the consent of all the participants, and afterward these responses were examined.

Group Boundaries

Groups develop norms and procedures for including new members in the group, defining the existing membership, and terminating the membership of group members when the group, itself, continues. The worker will assess these boundary issues to understand how to respond when members are added or discontinued. The worker and group members may be in agreement or disagreement on how these issues are to be handled, which also makes it important to understand this group dimension.

Even when the specific process of adding or subtracting members does not occur, the definition of membership has significance. Is a person who has missed a number of meetings or violated an important group norm or resigned and then reapplied considered a member? Can people be temporary members? Does a person become a member immediately, or is there a probationary period for membership?

These phenomena can be assessed in several ways: the worker can observe the members' reactions on occasions when individuals enter or leave the group; and greater details can be obtained by asking the members how they have handled these circumstances or wish to handle them. This type of question, however, can "force" the group to develop norms (or to rigidify them) when this was not previously the case.

Group Climate

As in other systems, the group may develop a climate that persists over time. In addition to the worker's own subjective judgment of the group's climate, the worker can ask the members the following types of questions: (1) What kinds of feelings do you believe most of the members had today? (2) How did you feel during today's meeting? In addition, if the worker wishes to have less influence on the response, he or she can use a "projective" approach by asking members to associate colors, songs, or adjectives (sometimes from a list of adjectives) to the group. Under these circumstances, the worker makes inferences about group climate from these responses.

Organizational Assessment

There are two major reasons why organizational assessment differs from family and group assessment. First, in our definition of interpersonal practice, the family and the group can be client *or* action *or* target systems, depending on the nature of the social work contract and the kinds of goals the client system seeks to attain. For the interpersonal practitioner, the organization is always either an action system or a target system—that is, a system that the client or worker or both may seek to change to achieve client goals. The dimensions that are assessed, therefore, are described with this in mind. For example, an individual client may seek to change the rules of the service agency itself, of another agency such as a welfare department, or of a community institution such as a commercial establishment or church.

Second, organizational analysis differs from small-group analysis because organizations are of larger size, have more formal structures, and engage in communications that may not be face to face but occur also through written channels. Many organizations are organized along bureaucratic lines, and the characteristics of bureaucracies, therefore, must be understood by workers.[23]

When workers seek to assess organizational conditions, they should also recognize that a distinction should be made between human service organizations, such as the service agency itself, and other organizations such as the place the client works. Some of the studies of organizations pertain to the latter, some the former, yet organizational conditions differ between these two types. As we discuss how the system variables we have listed apply to organizations, we shall further note how they apply to human service organizations, as these are the most frequent ones on which the worker focuses.

The major reason that human service organizations differ from other types is that their "raw material" is human beings with all the opportunities, complexities, ethical issues, and constraints that this implies. In addition, the goals of changing individuals are more difficult to specify and their achievement more difficult to measure than are changes brought about in an inanimate object.[24]

Organizational Purposes and Goals

These are the targets of change efforts when the client's needs are not met because the organization's goals do not incorporate them. This is not meant to imply that the client has a right to demand that every organization meet his or her needs. Nevertheless, when the client (usually together with others) believes that an organization has a social obligation to declare goals that are helpful to the client, this area is targeted. An example of this is a Chicano client who believed that a mental health center in her community should have as a goal meeting the mental health needs of Chicano members of the community. The agency did not state this and did not employ staff who had a knowledge of Chicano culture and language.

Organizational goals can be either explicit or implicit. Explicit goals are embodied in published agency documents. Implicit goals may be present in verbal understandings that exist among staff members that govern their practice. As we have stated earlier, the goal of human service organizations may be difficult to state in clear and operational forms, and, therefore, it may be hard to tell whether they are followed or not.

Organizational goals and purposes are assessed by examining organizational documents such as agency descriptions. They are also embodied in minutes from boards or staff meetings, and these can be requested. Implicit goals can be identified through interviews with organization staff and administration. They can also be inferred from the actual operations of the organization such as whom it serves and what it seeks to accomplish with its clientele.

Organizational Culture

Organizational norms and beliefs are targets of change when they conflict with client beliefs and inhibit client goal attainment. An example was an agency that acted on the basis of the belief that the traditional two-parent family, in which the husband is employed, is the "healthiest" family. The agency staff regarded one-parent families as "deviant."

The culture of the organization is a product of its history, the population from which it draws its staff, and the ideas held by powerful individuals such as its board of directors and administrators. This is difficult to assess because it is usually not embodied in official documents but rather in the beliefs and practices of staff. These can be documented through interviews. In addition, however, inferences can be drawn from other available data. For example, whose pictures hang on the walls? How is the agency decorated?

The technology the organization employs may also be indicative of its norms and values. In a human service organization, the use of a behavioral technology may indicate a value placed upon scientific approaches and accountability. Educational approaches are employed when clients are viewed as learners rather than as deviants or sick persons. The assessment of organizational culture will, therefore, include an examination of the values that are intrinsic to the technologies employed.

Organizational Structure

The same kinds of structures we presented in our discussion of groups are relevant to organizations. Thus, organizations will have communication, role, and power struc-

tures. Because of the size and complexity of the system, however, the distribution of power and the location of decision making will be more formalized than it will be in small groups. These variables are important to assess because the client system often seeks a change in the organization and must have access to sources of power.

The location of an important source of power is the governance structure of the organization. In governmental organizations, power may be located in a legislative body and delegated to departments of the executive branch of federal, state, and local governments. In nongovernmental organizations, a board of directors may fulfill the same function. Power will then be delegated to executive leaders of the organization, and they may further delegate power to department heads, supervisors, and the like.

The amount of delegation of power that takes place will vary, and this is also assessed. One source of data is the official policy documents of the organization. Often, however, these documents do not describe how the organization "really" functions. Data must be secured from interviews with informants such as the executive (and also others) to determine how power is exercised and how decisions are actually made. (It may not be practical for line workers on an individual basis to do this. In some agencies, agency self-study groups have been formed to secure such information.) It is common for people to deny the power they possess so as to avoid accountability. In addition, people lower in an organization hierarchy often have unspoken ways of controlling organizational behavior. For example, a nurse, social worker, or other health professional in a hospital can control the behavior of the "powerful" physicians by the information they supply.[25]

Closely related to the power issue is the

location of decision making in the organization. Some organizations require all decisions to be approved at an executive level; others define only some decisions as requiring this. Some require participation of several persons; others delegate authority to single individuals. The worker should assess how decisions are made relevant to the client's concerns.

Organizations will often have a written table of organization that indicates how organizational tasks are divided and how power is allocated. The worker will find this an excellent tool for assessing organizational structure, but with two cautions. One is that the table of organization may not represent the true state of affairs, and this possibility must be ascertained. Second, in many organizations the table of organization is often in the process of reconsideration and change, and the worker should also inquire as to this possibility.

The interaction of two kinds of roles in human service organizations is of particular interest: bureaucratic and professional.[26] The former are those that relate to maintaining the functioning of the organization, the latter to carrying out technical procedures to attain client goals. Thus record keeping, budgeting, and allocating of resources are bureaucratic activities, and assessing clients, planning treatment strategies, and evaluating client change are professional activities. Sometimes these two roles are both assumed by the same person; at other times they are not. An important part of organizational assessment, therefore, is to ascertain the nature of bureaucratic and professional requirements and how they are allocated among staff members.

Organizational Processes

One set of processes in the organization is determined by the technology employed.

The technology consists of the procedures employed to create the organization's "product." In human service organizations, such as those utilizing interpersonal practitioners, these technologies include behavior modification, ego-psychologically oriented casework, social group work, and family therapy. Organizational processes such as intake processes, client allocation processes, referral processes, and termination processes will be adapted to these technologies. The kinds of problems related to technology that workers assess include whether the organization has committed itself to the technology, the extent of consensus on this commitment, what the organizational requirements are for the technology, and whether they are being met.

Another set of processes surrounds the steps the organization takes to secure conformity to its rules, that is, its "compliance system."[27] One type of compliance system is the normative, and it is operational when organizational participants conform because of their agreement with or recognition of the belief system of the organization. Another type is the utilitarian, which utilizes conformity based on an exchange of goods and services. The third type is the coercive, which operates through the capacity of the organization to harm participants.

Most processes in social work organizations are based on normative compliance; that is, clients and staff will support the rules of the organization because they believe that this is to their benefit. Some processes also are based on utilitarian compliance. Staff may offer services primarily for the salary offered, and clients may participate because they believe that this will be rewarded, such as by a welfare grant. In correctional institutions, certainly, but also in other settings with the power to punish, such as schools, clients may comply because of the potential punishment.

The worker, therefore, will assess the

compliance processes in the organization. In addition to observing organization activities, the worker can ask relevant persons why they adhere to particular rules and what they believe the consequence of failure to follow the rules will be. For example, a client in one agency said that she provided the information the worker sought because she believed that this was necessary for the worker to help her (normative compliance). In another agency, the client said she provided information because she was participating in a research project and was paid for this (utilitarian compliance). Still another client said that if she did not provide the informatlion, her child would be removed (coercive compliance).

Organizational Development

Organizations, like groups and families, have phases of development. A major difference from these other entities, however, is that because of their formal nature and function, organizations may continue indefinitely. Groups usually end when their purposes are attained, and families (at least nuclear families) end when their members die. Organizations do, at times, attain their purposes and may then either terminate or identify new purposes. They may also terminate when resources are discontinued if the organization is deemed ineffective or for other reasons.

Workers assess organizational phases, for example, to identify whether the client's problems with the organization are due to the phase or represent a more serious problem in organizational functioning. For example, a client may be confronted with a series of new rules. This is to be expected in a newly developing organization, but it may indicate mismanagement or a change in goals in an established one.

Thus, in the beginning phases of an organization, much attention will be paid to defining policy, the roles of staff and governing bodies, and the purposes of the organization. Efforts will be made to secure adequate resources for the organization, and these will be based on less than adequate information about organizational needs as the experience with actual costs is lacking. Staff and others will anticipate these issues as they are attributed to the newness of the organization. A certain amount of confusion will reign as to proper channels and procedures, and these problems may be resolved through either ad hoc decisions or appeals to higher authority.

In the subsequent stage of organizational development, procedures will have been established, lines of authority drawn, and purposes clarified, and the organization will be engaged in creating its "product." Nevertheless, issues will occur that force the organization to change, and these are often related to the following:

- Installation of a new executive
- Recruitment of a new group of staff who differ from the old in such areas as skill, purpose, or beliefs.
- A change in the allocation of resources to the organization
- A change in the systems with which the organization interacts
- A change in the client group
- Information that the organization is not accomplishing its purposes, often secured from an evaluation of organizational outcomes
- A change in the organizational structure
- Changes in the goals of the society (e.g., those due to recession, the civil rights movement, the energy crisis)

The worker, consequently, will seek to understand the forces that promote organizational change as well as those that impede it. The consequences of these for the ability of the organization to meet client demands should be identified. How the worker uses information to change organizations will be discussed in Chapter 13.

Organizational Resources

The ability of the organization to carry out its purposes will be correlated with its resources. These include money for staff, equipment, and physical plant. Organizational resources also include human ones such as volunteers, appropriately trained staff, and persons to serve on governing bodies and advisory committees. The resource question must also include an assessment of how resources are allocated within the organization and whether they are appropriately consumed. The resource issue is also interwoven with the issue of how the organization presents itself to secure resources, that is, its public relations and informational outputs.

One example of a resource problem is a long waiting list in an agency because of lack of staff; another is an agency with a room for a group or family therapy sessions that is not adequately furnished, that is too small, or that allows noises from other activities to interrupt sessions. Still another example is an agency that supplies financial assistance and must reduce allocations because of budgetary problems.

The interpersonal practice worker is seldom required to perform a study of the organization's budget. On the other hand, when resources are not forthcoming to meet the client's requirements, the worker should ask questions such as the following:

- Are the required resources unavailable to the agency?

- Does the agency have sufficient resources but has not allocated them according to some reasonable priority system?
- Has the organization failed to secure resources because its work is not recognized or valued in the community?
- Does the organization suffer from the society's economic situation? If so, how does it plan to cope with this?
- Has the client failed to make "a case" for his or her resource needs?

Interorganizational Relationships

Client problems can result from the way in which organizations interact with each other. For example, a welfare department social worker wished to refer his client to a family agency for marital counseling. The welfare department and the family agency, however, recently experienced conflict with each other because welfare department staff criticized the family agency for serving lower-income families inadequately. The family agency, in turn, criticized the welfare department for failing to provide quality services. In the face of these events, the worker received a cold reception when he contacted the family agency about the referral.

In these and similar circumstances, the worker must assess the nature of interorganizational relationships. The kinds of variables that the worker assesses include the domain of the two agencies, whether the agencies interact cooperatively or exhibit conflict, and the kinds of power the agencies employ in their interactions.

The issue in regard to domain is whether the organizations in question have clarity regarding their purposes and populations and whether these domain variables lead to competition or cooperation between the agencies. Thus, an agency that provides vocational guidance and another that provides child guidance have separate domains. Even if they serve the same neighborhood, they should be able to work cooperatively. On the other hand, a sectarian family agency and a nonsectarian family agency, in the same community, may compete with each other for some clients.

Conflict among agencies can ensue from other issues than domain conflicts. The agencies may compete for support from the same community fund; they may compete for scarce trained staff; or they may, when working with the same clients, disagree as to the kinds of service that should be offered or domains may overlap because of ambiguity. The worker, therefore, should assess these kinds of conflicting circumstances so that the necessary cooperation of agencies may be elicited. This task relates to broker and advocate roles that we shall describe in Chapter 13.

The relative power of the organizations should also be assessed. Organizations obtain power through forces such as the following: their relationships with powerful systems (an organization's relationship to a legislature or other funding body); power granted by governmental or other systems (a court with the power to remove children from their parents); control over resources (a state agency that can contract with private agencies for services); and power gained through access to media (good relationships with a local newspaper). The worker who seeks to have an impact on interorganizational relationships must recognize the power involved and, when necessary, plan a strategy for utilizing or changing it.

Organizational Boundaries

An issue highly related to organizational domain is that of boundaries. As in families and groups, this relates to how people are admitted to and discharged from the organizational system. The domain definition will determine who is eligible to become a client or staff member but not what the intake process is. An intake procedure must determine which persons meet the organization's definitions of domain and which do not. Additional requirements may then be established that people must fulfill so as to enter. Clients may be required to pay fees, provide information, or even undergo a probationary period. Additional systems such as courts may be asked to act.

Analogous processes occur to discharge a client from "membership" in the system. The client must be judged either to have improved or to be incapable of improvement. On the other hand, the client may decide to terminate against the desire of the organization, and each system will define this differently as well as whether the client is to no longer be considered an organizational participant. Additional approval for termination must sometimes be secured from courts, probationary departments, or medical and psychiatric authorities.

Boundary issues become important to interpersonal practitioners when clients are refused service or when services are terminated against the client's desires. The client may also wish other members of the family to be served, and this may be refused, or in contrast the client may not wish to have the family included as part of an organizational system, and this may conflict with agency definitions.

The worker will assess boundaries of organizations by examining official statements of eligibility for services as well as information on duration of services. At times, when the practices of the organization appear to contrast with its official statements, the worker may call for a study of actual agency practices. These "actual" experiences may sometimes also be inferred from agency service statistics, which are almost always public records.

Organizational Climate

Organizations also have "climates" in that morale of organizational participants may be high or low, their pace of work fast or slow, their behavior tense or relaxed. These conditions may also be affected by some of the other variables we have described such as the organizational facilities, which may be colorful or drab, comfortable or uncomfortable. Decorations and pictures may also convey different kinds of feeling tones; an agency filled with religious symbols "feels" different from one with scenes of children playing.

These climate variables may affect the client's readiness to participate in the organization as well as the kinds of personal material the client communicates. They may also affect the quality of the relationship with the staff. Workers who seek to assess these conditions will tour the agency and note their impressions. Clients can also be asked to describe the organization and to indicate their impressions of mood, decor, and style of work. Many organizations are insensitive to these issues, and feedback from clients is valuable. In contrast, in some organizations the climate is a reflection of executive leadership, organizational powerlessness, and the convictions of the governing body. In the latter instances, these issues should be confronted.

Summary

In this chapter, we have presented the variables that workers should consider in the assessment of families, groups, and organizations. These variables were identified first in general terms. They include system goals and purposes, the culture of the system, the structure of the system, the processes that occur in the system, the stage of development of the system, the resources available to the system, the interaction among systems, the boundaries of the system, and the climate of the system.

Following this description of system variables, we discussed separately applications to assessment of families, groups, and organizations. We pointed out similarities in the assessment of these systems as well as differences. Differences between families and small groups occur because of the varying functions of these two entities as well as the long-term nature of the family. Differences between families and small groups, on the one hand, and larger organizations, on the other, were seen as occurring because of the face-to-face and informal nature of the former and the impersonal, structured, and formal nature of many interactions in organizations.

At this point in the book, the reader has become acquainted with the ways in which clients and workers engage each other and identify the problems on which they will focus. The current chapter demonstrated ways that workers seek to assess these problems to establish goals and choose effective change strategies. In the next chapter, on "contracting," we shall discuss how workers and clients utilize the information they have gained to create an agreement on change goals and strategies.

NOTES

1. For situations in which the best outcomes for family treatment have been established, see Alan S. Gurman and David P. Kniskern, "Research on Marital and Family Therapy: Progress, Perspective, and Prospect," in Sol L. Garfield and Allen E. Bergin, eds., *Handbook of Psychotherapy and Behavior Change: An Empirical Analysis*, 2nd ed. (New York: John Wiley, 1978), pp. 834–845. A broad review of

group outcome studies may be found in Richard L. Bednar and Theodore J. Kaul, "Experiential Group Research: Current Perspectives," in *Handbook of Psychotherapy*, pp. 771–783.

2. See Charles H. Mindel and Robert W. Habenstein, *Ethnic Families in America: Patterns and Variations* (New York: Elsevier, 1976).

3. Salvador Minuchin. *Families and Family Therapy* (Cambridge, Mass.: Harvard University Press, 1974), pp. 51–52.

4. Ibid., p. 53.

5. Jay Haley, *Problem-Solving Therapy* (New York: Harper Colophon Books, 1976), pp. 110–111.

6. Minuchin, *Families and Family Therapy*, p. 127.

7. Carol Meyer, *Social Work Practice* (New York: Free Press, 1976), p. 18.

8. For an extensive discussion of these two instruments, see Ann Hartman, "Diagrammatic Assessment of Family Relationships," *Social Casework*, Vol. 59, No. 8 (October 1978), pp. 465–476.

9. Minuchin, *Families and Family Therapy*, p. 130.

10. Ibid.

11. Haley presents a comprehensive discussion of such sequences in Haley, *Problem Solving Therapy*, pp. 100–128.

12. For a social-psychological discussion of group goals, see Marvin E. Shaw, *Group Dynamics*, 2nd ed. (New York: McGraw-Hill, 1976), pp. 294–304.

13. Charles Garvin, *Contemporary Group Work* (Englewood Cliffs, N.J.: Prentice-Hall, 1981), pp. 120–121.

14. Margaret Hartford, *Groups in Social Work* (New York: Columbia University Press, 1971), pp. 40–42.

15. Sheldon Rose, *Group Therapy: A Behavioral Approach* (Englewood Cliffs, N.J.: Prentice-Hall, 1977), pp. 50–51.

16. For a discussion of social power, see J. R. P. French, Jr., and B. Raven, "The Bases of Social Power," in Dorwin Cartwright, ed., *Studies in Social Power* (Ann Arbor, Mich.: Institute for Social Research, 1959), pp. 150–167.

17. For an example of research on such role perceptions, see Charles Garvin, "Complementarity of Role Expectations in Groups: Relationship to Worker Performance and Member Problem-solving," unpublished doctoral dissertation, University of Chicago, 1968.

18. Robert F. Bales, "Task Roles and Social-Emotional Roles in Problem-Solving Groups," in E. E. Maccoby, T. M. Newcomb, and E. L. Hartley, eds., *Readings in Social Psychology*, 3rd ed. (New York: Holt, Rinehart and Winston, 1958), pp. 437–447.

19. Charles Garvin, "Group Process: Usage and Uses in Social Work Practice," in Paul Glasser, Rosemary Sarri, and Robert Vinter, eds., *Individual Change Through Small Groups* (New York: The Free Press, 1974), pp. 209–232.

20. Irvin D. Yalom, *Theory and Practice of Group Psychotherapy*, 2nd ed. (New York: Basic Books, 1975), p. 122.

21. Theodore Mills, *The Sociology of Small Groups* (Englewood Cliffs, N.J.: Prentice-Hall, 1967), p. 57.

22. Hartford, *Groups in Social Work*, p. 67.

23. For a discussion of the properties of bureaucracies, see Peter M. Blau and W. Richard Scott, *Formal Organizations* (San Francisco: Chandler, 1962).

24. See Yeheskel Hasenfeld and Richard English, *Human Service Organizations* (Ann Arbor: University of Michigan Press, 1974), pp. 1–24.

25. See David Mechanic, "Sources of Power of Lower Participants in Complex Organizations," *Administration Science Quarterly*, Vol. 7 (December 1962), pp. 349–364.

26. Eliot Freidson, "Dominant Professions, Bureaucracy, and Client Services," in *Human Service Organizations*, pp. 428–447.

27. Amitai Etzioni, *A Comparative Analysis of Complex Organizations* (Glencoe, Ill.: The Free Press, 1961).

eight
Contracting

The concept of "contract" has been extensively discussed in social work literature.[1] Contract is a generic term and applies to work with individuals, families, and small groups.[2] Contract approaches have been developed in various fields of practice (e.g., child welfare,[3] public social services,[4] family services[5]), and the concept has been the focus of several research projects.[6] Contract has also appeared as a central concept in a number of models of social work practice (e.g., task centered,[7] behavioral intervention,[8] life model[9]). From this voluminous literature, research, and practice, contract has emerged as an important concept that prescribes a useful structure for worker-client interactions.

Origins of the Concept

There is a misconception that "contract" is primarily a behavioral concept that entered social work practice when behaviorism began to influence the profession. In contrast, the notion of "contract" is utilized in most therapeutic approaches, including both psychodynamic[10] and behavioral,[11] and the concept has been discussed in both the casework and group work literature.[12] In fact, references to the contracting process can be found in the writings of Freud.[13] For the past two decades principles of contracting have extended into all areas of social work, and not one ideology, method, or approach is exclusively responsible for the concept's introduction into social work practice.

Some practitioners have voiced concern about the term "contract" itself. Their reservations reflect the realization that this term is frequently used in law,[14] yet social work has borrowed a term and applied it in ways that differ from legal usage. These critics prefer other terms such as "compact" or "working agreement" rather than "contract." These reservations should be seriously considered because the use of "contract" in social work practice is not fully analogous to the term's application in law. For example, in law, contracts are static, binding, promissory agreements between parties that are not easily renegotiated or changed; yet in social work practice, contracts are viewed as dynamic and flexible arrangements between parties. In law, the remedies for failing to follow through on contractual agreements are usually spelled out in the original agreement; yet in most social work contracts, remedies are rarely discussed or negotiated and in some cases do not exist.

Whether the term "contract" is popular, or fits legal theory, or has origins in any given ideology is not as important as is a clear description of what "contract" means and how this concept can be applied to interpersonal practice with individuals, families, and small groups. This chapter not only describes and applies the contract concept to social work practice, it also presents a rationale for its importance. A contract is often difficult to accomplish, and this chapter discusses ways in which contracts can be adapted to problematic situations.

Components of a Social Work Contract

In both literature and practice, "contract" has been viewed in two ways. First, it has been defined as a product (i.e., the service contract) in the form of a written or verbal agreement between worker and client. This agreement is usually negotiated in early sessions and spells out major terms of service (e.g., duration of service, fees, parties to be involved). The contract may also be seen as an ongoing, decision-making process (i.e., contracting) in which worker, client, and other service providers continuously negotiate and renegotiate terms as service progresses. From this perspective, contracting is a circular process of negotiation, implementation, evaluation, and renegotiation involving client, worker, and possibly other service providers.

In both perspectives, "contract" may be defined as a working agreement among parties (i.e., worker, client, others) about the terms of service. This definition of contract has three basic elements. In interpersonal practice, the *parties* are usually the people involved in the service process such as the client(s) (individual, couple, family, small group), the worker, and the other service providers involved in the service process. The *working agreement* indicates that each party is expected to have input into the agreement, to understand it, and to accept it. The *terms* are the specific conditions or particular decisions that determine how service will proceed.

In practice there is no end to what can be negotiated as terms in a social work contract (e.g., seating arrangements, length of sessions, refreshments). The literature, however, does suggest that there are several essential terms to a social work contract: purpose, target problems, goals or objectives, time limits, and actions and responsibilities of parties.

Purpose refers to the "why" or "rationale" for service in the first place. Purpose is usually the first issue that is raised in an encounter between parties. For example, "I came in today to get some help with personal problems" or "I'm here to tell you about our services and see whether there aren't things that we can do to help." The practice of social work involves many potential purposes. Social workers may be engaged in prevention, rehabilitation, protection, resocialization, or education, and sometimes these purposes seem so obvious to the worker that a particular purpose is not made explicit in the first encounter. Purpose is the most important term, and it should be recognized and agreed to early. Purpose shapes all other decisions, and without understanding and agreement, it is risky for parties to continue service. If parties cannot agree on a purpose for their encounter, there is no reason for them to continue.

"Corrupt" contracts can emerge in practice if purpose is not clarified or honestly addressed. For example, students are sometimes assigned "learning cases." In these cases there is no expectation that the client will be helped by the student, but instead the student is expected to learn from the interaction with the client. Should a student then, in his or her first encounter with such a client, say "I've been assigned to you because you will be a good learning experience for me"?

Similarly, clients can propose corrupt purposes. Prisoners may attend a group therapy session not for any benefits in self-understanding or improvement they may obtain but to interrupt the boredom of prison routine or to secure "brownie points" toward parole. Sometimes the purpose stated by one party is not believed by the other. A child welfare worker may state that he or she wants to help parents solve family problems to return their child, yet the parents may believe the worker is involved with them to collect evidence to remove their other children.

Target problems are identified, deleterious conditions facing clients that must be changed to improve their social functioning. (See Chapter 4 and 5 for a further discussion of the concept of problems.) As discussed in earlier chapters, a client may want help with personal problems (e.g., alcohol or drug abuse, physical disability, serious emotional or mental disturbances), or interpersonal problems (e.g., marital, parent-child, role performance), or situational problems (e.g., housing, money management, social isolation). In our contractual approach to service, the client's choice of problem is valued and

encouraged. Clients are not expected to be passive recipients of service nor is the worker expected to decide unilaterally what is wrong. The choice of target problem is a mutual decision. The client must want help with it, and the worker must be willing to work on it too.

But eliciting the client's point of view is in many cases easier said than done. Several factors work against the client's choices. Social agencies are usually directed toward particular problem areas. Intake is a sorting process in which some clients are accepted for service and others are rejected or are referred elsewhere.[15] Most people (clients included) do not like rejection, so when they come to an agency for help, they try to make the best case for it. Clients can size up the agency and intake worker's biases quickly and accordingly present problems to fit the agency's and worker's agendas. Thus, a client who came to a community mental health center reported his problems as "feeling depressed, anxious, and restless"; when this client entered a family agency, he spoke about "hassles with the wife and kids."

Besides the pressures to please and the desire to give the agency and worker what they are looking for, some clients enter service and are unclear about what is bothering them. These clients require help to review their present situation and to decide what should be addressed. Inevitably, assessment procedures tend to be biased (as well as the workers who employ them), and the process of leading the client through an assessment procedure may be highly suggestive. A worker who thought that most people's troubles were caused by personal psychopathology focused his assessment on psychopathology. On the other hand, another worker who thought that most troubles were caused by situational stress and pressures reflected this bias.

Negotiation of the target problem requires an approach that encourages the client to participate in the search for that problem.[16] Such an approach does not mean that the worker is nondirective and inactive in the search. The ideal is a balance between worker and client input. In a contracting process, the worker actively engages the client in assessment procedures to help facilitate the client's selection of a target problem. Problems that can only be perceived or inferred by the worker (e.g., "oedipal conflict," "narcissistic wound") should not be chosen as target problems.

As discussed in Chapter 5, when negotiating a target problem with the client, the worker should encourage the client to be very specific about the problems that are being explored.[17] A specific statement of a problem, as described in Chapter 4, consists of the performance discrepancy, frequency of performance discrepancy, people involved, the sequence of events associated with the problem, and how significant others perceive the problem. This amount of detail, however, combines aspects of both problem specification and assessment.

A more parsimonious statement of the problem is required for contractual purposes and certainly for a written contract. This detail will include the performance discrepancy, problem frequency, and people involved. Thus a problem stated as "my husband is always angry" is inadequate. An appropriate specification for contractual purposes is, "My husband refuses to speak to me when I ask for money. This occurs on the average of twice a week and began when I lost my job two months ago." Workers can be helped in their search for this kind of specificity by remembering some of the same questions required of newspaper reporters: who, what, when, where, and how.

Goals are future, desired end states for the client. Sometimes goals flow directly from target problems as when the "opposite" of a problem defines the goal: unemployment-employment; dependent-independent.[18] Goals at this level of generality are not useful, and the worker's task is to help the client's goals become more concrete.[19].

A concrete goal consists of a desired behavior (of the client or someone else), the circumstances under which the behavior will occur, and a criterion of acceptable performance. The following is an example of an acceptable goal statement: (a further discussion of negotiating goals is presented in chapter 9):

> John, when he finds a partner to whom he is attracted and who is attracted to him, will negotiate mutually acceptable commitments to the relationship. These commitments will minimally include an agreement regarding the exclusivity of the relationship.

In this example, the behavior is to negotiate a commitment to the relationship; the circumstance is the availability of a partner; and the criterion is that the commitment will deal with exclusivity.

The contract, if it is based on global or fairly long-term goals, should indicate some short-term objectives. A short-term objective differs from a long-term goal in the frequency of the behavior and the intensity of the behavior, or it represents another behavior that is required for the goal to be attained. The following are examples of these three types of short-term objectives:

1. (differs in frequency) The long-term goal is for Ted to turn in his homework every day; the short-term goal is for this to happen twice a week.
2. (differs in intensity) The long-term goal is for the father to refrain from the use of cruel ways of disciplining his child; the short-term

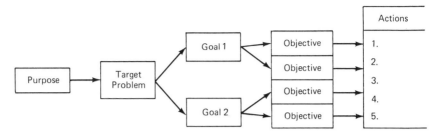

Figure 8-1. Contract Sequence

goal is to refrain from physical blows but to shout instead.

3. (represents another behavior that is required) The long-term goal for Anne is full employment; the short-term goal is attendance at a training program.

In a more complete example, a client determined to secure child care arrangements, enroll and complete a training program, and locate a job, apply for it, and be hired. While all these steps are specific objectives that may be stated in a social work contract, each of these objectives in turn can be specified farther. As the contract process unfolds, the terms become more and more specific and reflect actions and responsibilities of all parties.[20] Figure 8-1 graphically presents this contract sequence.

Because the objectives of a service contract are expected to be achieved during the service period, *time limits* are essential for all goals and objectives. In the example given, worker and client agreed to spend two weeks to secure child care arrangements.

It is impossible to predict with perfect accuracy how long it will take to attain a goal. Time limits are not strict, do-or-die requirements, but they do serve to motivate clients. Deadlines have other positive effects on goal achievement.[21] One is that they help people to rank the life tasks that face them. Students usually know weeks in advance when term

papers are due, yet most term papers are tackled in the last weekend or a few days before a deadline.

Goals and related time limits are terms in a social work contract that raise a thorny issue about the nature of "contracting." Contracts are promissory arrangements[22] that hold parties to certain conditions or actions; yet in a social work contract, goals, objectives, and time limits cannot be conceptualized as promissory in a binding sense. When worker and client establish a goal of "employment," the worker does not guarantee the client a job. When a worker establishes a goal with a marital couple to resolve marital problems, the worker does not promise the couple marital bliss.

This caveat about goals and deadlines in a social work contract concerns a basic dimension of contract negotiation. It is easy to think of all kinds of idealistic goals or desirable objectives; however, it is the *pragmatic, reality-based* goal that is most likely to be achieved in practice. Many low-income urban families need adequate housing, yet in most large urban areas, such a goal would be almost impossible to realize. In this example, a goal that is desirable and even reasonable is unlikely to be achieved in our present urban context.

One way of making goals more pragmatic is to avoid vague global goal statements that promise too much. Happiness, mental health, assertiveness, and so forth are global goals that may emerge in practice, but they are unlikely to be achieved unless they are specified and partialized with reference to particular events that are salient to the client's life. In one situation, a discharged mental patient wanted to be "mentally healthy," yet a more realistic goal upon discharge was to locate a structured living arrangement (halfway house) and a part-time job in a protected work environment.

Other time limits that may be negotiated in a social work contract concern the overall length of service (e.g., 10 sessions, 3 months), or the length of individual contacts (e.g., 50 minutes, 2 hours), or the frequency of contacts in a given time period (e.g., daily, weekly, monthly sessions). These time limits are more in the worker's and client's control than are deadlines on goals and objectives. Such limits can be more easily enforced than can deadlines on goals and objectives because they involve actions (not outcomes) that worker and client can take.

When goals, objectives, and time limits have been clearly established, the worker and client next contract on the *specific actions, activities,* and *responsibilities* that each party will assume to achieve the goals. Such a range of actions and activities is very wide in practice, yet it is limited by several considerations. Obviously the worker and client's knowledge and skill will affect the possible actions. Ethical considerations will also affect what the worker can and cannot do in a particular situation. Workers must not engage in sexual intercourse with clients no matter how willing clients may be. But even with these limits, the worker and client have a wide range of actions that can be taken to achieve their goals.

In an ideal world those actions and interventions that are most effective in achieving goals with a particular client will have been empirically validated so that the negotiation of actions in the contract can be guided by empirical knowledge. But this level of technical, prescriptive knowledge often does not exist except to a limited degree in social work. Even if this kind of systematic knowledge did fully exist, actions, interventions, and responsibilities will also be shaped by other variables in practice such as the client's values and preferences, agency policies, and worker expertise. Some clients may refuse to take actions that research demonstrates are important (e.g., parents may refuse to visit their child who has been removed to temporary foster care even though visits are important to restoration[23]).

A major value of contracting is to ensure that all parties are clear about what is expected of them. Such clarity is especially important when several professionals are involved with one client. When good coordination exists, duplication of effort can be avoided, actions are consistent and supportive of each other, and clients are not caught in the middle of conflicting agency agendas.

In some writings references are made to "behavioral contracts,"[24] "tasks,"[25] or "secondary contracts."[26] Whichever term is used to describe these activities, it is important that all individuals who are engaged in the service process have an understanding and acceptance of what each person is expected to do. This level of contracting becomes even more critical as the numbers of people involved increase.

Characteristics of a Social Work Contract

There are four basic characteristics of a social work contract: explicitness, mutuality, flexibility, and pragmatism. A service contract is *explicit and clear* so that all parties (worker, client, other professionals) understand all terms and little is taken for granted. Preferably, the terms of the contract are expressed in concrete, specific, and simple language. Professional jargon and legalese are avoided, and the client's own words are used so that ambiguity, vagueness, and confusion between parties are minimized.

To assure explicitness, some agencies use written contracts.[27] However, a written contract does not ensure that it will be understood by all parties. Many people sign legal contracts (loan agreements) without reading or even comprehending what they are signing. But simple contract forms have been developed that require workers to compose contracts in the client's own words (see the written contract in Figure 8-2).

It is not necessary, desirable, or possible to use written contracts with all clients. With some clients, an informed agreement can be achieved verbally, and a written contract is redundant and unnecessarily time consuming. With other clients, a written contract is threatening and intimidating because it resembles "legal devices" that have placed them in jeopardy with other agencies or authorities in the past. Still, with other clients (e.g. illiterate, psychotic, severely retarded, small children), a written contract would be meaningless as well as impossible to complete.

Written contracts can be valuable, though, with impulsive clients who should be held accountable for decisions they have reached. Written and signed contracts allow parties to hold each other more accountable for following through on agreements. Some social workers have also used written contracts to hold other professionals accountable for services they have promised their clients.[28]

Ideally, a social work contract is *mutually* established between worker and client and other parties. Not only must contracts be un-

derstandable, but they must also be *acceptable* to all parties. All parties participate in negotiating terms and should be given an opportunity to participate in decision making. The client's opinions and perspective are seriously considered and solicited, and the worker does not intimidate the client into accepting the "worker's wisdom." This is most likely to occur if the idea of a contract is fully explained to the clients and they are given oral or written examples.

Although mutuality is clearly consistent with the social work value of client self-determination, in practice mutuality can be difficult to achieve. For some clients, service is imposed by a higher authority such as a court, parent, or spouse. In these situations, the client may enter service reluctantly. A court may remove a neglected child from a parent and order the parent to seek services before the child can be returned, or the parents may force a youth, who is having problems at school and home, to come to an agency. Although mutuality may seem unlikely on these occasions, both youth and parent can be engaged in service with a chance to shape it so that the individual's willingness to participate emerges.

A worker may establish a trial contract with some clients, such as adolescents. This is an agreement to try out service for a few interviews.[29] The worker in one instance asked an adolescent if she would agree to return for two more sessions and to explore "what's going on" in her life before deciding whether she wanted service. During the few trial sessions, the worker had the opportunity to explore the client's situation in greater detail and convey to her the value of the service. A worker also has an opportunity to provide services, and in some trial periods, clients will constructively use the time to make changes. For clients who come in with crises, one or two sessions may be all that is required to elicit adequate coping behavior.

AGREEMENT WITH NATURAL PARENTS OR GUARDIANS

THIS AGREEMENT is a contract between __Nancy   Dunham__ , Social Worker, Hampton Department of Social Services, and __Robert__ and __Sally Smith__ parent(s) of __Alvin and George Smith,__ . The purpose of this Agreement is to make permanent plans for __Alvin and George Smith__ whose custody is with the Hampton Department of Social Services. It is the wish of the parent(s) to have the child(ren) __returned   to   their   custody.__

In order to accomplish the above goal the following conditions must be met:

1. Parenting skills must be improved.

2. Mr. Smith's employment must be maintained.

3. Household bills must be paid up to date.

4. Household furniture must meet children's needs.

5.

The parent(s) and the social worker will be responsible for doing the following things during this part of the Agreement:

Parent(s)

1. Buy baby crib by 1-27-78.
2. Mrs. Smith will attend weekly parenting class through 3-14-78.
3. Mr. Smith will continue present employment through 3-21-78.
4. Household bills (rent and utilities) will be paid on time through 3-21-78.

Social Worker

1. Register Mrs. Smith for parenting class by 1-24-78.
2. Arrange weekend visits between parents and children every other weekend from 1-20-78 to 3-21-78.
3. Make home visit every other Friday until 3-14-78.

This Agreement will be reviewed on __3-14-78__ in order to plan the next steps in the completion of the goal. The total period of time for the accomplishment of the goal of __return of custody__ is from __1-17-78__ to __3-21-78__

_____

_____

_____
Social Worker

1-7-78

Figure 8-2. A Written Contract

Not all clients decide that they need or want services; thus, at the end of the trial contract, some clients will decide not to return. This decision should be respected by the worker who closes the case with the understanding that clients can always return if they change their minds.

Parents who are ordered to use a service by the court, can be offered a dual contract approach.[30] The worker offers to help the client separate court-mandated terms from terms negotiated with the worker,[31] and the worker explains that court-mandated terms cannot be renegotiated with the worker and can be changed only through a legal proceeding. But even court mandates may give the client some discretionary power about how they will be operationalized in the service contract. For example, the court may demand improvements in child care arrangements but not specify what these improvements are or how they are to be accomplished. In this situation the worker and client will discuss a range of alternatives (e.g., day care, involvement of relative, child care classes). While contracting with the worker, the client has had a chance to determine alternatives that were not stated by the court.

A social work contract is *dynamic* and *flexible* so that decisions may be renegotiated as service progresses. Unlike a signed legal contract that is static and binding, a social work contract usually is tentative and represents a plan rather than a set of rigid rules. Most social work contracts will be renegotiated when the client or worker concludes that the terms are unfair, unacceptable, nonproductive, or noninclusive. When contract terms are not achieved, worker and client will evaluate the impasse and plan alternative terms.

A dilemma concerning flexibility is how much flexibility is appropriate? Too much leads to a meaningless contract that is always changing, and, thus, there are no boundaries to service. Too little flexibility creates a contract that rapidly becomes outdated.

Some clients fall into a pattern in which they agree to a responsibility but then fail to follow through. Verbally they agree to a particular action, yet behaviorally they do not comply. This lapse between intention and action is common to us all. It is much easier to agree to do something than it is to apply the time and energy actually to carry it out. This kind of common failure to follow through on a particular task or responsibility is a problem for a contractual approach.

How much flexibility is to be permitted in the service contract? When client and worker do not follow through on terms, should these terms be automatically renegotiated or should some form of sanction or remedy (pressure) be applied to encourage compliance with the original terms? How can a worker judge when terms should be enforced and a client not allowed to renegotiate prior agreements? When is enforcement or pressure unproductive and renegotiation a more plausible solution?

Some clients need the limits provided by a contract to produce significant changes in their lives. When these clients do not follow through, the worker should firmly encourage the client to try again until the action is completed. An excellent procedure has been developed that workers can employ to help clients follow through on tasks that they have trouble completing. The Task Implementation Sequence (TIS)[32] is designed to help clients discuss, plan, and practice a particular task or responsibility before attempting to carry it out. The TIS procedure effectively increases the likelihood that a client will follow through on an agreed-upon task or action. The TIS does not create motivation to complete tasks to which clients are opposed.

In fact, it is impossible to complete the TIS when clients are under this constraint.

Developing the TIS is not a time-consuming procedure. It may be completed in as little as 15 minutes, although it can require a full session. It is important that all steps (described next) be completed even though the order of the sequence may be rearranged. During the first three steps, it is best for clients to generate their own examples or ideas first; then the worker may suggest other possibilities. The steps in the Task Implementation Sequence are:

1. *Enhancing Commitment.* The worker asks the client to consider the potential benefits of carrying out the task or action in questions. "What good will come from it?" "How will the client benefit?" The worker reinforces and encourages realistic benefits. After the client has exhausted ideas, the worker may present positive consequences that have not been discussed.

2. *Planning Task Implementation.* The client is helped to specify the task and to develop a detailed plan for carrying it out. The worker may ask questions that enable the client to spell out exactly when, where, and with whom the task will be carried out. For example, the client will decide the day, time, place, main actors, and specific actions that will be involved in completing the task. The worker also helps the client to explore alternative ways of doing the task.

3. *Analyzing Obstacles.* The worker asks the client to consider problems or barriers that may be encountered in carrying out the task. If the client has trouble identifying obstacles, possible contingencies can be suggested. For example, "What if this happens?" or "What if that occurs?" situational obstacles such as lack of reliable transportation as well as psychological barriers such as fears associated with the task should be discussed. The worker should also explore possible negative consequences that the client may face if the task is carried out.

4. *Modeling, Rehearsal, Guided Practice.* In this step the worker helps the client in the inteview to practice parts of their task. Usually those aspects that are practiced involve interactions with others or difficult parts of the task. The worker may model possible task behaviors by demonstrating what he or she might say and do in the task situation, or the client may rehearse what to say or do. Modeling and rehearsal may be carried out through role play, and situations may be role played several times until the client feels some mastery. Practice can also be accomplished by having the client imagine or fantasize in the interview the actions of the task.

5. *Summarizing.* The worker restates the task and the plan for carrying it out. This review helps to assure that the client has a clear idea of what is to be accomplished, and the worker completes the sequence with a strong expectation that the client will complete the task. For example, a worker might say, "I look forward to hearing how the interview went at next week's session."

As good as TIS is as a practice procedure to encourage clients to complete tasks, some clients will simply fail to complete them even when TIS is employed. When repeated noncompliance occurs, it is not productive to push the client. Clients should not be pressured into situations of failure; on the contrary, successful situations are much more desirable. Renegotiation of terms is more sensible so that clients can plan actions that they are likely to accomplish. When the worker has carefully involved the client in decisions and planning and the client fails to complete negotiated responsibilities, the worker should question the client's desire to continue service, and the original purpose of service should be discussed.

A social work contract is *pragmatic* and *realistic*. The terms of a contract do not demand actions, tasks, or responsibilities that are beyond the capacity of either worker or client. Workers do not make promises that are beyond their own expertise or agency resources, and clients are not pushed or intimidated into accepting terms that demand more than their skills and resources can deliver. Unrealistic goals no matter how desirable may lead to failure and frustration. A contract based on false hope or intimidating demands may be more harmful than no contract at all.

How can a worker and client know in advance how realistic a given term is? One technique to test the reality of terms is for the worker to take a conservative stance. For example, after an objective and deadline have been planned, a worker might say to the client: "Fine, we've agreed to get you enrolled in a training program in two weeks, but tell me honestly, how far will you really have gone on this in the next two weeks?" And the client may answer, "Well, if I have even located a training program in two weeks, I'll feel I've done something!" Such a question helps clients to consider the objective realistically in the light of their own knowledge of their capacity to complete the objective. The client may then be in the position, also, of pushing the worker toward a more difficult goal instead of the worker doing so.

Another tactic that the worker may use to test the reality of terms is to "play the devil's advocate," basically a use of a "therapeutic paradox." Once the client and worker have agreed on a term, the worker may deliberately raise doubts or question its value. The worker might say, "I can't see why you would really want to do that." This allows the client to express doubts that he or she may not have raised and also tests the client's commitment to a term. "Playing devil's advocate" is not intended to talk the client out of a given term but, rather, to help the client consider all aspects of what is being agreed to in the contract.

One of the values of a Goal Attainment Scale (GAS),[33] besides its use as an evaluative measure, is that when goals and time limits are set up on a GAS, the worker and client are much clearer about what can be realistically expected of a given objective. (See Chapter 10 for a further discussion of this measure.) When goals and objectives are set up in a GAS and the client is encouraged to honestly express how far he or she will be at a given deadline, a realistic view of objectives is achieved.

Value of the Contract Approach

The contract approach is valuable to interpersonal practice for both empirical and ethical reasons. Ethically a contract approach is clearly consistent with social work's professed value that all clients have worth and deserve to be treated with dignity.[34] A contract approach requires that the worker deliberately encourage the client to participate in decisions about service. Even though a worker may not agree with the client's input, the client's opinion is important, and the worker has a responsibility to cultivate it.

Contract approaches thus reflect the professional ethic of client self-determination. Contract approaches encourage clients to be active participants in service, not passive recipients. This supports and demands client self-determination in the service process. When a client is not aware of what is being planned or is not in agreement with it, there can be no self-determination or contract as described in this chapter.

Contract approaches also provide a mechanism for accountability. When parties have reached agreement on a given arrangement, each individual is clear about what is expected of him or her and others. This allows parties to question actions that are inconsistent with objectives and to hold others responsible for what they have agreed to deliver. This kind of accountability is two-edged and can be used by both workers and clients.[35]

Because the social work profession is committed to serving all people in need, social workers are not only concerned about providing effective service to those they serve, but are also concerned about developing services for those who have trouble finding and using services. "Discontinuance," as discussed previously, is seen in the high dropout rates of clients who seek service and who fail to remain long enough for service to have much effect.[36] Some evidence suggests that discontinuance rates can be lowered by employing a contract approach to service.[37] Because contracting helps to clarify expectations about service, clients feel less anxious and confused about what to expect and therefore are more likely to continue.

There is a growing body of research on contract approaches that suggests that contracts have a positive impact on both the process of service and its outcome. In a controlled study, patients who were given a special interview to orient them to service and explain what to expect were judged to have a better relationship with their therapist, a better attendance record, and a more favorable response to treatment than did those who did not receive this orienting interview between intake and treatment.[38] In child welfare services, contracts have been demonstrated to reduce significantly "foster care drift" by facilitating planning and the restoration of children to their natural parents.[39] The evidence from agencies that have instituted contract approaches seems clear. Contracts help workers to be more systematic and organized in their approach with clients and to be more responsive to clients' needs. Contracts also strengthen the worker-client relationship and encourage clients to be more actively involved in service.[40]

Limits of Contracting

Contracting, as does any approach to practice, does not work in all situations with all clients. There are some practice situations in which contracting is impossible because it is unlikely that worker and client will reach an agreement about the terms of service. Contracting is primarily a verbal enterprise, whether spoken or written, and it requires that all parties be competent and rational at the time of negotiation. Therefore, extremely disturbed, retarded, brain-damaged, or intoxicated people are not fully able to engage in a contract process. Usually, in these situations a worker will establish a contract with a close family member or friend on behalf of the client.

Contracting is also impossible when a client seeks an objective that violates the values of the worker. Violence against others is not allowed in a worker's code of ethics even though there are clients who view violence as a way of solving problems. Although it may be desirable to be nonjudgmental in a social work relationship,[41] there are limits to how much so a worker can be. For example, a Catholic worker in a Catholic agency might find it impossible to work with a client who seeks help to terminate an unwanted pregnancy.

When there is a fundamental clash in values, the worker has a responsibility to inform the client of the conflict. When there is no chance that the conflict can be resolved, the worker has a responsibility to help the client locate another worker or service that can be responsive to the client's perspective.

Besides impossible situations, there are

times when contracting is *contraindicated* because a contractual approach will be detrimental to clients or to others. Although contracts are intended to facilitate service, with some clients in crisis, time is critical, and the worker does not have the luxury of discussing each decision to gain the client's acceptance of it. In fact, to clients who are in suicidal or homicidal crises, it may be absurd for a worker to say, "I'm here to talk you out of blowing up yourself and your family any way I can; and while we are talking, the police are sneaking your family out the back door!"

Life and limb considerations must always take precedence over a client's desires or perspectives, and a worker may have to overrule a client's decision and even act against a client's will. For example, a mother in an intake interview wanted help with her "blackout spells." The worker then learned that the client had an infant at home who had had severe vomiting and diarrhea and high fever for several days and had not received medical attention. Even if the mother does not want help for her infant, the worker cannot ignore the risks in such a situation and must act to protect the child. In another practice situation, an individual client and worker agreed that information the client shared with the worker was not to be told to family members. When that client became suicidal, this agreement was broken by the worker to protect the client, and the family and the client were told this.

Another contraindication to contracting involves social workers less directly. Contracting is a demystifying approach to practice because the worker's efforts involve the client in an explicit, pragmatic, and planned approach to service. Contracting increases the power a client has and concomitantly reduces the perceived power a worker has. There are clients, however, whose special

problems might be approached entirely differently. Rather than clarifying service and giving the client more control and responsibility, intervention is deliberately mystified and a healer is given special "magical powers" (that only the healer can control and understand). This "healer" may be a special person within the client's culture.

This approach is antithetical to a contract approach but should not be discredited. "Magic" is a powerful phenomenon and should not be underestimated as a force for change.[42] It can be successful with some people because it builds a powerful expectancy that one's problems can be solved, and research has demonstrated that expectancy is important to the success of therapeutic intervention.[43] This approach to helping is not likely to be used by social workers, yet social workers may help clients locate practitioners from the culture (e.g., spiritualist, *curandero,* shaman)[44] who effectively employ this approach with positive results for their client.

Because contracts are impossible or contraindicated in some practice situations does not mean that service cannot be delivered. The reason for discussing these situations is that the worker should attempt other approaches rather than waste time and energy struggling to apply a contract approach.

There are practice situations in which contracting is *problematic,* and the worker and client achieve only a marginal working agreement. Although there are numerous problematic situations in contracting, this discussion will focus on three common problems: The hidden agenda, the corrupt contract, and sabotage.

The Hidden Agenda.   Either client or worker or other service providers may engage in contracting while maintaining a hidden agenda. When parties have a hidden agenda during contract negotiation, they deliberately withhold information, an opinion, or a perspective. Even though the term is not fully discussed, secretly the party hopes that some kind of implicit agreement on the hidden agenda can be achieved. For example, a worker may agree with a client that the target problem is social isolation from family and friends, yet the worker may secretly believe that the problem that should be addressed is the client's low self-image. In this situation the worker may never have shared the view that self-image is important to the client, yet the worker may subtly try to direct service or interventions into this area. The confusion that may arise with such a hidden agenda is that the client may be working on the agreed-upon agenda, while the worker is working on the hidden agenda. The client and worker end up working at cross-purposes.

Individuals engage in contracting with hidden agendas for a number of reasons. Sometimes clients are simply too embarrassed, anxious, or threatened to share honestly what is important to them. The client may want service to begin with a safer agenda before moving into heavier issues. Worker and client sometimes can make this kind of entrée into service work—that is, move from simpler to more serious issues. But this is a risky way to proceed because some clients do not remain in service long enough to fulfill serious goals.

Sometimes individuals use a hidden agenda as a power tactic when contracting. Instead of discussing the hidden agenda openly and risking having it rejected outright, the hidden agenda is withheld so that it can be subtly employed as time goes on in the hope that the other party will be persuaded that it has merit. For example, in some family treatment situations, the child may be seen as the target (and having the

problem) by the parents, yet the worker may view the parents as the targets because they contribute to the problem. To work with the whole family, the worker may contract with the parents to participate as "information givers" yet maintain a hidden agenda that as parents become more involved, their problems will emerge and they will accept the need to change.

The dilemma with hidden agendas is that they do not always work out the way parties intend. As the hidden agenda becomes clear, the other parties may feel outraged at the deception and break off contact without considering the merits of the hidden agenda. The decision to hide the particular agenda for later discussion only dooms it to failure: a more open discussion in the beginning would have produced the desired response by the other party. In the example presented, if parents had been informed from the beginning that they too must be a part of the change if they are to help their child, they might not have liked the idea, but at least they could have negotiated a trial contract to test this out. Even if parents reject the idea that they are to change, time is not wasted manipulating them into accepting something they will later reject. It is difficult enough to change people when they agree to change. It is close to impossible using social work approaches to change people against their will, especially when they recognize that they have been deceived.

The Corrupt Contract. Another kind of contract problem arises when several individuals are involved in the service process (e.g., several clients and several professionals). A corrupt contract[45] may emerge when the various agreements among different individuals are not coordinated or are deliberately negotiated to be inconsistent. With some couples who experience marital problems and blame the other, a worker might have both spouses agree to come in and help the other spouse with his or her problems. Both spouses then enter service with the worker with two conflicting contracts—each believes it is the other who is to be changed.

Workers are not the only ones who engage in this kind of corrupt contracting. Some clients who use different services may engage in a similar duplicity by making agreements with one professional that contradict agreements with the other. The results of this behavior can be disastrous as agencies work at cross-purposes and the client is caught in the middle.[46]

The problem with a corrupt contract (as with a hidden agenda) is that sooner or later the contradiction in agreements is discovered. Parties may terminate their relationship together, and the progress already gained may be quickly destroyed.

Corrupt contracting can be avoided if all significant individuals in the service process are brought together in the beginning and periodically thereafter to discuss their various impressions, intentions, and responsibilities in the case. If face-to-face discussion is not possible, then someone (preferably the worker) must take responsibility for monitoring and coordinating the service process.

Even with face-to-face coordination, corrupt contracts occur when some or all of the people involved fear that explicitness will lead to conflict. Some individuals avoid conflict at all costs because they view interpersonal conflict as "bad," "unpleasant," or "unresolvable." There is nothing inherently bad about interpersonal conflict, and attempts to avoid conflict during contracting are self-defeating. Expressing differences early in the contract process requires parties to be honest[47] so that each has a better chance to engage in a frank negotiation of contract terms. When contracting goes too

smoothly, it may be a sign that one party is "selling out" to the other too quickly.

Sabotage.   Another problem is "sabotage." This involves actions that are designed to keep contract terms (especially goals and objectives) from being realized. Sabotage can be active and deliberate (a team member may disagree with a discharge plan and actively encourage the patient to act out so that the discharge plan will fail), or it can be subtle such as in passive resistance or marginal compliance (parents may periodically "forget" to bring a child to a scheduled appointment).

Workers, clients, other service providers, and significant others in the client's world are all capable of engaging in sabotage. Whenever individuals are strongly committed to a position (they believe they know what's right or best), sabotage may appear when they are overruled or outvoted in the negotiation of a service plan. Sabotage may also result from being left out of decision making or in other ways ignored. The point of this discussion is that anyone may engage in sabotage and that, when sabotage occurs, it does not mean that the person is evil—although this is often how sabotage is viewed by those it affects.

Sabotage can be prevented or at least minimized by carefully involving all parties who will be participating in the service plan in the planning and negotiation process. It may be time consuming to encourage maximum participation, yet such effort is invaluable if sabotage is to be avoided. This means that people are not just invited to participate in a conference or session, but during the meeting their opinions and perspectives are elicited; the final plan takes into account what all parties bring to the session. Although it may be difficult to involve a particularly contrary individual in some case conferences or planning sessions, deliberately leaving the contrary individual out may invite disaster if the plan is implemented and the contrary individual sabotages it.

Contracting with Families and Groups

This section focuses on selected issues of contracting with families and small groups. These issues are singled out because they represent contract issues that are particular to multiperson client systems.

The first issue involves *time* and applies to both families and small groups. When there are several people in the client system, negotiating contract terms will take *longer* than it will with an individual client. It takes more time to hear everyone, share perspectives, and agree to a common ground. Another reality is that the greater the number of people involved, the greater the chance for differing perspectives and the longer it takes to work toward a consensus or compromise. Because of these realities, the worker may spend too much time negotiating terms; and individuals may feel that service is dragging because too much time is spent on planning service rather than receiving it.

One way of avoiding these feelings of frustration is for the worker to structure these first sessions to facilitate contracting. For example, with some formed groups it is possible to have pregroup interviews with each prospective member.[48] These pregroup interviews are not only useful as a screening mechanism in selecting group members, but they also can be used to discuss with individuals what they want from the group and what they can expect from the group. When members arrive at the first session, they have completed some preliminary contracting, or at least a definition of terms, and groundwork has been laid for the group's

efforts to reach an agreement. This approach can be applied with families. Each member of the family may be seen in individual sessions before a conjoint session with the whole family is planned, although this is, for reasons to be discussed later, *not* typically how family treatment begins.

Another way of speeding up contracting in early sessions is to assign some of the tasks involved in contracting as "homework" between sessions. For example, members of a family may be requested to think about what they hope family sessions will do for them and the family, to write these thoughts down, and to bring them in to share at the next session. Group members can be assigned similar tasks that relate to contracting such as deciding how the group might help them or what things they might do in the group to help other members. By using the homework structure, individual members are given a chance to do some of the preparatory thinking, and this will be helpful to good contracting.

There are also activities that a worker can employ within the session to facilitate contracting. For example, individuals can be asked to write on cards what they think is important about a particular contract term (target problems, goals). The cards are collected and the worker reads or paraphrases each card.[49] This activity facilitates contracting because it encourages maximum participation; individuals are more apt to listen to what the worker says; and it is easier for all participants to see commonalities or patterns in what the worker reads because the participants are not focusing as much on their own perspectives.

Another way to minimize the feeling that nothing is happening in early sessions is for the worker to use early sessions for a broader array of activities that includes contracting. Workers may include group activities or experiences that make participants see that service has begun. For example, in an early group session, time may be set aside for one individual to bring up an issue that he or she hopes the group will help to resolve. If the worker can facilitate the ensuing discussion so that other members share information or at least give moral support, all members of the group experience how the group can be helpful to individuals, and thus they will feel that something more than "planning" has been accomplished.

There are many other procedures that workers employ to facilitate contracting with families and small groups. Contracting can be time consuming in a group. To avoid losing members who drop out in frustration because "All we did was talk about what we were going to do but never did it!" a worker must take responsibility for speeding up the process.

An issue that occurs when contracting with families involves the basic elements of contracting itself. Good contracts require honest sharing and mutual agreement, yet some families seek help with problems that do not lend themselves to successful contracting. Families may be unwilling to share or exchange information honestly or incapable of listening or responding to information that is offered by other family members. Some families cannot reach mutual decisions involving all family members. Therefore, contracting with the worker to reach mutual agreements is incompatible with their way of relating. When a worker asks such a family what it considers its biggest problem, chaos may break out as each family member presents a different problem and argues with the others about it.

When families have problems communicating and making decisions as a group, the worker should structure the early sessions to help the family formulate a contract. The Structured Family Interview (SFI)[50] offers a way of building structure into these early sessions. Although the SFI was developed as a diagnostic procedure, elements of SFI can be adapted to help families make decisions about contract terms. For example, the exercises in SFI require the family to talk to each other in pairs or other subgroups and then regroup to discuss what was accomplished. This patterning interrupts the usual communication patterns that such families use. The process of helping these families to contract with the worker about service may, in fact, be the most important technique the worker uses. Once the family has reached a mutual agreement with the worker, it may have accomplished a fundamental and essential change.

Another family contracting issue relates to the approach to family treatment chosen by the worker. In some approaches, the family is told that problems of individuals are maintained by family conditions. The worker contracts with the family to seek a change in such conditions as family communications, family consensus on goals, or family structures. In other approaches, the problem of an individual, such as delinquency, psychosis, or depression, is assumed to be legitimate, and a contract is made in which individual change is a goal. More discussion of this issue is presented in Chapter 11.

An issue that is particular to formed groups relates to the dual responsibility of group members to be both helpee and helper. This responsibility must be clearly understood and accepted by them. There are many ways in which a group member can be helpful to other members (for example, as support or model). Each member must not only take from the group but also give to it. When the "self-help therapy principle"[51] works, it is often the giving that means the most for a member.

At this point, the reader should recognize that there are five types of contracts in work with families and groups. To clarify this range of contractual possibilities, we list each type with appropriate examples of some contractual terms (see Table 8-1):

While this range of possibilities may appear confusing at first to workers, it should be recognized that each one has its value. When used at the appropriate time, each type of contract can help to unify the efforts of workers and family or group members toward the achievement of mutual desired goals. Work with multiperson client systems is a complex matter and devices such as contracts help to make it efficient and effective.

Summary

We began this chapter with a discussion of the origins of the contract concept in social work and the advantages and disadvantages of referring to the agreements between client and worker as a "contract." We subsequently indicated that the components of contract in-

Table 8-1. A Written Contract

1. **Between the family or group and the agency.**
   Examples: The group members agree to pay a fee for 12 sessions, even if a session is missed.
   The family members agree that all will take responsibility to see to it that all family members are present at sessions.

2. **Between the family or group and the worker.**
   Examples: The group members agree that they will try to complete homework assignments made by the worker.
   The family members agree to discuss among themselves the worker's recommendations.

3. **Between a member of the family or group and the worker.**
   Examples: Frank, a group member, agrees to make no suicide attempt without first discussing this with the worker.
   Alice, a single parent, agrees to call the worker when she feels so angry that she will not be able to restrain her violence toward her daughter.

4. **Between one member of the family or group and another member.**
   Examples: Two group members agree to become "buddies" and to call each other when they need support.
   The spouses in the family agree to discuss with each other how they will discipline their child before imposing the discipline.

5. **Between one member of the family or group and the entire family or group.**
   Examples: Carol, a group member, agrees to take notes of conclusions reached in the group and use them to provide feedback to the group.
   Bob, a teen-age son, agrees to discuss his plans to leave home with the entire family, including parents and siblings.

clude the purposes, the problems to be worked on, the goals, and the objectives of the service. In addition, the contract incorporates the actions to be taken by the worker and by the client to attain these purposes, goals, and objectives. Contracts also incorporate time considerations, the frequency of sessions, and fees.

In developing effective contracts, the worker must help clients to create terms that are explicit, mutual, and pragmatic. A desirable degree of flexibility must also be assured. One procedure, termed the Task Implementation Sequence, was presented as a way of securing this type of agreement. Such approaches to contracting were described as leading to both more effective outcomes and more ethical practices.

At times, a contracting approach is contraindicated. This occurs when the client is in crisis, when the worker does not seek to demystify service, and when the client is not competent to negotiate a contract. Some common problems in contracting are hidden agendas, corrupt agreements, and sabotage. Ways of identifying these problems as well as solving them were presented.

The chapter concluded with a discussion of issues for workers and clients when the client system is composed of several individuals as in family and group services. The contract differences in these situations stem from the fact that contracts must achieve a degree of consensus among participants and must occur between clients and workers singly or collectively as well as among the members of the client system. This complexity may at first appear to make work with such client systems more difficult, but contracts actually reduce such complexity when used appropriately and skillfully.

NOTES

1. John Collins, "The Contractual Approach to Social Work Intervention," *Social Work Today*, Vol. 8 (February 1977), pp. 13–15; Anthony Maluccio and Wilma Marlow, "The Case for Contract," *Social Work*, Vol. 19 (January 1974), pp. 28–35; and Brett A. Seabury, "The Contract: Uses, Abuses, and Limitations," *Social Work*, Vol. 21 (January 1976), pp. 16–21.

2. Allen Pincus and Anne Minahan, *Social Work Practice: Model and Method* (Itasca, Ill.: F. E. Peacock, 1973), pp. 162–193; Howard Goldstein, *Social Work Practice: A Unitary Approach* (Columbia: University of South Carolina, 1973), pp. 130–137, 191–193; Beulah Compton and Burt Galaway, *Social Work Processes* (Homewood, Ill.: The Dorsey Press, 1979), pp. 317–336; and Lawrence Schulman, *The Skills of Helping Individuals and Groups* (Itasca, Ill.: F. E. Peacock, 1978).

3. Grace E. Harris, *Training of Public Welfare Staff in the Use of the Service Contract in Preventing and Reducing Foster Care* (Richmond: Department of Continuing Education, School of Social Work, Virginia Commonwealth University, 1978), and Theodore Stein, Eileen Gambrill, and Kermit Wiltse, "Foster Care: The Use of Contracts," *Public Welfare*, Vol. 32 (Fall 1974), pp. 20–25.

4. Dorothea Hosch, *Use of the Contract Approach in Public Social Services* (Los Angeles: Regional Research Institute in Social Welfare, University of Southern California, 1973).

5. Richard Lessor and Anita Lutkus, "Two Techniques for the Social Work Practitioner," *Social Work*, Vol. 16 (January 1971), pp. 5–6, 96; and *Special Family Services Project: Final Report* (Lansing: Office of Individual and Family Services, Michigan Department of Social Services, September 1981).

6. Theodore Stein and Eileen Gambrill, "Facilitating Decision Making in Foster Care," *Social Service Review*, Vol. 51 (September 1977), pp. 502–513; Sonya Rhodes, "Contract Negotiation in the Initial Stage of Casework Service," *Social Service Review*, Vol. 51 (March 1977), pp. 125–140; Helen Harris Perlman, *Persona: Social Role and Personality* (Chicago: University of Chicago Press, 1968), pp. 172–176; and Carol Knapp, *Service Contract Use in Preventing and Reducing Foster Care: Final Evaluation Report* (Washington, D.C.: Administration for Children, Youth and Families, Department of Health, Education, and Welfare, December 1, 1980).

7. William J, Reid, *Task-Centered System* (New York: Columbia University Press, 1978).

8. Sheldon Rose, *Group Therapy: A Behavioral Approach* (Englewood Cliffs, N.J.: Prentice-Hall, 1977); Sheldon Rose, *Treating Children in Groups: A Behavioral Approach* (San Francisco: Jossey-Bass, 1972); and Arthur Schwartz and Israel Goldiamond, *Social Casework: A Behavioral Approach* (New York: Columbia University Press, 1975).

9. Carel Germain and Alex Gitterman, *Life Model of Social Work Practice* (New York: Columbia University Press, 1980).

10. Karl Menninger, *Theory of Psychoanalytic Technique* (New York: Basic Books, 1958). pp. 15–40.

11. See note 8.

12. For casework examples, see Lessor and Lutkus, "Two Techniques for the Social Work Practitioner"; Perlman, *Persona*; Rhodes, *"Contract Negotiation is the Initial Stage of Casework Service"*; and Brett A. Seabury, "Negotiating Sound Contracts with Clients," *Public Welfare*, Vol. 37 (Spring 1979), pp. 33–38. For group work examples, see Louise Frey and Marguerite Meyer, "Exploration and Working Agreement in Two Social Work Methods," in Saul Bernstein, ed., *Explorations in Group Work* (Boston, Milford House, 1973), pp. 1–16; Sue Henry, *Group Skills in Social Work: A Four-Dimensional Approach* (Itasca, Ill.: F. E. Peacock, 1981); Diane Kravetz and Sheldon Rose, *Contracts in Groups: A Behavioral Approach* (Dubuque: Kendall/Hunt, 1973); and Charles Garvin, "Complementarity of Role Expectations in Groups: The Member-Worker Contract," *Social Work Practice, 1969* (New York: Columbia University Press, 1969).

13. Sigmund Freud, "On Beginning Treatment: Further Recommendations on the Technique of Psychoanalysis," in James Strachey, ed., *The Complete Psychological Works of Sigmund Freud* (London: Hogarth, 1958), pp. 12, 123–124.

14. Tom Croxton, "The Therapeutic Contract in Social Treatment," in Paul Glasser, Rosemary Sarri, and Robert Vinter, eds., *Individual Change Through Small Groups* (New York: Macmillan, 1974), pp. 169–185.

15. Stuart Kirk and James Greenley, "Denying or Delivering Services," *Social Work*, Vol. 19 (July 1974), pp. 439–447.

16. See William Reid and Laura Epstein, *Task-Centered Casework* (New York: Columbia University Press, 1972).

17. Marlin J. Blizinsky and William J. Reid, "Problem Focus and Change in a Brief Treatment Model," *Social Work*, Vol. 25 (March 1980), pp. 89–93.

18. Frank Maple, *Shared Decision Making* (Beverly Hills, Calif.: Sage Publications, 1977), pp. 44–45.

19. Juliana T. Schmidt, "The Use of Purpose in Casework Practice," *Social Work*, Vol. 14 (January 1969), pp. 79–84; Weiner Gottlieb and Joe Stanley, "Mutual Goals and Goal Setting in Casework," *Social Casework*, Vol. 48 (October 1967), pp. 471–477; and Compton and Galaway, *Social Work Processes*, pp. 317–323.

20. Croxton, "The Therapeutic Contract in Social Treatment," and Rose, *Treating Children*.

21. Reid and Epstein, *Task-Centered Casework*, pp. 78–93.

22. Croxton, "The Therapeutic Contract in Social Treatment."

23. David Fanshel, "The Exit of Children from Foster Care: An Interim Report," *Child Welfare*, Vol. 50 (February 1971), pp. 65–80.

24. See, for example, Rose, *Treating Children*, p. 99.

25. Reid and Epstein, *Task-Centered Casework*.

26. Croxton, "The Therapeutic Contract in Social Treatment," and Seabury, "Negotiating."

27. Stein, Gambrill, and Wiltse, "Foster Care," and Knapp, *Service Contract Use*.

28. Sherida Bush, "A Family-Help Program That Really Works," *Psychology Today*, May 1977, pp. 48–50, 84–88.

29. Croxton, "The Therapeutic Contract in Social Treatment," pp. 180–181, and Kravetz and Rose, *Contracts in Groups*, p. 21.

30. Luke J. Fusco, "Power, Authority, and Influence in Social Work Treatment and the Two-Contract Model of Practice," paper presented at NASW Fifth Biennial Professional Symposium, San Diego, California, November 1977.

31. Seabury, "Negotiating Sound Contracts with Clients."

32. William J. Reid, "Test of a Task-Centered Approach," *Social Work,* Vol. 20 (January 1975), pp. 3–9.

33. Compton and Galaway, *Social Work Processes,* pp. 408–421.

34. See NASW Code of Ethics.

35. Seabury, "The Contract."

36. George Levinger, "Continuance in Casework and Other Helping Relationships: A Review, *Social Work,* Vol. 5 (July 1960), pp. 40–51.

37. Perlman, *Persona,* pp. 172–176.

38. Saric Hoehn et al., "Systematic Preparation of Patients for Psychotherapy," *Journal of Psychiatric Research,* Vol. 2 (1964), pp. 267–281.

39. Stein and Gambrill, "Facilitating Decision Making in Foster Care."

40. Knapp, *Service Contract Use.*

41. Dale Hardman, "Not with My Daughter You Don't!" *Social Work,* Vol. 20 (July 1975), pp. 278–285, and Felix Biestek, *The Casework Relationship* (Chicago: Loyola University Press, 1957).

42. Louise Frey and Golda Edinburg, "Helping, Manipulation, and Magic," *Social Work,* Vol. 23 (March 1978), pp. 88–92.

43. Russell A. Jones, *Self-fulfilling Prophecies* (Hillsdale, N.J.: Lawrence Erlbaum Associates, 1977).

44. Melvin Delgado and Denise Humm-Delgado, "Natural Support Systems: Source of Strength in Hispanic Communities," *Social Work,* Vol. 27 (January 1982), pp. 83–89.

45. Lynette Beal, "Corrupt Contract: Problems in Conjoint Therapy with Parents and Children," *American Journal of Orthopsychiatry,* Vol. 42 (January 1972), pp. 77–81.

46. Lynn Hoffman and Lorence Long, "A Systems Dilemma," *Family Process,* Vol. 8 (September 1969), pp. 211–234.

47. Harris Chaiklin, "Honesty in Casework Treatment," *Social Welfare Forum, 1973* (New York: Columbia University Press, 1974), pp. 266–274, and Seymour Halleck, "The Impact of Professional Dishonesty on Behavior of Disturbed Adolescents," *Social Work,* Vol. 8 (April 1963), pp. 48–55.

48. See Glasser, Sarri, and Vinter, eds., *Individual Change Through Small Groups.*

49. William G. Hill, "The Family as a Treatment Unit: Differential Techniques and Procedures," *Social Work,* Vol. 11 (April 1960), pp. 62–68.

50. The Structured Family Interview was developed in Palo Alto, California, as an intake procedure on families. Paul Watzlawick, "A Structured Family Interview," *Family Process* 5 (1966), pp. 256–271.

51. Frank Reissman, "The 'Helper' Therapy Principle," in *Community Action Against Poverty,* George Brager and Francis Purcell, eds., (New Haven, Conn: Yale College and University Press, 1967), pp. 217–226.

nine
Planning and Preparation

We have presented a strong bias toward action and quick service for clients who for the most part will not be in the agency very long. In spite of our emphasis that service should be delivered with alacrity, we recognize that planning is essential to success. Poorly thought-out or impulsive actions may be ineffective, or even worse, they may be counterproductive. Therefore, this chapter discusses the essential elements of planning that should occur before worker and client attempt to implement change strategies.

Although we devote an entire chapter to planning placed between chapters on contracting and evaluation, in practice planning is not such an obvious "middle phase" but actually begins during engagement and carries over into implementation phases. In fact, in most practice models, planning and implementation happen concurrently as service unfolds. For example, in the task-centered model, service is a repetitive cycle of planning and implementation, and planning is not a discrete phase that is completed somewhere in the middle of service.[1]

Although planning is important to effective action, the worker and client should avoid becoming bogged down in this activity. Planning can be overdone! Too much time and energy can be expended on decisions about what to do leaving little energy for the actual "doing." For example, a group may expend several sessions and hours of preparation for a particular group activity only to have low attendance and poor participation on the day of the activity.

This chapter has been divided into four areas that are critical to the planning process in interpersonal practice. *Goal formulation* concerns the steps that worker and client take to develop specific objectives for their work together. The next session concerns the *identification of the target system*, which is that part of the client's world that should be changed if the objective is to be achieved. The third section concerns the *development of the action system*, which are those decisions that go into determining who might be recruited or mobilized to help the clients achieve their objectives. The fourth area of this chapter introduces *monitoring procedures*, which can be employed to help worker and client to evaluate whether the objective has been achieved as well as the results of various actions that were implemented. (Monitoring will be discussed again in more detail in Chapter 10 devoted to monitoring and evaluation.)

Goals and Objectives

We use the term "goal" as a general, global, long-range concept and the term "objective" as a more specific, short-term one. Objectives are the building blocks of goals and represent the immediate steps that must be accomplished to achieve long-range circumstances.

As we discussed in the chapter on contracting, objectives should be explicit and clearly identified so that all parties understand what they are trying to accomplish. Explicitness helps to minimize confusion and hidden agendas that may develop in the planning process. It is also important for objectives to be specific and focused on a particular aspect of the target problem. "Partializing"[2] is an important practice principle that should shape the plans that worker and client develop. Objectives should also be realistic or feasible. Although in the beginning it is not always possible to know for sure what is feasible, highly idealistic or extremely unlikely suggestions should be avoided in planning. Finally, mutuality between parties is important to a successful plan so that objectives are acknowledged as worth pursuing. In practice it is not always possible to have all parties agree to a plan. Consensus must sometimes give way to compromise, "deals," or even recognition that agreement cannot be reached. While such consensus is not always possible in some planning processes, it surely is desirable and makes planning and future action much easier to accomplish.

Generating Meaningful Objectives

The first step in developing a service plan is for the worker and client to discuss the aspects of the target problem they think can be addressed. Questions such as, "Where would you like to be in two weeks on this problem?" may help the client generate some ideas about objectives. Numerous objectives may be generated at this point, and the worker helps the client to specify each objective. For example, some clients may want to work on improving the poor relationships they have with others (marital, parent-child, supervisor-supervisee). The worker can help the clients to focus on aspects of such relationships they wish to change, such as the amount of time they want alone, or the topics they wish to discuss, or the conflicts they wish to reduce.

A large number of objectives can be generated from any given target problem. No "correct" objective can be stressed at this point in the planning process. What is important is that the client participate in the discussion and that the worker help the client to be specific and focus on desired changes.[3]

To assure the client's participation, the worker should encourage the client to make suggestions about possible outcomes. No matter how trivial, absurd, or impossible the client's suggestions may be, the worker acknowledges them as possible alternatives before recommending others. When the client has been allowed to initiate suggestions and the client's ideas have been taken seriously by the worker, the client is more likely to follow through later when actions are being implemented.

We live in the age of plans. There are plans to move people, employ people, school people, serve people . . . in every case, people are the objects of the plans, never the SUBJECT. We find out how we are to be moved, employed, schooled, or served only through the generosity of the institutions who plan for us, and usually too late even to protest. Protests more and more often take the form of demands for community control, for the right of people to make decisions which affect their lives. The protest wells up out of the last impulses of dignity left in people who have been the passive objects of plans and non-plans, systems and nonsystems, long enough to know that the master plans are the master's plans.[4]

As this quotation clearly suggests, the worker should not try to develop a master plan with the client as object but instead should involve the client in the planning process.

Selecting an Objective

After several potential objectives are identified, the next step is to rank, or place some kind of value on, each potential objective. One important way to establish priorities is to let the client decide what to tackle first.[5] This may work well in many practice situations, but the worker cannot always be so "client centered," and other factors must be taken into account.

Behind each client choice or decision is some evaluative scheme. It is important for the worker to find out what this evaluation scheme is so that nonproductive decisions can be challenged. The value of having two or more individuals involved in planning is to avoid the narrow-mindedness of a unilateral decision based on a rigid or faulty evaluation scheme.[6] Suppose that a client ranks his or her objectives by what the worker or some other important person wants. That choice then may not be the client's own aspiration but instead a choice to please others. There is nothing wrong with a choice to please others, but the danger in this is that the client tries

to second-guess (or mind read) what others prefer without carefully checking the others' positions. This kind of faulty evaluation can be easily explored by the worker with a simple question, "I'm curious! With all the choices, why did you pick that one?"

In addition to the aspirations of the client, another important criterion in selecting an objective is feasibility. Feasibility involves a number of dimensions: one concerns "effort." How much time, money, energy, and resources must be expended for the client to achieve a given objective? In practice some objectives can be achieved quite rapidly, whereas others require a great expenditure of time and effort. For example, a parent may want help with a parent-child problem, and the objective might be for the parent and child to obtain services at an appropriate agency. In the community there may be several possible agencies to consider. Some programs may require extensive prescreening (psychological tests, psychiatric evaluations); others may require less documentation before service can begin. If "effort" were an issue, the referral involving easy entry would be the appropriate one.

Feasibility also involves the likelihood of "success." Some objectives, no matter how desirable, may be very difficult to achieve, while others may have a good chance of succeeding. A bag lady may want to become a receptionist. This is an improbable objective. Obviously worker and client should pursue objectives that have a high probability of being achieved and avoid those that seem likely to fail. There is no value in service to plan a process that has little chance of success when failure is already such a predominant characteristic of many clients' lives.

A worker and client do not have a crystal ball, so how does one predict which objective has the greatest likelihood of succeeding? Nevertheless, they can make an educated guess about their plans by weighing the forces toward and away from a given objective. Worker and client can discuss each objective as though it existed on a "balance sheet." On one side of the sheet can go considerations that are in favor and support the objective; the other side of the sheet can list obstacles or considerations that go against the objective. Figure 9.1 illustrates how a mother's desire to place her young child in day care might be assessed.

The balance sheet is a useful way of highlighting objectives that either have a lot or very little going for them. Even objectives that have many barriers may be pursuable if client and worker agree to pursue prior objectives that are aimed at removing barriers to the original objective. Thus, objectives with many barriers may be redefined as long-range goals that will be pursued once obstacles are removed. In the example given, the worker and client may decide to work on transportation and the grandparents' attitudes before working on child care services.

Feasibility cannot be taken too literally by client and worker because often the most achievable objectives are the most trivial. Those objectives that most fundamentally affect the client's life are often the most difficult to achieve. Simply pursuing an "easy objective" may not be in a client's best interest. This point is well presented in Epstein's critique of behavioral overspecification.[7] A client with serious economic, social, and interpersonal problems is placed on a successful regimen of reducing her "crying spells" with little attention paid to her deleterious living conditions. Success is an important criterion, but as with client aspirations, it cannot be the only determinant in ranking objectives.

A final consideration for ranking objectives concerns "life and limb" issues. Sometimes clients or people close to them are in situations where serious harm and injury may result if conditions are allowed to continue. A worker cannot ignore suicidal or homicidal ideas or situations in which the life and limb of others in the client's immediate life space are in jeopardy. All states have legislation that requires human service professionals to take action when child abuse or neglect is suspected. In the example given, the mother may be interested in placing her child in day care but is unconcerned about her child's severe diarrhea, which has persisted for several weeks. A worker must be concerned about this child's health status (possible dehydration), and an objective will have to be to get this child to a health care setting for immediate evaluation.

In this discussion of the factors involved in ordering objectives, we do not intend to discourage the worker from being client cen-

Objective: Place 3-Year-Old Daughter in Day Care

Figure 9-1.
Balance Sheet

Pros (+, support/resources)	Cons (−, obstacles/barriers)
1. Mother is strongly motivated to pursue placement.	1. Mother has no way to transport child.
2. Several day care centers have openings.	2. Parents of mother are opposed to placing child in day care.
3. Mother has financial resources to pay for services.	

tered. Consideration of the client's aspirations is very important during planning and is too often ignored; but the client's wishes are not the only considerations that should be discussed. The objectives that are finally pursued must be the product of client aspirations, feasibility, and life and limb considerations.

This section of the chapter concludes with a brief case example that highlights how these various considerations enter a practice situation. In this case example, there are at least a dozen problems facing the mother, and many more objectives can be suggested than can be pursued. An objective to help this mother to be at the hospital with her 6-year-old son may be most responsive to her aspirations, but it would ignore the health and safety risks to her younger children. Even though this woman's problematic relationship with her husband has "caused" the present crisis, objectives aimed at resolving this severe problem will have to take low priority because of their low feasibility and chance of success.

Example

The worker is located in a community action agency storefront office in an inner-city community. A white, 25-year-old woman entered the agency. She was wringing her hands and crying.

The social worker brought the woman to her office and gave her a glass of water. The woman began to explain why she was so upset. She stated that she lived around the block in a condemned walkup. Upon returning home that afternoon, she learned from a neighbor that her 6-year-old son had fallen off a broken fire escape and had been taken to the hospital. She called the hospital and talked with the doctor in the emergency room. Her son was in fair condition but must remain in the hospital for a 48-hour observation period. Because her son had been very upset, the doctor requested that she spend as

much time with him as possible. She wants to be with her son but does not know what to do with her other children (ages 4, 2, and 3 months).

Mrs. S gave her name and explained that she had left her 6-year-old son to babysit for her other three children while she was out trying to "hustle" for more money because there was no food in the apartment. She was very short of cash this week because her husband, from whom she is separated, came two nights ago, beat her up, forced her to have sexual relations in front of the children, and then took what was left of her welfare money for this month. She explained that this was not the first time her husband had come in drunk and abused her. In fact, she had separated from him because he was "abusing" the children, and about six months ago the parents had been brought into court by protective services to remove their children. Mrs. S was able to keep the children on the understanding that she would not allow her husband to associate with them.

Mrs. S is concerned about the health of her two youngest children. The baby has been throwing up and has had diarrhea for the past week, and the 2-year-old has had a severe sore throat and earaches for the last three days. She states that they have come down with these "colds" because the weather has gotten colder and the only way she can heat her apartment is with an old electric heater and by lighting the gas oven and leaving the door open.

Mrs. S states that she is not in good health herself because she has begun to have "blackout spells" again. For the past few months she has found herself walking around on the street and not remembering how she got there. These "blackouts" had happened before, after the birth of her second child.

Mrs. S is worried about her living arrangements because the building she occupies is scheduled to be torn down in a few weeks. In her search for a new apartment, she has not been able to find a place that she can afford on her present welfare allotment. She has had to put aside as much money as possible to pay the funeral expenses of her mother who died about two months ago. Mrs. S prefers to remain in her present neighborhood because she has become close to a neighbor who is also on welfare, and this neighbor helps her with her bills and mail because Mrs. S cannot read or write.

Identification of Target Systems

Once the client and worker have agreed on an objective, the next planning step is to decide what part of the client's life space should be changed for the objective to be achieved. Even though clients and their social contexts are complex, interlocking systems[8] and many social problems have a large number of contributing and sustaining factors, a worker and client cannot be expected to tackle all the complexities in the client's world.[9] "Biting off more than they can chew" is bound to choke both worker and client, but a focused, partialized approach is more likely to result in identifiable change.

Potential Target Systems

The first step in selecting the target system is to identify *all* potential target systems that are somehow implicated in the planned objective. (See Chapter 2 for a definition of target systems.) At this point the worker and client should think broadly about parts of the client's life space that can be changed—some personal aspect of the client, some part of the client's family or immediate household or social network, or some aspect of the client's organizational life.

The point we emphasize here is that social work is boundary work, and the client is not necessarily the target system as is usual in psychotherapy. The worker and client may select a target system that is distinct from the client such as an organization in which the client is a consumer. For example, the client may be a patient on a ward and the ward procedures may be a target for change. In other target systems, the client may be a component part, such as an individual client and an important relative, who together are the target system if their relationship is to be changed.

Selection of Target Systems

Once potential target systems have been identified, the worker and the client should identify at least *one* target system on which to focus their change efforts. Any given objective probably has several plausible target systems that can be designated, and the task in this phase of planning is to select *one*. Many factors will influence which target system is chosen. The experience and theoretical biases of the worker will affect the worker's preferences; the client may be influenced by concerns that some targets might be displeased and retaliate; and both might be influenced by the relative availability or complexity of target systems.

In the case example presented next, there are a number of potential target systems: family, landlord, city housing authority, tenants, city council, federal and state governments, and police. The actions that must be taken to influence an elected body such as a city council to change eviction laws are very different from the actions taken to mobilize tenants to engage in a legal rent strike.

Example

There is a severe housing shortage and the law allows landlords to evict tenants forcibly if their rental payments fall two months in arrears. The worker is employed in a "model cities" storefront agency. An 11-year-old boy comes running into the agency in tears and relates the following story:

He explains that his mother has just been arrested by two police officers for stabbing their landlord. While his family (mother, self, three younger sisters) were eating breakfast this morning, the landlord and two other men opened the door to the family's two-room apartment and began moving what little furniture they owned out onto the street. His mother pleaded with the landlord not to evict them, but the landlord said he was "fed up with their kind" and they would have to leave. His mother told the landlord that she would stop withholding the rent and would pay up her back rent today, but the landlord refused to accept the back rent. The mother pleaded that she would never again refuse to pay rent. The landlord refused to listen to the mother and continued to remove furniture from the apartment. In blind rage, his mother grabbed a pair of scissors and stabbed the landlord in his shoulder when he removed a crucifix from the wall. This is the third family to be evicted from this four-floor walk-up in two months.

In this case example there are many potential target systems that can be identified, but some will have priority over others. Because of the crisis situation in this family, the children, mother, and furniture are the most pressing targets to be addressed. The landlord, city council, or tenants, though important potential targets too, have lower priority at this point.

Designating the target system is important to the change effort so that various forms of resistance can be anticipated and managed. In a change situation, it is normal to expect resistance to arise.[10] There are many sources of resistance in social work practice. Some emanate from the worker (workers may be reluctant to pursue objectives that test their limited expertise or that they themselves have difficulty accomplishing); some resistances emerge from members of the action system; and some come from the target system (a decision maker in an organization may be against the proposed change objective). It is important to understand what kinds of resistances the target may display in response to the change objectives as an aid to further planning.

Common Resistances in Target Systems

There are a number of common resistances that a target system may display when change efforts are initiated. Sometimes target systems may believe that change is impossible and effort is futile.[11] These individuals or families may feel hopeless, apathetic, and fatalistic. They have been powerless to affect their circumstances and as a result are unable and unwilling to act even when opportunities for mastery do arise. Such individuals often live in families who have become highly disorganized and are barely able to perform even the limited role requirements of a functioning family[12]; other individuals may adopt alienated, self-destructive life-styles through abuse of drugs and alcohol. These kinds of resistance in a target system are some of the most intransigent. The most common strategy used in practice to deal with this form of resistance is "persistence." The boundary between "persistence" and "harassment" is narrow so that the worker must be careful not to pursue the target system too overzealously.

Some target systems are hesitant to change because they perceive no need to change, even though they may be surrounded by trouble.[13] Even when problems are finally acknowledged by these target systems, they make take no responsibility for the trouble and blame others for them. Individual targets may blame other family members, neighbors, the community, or society for the problem. Organizational target systems may engage in "blaming the victim,"[14] usually the consumer, for the problem. If this fails, some organizations may try to minimize or redefine the problem so that it does not appear to exist.[15] For example, it has been a common tactic in this period of high unemployment to point out that many unemployed workers have access to other benefits or have a spouse who is still employed. Those who use this tactic have even suggested that it is desirable to have high unemployment rates.

No simple strategies can be employed when a target ignores, denies, or minimizes problems. When the target system is an individual, sometimes the worker can employ the following strategy. Instead of trying to get the target to admit culpability or partial responsibility, the target system is recruited as a "helper" and is encouraged to identify as part of the solution—not the problem. For example, some parents are defensive about their part in the behavior of a problem child, but they can be influenced to change when they are encouraged to participate in service as part of the solution to their child's troubles. Even a self-help group like "Tough Love," designed to help parents cope with problem teenagers, is strongly pro-parent and denies that parents are responsible for their problem teenagers yet still changes members' behaviors and encourages better parenting.

Some target systems are resistant to the change process because their particular values or past life experiences mitigate against receiving help from an "outsider."[16] In this situation the formal authority or expertise of the worker is not legitimated by the target system. A cohesive, juvenile gang may be suspicious and hostile of the intrusions of a street worker; or a family in a cohesive, ethnic neighborhood may be reluctant to receive help from a worker who does not live on their block and is not from their same ethnic group.

Matching[17] is a common strategy for this form of resistance; that is, the worker should have a similar background to the target system. In some situations intermediaries between worker and target systems may be employed (indigenous helpers) to help bridge the gap. But sometimes the worker must simply forbear and struggle to "pass the test" before the target will begin to accept what the worker can do!

Resistances often arise within family target systems when the change objective involves areas of family life that are sacrosanct or taboo.[18] For example, a parent's excessive indulgence in alcohol or incestuous relationship with a child may be a carefully guarded family secret. Change objectives directed at these areas will be met with strong resistance. A common strategy that is employed with this kind of family resistance is to be "up front" with family members. Honesty,[19] clarity about issues, and confrontation will not avoid pain and conflict in these areas, but it will establish the worker as a serious and concerned change agent.

Within the life of a living system, certain tasks continuously appear and require management. To handle their repetitious demands, systems develop habitual patterns of behaving and functioning. These habitual patterns become comfortable for the living system because they are automatic and do not require energy to be expended in remaking a decision. When change objectives are directed toward these automatic, habitual patterns of behavior, resistance may appear as an equilibrium force.[20] Even when these habitual patterns are potentially destructive or painful, they are not easily abandoned because of their energy-saving function. Reminders of negative consequences, appeals to conscience, and doomsday scenarios are all tactics that might be employed to move highly resistant targets.

Some sources of resistance in target systems emanate from the target's environment or from the interdependence the target system has with other systems.[21] Sometimes systems external to the target system are threatened by the change objectives and place a counterforce on the target not to change. Other family members or friends may not support or may even sabotage the efforts of an individual to change some aspect of behavior or functioning. These significant others may fear that they will lose something if the target individual changes, or they may be jealous of, or threatened by, the change relationship that the individual target has developed with the worker.

Other examples are parents who might remove a child from psychiatric treatment because they are threatened by the relationship that a worker has with their child or information about the family the worker collects. Administrators in agencies are influenced by policymaking boards, funding sources, and other organizations, and they, therefore, cannot be totally responsive to their consumers or employees.

A common strategy for dealing with this kind of resistance is to change the size or focus of the target system and to include those other systems in the target system. For example, a worker might shift the target from one member of the family to include all members of the family.

Finally, a common form of resistance that arises in a target system results from the perceived threat that the change may have on the target's esteem or position.[22] Some individuals react to a change in the status quo as though it personally threatens some present satisfaction. Administrators may see a change as a threat to their "turf" or responsibility. Other targets may fear that the change objective reflects negatively on their capabilities. Parents may ignore problem behavior in their children until it becomes intolerable because a "bad child" will reflect negatively on them as parents. Similarly, decision makers in organizations may not want their weaknesses exposed through becoming a change objective. The organizational climate of some agencies is so punitive and intolerant of mistakes that employees must be careful to "cover themselves" and avoid calling attention to organizational blunders.

Some targets may want to avoid the awkwardness that accompanies the initiation of a new behavior or procedure. Individuals may want to master the new procedure before they try it out in the real world. Other targets may be aware of the risks and uncertainties that accompany any change effort, and they fear such uncertainty more than they dislike their present reality. An individual may tolerate a painful, debilitating medical condition rather than chance the uncertainty of a surgical procedure.

There are many strategies designed to overcome these kinds of resistance. Workers may be supportive and reassuring, or they may mobilize others in the target's environment to be supportive of the change efforts. They may focus on small changes first so that the target can experience success, or they may provide a protected environment in which the target can practice and try out new behaviors.

There are additional forms that are unique to organizations as target systems.[23] Change goals that address the entire organization are more difficult to achieve than are those that focus on its subunits. Changing a procedure in one unit is much easier to accomplish than is changing a policy that affects the entire organization.

Timing may also be an important factor in how organizations respond to change pressures. When an organization is battered by many competing demands or is struggling for its survival, any change goal may be perceived as an unfriendly, threatening demand. Organizations as well as individuals can be overloaded and unable to respond rationally to even reasonable requests. "Sunk costs" are another factor that contributes to organizational resistance.[24] If an agency has just spent a lot of time, money, and energy changing part of its services, then any change suggestion in that area will be met with automatic resistance. Most of these forms of organizational resistance can be managed by focusing on small aspects of the organization and recognizing that some changes have to be postponed.

In practice, planning is not a lockstep, linear process as presented in this chapter. After exploring target systems and discussing various resistances and obstacles, it may be necessary for worker and client to reconsider their change objectives. Revision of the change objective is necessary when it is apparent that worker and client are facing a target system that has overwhelming resistance to the change objective. It then may be more realistic to develop change objectives that are directed at the resistances in the target system before moving on to pursue the original change goal. In some situations a worker and client may have to abandon an objective altogether because their limited resources would never allow them to change the target system in question. Such revisions represent good planning and should not be considered a failure. In fact, as we discuss in the next section of this chapter, revisions are an expected, desirable element of the planning process.

Developing Action Systems

Because interpersonal practice is *social* work, we do not expect the client alone or the worker and client together to be the only actors involved in the change process. Although there may be situations in which worker and client exclusively make up the action system (defined in Chapter 2), as is usual in dyadic counseling, most practice involves a network of resources and helpers that are enlisted, orchestrated, and encouraged to work, on the client's behalf, to achieve the change objectives.

There is no such thing as an "ideal" action system. An action system is determined by the client's objectives and the target systems that have been identified; but it will also be determined by the availability of resources that worker and client can mobilize. In most practice contexts, resources are scarce, and in others, even though ample resources exist, the client and worker may not be able to utilize them effectively. Rural social workers often lament the lack of resources in rural areas[25] but overlook the reality that even a broad network of services does not guarantee that resources will be utilized effectively. Social work literature abounds with case examples of clients who are caught in dysfunctional networks of uncoordinated and competing service programs.[26] This section of the chapter presents ways in which the client and worker can develop as well-coordinated and effective action systems as possible.

Another important feature of the action system is its transiency. Of all the practice systems (client, worker, target, and action), action systems are the most changeable. From week to week or even day to day, membership in the action system may change. This flexibility is both desirable and necessary for effective practice because worker and client inevitably rely on different resources or helpers depending on what they are trying to accomplish.

Knowledge of Resource Systems

To build effective action systems, the worker should have an understanding of the many kinds of helping resources that may be mobilized as part of the action system. The worker should have knowledge of the formal network of services, as well as of indigenous helping resources. At a bare minimum a worker must know *how to* locate and find out about resources so that this information can be shared with the client system when deciding what to mobilize in the action system.

Formal resource systems are those agencies, programs, and services that comprise the public, voluntary, and private sectors of the service delivery system. These resources are staffed by various helping professionals who have degrees and credentials that have been sanctioned by society. Many other professions besides social work (medicine, law, nursing, psychology) operate in these organizations. Hospitals, psychiatric outpatient clinics, substance abuse clinics, public welfare, public schools, family agencies, community action agencies, legal aid programs, courts, and private therapists are examples of the services that are available in the formal resource system.

Most counties or metropolitan areas print a listing of these formal resources to identify and briefly describe the programs in their particular catchment area. Besides the Yellow Pages, some areas have information and referral "hot lines" that can be called. The problem with these printed guides is their inaccuracy. Some of the descriptions in guides are public relations statements of what the agency "would like to do" and are not, in fact, representative of what agencies actually do. Some information in guides is out of date, so that agency location, phone number, and contact person may have changed. Another problem with guides and referral services is that they inevitably overlook and omit potential resources that may be unknown to the authors of the guide or referral service. A final problem with guides reflects the reality that just knowing about a service does not guarantee that a client will be able to make use of it. Information about a service is not enough to assure a successful referral.

Indigenous helping resources refer to practitioners, groups, and institutions that the formal resources may disparage, yet to which individual clients tend to turn first in time of trouble.[27] Troubled individuals often try to solve problems on their own or turn to family and friends for help. If these efforts bring no relief, the individual may move into the indigenous healing system and seek help from a culturally idiosyncratic practitioner who is not formally recognized or legitimized by society at large.

Even though practitioners in the indigenous healing system may be rejected by the formal helping system as nonscientific, superstitious charlatans, the indigenous healing system is much larger and more significant to many clients than most professionals acknowledge.[28] In fact, the formal helping system may be only the tip of the iceberg of helping resources, and many more resources lie in the invisible, indigenous healing system.

The indigenous healing system is composed of many kinds of helpers. There are spiritual or religious practitioners. The more legitimated helpers such as ministers, priests, rabbis, and pastors are associated with institutional religion; but there are also *curanderos* in the Chicano community, spiritualists and *santeros* in the Puerto Rican community, shamans and medicine men in American Indian communities, voodoo practitioners in certain rural black communities, and faith healers in both the urban black and rural white communities. Besides spiritual healers there are also such forms of medicine as acupuncturists, Oriental herbalists, root doctors, Hispanic herb shops, and holistic health food stores.

For specific ethnic groups, indigenous healing is a healing system parallel to the

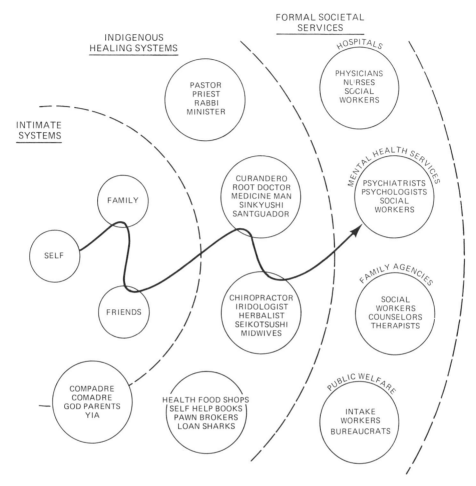

Figure 9-2. Help Seeking Journey

formal one.[29] For example, the herbalist supplies various remedies, potions, and salves in the same way a pharmacist supplies prescription drugs and medicines. Many of the modern wonder drugs of the pharmacist were once the secret folk remedies of indigenous healers. Many tranquilizers, antibiotics, anesthetics, and even aspirin have their origins in "folk medicine."

Table 9-1 is presented as a guide to the many kinds of indigenous helpers who practice in various ethnic communities. The table is by no means comprehensive, but does demonstrate a broad range of indigenous practitioners that is often ignored and little understood by professionals.[30]

The indigenous helping system is also permeated by numerous self-help groups and associations.[31] Americans are a self-help, do-it-yourself culture. There are self-help books for almost any conceivable human condition—divorce, sexuality, handicaps, parenting, dieting, nutrition, exercise, and so on. There are also numerous opportunities

Table 9-1 Indigenous Practitioners

PRACTITIONER	CONSUMER POPULATION	COMMON HEALING PROCEDURES
Priest	Catholic parishioners	Ceremonies, rituals, counsel/advice
Minister	Protestant parishioners	Ceremonies, rituals, counsel/advice
Rabbi	Jewish	Counsel/advice
Pastor	Local parishioners	Ceremonies, rituals, counsel/advice
Espiritist	Hispanic (Puerto Rican)	Diagnosis & prescribe rituals, herbs, ceremonies, salves
Curandero	Hispanic (Chicano)	Diagnosis & prescribe rituals, herbs, ceremonies, salves
Santero	Hispanic (Cuban)	Diagnosis & prescribe rituals, herbs, ceremonies, salves
Santguador	Hispanic	Treats mostly physical ailments
Compadrazgo (Compadre/comadre)	Hispanic	Family responsibility
Yia	Greek-Americans	Advice/counsel
Root doctor	Rural Black	Diagnose & prescribe herbs & home remedies
Voodoo practitioner	Rural Black	Rituals & ceremonies
Sinkyushi	Oriental community	Acupuncture, massage, counsel/advice
Seikotsushi	Oriental community	Skeletal & muscular adjustments, counsel
Shiatsushi	Oriental community	Skeletal & muscular adjustments, counsel
Herbalist	Hispanic/Oriental	Herbal remedies, salves, medicines
Chiropractor	Rural communities	Skeletal adjustments, some body work
Iridologist	Urban/suburban community	Diagnosis & prescribe purgatives & natural foods
Shaman/Medicine Man	American Indian	Ceremonies, rituals, counsel/advice

for individuals to meet in groups with other individuals who face similar problems or life transitions.

Table 9-2, a list of self-help groups, is offered as a guide to the numerous, indigenous associations that may exist in a given community. The list is not exhaustive, and all groups appearing here will not always be found in every community. As the list clearly demonstrates, there are many self-help groups, and some such as "Tough Love" are fairly hostile to the "professional" community. An effective interpersonal practitioner will know where, when, and how each group operates in the community.

Building and Maintaining Action Systems

Knowledge of available resources is critical to developing an effective action system, but knowledge itself will not guarantee that a successful action system can be developed. The worker must also be able to perform four basic functions to assure that an effective action system is created: linking, cementing, coordinating, and monitoring.

Somehow resources must be *linked up* with the client and the target systems. The worker should develop expertise in connecting and joining various parts of the action system. One important aspect of successful linking is the worker's ability to develop contacts or cultivate relationships with others associated with resources. It is easier for a worker to connect a client to a formal or indigenous resource when that worker knows somebody in that system. Such a prior relationship between worker and contact person may be critical in some linking situations in which the client may not exactly "fit" the resource's eligibility requirements or the client is ambivalent and unsure about establishing

Table 9-2. Self-Help Groups

1. Adoption Search and Research Group	Support group for those searching for relatives
2. Al Anon (Ala Teen)	Support group for families with an alcoholic member
3. Alcoholics Anonymous	Support group for alcoholics
4. American Cancer Society "I Can Cope Group"	Support and education for individuals with cancer
5. Dawntreader, Inc.	Support group for those who have received or are presently receiving psychiatric care
6. Families Anonymous	Support group for parents of teens with substance abuse and behavioral problems
7. Gay Alliance	Support and advocacy group for lesbian women and homosexual men
8. Grey Panthers	Advocacy group for the elderly
9. Hospice	Support group for individuals or family members facing terminal illness
10. Informed Birth and Parenting	Educational and support groups for new parents
11. LaMaze Childbirth Preparation Association	Educational classes and support group for expectant and new parents
12. Multiple Sclerosis Society	Educational and support group for individuals with MS and their families
13. New Beginnings	A grief recovery group for persons experiencing a recent loss
14. Overeaters Anonymous	Support group for fatties who want to be thin
15. Parents Anonymous	Support group for parents who have trouble controlling their anger when dealing with their children
16. Parents Without Partners	Support group for single parents
17. Reach to Recovery	Support group for women who have had mastectomies or breast surgery
18. Recovery, Inc.	Support group of former mental patients designed to prevent relapses
19. Resolve	Support group for people who have infertility problems and have experienced miscarriages
20. Singletarians	Adult singles socialization group
21. Tough Love	Support group for parents with a problem teenager
22. Widowed Person's Group	Support group for widows and widowers
23. Women for Sobriety	Support group for alcoholic women

the linkage. The worker's prior relationship with a contact person in the organization can be used to smooth the way so that a successful connection can be formed.

Linking clients to resources is such a common activity of social workers, it is surprising that this area of practice has received so little attention, and those few studies that have addressed this area show a low success rate.[32] In some studies, less than half the referrals are accepted or make it to the designated resource. "Referral fatigue"[33] is an unfortunate reality for many clients.

Weissman[34] has suggested a number of procedures that a worker can employ to improve the chances of a successful link. These procedures are presented in a hierarchy with the most intrusive and active interventions by the worker presented last.

The first level is to write down the critical information about the resource (name, address, telephone number, hours of operation) and let the clients make the connection on their own. With those clients who have the motivation and capacity to negotiate the linkage with the resource, basic information will be enough to promote a successful link.

With other clients, it may be necessary to provide the name of a particular contact person whom they should seek out in the resource or the name of individuals they should avoid in the resource. In large organizations there are numerous "gatekeepers" who have a great deal of discretionary power about who is served or rejected, and clients should be helped to locate responsive gatekeepers. In some situations, a written description of the client's particular problem or concern should be sent along. This kind of advanced preparation allows the worker to help the client build a good case with the gatekeeper.

In some situations, it may be necessary to introduce the client to an intermediary who can help to arrange the connection with the resource. Some indigenous healing systems cannot be approached directly by either clients or worker, and the worker will have to connect the client with an intermediary who in turn will help the client make contact with the resource.

It may be necessary to begin the linkage by phoning the prospective resource and making prearrangements before the client does anything. Such prearrangements allow the worker to initiate the link and also help the resource to understand what to expect when the client arrives. Finally, in some situations the worker will have to accompany the client to the resource to facilitate the client's entry or acceptance into the organization.

The Lower East Side Family Union in New York uses this linkage strategy to connect poor, multiproblem, ethnic families with the large service agencies that would normally ignore or reject such applicants.[35]

The worker will have to decide what level to choose to facilitate a successful link. If a linkage does not result from one level, it may be necessary to move to successively more intensive linkage strategies.

Linking only gets the connection started, and often a weak or fragile link can be easily dissolved unless the worker takes further action to strengthen the tentative connection. Weissman[36] offers a number of *cementing strategies* that are designed to reinforce and maximize the linkages established between client and resource. Essential to all cementing strategies is *follow-up*, which should be built into all referral activities. Not only does follow-up provide information to the worker about the success or failure of the referral, but it also provides information to the worker about what various resources are actually doing (screening procedures, new programs). Follow-up is basic to monitoring, which will be discussed in more detail at the end of this chapter.

There are five basic cementing procedures: checkback, haunting, sandwiching, alternating, and individualizing. In checkback, the client is requested to call back the worker and inform him or her how the referral went. The responsibility for the follow-up is placed on the client's shoulders. In haunting, the worker is more active and takes responsibility for the follow-up. The worker asks the client's permission to call either the client or the resource to find out about the results of the referral.

In sandwiching, a follow-up interview is scheduled for worker and client to discuss how the referral process went and to plan other strategies that may be necessary to make a successful connection to a resource. In alternating, the worker and client plan a series of contacts following each contact the client has with the resource. This strategy of alternating interviews is intensive because the client and worker remain engaged while the client receives help from the resource. Clearly these last two strategies are employed when the client's motivation or capacity is limited or the resources are difficult to utilize and the worker must remain involved in supporting the client's connection to the helping resource.

In some situations the worker will have to be intensively involved in encouraging the client to use a formal resource, as well as working with the resource to help it "bend" to the client's special needs. *Individualizing*[37] refers to the process of trying to improve the match between the client's individual needs and the agency's requirements. Individualizing requires the worker to engage both the client and resource if a successful connection is to be maintained. As was discussed in the chapter on clienthood (Chapter 4), there are many barriers that applicants face in trying to become clients in a large, formal organization. Workers should be able to educate and even coax clients so that clients can present themselves in the best light. For example, some agencies are

reluctant to serve clients (who could benefit from their services) because the client has an "undesirable" condition associated with the problem the agency is organized to tackle. Therefore, some clients are warned to avoid discussing, at least initially, their alcoholism and instead focus with the gatekeeper on their family conflicts. At the same time, the worker may have to bargain, persuade, or gently push the gatekeeper in the agency to bend policies and procedures to meet the client's individual needs. Sometimes workers make "deals" to accept each other's difficult clients on the promise of future reciprocity.

As Figure 9-3 illustrates, the connection between client and resource is the focus of the individualizing process. Individualizing is a mediating strategy[38] and will require the worker to be actively engaged with both the client and the agency if a successful link is to be nurtured and maintained.

With some clients a number of linkages may be developed with different resources or there may be existing linkages that need to be modified or improved. In the case that is presented in Figure 9-4, a 15-year-old boy is caught in a web of connections with many service organizations. With some agencies, he is a target system; with others, he is a client system. The problems that emerge in such a case situation are that agencies end up

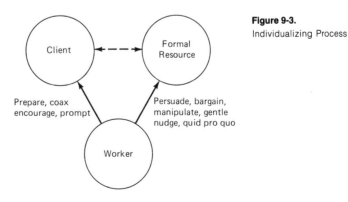

Figure 9-3.
Individualizing Process

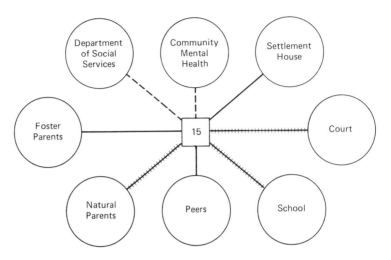

Figure 9-4   Ecomap of 15-Year-Old-Youth

duplicating each other's service or working at cross-purposes, and service providers are not clear what other service providers are trying to accomplish.

In this case example, not only were some service providers unaware of other services that were involved, but there also were inter-agency hostilities that pitted one service against the other, and this youth was caught between them. The courts did not get along with the settlement house and community mental health clinic, and the latter agency and school had poor relationships with the Department of Social Services. Because of these interagency conflicts, the 15-year-old youth was given mixed messages about what was expected of him, and these compounded his problems with the law and school. As the ecomap also shows, this youth has conflicted relationships with the court, school, and natural parents; weak relationships with the Community Mental Health Clinic and the Department of Social Services; and a positive relationship with his foster parents, peers, and the settlement worker.

This case is presented to demonstrate

how great the need for *coordination* is in many practice situations. The action system must be planned with coordination in mind, or whatever change strategies are implemented may be neutralized or vitiated in a network of competing services. Another negative consequence of uncoordinated action systems is that lack of communication between professionals may allow some client or target systems to avoid making changes by triangulating (that is, playing off) one professional against another. Inconsistency in the action system may allow a "systemwise" manipulator to pit one part of the action system against another and thus keep services from having any influence or producing any significant change.

Coordination can be accomplished through a variety of processes, but it is essential that someone in the service network take responsibility for these activities. In some settings these activities are performed by case managers[39] whose job it is to oversee all planning and to be responsible for coordinating various action systems. The case manager is similar to an orchestra conductor. No matter how proficient each individual player may be, the conductor must take responsibility for organizing and coordinating each of the individual instruments if a successful "piece" is to be performed.

Some forms of coordination may require telephone contact, memos, letters, or even formal hearings; others may require face-to-face contact between all parties involved. What type of coordination is best will depend on the particulars of the case situation, what is feasible for the resources involved, or what may be required by law or agency routine.

In this section of the chapter, we discuss the case conference as a coordinating activity that workers use to plan and improve existing linkages in a case situation. The case conference usually occurs at some decision or transition point in service such as discharge or admission planning. In some organizations a case conference is required before a change in the client's service plan can be implemented. For example, in some school systems, an Individual Educational Planning Committee made up of teachers, principal, parents, and school social worker must meet before changes are made in a student's special education services. In some mental health systems, a Placement Review Committee made up of hospital staff and community caregivers must meet before a patient is discharged to the community.

Most case conferences attempt to accomplish two tasks. All resources and service providers should understand and agree on an overall objective for the client or target system. Although each provider may be working on a particular piece, each piece must fit together into some general objective. Each provider should recognize how a particular effort fits together with that of others. Second, a case conference should also clarify and attempt to achieve some agreement about the role responsibilities of each member of the action system. Ideally, a case conference should also generate some commitment among members to carry out their respective responsibilities.

There are three parts to a successful case conference: calling the meeting, conducting the meeting, and following up the meeting. What happens in the meeting is only a small part of a successful case conference. In fact, without careful planning and follow-up, a good decision-making conference may go nowhere.

The worker must accomplish a number of decisions and tasks before the meeting or case conference occurs. First and foremost must be consideration of purpose. There must be a good reason for calling members of the action system together. The worker should be able to clearly articulate this reason to all who are invited. "We need to meet to discuss the patient's discharge plans" or "We need to get everyone together to clarify what each of us is doing in this case" or "We need to get all parties together because it seems that there are several disagreements about what should happen next in this case."

Once purpose has been established and there is a good reason for calling the conference, the client should be informed of the conference. Whether the client or family representative plans to attend the conference or not, permission for release of information must be obtained prior to the conference.[40] In discussing the release of information issue with the client, it may also be useful to discover whom the client feels should attend the case conference. Sometimes the worker overlooks members of the action system whom the client feels should contribute to the decisions in the conference.

The next step in planning the conference is most critical and is influenced by many factors. Who should be invited to the case conference is a complex decision. Should everyone in the action system be invited? Should the client be invited or should the meeting be for "professionals only"? Decisions to include or exclude potential members will depend on the purpose of the conference, which is why clarity of purpose is so essential. Obviously there is no reason to invite a resource person who has nothing to do with the purpose of the conference. There may also be no reason to invite several people from the same service or agency when this involves duplication.

Case conferences should not be too large, or they become unmanageable. In large meetings it is impossible for everyone attending to have an opportunity to present perspectives and opinions. How large is too large will depend on the worker's skills at managing and facilitating the group as well as the particular issues for the conference. It is easier to mediate highly contentious issues when fewer parties are present.[41] No matter how skilled the worker may be, a case conference with 10 or more members will be unwieldy and allow limited time for each member to present and interact.

A common way of reducing the number of members in the conference is for the worker to contact less essential resources before the conference and to represent their perspective in the conference. Five or six members is probably the optimal size for a case conference.[42] Full attendance is rare in small groups, and the worker should expect some members to be unable to attend when the conference actually occurs.[43]

Because there are many factors that will determine who should be invited to a case conference, it is almost impossible to generate firm rules about inclusion. Our bias is that it seems best to err on the side of inclusion rather than exclusion. Inviting too many members to the conference is a lesser evil than inviting too few.

Our position for inclusion is based on two important considerations. Too often in practice the client is excluded from case conferences, yet we strongly believe that clients should be included. Clients are not only a good source of information, but they also have a right and a responsibility to participate in decisions that affect their lives. It may be easier for professionals to meet without clients present, and some professionals may find it discomforting to share negative information in the client's presence; yet the client's presence will eliminate unsubstantiated character assassination and inferences that cannot be supported by facts and observation.

One of the biggest problems that occurs in action systems is sabotage,[44] as when one party deliberately works against the plans of other parties and contributes to the failure of the plan. A way to minimize sabotage is not to overlook any member of the action system and to include as many members as possible in the case conference. Action system members who are left out of the case conference may retaliate by not supporting the decisions of the conference. Even though some individuals may be obnoxious, contentious, or disagreeable in a conference, these are not viable reasons for excluding them. It is better to have a stormy planning session than to have the case conference go smoothly and later to have the whole plan defeated by one action system member who was excluded from the meeting.

A case conference that is planned to avoid conflict is an example of faulty decision making. The different perspectives and interests of members of the action system make conflict inevitable, and it is naïve (and maybe even impossible) to try to plan an effective case conference that does not have conflict. The worker should expect conflict and be able to mediate differences, not try to avoid them. In fact, if there is no conflict in a case conference, there probably was not much need for the conference in the first place.

Once members have been selected for the case conference, each should be contacted and invited. This step sounds much easier than it actually is. Trying to arrange a common time and an agreeable place in which to meet may require patience and persistence. Individual calendars are usually crowded, and not all meeting places are convenient or desirable for each individual. The worker may spend more time and energy on just this step (making phone calls to arrange a time and place for the conference) than the actual conference itself.

Once a time and place have been arranged, the worker should follow up the phone call with a letter. This letter should remind each participant of the time, date, place, and purpose of the conference. It is also desirable to include a brief, tentative agenda for the conference in the form of a short list of the major issues or decisions that will be addressed. An agenda will give participants a chance to prepare for the conference, and advanced preparation is an important way in which to increase the efficiency of the meeting.[45] A copy of the letter should also go to the clients, whether they plan to attend or not.

The primary responsibility of the worker who called the meeting is to facilitate decision making and group interaction. The basic task of this worker will be to clarify and mediate the various positions and perspectives of each participant. A good mediator should allow each party a chance to present his or her perspective and must keep any one party from dominating the meeting. The best conference plan is one for which everyone has input and can come to some agreement. No one party knows what is best, even though

some usually think they do! In practice some case conferences will not result in a common plan to which all parties can agree, but even this ending to a conference is valuable because the divergent positions of members will have been clarified.

In conducting the meeting, the worker should ensure that all members are introduced to each other in the beginning. Everyone should have a chance to state what his or her interests are in the situation (how long and in what capacity each knows the client). As the discussion progresses, the worker should try to identify the common ground between all parties that will form the basis of the conference plan.

When a common plan finally emerges, the worker allows each party a chance to comment on the respective actions they will have to carry out for the plan to be realized. Both the plan (decision) and specific responsibilities of each party should be briefly recorded as minutes. The worker may also take responsibility for arranging a time and place for subsequent conferences if they are deemed necessary by the group.

To assure that decisions reached during the case conference are operationalized later in practice, the worker should take responsibility to follow up the conference. A simple way of following up is to send each member of the action system a follow-up letter that includes the minutes of the case conference. At a bare minimum, the minutes should reflect the date of the meeting, members present, and all major decisions reached by parties at the conference, that is, major objectives, plans, and responsibilities of each party. In a sense the minutes become a written contract of what members agreed to in the case conference and can be used by the worker to monitor individual activities.

Workers should have made it clear in the meeting that they will follow up the conference by contacting each member of the action system. Follow-up does not have to be in person, but it should be accomplished by phone call or letter at least. This kind of "haunting" is essential for the worker to reinforce decisions made in the conference and to work out impasses that may arise when the plan is implemented.

At this point in the planning process, both planning and intervention are going on at the same time. Conceptually, the differences between planning and intervention are slight when the operations of the action system are considered. The point that should be emphasized is that interpersonal practice involves lots of work "in the wings," and this work is essential to successful interventions.

Monitoring Procedures

This final section of the chapter concerns monitoring processes. Some of these activities are discussed more fully in Chapter 10. Monitoring is a form of feedback that is immediate and short range and is designed to reinforce or raise questions about interventions that are carried out by members of the action system. Monitoring processes are not focused on the ultimate outcomes of service

but on specific actions and activities. They should be simple and built into planning. Long, elaborate, or detailed evaluation mechanisms should be avoided in monitoring processes, although these mechanisms may be essential to evaluating the overall outcomes of service.

Most monitoring involves two dimensions: process and outcome. Process monitoring concerns feedback about whether the action has been completed, or is still in the process of being carried out, or has not yet been attempted. Outcome monitoring concerns feedback about the effects or results of specific actions. Outcomes of actions may be rated as intended, desirable, or successful through a midpoint of "no apparent effect" to "unintended," "undesirable," or "unsuccessful" effects. These two dimensions of monitoring can be seen as scales on continuums (see Figure 9-5).

Any action, activity, or intervention planned by members of the action system can be monitored along these two dimensions. For example, one case conference produced the following decisions: vocational rehabilitation counselor is to perform vocational preference testing; social worker is to take client on a previsit to a group home; client is to locate time and place of Recovery Incorporated

Figure 9-5
Simple Monitoring Scales

Effort Toward Action

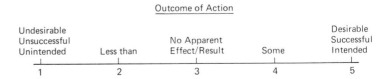

Outcome of Action

meetings; and psychiatrist is to prepare discharge planning papers. Each of these actions was monitored at a later point to see whether it had been completed. The vocational rehabilitation counselor had completed part of the test battery, but another appointment with the client was scheduled to finish the battery. The social worker had arranged a date for the visit, but it had not taken place. The client had located Recovery Incorporated and had attended his first meeting. And the psychiatrist had completed the discharge papers. Each of these actions is in various stages of completion, and those that have been completed can be evaluated to determine how successful they were. In this case, the client felt very positive about his contact with Recovery Incorporated but not very hopeful about the vocational preference tests.

The information that is collected in monitoring may be gained from the client or other service providers, or by direct observation, or any combination of these. The worker may use all three sources of information to monitor the activities of the action system. One worker went with the client to an initial interview and then followed up later visits with a phone call to both agency and client to discover how this particular interaction was progressing.

Whenever monitoring procedures are initiated, the worker should be clear on the time frame for monitoring. Whether monitoring will immediately follow the action or occur at weekly or monthly intervals, the time frame should be clear to all parties involved in the action and established before the intervention begins. There is no precise, a priori way of determining an appropriate time interval for monitoring. This decision will be determined by the particulars of the case, the type of intervention planned, and the members involved. In some service systems, the worker may be required by law or administrative procedure to engage in periodic monitoring, for example, 90-day intervals. These routine intervals should be clearly established in advance with all members of the action system and such intervals may help the worker to diffuse the sensitivity of some practitioners to monitoring activities by treating them as "routine requirements" of practice.

Summary

This chapter presented the major planning and preparation tasks. The first of these is the formulation of goals and objectives. We described goals as long-range end states to be obtained through interpersonal helping and objectives as immediate steps taken to achieve goals. We discussed the ways in which goals and objectives can be specified and how clients and workers join together to obtain a consensus on their selection. We described a "balance sheet" procedure to help in this process.

Second, we discussed how clients and workers identify and select a target system, namely the entity that is to be changed for goals to be achieved. We pointed out that target systems can include the clients themselves, the service agency, or other institutions. We described a series of considerations for the selection of target systems, one of the major ones being the kinds of resistances to change present in such systems. Since the likelihood of change is dependent on plans to deal with resistance, this topic was emphasized in this section of the chapter.

The third section of the chapter was devoted to developing action systems. These consist of the systems with which the worker will interact to help the client achieve goals. Since we shall devote later chapters to one-to-one, family, and group action systems, we focused here primarily on action systems that exist in the community and that will be used to provide services and other resources to clients. Such resources are often those that are indigenous to the client's community and are not well known to workers; thus, we devoted considerable space to listing these. Clients may need help in the planning period to gain access to resources, and this was also given consideration.

While we devote considerable attention to monitoring in Chapter 10, we recognize that monitoring procedures must be established during the planning period. We, consequently, introduced this topic as the final one for this chapter.

NOTES

1. William J. Reid, *The Task-Centered System* (New York: Columbia University Press, 1978), pp. 138–178.

2. Helen Harris Perlman, *Social Casework: A Problem Solving Process* (Chicago: University of Chicago Press, 1957), pp. 144–149.

3. William J. Reid and Laura Epstein, *Task-Centered Casework* (New York: Columbia University Press, 1972), pp. 121–175, and Frank Maple, *Shared Decision Making* (Beverly Hills, Calif.: Sage Publications, 1977).

4. *Health Pac*, New York City, December, 1969. (This citation is an editorial from a consumer advocacy group's newsletter).

5. Reid and Epstein, *Task-Centered Casework*.

6. The accuracy of some decisions can be significantly improved when planning is carried out in small groups rather than by individuals.

7. Irwin Epstein, "The Politics of Behavior Therapy: The New Cool-Out Casework," in Howard Jones, ed., *Towards a New Social Work* (London: Routledge and Kegan Paul, 1975), pp. 138–150.

8. Ben Orcutt, "Casework Intervention and the Problems of the Poor," *Social Casework*, Vol. 54 (February 1972), pp. 85–95.

9. We disagree with some "systems" texts that suggest that the worker should address all the complexity of a social problem. See, for example, Howard Goldstein, *Social Work Practice: A Unitary Approach* (Columbia: University of South Carolina, 1973).

10. The concept of resistance is central to a number of practice models. See Ronald Lippitt, Jeanne Watson, and Bruce Westley, *The Dynamics of Planned Change* (New York: Harcourt Brace Jovanovich, 1958), pp. 71–89.

11. Charlotte Henry, "Motivation of Non-Voluntary Clients," *Social Casework*, Vol. 39 (1958), pp. 130–138.

12. Louise Bandler, "Family Functioning: A Psychosocial Perspective," in Eleanor Pavenstedt, ed., *The Drifters* (Boston: Little, Brown, 1967), pp. 225–253.

13. Goodwin Watson, "Resistance to Change," in Warren Bennis, Kenneth Benne, and Robert Chin, eds., *The Planning of Change* (New York: Holt Rinehart and Winston, 1969), p. 491.

14. William Ryan, *Blaming the Victim* (New York: Pantheon, 1971).

15. Benjamin Singer, "Assessing Social Errors," *Social Policy*, September–October, 1978, pp. 27–34.

16. Herbert Gans, *The Urban Villagers: Groups and Class in the Life of Italian-Americans* (New York: The Free Press, 1962), pp. 142–162; Alice Overton, "Serving Families Who Don't Want Help," *Social Casework*, Vol. 34 (1953), pp. 304–310; John Spiegel, "Some Cultural Aspects of Tranference and Countertransference," in Frank Riessman et al., eds., *Mental Health of the Poor* (New York: The Free Press, 1964), pp. 303–320; and John M. Martin, "Social-Cultural Differences: Barriers in Casework with Delinquents," *Social Work*, Vol. 2 (July 1957), pp. 22–25.

17. Ted B. Palmer, "Matching Worker and Client in Corrections," *Social Work*, Vol. 18 (March 1973), pp. 95–103.

18. Watson, "Resistance to Change," p. 495.

19. Harris Chaiklin, "Honesty in Casework Treatment," *Social Welfare Forum, 1973* (New York: Columbia University Press, 1974), pp. 266–274.

20. Judith Nelsen, "Dealing with Resistance in Social Work Practice," *Social Casework*, Vol. 56 (December 1975), pp. 587–592, and Watson, "Resistance to Change," p. 490.

21. Alfred Kadushin, "Opposition to Referral for Psychiatric Treatment," *Social Work*, Vol. 2 (April 1957), pp. 78–84; George Levinger, "Continuance in Casework and Other Helping Relationships: A Review of Current Research," *Social Work*, Vol. 5 (July 1960), pp. 40–51; Jona Rosenfeld, "Strangeness Between Helper and Client: A Possible Explanation of Non-Use of Available Professional Help," *Social Service Review*, Vol. 38 (March 1964), pp. 17–25; and Watson, "Resistance to Change," pp. 493–494.

22. Yona Cohn, "Channeling the Probation Interview," *Crime and Delinquency*, Vol. 4 (July 1968), pp. 226–232; Kadushin, "Opposition to Referral for Psychiatric Treatment," p. 79; Lippitt et al., *The Dynamics of Planned Change*, pp. 82–85; Nelsen, *"Dealing with Resistance in Social Work Practice,"* p. 580 and Watson, "Resistance to Change," p. 493.

23. Rino Patti, "Organizational Resistance and Change: The View from Below," *Social Service Review*, Vol. 48 (September 1974), pp. 367–383.

24. Ibid.

25. Richard J. Margolis, "Rural Health and the Politics of Neglect," *Human Services in the Rural Environment*, Vol. 2 (August 1977), pp. 3–6, and "Report from the Rural Social Work Caucus," *Human Services in the Rural Environment*, Vol. 2 (January 1977), pp. 1–5.

26. Lynn Hoffman and Lorence Long, "A Systems Dilemma," *Family Process*, Vol. 8 (September 1969), pp. 211–234.

27. James Green, *Cultural Awareness in the Human Services* (Englewood Cliffs, N.J.: Prentice-Hall, 1982), and Naomi Golan, "Intervention in Times of Transition: Sources and Forms of Help," *Social Casework*, Vol. 61 (May 1980), pp. 259–266.

28. Ibid.

29. Melvin Delgado and Denise Humm-Delgado, "Natural Support Systems," *Social Work*, Vol. 27 (January 1982), pp. 83–90.

30. Emma Gross, "Curanderismo, Espiritismo, Shamanism and Social Work," unpublished paper, University of Michigan, December 1979.

31. Alice Collins and Diane Pancoast, *Natural Helping Networks* (Washington, D.C.: NASW, 1976), and Thomas Powell, "The Use of Self-help Groups as Supportive Communities," *American Journal of Orthopsychiatry*, Vol. 45 (October 1975), pp. 756–764.

32. Stuart Kirk and James Greenley, "Denying or Delivering Services," *Social Work*, Vol. 19 (July 1974), pp. 439–447, and Andrew Weissman, "Industrial Social Services: Linkage Technology," *Social Casework*, Vol. 57 (January 1976), pp. 50–54.

33. James Lantz and Beverly Lenahan, "Referral Fatigue Therapy," *Social Work*, Vol. 21 (May 1976), pp. 239–240.

34. We have somewhat modified Weissman's list, but the main ideas are his.

35. Sherida Bush, "A Family-Help Program That Really Works," *Psychology Today*, May 1977, pp. 48–50, 84–88.

36. Again we have modified Weissman's list, but the main ideas are his.

37. Carol Meyer, *Social Work Practice: The Changing Landscape*, 2nd ed. (New York: The Free Press, 1976), Chaps. 2 and 5.

38. William Schwartz and Serapio Zalba, *The Practice of Group Work* (New York: Columbia University Press, 1971).

39. Ann Bertsche and Charles Horejsi, "Coordination of Client Services," *Social Work*, Vol. 25 (March 1980), pp. 94–98; Charles Rapp and John Poertner, "Public Child Welfare in the 1980's: The Emerging Case Management Role," paper presented at the NASW Professional Symposium, San Antonio, Texas, November 1979.

40. Suanna Wilson, *Recording: Guidelines for Social Workers* (New York: The Free Press, 1976), pp. 189–191.

41. Claire Gallant, *Mediation in Special Education Disputes* (Washington, D.C.: NASW, 1982), pp. 25–34.

42. Margaret E. Hartford, *Groups in Social Work* (New York: Columbia University Press, 1971), pp. 159–169.

43. Attrition is a fact of life in groups. Members will drop out before a group gets going, and 100 percent attendance is the exception rather than the rule.

44. Brett A. Seabury, "Negotiating Sound Contracts with Clients," *Public Welfare*, Vol. 37 (Spring 1979), pp. 33–38.

45. John E. Tropman, *Effective Meetings: Improving Group Decision-making* (Beverly Hills, Calif.: Sage Publications, 1980).

ten
Monitoring and Evaluating Change[1]

We have deliberately placed this chapter on monitoring and evaluating change in the part of this book devoted to the initial stages of work with clients. This is in contrast to many other texts that include this topic as part of a discussion of termination. Our reason for this is that workers and clients should plan at the beginning of their interaction how they will determine whether the helping process is effective and what is actually done during the process.

This chapter has the modest objective of *introducing* the reader to the topics of monitoring and evaluation. This introduction includes a recapitulation of how our practice model incorporates empirical elements, as well as a brief survey of some of the major tools of empirical practice. The actual work of monitoring and evaluation demands a full study of evaluative designs and instruments, which requires a volume devoted to that topic alone.[2] We, therefore, intend this chapter to be a bridge between this text and those devoted to clinical measurement. We have additionally, as the reader is now aware,

sought to accomplish this goal through references throughout to measurements that can be used in relationship to many of the procedures we have described.

When we state that change in the client or the client's situation should be measured, we recognize that such measurement of the client and his or her circumstances may, in itself, produce changes and that a clear-cut delineation of when the actual change process begins is not always possible. The decision itself to come for help can alter people and their circumstances. The process of measurement also can have similar effects. For example, one client who wished to lose weight began to eat less when she wrote down everything she consumed. Later in this chapter we shall describe an aspect of measurement referred to as a baseline. This aspect helps the worker to determine both what the effect of measurement itself was as well as what changes occurred after the helping process began.

We introduce two separate but related topics when we refer to monitoring and evaluation. By monitoring, we mean identifying and recording events that occur during social work helping. These include the activities of the worker as well as of the client. If the action or client systems includes a family, group, or organization, then monitoring also includes a record of events in these multiperson systems. By evaluation, we mean an analysis of whether the client has attained his or her goals and whether changes can be attributed to the help offered. As we have implied, however, determining whether changes have occurred in the client or the situation or both is easier than ascertaining what has "caused" the change. We will elaborate further on this issue in this chapter.

Purposes of Monitoring and Evaluation

Although we have referred to evaluation and monitoring as separate, in practice they are usually inseparable. Thus, any approach to evaluation requires the practitioner to determine whether the intervention actually occurred, a monitoring topic. Many evaluative designs also require repeated measurements, and this incorporates monitoring activity.

The social worker should monitor and evaluate the helping process for several reasons:

1. To determine and report to the clients whether they have been helped to attain their goals. The clients should use this information to decide whether to terminate the service, continue with the service for other reasons, or seek a new service.
2. To engage in a self-correcting practice, that is, to continue to use procedures that are effective and to discontinue procedures that are ineffective. This kind of information should be used by the worker and also should be

shared with colleagues so that the entire profession moves toward more effective practice.
3. To supply effectiveness data to the agency so that the agency can determine whether it is accomplishing its purposes. The evaluation of work done on each case should, therefore, be accumulated so that the agency's program can be evaluated. The agency, in turn, has the obligation to inform its funding sources of its effectiveness, so that public funds will be spent in an accountable manner.

In this chapter, therefore, we shall briefly survey how workers monitor practice and assess outcomes. In the latter instance, we shall note a few of the instruments workers use as well as the designs employed to relate outcomes to social work interventions. Because workers monitor changes in individual, family, group, and organizational conditions, we shall also illustrate our discussion with a few of the measures appropriate to these entities. The worker should, in addition, not only examine whether desirable outcomes are attained but whether undesirable ones are avoided, and this issue of "side effects" will be discussed also.

Relationship to Practice Model

The reader will be helped to assimilate this information on monitoring and evaluation by the following restatement of empirical aspects of our practice model. Later we shall conclude the chapter with an illustration of these stages.

1. The problem of the client is specified in such detail that a measurement approach regarding the state of the problem can be devised and utilized prior to, during, and subsequent to the change activity to determine a change in the state of the problem.
2. Goals for change are also specified in enough detail so that worker and client can determine whether the client is moving toward or

away from the goal and when the presence or lack of goal attainment requires a change in the intervention plan, termination, or referral to another change agent system. A time frame is part of this goal statement.

3. A plan is made for measurement of goal attainment and problem change that includes selection of instruments, time of their administration, and what responsibility the worker, client, and significant others have for carrying this out.

4. A change plan is made and specified in enough detail that worker and client can determine whether the plan has been put into effect.

5. A means has been devised for monitoring the worker and client activities directed at change.

6. The worker and client identify possible side effects: these may be either beneficial or harmful changes in aspects of the client and his or her life space that occur as a result of the social work intervention.

These steps may, and in fact usually will be, redefined and renegotiated as the interpersonal practice process unfolds.

Monitoring

Process Records

The traditional way to monitor what the worker has done and what the immediate effects of worker activity are has been the process record. In this record, the worker indicates the individual or group of individuals that constitute the action system as well as other identifying data such as the date and location of the session and who was present. Workers also record their goals for the session. In group situations, these goals are expressed in terms of both the individual and the group.

The bulk of the process record presents a chronological recounting of the events of the session. The worker indicates his or her own part in these events but does not record every word that was spoken or action that was taken. Instead, the worker records those events that appear pertinent to attaining the social work purposes of the session. Thus, a client's sneeze is usually ignored unless it indicates a substantial emotional reaction to the content of the session or, in some other way, contributes significantly to the events that follow. The record ends with the worker's reflections on the events and plans for further work.

One difficulty is to determine what material to place in the process record so that it does not become overly burdensome. Writing the record has value as it forces the worker to reflect on the events of the session and to assess their relative importance. The main beneficiary, therefore, of the process record is the worker. Training and experience in the writing of process records should be included in professional education as practice makes the preparation of such a record progressively easier. Process records are used in supervision of workers as they provide the supervisor with information on the worker's use of self as well as on the forces present in the situation.

Supervisors will often ask beginning workers or students to write at least one process record a week both to train the worker in the preparation of such records as well as to promote self-awareness. While some years ago supervisors required workers to prepare process records on all their contacts, this practice is a rare one today. For details as to how workers acted and clients responded, workers can now use audio and audiovisual recordings. For an efficient means of recording worker interventions and client responses, workers can now also use coded recording forms.

Electronic Recordings

Workers increasingly use small portable tape recorders to record sessions. Many agencies also have audiovisual equipment. Clients are always asked for permission to record sessions in this way and may terminate permission at any time or may ask that the tape be erased.

These recordings provide an accurate portrayal of the session. The problem lies in their use to monitor worker and client activities. Whether the recordings are stored in their original form or are transcribed, it takes many hours to review them. They are most useful, therefore, immediately after the session to identify events for training purposes or to establish the occurrence of these events.

Another advantage of electronic recordings is that the worker can monitor classes of events after the session that were not identified before. Rating scales, content analysis categories, and other approaches can be used to improve the worker's and client's understanding of what occurred in the sessions.

A related approach is observation of the session by others through a one-way window. These observers, whose presence is always known to the clients and approved by them, can perform a number of functions. They can code the actions they observe, and they can advise the worker on desirable interventions during or after the session. Some workers have received such feedback during sessions through a telephone line to the observers or through consulting with them in person.

Critical Incident Recording

The critical incident record is a modified form of process recording in which only a portion of the session is recorded. The portion referred to as a critical incident is one during which either an issue presented by the client or an intervention of the worker demands thorough analysis. The recording of the incident must be sufficient to indicate all the relevant information about the client's and the worker's behaviors with reference to the issue.

Coded Recording Forms

Forms have been developed on which the workers utilize codes to record the client's actions and their own. One such system, reported by Seaburg, was developed for a project at the Seattle Atlantic Street Center.[3] This form incorporates the following elements:

- The case number, client name, and worker.
- The date of the contact.
- The person contacted (whether the client or another person relevant to work with the client)—for example, mother, father, sister, grandmother, teacher, lawyer.
- The mode of contact—for example, individually at home; individually, in community, at a group meeting; over the telephone; in a family interview.
- Duration of the contact.
- Diagnostic category—the type of problem behavior or attitude focused on in the episode. The substantive content, therefore, of the episode is represented by the category. The first digit of a four-digit code refers to the person who is discussed, and the remaining digits refer to the situation. The categories of situations include goals, self-concept, social control, social interactional issues, personality characteristics, and norm violations. Each of these is further subdivided so that a high level of specificity is attained.
- Interventive techniques—the categories that are coded are interpersonal, group, and programmatic techniques. Subcategories of interpersonal techniques include such items as confrontation, clarification, advice giving, and logical discussion. Subcategories of group techniques include those that support a member's viewpoints and those that discredit them. Programmatic techniques, used with

either individuals or groups, are those directed at involving clients in experiences.

Fischer describes a similar instrument, which he calls "systematized recording."[4] He codes some of the same aspects as Seaburg but also includes the following:

- Target problems
- Specific objectives
- Worker roles
- Client tasks

The work at the Seattle Atlantic Street Center was a pioneering one in its efforts to create such categories. Since that time, worker interventions in group situations have been explicated to a greater degree. We use the following categories, for example, to code worker behaviors in the group when directed at the entire group: teaches the group a specified group approach, limits behavior of group members, introduces group problem solving, facilitates group problem solving, assigns members to roles, introduces a group task, comments on process, restructures group, and redirects communications among members.[5]

Other Monitoring Techniques

There are other techniques for monitoring changes in individuals, for example, behavioral counts; rating scales applied by clients to themselves, family members, or staff members; and observations of a qualitative nature. These techniques are employed both for monitoring and evaluation and are described later in this chapter when evaluation is discussed.

In addition, group workers will monitor changes in group conditions. These data are used to assess problematic group conditions and to determine whether interventions have been effective in changing them. The following are some of the techniques that are useful for this purpose:

1. Changes in the pattern of who associates with whom can be monitored by charting the seating pattern of the group or administering a questionnaire in which members indicate their choices of other members as co-participants in designated activities.

2. Changes in commujication patterns can be monitored in several ways. One is by designing a form in which members' names are placed on both column and row headings. Column spaces are also designed to show that the individual spoke to more than one person or that it was unclear who was spoken to. The rater places a slash (////) for each remark. This simple instrument, when the rows and columns are totaled, presents information on who speaks most, who is most spoken to, and who speaks most frequently to whom. Another simple device is a record of when a member speaks and when a worker speaks in the form of M M M W M W M M M. This will indicate when members speak to each other as compared with the worker. The overall ratio of member comments to worker comments can also be easily computed by counting the W's and M's.[6] (These procedures were also discussed in Chapter 7.)

3. Changes in the distribution of power can be monitored by recording the responses of members to other members' ideas or suggestions. The responses so recorded are supporting, disagreeing, or ignoring these ideas.

4. Changes in roles can be monitored by asking the members at different points of time to "vote" as to which members exert the most leadership in the group, which mediate disputes, which reduce tensions, or which perform such specific tasks as securing information or planning group events. Other categories appropriate to the given group can be employed. Since one view of role behaviors

is that they are socially assigned, this "subjective" view of role behaviors is appropriate. Workers will be careful in the kind of feedback given after this procedure so as not to reinforce assignment to dysfunctional roles in view of the members' goals.

5. Changes in the group's effectiveness in utilizing a problem-solving process can be determined by the use of a scale during specific problem-solving episodes. One such scale rates the problem-solving during the episode on a five-point scale ranging from "problem completely resolved" to "the movement was completely away from the problem in that the issue was abandoned."[7]

Changes in family conditions can be monitored using some of the same instruments as those used for monitoring group conditions. In addition, the ecomap presented in Chapter 7 can be used to describe changes that occur in the interactions of families with other systems. Diagrams of the family's internal structure (also described in Chapter 7) can also be used to monitor changes in that dimension.

As with any form of measurement, those used for monitoring will involve the worker in resolving issues of reliability and validity. Reliability refers to whether the measure is stable, for example, whether several observations of the same phenomenon display the same results. Validity refers to whether the measure does what it is purported to do. Even a process record would be unreliable if several people observing the same session saw different events. It would not be valid if it were intended to show something about the quality of relationships in the session and it failed to do so. For this reason, workers should periodically seek to use at least two measures that might consist of contrasting a client's account to their own.

On the other hand, the amount of time spent on monitoring activities will always be an issue, at least for full-time staff. Students, in contrast, will spend time on monitoring during internship experiences as part of their training. We estimate that workers who take monitoring seriously will spend about 20 percent of their time on a case on monitoring.

As we noted earlier, an important aspect of monitoring is to determine whether the planned intervention did, in fact, occur—including both the actions of the worker and the client. The worker's actions can be demonstrated by a log of worker activities or an electronic recording of the same. Client activities such as homework assignments should also be noted in a log or journal. In some cases these client activities should be attested to by another person. This does not necessarily mean that the worker distrusts the client. Clients, themselves, often want this as a stimulus or reinforcement to their completing tasks. An example of this was a client who assumed the task of writing a letter to his estranged father. He promised to show the letter to his wife before it was sent to see if he had expressed the ideas and feelings he hoped to communicate.

Evaluation

The Design of the Evaluation

The *design* of the evaluation refers to the overall strategy utilized by the worker to ascertain what changes have taken place in the client and whether such changes are likely to have been brought about by the service offered. We shall now consider some approaches to the design of such an evaluation, and later in the chapter we shall indicate some ways in which the worker can measure change.

Interpersonal practice in social work has

long incorporated the idea that workers should determine whether clients have achieved the purposes for which service was offered. The traditional means of accomplishing this was to use the case record to qualitatively describe changes in the client. For example, a record indicated that Johnny, who did not attend school, was now doing so or that Mr. and Mrs. Jones, who were dissatisfied with their marriage, were now happier together. This approach had several deficiencies. First, the judgments of the worker were often subjective and unreliable. Second, the time frame was imprecise in terms of the sequence of events that took place related to the worker's intervention. Third, it was unclear what the status of the client was prior to the intervention and, therefore, whether any change had taken place at all.

In recent years, a number of changes have taken place to improve this evaluative process. First, workers have striven to employ valid and reliable measurement procedures, and most agencies now require workers to utilize such instruments. Agencies, often utilizing coded forms, may also require workers to indicate client goals as well as the techniques that were employed to help the client. In large agencies, research departments utilize these data to aggregate information so as to show overall agency effectiveness with different types of clients and with different treatment approaches.

These kinds of agencywide data may or may not be shared with workers and subsequently used by them to improve practice. In addition, the categories utilized on agency forms may not have been developed cooperatively with workers and may not correspond with how the workers, themselves, view their clients and their work. In this event, workers sometimes complete forms in a perfunctory way, and the resulting data are consequently not very helpful to anyone.

Such agency data systems can be made more useful when they are devised jointly with workers and provide the information that workers would like to have about their practice and its consequences.

While agency systems for the evaluation of practice have their use, they often obscure the meaning of events in the particular case because data from so many cases are combined. This can be prevented by the introduction of means for careful scrutiny of events that occur with each client. This has been done by the careful preparation of case studies. We believe that this still has an important role in the evaluation of practice because the availability of this kind of narrative allows the worker, as well as colleagues of the worker, to generate alternative hypotheses about changes in the client and the forces that contributed to such changes. This, however, is a time-consuming process and is often not done because case records often contain so much data and data of such dubious reliability and validity as to pose strong barriers to rigorous case study. The alternative that has recently been introduced into interpersonal practice is the *single subject design*.

The central idea of the single subject design is that it encompasses a series of measurements before, during, and after an intervention.[8] An example is that of a student who has been a truant from school. The worker measured how frequently the student attended school by an examination of attendance records prior to offering an intervention. The student in each two-week period, that term, missed an average of four days. The worker's intervention consisted of planning with the student how to complete his homework. During the intervention, the amount of homework done increased, and after the intervention, for a period of three months (the period of follow-up) the student averaged one day absent during each two-week period.

An important feature of all single-case designs is the "before" measure, referred to as the *baseline*. The purpose of this measure is to determine what the situation is prior to any intervention. This information then facilitates both goal setting and the evaluation of change. The former emerges because when the worker and client know exactly what exists in the present, what will constitute improvement can be seen. Changes from the baseline both in the direction of improvement as well as deterioration can be measured using the same approach as that employed to secure the baseline.

When the baseline measure is related to the frequency of some event (such as how frequently one person says something to another), some care must be taken to ensure that the measure is, in fact, representative of the situation. The worker may ask the client to keep a record of the event for several days (or even longer) to identify a typical frequency. This can also be done by securing a series of averages that do not significantly vary from one another. A good deal of technical information has been created so that workers can have confidence in baseline measures.[9]

A number of different single-case designs have been utilized to evaluate the effectiveness of interventions.[10] One of the simplest is the AB design in which a baseline is established (A), an intervention is carried out, and a measurement is made of the problem behavior after the intervention (B). Similar to the AB design is the ABC design. This represents a practice situation in which the worker utilizes more than one intervention. A baseline is established (A), after which an intervention occurs, the behavior is measured (B), another intervention occurs, and another measurement of behavior is taken

(C). This sequence is potentially continued until the clients attain their goals or terminate for other reasons. Again, by incorporating before, during, and after measurements, this type of design combines monitoring and evaluation components.

A design that is less frequently used in social work practice is the ABAB design. In this situation, a baseline is established (A), an intervention occurs, and a subsequent measurement is taken (B). In the event that the behavior has improved, the intervention is withdrawn. If the behavior returns to its preintervention level, this is evidence that the behavior is under the control of the intervention. For example, a child might do his homework when he is awarded "stars" and discontinue doing homework when the "star" system is discontinued. A decision might then be made to continue the star system or find some other means of sustaining attention to homework. The design has the advantage of demonstrating causality, but in the "real world," the existence of many "causes" together with the possible risks in reestablishing undesired behavior makes this design of less use to social workers. There are times, nevertheless, when the factors that control behavior must be ascertained in this way.

It is frequently desirable to determine what types of events *do* control the client's behavior. This is one of the reasons for the use of a multiple baseline design. When this is employed, the worker identifies two or more behaviors in which change is sought by the clients.

Fischer, in his discussion of this design, states:

> The multiple baseline design also is used to minimize the possibility that behavior changes are due to chance, but does so by either (1) collecting baseline data on more than one target behavior, (2) collecting baseline data on the same target behavior but in more

than one setting, or (3) collecting baseline data on more than one but similar clients. Then intervention techniques are applied and focused either on one of the behaviors or the behavior in one of the settings, or on one of the clients, while continuing to record data on all the behaviors or from all the settings and/or on all the clients. Once the initial target behavior is seen to change, intervention is systematically introduced with the next target behavior or in the next setting.[11]

The worker will not necessarily utilize statistical procedures to identify the probability that changes identified through these designs were due to chance. The fact that changes sought by the client were or were not attained may be enough. On the other hand, there are occasions when the workers may wish to employ such tests when the results appear ambiguous or when the worker plans on presenting the results to colleagues. Fischer, Gottman, and Leiblum; Hersen and Barlow; and Jayaratne are some of the writers who can be consulted further on this.[12]

Control group designs are also employed by practitioners at times, usually when they are involved in research projects, as such. These are the types of designs found in studies in which two or more groups of people are compared when one was exposed to an experience that the other was not; a variation of this is to compare groups that have had different experiences. The groups are presumed to be similar because individuals have been assigned to them by a random process or have been matched on salient characteristics.

The practitioner who uses control group designs must have a sufficient pool of clients to use the randomized or matched approach and must be able to take other precautions to avoid a contamination of the results. For this reason, they are usually employed when the practitioner is involved in a research study on

practice. These designs, nevertheless, have the advantage of enabling the investigator to rule out a number of alternative causes of change beyond the intervention under consideration. The research-oriented practitioner may, however, consider these designs after an intervention has been tested and retested through single-case approaches.

We have made references in this chapter to being able to detemine causality, particularly whether changes in clients or situations or both occur as a result of social work intervention. There are at least three conditions that must be established to assert causality. One is that the event that is hypothesized to be the cause precedes the event that it presumably has caused (A precedes B). This is one of the easiest criterion to determine, as the worker knows when the intervention has occurred as well as changes that were sought if proper monitoring has been in place.

The second criterion is that these two events vary together: that is, when A occurs, so does B; as A increases, B increases commensurately; and vice versa. This type of determination is a more difficult one to make in a rigorous manner as it requires knowledge of statistics that indicate associations between variables.[13] Nevertheless, the practitioner will often use judgment regarding the magnitude of changes or will secure statistical consultation if a more rigorous declaration is required.

The third criterion is that other possible causes are ruled out. This can most easily be achieved when work is done under laboratory conditions. Otherwise, the worker can conduct interviews with the client and relevant others to learn if there were other events that may have caused the change.

As can be seen, single-subject designs are very helpful in determining whether the intervention was likely to have produced the outcome. Through baselining and subsequent measurements, the practitioner can determine the magnitude of changes at different points of time. The careful timing and monitoring of the intervention identifies the time sequences of intervention and change. The monitoring of changes throughout the helping process serves to draw attention to other causal events, although the careful worker will make other efforts to learn of these. The precision of measurement will allow for determinations to be made of the magnitude of changes as related to interventions.

The single "case," it should be remembered, can be groups, families, and organizations as well as individuals. When this is the situation, however, the worker will utilize measures of systems change rather than measures of individual change. For example, the number of affectionate messages in a family, of reinforcing communications in a group, or of ratings of a positive organizational climate can be recorded before and after interventions and analyzed through the single-case approach.

The Measure of Change

The following are some of the approaches currently employed to measure changes in individual clients.[14]

Behavioral Counts. These consist of counting the number of times a client acts in a specified way. Such counts are often maintained by the clients themselves or by others with whom they associate such as parents or spouses. The worker will suggest a chart to the client and will negotiate the time period for recording events. If the event is relatively infrequent, such as the number of days a week clients have sexual intercourse, the period may be the entire time between sessions. Frequent behaviors such as a client's tics may be counted during time segments such as four quarter-hour periods between social work sessions.

Goal Attainment Scaling. This is a way of measuring a client's goal achievement. To do this, a chart is developed in which each column in the chart represents a different client goal. Each row of the chart represents a different level of possible attainment of the goal. Five levels of attainment are generated: "most unfavorable outcome thought likely," "less than expected success," "expected level of success," "more than expected success," and "most favorable outcome thought likely." Kiresuk and Garwick have developed statistical approaches to generate goal attainment scores for clients.[15] Some question has been raised as to the validity of these statistics, yet we believe that this issue does not preclude the use of goal attainment scales to evaluate changes in individual clients. These criticisms are more likely to apply to the uses of the goal attainment scores to compare intervention approaches.

Self-ratings on Emotional States. Difficulties of clients are often expressed in emotional terms: thus, sadness, anxiety, or even lack of pleasure are stated as presenting problems. One way of measuring these is to ask the client to imagine a scale from 0 to 100 on which 0 represents a total absence of the emotion and 100 represents the most intense experience of the emotion.[16] This approach can be used to baseline the emotion, determine the levels of the emotion induced by various experiences,[17] and measure the improvement after intervention.

Value Ratings. As the preceding discussion indicates, workers will sometimes seek ratings of behavioral change, sometimes emotional change, and sometimes movement toward more complex goals. Another dimension that may be evaluated is the client's attitude. For example, a parent may wish to be accepting of new sexual mores governing adolescent behavior, or, in contrast, may even wish to be more comfortable asserting his or her traditional values while permitting a youth to seek a different value system.

Some approaches that have been developed to help people determine their values can also be used for measurement. Simon, Howe, and Kirschenbaum, for example, present a value grid in which individuals rate the following dimensions associated with a value[18]:

1. Are you *proud* of (do you prize or cherish) your position?
2. Have you *publicly affirmed* your position?
3. Have you chosen your position from *alternatives*?
4. Have you chosen your position after *thoughtful consideration* of the pros and cons and consequences?
5. Have you chosen your position *freely*?
6. Have you *acted* on or done anything about your beliefs?
7. Have you acted with *repetition,* pattern, or consistency on this issue?

We have used these items to evaluate changes in value positions by asking the client to respond to each item on a three-point scale as follows: (3) frequently, (2) occasionally, or (1) seldom or never. For some clients, the use of the seven different scales is burdensome, and, in these cases, we have used the items that appeared most appropriate for that client.

Rating Problem-Solving Skills.   Cognitive dimensions also exist in relationship to the client's problems, and one such dimension is whether the client uses logical processes to solve problems. If the worker has taught or helped the client, in some other way, to learn an approach to problem solving, the use of this approach can be measured. The client can tell the worker (or in a group or family, can tell the other members) how he or she approached the problem. A rating scale such as the following can then be used to evaluate problem-solving skills[19]:

1. Has the client sought information relevant to the problem? For example, if the problem is finding a job, has the client found out about the types of jobs most available for persons with his or her training or abilities?
2. Has the client identified the alternatives available to him or her? Do these alternatives include all the most important or relevant ones? Has the individual used the information generated in question 1 to identify alternatives?
3. Has the client evaluated the alternatives using criteria such as the following?
   a. The alternative with the most likelihood of helping the client to achieve his or her goal to the optimum degree
   b. The alternative with the fewest disadvantages or costs
   c. The alternative most consistent with the client's values
4. Has the client chosen the alternative that he or she evaluated most favorably?
5. Has the client developed or begun to develop a plan to implement the alternative?

As written, these questions can be answered with a "yes" or "no," or they can be rated on a zero to five-point scale with a zero representing the absence of the step and five representing its full utilization.

Rating Interpersonal Behaviors.   A major focus of social work practice, as we have seen, is on the interpersonal relationship of clients. It is not surprising, therefore, that social workers have contributed to the measurement of changes in interpersonal behaviors. Thomas, for example, has done extensive work on improving marital communication and has developed scales for measuring this dimension.[20] Rose has worked to improve interpersonal competence of children and adults and presents suitable measurement scales for this.[21] Hudson has also pioneered in the generation of instruments that can be used and scored by social workers, many of which measure interpersonal behaviors such as marital satisfaction, parental attitudes, and child attitudes toward parents. Scales for measuring self-concept and sexual satisfaction have also been developed by the same author.[22]

Evaluation of Family Change. Some family therapists will measure changes in individual members of the family and will employ the standard approaches that are used when one-to-one help is offered. The problem is more acute when investigators seek to measure family-level changes. This is because there are no generally agreed-upon criteria as to what a good outcome is for the family as an entity. Even when specific writers state what *their* criteria of success are, they may not have developed appropriate instruments, or the instruments may not have been well validated.

There are several works, however, that describe the state of knowledge of measurement of family change, notably those of Straus[23] and of Cromwell, Olson, and Fournier.[24] Some of the variables that have been used to evaluate family change are the following:

1. Marriage quality[25]
2. Marital relationship[26]
3. Family interaction[27]
4. Family functioning[28]
5. Communication behaviors[29]

Some of the instruments used to monitor change can also be used to evaluate outcomes. When the worker, for example, is interested in restructuring the family, diagrams of family structure should be used to evaluate progress. Similarly, assessment devices such as the ecomap can be used in the same way when changes in the family's relationship to external systems are sought.[30] When clients are involved in creating their own diagrams, a kind of "face validity" is present when the clients *perceive* that their family situation has changed.

In the model of group work employed in this book, we view the group as a means and a context for helping individuals, and thus, the group is seldom the client system. Workers, therefore, will wish to monitor change in group conditions when they seek these changes to help the individual members. The evaluation of the success of the group work effort, however, will be based upon the degree to which members have achieved their individual goals. This is in contrast to work with the family when, according to our model of practice, it is legitimate to set ultimate goals in terms of changes in family conditions. This does not preclude, however, an assessment of changes in individual family members when these have been sought by the family.

Evaluation of Organizational Change. As we have stated throughout this text, the objective of interpersonal practice is to help clients achieve their goals. At times these goals are to change some organization that has a negative impact upon the client. The evaluation of practice under these circumstances will depend on an assessment of changes in some organizational condition. Examples of this are a client who wished to change a school policy that denied special services to her deaf son, a client who sought to change the fee structure of the service agency, and a client who opposed the educational plan that her child's teacher utilized with the child.

The evaluation of a change in the environment is sometimes self-evident. In all the examples given in the previous paragraph, this was the case. The school policy affecting the deaf son was changed, and this was manifested in the enrollment of the boy in the desired programs; the client who opposed the fee structure was notified in writing of the new fee; and the parent who opposed the educational plan was informed by the teacher at a conference of the new approach she will use.

At other times, however, a more valid and reliable confirmation of a change in organizational conditions is sought. The following are some ways that this can be accomplished.[31]

1. *Documentation*. Most organizations issue a variety of written documents that describe their policies and services. Reports are also regularly issued to their governing bodies and other constituencies. Workers and clients can secure these documents to determine whether the organizational change has occurred. For example, a group of clients visited a legislator to ask his support for legislation to increase the size of the welfare appropriation. They then examined the published proceedings of the legislature to see if the legislator provided the promised support. They also noted the ultimate vote on this budgetary issue.

In some situations, the organization does not provide the desired data, and the clients, themselves, may have to secure this. In one group of parents, a problem that was perceived was that the school was viewed as administering a discipline policy unfairly in that more black children were suspended than white. The members kept a record of the number of complaints leveled against their children and the disposition of the complaints. Since the group was composed of both black and white parents, this gave them

a rough measure of the type of complaints against their children and the punishment that was decreed.

2. *Interviews*. There are two types of occasions when clients and workers may seek to interview staff or administrators of an organization. One is when policies and procedures are of interest but are not embodied in official documents as is often true in small organizations. In these circumstances, the worker or the client will interview the appropriate person in the organization to determine if the desired changes have been achieved.

The other occasion is when the desired change is not of the type that is reflected in official statements. One example of this is the labeling of clients in ways that are detrimental to them. Another is when the problem condition is idiosyncratic to one staff member and is not a matter of agency policy, such as a teacher who gives inappropriate assignments to students. In these cases, the worker or client or both will interview agency personnel to learn if the desired changes have been accomplished.

In the example of harmful labeling, the worker will have to understand how this type of information can be secured. For example, in a mental health center, several staff members viewed homosexuals as "sick" and, on the basis of this, recommended long-term psychotherapy regardless of the presenting problems that brought the clients to the agency. The administrator of the agency received complaints from several homosexual clients and, on the basis of this, instituted a staff training session on homosexuality conducted by several members of a university support system for gay students. Afterward, an effort was made to evaluate change through interviewing staff members as to their assessment and treatment of homosexual clients.

3. *Measurement Scales*. At times, the worker or clients will evaluate changes in an

organization that represent more complex variables than a change in policy, labeling, or behavior toward a client. Examples of these variables are organizational climate, the freedom felt by participants to express their beliefs, and the amount of conflict expressed, the openness of communication among persons, and the tolerance of diversity in the organization. An example of an instrument that can be used to evaluate these conditions is that devised by Moos and his colleagues.[32] This instrument has been used in many organizations and can be presented to different sets of persons such as staff and clients to determine the similarity and differences of perceptions of organizational conditions within and between these groups of people.

Side Effects

An evaluation of change should have two major components: (1) whether the planned intervention accomplished what it set out to do and (2) whether it caused things to happen that were *not* part of the plan. These unanticipated consequences can either be desirable or undesirable. An example of a desirable, but unplanned consequence was work done with a woman to help her to leave a mental hospital. A major component of this work was to change aspects of her marital relationship that were stressful for her and that were associated with her "breakdown." Her behavior as a parent was not focused upon, yet the worker observed in a follow-up that the wife's skills in negotiating with the husband were now also being used by her with her children, and this resulted in a better relationship between mother and children.

An undesirable consequence in another situation was when work was done with a wife to help her reduce her periods of severe depression. While this work was successful,

her marriage terminated. A later interview with the husband suggested that he wanted to be more adequate than his wife, and her improved functioning created a great deal of anxiety in him. While he desired an end to the marriage, his wife did not.

The worker should be aware, therefore, of the effects of intervention that are not anticipated, particularly those that may be viewed by the client or others as undesirable. These "side effects," as they are called in medicine, can be avoided under some circumstances, and in others, at least anticipated. Perhaps research will eventually help practitioners to know which side effects are most likely to occur with which interventions. At present, however, we can list major categories of side effects.

One set of side effects directly affects the client. This includes the following:

1. *The client improves in regard to some behaviors but deteriorates in regard to others.* In one case, a client became more assertive toward her employer but afterward had bouts of anxiety; in another, the client began to work on problems that she previously had denied but became so dependent on her social worker that she felt she had to consult her before making major decisions.

The worker should understand that these types of difficulties can often be predicted. A treatment situation that can create anxiety for the client sometimes requires changed behaviors that are unacceptable to others. Another requires testing out new ways of coping with situations, yet the client risks a great chance of failure. Revealing one's problems in front of others can also produce anxiety, even when the "other" is a social worker. A client may also become anxious when discussion of a problem forces the client to confront material about himself or herself that the client has not been aware of or that the client has "repressed." Whenever these events are likely to occur, the worker will watch for the occurrence of client anxiety and will be prepared to help with it.

An increase in client dependency can occur in interpersonal helping under several circumstances. Clients will often feel vulnerable because of the problems that brought them to the agency. Work on problems can increase this sense of vulnerability. Under these circumstances, the client may revert to a form of coping with this feeling that was used earlier in life, namely, to turn to a more powerful figure (such as a worker) for help. In addition, the emergence of the kinds of anxiety we noted may also cause the client to become dependent on the worker as a way of warding off this anxiety.

Other kinds of deterioration of behavior can also occur as a result of helping. The worker's attention to some client problems may cause the client to maintain, rather than to change, problems as a way of retaining the worker's attention. The client may also generate problems as a way of avoiding the termination of the worker-client relationship. Later (in Chapter 14), we shall discuss means of dealing with these issues.

The reader should recognize that there are many reasons why the client might suffer negative outcomes in addition to the association of some negative outcomes with positive ones. Stuart has reviewed the range of events that can occur to produce negative outcomes for clients, which he calls *iatrogenic illness*, a term used in medicine to denote an illness that was created as a result of treatment.[33] Stuart deals with negative outcomes that result from psychiatric hospitalization, diagnosis, labeling, and psychotherapy itself.

2. *The client improves in regard to the targeted behaviors but then suffers from the reactions of others to this change.* This is a phenomenon that is predicted by a systems approach to practice, which sees behavior of an individual as contributing to the maintenance of some system. One example of this is the treatment of a wife whose phobic behavior was a fear of going outdoors. When this behavior was changed, her husband became anxious about what would happen to her, and he sought to prevent her from leaving the house. Another example is a child who had a heart condition and who refrained from social activities with other children to a greater degree than that required by the disability. When the child was helped to plan an appropriate activity schedule, the parent became overprotective of the child.

The implication of such responses of others is that they must be anticipated or at least monitored. The worker should identify those persons who will be affected by changes in the client and should discuss with the client how they are likely to respond to such changes. At least the client should be helped to cope with his or her reactions. Often the most desirable plan is to involve these other people in the helping process, either together with or separately from the client as the situation requires.

3. Another set of side effects are the *client changes that affect other people, even when these others do not retaliate.* We believe to a reasonable degree the social worker has a responsibility for the effects of his or her work with the client on others. Obviously there are limits to this responsibility because in at least a theoretical sense a change in the client may be like a stone thrown into a pond that produces ever-widening ripples. What we have in mind here are serious or immediate effects on those closest to the client. An adult daughter, for example, was helped to see her duty to herself to lead her own life and to move away from her widowed mother. The mother did not resist this move as she understood her daughter's wish to become

more independent. Nevertheless, the mother was very lonely and was likely to become depressed when the move occurred. The worker anticipated this "side effect" and offered services to the mother.

The worker, therefore, should think about the consequences of client changes on other people who interact frequently with the client and should discuss these with the client. In cooperation with the client, decisions can be made as to the likelihood these people may need social work or other services and what the worker's and the client's responsibilities may be to facilitate obtaining services for such people.

Earlier in this chapter, we described the worker's tasks, and their sequence, in relationship to monitoring and evaluation. We shall now present a case example of the accomplishment of these tasks.

Case Example

John W came to the counseling office of his university because of his loneliness and lack of friends. When he told this to the social worker to whom he was assigned, the worker helped him to be more specific by asking him to tell about his current relationships and his feelings about them. John indicated that he had phoned four people during the previous week to arrange to meet to do something together; all except one person had "made excuses" and that individual had phoned later to cancel the date.

The worker asked John to complete a questionnaire, the Index of Peer Relations (IPR). This instrument is included in Hudson's "Measurement Package for Clinical Workers,"[34] and consists of 25 items rated on a five-point scale. These items refer to experiences with and attitudes toward peers. A few examples of these items are the following:

8. My peers seem to like me very much.
9. My peers seem to look up to me.

On this instrument John received a score of 85 out of a possible 100, in which the higher the score, the greater the extent of peer relationship problems.

The worker discussed with John that it was important that he answer the questions thoughtfully and honestly so that the instrument would be helpful to him. The worker also indicated he would go over the results with John. John proceeded to complete the questionnaire, after which the worker scored it and discussed the score with John. The worker also did an assessment of John and his situation in the ways described in Chapter 6. (We shall not present this information here as it does not immediately bear upon our discussion of monitoring and evaluation.) At this point, the worker indicated tht he and John should evaluate their work as it proceeded. This would require John to complete the questionnaire every two weeks. The worker also explained that if their work together was successful, the scores should go down. If this did not happen, they should discuss whether alternative approaches or even John seeing another worker should occur.

The worker used John's responses on the questionnaire as well as the other information he obtained as the basis for a discussion of the goals for their work together. As a result of this discussion, the following long-term goals were agreed upon:

1. John will be successful in making "dates" with friends at least two nights a week.
2. John will discontinue comments that he makes that are disparaging of peers and instead will make complimentary comments to them.
3. John will feel less anxiety when peers communicate feelings of closeness to him.
4. John will score 40 on the IPR.

A number of short-term goals were also discussed. One, for example, was that John would negotiate a mutually attractive activity when arranging a date.

The worker determined several types of interventions to attain the long-term goals. For (1), the worker decided to use a role-playing technique that involved behavioral rehearsal and role reversal. For (3), the worker decided to use a relaxation procedure. The use of these procedures was to be monitored by a log kept by the worker that incorporated feedback responses on these procedures secured from John at the end of the sessions in which they were employed.

The worker was concerned about side effects. One stemmed from the fact that John's mother, a widow, was very dependent on John. She succeeded, at times, in keeping him from friends by her criticism of them. The worker thought that she might resent the changes in John and that she would increase her demands upon him. The worker during the early part of the helping process continued to ask John questions about his mother's reactions. These did, in fact, become problematic, and the worker was successful in meeting with the two of them and referring the mother to another agency to consider other ways of meeting her own needs.

The worker and John met together on a weekly basis for five months. While the worker did employ several instruments, in addition to the IPR to monitor progress, that questionnaire was the one the worker used to measure overall progress in the area of peer relations in evaluation discussions with John. The graph in Figure 10-1 shows John's scores on this instrument over the period. The period during the sixth to eight week, when the score went up again, was the period in which John's mother was creating the most difficulty. Another rise at the fourteenth week appeared to be associated with the fact that John felt more confident socially at that time and made a number of calls to peers. One of

these was received very negatively, and John went through a period of discouragement about that.

Summary

In this chapter, we have stressed the idea that an evaluative plan must be generated at the beginning of the social work process rather than its ending so that clients and workers alike know how service will be evaluated and collect information throughout the process to produce a valid assessment of it. Two interrelated procedures were described: monitoring and evaluation. Monitoring consists of those activities that provide information on the actions of the worker, the client, and other relevant systems. Under this heading we described process records, recording by code, and electronic recording. We also discussed how to monitor changes in group conditions.

Under the heading of evaluation, we discussed possible designs of evaluation that also incorporate monitoring such as the "single-case" designs. Ways of measuring changes were enumerated such as behavioral counts, goal attainment scaling, and ratings of emotional states, attitudes, problem-

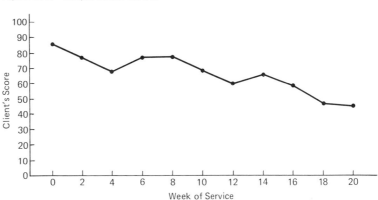

Figure 10-1. Sample Scores on IPR

solving skills, and interpersonal behaviors. A separate section was devoted to the evaluation of organizational changes sought by interpersonal practitioners and their clients.

An important topic that was also discussed was "side effects" because interpersonal change processes may produce effects on the client and significant others that are undesirable. To the extent that side effects are predictable, plans should be made to cope with them, or, at the least, the client should be warned that they are possible. At times, the worker may also seek to offer help to people who may be affected by procedures used with, or changes effected in, clients.

NOTES

1. The authors wish to express their appreciation to Tony Tripodi whose comments on an earlier version of this chapter were very valuable in its revision.

2. See, for example, Tony Tripodi and Irwin Epstein, *Research Techniques for Clinical Social Workers* (New York: Columbia University Press, 1980), and Srinika Jayaratne and Rona L. Levy, *Empirical Clinical Practice* (New York: Columbia University Press, 1979).

3. See James R. Seaburg, "Case Recording by Code," *Social Work*, Vol. 10 (October 1965), pp. 92–98; also, see "Seattle Atlantic Street Center Recording Form and Coded Recording Manual," in *Effectiveness of Social Work with Acting-out Youth: Third Year Progress Report: September 1964 to August 1965* (Seattle: Seattle Atlantic Street Center, 1965), mimeographed.

4. Joel Fischer, *Effective Casework Practice* (New York: McGraw-Hill, 1978), pp. 120–124.

5. Charles Garvin, *Contemporary Group Work* (Englewood Cliffs, N.J.: Prentice-Hall, 1981), p. 139.

6. This device was developed by Sheldon Rose; see his *Group Therapy: A Behavioral Approach* (Englewood Cliffs, N.J.: Prentice-Hall, 1977), pp. 138–140.

7. Garvin, *Contemporary Group Work*, p. 139.

8. John M. Gottman and Sandra R. Lieblum, *How to Do Psychotherapy and How to Evaluate It* (New York: Holt, Rinehart and Winston, 1974), p. 138.

9. See Srinika Jayaratne and Rona L. Levy, *Empirical Clinical Practice* (New York: Columbia University Press, 1979), pp. 114–223, for an extensive discussion of the use of these designs as well as the strengths and weaknesses of each one.

10. Ibid., pp. 95–113.

11. Fischer, *Effective Casework Practice*, p. 98.

12. Ibid., pp. 100–103; Gottman and Leiblum, *How to Do Psychotherapy*, pp. 141–150; M. Hersen and D. H. Barlow, *Single Case Experimental Designs* (Elmsford, N.Y.: Pergamon Press, 1976), Chap. 8; and S. Jayaratne, "Analytic Procedures for Single Subject Designs," *Social Work Research and Abstracts*, Vol. 14 (Fall 1978), pp. 30–40.

13. See Michael S. Kolevzon, "Bivariate Analysis: Correlation," in Richard M. Grinnell, Jr., ed., *Social Work Research and Evaluation* (Itasca, Ill.: F. E. Peacock, 1981), pp. 481–499.

14. This section draws heavily on Garvin, *Contemporary Group Work*, pp. 190–195.

15. Thomas Kiresuk and Geoffrey Garwick, "Basic Goal Attainment Procedures," in Beulah Roberts Compton and Burt Galaway, eds., *Social Work Processes*, 2nd ed. (Homewood, Ill.: The Dorsey Press, 1979), pp. 412–421.

16. See T. M. Sherman and W. H. Cormier, "The Use of Subjective Scales for Measuring Interpersonal Reactions," *Journal of Behavior Therapy and Experimental Psychiatry*, Vol. 3 (1972), pp. 279–280.

17. The determination of levels of anxiety, for example, induced by various situations is a central procedure in the behavioral treatment known as systematic desensitization. For an application of this, see R. P. Liberman and V. Smith, "A Multiple Baseline Study of Systematic Desensitization in a Patient with Multiple Phobias," *Behavior Therapy*, Vol. 3 (1972), pp. 597–603.

18. Sidney B. Simon, Leland W. Howe, and Howard Kirschenbaum, *Values Clarification: A Handbook of Practical Strategies for Studies and Teachers* (New York: Hart 1972), p. 35.

19. Garvin, *Contemporary Group Work*, p. 194.

20. Edwin Thomas, *Marital Communication and Decision-making: Analysis, Assessment, and Change* (New York: The Free Press, 1977).

21. S. D. Rose, J. Gayner, and J. L. Edleson, "Measuring Interpersonal Competence," *Social Work*, Vol. 22 (1977), pp. 125–129.

22. These scales are available in Fischer, *Effective Casework Practice*, pp. 110–115.

23. Murray Straus, *Family Measurement Techniques* (Minneapolis: University of Minnesota Press, 1969).

24. R. Cromwell, D. Olson, and D. Fournier, "Diagnosis and Evaluation in Marital and Family Counseling," in D. H. Olson, ed., *Treating Relationships* (Lake Mills, Ia.: Graphic, 1976).

25. G. R. Reding, L. A. Charles, and M. B. Hoffman, "Treatment of the Couple by a Couple: Conceptual Framework, Case Presentation, and Follow-up Study," *British Journal of Medical Psychology*, Vol. 40 (1967), pp. 243–251.

26. David Fanshel, *An Overview of One Agency's Casework Operations* (Pittsburgh: Family and Children's Service, 1958).

27. R. Postner et al., "Process and Outcome in Conjoint Family Therapy," *Family Process*, Vol. 19 (1971), pp. 451–473.

28. Murray Bowen, "The Family as the Unit of Study and Treatment," *American Journal of Orthopsychiatry*, Vol. 31 (1961), pp. 40–60.

29. D. A. Cadogan, "Marital Group Therapy in the Treatment of Alcoholism," *Quarterly Journal of Studies on Alcoholism*, Vol. 34 (1973), pp. 1187–1194; and N. S. Mayadas and W. D. Duehn, "Stimulus-Modeling Videotape for Marital Counseling: Method and Application," *Journal of Marriage and Family Counseling*, Vol. 3 (1977), pp. 35–42.

30. See Chapter 7 for a discussion of the ecomap.

31. This discussion draws from Garvin, *Contemporary Group Work*, pp. 199–201.

32. Rudolf Moos, *Evaluating Treatment Environments: A Social Ecological Approach* (New York: John Wiley, 1974).

33. Richard B. Stuart, *Trick or Treatment: How and When Psychotherapy Fails* (Champaign, Ill.: Research Press, 1970).

34. Walter W. Hudson, "A Measurement Package for Clinical Workers," paper presented at the Council on Social Work Education, 23rd Annual Program Meeting, Phoenix, Arizona, March 1, 1977.

eleven

The Change Process

APPLICATIONS WITH INDIVIDUALS

This chapter is the first of three devoted to how workers help to bring about change. As the previous chapters indicate, our approach is both goal oriented and systemic. We have described our goal orientation as emphasizing that the worker and client should strive for a clear idea as to the ends to be sought through the change effort. As the change process occurs, however, and as other events unfold, the goal is often renegotiated.

Our systemic orientation provides an awareness that individuals and systems are constantly in interaction and that it is almost impossible to change one without the other. We do recognize, nevertheless, that at times, the worker and client focus on changes in the individual client and at other times on those in the family, group, or larger environment—even though the former and latter are inseparable. We, consequently, devote this chapter to ways of facilitating individual change and subsequent chapters to ways of facilitating change in other systems. Ultimately the worker must integrate these proc-

esses in ways that are appropriate to each practice situation.

There is an additional difference in how we present material on individual, family, group, and environmental change. As we also indicated earlier, our model of interpersonal practice views the individual and family and sometimes the natural group, such as a residential treatment cottage, as *client systems* and other groups and organizatons as *target systems* in which change is sought as a means of attaining family or individual change or both. This chapter is unique in that its subject matter, the individual, is both the entity on whose behalf change is sought as well as the entity *in which* it is sought. This has ethical and procedural implications that we shall refer to at various points in our discussion.

Since we focus in this chapter on the individual as both client and target, it is also important to remind the reader that change in the individual is part of a process that begins with the way in which the individual and social worker make contact, begin to work together, specify problems and goals, assess the client and the situation, choose targets of change, form action systems, pursue changes, and measure them. All these steps are inextricably interwoven through a continuous process that can change direction a number of times before service is terminated. While we focus here on how change is to be attained, this represents something of an artificial separation from those other stages of the process. Even with such a separation, however, the worker should always strive to maintain a logical correspondence between phases. For example, an intervention should make "sense" in terms of the assessment and should flow from it.

Background

Although the early writers on social work practice recognized the value of interventions in family and group situations on behalf of individual clients, an individual focus in social work practice was (and is) strong, and approaches to work with individuals have always been a central topic in social work writing and teaching. (This may be both the strength and the failing of the profession.) A glimpse of the history of social work with individuals, therefore, will help the reader to place this practice into a broader perspective. We shall focus here only on the background of work with individuals; the background of work with families and groups is presented in the following chapter.

One-to-one social work emerged out of the activities of a group of people, mostly volunteers, who served in agencies established to aid the poor. The most influential of these agencies in the development of casework were the Charity Organization Societies (referred to hereafter as the COS). This type of service began in London in 1869 and in the United States in 1877. In the early part of this century, these workers came to be known as social caseworkers as their work became more systematized and as paid workers replaced volunteers. It was not long before the methods practiced by the COS workers were also being used by practitioners in hospitals, child welfare agencies, psychiatric facilities, schools, and correctional programs.

As casework spread to a variety of settings, workers sought an intellectual foundation and discovered it through a close association with people in the psychiatric and mental health fields. While all casework was not psychiatric, for many years of practice, this aspect had more prestige than the others. This was associated with the strong impact that psychoanalytic theory had upon casework. As Briar states,

> By 1930 when Virginia Robinson published *A Changing Psychology in Social Casework*, the psychiatric perspective had become central to the training of caseworkers in many schools of social work. Consequently Robinson could confidently proclaim a new era in casework, one in which the important reality is psychic, the caseworker is a psychotherapist, and his primary tool is the therapeutic relationship.[1]

For several decades following Robinson's 1924 statement, the psychiatric perspective dominated social casework. This was strengthened in the 1929 report of the Milford Conference, which concluded that casework as practiced in different settings drew from a common base. Nevertheless, during this early period there was a theoretical division between the diagnostic and functional approaches, the former drawing on Freud's thinking and the latter on Rank's.

By the 1950s, however, social science

began to have a greater impact on casework as social scientists, particularly sociologists, took more interest in mental health and mental health services. This contribution was enhanced when the Russell Sage Foundation supported several projects at universities to introduce social science into social work education. Helen Perlman, in her important paper "Putting the 'Social' Back in Social Casework,"[2] provides a good example of this kind of development. Her later book, *Persona*, is a further demonstration of the usefulness to social casework of social science ideas, in this instance role theory.[3]

The decade of the 1960s was characterized by many attacks on social casework because of its psychological emphasis, its lack of development of approaches directed at serving the needs of poor people, and its presumed lack of effectiveness. Among the developments that can be considered responses to these charges were (1) the introduction of approaches emphasizing research evidence of effectiveness such as behavior modification and task-centered practice, (2) a new emphasis on ways of intervening in the environment to fulfill such roles as advocate and broker, and (3) a movement of social caseworkers into working also with families and groups.

Models of Practice

So many writers have presented their ideas about social casework that it would take many pages to analyze similarities and differences among them. For a comprehensive analysis, the reader is referred to Simon's comparison of casework approaches presented at a conference on models of social casework.[4] For our purpose—to present the reader with some idea of the range of thinking in social casework—we shall comment on the following: psychosocial, functional, problem-solving, task-centered, behavioral, and competency-based ecological approaches.

Psychosocial. This, along with the functional approach, clearly has the longest history in that its ideas were enunciated by such writers as Gordon Hamilton in the 1930s.[5] Florence Hollis has done a great deal in recent years to expand on and update this approach as well as to stimulate research on its processes and outcomes.[6] Psychosocial casework has drawn heavily from psychoanalytic theory and ego psychology. While recent writings of Hollis and others have incorporated systems and famiy concepts to portray the individual-in-situation, the techniques of this approach clearly reflect its psychoanalytic origins.

These techniques include assessment procedures to be used in early interviews that incorporate a comprehensive inquiry into aspects of person and situation that go beyond the initial statement of the problem by the client. Treatment considerations include a considerable emphasis on understanding and modifying the client-worker relationship. Hollis has developed a typology of the treatment process that has been well tested for reliability. The typology consists of supportive measures (sustainments): direct influence, exploration–description–ventilation, and several types of reflection. Reflection is a significant part of the work with clients and includes three levels: one focuses on the person and his or her current situation, another focuses on patterns of reactions that are recurrent, and the third focuses on patterns that have emerged in relationship to the client's development. Hollis's recent writings have sought to attain a similar level of specificity regarding the worker's attention to the client's environment.

As can be seen from this brief discussion, Hollis and other psychosocially oriented workers are mindful of client-environment interactions. They seek to enhance the ways in which the client copes with that environment through enhancing the client's self-understanding and through a close attention to the client's feelings in attaining that understanding.

Functional.   We do not think it likely that "functional" casework is taught or practiced in as distinct a form as was the case a few decades ago when it was the main orientation of the School of Social Work at the University of Pennsylvania. Nevertheless, it has represented a significant proportion of casework thinking and is invariably included in lists of casework approaches. If it is not currently as separate a model, it is because some of its important ideas, such as the impact of agency function, and the way in which time is used in the helping process, and its views of that process itself, have largely been incorporated in much of social work thought.

Another reason, perhaps, for the lesser role of functional approach is that it was derived from the teachings of Otto Rank who was an early associate of Freud's but broke with him over ideological differences. As is well known, the teachings of Freud, at least to date, have been much more widely disseminated than have those of Rank. One of Rank's key concepts was that of the "will," and his use of this term was meant to counter what he thought was a strong deterministic thrust in Freud's thinking. It is interesting that such writers as Yalom who have sought to develop an existential approach to psychotherapy have returned to Rank's ideas to understand better how to enhance the autonomy and self-direction of the client.[7]

Some of the central ideas of the functional approach as shown in the writings of Taft and Robinson, who sought to apply Rank's teachings to social work, are the following[8]: the worker must have a clear understanding of agency purpose, as an essential skill is to help the client to make use of the agency purpose to accomplish his or her purpose; the function and process of the social work situation will result in structure, and the worker will make a conscious use of this; and all social work processes require the use of relationship "to engage the other in making and acting on choices and decisions."[9]

In our opinion the functional approach anticipated a number of developments. These include the incorporation of systems ideas, an understanding of the effect of the agency, and the use of short-term contracts. Perhaps the value of functional concepts, as such, today is to give philosophical meaning to what have now become empirically validated procedures.

Problem Solving.   Perlman, the major contributor to the early development of the problem-solving approach, began this work in the 1950s. She saw it as having roots in psychodynamic theory but also incorporating ego psychology, the psychology of learning, and concepts from the functional approach. In addition she sought to incorporate social psychological concepts, particularly role theory, to enhance our understanding of human development.

As the title of the approach implies, it presents casework as a problem-solving process. This focus has been adopted for several reasons. One is that human adaptation itself is seen as a problem-solving process. Such problem solving is, in psychodynamic terms, a function of the ego as it is affected by other aspects of personality as well as the social situation. Second, the people who come for casework services are likely to be those whose problem-solving capacities or resources have broken down.

The techniques of the problem-solving

approach are directed at the client's motivation for problem solving, his or her capacity for such work, and the opportunities provided by the service agency as well as the broader environment for assistance and support for problem solving.

Because of its emphasis on problem solving, this approach is likely to be more focused than the psychosocial one and in this respect has some similarities to the functional stance. The client's problem serves as the basis of the worker's assessment, and while the worker seeks to understand the person and situation, these are examined in the light of the problem. The client is encouraged to select a problem area(s) and to focus on and cope with it. The client may, through this process, become strengthened in his or her problem-solving capacities and, therefore, better equipped to cope with future events.

Perlman in her writings on treatment, in the light of the focus on problem solving, has a great deal to say about the worker-client relationship and how it can enhance the process. She also sees the basic procedures of treatment as similar among the various approaches, such as clarifying perceptions, creating an understanding of the problem, and strengthening the linkages between the client and significant others "through whom he can find greater fulfillment."[10]

Because of her emphasis on reality factors, concrete problems, and enhancing relationships, Perlman's ideas have had wide circulation in social work as these are central social work concerns. The specificity of her model and its eclecticism have enabled workers trained in it to incorporate new technological developments. For example, Reid and Epstein, the creators of the task-centered approach, to which we now turn, were colleagues of Perlman at the University of Chicago, and they acknowledge their debt to her problem-solving ideas.

Task Centered.   Reid and Epstein, the creators of the task-centered approach, developed it out of Reid and Shyne's earlier research on short-term work as well as the ideas of people like Elliot Studt who saw task accomplishment as an essential process in human coping endeavors.[11] Their work is quite recent: the first book on the approach appeared in 1972. There was a clear linkage, as we have stated, to Perlman's work because the process of choosing and accomplishing tasks was seen as one way of solving problems. What Reid and Epstein did was to develop a well-specified set of procedures to be used in an orderly fashion to accomplish this. Unlike some of the other approaches, Reid and Epstein sought to specify the approach and its outcome concretely so that the effectiveness of the approach could be scientifically demonstrated. In this respect, their work has some affinity for behavioral methods.

The task-centered approach begins with a careful specification of the problem for which the client wants help. A strong ethical stance is taken regarding the client's autonomy in selecting the problem. Because of the empirical emphasis of this approach, the authors provide a problem typology so that outcomes and techniques can be linked to types of problems.

After the problem is specified, the worker helps the client to identify goals that he or she will seek to attain through accomplishing the tasks selected. These goals serve as the basis, consequently, for the choice of such tasks. A task is simply "what the client is to do."[12] Both the client and the practitioner have tasks, and the latter has "commitments to clients for actions to be taken on their behalf."[13] At the time that these decisions are made, the worker and client also contract for time limits, which normally include 8 to 12 sessions over a two- to three-month period. (Later in this chapter, we provide more details on tasks as one of the major vehicles for individual change.)

Reid, Epstein, and colleagues in many countries have developed details as to how these processes are to be accomplished as well as monitored. Outcome measures have also been created, and this approach is clearly related to empirical considerations.

Behavioral.   The introduction of behavioral approaches into social work practice preceded the task-centered approach by a few years. The first comprehensive treatment of this subject in a social work journal was Thomas's 1968 article "Selected Socio-behavioral Techniques and Principles: An Approach to Interpersonal Helping."[14]

This diffusion into social work, however, occurred much later than it did into such fields as clinical psychology where texts and journals devoted to behavior therapy had already been in existence for more than a decade. The influence of behavioral ideas on social work has continued to grow, and this has been true for all the human service professions. Thus, most social workers and social work students are now taught basic behavioral concepts.

Fischer, in introducing these concepts in a recent text, defined behavior modification as follows:

> In essence, behavior modification can be defined as the planned, systematic application of experimentally established principles of learning to the modification of maladaptive behavior, specifically to decreasing undesired behaviors and increasing desired behaviors. Moreover, the behavioral approach is a parsimonious one. Most of its procedures are derived from only three basic perspectives on human learning—the fields of operant learning, respondent learning, and imitative learning (modeling).[15]

The reader is encouraged to consult any of the numerous books on behavior modification for a detailed explanation of behavioral theory.[16] While we do not expand on this to any great extent here, we shall define the three perspectives to which Fischer refers. We shall also describe a number of procedures for individual change later in this chapter that stem from behavior modification as well as from the other approaches we have enumerated.

The field of operant learning stems from the finding that behavior occurs in relationship to existing circumstances (antecedents) and will be more or less likely to reoccur as a result of the consequences that follow the behavior. Thus, behavioral assessment lies in identifying antecedents and consequences, and behavioral change lies in modifying them. We shall discuss this approach in more detail later in the chapter in reference to the topic of reinforcement.

The field of respondent learning stems from another finding that when behavior occurs involuntarily as a result of some stimulus (for example, a fear reaction results from a frightening object), other stimuli can become associated with the initial stimulus. Such other stimuli are then capable of eliciting the same reaction. Thus, a person who is in the room at the time of a frightening event may cause other persons present to become frightened in the future when they see that person and associate him or her with the fright.

The field of imitative learning evolved from the observation that under specifiable circumstances, people are likely to imitate the behavior they observe in others. These circumstances include, for example, occasions when the person imitated is rewarded for the behavior. Imitation is another basic individual change process to be discussed later in this chapter.

The introduction of behavioral approaches into social work has occurred, we believe, because behavioral techniques have been demonstrated in many cases to be highly effective; they are specific; and their use is often less expensive in time and effort than traditional approaches. As with any other innovation, behavior modification was met both with considerable enthusiasm on the part of some and hostility on the part of others. We believe that as social workers gain experience with behavioral procedures, they will select many of them for a firm place in their practice repertoire. The requirement that any procedure be in conformity with social work values and roles is, of course, a given.

Competency-Based Ecological.   As we have indicated throughout this book, one of the oldest ideas in social work, and one that is still central to the profession, is that social work practice is aimed at enhancing the way in which people interact with their environments to meet their needs. Recent knowledge developments have led to a model of practice that reaffirms this traditional commitment while bringing it new perspectives and techniques. These knowledge developments relate to how people develop competence in coping with or changing their environments and how workers can facilitate the development of competence in people while working to create environments that are supportive of this effort. A competency-based ecological model, therefore, emphasizes the idea of competence in dealing with environmental demands and opportunities.

Anthony Maluccio, one of the leading contributors to the development of this model, describes ecological competence as including capacities and skills, motivational aspects, and environmental qualities.[17] He indicates that these capacities and skills include how one acts in interpersonal situations as well as aspects of one's cognitions and per-ceptions. Motivational aspects relate to one's interests and aspirations; environmental qualities include social networks and other environment resources for establishing competence.

Maluccio states that assessment should be directed at these dimensions of ecological competence and that the social work process should be used to enhance them. A related philosophy of practice defines the client as a resource and partner rather than as a "carrier of pathology." The worker is an enabler rather than a therapist and uses feedback from the client to maintain the partnership quality of the work. In most ways this model is highly compatible with the one we present, and we believe that the procedures we describe later in this chapter can be employed to increase client competencies. Our idea of enhancing individual functioning through one-to-one, group, and environmental action systems is also compatible with this ecological concept.

Procedures

This information provides the context for our discussion of the procedures that workers use to help individuals to change. The approaches that we have described offer their adherents a rationale for the selection of specific procedures and, at times, their sequence. Approaches overlap in their use of procedures but may employ them for different reasons, in different sequences, or with different styles of presentation. Thus, a procedure, such as training the client to perform some action, or giving the client advice, or reinforcing the client's behavior, may be utilized by practitioners who adhere to different sets of practice ideas.

While our model of practice offers broad guidelines as to how to conceptualize interpersonal helping, it is eclectic in the choice of procedures. We believe that in many practice situations, there are several procedures that can be used to attain a similar outcome. For this reason, we shall devote much of this chapter to a description of such procedures. To help the worker to select from among this array of interventions, we have employed two ways of categorizing them. The first set of categories, one that will constitute major subject headings of the chapter, is the *action systems* the worker interacts with when promoting *individual change*. These consist of (1) the individual himself or herself, (2) a small group (including the family), or (3) some aspect of the environment outside of the group or family.

The second set of categories describes the *aspects* of *human functioning* at which the intervention is directed. These aspects are the individual's *cognitions, affects,* and *behaviors.* Various approaches to interpersonal helping emphasize one or another of these aspects, and none adheres to one aspect exclusively. It is also likely, in our opinion, that an effective helping process must involve all three. We thus agree with Garfield, who states that:

> [O]ur therapeutic procedures in many respects may be less efficient, and less successful than they might be if we were to enlarge our understanding of the variables that are important in the therapeutic process and develop our procedures accordingly. In order to accomplish this goal, we shall eventually have to give up our segmental and partisan approaches to psychotherapy, and to recognize clearly that progress can only be made if we give proper attention to the totality of human functioning. Man and woman are organisms in which cognitions, emotions, and behaviors are interrelated and integrated aspects of their being and, although particular aspects may be pronounced in certain types of psychopathology, an effective approach to psychotherapy has to be aware of this interrelationship and be able to utilize this

awareness constructively . . . in the final analysis, psychotherapy is best viewed as a complex cognitive, affective, and behavioral learning process.[18]

As Garfield indicates, cognitive, affective, and behavioral functioning must be enhanced to help people to cope with their problems; nevertheless, specific procedures may be directed more at one of these dimensions than another, and we have used this as the basis of the second way of categorizing such procedures. Thus, for example, teaching a client a problem-solving process is a procedure in which the individual is the action system and the procedure is directed at that individual's cognitions. Assigning a group member a role to play in a group exercise is a procedure used when the group is the action system and the procedure is directed at the member's behavior. Advising a teacher to provide a different kind of reinforcement for a student (when the student is the client) is a procedure used when the teacher is the action system and the procedure is also directed at the client's behavior. We shall now proceed to use these categories to describe a variety of procedures to attain individual change.

Procedures Used When the Individual Client is the Action System

Procedures That Emphasize Client Cognitions

In this section, we shall describe a set of procedures used primarily to affect the client's cognitions, that is, the clients' views of themselves and their significant others. The procedures to be discussed are those to enhance the client's sense of self-worth, ability to problem solve, awareness of aspects of self and others, and ideas about causality. These procedures obviously also affect behaviors and feelings but do this with a primary emphasis on cognitions.

Enhancing a Sense of Self-worth. As Eisenberg and Delaney state, "People who like and respect themselves are more likely to relate well to others, to develop deep versus superficial relationships, to set attainable goals, to have well-developed ideas for achieving the goals they set, and to make decisions that are in the best interests of both self and others."[19] Workers encounter many situations in which the client has failed to attain his or her goals because of such a lack of self-respect: one client, for example, may fail to initiate a friendship because he believes that he is not likable; another may do poorly at work because she falsely believes that all other employees are superior to her.

Rational-emotive therapy offers one of the most effective systems for enhancing a sense of self-worth.[20] The basic idea behind this system is to help the client to recognize the negative idea behind self-destructive behavior and to replace it with its converse. Some of the negative ideas that are frequently found are that one must be loved by everyone, it is easier to avoid responsibilities than to face them, one must be thoroughly competent to achieve, and one has no control over one's emotions.

Ellis and Harper have developed a series of specific steps for the worker to use in modifying such self-defeating statements.[21] The first step is for the worker to explain to the client the rationale for the use of the approach. The importance of self-statements is stressed, and examples of them are given. The second stage involves educating the client about the kinds of irrational statements that interfere with goal attainment, such as the examples given.

After this introductory period, the client's problems are analyzed in rational-emotive terms. The worker contributes his or her awareness of the explicit or implicit self-statements that hinder the client, and the client is helped to do the same. Finally, and most important, the client is taught to modify such statements. The client and the worker engage in logical discussion of these alternatives, and the client may be helped to visualize them in the actual anxiety-provoking situation.

In addition to such explicit procedures as those developed by Ellis, the worker should make statements in each session to enhance the client's self-concept such as those that show respect for the client, that confirm the client as a person of worth, and that state the belief that the client is capable of further development of his or her capacities. Without these, any procedure that targets self-concept would be a hollow gesture.

Enhancing Problem Solving and Decision Making. A major part of the time in one-to-one sessions with clients is spent on solving problems and making decisions. An approach to practice that emphasizes client autonomy must support the client's own problem-solving efforts as this runs counter to the client either engaging in impulsive actions or becoming overly dependent on decisions made by others.

Writers on problem solving and decision making recommend the following steps. These serve as guidelines to the worker and also can be taught to clients.

1. *The problem is specified in detail.* This specification includes the amount of discomfort felt about the problem, how severe the problem is, how frequently the problem is experienced, and in how many situations it occurs. These details prepare the worker and the client for the next phase of the process in

which goals in relationship to the problem are generated.

2. *Goals to be attained through problem solution are specified*. For many clients this step may be a difficult one. This is because some clients do not know what they are capable of attaining, they may not be sure of environmental opportunities, and they may be unclear as to what they "really" want. Thus, for example, one client started with the problem of being very lonely. His description of the problem provided information that he did not "share" personal information with friends, he rarely had dates with women, and he spent most of the time in solitary activity when he was not working. He worked during a number of sessions to determine what his desires were regarding heterosexual contacts as well as whether he wanted a different type of life-style. He ultimately decided that he did seek heterosexual marriage as a long-term goal and weekly dates with a woman as a short-term one.

3. *Information is then sought to help the client generate possible solutions*. This includes information about aspects of the client's personality as well as situations that relate to the viability of one solution as opposed to another. This examination of and reflection upon person and situation also helps to uncover potential solutions. Sometimes this process includes "brainstorming" in which ideas are generated on the premise that none will be rejected until a sufficient number has been developed.

4. *Alternative solutions are evaluated*. The c) teria that are used for evaluation include the benefits for the client, the costs to the client, and how the alternative relates to the client's values as well as those of significant others. The consequences that will occur if each alternative is adopted are exam-

ined including those that are negative as well as positive for the client and others.

5. *One alternative is chosen*. The basis for this choice should stem from the evaluation described in (4) with special emphasis on whether it can be accomplished in the light of existing resources.

6. *The final stage, once an alternative has been chosen, is to plan the details of how to carry out the alternative and then act on the basis of this plan*. The worker may have to help the client determine these details and secure necessary resources and reinforcements. During the implementation of the plan, the worker may have to provide support and coaching for the client. If major obstacles occur, this may necessitate a return to stage 4 to select another alternative or even the initiation of a new problem-solving process.

Some clients should literally be taught these steps. Other clients have acquired problem-solving skills but are unable to use them. One reason for this is emotional factors. The client may be too anxious, angry, or depressed to participate in problem solving. Under these circumstances, the worker must respond to the strong emotions that hinder the client from using his or her rational powers. This response may be in the form of providing for catharsis, and we shall describe this technique when we discuss emotional changes. The client may be helped to relax, if he or she is too tense, or the client may be helped with feelings of depression. The client may need to resolve the situation that evoked anger before continuing with problem solving.

Another situation in which problem solving may be difficult arises when the client encounters a crisis that makes his or her use of rational thinking impossible for the moment. The worker should respond to the crisis with appropriate uses of catharsis, support, and directiveness and return to the problem-solving work when it is again possible. This is true for many situations when problem-solving work is interrupted by some event in the life of the client. The event can be handled and the problem-solving work then resumed.

Enhancing Awareness. Clients can be hindered in their problem-solving efforts by a lack of awareness, or of attention, to information about themselves or others. Such information can be a prerequisite for arriving at an effective solution to the problem. Thus, one client talked about pursuing a career as an accountant despite the fact that he disliked working with numbers as well as all his mathematics classes. Another client was hostile toward a potential boyfriend who in some ways reminded her of a feared brother. A third client continued to try to date a woman despite her consistent refusal of his invitations. In all these examples, the worker was able to help the client only when she promoted his or her awareness of these "facts." Two of the most frequently used procedures to accomplish this are *confrontation* and *interpretation*.

Confrontation involves making a firm statement to the person confronted about the person, situation, personal attribute, or event that is blocked from awareness. Because this "blockage" involves some type of active denial, nonattention, or repression on the part of the client, the confrontation will evoke discomfort. This presents the worker with the responsibility of handling the confrontation in such a way that the negative aspects of this discomfort are addressed. Otherwise, the client will experience needless pain and is likely to leave the social work situation or more intensely deny the information presented.

Eisenberg and Delaney have suggested useful guidelines as to when to confront as well as for the actual confrontation.[22] The rules of preparing for a confrontation are, first, to confront only when the worker intends to remain involved with the client. This is so that the worker can help the client deal constructively with the information and the emotions that are aroused. Eisenberg and Delaney view confrontation in a noncontinuing relationship as an act of hostility.

Second, a worker should confront only when he or she experiences feelings of caring for the client. As Eisenberg and Delaney state, "If the caring is not present, the purpose for confronting is not to help, but to express or ventilate hostility."[23] Third, a confrontation should only be attempted in stages of helping when trust has been established between worker and client. Despite the worker's intentions to continue in the relationship and feelings of caring, the client has to be convinced of these things to face painful information.

Fourth, the client should have acquired some capacity to react to painful information nondefensively. This means that the worker should have made progress in helping the client to recognize his or her characteristic ways of acting defensively so that this information can be drawn upon when defenses are mobilized by the confrontation.

When this preparation has occurred, confrontation can be a constructive strategy if enacted skillfully. This enactment, according to Eisenberg and Delaney, consists of the following.[24]

1. The data on which the confrontation is based should be stated prior to the actual confronta-

tion. Unless this is done, the client may believe that the conclusion reached by the worker is not objective. A worker, for example, who wished to confront a client in a group situation about her hostility to other group members restated the client's most recent responses to them.

2. The worker should distinguish between observations and inferences. This is because the client should participate in the process of determining the validity of the inference. In the example cited in (1), the worker, after summarizing the client's responses to other group members, was tentative in indicating her conclusion that these were hostile by stating that "it seemed" that way to her. This invited the client to be a co-participant in the process of promoting her own awareness.

3. The worker should phrase the confrontation in terms of "I" messages. Thus, in the example cited, the worker's statement that "I experienced your comments as hostile" was in the spirit of "owning" her own perceptions and acknowledging that they were subjective.

A type of worker response that is, in a sense, a confrontation is to help the client become aware of emotions that he or she is experiencing, or expressing, or both. Because this falls more in the affective realm, we shall discuss this type of confrontation later in our consideration of the modification of affect.

Another way in which awareness is promoted is through the use of *interpretation,* which we define as helping the client to uncover relationships among actions, cognitions, and/or affects of which he or she was unaware. Some practitioners confuse confrontation and interpretation and label anything that is pointed out to the client as an interpretation if the client was unaware of it. In contrast, we use the term interpretation to refer to a procedure to help the client see the relationship between *two sets* of events that had been regarded as unrelated previously.

Moreover, we do not limit the use of the term interpretation, as in psychoanalytic theory, to the content of which the client was unaware because of unconscious processes. Psychoanalytic writers refer to the interpretation of dreams, of transference phenomena, and of "accidental" events, such as slips of the tongue or forgetting. We believe that many phenomena that are not perceived can be "interpreted" without assuming that an unconscious process was at work.

As we have stated, an interpretation promotes the client's awareness of the relationship between two or more sets of events. Some examples of awareness promoted through interpretation are the following:

• The client became aware that his dependent responses toward his wife (one set of events) were similar to his dependent responses toward his mother (another set of events).

• The client (a teenager) became aware that when he came home late at night (one set of events), he actually enjoyed the attention he got from his mother as she quizzed him about his whereabouts (another set of events). It was explained to the son and his mother that the mother was reinforcing his behavior.

We believe that many of the conditions that Eisenberg and Delaney state should be present for a confrontation should also be present for an interpretation. The interpretive experience can be anxiety provoking and requires that the client and worker (whether individually or in a group setting) trust one another and be able to work together on the implications of the interpretation after the interpretation is made and understood.

Before we discuss some of the steps in offering an interpretation, we shall note some of the reasons why interpretations may be useful. One is that they can help the client to distinguish among events to which he or she is responding similarly yet inappropriate-ly—in a behavioral sense, learning to discrimiate among stimuli. Another is that they produce cognitive dissonance. Levy, in an early yet still important study of psycho-logical interpretation, arrives at the conclu-sion that this is one of the main functions of interpretation: to produce an understanding of events that is contrary (dissonant) to the one held as this conflict can initiate a process of change.[25] The psychoanalytic idea that in-terpretation is a way of bringing the uncon-scious to awareness and freeing mental en-ergy bound up in repression may be a valid procedure but one not appropriate to most social work interactions.

An interpretation should not be seen as an intervention that takes place in only one episode between worker and client but rather as a process that requires a number of episodes to complete.[26] The process usually begins with the worker or client hypothesiz-ing a relationship between two (or more) sets of events; this may be expressed in general terms such as, "There seems to be some rela-tionship between your difficulties on this job and the ones you had on the last job."

The next step is to identify clearly the ex-act details for each set of events. This might be elicited through such questions as, "Tell me more about what led to your loss of your last job?" Sometimes, the worker will draw the client's attention to the nature of these events through a confrontation such as, "You reported to work late every day for your last two weeks on that job!"

When the two (or more) series of events are specified, the worker may either tenta-tively suggest the relationship between the sets of events or ask the client if he or she perceives one. If the timing of this is right, the client-worker relationship is a trusting one and the client is prepared to reflect on his or her behaviors, the interpretation will

be seriously considered by the client. The value of the interpretation, subsequently, will depend on the implications it holds for further exploration or for arriving at deci-sions. Clients and workers seldom seek the understanding obtained from an interpreta-tion solely for its own sake but rather for the changes in behavior that may be initiated through changes in cognitions.

Related to these procedures for enhanc-ing awareness are processes referred to by Hollis as those designed "to encourage re-flective consideration of the person-situation configuration," to encourage "the client to think about the psychological patterns in-volved in his or her behavior and the dynam-ics of these patterns and tendencies," and to encourage "the client to think about the de-velopment of his or her psychological pat-terns or tendencies."[27] Hollis describes these processes as including the client's re-flection on the perceptions that he or she has of the situation, the consequences of deci-sions that he or she has made, the thoughts and feelings that he or she has in specified situations, his or her self-evaluation, and his or her reactions to the worker and to treatment.

Hollis, using psychoanalytic terms, sees reflection on psychological patterns as including consideration of ego defenses, su-perego manifestations, and ego functioning. Reflection on developmental patterns in-volves an examination of the relationship be-tween reactions to historical events and cur-rent ones. Commenting on this type of developmental reflection, Hollis states:

> There are times, however, when the client can be helped greatly in understanding un-healthy and unprofitable ways of acting by coming to understand some of their historical sources . . . . The client's attention is drawn to inappropriate or inconsistent behavior. Sometimes the client makes the choice of

seeking further understanding, reacting in one way or the other to the worker's pointing up of the problem. At other times the worker takes the lead in steering thinking toward his or her earlier life. "Have you had feelings like this before?" "Does this make you think at all of similar things that have happened to you?"[28]

Modifying Attributions. The concept of attribution, as used in social-psychological theory, refers to people's beliefs about causality. Heider, the originator of attribution theories, proposed that people are likely to think in consistent ways about the causes of events in themselves and the environment.[29] The importance of such attributions is that they are hypothesized to affect how we are likely to act under various circumstances. Thus, if I am having difficulty in a class I am taking and I attribute this to my lack of effort, if I do anything at all, it will be to increase my level of effort. If I attribute the difficulty to the instructor's input, I will be most likely to seek to affect that.

Brehm, in a comprehensive discussion of the clinical applications of attribution theories, suggests a number of occasions when it is appropriate to encourage clients to attribute changes to themselves[30]:

1. When a desirable behavioral change has taken place, it is more likely to be maintained or increased when the person believes he has caused the original change than when the change is attributed to an outside agent, such as a medication."[31]
2. " . . . when the therapist desires the client to experience his arousal as a spontaneous emotional response to environmental stimuli. Whether this desire is related to wanting the client to experience guilt so as not to behave in an antisocial fashion, or pleasure so as to behave in a prosocial fashion, or discomfort so as to reduce dissonance . . . . That goal is for the client to believe, for example 'I feel guilty about cheating,' rather than 'The pill/

weather/therapist makes me feel uncomfortable.'"[32]

In contrast, clients are discouraged from attributing change to themselves as follows:

1. " . . . when a therapist anticipates a client's experiencing deleterious emotional arousal, it may reduce undesirable behavioral consequences of this arousal if the physiological arousal can be accounted for in other terms . . . . 'You always feel restless on rainy days.'"[33]
2. "If symptomatic behavior seems to be increased by the client's worrying over its occurrence, it may help, at least for an initial period, for the therapist to reduce the client's tension and anxiety by having him believe that some external force (e.g., medication or therapeutic procedure) will ensure that the symptomatic behavior will in fact take place. This approach has the benefit of allowing the client to avoid obsessive ruminations about whether or not the symptomatic behavior will occur; he can assume that it will and that control over it has been taken out of his hands."[34]

Brehm points out that another use of attributions lies in converting abnormal attributions into normal ones. This technique has often been used by workers who do not realize that they are modifying attributions when they relabel a mother's overprotection of her child as "concern" or a wife's demand for more of her husband's time as "caring."

Still another category of attributions is referred to as "dispositional." This refers to attributing the behavior of others to presumed traits of the person. Thus, a client may assume that another person has acted on the basis of his or her dislike of the client or "craziness" or "meanness." This assumption of the client may lead to his or her subsequent dysfunctional responses.

In general, workers can seek to change client attributions by stating the attribution that the worker believes will be beneficial and by presenting evidence in support of that attribution. In regard to dispositional attributions, Brehm further suggests the following: when the client makes too few self-attributed dispositions, the worker can videotape the client during a session and replay the tape while pointing out the continuity in the client's behavior; when the client makes too many self-attributed dispositions, the therapist can record the client in interaction with others and then point out how the client's behavior was affected by other people.

When the client makes too many dispositional attributions to others, the worker can track the behavior of the other person while pointing out the many situational events to which that person is responding. Finally, when the client makes too few dispositional attributions to others, Brehm suggests that the client be urged not to empathize with the person and not to project how he or she feels onto the person in question.

This discusssion constitutes a brief review of some of the practice implications of modifying attributions. This is still a relatively new arena from which to derive useful practice principles. As we develop more research as well as clinical evidence for the influence of cognitions on behavior, we are likely to utilize attributional concepts to explain these findings. It is probable that current theories will be reinterpreted in attributional terms because of the simplicity yet power in the idea that our actions are based largely on the explanations we offer ourselves for what we perceive.

Procedures That Emphasize Client Behaviors

The procedures we shall discuss are reinforcement, modeling, and task assignment.

Reinforcement. The principles of reinforcement are derived from a body of knowledge about *operant behavior*. This category of behavior is the one that includes all the actions that we take voluntarily both through body movement (dancing, running) and through communication (talking, gesturing). These types of actions are viewed in behavioral theory as produced by the context existing immediately prior to the act (antecedents) and by the consequences that that type of action has produced on previous occasions. These relationships are expressed simply as A (antecedent)–B (behavior)–C (consequences). In the view of at least some theorists, the antecedents and consequences can exist within the person or in the environment or both. For example, either I can be told or I can tell myself that I am ready to begin a project (external and internal antecedents), and after the project is completed, I can be told or tell myself that it has been done well (external and internal consequences).

The effects of different types of consequences are stated in the following principles:

1. A behavior has been *positively reinforced* when the presentation of some stimulus leads to an increased likelihood that the behavior will reoccur. These stimuli are usually experienced as pleasurable.

2. A behavior has been *negatively reinforced* when the removal of some stimulus leads to an increased likelihood that the behavior will reoccur. These stimuli are usually experienced as unpleasant.

3. A behavior has been *positively punished* when the presentation of some stimulus leads to a decreased likelihood that the behavior will reoccur. The stimuli are usually experienced as unpleasant.

4. A behavior has been *negatively punished* when the removal of some stimulus leads to a decreased likelihood that the behavior will reoccur. The stimuli are usually experienced as pleasant.

5. A behavior has been *extinguished* when the consequence that is maintaining the behavior is withdrawn and the behavior diminishes.

The following are some practice examples of the application of these principles:

- *Positive reinforcement*—The school worker for John, age 8, awarded him "points" for completed homework assignments. When John earned 30 points, the worker contracted to take him bowling.
- *Negative reinforcement*—The school social worker contracted with John that if he completed his assignments regularly for a month, John could discontinue his attendance at the remedial class that he dislikes.
- *Positive punishment*—The school social worker criticized John's fighting behavior on the playground, and as a result of this criticism John's fighting decreased.
- *Negative punishment*—The worker also indicated that if John continued to fight on the playground, John's opportunity to play there during recess would be restricted by the teacher.
- *Extinction*—When John fought on the playground, the other children stood around and "cheered him on." The social worker held a meeting with the boys who were most likely to do this and convinced them that their actions were harmful to John and should cease.

The opportunities that workers have to use reinforcement with clients are manyfold. The worker can provide the reinforcement or the worker can encourage others in the environment to do so. The reinforcement can be in the form of material objects or can be "social" such as praise. Similarly, punishment from social workers can be either verbal through the use of criticism or "negative" through the withdrawal of pleasurable consequences. Social workers, in our opinion, should never use painful *physical* consequences.

Clients can also be helped to reward or punish themselves. One client who was having trouble doing his homework was helped to develop a plan whereby he rewarded himself with a specified amount of television time (which he enjoyed) for each completed homework assignment.

A good understanding of the use of reinforcement must include a knowledge of schedules of reinforcement—that is, how frequently the reinforcement is to be administered. Such schedules may either be ratio schedules in which the reinforcement is supplied after a specified number of responses or interval schedules in which the reinforcement is supplied after the elapse of specified time periods. These schedules may also be continuous in which reinforcement occurs after every response or intermittent in which the reinforcement occurs less frequently. The scheduling of reinforcement is a complex topic. Fischer and Gochros, however, have reduced this complexity by offering the following principles[35]:

1. For the development of new behavior, and to achieve the highest frequency of occurrence, use a continuous schedule.
2. For the highest resistance to extinction . . . use a variable schedule, preferably a variable interval schedule.
3. If you cannot keep a count of the number of responses (which is required for the use of a ratio schedule), use an interval schedule.
4. If you cannot keep track of the passage of time (required for the use of an interval schedule), use a ratio schedule.
5. Generally, interval schedules are easier to administer than ratio schedules because timekeeping is easier than is counting specific behaviors.
6. For increasing or maintaining a certain number of responses a client is to perform (the rate of responding), use a ratio schedule.
7. For strengthening certain behaviors performed over a period of time, use an interval schedule.
8. Use a variable ratio schedule if the goal is to develop a high, sustained rate of behavior (i.e., when performing a certain number of responses is the crucial criterion).
9. Use a variable interval schedule for a low, sustained rate of behavior (i.e., when the number of responses, per se, is not the crucial criterion).

10. For all intermittent schedules, start with low-performance requirements for behavior to be reinforced and gradually increase the performance required to receive reinforcement.

The material we have presented here merely hints at the array of procedures available to the practitioner based on operant conditioning. The reader is referred to works by such writers as Kazdin, Krasner, and Fischer and Gochros for more information on this subject. An excellent review by Kazdin summarizes a great deal of research evidence on the effectiveness of this approach.[36]

Modeling. Practitioners are sometimes surprised when the suggestion is made that clients should be encouraged to imitate the behavior of others, and yet this is one of the most important ways in which people learn. Whether or not this conforms to the abstract ideals of self-determination or "do your own thing," everyone—including clients—imitates behavior, even the behavior of social workers! It is not unusual or undesirable for a client to say "I wonder how my social worker would have handled this situation?" The term "imitation" refers to this type of learning, and "modeling" refers to the intentional offering of a person as a model.

Modeling is often utilized in interpersonal practice when the client lacks social skills, although almost any response can be modeled. A customary way of staging a modeling session is through a role play in which the worker, or others who are appropriate, demonstrate such skills as applying for a job, making an acquaintance, or confronting a child about misbehavior. Other ways include playing tape recordings or describing the behavior. Modeling is also utilized when the client feels some inhibition about performing the behavior. Observing others can have the effect of diminishing this inhibition.

Marlatt and Perry present a series of principles to increase the likelihood that the modeling procedure will be effective.[37] One set of principles prescribes the selection of a model who is seen as competent and prestigious and is similar to the observer. The model, on the other hand, should not be viewed by the client as *too* superior.[38] Once the model has been selected, the worker must ensure that the client will pay attention to the model. This can be accomplished through the worker directing the client's attention to some aspect of the model's behavior. If the client is anxious while observing the model, his or her attention may stray; it is, therefore, desirable to help the client to relax before a modeling session.

After the client has observed the model, the worker should help him or her to retain this information. This is facilitated by reviewing with the client what has been observed. If the client rehearses the behavior shortly after observing the model, retention is also more likely to occur. Another factor promoting retention is to show the model being rewarded for performing the desired behavior. The client also should receive reinforcement when he or she performs the behavior.

Task Assignment. Client behaviors may also be modified when the client and worker agree on tasks that the client will perform, usually between sessions. In some approaches to practice, these are termed "tasks," while in others, they are called "homework assignments." Reid, together with others, has devised a comprehensive approach to interpersonal helping referred to as Task-Centered Practice.[39] That approach uses task assignments as a primary intervention but also has other components such as limiting helping to a short term, basing the process on a clear statement of problem and goal, and utilizing a variety of research tools to monitor process and outcome. We are interested at this point, however, only in the ways that tasks are generated and carried out.

Reid conceives of two types of tasks: *general tasks* that "give the client a direction for action" and *operational tasks* that "call for specific action the client is to undertake."[40] An example of the former is that Mr. J is to look for work; an example of the latter is that Mr. J is to visit an employment counselor within the next week.

Reid has identified a series of stages in the "task planning and implementation" process. The first stage includes a specification of the problem and the goals that will help to resolve the problem. The next stage involves task selection and begins with generating task alternatives. The question to be answered is "What can the client do to obtain what he wants?" The answer to this may, under some circumstances, be obvious, but under others, it may require difficult thinking as well as brainstorming. Some clients are well able to generate ideas for tasks; others require more input from the worker. As in any problem-solving process, the alternatives must then be evaluated and the best ones chosen.

Once a task has been chosen by mutual agreement of worker and client (although with a major emphasis on the client's desires), the next stage is to plan the details of task implementation. This may involve breaking the task down into a "sequence of operations" and, depending on the complexity of the task, one or all these operations should be performed before the next session.

One of the worker's tasks is to determine the kinds of help that he or she will have to provide clients so that they can perform their tasks. This help can include offering reinforcement for task accomplishment or models of task performance. The worker should also help the client to predict some of the obstacles that might stand in the way of task accomplishment and how these can be overcome. Obstacles might result from the client's attitudes as well as those of others, and overcoming these can represent additional client tasks or worker tasks, or both.

At the session(s) after the task is determined, the worker and client should work together to promote task attainment. If the task has been accomplished and the goal attained, either additional tasks related to other goals will be generated or service will be terminated. If the task has not been completed, the worker will help the client to continue his or her efforts to finish the task and to identify obstacles that have been encountered. The worker and client may both have responsibility to remove these obstacles so that the task can be completed.

Procedures That Emphasize Client Affects

The procedures to be discussed are ventilation, relaxation, and overcoming depression.

Ventilation.   We refer here to procedures that the worker can use to help the client to express strong emotion that the client has held back. We use the word "ventilation" instead of the word *catharsis* to avoid some of the theoretical assumptions implicit in the use of the latter term. We do not assume that expressing feelings is always a necessary or sufficient condition for change to take place in the client; nevertheless, all workers have worked with some clients who obtained a great deal of relief when pent-up sorrow was released through tears of anger or through shouting during a session.

We are not referring here to the efforts workers should make to understand the feelings associated with the information the client presents. At times, these client feelings are clearly expressed, and the worker, as we stated earlier in this book, will empathize with such feelings to enhance the worker-client relationship and to facilitate the client's work on his or her problems. At other times, the worker will enhance the client's awareness of feelings to learn more about, as well as to promote the client's awareness of, his or her motives, perceptions, hurts, or experiences.

The worker becomes aware that a strong pent-up feeling is present when clients fight to hold back tears, anger, or other feelings. Such "fighting" is manifested in blinking back tears, clenching and unclenching fists, making facial grimaces, and exhibiting similar kinds of "body language."

A precondition to the client's expression of such feelings in a session is a trust in the worker as an accepting person who does not share negative stereotypes about the expression of feelings. For some clients with a strong desire to "unload," it does not take long to release such emotion when an accepting atmosphere has been established.

In one session conducted by an author of this text, a young black man was seen in an army mental hygiene clinic. This man was highly educated and had been drafted into the army. His skin color was very light so that he was not clearly identifiable as black. He had been present during many racist discussions in his barracks when it was clear to him that the other men did not know of his ethnic identity. He was being given opportunity for a leadership assignment and he thought that this would not have been offered if his identity were apparent. He felt a great deal of frustration and rage that he had not felt before because of the protection he had experienced all his life through having a wealthy family and having been educated by

a prestigious school. As he discussed these matters, he showed signs of tears. He was encouraged to allow these feelings to come out, and he cried bitterly for a few minutes. He stated that he had not cried since he was a young child but that he felt much better. In this more relaxed frame of mind, he discussed his alternatives and decided that he wanted to let his barracks mates and officers know that he identified as black, no matter what the consequences. His entire bearing as he left showed that he felt a burden had lifted from him. A later check indicated that he had carried through on his intent and did not need further services.

All interventions of this sort do not take place in one session alone. With many clients, however, this kind of release often marks a turning point in the helping process. Garfield even describes a person being treated through behavior therapy in which this occurred as follows:

> The client insisted on talking about a particular event to the therapist and not following the particular instructions for that session. The therapist, however, allowed the client to express himself, and there was considerable emotional release which was followed by significant forward movement in therapy.[41]

We conclude this section with two points, one theoretical and the other practical. Emotions are complex phenomena and to understand them requires more than a simple ability to identify "feeling words." They represent both physiological changes in the individual as well as the way in which the individual, as well as others, labels these changes. There is no doubt that the individual who "feels" some emotion usually experiences some physiological changes such as perspiration and muscular tension. Sound research has shown that the words the individual uses to describe this (such as fear or anticipation) depend in part on the context. The worker, therefore, must take into consideration both how the individual describes his or her feelings as well as the antecedents and consequences of such statements.[42]

Second, it is possible for the therapeutic experience to promote both emotional labels and intense states of physiological arousal not "brought in" by the client. Some research on encounter-type experiences that promote these states has indicted that they are potentially harmful rather than therapeutic.[43]

Relaxation. There are many occasions when the worker will seek to help the client to relax: one is when the client is undertaking a task, such as forming a new relationship, about which he or she is anxious. Another is when the worker uses a procedure such as systematic desensitization in which the client is helped to relax as he or she experiences progressive levels of anxiety related to approaching closer and closer to a behavioral goal. This is a classic behavioral treatment of phobias (fear of heights, fear of going outdoors, fear of a pet animal, etc.).

Fischer describes the process of muscle relaxation as follows:

> Based on the work of Jacobson, the procedure developed by Wolpe involves selecting one muscle group (e.g., lower arm group) and illustrating the contrast between tension and relaxation. In a comfortable chair, the client is asked to sit in the most relaxed position possible. Next, the client is instructed to make a tight fist with one hand, hold it fifteen to twenty seconds, then relax it, drop it to the side, and notice the pleasant tingling sensation as the arm relaxes, in contrast to the previous feelings of tension. This is repeated until the client reports that muscle group completely relaxed with no tension. The same process is then repeated with all the muscle groups of the body, including extensor muscles of the arms and legs, abdominal muscles, facial muscles, and upper trunk and

neck muscles. This period of instruction can last from one to six sessions, with the client requested to practice deep muscle relaxation fifteen to thirty minutes a day at home.[44]

Another approach, one that requires less training of the worker than deep muscle relaxation, is the use of fantasy. The client is encouraged to imagine a peaceful scene (usually with eyes closed) and to remain with this image until the desired state of relaxation is achieved. The worker helps the client to maintain this state by directing him or her to "return" gradually to the session. Sometimes workers can also help clients to relax by noticeably relaxing during the session (leaning back, extending legs, relaxing the body). The client will often, without realizing it, imitate the worker.

Overcoming Depression. Although we do not intend for this section of the chapter to be a comprehensive discussion of working with specific emotional states, a few comments on depression are appropriate in view of the frequency with which practitioners interview clients who are depressed. This is especially true of social work as many clients are poor, oppressed, handicapped, or for some other reason limited in opportunities for the "good life," and it is not hard to understand why such clients may be sad, pessimistic, or lethargic. We refer here to clients who despite their depression are likely to be cognizant of their realities as compared with clients whose depression is part of a psychosis. We also refer to clients whose depression is reactive to their situation rather than a result of internal physiological processes.

When people are depressed because of the reality of their situation, it is apparent that a major step in alleviating that depression is doing something about that reality. This may be to help them to locate housing, additional income, or other resources. People may also be depressed because of mental processes. There is research evidence that one of the most effective treatments for such depression is "cognitive therapy." Beck, who developed this approach, sees depression as stemming from persistent thoughts related to a devaluation of self, a negative view of life experiences, and a pessimistic view of the future.[45]

Cognitive therapy of depression, as presented by Beck, involves the following stages:

> First he has to become aware of what he is thinking. Second, he needs to recognize what thoughts are awry. Then he has to substitute accurate for inaccurate judgments. Finally he needs feedback to inform him whether his changes are correct.[46]

Workers adopting a behavioral approach to depressed people will encourage them to engage in activities (going to work, attending meetings, going shopping) that are incompatible with remaining inactive and dwelling on sad thoughts. Psychodynamic workers also recognize that it is essential to enhance the ego strengths of depressed clients by furthering their coping capacities—in effect, helping them to resume or increase their involvement with family, work, and community tasks.

Clients will also become depressed when they experience separation from loved ones, as when a family member dies. Helping people to cope with a grief process is an important topic but one that is beyond the scope of this volume. Such writers as Elizabeth Kübler-Ross have extensively discussed the emotional stages that people experience when they learn of the impending death of themselves or others.[47]

Social workers in their practice (as well as life) will inevitably encounter clients who must deal with death and loss; workers must be able to confront their own feelings about this issue to help clients. Yalom views death as one of the most important issues that we must come to terms with to lead satisfactory lives. He indicates many kinds of dysfunctional behavior patterns that are related to self-defeating ways in which we face the fact of our own mortality.[48]

In this section, we have described many of the procedures that social workers use to help individuals to change through one-to-one interactions. It is important to remember that in our framework, workers should use group, family, and environmental situations as the means and context of individual change when these will be more effective and efficient in helping clients to achieve their goals. At this point, we turn to the use of these systems for this purpose. In the next two chapters, we discuss how workers achieve changes in those systems as such rather than primarily as a means of individual change.

Procedures Used When the Group or Family is the Action System

In the preceding section, we described procedures that workers use to help clients in one-to-one sessions to modify their cognitions, affects, and behaviors. In this section, we shall use a similar typology to describe how workers enlist group and family forces for similar purposes.[49] (We shall refer in this discussion to "group" but intend this always in the sense of group *and* family.)

Procedures to Modify Client Cognitions

It is a well-established fact that group and family conditions are very powerful determinants of the beliefs, perceptions, and attitudes of their members. This does not, of course, mean that groups when they arrive at a consensus will always be accurate, but it is often likely that if several persons perceive something in the same way, that perception represents the truth of the matter. For this reason, when a group or family member makes a statement about an event or his or her understanding of the event, the worker frequently asks other individuals who have relevant information to indicate whether they view things in the same way. This can be an effective procedure in "changing the member's mind" if his or her views are distorted or reinforcing these views if that is what is called for.

Elsewhere we presented the following examples of this process:

> A group of socially inadequate young adults had recently taken an outing to a restaurant. A member was convinced that she had been singled out by the waitress for poor service. She attributed this to her lack of attractiveness. The other group members, when asked by the worker, had all noticed that the waitress was very busy and she had not given any of the members enough attention.
>
> Another example, related to the same member, occurred at a meeting when she again referred to her physical appearance. The worker suggested that members report to her what they "saw." One commented on her attractive eyes, another on her pleasant smile, and a third on the way she managed to convey a sense of personal energy in her movements. These comments were very helpful in changing this woman's image of herself.[50]

Another example of this type of process occurs frequently in family treatment where it is called "relabeling." The worker in this procedure selects a behavior of a member that is labeled one way by the others and labels it differently. An example of this was a mother who was seen as overprotecting her children. This was termed by the worker as being responsible and caring.

The purpose of this relabeling is not to reinforce the behavior but to allow the person in question to explore ways of being caring other than the dysfunctional one of "overprotection"; this exploration is made more likely because the person is valued rather than rejected through the relabeling process. In this example, the entire family's participation in the process makes it a more powerful one than the same type of cognitive approach used in a one-to-one context. Relabeling has effects, also, on the entire system, and so we shall refer to this process again in the next chapter.

Groups have strong effects on other kinds of attributions, particularly whether the member is likely to locate the causes of his or her behavior in self or environment. The group's effect on this is as follows:

1. When the group members point out to an individual that he or she has acted in a similar manner in a variety of circumstances, the individual is likely to attribute the cause of the behavior to himself or herself.
2. When the group members point out to an individual that he or she has not acted in a similar manner in other circumstances, the individual is likely to attribute the cause of the behavior to something or someone in the environment.

Since the individual is likely to act to change what he or she perceives to be the source of the problem, how this is attributed is important. The following examples illustrate the use of these principles:

> In a group of adult parolees, one of the members complained that his employer did not listen to "his side" of an argument. The worker asked the group if they recalled other similar complaints from this member. Several members pointed out that he had made such complaints about his wife and even about other members of the group. The member then moved to a personal attribution of the

causes of the problem and was open to the worker's observation that it may have had something to do with how he presented his "side."

In contrast, in a group composed of couples working on marital problems, a wife stated that she believed her problem was due to the fact that she was not as intelligent or articulate as her husband. The members pointed out to her the many occasions in the group when she had made well-stated and insightful comments. This led to a change in her attributions in the direction of considering her husband's attitude to her rather than her sense of personal inadequacy. She and her husband became more open to considering the sexist roots of their troubles rather than blame them on the wife.[51]

Another kind of awareness promotion for the individuals in families and groups occurs when the worker asks the group to give feedback to a member regarding the impact the member has on the group. This can occur through informing the member about the nature of his or her own actions or of their effects on others. The worker either asks several (or all) members to provide this or asks the member to select others from whom he or she wishes such a response.

Procedures to Modify Client Affects

We have in mind here primarily the ways in which the worker can help the group to help the member to express affects rather than to change them. We note, however, that it is possible for group members to change each other's affects in that one member can help another member to relax, to ventilate, or to deal with emotions in the same way as we previously described workers doing this. In fact, a member may, at times, trust another member and be more willing to take such help from that person than from the worker.

Since the group usually comes to represent what has been termed a microcosm that represents the society, members are likely to encounter other members who arouse the same feelings in them that significant people outside the group do; they are also likely to deal with those feelings as they do elsewhere such as disguising or denying them, as in the following example:

> In a group of recently divorced people, one member, Jack, denied that he was angry when another member criticized him. Several members then told him that he had said this with clenched teeth, loudly, and while "jabbing his finger" at the group. Jack smiled and said that "I guess I have a hard time admitting what I felt."[52]

It is not only negatively evaluated feelings such as anger or fear that members deny. Many people hide caring and affectionate feelings and, thus, distance themselves from others. A great deal of time is spent in many groups helping members to recognize that they care for one another and to be able to tell this to each other.

Procedures to Modify Client Behaviors

We noted in our discussion of the group's effect on the emotions of individual members that members can be helped by the worker to employ some of the same techniques that workers employ. This can enhance the member's abilities to help others outside the group and to function more competently in social interactions. The same is true of behavioral measures.

Members can learn in either structured or spontaneous ways to reinforce the behavior of others in the group. Thus, if a member of a group is trying to change a response (express caring to others, avoid threatening others), he or she can "contract" with all or some other members to receive reinforcement from them when the change is manifested in the group. Members sometimes choose buddies in the group for this purpose. This reinforcement might be "social" such as praise or material such as receiving a token.

Members will usually vary in the kinds of coping skills they possess and, thus, modeling can be used with good effect in the group. Members can demonstrate to each other through role plays how they handled specified situations. This can also be approached vicariously as members describe to each other how they responded to such situations.

Last, members' behavior can be modified through roles that they assume in the group. There are three types of roles that can be used in this way: (1) roles of "officers" in the group such as chairperson or secretary, (2) roles that are created through activities such as scorekeeper in a game or the designer of a mural to be completed by the group, and (3) roles that grow out of specific social interactions such as the mediator of a dispute or the tension reducer who "cracks a joke" at the right moment.

The worker should be aware of the fact that all such roles have behavioral expectations associated with them that are known to the members. "Placing a person" in a role brings these expectations and consequent reinforcements for role performance into play and is, consequently, a powerful strategy.

It is also possible that an individual's "problem" is related to some role that elicits dysfunctional behavior such as the role of "fool" or "mess-up." In family situations, one can view the label of "schizophrenic" (as well as many other psychiatric or medical terms) as creating a role that maintains behavior patterns that have very severe consequences for the individual. Family therapists have preferred, for example, to label anorexia as "stubborn" behavior or schizophrenia in a young adult as "failure to leave home" behavior to help individuals move out of roles that

maintain destructive (and even fatal) behavior patterns.

These points should be viewed as an introduction to how group and family forces can be enlisted to modify individual behavior. Although the next chapter is primarily devoted to changing group and family conditions in their own right, the procedures to be described there do have effects on individuals and provide the reader with additional information on the way to use group and family forces for the benefit of individual members. We now turn to the third set of procedures for facilitating individual change—the enlistment of people and systems in the environment beyond the family and peer group association of clients.

Procedures Used for Action Systems in the Environment

An individual's responses are molded by the events taking place in the various environmental systems of which he or she is part. These include the following:

1. The social networks with which the individual is associated, such as extended family, friends, and neighbors
2. The social agency in which the interpersonal practitioner is located
3. Other social agencies and service institutions, including schools and hospitals
4. Community institutions, such as churches, commercial establishments, and recreational facilities
5. The workplace

These systems affect the behavior of the individual in several ways. They supply the resources that are required for all daily activities; they provide opportunities to learn new roles and to develop the skills to acquire additional resources; they either reinforce or punish behavior; they furnish models for behavior; they assign roles; and they define tasks.

These effects can be beneficial to the client, in which case they should be maintained; they can be detrimental, in which case they should be changed; and they can be absent, in which case they should be created. The following are illustrations of this:

> When John was having trouble completing his homework assignments, his teacher assigned another student as a tutor to him. The social worker saw this as a beneficial move and encouraged the teacher to continue this plan.
>
> Every time that John misbehaved in class, the teacher called the assistant principal who took John to his office. The worker noted that John's behavior became worse after this consequence was introduced. The worker hypothesized that being taken to the assistant principal's office actually functioned to reinforce John's misbehavior. The worker suggested that John be placed on a "point system" in which certain behaviors were rewarded by the award of points and others by the withdrawal of points. When John earned enough points, he could use them to "purchase" extra gymnasium time, which he liked.
>
> John did not like to recite in class because he had a speech defect and the other children laughed when he spoke. Not enough time was being spent at the school by a speech therapist. Using this as an illustration of a need, the social worker convinced the school district's administration to assign another speech therapist to the school.

The interpersonal practitioner has a number of different roles that he or she can fulfill in modifying the environment so as to affect the behavior of a specific client. The ones that we shall discuss here are networker, consultant, and placement facilitator. The roles of advocate and mediator will be discussed in Chapter 13 because they are used to change systems as such as well as to promote individual change.

Networker

We assume that virtually everyone who functions adequately lives his or her life with the support of immediate family, extended family, and friends. Individuals in our society who require the services of a social worker often do not have a linkage with such networks, or their networks are deficient in some way. Examples of this are the many former psychiatric patients who live in inner-city hotels in isolation, abusive families who are in conflict with their kin, and people who have moved to new areas where they have no one to turn to for the relief of stresses.

Social workers are developing skills in remedying these types of problems involving networks. One approach, referred to as network therapy, involves bringing together people from the various systems that impinge upon the client such as neighborhood leaders, school personnel, physicians, and representatives from the church. These people are helped to interact with the client around various problems and to take roles in problem-solving and resource provision. For some ethnic groups, such as native Americans, this gathering represents the tribe and is actually a "natural" approach to problem solving that is already present in the culture.

Another approach is to seek to create a network. This involves bringing together people with similar or even different concerns who can help each other through a pooling of resources. This has been an effective tool in working with people who are experiencing oppression, such as women who are seeking a way to move from confining family situations into work and community involvements. Women have helped each other to locate jobs, prepare for jobs, and secure resources such as babysitting, educational scholarships, and even housing if they are planning to separate from a spouse.

Consultant

At times the worker can secure environmental change to promote individual change by offering consultation to individuals in the environment. Such individuals have included teachers, employers, medical personnel, and clergy. The worker may be part of the same organization as the individual (school social worker and teacher) or may be an "outsider" (mental health worker and minister). The worker sometimes reaches out to that person but at other times is "called in."

The worker should bear in mind that he or she is neither the therapist nor the supervisor of the other person. This requires the worker to couch ideas as suggestions rather than as demands and to empathize with the difficulty the other individual may be having in carrying out his or her role.

An example of the role of a consultant was a worker who worked with clients in an after-care program for mentally ill people. One client gave the worker permission to talk with his employer as he was in danger of losing his job. The worker had assessed the situation and concluded that the client was not functioning well because of a deficiency in the clarity with which the job was structured and a lack of feedback from the supervisor. The employer was interested in working with the social worker to make this job experience a successful one. When the problems were identified, the employer used the worker to help determine ways that these aspects of the job could be changed. This took several conferences, but ultimately changes were made and the client improved his job performance.

Placement Facilitator

The improved functioning of clients sometimes requires removal of the client from one environment to another. Typical instances of this are changes in living arrangements for children or adults, changes in jobs, and the termination of a marriage. All these topics require extensive discussion beyond the scope of this text, but it is important for the worker to recognize these situations and to realize the amount of knowledge and skill required to work with them.[54] We wish at this point to summarize some of the dimensions that workers must understand to work effectively with helping clients change from one environment to another. These include the following:

1. *How to assess situations so as to determine when they can be improved or when improvement is so unlikely that the continued development of the person will be severely impaired without a change.* There are many value components related to this topic in social work. Some "family-oriented" workers will almost never recommend the placement of a child because of the high value placed on family continuity and the belief that almost all families can become functional if the right resources are supplied. Other workers, including many in the child welfare field, while supporting the principle of strengthening families, believe that the reality for some families is such that change will not occur and the child will be severely damaged or even killed unless placed.

2. *An understanding of the importance of the client's situation to the client with reference to identity, continuity, and emotional investment.* Thus, when a change is required by the severity of circumstances, a great deal of preparation is required to help the client deal with feelings of loss, rejection, and fears for the future. When this is not accomplished, the client may spend a lifetime trying unsuccessfully to deal with these issues. Admittedly, crises do occur when a person, usually a child, must be removed without such planning. Such situations require even

more extensive services afterward to offer any chance of avoiding serious emotional damage to the client.

3. *An understanding of how to work with the client and with other people in the "new" environment to enhance the likelihood of sound relationships emerging in that environment.* This involves understanding how people test out the properties of the new environment while inappropriately carrying over to the environment ways of coping that were functional in the old situation but not the new. Again, working out these issues may not be a matter of days or weeks but of months or years, particularly in the case of child placement. It is an adage of the placement field that how quickly the person adapts to the new environment is an indicator of the individual's abilities to test reality and cope with change as personality components.

Summary

This chapter was devoted to a discussion of the ways that social workers facilitate changes in individuals through one-to-one interactions with the individual, through working with the individual in the context of his or her family or small group, or through changing the impact of the environment on the individual.

We began the chapter with a discussion of the evolution of individually oriented services in social work, an approach that has been one of the dominant ones in this profession, perhaps even too dominant as it has operated at times to the exclusion of attention to negative environmental forces. In this introductory material we also described some of the practice models used by social workers to facilitate individual change, namely, the psychosocial, functional, problem-solving, task-centered, behavioral, and competency-based ecological models.

The largest part of the chapter was devoted to describing procedures for individual change. In the section devoted to one-to-one interactions, we described procedures by categorizing them as directed at cognitive, affective, and behavioral aspects of human functioning. We recognized that few procedures are so narrowly constructed, but, on the other hand, we contended that procedures often are directed more at one aspect of behavior than at another.

In the section devoted to family and group interventions utilized to achieve individual change, we indicated that here (as well as in the next chapter) we integrated this discussion because families and peer groups are both small groups and similar procedures are often used with them. We utilized a similar set of categories as we did in describing one-to-one interventions, namely, that interventions can be analyzed in terms of the way they impact on cognitive, affective, and behavioral functioning of individuals.

The last section of the chapter reviewed some of the procedures utilized by workers to modify the impact of the environment on individual functioning. We were somewhat briefer in this discussion as well as in that on family and group interventions than we were in our treatment of one-to-one techniques as the next two chapters have a great deal of bearing on these topics.

NOTES

1. Scott Briar, "Social Casework and Social Group Work: Historical and Social Science Foundations," *Encyclopedia of Social Work*, Vol. II (New York: National Association of Social Workers, 1971), p. 1240.

2. Helen H. Perlman, "Putting the 'Social' Back in Social Casework," in Helen H. Perlman, ed., *Perspectives on Social Casework* (Philadelphia: Temple University Press, 1971), pp. 29–34.

3. Helen H. Perlman, *Persona: Social Role and Personality* (Chicago: University of Chicago Press, 1968).

4. Bernice K. Simon. "Social Casework Theory: An Overview," in Robert W. Roberts and Robert A. Nee, eds., *Theories of Social Casework* (Chicago: University of Chicago Press, 1970), pp. 355–395.

5. Gordon Hamilton, *Theory and Practice of Social Casework* (New York: Columbia University Press, 1940).

6. Florence Hollis and Mary E. Woods, *Casework: A Psychosocial Therapy*, 3rd ed. (New York: Random House, 1981).

7. Irvin D. Yalom, *Existential Psychotherapy* (New York: Basic Books, 1980), pp. 293–297.

8. Virginia Robinson, *A Changing Psychology in Social Casework* (Philadelphia: University of Pennsylvania Press, 1930) and Jessie Taft, "The Relations of Function to Process in Social Casework," *Journal of Social Work Process*, Vol. 1 (1937), pp. 1–18.

9. Ruth E. Smalley, "Social Casework: The Functional Approach," in *Encyclopedia of Social Work*, Vol. I, p. 1204.

10. Perlman, "Social Casework," p. 1215.

11. William J. Reid and Laura Epstein, *Task-Centered Casework* (New York: Columbia University Press, 1972).

12. Laura Epstein, *Helping People: The Task-Centered Approach* (St. Louis: C. V. Mosby, 1980), p. 13.

13. Ibid.

14. Edwin J. Thomas, "Selected Socio-behavioral Techniques and Principles: An Approach to Interpersonal Helping," *Social Work*, Vol. 13 (January 1968), pp. 12–26.

15. Joel Fischer, *Effective Casework Practice: An Eclectic Approach* (New York: McGraw-Hill, 1978), p. 157.

16. Martin Sundel and Sandra Sundel, *Behavior Modification in the Human Services* (New York: John Wiley, 1975), and Joel Fischer and Harvey Gochros, *Planned Behavior Change: Behavior Modification in Social Work* (New York: The Free Press, 1975).

17. Anthony N. Maluccio, "Competence-Oriented Social Work Practice: An Ecological Approach," in Anthony N. Maluccio, ed., *Promoting Competence in Clients* (New York: The Free Press, 1981), pp. 1–26.

18. Sol L. Garfield, *Psychotherapy: An Eclectic Approach* (New York: John Wiley, 1980), p. 222.

19. Sheldon Eisenberg and Daniel J. Delaney, *The Counseling Process* (Chicago: Rand McNally, 1977), p. 180.

20. A. Ellis and R. A. Harper, *A New Guide to Rational Living* (North Hollywood, Calif.: Wilshire, 1975).

21. Ibid., pp. 202–230.

22. Eisenberg and Delaney, *Counseling Process*, pp. 100–112.

23. Ibid., p. 103.

24. Ibid., p. 105.

25. L. H. Levy, *Psychological Interpretation* (New York: Holt, Rinehart and Winston, 1963).

26. R. J. Langs, *Resistances and Interventions: The Nature of Therapeutic Work* (New York: Jason Aronson, 1981), pp. 157–202.

27. Hollis and Woods, *Casework*, pp. 100–101.

28. Ibid., p. 154.

29. F. Heider, "Social Perception and Phenomenal Causality," *Psychological Review*, Vol. 51 (1944), pp. 358–374.

30. Sharon S. Brehm, *The Application of Social Psychology to Clinical Practice* (New York: John Wiley, 1976), pp. 164–171.

31. Ibid., p. 168.

32. Ibid.

33. Ibid., p. 169.

34. Ibid.

35. Fischer and Gochros, *Planned Behavior Change*, p. 93.

36. Alan E. Kazdin, "The Application of Operant Techniques in Treatment, Rehabilitation, and Education," in Sol L. Garfield and Allen E. Bergin, eds., *Handbook of Psychotherapy and Behavior Change*, (New York: John Wiley, 1978), pp. 549–590.

37. G. Alan Marlatt and Martha A. Perry, in Frederick H. Kanfer and Arnold P. Goldstein, eds., *Modeling Methods in Helping People Change: A Textbook of Methods* (Elmsford, N.Y.: Pergamon Press, 1975), pp. 117–128.

38. Ibid., p. 122.

39. Reid and Epstein, *Task-Centered Casework*.

40. William J. Reid, *The Task-Centered System* (New York: Columbia University Press, 1978), p. 139.

41. Garfield, *Psychotherapy*, p. 141.

42. S. Schachter and J. E. Singer, "Cognitive, Social, and Physiological Determinants of Emotional State," *Psychological Review*, Vol. 69 (1962), pp. 379–399.

43. M. Lieberman, I. Yalom, and M. Miles, *Encounter Groups: First Facts* (New York: Basic Books, 1973).

44. Fischer, *Effective Casework Practice*, pp. 298–299.

45. A. T. Beck, *Cognitive Therapy and the Emotional Disorders* (New York: International Universities Press, 1976).

46. Ibid., p. 217.

47. Elizabeth Kübler-Ross, *On Death and Dying* (New York: Macmillan, 1969).

48. Yalom, *Existential Psychotherapy*, pp. 110–158.

49. This part of the chapter draws from Charles Garvin, *Contemporary Group Work* (Englewood Cliffs, N.J.: Prentice-Hall, 1981).

50. Ibid., p. 153.

51. Ibid., pp. 154–55.

52. Ibid., p. 155.

53. Alice Collins, and Diane L. Pancoast, *Natural Helping Networks: A Strategy for Prevention* (Washington, D.C.: National Association of Social Workers, 1976).

54. See, for example, Lela Costin, *Child Welfare: Policies and Procedures* (New York: McGraw-Hill, 1972).

twelve

The Change Process

APPLICATIONS WITH GROUPS AND FAMILIES

In this chapter we consider work with both families and groups because both these entities are small social systems. The family can be considered a small group and in many ways can be analyzed and worked with as any other small group. On the other hand, workers interact with families or other "natural" groups in some ways that differ from how they work with groups that are "formed" to help individuals and then disband. Differences between these two types of groups also stem from the fact that groups such as the family differ from other groups because they have a history, a high degree of intimacy, and considerable interdependence due to the many functions they perform for their members.

While many workers think of formed groups as vehicles for individual change, they usually think of the family as an entity in its own right and emphasize goals of improved family functioning as such. In contrast, many workers with groups give equal or even greater weight to goals of improved *individ-*

ual functioning and create group goals that contribute to this.

The degree to which the differences in family and other groups lead to differences in practice procedures has not been adequately explicated in the practice literature, and we seek to clarify this issue in each section of this chapter. Before we discuss group and family matters, however, we present the history of work with groups and families in social work, as this illuminates many of the issues of concern to us today.

Introduction

Family Therapy in Social Work

Social work has identified itself with the welfare of the family since its beginnings. One of its pioneers, Zilpha S. Smith, wrote in 1890 in reference to her colleagues, "Most of you deal with poor persons or defective *individuals* removed from family relationships. We deal with the *family* as a whole, usually working to keep it together, but sometimes helping to break it up into units and to place them in your care."[1]

While the work of Smith may be recognized only by social work historians, that of Mary Richmond is better known as she was one of the first to conceptualize social work practice. In her often-cited work, *Social Diagnosis*, she stated, "in some forms of social work, notably family rebuilding, a client's social relations are so likely to be all important that *family* [our emphasis] caseworkers welcome the opportunity to see at the very beginning of intercourse several members of the family assembled in their own home environment, acting and reacting upon one another, each taking a share in the development of the client's story, each revealing in ways other than words social facts of real significance."[2]

Following upon this beginning, social workers were invariably taught that improved family functioning was a major objective of social work practice and that the client's family was an essential component for understanding the client. For many years, ones of the major journals for social work practice, now called *Contemporary Social Work* (and previously *Social Casework*) was called *The Family*.

Despite this kind of commitment, social workers have worked primarily on a one-to-one basis, although there has undoubtedly been an increase in the frequency with which several members of the family have been seen together. While this emphasis on one-to-one work was undoubtedly related to the strong influence of psychoanalytic ideas on social work, it was also due to the fact that the techniques and theories of family therapy have been developed only fairly recently. The 1950s were the years when this technological development began to take place as a number of individuals, working alone or in teams, almost simultaneously began to work with families and to conceptualize this activity. The people that are most often cited, and their locations at the time, are John Bell at Clark University; Nathan Ackerman at Jewish Family Services in New York City; Theodore Lidz at Yale; Lyman Wynne and Murray Bowen at the National Institute of Mental Health; Carl Whitaker in Atlanta; Gregory Bateson, Jay Haley, John Weakland, Don Jackson, and Virginia Satir in Palo Alto, California; and Ivan Boszormeny-Nagy, James Framo, and others at the Eastern Pennsylvania Psychiatric Institute.

As can be seen, the widespread geographical distribution of the development of family therapy indicated that this was an idea whose time had come. Most of the people cited were psychiatrists, yet social workers were associated with almost all these programs, and such social work trained people as Virginia Satir, Lynn Hoffman, and Harry Aponte are recognized as leading theoreticians of family therapy.

The current situation, therefore, is that family therapy has become a significant part of education for interpersonal practice. Practitioners who were educated before this development, consequently, are flocking to continuing education programs to learn about family therapy. Exactly how much this has changed agency practice is less clear.

We should stress at this early point in the chapter that in our idea of the "family" we include a great variety of forms. We define the family as a set of individuals who have economic and other commitments to each other, who are likely to meet each other's needs for intimacy, and who usually maintain a joint household. Thus communes, adult siblings living together, and homosexual couples are some of the many types of families.

Group Work in Social Work

The use of groups to help people began early in the profession's history. Social workers, for example, worked in agencies such as settlement houses, "Y's," and youth serving organizations where they sought to draw upon the effects of group experiences to socialize individuals to urban environments, to maintain their cultured identities, and to encourage their participation in a democratic society.[3]

Mary Richmond whom we cited regarding her emphasis on families also encouraged the interest of social workers in groups as, for example, through her oft-quoted reference to "the new tendency to view our clients from the angle of what might be termed small group psychology."[4] Early social workers interested in groups, however, had very broad theoretical foundations. Their interests included political ideas such as those of Follett and Lindeman[5] that related small-group processes to the growth of democracy in society as well as the progressive education ideas of John Dewey who realized that group processes focusing on life issues have a significant educational impact.[6]

By the late 1920s, group work training was available in several schools of social work, although controversy existed among group workers as well as other social workers as to whether social work methods included group work. This issue was settled to a degree by the mid-1930s, and this was reflected in several papers presented at the 1935 National Conference of Social Work. The conference that year created a section on group work and Grace Coyle and Wilbur Newstetter described the philosophy and methods of group work as linked to those of social work.[7]

The theoretical base for social work with groups continued to develop throughout the next decades as group work writers sought conceptual inputs from the social sciences, particularly from social-psychological investigations of small-group phenomena. Some of the ideas that evolved within social work were that the worker was a facilitator of group process, that the activities of the group were important tools that the members could use to enhance group processes, and that the limits imposed on the group by the worker and the agency, as related to the realities of the situation, will produce growth in the members and strengthen the group. These and many other conceptions were discussed and analyzed at many conferences and through a substantial number of publications that emerged during those years.

Theory and practice changed during the 1960s, however, in ways that continue to have a great impact. This consisted of the effort, in line with that to which this book is devoted, to integrate practice theory related to work with individuals, families, and groups and to create a body of knowledge that relates to all these systems. In addition, some workers saw their practice as generic and offered their clients a full range of services as dictated by client need rather than worker specialization. This, unfortunately, has lessened the attention paid to theory for practice with groups.

In this chapter, we shall present theory for practice with families and groups as linked to theory for all of interpersonal practice yet possessing unique elements that both professionals and theorists should continue to explore. The reader should be aware, nevertheless, that this view of group work is a controversial one as some group work authorities perceived group work as a unique mode of practice,[8] without linkages to other approaches and action systems such as two persons (worker and client) and families. Despite this controversy, almost all professional training programs incorporate content on group approaches. Groups are also utilized as a means of helping clients in all types of interpersonal settings, and the terms "caseworker" and "group worker" are often replaced by the broader designation of "social worker" or "clinical social worker."

As we proceed to discuss change processes in groups and families, the types of groups served by interpersonal practitioners should be borne in mind. These include groups in psychiatric settings to help clients acquire social skills, cope with interpersonal conflicts, and improve their ability to perceive social circumstances correctly; groups in child welfare settings to help clients deal with problems associated with separation; groups in school settings to help children cope with impediments to learning; groups in correctional settings to help clients offset forces that promote lawbreaking; and groups in family settings to help individual clients or even several families or couples work together to help each other to fulfill family roles or to change them.

In addition, the agencies that originated group work, namely, the settlement houses and community centers, still exist and sponsor group services. These services emphasize socialization activities to help members fulfill their social roles. Recently, however, many such agencies have offered group services to such populations as retarded people, former mental patients, and the handicapped.

A point of view we wish the reader to consider in this chapter is that the wide range of group services offered by social workers requires many different approaches to facilitating the group experience. While some social work writers argue that social work with groups is a single approach, we believe this to be unrealistic.[9] Social work purposes and settings do set some limits on the

kinds of techniques that social workers should use in group situations. We should, therefore, devise research to determine what these limits are rather than set boundaries by ideological positions.

The Group and Family as Target Systems

Occasions for Family and Group Interventions

The idea that workers should intervene directly in the systems in which the client's presenting problems are embedded is becoming a well-established one in social work. Thus, when an individual's problems are maintained by family conditions, the worker should become involved with the family or in other ways seek to change those conditions; a similar principle will apply in regard to group associations. Since many, if not most, of the problems that people bring to social workers have these aspects, some conclude that work on a one-to-one basis should be the exception.

We do not take as strong a position. The individual may be unable or unwilling to work together with others. The individual may also wish to focus primarily on his or her cognitions and feelings, although, again, one can argue that even this goal will be more easily achieved if the individual secures feedback from people who are significant in his or her life. It is also possible that clients on a one-to-one basis with the worker can develop ways to reshape their own situations.

We believe, nevertheless, that even one-to-one practice should have a group and family perspective. Clients' problems should be understood as they are related to social interactions, and goals should be developed regarding changes in these interactions. We should, however, seek to advance our knowledge about the relative effectiveness of one-to-one, family, group, and environmental interventions for different people with different kinds of problems, from different cultures, of different genders and sexual preferences, and in different social situations. Practitioners should become familiar with such reference works as the *Handbook of Psychotherapy and Behavior Change*[10] that contain extensive reviews of the effectiveness of group and family approaches along with many other dimensions of interpersonal helping.

Additional principles exist when practitioners target group circumstances. One of these arises when the worker functions professionally with a *group whose purpose is to help the individual members enhance their social functioning*. Some of these groups are appropriately termed "treatment groups" because they function in therapeutic settings such as psychiatric clinics and community mental health programs. Groups, however, in community centers, settlement houses, and sometimes schools are not thought of as "treatment" or "therapy" but as socialization experiences that facilitate the group's members "normal" social development. Nevertheless, these groups are also intended to enhance the social functioning of individual members and do not exist for the sake of the group as an entity.

Another type of group that might use a social worker is a *self-help group*. In most cases, the worker does not become the ongoing facilitator of the group. The group instead seeks the worker's help in securing resources, resolving a current problem, or training the group's indigenous leaders. One exception is an organization, Parents Anonymous, established to help parents who are actually or potentially involved in child abuse.

The "sponsor" of these groups may be a professional social worker, although the emphasis is still upon the self-help component.

The worker will draw upon his or her understanding of group phenomena to fulfill the specific request of the self-help group. In addition, members of self-help groups may also be clients of social workers in other contexts such as one-to-one or family treatment. An understanding of the impact of the group experience is necessary for the worker as part of the support the worker provides for the client's use of group resources.

The worker also draws upon knowledge of group phenomena in reference to groups in which the client holds membership and that constitute either resources for or barriers to client change. These groups constitute target systems in that the worker helps the *client* to have an impact on them. An example of this is work done with an adolescent who sought to fulfill a constructive leadership role with a group of friends. The worker helped this client to understand some of the group processes that occurred among her friends and what she might do about these. Workers have fulfilled similar functions when clients have discussed their memberships in church groups, cottage groups in residential institutions, and fraternal orders. This is not to deny the fact that at times the worker may offer to meet with such groups, thus defining them as action systems.

Finally, while we do not intend in this chapter to draw connections to groups in which the worker functions on behalf of clients (such as staff teams and case conferences), many of the processes we discuss in this chapter are relevant to these. The workers will be called upon to be sensitive to his or her impact on these groups and how their processes can be enhanced so as to secure better services for clients.

Approaches to Changing Group and Family Conditions

Points of Entry

In Chapter 7 we described various system dimensions, and this information should help the reader to assess the conditions in the group or family that enhance or hinder the resolution of problems experienced by individuals. When the worker and the members desire, consequently, to maintain some conditions and change others, a strategic decision must be made as to how to do this. A systemic principle, that of equifinality, implies that there may be several ways in which to affect a system, and the question is which one is accessible to the worker and members. One way of analyzing this is to conceive of the situation as comprising systemic levels of the individual, several individuals in interaction (a subgroup), the system as a whole, and the systems outside the family or group that interact with it.

Change in any one of these levels may have the desired impact. One example of this is a family or group in which a few individuals do all the talking. This can be changed by encouraging nontalkers on a one-to-one basis, by confronting a subgroup of "talkers" with the effect they have on the others, by presenting the problem to everyone and helping all to work together to devise a solution, or by interacting with some person in the environment (such as an individual who punished some family or group members for what they said in the group).

Models of Interpersonal Practice with Groups and Families

Almost all approaches to practice with groups devised by social work writers prescribe in some way the role of the worker in relationship to individual members, subgroups, the group as a whole, and the environment outside the group. These prescriptions vary, however, depending on the writer's model of practice. In one effort, for example, to identify the similarities and differences among models, Schwartz wrote,

> There was a kind of "medical" model on which "the steps of the helping process are described by assuming a sequence of movements through which the worker investigates, diagnoses, and treats the problem under consideration." There was a "scientific" model "in which the steps in the helping process resemble closely the problem solving sequence by which the scientific worker moves from the unknown to the known." And there was a "model of the organic system" in which "the total helping situation is viewed as a network of reciprocal activity, and in which it is impossible to describe accurately any part of the system without describing its active relationship to the other moving parts."[11]

Papell and Rothman also sought to delineate group work models.[12] They described three models: the *social goals model*, the *remedial model*, and the *reciprocal model*. The social goals model draws from the ideas of the early group work writers who conceived of groups as enhancing the participation of members in a democratic society. The remedial model is similar to Schwartz's medical and scientific models as it is based on a diagnosis and treatment paradigm that draws upon the problem-solving process. The reciprocal model emphasizes the transactional processes among individuals, groups, and environments as each entity seeks to fulfill its purposes. In the reciprocal model, the worker is described as facilitating these transactions through "mediation."

Sharp philosophical differences exist between the remedial and reciprocal models. The remedial model manifests a scientific and positivist bias in its attention to individual and group goals in which the latter are consistent with the former. The model directs the practitioner to use social science and social work research findings to create practice procedures that lead to the attainment of individual and group goals. The reciprocal model is an existential one, as Schwartz states, because of its "curiosity about processes, the nature of experience, the influence of feelings on human behavior, and the conduct of people in interaction."[13]

Another approach to the identification of models of group work was the volume edited by Roberts and Northen, *Theories of Social Work with Groups*.[14] This work included articles about the reciprocal and remedial (called in that volume the "organizational") models. The book followed the tradition established in the *Encyclopedia of Social Work* in two consecutive editions in which a *developmental* model was seen as the third model. In addition, Roberts and Northen included approaches associated with generic practice, psychosocial practice, functional practice, task-centered practice, socialization through groups, and crisis intervention. Chapters on group work history and on approaches to problem solving in groups were also included in that volume.

In a final chapter, Roberts and Northen compared the various approaches. In their analysis, the editors concluded that the authors did not represent distinct theoretical postures as there was a good deal of overlap. Thus, authors create internally consistent models by assembling elements of practice in different ways. All approaches share the values common to social workers, use similar small-group concepts (e.g., group structure, group leadership), and envision groups as proceeding through phases. Worker tasks differ, according to all writers, depending on whether the group is in the beginning, middle, or ending phase of the group experience. The major difference, it seems to us, is found

in how workers interact with individuals, the group as a whole, and the environment and interactions among these entities. Theoretical underpinnings are also not identical. Controversy exists as to how social science should be used in group work and whether ego psychological, behavioral, role, socialization, organizational, or other concepts should be added to those drawn from small group theory.

In the same way as there are commonalities among models of group work, there are also similarities among approaches to family treatment. All present individual problems as embedded in family conditions and as requiring changes in such conditions for their solution. All see such conditions as including the family's interactions with its environment, the family's structure, the nature of communications in the family, the family's processes, and the roles fulfilled by family members. While all seek to change these dimensions, each approach to family therapy directs interventions at one dimension more than another. All approaches also recognize that families develop repetitive ways of coping with stresses that are difficult to change—that is, that there are forces that maintain an equilibrium in the family that must be displaced.

Unlike group work, however, there is no clear delineation of social work approaches to family treatment as distinguished from nonsocial work approaches. Social workers in the same way as other professionals divide themselves among the various schools. We hope, nevertheless, that since we view social work as focused on individual-environmental transactions, social workers will be drawn to models of family therapy that give the greatest consideration to the role of the environment beyond the nuclear family.

Different authorities may subdivide the field of family therapy differently. We choose to utilize the typology presented by Gurman and Kniskern because of its clarity and simplicity. They view the schools of thought in family therapy as (1) psychoanalytic-object relations, (2) intergenerational, (3) systems theory, and (4) behavioral.[15]

Psychoanalytical-Object Relations

Much of psychoanalytic theory has been devoted to the mental processes of the individual while the emphasis in family approaches is on transactions among family members. Nevertheless, some family therapists seek to integrate a psychoanalytic understanding of mental processes into a family systems perspective. Systems concepts can be used in this way as they portray the individual as a system interacting with social systems. The personality of the individual can be examined for its effect on social systems, and vice versa. For example, a psychoanalytic family therapist who looks at such a phenomenon as insight, unlike more traditional psychoanalysts, will see it as a consequence of systems change as much as an antecedent of it. It is interesting to view the development over the course of their professional lives of such psychoanalysts as Ackerman as they shifted their perspectives from an individual psychological to a systems perspective under the impact of their work with families.

Intergenerational Considerations

This approach is distinguished from the others in that family problems are seen as arising from experiences in the individual's families of origin. Parents in a family with problems may create these problems because of the ways in which they try to force other people to fit into preestablished molds developed in those earlier family circumstances. A major treatment issue, consequently, is to require adults to have sessions with their families of origin to resolve issues where they were originally created and where they are presumed to continue to exist.

Systems Theory

It may seem odd to label some approaches as stemming from systems thinking when it is scarcely possible to find a writer on family therapy who does not use some systems concepts. Nevertheless, some approaches emphasize the following to a greater degree than others:

1. The goals of family therapy are expressed as a change in family functioning even though the therapist may contract around the problem of an individual.
2. The cognitions of family members are seen primarily as products of systemic conditions and are worked with as such.
3. Strategies of change are primarily derived from system ideas.

In Gurman and Kniskern's typology, a number of approaches are subsumed under the system's label that are categorized separately by other writers. This includes the work of those who had been associated with the work of Bateson on communications and family systems at Palo Alto, with the structural thinking of Minuchin, and with the "strategic approaches" stimulated to a great degree by the work of Milton Erickson. Erickson was a psychiatrist who had highly innovative ideas about forms of psychological influence such as hypnotism; "strategic" therapists whom he has influenced are marked by a very directive posture and the use of this to design strategies uniquely for each family to achieve systemic changes.

Behavior Modification

Family therapy applications of behavior modification are similar to other behavioral approaches in that they constitute applications of behavioral learning theory to family contexts. Thus, such therapists will identify specific behaviors exhibited by family members and modify these by helping them to communicate or otherwise act differently with each other. Techniques used by such practitioners include communications training, training in the use by family members themselves of behavioral approaches, and establishing contracts among family members. Many sexual dysfunctions are treated in this way, and such treatment may also incorporate behavioral procedures to reduce anxiety related to sexual performance.

Procedures to Change Group and Family Conditions

As indicated, we categorize procedures for changing group and family conditions into those in which the worker interacts with individuals, subgroups, the system as a whole, or external systems. In utilizing these categories, the worker should remember that interventions with any of these systems can have expected or unexpected effects on other systems.

Changing Family and Group Conditions Through Work with Individuals

Single persons can have effects on group or family conditions under several circumstances: (1) when they have tasks to perform, (2) when they exercise power, or (3) when their behavior fulfills a systemic function. Examples of tasks that individuals perform are doing chores, securing resources, and acting as a leader. The worker can affect the system by helping the members perform these tasks. One of the procedures the worker can use for this is "coaching the member." Coaching involves giving support as well as "feedback" to

the member on how well the member is doing. The worker may also suggest actions to the member that will enhance task performance such as rewarding other members or empathizing with them.

The worker may also use behavior modification procedures to help members perform tasks. These include helping the member select a role model who has performed the task well. The same procedures we described in Chapter 11 for modeling can be used. The worker can also supply reinforcement in the form, for example, of praise for aspects of the job that are well done. If the individual has a high degree of anxiety about performing a task, the worker can help him or her to relax.

Workers often provide leadership training for group members who are in leadership positions, and this has its family analogue in parent training. There are many formats for such training for group leaders, but they usually include information on how to moderate discussions, facilitate equity in group participation, mediate conflicts, and structure group tasks. Parent training includes information on how to assess family circumstances that create child problems, how to limit child behavior through appropriate use of discipline and rewards, and how to communicate effectively with children.[16]

The second reason for working with individuals to modify group and family conditions is that individuals with power may use this to change the system. The worker can facilitate this by interacting with powerful group members or by increasing the amount of power of those who do not possess it. An example of this condition is a group of patients in a psychiatric facility. The worker sought to encourage the group to plan some trips outside the institution so that the members could learn skills that are useful in returning to the community. The worker discussed this idea with several of the members whom she thought were listened to by the others. When the idea was presented at a meeting, these members supported it. In an analogous way, a worker with a family discussed a family project with the parents first.

An example of the second condition is another group in the same institution. In that group, the worker sought to encourage trips into the community. The members who supported this, however, were the least influential in the group because they had been in the group the shortest time and were not well known to the other members. The worker encouraged them to present their plans at the group meeting. When the other members realized the newcomers' competence in planning such activities, they gave more attention to their opinions, and this moved the group toward a decision to take the proposed trips. Similarly, in one family, a worker helped the mother, who was seen by other family members as ineffective, to determine what rights she wanted to insist upon and then to carry through on this.

In the interactions just cited, the worker is modifying the power structure of the system. The worker sometimes does this by encouraging powerful individuals to relinquish their influence or to use it sparingly. This is accomplished by helping people to be more caring for others as well as to understand that domination of others can interfere with developing one's self as a person who is concerned about, helpful to, and respected by others including family members.

At other times, as in our illustration, the worker seeks to increase the power of the less influential members by increasing their expertise, their contribution to group tasks, their ability to reward others, and their likability. Likability is, in part, a function of the ways we listen to and provide gratification to others and can, thus, be enhanced.

The third reason for working with individuals to modify system conditions is when the individual's behavior maintains problematic group conditions. In these circumstances, the condition is preserved by both the individual's behavior and the system's response to it. In view of the equilibria that systems seek to maintain, a change in this equilibrium can be initiated by an intervention with an individual or the other members of the group or with both in close order. Family therapists have developed many ways of implementing this principle, such as giving directives or tasks to one family member not given to others.

One example of the way in which an individual acts to maintain or change a systemic condition arises when the individual is regarded by group members as a "deviant," that is, as departing in some way from behaviors regarded as normative. The phenomenon of deviance is a complex one, as the consequence of deviance may be either to reinforce the system's commitment to its norms or to change them.[17] The worker can work with the deviant individual in a number of ways to influence this process. The worker may help such an individual to accept and conform to system norms. On the other hand, the individual may be helped to present his or her "case" in the most effective manner, thus seeking to change such norms. Which course the worker takes will be governed by the purposes of the system and the effect of the norm on the achievement of those purposes.

Changing Family and Group Conditions Through Work with Subgroups

Groups tend to create subgroups in that members may be attracted to and interact with some individuals more frequently than others. Subgroups may be perceived as "cliques," and their existence may be supported or criticized. At times the existence of such subgroups is appropriate as members with interpersonal relationship problems, for example, can test out their interpersonal skills with selected others in the group. Subgroups may be dysfunctional, as when one clique destructively dominates others or when a pact is made within a subgroup that the members will protect each other from even the beneficial influences of the group and its worker. All these alternatives can be found in families where subgroups typically consist of the parents in one and the children in another. It is possible for a subgroup of a parent and child to form with the other parent as an isolate or in another subgroup with another child or a grandparent. This type of structure is often the source of family problems.

In a manner analogous to the one the worker uses to work with individuals, the worker can modify a subgroup and, through it, the whole group. The worker can make assignments to the subgroup and ask it to perform tasks for the whole group. Thus, a subgroup might constitute a "committee" to secure resources or arrange for group events. Subgroups can also be given problem-solving tasks in which they report on their conclusions so that all members can give further consideration to the matter. In the family, the worker often works with the parents to solidify their existence as a subgroup and to reduce conflicts between them.

Under other circumstances, the worker wishes to affect processes occurring within the subgroup. Thus, in some subgroups one member dominates the situation or in other ways diverts others from reaching their goals. The worker may ask the members of the subgroup to examine their relationships to one another, and relevant observations of members outside of the subgroup can also be secured. Members of other subgroups may recognize that similar patterns exist in *their*

subgroups; thus, an understanding of one subgroup's patterns may have a "ripple" effect throughout the group. This process is one that has been helpful in groups composed of several families or couples in which each family constitutes a subgroup. It also represents a major task in family therapy, that of resolving problems within each generational group.

At times the worker wishes to change the subgroup pattern as well as the structure of the whole group. This is the case when subgroups maintain members in high and low status in a rigid manner or when subgroups are antagonistic to one another in ways that interfere with the development of the group. Under these circumstances, the worker will often introduce activities or subgroup assignments that require realignments that differ from the existing subgroup pattern. In a group of children, for example, in which two hostile subgroups emerged, the worker introduced several games. In each game, a different principle for choosing team members was used (such as counting off by fours) so that the members experienced alternative subgroup patterns.

We have noted that work with a marital couple, in small-group terms, is the same as working with a subgroup. The reader is undoubtedly aware, however, that the kinds of issues raised in marital counseling are usually more intense and more significant to the outcome of the interpersonal helping process than is work with a subgroup of a formed group. The marital partners have made a lifetime commitment to one another; the range of needs each is expected to meet for the other is broad; the interaction between the partners includes sexuality as a major component; and the marital subgroup has responsibilities for the other subgroup(s) (such as the children) that subgroups in a formed group do not have.

As a consequence of this, the entire course of interpersonal helping may be devoted to the marital subgroup, and in work with the entire family, this subgroup may be the major focus. Some of the interventions used in work with the marital subgroup are the following:

1. *Communications training and enhancement.* Couples are taught to avoid exaggerated accusations ("You *always* lie to me"), to state directly how they feel ("When you shout, I become frightened"), to proceed in a rational fashion to solve problems (gather information, examine alternatives, choose the alternative with the most benefits and the least costs), as well as other communication styles required by their specific problems.[18] This kind of training is often done in couples groups.

2. *Marital contracts.* Couples are helped to identify their expectations of each other and to negotiate with each other to meet them.[19]

3. *Cognitive and insight-oriented techniques.* Spouses are helped in the presence of each other to work on distortions in their perceptions of each other, conflicts because the nuclear family differs from the family of origin, and reactions to changing family and sex roles.

4. *Sex therapy.* Couples are helped through a variety of training techniques to reduce such problems as differences in the frequency with which sex is desired, impotence, frigidity, and delayed or premature orgasms. This topic is well beyond the scope of this book, but the reader can consult works by Kaplan, Masters and Johnson, and Heiman et al.[20]

Changing Family and Group Conditions Through Work with the Entire System

The worker has several decisions to make in seeking to modify directly a condition of the entire group or family. The first is the choice of which variable to change. This choice can be made collaboratively with the group or family members: their help in any case should be elicited to determine the nature of the system's problems and which variables contribute to this. We discussed in Chapter 7 the variables that can be used to assess group and family conditions, and these should be considered when a change in such conditions is sought.

One of the variables that should be considered first in any effort to change the system is the stage the group or family has reached in its development because a condition required at one phase may be dysfunctional at another. For example, in the formation phase of one formed group, a thorough discussion of group purpose was a necessary condition for the further development of the group. On the other hand, in another group that was proceeding in a manner that was satisfactory to most of its members, one individual sought to open the group to rediscussion of purpose. This was an obstructive act on his part and stemmed from his competitive feelings toward other members. The worker helped the members discuss the issue in that context rather than that of group purpose. Similarly, a couple with a newborn child was helped to renegotiate roles so as to integrate the child into the family, while a couple with a young adult was helped to renegotiate roles so as to be less dependent on the presence of this youth to maintain family stability.

In a formed group's formation phase, the variables that the worker most seeks to affect are (1) the group's definition of its purpose, (2) the members' clarification of their individual purposes and goals, (3) how these relate to the group's purposes and goals, (4) the quality of the relationships among the members and between the members and the worker, and (5) the level of commitment the members wish to make to the group. In a formed group's middle phases, the worker seeks to help the members plan group activities that will aid the members to reach their individual goals through the pursuit of group goals.

The worker also is aware that during the middle phases, conflicts are likely to arise in the group as members compete with each other for positions of influence in the group and as disagreements arise regarding the program of the group and the solutions to group problems. The worker, therefore, will provide emotional support to the members during these group "crises" and will help the members to solve group problems with as much consensus as possible. During the final stages of the group, the worker will help the members to lessen the emotional hold the group has upon them and to transfer both the new forms of adaptation they have acquired in the group as well as any dependency they may have developed on the group to other systems in the environment.

These phases have their analogues in family phases, although family phases are more complex and have greater impact on the individuals than group phases. The times when families are adapting, for example, to the birth of the first child, the child's entry into school, the child's adolescence, and the child leaving home can be experienced as major family crises.

When the worker decides to alter, or help the group to alter, some group condition—and after due consideration of the stage of system development—this is done through the use of a number of procedures. We have organized these procedures into five categories of behavior. These categories are (1) cognitions, (2) action patterns, (3) activities, (4) norms, and (5) emotional states. We will now consider each of these in turn and describe the related family and group procedures used by the worker.

Cognitions

Under this heading we include views that are shared by members of the system as a result of communications among them about events and their causes. The worker can help to change system conditions by initiating a change in these understandings. One way that this is done is through the initiation of a problem-solving sequence in which the problem is the condition. An example is a group that was concerned about some members who considered leaving the group because they were not involved in group decision making. The worker suggested that the group study the problem and arrive at its own conclusions about it. The members decided to keep a record of how often each member spoke during the meeting. The record was maintained for two meetings, and this information supported the contention that participation in group discussions was uneven as some members spoke much more and some much less than others. The worker suggested that the group choose a method of changing this pattern. This led to an animated discussion of various techniques for doing this; ultimately one was chosen and implemented. This process led to changes in the views of the members about their group and had consequences for a change in group conditions.

Members have also learned other ways to examine their group based upon one or another models of group phenomena. For example, Bion's idea that group members develop various forms of emotional resistances to the work of the group has been taught to group members together with ways of identifying these resistances.[21] They consist of "basic assumptions" that the members share, namely, a *dependency* upon the leader, *fight or flight* in which emotional issues are handled through either conflict or digression, and *pairing* in which two persons focus their attention upon each other rather than upon the work of the group.

Several techniques for changing shared cognitions in systems have been developed by family therapists. We shall describe these here as "family therapy" techniques, although we believe that they also can be used in formed groups. Using Minuchin's terminology, they are reframing, realities, and constructions.[22]

Reframing.   Families have a view of their situation that was created by their experiences together. As Minuchin states,

> They have made their own assessment of their problems, their strengths, and their possibilities. They are asking the therapist to help with the reality that they have framed. . . . Therapy starts, therefore, with the clash between two framings of reality. The family's framing is relevant for the continuity and maintenance of the organism more or less as it is; the therapeutic framing is related to the goal of moving the family toward a more differentiated and competent dealing with their dysfunctional reality.[23]

Examples of reframing are declaring that a mother whom the family labels overprotective is "caring;" that a father whom the family labels as uninvolved is a "workaholic;" and that a child whom the family labels as a troublemaker is keeping the number of family rules within reasonable limits.

Realities.   While reframing relates to the definitions that the family places on situations, realities relates to what the family regards as factual. Realities also includes the family's world view that involves the proverbs, maxims, legends, and folktales learned by the family. The worker may decide either to use the family's realities or to change them. An example of the former was a worker who worked collaboratively with a *curandero* to help a Chicano family. A *curandero* is a practitioner of procedures to restore health (as a holistic entity) that have been developed for centuries out of Spanish and Indian traditions and experiences. An example of the lat-

ter is a worker who engaged in several discussions with a family in which she challenged the sexist beliefs of the family that were creating severe stress for the female family members in one way and for the male members in another.

Constructions.   This technology relates to how the family explains events as opposed to the definitions they use and the "facts" they accept as true. In one family, for example, the worker explained that a teenager's misbehavior was his effort to establish his own identity as separate from the family. This led to problem solving regarding alternative ways of establishing such an identity that did not result in punitive legal action.

Action Patterns

Under this heading we include changing behaviors of members when these behaviors are embedded in a repetitive sequence of actions. We shall now describe some of the techniques that can be used to alter these.

A procedure to alter the amount of participation was used with the children in one boy's group who said very little when the worker introduced a discussion topic. The worker awarded each boy a peanut each time he spoke, and this led to an increase in this type of behavior. In groups of people of other ages, this approach can be varied so that the consequences of participation can be verbal support, an entry on a chart, or a caring touch from an adjacent member.

A concern in groups is that while some members participate responsibly, others tend to stray from the topic. Contingencies can be used with reference to the content of verbalization as well as the amount. An example of this approach, as suggested by Rose, was used in a group where members made too many critical or otherwise unpleasant remarks to one another.[24] Each time a member felt abused, he put a white poker chip in a can in the center of the room; a red chip was placed to indicate the member felt supported. This procedure for signalling feelings to other members led to a decrease in abusing statements and an increase in supporting ones.

Another approach to modifying action patterns in addition to utilizing reinforcement contingencies is to *interrupt* or *modify directly* a sequence of actions. One example of the need for this occurred in a group of adults whose purpose was to help the members with problems in interpersonal relationships. Whenever Sue, one member, sought to relate the group's discussion to her own problems, Fran interacted with her in a maternal fashion. Bill then addressed his remarks to Fran in an effort to have her direct this nurturance to him. Fran became impatient with Bill who then attacked Sue in a jealous fashion. Sue withdrew from the discussion until this sequence was repeated on another occasion when she again sought to relate a group discussion to herself.

There are many ways in which the worker can target this type of interaction, including helping the members to approach it *cognitively* in one of the ways we have previously described. The worker may seek instead to *interfere directly* with the sequence of behaviors. In the group just cited, this consisted of instructing another member (other than Fran) to respond to Sue and instructing Bill to address his remarks to someone else besides Fran. This type of intervention can have the effect of initiating a change in a pattern that is dysfunctional to someone such as Sue and may be the only thing that will "work," when cognitive approaches fail, because of the strong forces that maintain recurrent group patterns.

Interfering with a repetitive sequence is also frequently a requirement for effective family therapy, and, therefore, family therapists have developed many strategies to achieve this. One such approach is *"unbalancing,"* in which the worker, for the moment, casts his or her lot with one individual or subgroup in the system.[25] This may lead to a change in the behavior of all parties. In one situation, the worker stated that the wife in the family was engaging in very jealous behavior when she questioned her husband about his previous relationships. The husband saw his wife as being attacked and rose to defend her. This was a change from a previous pattern in which the husband attacked his wife on a number of scores and the worker was the one to defend her. The worker, after this intervention, gave suport to the husband's subsequent defenses of his wife and the wife's expressions of appreciation for these.

Another type of intervention used in families to interfere with sequences is to *replace* one type of dysfunctional sequence with another. This strategy can have the effect of initiating a change process that culminates with a more functional set of behaviors. An example of this occurred in a family in which the mother was overinvolved with a child and the father was excluded. A grandparent was critical of the mother's handling of the child and the worker assigned her to take charge of the child for a week. The father was critical of the grandmother's handling of the situation, and this ultimately led to his greater involvement.

Yet a third approach is the use of a *paradoxical instruction*, in which the worker urges a behavior that is contrary to the initial set of goals.[26] In a case of this type in which a child would not go to school, Haley describes the worker as suggesting that "it might be better if the boy just stayed home" and giving such reasons for this as the family becomes too upset when the boy goes to school.[27]

This type of intervention requires great thought and skill and should not be attempted by an inexperienced worker. As Haley states,

> The therapist is communicating a number of different things at the same time. He is saying "I want to help you get better" and he is saying, "I am benevolently concerned about you." He is saying things to the family that are on the edge of being insulting: he is saying he thinks the family members can really tolerate being normal, but he is saying perhaps they cannot.[28]

Restructuring is another frequently used family therapy approach to change a behavior pattern. This involves a direct manipulation of the family's interactions, physical space, or tasks so as to change the coalitions among family members.[29] Three examples of this follow:

1. The worker directed the father to speak directly to his son rather than talk to the mother about the son (manipulation of interactions).
2. The worker asked the mother and John to change chairs so that the mother was seated next to the father. The worker then moved the mother's and father's chairs into a position in which they sat facing one another (manipulation of physical space).
3. The worker assigned the father to be responsible for all child discipline for one week (manipulation of a task).

While these techniques have been closely associated with the family therapy process, they can also be used in groups. This is an additional example of how family therapists and group workers might learn from each other, because of their common interest, which is to enhance the functioning of small social systems. We shall now move on to a full discussion of the manipulation of the tasks (activities) of the system, which, while considered briefly already, represent a major contribution that group work practice has made to work with small systems.

Activities

Another set of procedures for modifying small social systems is that in which the members select and participate in an activity. In the group work literature, this is referred to as the *use of program*. Group workers have typically drawn upon games, crafts, music, dramatics, and other creative endeavors to help group members achieve their purposes. In one of the classic texts, for example, that of Wilson and Ryland, several chapters are devoted to each of these media.[30]

A major advancement in the conceptualization of program was made by Vinter when he identified a series of program dimensions.[31] Vinter states that all activities occur in a *physical field*, which "refers to the physical space and terrain, and the physical and social objects characteristic of each activity." The physical field of a group discussion is the persons in the room, the chairs and table around which they sit, and other objects in the room such as pictures and lamps. The physical field of a baseball game, in addition to the players, includes the spectators, baseball diamond, and the bat and ball.

Second, Vinter states that all activities consist of *constituent performances*, which are "behaviors that are essential to the activity and thus are required of participants." A discussion requires that the members express their ideas to each other and listen to each other. The baseball game requires the participants to follow the rules of baseball and to engage in such behaviors as batting, running bases, and catching the ball.

According to Vinter, the physical field and the constituent performances compose the *activity setting*. The activity setting produces the third dimension, which is the *re-*

spondent behaviors defined as "individual participant actions evoked by, but not essential to, participation in the activity." Thus, in a discussion, some of the respondent behaviors were a realignment of subgroups based on positions that emerged in the discussion as well as new information and insights that several members acquired in the discussion. In the baseball game, some of the respondent behaviors were a greater sense of cohesiveness in the group, a feeling of accomplishment among members who had improved in skill, and a relaxing of tensions brought on by the actions of the game.

As can be seen from Vinter's ideas, workers and members should choose activities in light of the activity dimensions involved. The "outcomes" of the activity, the respondent behaviors, are the changes in group conditions (as well as individual conditions) that the worker and members seek to attain group and individual goals. For example, a worker, with a group of clients in a community mental health setting who had been previously hospitalized, introduced the idea of planning a Halloween party to the group. She hoped that as a result of planning for the party, the members would become more committed to the group, all members would be assigned tasks that they realized would contribute to the success of the party, and the members would also come to see themselves as competent to plan social events.

Vinter provides a way of analyzing the activity setting of a program. The concepts that he uses for this are as follows:

Prescriptiveness of the Pattern of Constituent Performances. This is the degree and range of rules or other guides for conduct. Thus, baseball is more prescriptive than is "playing catch," and painting an individual's accurate likeness is more prescriptive than is finger painting.

Institutionalized Controls Governing Participant Activity. This is the "form and source or agent of controls that are exercised over participants during the activity." In a social work group, the controls over members might be exercised by someone outside the group (the agency director who enters the room when the group is out of order), the group worker, other members, or the members over themselves through internalized factors (such as internalized norms). In one group, for example, the group worker restrained a child during a game of baseball when he started to attack another child who had "struck out." Later in the life of the group, when the child in a similar situation became very angry, the other members told him to "cool it." Even later, this child told the worker that when he felt like attacking another child during a game, he remembered that each had been following the rules and had been playing his or her best. The worker was aware that this progression of behavior related to controls was likely to occur and he planned this group activity for that reason.

Provision for Physical Movement. This is "the extent to which participants are required or are permitted to move their bodies in the activity setting." A ball game allows for a great deal of physical movement; an art activity does not. The worker may alter the amount of physical movement, through modifying an activity setting, when required by the members' built-up tensions, their desires to interact with an increased number of other members, or their ability to accept controls.

Competence Required for Performance. This is "the minimum level of ability required to participate in the activity." Group workers will seek to define the level of competence in relationship to the needs and abilities of the members. Thus, a regulation baseball game will require a high level of ability to catch, bat, run, and make a variety of split-second decisions. Workers with groups of physically handicapped youngsters have changed certain rules, for example, how far the pitcher stands from the batter and how far the batter runs (or moves a wheelchair) after hitting the ball. Norms regarding competence will affect other group conditions. They will determine whether some members will be singled out because they are over or under the required competence level and also whether some subgroups will form because of the similar levels of competence among subgroup members.

Provision for Participant Interactiveness. This dimension consists of "the way the activity setting locates and engages participants so that interaction among them is required or provoked." In reference to the baseball example, if the worker trains the members in the skill of batting by having each child take a turn at batting balls pitched by the worker, the interaction is primarily with the worker. A game in which half the group plays against the other half will produce interactiveness within each half. Analogously, a discussion in which most of the remarks are directed to the worker will be less interactive than will one in which members are reinforced for speaking to each other.

Reward Structure. This consists of "the types of rewards available, their abundance or scarcity, and the manner in which they are distributed." While activity dimensions all affect one another, the reward structure may be the one that has the most effect on how receptive the members are to the other activity variables. The reward pattern includes the nature of rewards, the schedule for the presentation of rewards, and the distribution of rewards among the members. Thus, in some activities, all members are rewarded (eating some food prepared by the group); in others, some members are rewarded and others are not (the winner in a game). Sometimes the individual is rewarded because of his or her own efforts (a token awarded for participation in a discussion), while at other times the individuals are rewarded if the group attains some goal (a group was provided with a party when *all* members had reached their first individual treatment goal).

Members are likely to accept an increase in prescriptiveness, a decrease in physical movement, or an increased demand for competence when these requirements are followed by rewards. Rewards may be extrinsic (such as tokens) or intrinsic (as the member gains satisfaction from conforming to a requirement that the member believes will help him or her attain a personal goal).

An example of a worker who used program procedures to modify member action patterns occurred in a group of adolescents meeting in a child guidance clinic. The worker wished to establish an initial group pattern in which members maximally interacted with one another. He, therefore, suggested that members divide into pairs and learn something about each other, after which one member of the pair introduced the other to the group. Later in the meeting, the worker divided the group into subgroups of four members each to discuss what the group's purposes should be. This structure encouraged members to relate to several others at the same time.

The movement from the pairing activity to the four-person one increased the levels of required interactiveness and competence. Before the meeting ended, the worker suggested that the members "mill around" and talk to at least one other person with whom they were not acquainted. This third "program" had a higher level of physical movement, a lower level of competence (members can stop talking whenever they wish), and less prescriptiveness than the previous two. Each of these events had effects upon other group conditions, including climate, norms, structures, and group developmental characteristics, and the worker analyzed each of these in preparation for the next meeting.

Although this scheme was developed for group work, it can be utilized when activities are prescribed for families. The approach of using a wide range of activities has not been widely used in family therapy and this is likely to be an area where family work can borrow from group practice.

Norms

Systemic conditions are also maintained by norms that are shared beliefs about what is desirable and what is undesirable. One way, therefore, to induce a change in group and family conditions is through a change in such norms. For example, in a group of teenage boys, a subgroup of those who were considered the best athletes formed. The norm that athletic skill was the most desirable trait and that it should be sought at the expense of other skills supported this development. This subgroup, however, dominated other subgroups and ridiculed the efforts of other members to work on their "problems." The worker held several discussions on what the boys valued, and this led to a change in the subgroup patterns as well as the dominance of the powerful subgroup. In one family, a normative issue the worker sought to change was that it was desirable for the sons but not the daughters to receive an education. In another family, the worker challenged the members' belief that it was all right to engage in petty stealing if you did not get caught.

One set of techniques for altering norms is value clarification. "Exercises" can be chosen to help individuals identify and change their values. The following are examples of these:

1. *Forced Choice Ladder.*[32] In this exercise, the worker helps each participant to draw a ladder. This ladder consists of a series of steps with each step numbered consecutively to some number (such as eight) selected by the worker. The worker reads aloud descriptions of the behavior of persons in controversial, value-laden situations that are relevant to the members. Each member places the situation at the "step" of the ladder that represents how strongly (either for or against) the member reacts to the behavior. After this is completed, members share and discuss their "ladders."

2. *The Pie of Life.*[33] For this activity, the worker asks the members to estimate the number of hours each day they spend on sleep, work, school chores, friends, family, and alone. Members draw a circle (a pie) in which each "slice" represents an activity and is proportionate in size to the portion of the day spent on the activity. Members may also draw another "pie" that describes how they would *like* to spend their day. Following this, members share their pictures with each other and discuss how these portrayals illustrate their values as well as how well their values and their behaviors coincide.

In addition to the exercises such as those described, workers will sometimes discuss their own values with members. Schwartz refers to this as "lending a vision" to the client: the worker reveals himself or herself as "one whose own hopes and aspirations are strongly invested in the interaction between people and society and projects a deep feeling for that which represents individual well-being and the social good."[34] The worker's beliefs will have a strong impact on members because of the emotional meaning attached to the worker through his or her prominent position in the helping process, a position with which the worker is endowed despite strong efforts to foster system autonomy.

Some of the values that workers state to members are those of the social work profession as discussed earlier in this book: respect for persons, self-determination, and social responsibility. In addition, other values expressed by workers will bear directly on systemic conditions, namely, those associated with openness among members, appropriate self-disclosure, and the responsibility of members for each other.

The worker may also present values relating to how decisions are made in the group or family, for example, by majority rule or by consensus. The consensus rule is usually invoked when the worker is concerned about a decision that might harm a member; as a worker's guiding principle should always be that decisions may be made that do not help all individuals as long as no one is harmed. This principle is used, for example, when the worker thinks that discussion of a sensitive issue may harm a member who is not yet ready for such a discussion. A related norm is that, even when a discussion takes place by agreement among members, no member should be pressured to give personal information or to take part in an exercise. The worker has a responsibility to maintain a "safe" atmosphere, and this responsibility is shared by the members as well.

Closely associated with the worker's role in establishing norms that support therapeutic conditions is the worker's responsibility in formed groups to implement these norms through appropriate limit setting. This is essential in some groups such as those of young children or adults who lack reality testing skills. The worker in these groups will have to at times restrain members from attacks on one another as well as upon objects in the physical setting. Workers in such groups sometimes employ items such as pillows upon which members may vent their angry feelings. In families, the worker will usually turn to the parents to set limits on children. When a parent, however, is likely to harm a child, the worker will stop that act. On some occasions, the worker may model limit setting for a parent.

Members, particularly children in formed groups, may also have to be restrained from running in and out of the room when this disturbs other activities in the agency. Even the use of obscene language is sometimes restrained when its expression is too stimulating or anxiety provoking to other members. The worker may offset these behaviors through the use of program activities that drain off tensions, offer limits that members will observe, and provide members with gratification.

Redl and Wineman list techniques they have used in groups to limit behavior.[35] They use terms to describe such worker responses as ignoring the behavior, using humor, appealing to the member, telling the member to leave the situation (antiseptic bouncing), physically restraining the member, and telling the member in a highly authoritative manner to stop (authoritative verbot).

These kinds of issues regarding the control of behavior may also occur in adult groups, even those that are not composed of severely dysfunctional people. Groups where this may happen are those in which the emotions of members have been intensely aroused as highly charged experiences are dealt with or intense conflicts arise. Even minor physical encounters are the subject of much controversy among group facilitators. Some make a blanket rule that no aggressive physical contact can take place. Others allow for discharge of such tensions through such controlled means as arm wrestling. The value of either of these approaches has not been rigorously ascertained. We, therefore, enjoin the practitioner to make sure that no physical or emotional harm will come to a member if this can be anticipated and avoided. This principle requires a very cautious approach to any physical contact among members, particularly of formed groups.

System Emotional States

The final set of procedures we shall discuss for modifying system conditions are those related to modifying emotional states. By an emotional state, we mean occasions when members express similar emotions. Thus, one might observe a group or family in which all the members appear elated or anxious or depressed. The shared emotion may be a product of "contagion" among the members or a common stimulus such as a story told by a member or an action of an individual within or outside of the group.

One approach to modifying an emotional state, if this is desirable, is to bring the emotion to the awareness of the members, if it is not already evident, and then explore its sources. An example of this was a discussion of an untrue rumor that the worker planned to leave. During such discussions, when the worker approaches an issue in a relaxed manner, this may be imitated by the members.

Various phases in the life of the group may also stimulate emotions with which the worker must help members. We shall discuss, for example, termination of the helping process later in this book. In group situations, termination induces feelings of loss among members with regard to the other members, the worker, and the group as an entity. The worker should plan approaches to dealing with each of these loss dimensions. Other types of events that arouse emotions include the loss of a single member when the group continues, the loss of one worker and the acquisition of another, the loss the group

may suffer in a competitive event, and a change in the indigenous leadership pattern among members.

There are procedures that can be used in groups to change member emotions directly. One is a group relaxation procedure. A simple example of this is to ask members to be conscious of their breathing and to breathe deeply several times. Another is to suggest that members select some peaceful scene in their lives and imagine returning to such a scene. A more complex approach is a progressive relaxation exercise. According to Rose, this consists of "the alternation of tension of the muscles in each large muscle group with the relaxation of that tension . . . ."[36] Each member can be helped by another member to pace the exercise, and Rose does this through pairing the members. The member who guides the other, after appropriate training from the worker, can call upon the worker when a problem arises in the procedure. The workers, of course, should have received training in the procedures.

So far, we have discussed procedures for the reduction of such emotions as anxiety in the group. On some occasions, the worker will wish to increase the expression of a "positive" emotion related to caring for or supporting other members. One way of doing this is through an exercise such as "giving and receiving compliments." As described by Lange and Jakubowski, this exercise begins with the worker pointing out behaviors to members that discourage compliments, such as stating that they are not valid. Another behavior that is targeted for change is presenting a compliment in which the complimenter depreciates himself or herself in the process.[37] The worker can demonstrate, and the members can practice giving brief, unqualified compliments. The next stage of the exercise consists of each member giving a compliment to the person on his or her right and receiving an appropriate response. In the final stage of the exercise, each complimenter expresses something that he or she liked about how the compliment was received by the person complimented.

The worker often has the objective of helping members become more aware of their feelings. This can be accomplished by asking members to share with each other their feelings at a given time or their reactions to group events. The worker can also utilize a program activity to elicit or heighten some group emotion. Thus, some games reveal competitive feelings; some art projects, feelings of elation or depression, and some discussions of member strengths, feelings of jealousy.

Changing Group Conditions Through Systems Outside the Group

The final category for changing system conditions is producing such change through the use of forces from outside the group. One of the primary sources of such forces is the agency. An input from the agency that has this effect is a statement of the agency's purposes. Presumably, this was clarified before service began, but the agency can also restate its purpose or make it more evident. For example, the agency can ask a group to evaluate how well it is achieving its purpose, therefore drawing the group's attention to this dimension.

The agency can seek to change a formed group's composition by referring new members. In some situations, the members will contract for the right to make the final decision on this matter, but, in any case, the group should be consulted on the ways in which members are added. When the new members join the group, they bring new approaches to problem solving and new patterns of relationship to the group as they incorporate themselves in its structure and process. A similar process occurs if an agency seeks to bring several families together for several sessions.

Still another way the agency affects the group or family is through a change in the resources supplied. This includes a change in the meeting room, the equipment the system has available, the kinds of consultation or training the system receives, and the reinforcers available to members. The agency can also affect the system through interactions with selected members outside the group. Some agencies do this through forming an advisory council composed of "representatives." This creates two-way communication in that the agency, itself, may change as a result of inputs from a council. On the other hand, the council may develop norms or receive information that, when transmitted to the group, can also affect its structure and process.

Agencies may have preferences for how the worker will work with the system, and this will affect it to the degree that the worker accepts the agency's ideas or they are otherwise transmitted. One agency, for example, believed that clients should be alerted to the dangers of alcohol abuse. Posters were placed on the walls that warned of this danger, and workers were instructed to be sensitive to alcohol-related issues.

At times, the worker seeks to help systems to interact with others in the agency when this is likely to be beneficial. For example, in one agency members of one group were invited to visit another group to describe how the former's group dealt with a conflict between subgroups as the latter group had a similar problem. Another agency input is that group or family members may receive one-to-one services from staff members other than their own worker, and the consequences of this service may have effects upon the system. An example of this is a group that contained several members who were anxious when sexual matters were discussed in group meetings. Some of their anxieties were reduced in their extragroup sessions. This led to a shift in the group's program as members felt more comfortable dealing with this subject matter.

A type of intervention with families that should be mentioned here is the use of an agency team. Because of the likelihood of the worker losing his or her objectivity by becoming too enmeshed in the family system, family therapists are frequently likely to work with a team composed of colleagues. The team may observe sessions and may send communications to the worker or even to the family, usually transmitted by the worker. This, in addition to allowing the worker to have the benefit of multiple experiences, presents the family with a communication that is difficult to ignore.

The group worker should not simply be cognizant of the agency's effect but should usually initiate or approve it. Otherwise, the effect on the worker is demoralizing. The value of input that comes from the agency, rather than only from the worker, is also that the worker's role becomes a mediating one. The worker is not so much a symbol of authority but of a "helpful person who assists the system to cope with reality." This type of process can often be highly facilitative of change because the member's response to the substantive issue is not confused with authority conflicts with the worker. The worker, therefore, should be active in helping the agency create conditions that will confront systems in ways that are beneficial to them.

Group and family conditions are also affected by systems that lie outside the agency. One of the most frequent of these in formed groups is the members' families. An example of the use of this is meetings that are arranged with the parents or spouses of group members. There may be good reasons why groups are composed of persons who fulfill the same role in the family (mother, child) rather than of entire families. One such occasion is when the family member included in the group strengthens his or her position or discovers it before confronting other family members. This can be because of inequalities in power that may exist.

An example of a group composed of persons with similar family roles was a husbands' group established in a shelter for abused wives.[38] This group was created because the husbands did not accept any responsibility for their violence and were not likely to without preliminary support from other people who are most likely to offer it, namely, men with a similar "problem." Ultimately, through this support, the men accepted responsibility and a later joint meeting with the wives was a productive one.

Workers also can effect changes in system conditions through their influence on other agencies in the community. Examples of this are work done with authorities in a school attended by children in a group or family, with leaders of a community recreation program utilized by members, with a staff member in a welfare department of which members were clients, and with a nurse in a hospital serving the members.

Another community target with which the worker may interact on behalf of the group, is indigenous community groups. Spergel, for example, describes many examples of this in reference to work with adolescent gangs.[39] Gang work has diminished because of its presumed ineffectiveness and because of doubt as to whether gangs existed in the way workers thought they did. Nevertheless, the model of helping adolescents in groups through changes in the way they are perceived and responded to in their community is still a valid idea. This includes helping group members find jobs, interact with parole officers, and secure the educational programs they need.

Another significant way the environment impacts upon groups and families is through culture and ethnicity. The worker should be aware that different cultural groups exert influence in terms of what may be said in sessions, who should be given the most respect, and what public behaviors should be. In some cultures, for example, members are enjoined not to discuss family issues outside the family. In other cultures, some persons are accorded higher or lower status in terms of their family's position in the culture.

Knowledge of these dimensions will help the worker to know how what is permitted or forbidden will affect system structure and process. The worker can incorporate this into planning for the system. At times, the members' culture will be a barrier to their attaining their goals, and members will have to be supported when they decide to violate cultural norms or seek to change them. An example of this is a group in a school in which several young women came from an Arab Moslem culture. They wished to consider careers outside of the home even though this was against their parents' wishes and the norms of their culture. The worker, in addition to helping these group members to evaluate their plans and the implications of these plans, also sought to influence the group through actions in the environment. These consisted of meetings with the parents so that the parents might discuss their efforts to cope with American culture. One meeting included women from the culture who had chosen vocational careers and who could, consequently, discuss these issues from the point of view of people who had personally faced them.

Summary

We began this chapter with a brief discussion of the evolution of service to groups and families as an interpersonal practice modality in social work. This was followed by a discussion of some of the differences between family and formed groups that have implications for practice. The issue of selecting clients for group or family services was also raised.

Because of conditions that emerged as well as the existence of several philosophies in the profession, a number of "models" of group work and family therapy have come into existence. These models were identified and described. We do not see these models as discrete entities but rather as overlapping so that each one is similar to several others. Some have even suggested that all the models, when employed in practice, lead to interventions that are much more alike than they are different.[40]

The remainder of the chapter was devoted to a discussion of ways that workers can have an effect on group and family conditions. These ways consist of interventions with individuals, subsystems, the whole system, and external systems. Individuals, for example, can affect the system through the tasks they perform, the power they exert, and the functions they fulfill. Similar conclusions were drawn about the effects of subsystems on the whole system as subsystems can perform tasks and fulfill functions for the larger entity.

The ways in which the worker can directly affect the entire system were described. These include facilitating its development and influencing the shared cognitions of members, member's action patterns, and their activities, norms, and emotional states. Finally, the worker can affect the group or family system through modifying environmental conditions that in turn impact upon it. Some of the ways this is done are to modify agency conditions, the actions of people who are not members of the family or group, the responses of other agencies, the impact of the community, and the influences stemming from the members' culture and ethnicity.

NOTES

1. Cited in M. E. Rich, *A Belief in People: A History of Family Social Work* (New York: Family Service Association of America, 1956), p. 95.

2. Mary Richmond, *Social Diagnosis* (New York: Russel Sage, 1917), p. 137.

3. For details of this history, see Chapter 2 of Charles Garvin, *Contemporary Group Work* (Englewood Cliffs, N.J.: Prentice-Hall, 1981), pp. 30–37.

4. Mary Richmond, "Some Next Steps in Social Treatment," in *Proceedings of the National Conference of Social Work, 1920* (New York: Columbia University Press, 1939), p. 256.

5. See Mary Parker Follett, *The New State*, (New York: Longmans, Green, 1926), and Edward C. Lindeman, *The Community*, (New York: Association Press, 1921).

6. John Dewey, *How We Think* (Lexington, Mass.: D.C. Heath, 1933).

7. Grace Coyle, "Group Work and Social Change," *Proceedings of the National Conference of Social Work, 1935* (Chicago: University of Chicago Press, 1935), pp. 393–405, and Wilbur I. Newstetter, "What Is Social Group Work?" in ibid., pp. 291–299.

8. See, for example, Emanuel Tropp, "A Developmental Theory," in Robert W. Roberts and Helen Northen, eds., *Theories of Social Work with Groups* (New York: Columbia University Press, 1976), pp. 198–237.

9. Norma C. Lang, "A Broad Range Model of Practice with the Social Work Group," *Social Service Review*, Vol. 46 (March 1972), pp. 76–89.

10. Sol Garfield and Alan Bergin, eds., *Handbook of Psychotherapy and Behavior Change*, 2nd ed. (New York: John Wiley, 1978).

11. William Schwartz, "Social Group Work: The Interactional Approach," in *Encyclopedia of Social Work*, Vol. II (New York: National Association of Social Workers, 1971), p. 1255.

12. Catherine P. Papell and Beulah Rothman, "Social Group Work Models: Possession and Heritage," *Journal of Education for Social Work*, Vol. 2 (Fall 1966), pp. 66–77.

13. William Schwartz, "Between Client and System: The Mediating Function," in *Theories of Social Work with Groups*, p. 175.

14. Roberts and Northen, eds., *Theories of Social Work with Groups*.

15. Alan S. Gurman and David P. Kniskern, *Handbook of Family Therapy* (New York: Brunner/Mazel, 1981).

16. For a discussion of these procedures, see Steven B. Gordon and Nancy Davidson, "Behavioral Parent Training," in *Handbook of Family Therapy*, pp. 517–555.

17. For a discussion of the function of deviance in groups, see Howard L. Nixon II, *The Small Group* (Englewood Cliffs, N.J.: Prentice-Hall, 1979), pp. 142–156.

18. For a fuller discussion of communication training, see Luciano L'Arate, "Skill Training Programs for Couples and Families," in *Handbook of Family Therapy*, pp. 631–661.

19. See Clifford J. Sager, "Couples Therapy and Marriage Contracts," in *Handbook of Family Therapy*, pp. 85–132.

20. Julia R. Heiman, Leslie LoPiccolo, and Joseph LoPiccolo, "The Treatment of Sexual Dysfunction," in *Handbook of Family Therapy*, pp. 592–630, and W. H. Masters and V. E. Johnson, *Human Sexual Inadequacy* (Boston: Little, Brown, 1970).

21. W. R. Bion, *Experiences in Groups* (New York: Basic Books, 1959).

22. This discussion draws upon Salvador Minuchin and H. Charles Fishman, *Family Therapy Techniques* (Cambridge, Mass.: Harvard University Press, 1981).

23. Ibid., p. 74.

24. Sheldon Rose, *Group Therapy: A Behavioral Approach* (Englewood Cliffs, N.J.: Prentice-Hall, 1977), p. 142.

25. Ibid., pp. 161–190.

26. Jay Haley, *Problem Solving Therapy* (San Francisco: Jossey-Bass, 1976), p. 68.

27. Ibid.

28. Ibid.

29. Minuchin and Fishman, *Family Therapy Techniques*, pp. 142–145.

30. Gertrude Wilson and Gladys Ryland, *Social Group Work Practice* (Boston: Houghton Mifflin, 1949).

31. Robert Vinter, "Program Activities: An Analysis of Their Effects on Participant Behavior," in Paul Glasser, Rosemary Sarri, and Robert Vinter, eds., *Individual Change Through Small Groups* (New York: The Free Press, 1974), pp. 233–243.

32. Adapted from Sidney S. Simon, Leland W. Howe, and Howard Kirschenbaum, *Values Clarification: A Handbook of Practical Strategies for Teachers and Students* (New York: Hart, 1972), pp. 98–111.

33. Ibid., pp. 228–231.

34. William Schwartz, "The Social Worker in the Group," *The Social Welfare Forum, 1961* (New York: Columbia University Press, 1961), p. 157.

35. Fritz Redl and David Wineman, *Controls from Within* (New York: The Free Press, 1952), pp. 153–245.

36. S. Rose, *Group Therapy*, pp. 120–123.

37. Arthur J. Lange and Patricia Jakubowski, *Responsible Assertive Behavior* (Champaign, Ill.: Research Press, 1976), p. 74.

38. Janet A. Geller, "Reaching the Battering Husband," *Social Work with Groups*, Spring 1978, pp. 27–38.

39. Irving Spergel, *Street Gang Work: Theory and Practice* (Reading, Mass.: Addison-Wesley, 1966).

40. This conclusion was implied in a lecture presented by Gisela Konopka to a doctoral seminar on group work at the University of Michigan in October 1980.

thirteen
Organizational and Environmental Change

We have endeavored throughout this book to consider organizational and environmental issues. In our first chapter we indicated that the purpose of social work is to improve or change the transactions between people and their environments so that human needs can be fulfilled. In the second chapter we discussed our model of social work practice and the importance to it of an understanding of systems. We defined, in particular the concept of target system and stated that this system will often be some component of the service agency, other organizations in the community, or even in the larger society. Subsequently, in Chapter 7, we explained how systems are assessed, and part of that chapter was devoted to the assessment of larger systems such as organizations.

In Chapter 11, we discussed how individuals are helped to change and included there an analysis of how changes in environments can bring about changes in individuals. In the next chapter, on changing families and groups, we showed in a parallel fashion that changes in the environment can also fa-

cilitate change in those entities. In this chapter, we shall discuss organizational and environmental changes in detail, as these are often sought to create more advantageous and humane situations for people as well as to stimulate immediate changes in individuals, families, or groups.

Targets of Change

It may help the reader to visualize these types of changes if we present examples of some of the most typical types of organizational and environmental changes sought by interpersonal practitioners. First on such a list should be the families and formed groups to which individual clients belong. Since, however, the preceding chapter was devoted to these as both action and target systems, it would be redundant to say more about them here.

Next on the list are the friendship groups, peer groups, and similar aggregates within the client's social network. For many clients, these are conflictual, inadequate, or even totally missing. People who have had long periods of hospitalization in mental health facilities are often totally alienated from their families. Too often, when they are placed in the community, they take up residence in "hotels" filled with other isolated people. Any possibility of their successfully remaining in the community will be dependent on an environmental effort to create a social network for them. Another example of an environmental effort of this sort is that on behalf of people who have abused their children. They are often devoid of supportive social networks, and the creation of these is essential to reduce this type of family violence.

The workplace is another environmental target that should be considered by interpersonal practitioners. A substantial amount of the stress we experience in life is a consequence of conflicts in expectations among our colleagues and superiors, ambiguity of such expectations, lack of job security or opportunity for promotion, and even a sense of meaninglessness in what we do. Social workers increasingly are developing an understanding of the "world of work," and industrial social work is becoming a major arena of service delivery.

The service agency itself should always be thought of as a target of change. Aspects of our own agencies that are detrimental to clients include intake policies, agency resources (adequate staff, physical space, emergency funds), negative responses to clients from other staff (such as receptionists, maintenance workers, and even other professionals), and the acts of agencies that stigmatize clients (the way clients are spoken of, the way confidentiality may be abused).

Beyond social networks, there may be other aspects of the client's community that affect clients adversely. Some neighborhood

institutions practice racism, sexism, and ageism. Vital services such as transportation, refuse disposal, and street maintenance may be deficient. Some human services may also be missing such as adequate child care, health care, and educational programs. The power structure of the community may be faulty, and the client may be excluded from political processes, participation in decision making about the future of the neighborhood, and representation on governing bodies of schools, social agencies, and religious institutions.

It is impossible for the interpersonal practitioner to undertake activities to change each national social policy that affects every client who suffers from such policies. We hope, nevertheless, that the practitioner, as a citizen, member of professional organizations, and dedicated social worker will devote time and energy to changing policies about which he or she feels most strongly. Practitioners have ample opportunities to see the negative effects of social policies on people. In given instances, however, social workers will help clients—frequently in groups, because of the power inherent in groups—to target social policies. Examples of this are workers who helped groups to join together with others to lobby for better welfare allocations, housing, job programs, and the Equal Rights Amendment and against the draft.

There are several general reasons to target these environments:

1. The environment may fail to provide the kinds of *social and material reinforcements* and resources the client requires. Examples are a student who is not given recognition by a teacher for work performed or an employee who is not given adequate compensation.

2. The environment may *punish* the client for desirable actions. Examples are a black student who is rejected when he seeks to make

friends with a white student or an employee who is fired when he makes suggestions for improving working conditions.

3. The way in which the environment is *structured* may affect the client in detrimental ways. This includes the roles created for the client, the labels attached to the client by virtue of these roles, and the positions created for the client in relationship to other organizational positions in the organizational hierarchy. Examples are in one agency, clients who were labeled alcoholics were subtly rejected from agency services; and in another agency, Hispanic clients were seen by staff as inferior, and they were allocated very little influence in determining agency policies.

4. Selected policies in the agency may be harmful to some clients. These include the kinds of procedures established in the agency as well as more subtle sequences such as a harmful chain of events that occurs repetitively. An example is in one youth serving agency, a staff member was seen by many youths as favoring a particular client, which led to the youths scapegoating the "favored" one, which, in turn, led to even more overprotection on the part of the staff member.

5. The agency *opportunity structures* may be deficient. By this term we refer to a stepwise series of resources and related roles that lead to specified types of goal attainment. Examples are in one school system, there was a dearth of learning opportunities for children with such special needs as the hearing impaired and the developmentally disabled; and in a large firm, members of many ethnic groups were denied opportunities for advancement.

A major decision confronting the worker and client is whether to target the environment and, if so, which environmental system to target. There are several criteria to use in arriving at this decision.

The first is whether the change the client seeks can be attained without a prior environmental change or whether environmental change is essential. This point is made even though our assumption is that a change in

one individual will *always* be associated with environmental changes because individuals are part of environmental systems. It is likely, nevertheless, that a change in an individual may precede and initiate environmental changes. An example of this was a father who developed a plan for a more humane approach to child discipline than he had used previously. This led to changes in his wife (she supported his actions instead of criticizing them) and his daughter (she became less defiant). The protective service worker also changed in that she recommended their case be closed. In a broad sense, this is always the process in a client-induced environmental change: that the client adopts a change strategy that itself represents a new behavior on the part of the client.

Another criterion is based on the principle, used in many other practice situations, that nothing succeeds like success. In this instance, this means that an environmental target should be chosen that is amenable to change. When several environmental targets are appropriate, the first chosen should be, again, the one where the most gains can be achieved at the least cost. In one instance, a woman who desired to change a series of sexist responses to her saw these as occurring in her marriage, her workplace, from her children, and from her parents. She decided to *initiate* her efforts with respect to her children and to ask both her sons and her daughters to share the same household chores. This decision was made based on where she thought she had the greatest power.

A related criterion is the client's estimate of where he or she will experience a favorable cost-benefit ratio. This means that the client will have to identify the likely gains from the action as well as the costs in terms of such matters as energy, punishment from the environment, and consequences for others. In one case, a black client wished to change some racist practices in his office as well as with his white fiancée. He recognized that his raising this issue at work might cost him his job. On the other hand, he knew that his fiancée wanted to work on this issue. He determined to handle the latter first and then to share the decision to change the office with his fiancée in terms of the costs to both of them as well as the benefits, which included a matter of great importance to him—his self-respect.

In assessing costs, we suggest the reader take note of our experience that the costs of environmental change strategies vary for the worker and the client depending on whether the target is internal or external to the service agency. When they seek to change some aspect of the service agency, it is likely to be the worker who assumes the greater risk. Workers can be accused of disloyalty to agencies when they seek to change them on behalf of clients while clients may merely be thought of as serving their own best interests. On the other hand, clients take greater risks than workers when they seek changes in *their* natural environments. The exception to this is when clients band together to seek changes that affect a great many people and, thus, will have significant effects on larger systems. A case of this was the Mobilization for Youth Program, which during the 1960s involved its constituents in seeking major changes in schools, housing, and legal processes. Ultimately, this stimulated a powerful backlash, and the program was reduced and changed as a result.

In addition to choosing the environmental system as a target, the client and worker must choose some *aspects* of the system as focal points of their efforts. To accomplish this, the reader should review the typology of system variables that we identified in Chapter 7. Different strategies and environmental targets will be chosen depending on whether

the problem is embedded in system goals, culture, processes, resources, boundaries, and so forth. A next step is to determine which "level" of the system to target. What we call levels refers to whether change is sought in (1) a specific individual, (2) a set of people such as workers within a work unit or all women employees, (3) structures and processes related to the entire system such as the power of one group compared with that of another, or (4) the system's ultimate authority structure such as the executive committee of a church or even its highest governing body.

As we have stated elsewhere, there are criteria for helping the worker and client choose a level of the system as the target of change.[1] These are

1. The (clients) must decide the degree to which the behavior of some individual . . . is determined by idiosyncratic factors or organizational ones. For example, is the individual following "orders" or is he or she creating them? This is sometimes a difficult assessment to make because people can perform in ways condoned by the "system" but not part of its official rules. Thus, a teacher might discriminate against some group of students when this is unofficially supported by the school yet is not part of its "official rules."

   When the behavior of the individual is idiosyncratic, the client should seek to have an effect on that individual's behavior. An exception to this is when the individual is intransigent; the member may then seek to have the larger organization exert influence on this person or even remove him or her. Thus, a teacher who was prejudiced against members of a minority group and who would not change was replaced after an appeal to school authorities.

2. The clients should also assess the aspects of the . . . system that are most amenable to change. In some school situations, for example, the teacher concerned might be the most responsive; in others it may be the principal, the teachers' union, or the superintendent. As a general rule, it may be easier to change

an individual or a few individuals than the whole system, unless such individuals are acting in clear conformity with the rules and procedures of their organization.

Involvement of the Client

Decisions to seek changes in some aspect of the environment should be made with the full participation of the client or of someone who can appropriately act on behalf of the client. A major exception is the responsibility of workers to seek changes in their own agencies to be able to offer better services to particular clients as well as clients in general.

This principle directly contradicts a practice, perhaps more typical of an earlier period in the history of social work, when some social workers contacted such institutions as schools and hospitals to secure information about clients (or some change in procedures with reference to particular clients) without the assent of the clients. When the approval of the client has been obtained, however, another decision must be made: whether the client will be helped to seek environmental change independently, whether the worker will act on behalf of the client, whether worker and client will act jointly, whether a group containing the client will be involved, or whether the services of another agency (such as a lawyer or civil rights organization) will be enlisted.

One factor in the decision as to the role of the client in the change effort is the motivation of the client. Some clients may be ready to engage in various forms of social action because they have had previous successes in such endeavors, role models who have acted in this way, or even some relevant training. Others may have had the opposite such as frequently frustrated attempts to secure environmental changes. In such cases, the worker's actions on their behalf, if successful,

may stimulate the clients' subsequent efforts on their own behalf.

Another factor is the client's capacity. As Glasser et al. have stated, this capacity consists of the client's ability "to understand the intent of the change effort, perform the actions required, and withstand the anxiety and stress which may be engendered by the effort."[2] The same authors concluded that young children, psychotics, or the retarded will not be able to contribute a great deal to environmental change but that public welfare recipients, inmates of correctional institutions and parents of schoolchildren will have capacity for such activity.

In arriving at the decision as to who will make the change effort, the worker will, if at all possible, emphasize the desirability of the client acting on his or her own behalf. The obvious reasons for this are that clients enhance their ability to act independently and to achieve greater power. This does not preclude the desirability for clients to work together in groups to seek social changes.

A second choice is for workers to join together with individual clients or groups to seek changes in the environment. This does not detract as much from the client's own experience as when the worker acts independently, and it offers many opportunities for the worker to coach clients in effective social change behaviors. An example of this was a worker with a group of people suffering from sickle cell anemia who invited hospital personnel to attend a group meeting where the personnel were confronted with the stereotyped manner with which they dealt with people with this disease.

We believe that in most cases workers who act on behalf of clients (outside of the service agency) should do so when the foregoing options have been ruled out. An example of this was a worker in a family agency serving the C family who contacted the social worker at a local hospital to report that the elderly parent of Mrs. C was receiving inadequate care in a nursing home where she had been placed by the hospital. The nursing home resident was too incapacitated to act on her own behalf, and the family was so preoccupied with their marital and child care problems they could not make plans for their relative.

Another exception to the principle of least worker involvement is when the worker is called upon to fulfill a broker role. This activity, to be described later in this chapter, is required so that the client can locate and secure appropriate resources.

Strategies of Change

In the preceding section, we listed the possible agents of change as the worker or client singly, the client and worker together, the clients in a group, or an outside organization on behalf of the client. Some strategies can be used by several types of agents; others are more appropriately used by one type. In the following discussion, we present strategies in relationship to these possible agents.

Workers on Behalf of Clients

One set of techniques used by workers on behalf of clients relates to the role of *advocate*. This role stems from the fact that social work clients are often in conflict with institutions. Workers frequently become partisans in such conflict, and they will "argue, debate, bargain, negotiate, and manipulate the environment on behalf of the client."[3] Workers who take on an advocate role can be effective only when they have done their "homework." They must be familiar with the policies and procedures of the institution in question so that demands on the institution are appropriately presented. A negative ex-

ample of this was provided by a social work student who sought to function as an advocate for a client at a hearing with reference to the client's complaint that she was denied welfare benefits to which she was entitled. The student was not familiar with welfare policies, so he reported to the instructor that he vehemently stated that the client's rights should be recognized even though he did not know what these rights were. Needless to say, this did not benefit the client or the reputation of the agency he represented.

In addition to pointing out to the institution the rights of the client, in as diplomatic manner as possible, the social worker, as advocate, will sometimes find it necessary to advance the case to another level of the hierarchy. Here the advocate must be familiar with the structure of the agency so that an appeal to a higher authority is an appropriate one. The worker should be cautious in this respect, as a premature appeal may turn a potential colleague into an enemy. A desirable process is one in which the "lower" authority sees it as helpful to have the issue clarified at a higher level rather than as a challenge to the higher authority's competence or integrity.

The worker who acts as advocate for the client should have a clear understanding with the client as to goals, procedures, and risks assumed by the client. Even with the most carefully executed advocacy plan, the client may end in a worse status than before as the targeted agency may decide the client merits even less service. There is also a possibility that the client may suffer retribution.

Another set of techniques stems from the role of *mediator*.[4] In this position, the worker seeks to resolve disputes between clients and others by helping them to negotiate to find a common ground for their respective interests. Some of the techniques employed by a worker in this role are helping the parties to communicate better with each other, to remain engaged with each other during this process, and to focus on the issue in dispute. At times the worker may also seek to conciliate the parties when communications break down such as persuading them to "back off" more extreme positions.

An assumption underlying an effort at mediation is that both parties have a complementary interest in resolving the dispute. An example is that of mediation of a dispute between a student and teacher in which the teacher has an investment in educating the student and the student has one in being educated. The dispute may involve a difference regarding the amount or quality of work expected of the student, and the worker can help the student to describe abilities to produce the work, the teacher to describe expectations, and both to agree to a reasonable compromise.

The worker as mediator must be able to avoid "taking sides" as this changes the role to one of advocate. The environmental target, as well as the client, must experience the worker as understanding the reasons for the stance of each. Both must trust the worker to play a facilitative rather than a directive role. It is the quality of the process that is the essential ingredient.

A third set of techniques is used in the role of *broker*.[5] In this role, the worker helps clients to determine the resources they need to ameliorate their problems and then identifies institutions that can supply these resources. In accomplishing this, the worker may have to help those institutions provide information to the client and facilitate the client's application for resources.

The worker in anticipation of the broker's role should develop a "catalogue" of information about resources and informal as well as formal information as to how they can be obtained. *Formal information* consists of statements from the institution's written policies, brochures, and announcements. *Informal information* includes the names of persons in the agency who can provide information or facilitate an application as well as how the application process "really" works as compared with formal, and possibly inaccurate, accounts. Unfortunately, in many agencies workers protect their "information" to benefit their *own* clients. It is the task of administrators to help workers to pool their information into an agency resource file so that all clients may benefit.

The process of fulfilling the broker role should not end when information is supplied to the client. The worker should continue to monitor the client's progress in obtaining the resource so that the worker can confirm or modify his or her knowledge of the institution to which the client has been referred. In some cases, the worker will subsequently have to assume the role of mediator or advocate because of an inappropriate denial of services. The worker may also have to assume a social action role to bring about changes in the institution or a community organization role to create institutions when unmet needs exist.

We shall not provide details on social action or community organization roles because, while these may be engaged in by interpersonal practitioners, they usually are "class" rather than "case" oriented. In this respect the worker moves beyond the array of roles usually identified with interpersonal practice into those identified with community organization and social policy activities. A discussion of these requires a comprehensive text devoted to that subject.[6] While we believe that these roles should at times be assumed by interpersonal practitioners, they often are accomplished as part of team work with "macro"-oriented social social workers. The task of the interpersonal practitioner is often to alert other kinds of workers to the needs identified in work with individuals, families, and groups and to supply those workers with information that will help them to make the case for meeting the need so identified. In this way, the interpersonal practitioner has helped the profession fulfill its function to relate "private troubles" to the social issues that gave rise to them. As we have implied, however, the job definition of some interpersonal practitioners encourages or requires them to participate in community organizations and social policy activities to meet the needs of the agency's clientele.

Clients on Their Own Behalf

In this and the following sections of the chapter devoted to ways that clients can seek to change their environments, we affirm that one of the tasks of the worker is to help clients to determine when they should seek to do this and how they should go about it. Any effort to change the environment may intensify the amount of conflict between the client and the environment, at least until the issue is resolved. We do not believe that conflict is desirable for its own sake as it subjects the client to costs such as expenditure of energy and the likelihood of punishment. We, therefore, propose that the client adopt a strategy that involves the least amount of conflict required to attain the environmental goal. An advantage of this principle is that the client can escalate the strategy to one that may produce more conflict if the lesser strategy is ineffective. This approach will also be seen as "just" by significant persons in the client's life space.

The approaches that can be taken only by individuals because they involve immediate ways of interacting with environments are (1) avoidance, (2) alternate reactions, and (3) manipulation of the social or physical situation.[7] In subsequent sections we describe approaches that can be used by individuals but can also be used collectively by groups of clients.

Avoidance. The least conflictive way of modifying one's environment is to remove one's self from it. This includes placing a child, securing a divorce, transferring schools, or changing jobs. While we state that this strategy may not be conflictive, we do not imply that its use is not stressful. It may also follow a period of conflict. Removing one's self nevertheless may diminish the conflict by separating from it. Major tasks of the worker lie in helping the client (1) to determine that leaving a situation is better than coping with it and (2) to select alternative situations to meet his or her needs.

Alternative Reactions. The client may choose to modify a situation through a change in his or her behavior in the situation with the expectation that this will lead to a change in the behavior of others, even when no request is made of the other. An example of this is a parent who resolved to model "polite" behaviors with the hope that the child would imitate these behaviors. Another example is a parent who ignored a child's tantrums with the expectation that the tantrums would diminish if that source of reinforcement were withdrawn. A third example is a spouse who resolved to discontinue criticism of the other spouse with the assumption that this would make it possible for the other spouse to become more affectionate. The worker's task in these situations is to help the client to analyze which changes in his or her own behavior will lead to the desired effects. The client may also need help in practicing changes as well as reinforcement for the new behaviors to sustain them until reinforcement occurs naturally through a change in the situation.

Manipulation of the Social or Physical Situation. Third, the client may alter an aspect of the situation that is within his or her control. A parent, for example, changed the seating pattern of the family at the dinner table to involve the other parent in family discussions to a greater degree. Another parent avoided leaving money around the house as part of a plan to help a child with a stealing problem. A client planned to take a vacation with his wife without the children in an effort to reestablish his bonds with her. The worker's task is to help the client to assess aspects of the physical and social situation that are barriers to attaining the client's goals. The client will also have to decide which changes should be made unilaterally as his or her contribution to resolving problems and which should be negotiated with the other people in the situation who might regard unilateral action as an abuse of power.

By Clients Individually or in Groups

The approaches that can be taken by individuals but that can also be strengthened by acting together with others are, in ascending order of the likelihood of promoting conflict, (1) interpretation, (2) education, (3) evaluation, (4) use of influentials, (5) bargaining, (6) confrontation, (7) use of mass media, (8) passive resistance, and (9) active resistance. All these approaches can be jointly employed, also, by a worker and client.

Interpretation. This involves explaining to others the causes or consequences of either the client's behavior or their own. The reason for doing this is that an awareness of the meaning of the behavior of one's self or others may lead to a change in that behavior. An example is a client who explained to a potential lover that he could not engage in sexual acts because he was recovering from surgery.

The companion had previously become angry and withdrawn because of feeling rejected but now responded warmly to the client. Another example is a parent who explained to a teacher that the child had recently been diagnosed as suffering from a perceptual handicap. The parent offered the teacher some interpretive material on this handicap. The teacher, who had accused the child of misbehavior and had punished the child, now altered his responses.

Education. This approach is based on the premise that new information can produce change in people. An example of this occurred in a group of clients about to leave a psychiatric treatment facility. They believed that prospective employers might reject them because of misunderstanding the nature of mental illness. They were successful in convincing a local educational television channel to institute a series of information programs on mental illness. These programs highlighted the employment successes of former mental patients.

Evaluation. This is an all too seldom used device in which the targeted persons are induced to gather more information and to guide their actions by it. One example is of a teacher who argued that a student "never" turned in homework and should be failed. The student asked the teacher to examine his workbook to establish that he had earned a passing grade. On another occasion an agency planned to maintain the payments to foster parents at the same level from one year to the next. A group of foster parents secured the agency's commitment to gather data on the costs faced by foster parents after several years of inflation. This study convinced the agency to raise their payments.

Use of Influentials. In this strategy, the client asks a third person to act on his or her behalf. The third party who is enlisted has the power to alter the situation. Examples of this are requests of a principal to override the policy of a teacher and of a supervisor to do the same with reference to a worker. This approach has the advantage of enlisting the greater power on the side of the client; the powerful person may have the authority that is not given to the line person to waive rules or to draw upon knowledge of policies that the latter does not possess. The disadvantages are that this approach may antagonize line persons and make them less cooperative in the future. It may also lock the line person into following procedures in ways that do not benefit the client.

Bargaining.   In this approach, the client system agrees to offer something in exchange for the benefit that he or she desires from the environment. A student, for example, promised to do more work on a classroom assignment if she were allowed to rewrite it and turn it in after the deadline. In another situation, an agency agreed to allow a group to hold a party after normal closing hours if it contributed some money to pay the maintenance worker for overtime.

Confrontation.   This strategy is employed when the client system insists that another person recognize that the latter's behavior is problematic to the client. The implication is that the other should find some way of modifying that behavior. An example is of a spouse who, by mutual agreement, recorded the number of critical comments made by the other spouse during an evening. The number was far in excess of what the "critical" spouse believed to be the case. In another situation, a group of black clients presented a list of complaints to an agency regarding the way in which black clients were responded to by the receptionists. The validity of the complaints was supported by observers of the incidents.

Mass Media.   This strategy requires the client or group to utilize newspapers, radio, television, or other forms of mass communication to achieve change in the target. Individual clients can write letters to the editor, interest reporters in their case, or volunteer to be interviewed. Groups of clients can document injustices and submit that information to the media in press releases. This approach is more likely to produce conflict than the previous ones because it exposes the target to sanctions from the community. An example of the use of this approach was a client who was refused employment when she had reason to believe that she was better qualified than the other applicants who were all men. She gathered information on the low number of women who were employed in the firm, and she got a reporter from the local paper interested in doing a feature on sex discrimination in employment. She presented her data to the reporter, who, after checking them, used them in the story.

Passive Resistance.   The intent of passive resistance is to cause a major disruption in the target system. The disruption results from noncompliance with the rules and procedures of the system. Examples of this kind of activity are hunger strikes, refusal to perform tasks either in one's community or place of employment, and failure to leave the premises when ordered to do so. People who use this strategy usually feel desperate about their situations because other, less extreme strategies have failed to obtain results. Such clients, therefore, feel extremely powerless as well as frustrated. Passive resistance as a political tool has been widely publicized through the writings and activities of Mahatma Gandhi[8] as well as of Martin Luther King, Jr., and other leaders of the civil rights movement in the United States in the 1960s.

Because passive resistance can lead to retaliation against clients, at least in the short run, clients should be helped to consider this and how they will cope yet still sustain their efforts for change in their situations. An example of a use of this strategy, in which social workers participated, involved the residents of an inner-city building who had used many other strategies to secure building repairs from their landlord without success. They ultimately withheld their rent, a form of passive resistance. The landlord tried to evict them, but the eviction was not upheld in court because the withholding of rent was ruled justifiable. The landlord subsequently made the requested repairs.

Active Resistance.   This strategy involves inflicting harm upon the target. This type of action can be illegal, which raises many ethical issues. Examples include destruction of property or the prevention of others from exercising their liberties. Helping clients to resist actively, except in a mild form, is contrary to the professional ethics of social workers.[9] Workers, however, can empathize with clients who, when subjected to extremely cruel conditions, engage in prison riots or destruction during industrial strikes. It is hoped that social workers can help clients to discover ways of coping with severe situations that do not result in harm to themselves or others. This can occur most readily when workers consistently draw the attention of society to inhumane social conditions, particularly those that exist in the institutions that employ social workers.

By Groups of Clients

The strategies described in the previous section can be utilized by individuals or by individuals acting together in groups. There are some additional processes that *require* a group. These are cooptation and alliance.

Cooptation.   This procedure requires a group of clients to interact with targeted individuals in such a way as to induce them to identify with the values or goals of the group. An example occurred in a group of Chicano youths meeting with a school social worker. The youths perceived that their Anglo teachers did not understand their needs and so invited a few teachers to attend several group meetings during which they discussed problems they had in school. As a result, teachers began to think of themselves as having a special interest in and commitment to meeting needs of Chicano students.

Alliance.   In this procedure, the client group forms a cooperative relationship with another group to attain an end sought by both groups. In one example, a group of adolescents at a settlement house contacted other youth groups to see if they were willing to join together to improve recreational facilities in the community. At the first meeting of the representatives of the groups, the participants discovered they had other problems in common such as police harassment and inadequate employment opportunities.

By Outside Organizations

We have already cited a strategy that we termed "use of influentials" and categorized it as one used by individuals and groups. We gave as an example of this strategy an approach to an influential individual. At times, the client can also be helped to solicit an organization to act on his or her behalf, and we believe that, under these circumstances, we should view that organization as the "agent" of change.

One such instance involved a client who was helped to contact a welfare rights organization because her complaint against the welfare department was similar to that of many others served by that system, namely, the adequacy of her assistance payment. Other members of that organization subsequently advocated for her with her assistance payments worker because of their greater experience with that type of action.

The use of outside organizations can also involve those staffed by other professionals such as lawyers. Many social work clients need help in locating legal services they can afford and using these services effectively. This is a good example of securing the help of outside agents to change some aspect of the environment.

Organizations acting on behalf of clients will use the same strategies employed by groups. In the case just cited, the client who contacted a welfare rights organization, that organization involved the client ultimately in picketing a welfare rights office (confrontation), presenting information to other organizations on the plight of welfare clients (education), and developing a letter-to-the-editor campaign (mass media).

Selection of Strategies

We have developed some principles for relating the strategies we have just discussed to changing aspects of systems as we presented these in Chapter 7. These principles are meant to be suggestive rather than definitive or comprehensive.

When the worker and client target the goals and culture of the system, we believe that the approach should have an impact on the information supplied to the system. The strategies that have this effect include interpretation, education, and evaluation. The mass media might be employed to convey this information, and influential people can also serve this purpose. These strategies can have an effect on structures, processes, and boundaries if the information shows that these aspects are dysfunctional to the system's goals.

If the system adheres to goals that are contrary to those in the best interests of the client, the more conflictual strategies will have to be employed if informational strategies are ineffective. These may include confrontation, bargaining, and even passive resistance. These latter strategies will also be appropriately employed if the organization is unresponsive to a demonstration that its structures, processes, and boundaries are in opposition to its avowed goals.

Two cases are cited to exemplify these principles. In the first, most staff members in an agency had the view that indigenous healers such as *curanderos* in the Chicano community and spiritualists in the Puerto Rican community were outdated and useless practitioners. A few workers with Hispanic clients, however, understood the value of these practitioners and planned, with the clients, to educate the staff. This education took the form of lectures and readings on these practices as well as presentations by a *curandero*, and it led to an acceptance of these resources and, ultimately, to collaborative efforts.

In another case, the agency had no black staff members in key agency positions. A large proportion of the clientele of the agency was black, and the agency had as an avowed purpose offering quality service to members of nonwhite groups. Nevertheless, the management of the agency did not recruit or promote nonwhite administrators or supervisors. Several staff members (who were white) believed that this occurred even though several black applicants were as well, or better, qualified as the people hired and promoted. Efforts to point this out failed. A confrontation strategy was chosen in which information was obtained on the qualifications of black applicants and presented to the agency's board of directors as well as outside organizations involved in either funding the agency or referring clients to it. This strategy succeeded, and the next two openings for supervisory staff were filled with nonwhite applicants.

Summary

This chapter presented information on the sequence of decisions required to accomplish environmental change. These consist of first determining whether or not the environment should be targeted. Considerations here include the likelihood of a supportive environment and the amenability of the environment to change. The next decision is to determine which system to choose when change in several is desired. We discussed in reference to this decision the likelihood of success and the balance of gains to costs.

The next decision is which level of the system to target. For puposes of simplicity we referred to two levels: the individual and the systemic. A consideration in this decision is an assessment of the degree to which the individual is acting alone as compared with being in compliance with policies and other agency conditions. A related consideration is to decide where the "problem" is embedded in regard to the system components we referred to in Chapter 7: climate, processes, boundaries and so forth. Decisions on levels and system components help the client and worker to choose from the array of change strategies we portrayed.

In choosing a strategy, a decision must also be made as to whether the worker and client will act individually or jointly and whether another agency such as a group or organization will be enlisted. We discussed a number of factors that should be considered in making this choice.

NOTES

1. Charles Garvin, *Contemporary Group Work* (Englewood Cliffs, N.J.: Prentice-Hall, 1981), pp. 174–175.

2. Paul Glasser et al., "Group Work Intervention in the Social Environment," in Paul Glasser, Rosemary Sarri, and Robert Vinter, eds., *Individual Change Through Small Groups* (New York: The Free Press, 1974), p. 297.

3. Beulah R. Compton and Burt Galaway, eds., *Social Work Processes* (Homewood, Ill.: The Dorsey Press, 1979), p. 342.

4. For further details on mediation, see Ruth Middleman and Gale Goldberg, *Social Service Delivery: A Structural Approach to Social Work Practice* (New York: Columbia University Press, 1974), pp. 59–65.

5. Ibid., pp. 65–72.

6. See, for example, Fred M. Cox et al., *Tactics and Techniques of Community Practice* (Itasca, Ill.: F. E. Peacock, 1977).

7. These sections of this chapter draw from Garvin, *Contemporary Group Work*, pp. 178–182, which, in turn, draws from Glasser et al., "Group Work Intervention in the Social Environment," pp. 292–306.

8. For a discussion of the implications of Gandhi's ideas on passive resistance, see Erik H. Erikson, *Gandhi's Truth: On the Origins of Militant Non-violence,* (New York: W. W. Norton, 1969).

9. See Harry Specht, "Disruptive Tactics," *Social Work*, Vol. 14 (April 1969), pp. 5–15.

fourteen
Termination

Workers must approach the end of the relationship with clients with as much understanding and skill as they did the beginning and the middle stages of service. Each period has its own impact and tasks. As we saw, clients approach the beginning of the process with mixed feelings. Some responses are positive as clients anticipate relief from the pain, deprivation, or conflict of their situations. Some are negative as clients experience fear that they will not be helped, that they may be harmed, and that, in any case, they will invest money, time, and other scarce resources for services that may or may not be worth this expenditure.

Clients approach the middle phases with analogous concerns. They have tentatively, at least, committed themselves to the service, identified problems and goals, and understood in general terms what the service will be. The hard work is to make these dreams come true. Even under optimal circumstances, changes will occur in the client and his or her interaction with systems that

will be both beneficial as well as troublesome. Rarely is any change an unmitigated blessing.

The end also brings with it a number of issues. These will be portrayed in this chapter along with the workers' tasks in relationship to them. Our contention is that in any phase of work, if the issues are well handled, the client will be able to proceed into the next phase. For termination, the next phase for the client is to invest himself or herself in living without the supportive and ameliorative inputs of the social work service. The client should also be able to bring to his or her life the strengths and skills that were obtained through the service, if it has been successful, and to retain these. On the other hand, no social work service (or any other one, undoubtedly) guarantees that the client will not have additional problems. The client, therefore, should feel able to return to the previous service facility (or even worker) for further help, if that becomes necessary.

On the other hand, the service may not

have been successful. Clients may terminate prior to the accomplishment of their goals, or the worker may be replaced. In group situations, some members may leave while others continue, and in family work, some family members may also do the same. In this chapter we shall, therefore, consider problems that arise through these and other events in the termination process.

As we have stated elsewhere, all endings have some common effects.[1] Whether the ending is the loss of a job, graduation from school, or a move to a new city, some degree of mourning and a feeling of loss will occur if the person was invested in the experience. These feelings and experiences occur more intensively with great or irreversible losses such as the death of another person or a disability to one's self or a significant other. This is because after the loss, one must withdraw the investment of energy in the person or object and establish a new equilibrium in which the person or object is no longer present except in memory.

Thus, coming to terms with endings is an inevitable experience in living. Endings, as one experiences them or anticipates them, are what create the sense that life has a tragic component. Life cannot be fully lived and new experiences accepted until one develops a way of coping with this. How the worker handles the ending of a one-to-one or group or family experience can add to or take away from the evolving ability of the person to cope with life's inevitable losses and changes.

Beginning with the "functional" approach to social work practice, many practice models have focused on the meaning of time in the social work process.[2] These models identify the way in which clients respond to beginning, middle, and ending phases and incorporate this into the way the worker facilitates the process. Such models often set time limits at the beginning of the service, and these may even be for a short term such as two or three months. As Smalley so well states,

> The "use of ending" as one aspect of skill in social work process has been much misunderstood. There should never be a practice of setting a rigid and arbitrary time limit at the point of entering on the giving of service as a "technique" unrelated to the needs and requirements of a particular situation of service. When the ending is *in the situation*, it can be used with sensitivity and skill, which involves not only technical capacity for dealing helpfully with what is involved in ending for the other but also the worker's own capacity to let go. Where there is no ending inherent in the situation, it can be psychologically helpful to establish one at the point of the beginning. The ending time established will be based on the time required for something productive to be done in a particular kind of situation. Setting an ending can alleviate a client's feeling of being trapped in something that may go on forever with his own will and self lost to the control of an outside force. It can serve as an incentive to him to use productively the present moment out of the recognition that the relationship and service are not going to last indefinitely. In developing capacity and courage to enter on something, use it, and let it go, he develops capacity and confidence in living with all things temporal, and in small degree with the fact of life itself, with its inevitable physical ending.[3]

We shall now turn to a consideration of the skills required of the worker during this period. In this part of the chapter, we shall discuss "nonproblematic" endings, that is, situations in which the termination occurs through the mutual agreement of the worker and client system when at least some of the client's goals have been attained. Later in the chapter, we shall discuss endings that are less satisfying.

We shall discuss these skills in relationship to a series of tasks that confront the client and worker during the termination phase. These are

1. To evaluate the experience in relationship to the goals established for it
2. To understand and cope with feelings about termination
3. To plan ways to maintain the beneficial changes that have occurred
4. To utilize these beneficial changes in a variety of situations
5. To seek out and engage one's self in new services when this is required

The order in which we have listed these tasks is an arbitrary one. The actual order in which they are accomplished will depend on the unique nature of each situation and the way in which the client wishes to proceed. The issues that arise as one task is undertaken will also affect this sequence. For example, as one client became aware that his goals were only partly achieved, he expressed feelings of discouragement, and these were dealt with by the worker. Another client, in contrast, became quite elated as she realized how much she had attained, and this feeling was appropriately responded to by the worker. For the client who was discouraged, one way the worker tried to help him to cope was to take up task "5," that of supporting his plan to return for more service in the new community to which he was moving.

The Tasks of Termination

Evaluation

In Chapter 10, we presented many of the ways that changes in individuals, families, groups, and organizations can be monitored and evaluated. We shall now consider how these tools are used by workers as part of the termination process. One important decision that should be made during termination is to select from among the instruments chosen in the beginning of the process or during it the one which should be considered at this time.

The instruments chosen for use during termination should be those that will show the client most clearly to what degree goals have or have not been achieved. This may not be the most valid and reliable instrument, from a research point of view, but should be the most graphic one from the client's standpoint. In addition, clients at termination should select the types of information they want most, and this will also govern what data are reviewed.

New information relevant to the evaluation of the interpersonal practice experience is likely to emerge at this time. Some of this will ensue from the discussion of the evaluative data as clients point out additional meanings of the data and, thus, generate more information. Part of the evaluation process at termination should also be an evaluation in the client's own words, independent of any formal evaluative procedure that has been employed. Formal measurement procedures are likely to present isolated bits of information such as the grades the child has received, the amount of satisfaction in a marriage, or the fact that a decision was reached on an important issue. The client's more qualitative response to an open-ended question such as, "In your own words, how do you think things are different now from the way they were when you began?" will suggest how a number of aspects link together as well as how the client may have benefited or been hurt by the experience along lines not elicited by the planned evaluation procedure.

This evaluation should also produce the client's perceptions of the "causes" of change. While these may or may not be more "true" than the worker's ideas of cause, they can suggest hypotheses of what is effective and ineffective in social work techniques that can then be tested in more systematic ways. For example, one client told her worker that she attributed her improvement to an explanation she received of the reasons why her husband treated her as he did. This led her to stop blaming herself for all her problems. This worker had attributed her progress to specific instruction she had given the client on how to be more assertive. There was no certainty in the worker's mind as to which factor was the most important, but she did rethink the strategies she will employ in similar situations.

Another important function that is fulfilled by evaluation is the reinforcement of changes that have taken place in the client. When the client recognizes, and receives, recognition for change, this may more firmly establish new behaviors. The client's perception that change has taken place may also reinforce clients' efforts to seek new changes on their own.

Another aspect of evaluation during termination should be the client's evaluation of the worker. This does not mean that workers should wait until termination to seek feedback on their behaviors, as this can be helpful throughout the process. Nevertheless, professional growth requires this kind of personal information. The fact that the worker asks for it can also provide a model to the client as to constructive ways to ask for and receive evaluative information about one's self.

The evaluation of the worker by clients can be written or oral. If it is written, the worker will usually discuss the client's reactions with them so that additional information can be secured. In group situations, the worker has to reach the additional decision with the group members as to whether the evaluation should be anonymous. Generally,

we favor evaluations for which the evaluators take responsibility and, therefore, to which they sign their names. This may be difficult in groups conducted in social control settings, such as prisons, where clients may fear the consequences of offering a negative evaluation, and this is a reasonable stance under those circumstances.

The following are some questions we have used in asking clients to evaluate the worker.[4]

1. What were some of my actions you found most (least) helpful?
2. What actions would you have liked me to take that I did not?
3. Were there personal qualities of mine you found helpful or not helpful (for example, ways of speaking, timing of comments, sense of humor, ways of expressing myself)?
4. How well did you think that I understood what you were thinking and feeling? In what ways did I communicate that?
5. How honest and open did you experience me as being?
6. In what ways did you (or did you not) experience me as supportive and caring?

It is not easy for clients to provide this kind of information because they may not wish to hurt the feelings of the worker; also many people have a sense that this kind of feedback is impolite, although it is hoped that the worker and client have a relationship that is based on honesty and openness. Our experience, however, is that when the worker unequivocally asks for such information, clients respect the worker's wishes.

Coping with Feelings

As we suggested in the beginning of this chapter, we react to all endings in some common ways, and this includes feelings about endings. We have found it useful, therefore, to draw upon the literature regarding how individuals cope with the ultimate ending, death, to analyze the feelings associated with termination.[5] We do not mean to imply that the intensity of feelings at all terminations is the same but rather their character. We also do not propose that the sequence with which people experience feelings regarding termination and deal with them occurs in a predictable order either.

One reaction associated with endings is that of *denial*. Clients may state that they do not have any feelings about ending. They also may "own" some feelings but reject others such as a client who said that he looked forward to ending his sessions but expressed no regrets about this. Denial of feelings about termination may be seen in clients who continue to work in sessions as if there is to be no ending. Still another manifestation of denial is the client who, when termination is broached, misses sessions or seeks to terminate earlier than the projected ending.

In group sessions, members may accept some feelings regarding termination and deny others. Thus, in one group, a member spoke about missing the other members, but he disclaimed any feelings about the worker. In other groups, members have experienced these feelings in reverse. In family sessions, the members do not usually terminate with one another unless the family sessions have led to a decision for the parents to divorce or for a child to leave. Feelings that are expressed, therefore, are usually directed at the worker. If the worker, as is usually the case, has become incorporated into the family system, the family members may feel toward him or her as they would toward any person who leaves the family, and the intensity of these feelings may be denied.

The process of denial may also affect the workers who underestimate the emotional impact that termination has on both the clients and themselves. This can lead to an underestimation of the value of the entire experience that is detrimental to the client's ability to maintain their gains and transfer them to new settings. Part of the workers' effective response to termination issues is to face their own feelings regarding loss of a client. Workers may experience both pleasure that the client has made gains and even relief that the client and his or her troubles will no longer be the concern of the worker. On the other hand, the worker may feel pain that a client whom the worker has cared for may never be seen again. The worker may have to begin with a new client with all the discomfort occasioned by a new beginning rather than a continuation of an accustomed pattern.

The worker who faces these feelings will provide a model for the client. More direct approaches are also possible. The worker can acknowledge with clients that endings are difficult and that they may find it hard to talk about them. Some clients spontaneously reflect on how they felt when other relationships ended and how they coped then as well as the implications of these past terminations for the present one.

In groups, workers have asked the members to move about the meeting room and to say goodbye to other members as individuals. Another procedure is to rotate around the group giving each member an opportunity to say farewell to others. These types of activities elicit many feelings. Members observe other members who are more expressive of feelings than themselves, and this helps the more reluctant members to express their reactions.

Another reaction associated with endings is that of *anger*. The anger may be expressed toward many different persons. It may be toward the agency that has established time limits, toward the worker who has implemented them or who has not met all the client's expectations, or toward one's self as a client for not having worked hard enough. In group situations, some of the anger may be directed toward other members or even toward the group as an entity for not being the kind of group the member wished.

There are many reasons why this manifestation of anger may occur. One is the clients' idea that they should reject the "other" first before being themselves rejected. A feeling of rejection is one of the most painful of experiences. Anger may also be a means of coping with the client's feelings of guilt for events that have occurred during the process. In many cases, the anger is a reaction to the pain of termination and a move to hurt the perpetrators of such pain.

The emotion of anger, at termination or any other time, is a very difficult one for members and workers to handle. Workers may feel guilty because of things they had done or not done to help the clients and may experience the client's anger and punishment for this. The clients, in turn, may fear that positive components of the experience will be lost if they express anger. They may also believe that anger during termination shows a lack of gratitude for what the worker has done or may cause the workers to experience feelings that are too painful for them to handle.

Workers, therefore, should indicate to clients that experiencing some anger is appropriate during endings. Workers can also reiterate that the principle that has governed all the work together has been an open and honest expression of feelings and that this is as important a component of the final stage as of all other stages. A feeling of anger has a legitimate basis, as all helping experiences are in some ways imperfect. The question regarding anger, in addition to expressing it in a constructive manner, is what to "do" with it. The anger must be channeled so that the clients consider how to make future situations more responsive to their needs and themselves more effective in those situations.

A third reaction associated with endings is bargaining. Clients show this response to termination when they seek to postpone the time set for ending. They may also try to create new experiences that are not appropriate. In group situations, some members may, for example, try to arrange get-togethers with other members when this desire is not reciprocated. *Bargaining* is one approach clients use to channel their anger and, therefore, is a beginning effort to cope with it. Workers can indicate an understanding of this desire to continue and can help the clients to understand that it is one way of coping with the feelings associated with termination. If the worker, along with this, is firm on plans for ending, more effective means of coping are likely to emerge.

Depression is another reaction to termination. In helping situations, we find that depression often follows expressions of denial and bargaining. This type of depression can be seen in a lack of energy for the tasks of termination such as evaluation and planning subsequent activities to maintain gains. The client may also display feelings of depression through talking of sad events and previous losses. This expression of sad feelings is occasioned by a withdrawal of energy from the social work experience and, like the other feelings we have described, is a necessary part of the termination experience. We find that when this feeling is not denied and is allowed full expression, it usually "runs its course," and the client regains the energy required to perform the tasks required for termination. Workers can help with this feeling, as with all others, through expressions of empathy and through sharing their own regrets about ending.

Another reaction found in some termination experiences is that of *regression*. This is also an effort on the part of clients to cope with the feelings associated with termination. Regression during termination usually consists of behavior that was typical of earlier stages of work. The client may experience a return of difficulties that were previously resolved or of interactions with the worker that had also been given up. The latter can consist of dependence on the worker, expressions of mistrust of the worker, or a withdrawal from interactions with the worker.

This type of regression can also be seen in family and group situations. Family or group members may also interact with each other in the ways they did earlier in the family treatment experience. These individuals may use this as ammunition for the argument that the process should not end.

One way for the worker to approach regression is to accept it as a temporary way of coping with the ending. The worker can even interpret this to the members with the "prediction" that it will continue until the clients accept the reality of termination. This use of a "paradoxical" instruction will relieve the oppositional quality that characterizes this phase of the relationship as the client cannot maintain the "regression" as a way of proving the worker wrong.

This discussion of feelings associated with termination is not meant to suggest that all feelings during this period are painful and must be defended against. Quite to the contrary, most clients have pleasurable feelings that the experience is coming to an end, particularly if the outcome has been satisfactory. These positive feelings can be increased when the worker reminds clients that they have continued in the service relationship and have invested their energy in it, even when the "going was rough." This fact can enhance the clients' conception of themselves as persons who have the strength to seek help when it is necessary and to commit themselves to the process.

Thus, the feelings at the time of termination will almost always be ambivalent ones. This characterizes any change in one's situation because of a simultaneous anticipation of the future and regret for the past. During the interpersonal practice process, this ambivalence is likely to be experienced and mastered around a variety of issues, and the worker utilizes these previous experiences to give the clients a broader perspective on their current transition.

Maintaining Change

For a variety of reasons, workers cannot assume that beneficial changes that the clients have attained will continue. One reason, for example, is that the environment may not be supportive of changes. Parents, spouses, employers, teachers, or others may be unwilling to make changes in their own reactions that complement changes occurring in the client. This may cause them to criticize or in other ways undermine the client's new ways of coping. Labels placed on the client such as "delinquent" or "poor student" may continue to be attached to the client orally, as well as in recorded materials. The client may also have received recognition and other forms of reinforcement from the worker (or from other individuals in family and group modalities) that are not forthcoming from other persons outside the social work experience.

For change to be maintained, therefore, one or more of the following factors must be present:

1. The individual, if he or she was the target of change, must have developed to the degree required by the actual life situation the knowledge, skills, and attitudes required.

The family, group, or other system, if they were the target of change, must analogously be composed of individuals who have acquired the essential knowledge, skills, and attitudes. In the case of a client who wished to do better in school, he acquired, through his work with a social worker, better study habits, an understanding of how to establish a good study environment (quiet, lighting, clear table), and a value that studying was important.

2. The individual (or individuals in a system) must continue to receive reinforcement rather than punishment for the behaviors associated with the change. In the example cited in (1), the student contracted with his parents to allow him to meet with his friends after he had spent a designated amount of time studying. He also decided to associate with friends who would praise him for studying rather than those who would criticize him.

3. The individual (or individuals in a system) must have access to the resources they will need to continue the behavior. The student in our example must be allowed to use a quiet room with adequate lighting and space for studying.

4. The individual must have a means of "self-control" for resolving problems that arise in the future that would prevent a continuation of the new pattern of behavior. The youth in our example was confronted with conflicts between his desire to study and a desire to see his girlfriend. He was able to assess the circumstances in which he most felt this conflict, using a framework taught him by his worker. As a result of this assessment, he contracted with himself and with his girlfriend to make seeing her contingent upon a specified amount of completed homework.

The worker, therefore, as termination approaches (if not before), must develop a plan with the client as to how change will be maintained. This plan will include some of the following procedures, each related to the principles just cited for maintaining change: overlearning, problem solving with regard to the environment, network interventions, creation of support groups, securing reinforcement, and self-control.

Overlearning is used to help clients practice the new ways of coping after they learn them initially. The clients are helped to plan ways to use their understanding and skills in a number of situations, often situations that are quite different from one another. For example, one client had worked to develop assertive behaviors. He was helped to act more assertively with his fellow workers as well as with his family before termination. Another client worked to form new relationships. Before termination was considered, she was helped to initiate new relationships with several neighbors as well as with co-workers. In group situations, overlearning can occur when group members role play their skills with one another.

Problem solving with reference to the environment begins with helping the client to predict the possible environmental opposition that will be generated. The worker helps the client to consider ways of responding to this opposition. These include negotiations with people in the environment who are unsympathetic to changes, recommendations that such persons also seek professional intervention, and actions to insulate one's self from such negative responses. In group and family modalities, the clients will help each other to identify and solve such problems.

The idea that others in the environment may also require professional help recognizes the frequent finding of interpersonal practitioners that, as the client improves, others, such as family members, develop dysfunctional behaviors. This is one of the strongest reasons for involving family members and others in the process from its beginning. Unfortunately, this is not always possible as the client, as well as the relevant others, may oppose this approach. Some family-oriented practitioners refuse to work with individuals on a one-to-one basis when problems are seen as family problems. We do not take as unequivocal a stand but on occasion do make such demands of clients when all the information supports the value of such an approach.

The third way we have listed of maintaining change is *network intervention*. We do not mean by this term the type of network therapy that enlists the participation in the process of all the people with whom the client interacts. While this may be valid in some cases, in others the worker interacts or helps the client to interact with such persons during the termination process specifically as a way of seeking to maintain changes. A school social worker, for example, worked with a boy to help him improve his classroom behavior as well as his completion of assignments. The worker, with the knowledge of the boy, had contact with his teacher during this period but also held conferences with the teacher and parents at the time of termination to discuss a plan for maintaining the child's excellent progress.

Another way of helping the client to maintain change is through the creation of *support groups*. When the form of helping has been the group, some or all of the members may decide to maintain contact with each other. In other situations, whether individual or group helping, a new group may be formed for this purpose. An existing group in the community may also be available. These formats are necessary for clients who do not belong to other networks that have the potential to provide necessary support. This may be true for isolated individuals who have been in medical, psychiatric, or penal institutions. Such support may also be required for people who seek to maintain a life-style that is regarded as deviant by many groups in the society. Examples are a gay life-style, single-parent status, or living alone as an emanci-

pated adolescent. It is incorrect to predict people who need such support will become chronically dependent. All of us are able to function in part because of the existence of supporting networks. For some people, such networks have not emerged "naturally" and must be created.

The principle associated with all these measures is that of ensuring the kinds of *reinforcement* the client will need to maintain change. Sometimes this issue must be confronted directly in these terms. For specified periods of time, individuals in the environment may be asked to guarantee reinforcement of change. In addition, the client can be taught to understand the kind of reinforcement he or she wants and to request it from teachers, family members, employers, and others. It is unfortunate that in our society many appear to find it difficult to offer praise or encouragement spontaneously for desired behavior, but instead focus on criticism or punishment of undesired actions. Clients can be helped through role plays and other simulated experiences to ask for recognition of their accomplishments. The anxiety that such requests cause clients (as well as all of us) and the assumption that such a request is immodest can be overcome. This is in some small measure a step toward the creation of a community in which norms favoring positive responses properly outnumber those favoring aversive ones.

A number of these processes are included in what is called *self-control*. This procedure is based upon the client's understanding of the process of change, usually from a behavior modification perspective. The client in a typical situation has learned on his or her own to state a problem in behaviorally specific terms, develop a baseline of the behavior, determine a goal, make a contract with himself or herself to secure and utilize reinforcements for steps toward the goal, and monitor change. The client may alternatively choose to modify some antecedent rather than consequence or to self-modify some disabling emotion, such as anxiety, through a relaxation procedure previously taught by the worker.

An example of a use of a self-control procedure that was taught during the termination process is the following. At the time of termination, Susan had attained her goal of making new friends. She had accomplished this through learning a number of techniques for initiating relationships, and she had also been helped to lessen her anxiety in social situations. Subsequently, she found that she was in danger of losing a new friend because she did not know how to roller skate and this was a favorite activity of the friend. She contracted with herself to learn to roller skate and was even able to set up a series of appropriate learning steps with the help of an attendant at the local rink. She engaged her friend to reinforce her for accomplishing these steps by having the friend agree to join in an activity of the client's choosing. One antecedent she changed was that she did not like the music or decor of one rink and she felt uncomfortable learning to skate there. She was able to locate another rink that did not have this effect on her.

Utilizing Changes in a Variety of Circumstances

Another task of the termination process, one closely associated with that of maintaining changes, is to use such changes in a variety of circumstances. Clients, at the beginning of the helping process, are helped to state their problems in terms of specific situations. Examples are discomfort in a *marriage*, anxiety while at *work*, nonperformance in *school*, or inability to act in desired ways in the *community*. When clients do not base their problems in such specific situa-

tions, the worker helps the client to select and focus on some so that problem solving and evaluation of changes may have an appropriate foundation.

Nevertheless, the solutions obtained by clients are likely to have relevance in more circumstances than the ones focused on during the helping process. The worker can aid the client in selecting these circumstances and handling them in ways that were acquired. For example, in a group the worker may take trips with the members to several different environments that require the members to adapt their skills to a variety of circumstances. Groups also offer the opportunity to simulate different situations in which the members can practice new behaviors. For this reason, even when the form of helping is on a one-to-one basis, the worker may help the client to join a group that has this potential.

In family treatment, the worker, as part of the termination process, may raise issues that have not previously been emphasized so that family members can practice new patterns of adapting. This procedure can also be accomplished with families during termination phases through a series of "homework assignments." Thus, one family had worked on learning better means of problem solving. The content of the discussions in which they acquired problem-solving skills was the use of money. The worker during the termination phase asked the family to select a problem around child behavior and subsequently a problem around responding to a troublesome relative to see if this approach to problem solving would "work" with those issues.

An important skill that helps clients to apply what they have learned to a broad variety of circumstances is the ability to analyze the relevant aspects of those situations. This ability enables the members to know how to employ the right skill in the right place. In a way, therefore, any social work process must add to the client's understanding of human behavior. Yalom expresses this well when he states:

> In part, however, explanation and clarification function as effective curative agents in their own right. Man has always abhorred uncertainty and through the ages has sought to order his universe by providing explanations, primarily religious or scientific. The explanation of a phenomenon is the first step toward control of the phenomenon . . . . Similarly with psychiatric patients: fear and anxiety which stem from uncertainty of the source, meaning, and seriousness of psychiatric symptoms may so compound the total dysphoria that effective exploration becomes vastly more difficult. Thus, didactic instruction, through its provision of structure and explanation, has intrinsic value and deserves a place in our repertoire of therapeutic instruments.[6]

An example of this was a client who in the beginning of the helping process tended to blame himself exclusively for any problem that developed in his interpersonal relationships. When he fought with his girlfriend, he felt very guilty and looked solely at his own present and past actions for the source of the difficulty. In the course of his social work experience, he learned to discuss such situations with his girlfriend and to work out with her what each one contributed to the problem and what each was willing to do to solve it. In the termination phase, the worker reviewed with this client the ways in which he could examine his actual behaviors in conflict situations as well as those of the other person, the goals of each, and the motivation of each to seek to change the interaction.

The way in which the worker helps the client to acquire cognitive skills for the assessment of situations will be heavily influenced by the theoretical bias of the worker. Behaviorists among social workers will teach clients to analyze antecedents and consequences; transactional analysts will do the same for ego states; and ego psychologists will introduce notions of the importance of feeling states, levels of awareness, and ways of coping. In addition to the issue of the truth or falsity of any of these ideas, clients are often strengthened by their sense that they have a "handle" on understanding the behavior of themselves and others.

Engaging in New Services

One interpersonal helping experience can be a preparation for another one. A client who used one service to determine whether or not she wished to place her baby for adoption decided to use another one to help her to seek a career after she placed the child. Another client used one group experience to prepare for leaving the mental hospital and a subsequent one to secure support when she returned to the community. A family that used family therapy at one time decided to seek a "preparation for retirement" program later.

While subsequent services are not always selected as part of termination, when they are, preparation for them should be part of the termination process. This should be more than a brief presentation of information. Clients should be helped to identify their subsequent needs, and the relationship of these needs to available services should be made clear. The worker should help clients to discuss their expectations of the new service as well as any barriers they see to its use. When barriers are anticipated, the worker should help the clients to plan ways of overcoming them.

An example of this process is a student in a school for adolescents with developmental disabilities. A social worker helped this student to plan for his future vocational training. The social work service was focused on the choices the student had to make. As part of the termination phase, the worker reviewed the kinds of services the client needed such as a counselor to provide support and help in problem solving. The worker helped him to consider what his expectations were for this type of counseling. The client and the worker knew that the counselors in the program were overworked and might spend their scarce time with less motivated students. The worker, therefore, helped this client to think of clear and direct ways for expressing his desires for services to the counseling staff.

Termination Issues in Group Work

All interpersonal practice situations share the tasks just described. Work with groups, however, involves some additional issues. One of these is that one member of the group may terminate while the other members continue. This can occur in any group, although some workers conduct "open" groups in which members enter or leave at any time. (The more typical group is "closed" in that all members start and continue together for a specified number of meetings.)

A termination process should occur with reference to the member who leaves. A contract that workers often suggest at the beginning of a group to ensure this is that if a member desires to leave the group, he or she will attend at least one meeting to deal with termination issues after the decision is reached. This (these) meeting(s) should be used to accomplish the same termination tasks, although in a briefer form, as when the entire group ends. Thus, the member is encouraged to evaluate what he or she has attained through the group experience and how the group has or has not been helpful. The worker and other members help the member to express his or her feelings about leaving.

The other members, in addition, are asked to state their feelings about the departure of the person terminating. These feelings, which can include both hope and anger, can impair the continued development of the group if they are not expressed at this time. The terminating member also uses knowledge of these feelings to deal with the reality of the group's response as well as to avoid the perception that the group members do not care for him or her.

All the tasks of termination noted for individual clients are also undertaken with individual members who terminate. They are aided to reinforce what they have learned as well to apply their skills as broadly as possible. They also should be helped to consider new resources, particularly if their termination is a result of dissatisfaction with this group experience. Another by-product of this process is that other members will learn about the termination process and will also be convinced that their presence matters to the group and their leaving will be appropriately responded to should it become necessary to resign from the group.

Sometimes a group begins to disintegrate and attendance falls off. When this occurs, the worker should ask the members to attend a formal ending to the group. At this time a decision on termination can be clearly made; feelings about this can be dealt with, and an evaluation that includes the reasons for the group's failure can be generated. Occasionally, the reasons for the group's failure are responded to in ways that allow for changes in the group to be made and the group proceeds in a more vigorous and successful way.

When the group members all terminate at the same time because the group itself is ending, members can help each other with each of the processes we have described. Members will evaluate the progress made by each individual, the effectiveness of the group as an entity, and the effectiveness of the worker. While the content of the first and last of these evaluations is similar to that in one-to-one terminations, the evaluation of the group is a new issue. This can include an evaluation of the tasks and programs the group undertook, the nature of interpersonal relationships in the group, the kinds of norms the group adopted, and the group's overall emotional atmosphere.

Members will also help each other to express feelings about termination. These feelings will not only be those regarding the loss of associations with other individuals, including the worker, but also the loss of the group as an entity. It should be remembered that even if a particular individual missed a meeting, including again the worker, the group was "there" if at least one other individual was present. Members should be helped to recognize this and deal with the empty space created by the disbanding of the group.

Regarding the remaining three issues of maintaining change, generalizing change, and planning future activities, members can also help each other. Since members often have similar problems or come from similar backgrounds or both, they may be more adept than the worker is at spotting future problems as well as support systems. If this does not violate a goal of termination, members may be encouraged to contact each other on a one-to-one basis to help with problem solving or to reinforce the use of a self-control procedure.

Termination Issues with Families

The unique aspect of family treatment is that the family remains together after it discontinues services from the worker. The exception is when family treatment ends with either divorce or child placement. Some family work also ends, when one member of the family continues to receive service from the same or a different worker while others do not. Each of these circumstances raises different termination issues.

When the family continues intact, the sense of loss of the worker may be less than in one-to-one treatment or even group work, as in the latter, termination is associated with the concurrent loss of other members. In some approaches to family therapy, also, the worker terminates when the family structure is more functional than it was when the family entered service. The worker assumes that the family has become equipped to resolve its own problems and is more likely to do so "on its own" than when it is dependent on the worker. Termination is associated, therefore, with greater problem-solving capacity rather than problem solution as such and the job of the worker is deemphasized. We hypothesize that this type of termination may be easier for the family than for other action systems although this proposition should be examined through research on family terminations.

If family work ends in divorce or placement of a family member outside the household, the worker should continue to offer service to the separated parties or ensure that they have access to services they need. Under these circumstances the feelings of loss from *both* the worker *and* other family members can be devastating. These clients will require the supportive presence of the worker (or other workers) as they embark on their new roles. The emotions associated with other types of termination will appear among the family members, and they will require help to cope with this separation process.

Worker Termination

In individual, family, and group work, it is possible for the worker to terminate, while the client system desires to continue services. The worker's termination may occur when the worker leaves for a new job, becomes ill or pregnant, is fired, or reaches the end of a student placement. Each of these reasons requires similar as well as different worker responses. The similarities include informing the client, if possible, several sessions in advance. The client should be helped to express and cope with feelings associated with the pending loss of the worker. These feelings can include sadness as well as anger that the worker is leaving when the client needs him or her. Workers should not minimize the likelihood that the client will have these feelings. The loss of the worker can recall other circumstances to the clients when important persons deserted them when they were in need. Clients who have experienced rejection from parents or other crucial persons in their lives will be particularly vulnerable to the loss of the worker. Children are also highly susceptible to worker loss because of their dependence on parental figures for security.

Clients will require reassurance that the worker's termination is not due to their own behavior as some will assume that if they had been "better" clients the worker would have remained. This reassurance will be a therapeutic one to those clients who have believed the loss of other persons was a consequence of their "bad" behavior and who continue to work on this issue. Workers should be aware of their own feelings about terminating from the agency, as these feelings can inhibit the practitioner from being sensitive to the feelings of the client. For example, a student social worker believed that he had not responded to some of the client's problems as skillfully as he should have. His guilt over this blocked him from accepting the fact that he also had been helpful to the client and had expressed a great deal of caring to him. He was unresponsive at first to the client's sense of loss and was unable to approach this until he had discussed his feelings with his supervisor.

At times it is wise to have the client's termination coincide with that of the worker, especially if the client's termination would have occurred soon after that of the worker. The amount of readjustment to a new worker in these cases may not be worth the additional steps toward goal attainment. On the other hand, the worker may leave when the client is nowhere near his or her appropriate termination time. Ideally, a new worker will be chosen prior to the departure of the previous one and can be introduced to the client. In this situation, both workers should be present for several sessions to create continuity.

Even under the best of circumstances, the client is likely to spend several sessions (or even more) with the new worker discussing feelings about the departure of the previous one. This helps the client to determine the degree to which the new worker can be empathetic but also is a test as to whether the new worker also has plans to terminate. The client may extoll the virtues of the previous worker or condemn his or her vices. The effect may be to hint at either the assumed superiority or inferiority of the new worker. This is often a repetition of how the client has coped with previous separation issues, and exploration at this time may help the client to gain new insights into his or her previous relationship patterns.

In all cases, the departure of one worker and the appointment of another can provide useful learning. Our lives are inevitably composed of shifts in our relationships in which loyalties must be transferred from one individual to another. A recognition of functional as well as dysfunctional ways of coping with this can develop in the social work context and can be generalized to other occasions where such changes must be coped with.

Problematic Terminations

Terminations can be more difficult when the worker or the clients or both view the social work process as having been unsuccessful in attaining the client's objectives. An absence, however, of efforts to fulfill termination tasks in these situations can increase their negative impact. This can be in the form of exaggerating the client's sense of failure, thus making it difficult for the client to seek out a new helping experience that can be more effective than the existing one.

Each of the termination tasks outlined earlier in the chapter can be appropriately adapted to times when the service has been a partial or complete failure. An evaluation of the experience can help to identify some success as well as failure. It can also determine aspects of the process responsible for the failure so that these may be avoided in the future. It is possible that the evaluation will produce material that is critical of the worker. This is always difficult for the worker, but the worker should seek to overcome feelings of guilt and regret. This is a valuable opportunity for the worker to identify ways of improving his or her practice skills. In addition, the way in which the worker copes with failure can provide an important model to clients as to how they can cope with occasions when they are not successful. Thus, the ways that workers help clients to deal with feelings when termination follows an unsuccessful service can, in itself, be one of the most valuable aspects of the

service. After all, the client has usually sought service because of unsuccessful coping and can learn from the worker how the latter responds to an analogous situation.

The worker may wish to help the client reach out to a new service that will be more helpful to the client. Because the client may fear a repetition of the present unsuccessful experience, the worker will have to handle this termination in such a way as to avoid this. As we have sought to demonstrate, the worker must use all the skills at his or her disposal to free the client from the emotional bonds of an unsuccessful helping experience so that the client's energies can go into locating and investing in a new one.

Another problematic situation related to the one that we have just discussed is the client's desire to terminate in opposition to the worker's recommendation for continuance. The client may wish to do this because of his or her resistance to change. The client's investment in "things as they are" or fear of new patterns may overwhelm the client's hope that a better life will be attained. The client may also meet with pressures on the part of "significant others" who cannot adapt to changes in the client, although workers should try to identify and ameliorate this type of response when it is identified, often through a redefinition of the client system.

If the client contracts to meet with the worker for a session after he or she has decided to terminate, such a "premature" termination can sometimes be avoided. On other occasions, no matter how skillful the worker is, a termination cannot be prevented. The client should still be helped to participate in the termination tasks we have outlined because this process will make it more likely that the client will reapply for some service when he or she has coped with internal or external sources of resistance or when the pain associated with dysfunctional life patterns grows more intense. The worker's understanding of and ability to work with the client's feelings in these type of terminations will be a vital factor in the likelihood the client will seek help again.

The issue of termination has been analyzed by some theorists as an extension of a social psychological concept referred to as the *comparison level of alternatives*.[7] This concept means that our choice of social affiliations is governed by a comparison of the rewards and costs associated with that affiliation as compared with alternatives. In cases of premature termination, the worker should explore with the client, therefore, the rewards and costs of remaining in the social work service, choosing an alternative service, or terminating formal service altogether. This can be an exercise in rational decision making that is a model for other occasions when the client must choose among alternatives.

Summary

We began this chapter with a discussion of the universality of the termination process as clients move through life because old attachments must be relinquished and new ones formed. The worker is helpful in this process through fulfilling a series of tasks that include evaluating the experience (including the worker's performance), coping with feelings about termination, planning ways to maintain beneficial changes, generalizing changes to a variety of circumstances, and engaging in new services when they are required.

The tasks of termination occur whether the client system is an individual, a family, or a group. There are, however, several issues around termination in multiperson client systems. Families will continue together although the worker who has "joined" the family, in an emotional sense, now drops out. On the other hand, the result of family treatment may be the departure of one or more family members. In contrast, group members must cope with the loss of each other, as well as the group. Some groups may continue as a support for the members. In groups, also, a member may terminate while the group continues.

Additional termination issues occur when the worker leaves, when the experience has been unsuccessful, and when the client terminates against the worker's advice. These latter situations were analyzed and suitable worker approaches were noted.

NOTES

1. Charles Garvin, *Contemporary Group Work* (Englewood Cliffs, N.J.: Prentice-Hall, 1981), p. 206.

2. For a "functional" approach to the use of time and its relationship to termination, see Ruth Elizabeth Smalley, *Theory for Social Work Practice* (New York: Columbia University Press, 1967), pp. 142–151; for a more research-oriented presentation, see William J. Reid and Ann W. Shyne, *Brief and Extended Casework* (New York: Columbia University Press, 1969).

3. Smalley, *Theory for Social Work Practice*, p. 149.

4. Garvin, *Contemporary Group Work*, pp. 210–211.

5. This discussion draws from Elizabeth Kübler-Ross, *On Death and Dying* (New York: Macmillan, 1969).

6. Irvin D. Yalom, *The Theory and Practice of Group Psychotherapy*, 2nd ed. (New York: Basic Books, 1975), p. 11.

7. J. W. Thibaut and H. H. Kelley, *The Social Psychology of Groups* (New York: John Wiley, 1959), p. 15. The application of this framework to termination issues in groups was demonstrated by A. Sagi in his Ph.D. preliminary examination in social work at the University of Michigan.

fifteen

Practice Effects of Settings and Cultures

Throughout this book, while we have included examples from many interpersonal practice settings, we have emphasized practice theory and principles that apply to all or most of them. There are practice principles, however, that are appropriate to some situations and not others. In a sense, each situation is unique and requires an idiosyncratic solution. In addition, issues tend to arise in some types of agencies and not others, among members of some ethnic groups and not others, among men as compared with women (and vice versa), and among some age groups and not others.

There are still other ways of classifying client populations that have merit for defining specific practice principles, but we will focus in this chapter on the ones listed. These represent some of the most important types of practice distinctions that can be made. Also a discussion of these variations is illustrative of how the practitioner should differentially approach members of other groups.

When we refer to the client as a member of a group such as youths, older persons, males, females, blacks, or Chicanos—to name a few—an issue arises as to whether the worker's actions are intended to benefit the individual client or other members of the group who are not in the client status. An example of the former is a black client whom a worker helped to overcome a racist response from his school. An example of the latter is a school social worker who sought to change the school's system of dividing students into tracks as this operated to the detriment of black students in the school.

While some of the interventions in the former (case) situation may be similar to those in the latter (class) situation, we shall focus in this chapter on the case situation. We believe that all social workers have social action resonsibilities that involve class actions, but these are usually analyzed and dealt with as community organization activities, and this method is beyond the scope of this book on interpersonal helping, albeit *not* beyond the scope of interpersonal practitioners.

Interpersonal practice with members of groups such as those just referred to involves efforts to change the environment as well as the client system. While we have stressed this dual emphasis throughout as a basic principle of interpersonal practice with all clients, it is a particularly valid point for clients from these groups. Many people in our society have been oppressed on the basis of their gender, their ethnicity, and their age, and this oppression accounts for many of their problems.

In the concluding chapter, therefore, we shall describe how the worker can assess situations related to the client's ethnic, sex, and age groups and vary practice procedures with reference to these groups. We shall also discuss the impact of the agency on clients and services so that readers may be made aware of ways in which this also affects practice. We begin this discussion with a consideration of ethnicity.

Ethnic Conditions

In discussing ethnicity, we utilize Gordon's definition of an ethnic group as "any group which is defined or set off by race, religion, or national origin, or some combination of these categories."[1] Gordon also notes that these categories have "a common social psychological referent, in that all of them serve to create, through historical circumstances, a sense of peoplehood."[2] This sense of peoplehood has many implications for social work practice. As Gordon goes on to say,

> [W]ithin the ethnic group there develops a network of organizations and informal social relationships which permits and encourages the members of the ethnic group to remain within the confines of the group for all of their primary relationships and some of their secondary relationships throughout all of the stages of the life cycle.[3]

As the reader can see, the ethnic group, as well as the worker's ethnicity, will influence all aspects of practice. Ethnic factors will influence where the client seeks help, how the client involves himself or herself in the helping process, and whether any benefits accrue from the process. Ethnicity will also help to determine whether change targets are chosen that are internal or external to the client and agency systems and whether these ethnic variables serve as resources or as barriers or whether or not they, themselves, will be targets for change.

Ethnicity in a complex society such as ours is not an easy topic to analyze. This is, in part, because ethnic groups constantly change. The black community, for example, is different now from that existing a few years ago. Ethnic variables also lead to stereotyping clients. All black, or Hispanic, or Jewish clients are not alike. All that one can assert is that the members of each group share a common history and are often treated the same (rather than as individuals) by social institutions. In addition, groups develop norms, and while individuals may deviate from these, these norms determine the consequences of this deviation. Another complexity is that ethnic factors may vary among geographic regions and social classes, and it is often difficult to separate ethnic effects from those of region and class.

Social work, we believe, should have a special commitment to serve people who are socially and economically oppressed. Groups such as blacks, Hispanics, native Americans, and Asian Americans fall into this category. For this reason, in this section, we emphasize ethnic issues related to these groups.

To help the reader to analyze ethnic variables and their effects on service, we have developed a typology based on one created by Valentine.[4] It consists of six dimensions: (1) communications, (2) habitat, (3) social structure, (4) socialization, (5) economics, and (6) beliefs and sentiments. This classification helps the worker to understand the behavior of members of an ethnic group as this behavior is affected by their group membership. It does not include historical circumstances, although an appreciation of such history helps workers to understand how the group entered its current situation and continues to cope with it. These variables, however, should be looked at historically as well as in the current context, and a worker who hopes to help members of any group should examine the group's history.

An extremely important fact to emphasize is that the ethnic group is profoundly affected by its interactions with the larger society, and this part is crucial when the group is oppressed by that society. As we define these variables, we shall endeavor to indicate also how they interact with conditions in the society.

Communications

Two issues that should be considered in analyzing communications related to ethnicity are (1) the language pattern prevalent within the group and (2) the rules as to who speaks to whom about what. We discuss each of these issues separately.

Distinguishable patterns of communication have arisen in most ethnic groups. One reason for this is that persons who live in close proximity to each other come to share and sustain language similarities. One example of this is the Chicano community in which members reinforce each other's use of Spanish. Another is the black community in which many members have developed over time a form of English that varies from "standard English" as described in textbooks and is referred to as "black English." Another reason for a group's sustaining a language difference is that this difference can function as

an identifying characteristic to promote cohesiveness among group members.

It is obvious that effective work with members of an ethnic group who use a language other than standard English requires an ability either to understand that language or to form a team relationship with someone who does. This may be apparent to the worker who works with a Spanish-speaking client but not to a worker who works with a black one. In the latter case, the issue is not only whether the worker correctly understands the client but also whether the worker understands the attitudes that he or she conveys about language. People who use standard English tend to regard those who do not as using an inferior means of expression. This leads to the implication that the speaker is inferior and disregards the fact that in terms of complexity and adequacy of expression, nonstandard dialects are "complex, valid, and adequate linguistic systems."[5] It is essential for a client to learn standard English to succeed in educational and occupational institutions, but this is another matter.

Educational institutions have approached this question more seriously than social work agencies. An example was a court order requiring Ann Arbor, Michigan, school teachers to learn black English so they could better teach standard English to their students. The judge "held that black English was a distinct dialect that required recognition and respect from teachers so that black children would not develop 'a psychological barrier to learning.'"[6] We believe that social workers should have an analogous perspective.

Workers should become familiar with the language of the client through study of resource materials along with as complete an immersion in the culture as possible. Beyond serious study of language, there is controversy as to whether the worker should communicate in the client's idiom. For some workers this would be a false and patronizing effort. For others, this is a natural move. The basic issues, however, are the worker's nonpatronizing attitudes, understanding of the client, and genuineness. All the worker's acts must be consistent with these.

The other communications dimension referred to is who communicates to whom and about what. Cultures vary as to what may be spoken about among people of the same sex or different sexes or generations or status levels. Examples are the negative reactions in many ethnic communities to people of one gender giving advice to people of another or to the discussion of sexually related matters in "mixed" groups. We do not contend that workers should not challenge these patterns; challenges occur through the changes taking place in American society. It is imperative, however, for the worker to understand these patterns and to plan interventions informed by this information.

Habitat

As we use this term, we refer to the way in which the ethnic group structures the physical environment and prescribes the way in which it will be used. The ethnic group creates aspects of its environment to reflect its cultural traditions, and the environment, in turn, has a reciprocal effect on behavior. This phenomenon occurs at three levels that have implications for interpersonal practitioners: the way in which the household, the neighborhood, and the environment beyond the neighborhood are utilized.

A few examples follow: the environment has an effect upon the locations that workers choose for interaction with clients. In some cultures a first contact with a stranger is usually held outside the household while in others, inside. This fact should influence whether the worker plans for home or office

visits. In some cultures, also, there are rules as to which room in the house is used for visitors (and this sometimes varies by the sex and age of the visitor) and where in a room the visitor should sit.

The worker's understanding of habitat will influence the worker's understanding of the meaning of many client communications. When the client talks to the worker about interactions with others, the worker's understanding of cultural norms regarding the "habitat" will sensitize the worker to the meaning to the client of where these interactions took place. For example, when a client told her worker that her boyfriend visited her home, the worker knew this relationship was "serious" because in the client's culture casual friends were not invited to the household.

The way the household is decorated will also inform the worker because of the specific meaning in the culture of such decorations. In one black household, for example, the worker observed pictures of such persons as Martin Luther King, Jr., and Malcom X. The worker later learned that the family was active in militant groups in the black community. In another black household, pictures of Jesus were hung in central locations, and the mother spoke of her active role in the church.

Workers will also seek to familiarize themselves with the ethnic aspects of the community habitat. This includes the nature of community facilities and how they are used: Which are meeting places and which are used for resolving social conflicts? Which are primarily used by one age or sex? For example, in describing local establishments in a west side Chicago area, Suttles wrote:

> The local taverns are considered unfit for a respectable girl. In a few places where food is served, girls or women may come with their family or male friends. . . . The single pool

hall in the Addams area is so thoroughly a male "hangout" that a women who entered for some purposes other than speaking to her brother or asking for her husband would be inviting sexual overtures.[7]

This analysis suggests several implications for interpersonal practice. Workers may develop serious misunderstandings if they conclude that a statement as to where events occur in the client's community has the same meaning as in the worker's. In addition, workers frequently make suggestions to clients as to how they might use their environments. Unless this advice is informed by a knowledge of the ethnic aspects of the environment, the worker's suggestions might be meaningless or even harmful.

Since most ethnic areas adjoin or even intrude on one another, another important issue is how the community habitat interacts with that developed by other groups. Suttles indicates that institutions have different functions in this regard[8]: first are those institutions not located at the boundary of the ethnic area that devote themselves to ethnic products and view outsiders with suspicion; second are institutions that are similar to the aforementioned except that they help to supply outsiders with a "product"; third are institutions that different ethnic groups take "turns" in using: a recreation center used by black youths on one day and Chicano youths on another is an example of this.

"Mutual tolerance" is a fourth type of institution, usually located on the boundary of an area, where the proprietor's ethnicity is not the same as the consumer. Finally are institutions in which conflict occurs over use, either among consumers or between proprietor and consumers.

Workers who are aware of the function played by the institutions we have described will better understand the way in which clients cope with ethnicity. One client, for example, spent most of his time in institutions where conflict with other ethnic groups occurred, while another client only utilized institutions that had a strong ethnic orientation and in which outsiders were largely absent. Both clients sought to resolve ethnic identity issues, but one coped with this through conflict and the other through avoiding conflict.

The use of the environment outside of the ethnic community is controlled by ethnic variables. An example is areas that are utilized or avoided by ethnic group members and how such areas are used. These patterns may be controlled by a combination of racist pressures from the larger environment, ethnic values and requirements, and client identity factors. Workers encounter these issues when helping clients to deal with problems regarding employment, transportation, recreation, and the use of commercial, welfare, and educational resources.

Social Structure

The ethnic group is one structural aspect of the larger society yet is itself structured internally, and this should be assessed. The concept *structure* refers to patterns that exist in social relationships. These patterns may be constituted in formal systems such as structures in family, economic, and other social institutions. The patterns may also be created through other ways in which a society is stratified such as social class, gender, and age.

For practitioners, one of the most important aspects of the social structure of an ethnic group is its family structure. In some ethnic groups the extended family is accorded a greater influence than in others. The respect, for example, that is extended to aging parents in many Asian-American groups should not be neglected when considering the influences of that culture on the nuclear family.

The complex family patterns that exist in many native American tribes and how these are used differently by each tribe to reinforce behavioral patterns must be understood when working with native Americans. The family for black Americans is so strong a source of social support that any practitioner who neglects this has eliminated a major resource.

Another structural aspect of ethnic life is the statuses that an individual occupies at various stages of life. Some of these statuses are present in all cultures such as childhood, adolescence, and adulthood. Others are entered into by only some individuals within the ethnic group such as those associated with the dominant religion of the group or its indigenous economic and social institutions. The client may experience difficulties related to these statuses that a social worker can ameliorate. Youths may have difficulty accomplishing tasks that are required for adult status in their culture, for example, or adults may wish to accomplish tasks that will admit them to the statuses they seek. Interpersonal practitioners must be able to add particular knowledge that is culturally relevant to their general knowledge of how to facilitate socialization into statuses. For example, a Chicano youth acted out her family conflicts by refusing to fulfill obligations in the church that her family required of her. The worker used knowledgeable informants to help her to understand the meaning of these religious obligations to the family as well as to the youth.

It is also likely, in an ethnically diverse society such as ours, that individuals will be exposed to conflicts among ethnic structures or between structures of the ethnic group and the larger society. Examples are youths who are defined as members of the adult community in their own culture but not in the larger society and individuals who occupy prestigious and influential positions in their ethnic culture who are not recognized as such in the larger society.

The worker must also consider that the external society often seeks to create or control ethnic group structures. This is part of the issue of internal colonialism that we shall describe later. These controls can undermine family strengths in the ethnic community as well as its social and economic institutions. An example is the unwilliness of the larger society to recognize family forms and institutions that are important within the ethnic society. The interpersonal practitioner may be required, in these instances, to help families to discover and build supports through their own social networks. It is hard to imagine, therefore, an effective interpersonal practitioner in an ethnic community who is not something of a community organizer.

Socialization

The ways in which members of various ethnic groups enter into social roles that exist within their culture and learn the behavior required for these roles is also important for interpersonal practitioners to understand. Workers can be enlisted to help with this process when problems emerge. An example is provided by Brewer who is an Oglala Sioux Indian and a trained educator and who seeks to integrate these two perspectives. Brewer notes that in her tribal society "children learned through family and community socialization in a very informal and unpressured way."[9] She gives an example of this as the bringing of children to pow-wows, feasts, and bingo.

Brewer contrasts the schooling required by the larger society to this indigenous approach to socialization as follows:

> The classrooms are not community wide, open to all and freely chosen by the

students . . . the leader is not the one they have chosen. He is usually an outsider to the culture . . . . The leader will not follow cultural cues and go away, even if ostracized . . . . All students may not participate in a given activity . . . . The choices belong to the teacher.[10]

These educational patterns are contrary to those of the tribe. As a consequence, the child is exposed to an unfamiliar *individual* competitive mode, although the culture is organized around *group* competitive modes. The child responds with what the educational system labels "shyness" and also shows other signs of stress. Brewer recommends ideas to teachers of these children that are appropriate to social workers serving similar populations:

> What can a white teacher do to "teach" Indian culture? A white teacher cannot *teach* culture. She can, however, help the Indian child appreciate his own cultural and value systems by showing her interest, respect, and appreciation for them. She can also provide the framework for the culture by inviting Indians who have first hand knowledge of the culture to be resource persons, for it is they who teach the culture. Secondly, she can provide an environment that is familiar to the child and reflects his own culture most authentically and genuinely as it was and, more importantly, as it is today.[11]

The worker who seeks to understand socialization processes within the culture should note the following variables identified by Henry. While they were intended to be used by educators, we believe that they also relate to the socialization processes with which social workers are involved.[12]

1. On what does the socialization process focus? Included here are the nonhuman environment, the world view of the culture, values, social skills, and "cultural fictions."
2. How is the information communicated? This consists of opportunities for imitation, formal instruction, problem solving, and gradation of tasks.
3. Who socializes? The choices of these persons are based on sex differences, peer influences, and the status of the educator (e.g., parent, expert).
4. How does the person being socialized participate? Henry identifies variations related to emotional responses, social distance, and interactions among individuals in the cohort of people to be socialized.
5. How does the socializer participate? This is affected by the willingness of the socializer to assume that role and his or her attitudes toward the learner's degree of spontaneity and creativity, ways of manipulating the cohort of learners, and use of sanctions.
6. Are some things taught to some and not to others? That is, among a cohort of people socialized at the same time within a culture, further differentiation may occur in view of the sex, social class, or other statuses of the culture.
7. Are there discontinuities in the educational process? This question considers the fact that some stages of the socialization process may require the individual to unlearn things they were taught at other stages.
8. Are there limits to the quantity and quality of what is taught to the socialized person related to the availability of resources? To institutional biases?
9. How is the behavior of the person being socialized controlled?
10. What is the relationship between the intent of the socialization process and its outcomes? In some ethnic groups, the intents of the socialization activity are not realized.
11. What forms of discipline are used?
12. How long does the socialization process last? The actual process, as it affects an individual, may take varying amounts of time, but whether an individual's experience is slower or more rapid than the norm will have implications for the individual.

These dimensions can be examined for the broad variety of roles for which members of a culture are socialized. These many include family, occupational, religious, leadership, ritual, political, therapeutic, and service roles that are prescribed by the culture and are affected by cultural norms and processes.

Economy

The interpersonal practitioner should analyze economic variables on several levels related to the ethnic group's experience. One level is the extent to which the ethnic group is affected as a group by economic practices and institutions in the larger society. For example, blacks, Chicanos, and native Americans have been systematically exploited and oppressed by the economic institutions of the United States. This process can be analyzed in terms of the concept of "internal colonialism," which has been described by Blauner as follows:

> Colonization begins with a forced, involuntary entry . . . there is an impact on the culture and social organization of the colonized people which is more than just a result of such "natural" processes as contact and acculturation. The colonizing power carries out a policy which constrains, transforms or destroys indigenous values, orientations and ways of life . . . colonization involves a relationship by which members of the colonized group tend to be administered by representatives of the dominant power. Here is an experience of being managed and manipulated by outsiders in terms of ethnic status. A final fundamental of colonization is racism. Racism is a principle of social domination by which a group seen as inferior or different in terms of alleged biological characteristics is exploited, controlled, and oppressed socially and physically by a superordinate group.[13]

The idea of internal colonialism is useful to interpersonal practitioners who seek to understand several issues. First, social welfare institutions are often those that Blauner states "tend to be administered by representatives of the dominant power." Thus, members of the ethnic group may not only see

agencies as staffed by persons of cultures other than their own but by persons who come from cultures that have controlled ethnic institutions for their own ends. This may also be the perspective drawn upon by members of ethnic minorities in approaching economic institutions as well.

Our use of this colonial analysis does not imply that all or even many members of the ethnic group are aware of this perspective in a full-blown ideological sense but rather that their experiences and reactions are compatible with it. The worker's understanding of this will help him or her to perceive the client's reality and to take it into consideration in practice. A crucial issue is that the client may perceive the agency as one of several that seek to dominate the ethnic community with the worker as the instrument of this domination. This can be offset if the agency accepts control from the ethnic community.

Another aspect of the ethnic economic dimension is the internal economy of the ethnic community. For example, ethnic communities can be the main source of support for economic institutions that supply goods and services used exclusively by members of the ethnic group. Of significance to interpersonal practitioners also is the way in which members of the ethnic group are distributed among occupations. Some better paid occupations, for example, may be restricted for members of ethnic groups because of racist practices in the occupation or in educational preparation for it. Affirmative action may have diminished this problem but the problem remains. In addition, for historic or other reasons, members of an ethnic group may be more likely to choose certain occupations or businesses than members of another group. Some occupations may exist solely to serve the needs of the ethnic group such as the indigenous healers in Puerto Rican, Chicano, and native American communities.[14]

Since one's occupation plays such a major role in satisfying personal as well as economic needs, occupational issues often enter into discussions between clients and interpersonal practitioners. Workers should understand the vocational opportunity structures available to clients and the barriers to their utilization. The meaning of various occupations to members of an ethnic group should also be understood as well as the status the ethnic group accords an occupation. These types of understanding will enable workers to facilitate clients' occupational planning. At times, workers should also advocate with economic institutions for the client as well as help the client to join with others in removing ethnic barriers to participation in occupations.

Beliefs and Sentiments

Ethnic groups create belief systems that support their structures and institutions. Some beliefs may seem outmoded because either the conditions that gave rise to them have changed or they "make sense" to the ethnic culture but not to the larger society. Nevertheless, these traditions are maintained through socialization processes. They are also embedded in religion, folklore, ethnic literature, and folk sayings. They control such behaviors as the selection of marriage partners, discipline of children, behavior toward other people, treatment of illness, use of contraception, and actions to maintain mental and physical health.

Papajohn and Spiegel, drawing upon Kluckhohn, present a framework consisting of five dimensions for analyzing the beliefs of ethnic groups.[15] They recognize, in presenting their conceptualization, that the full range of beliefs may be present in all ethnic groups but that ethnic groups have, nevertheless, a dominant profile.

The first dimension is *activity*. One belief about activity relates to "being" and favors spontaneous expression. Another favors "being in becoming" related to personal fulfillment aspects of any action. The last view is that of "doing" and relates to the pragmatic results of activity.

The second dimension is how relations among people are viewed. Such views may be "lineal," which emphasizes heritage; "collateral," which emphasizes group membership; and "individualistic," which emphasizes self-preferences. The third dimension is *time*. Some cultures have a profile oriented to the past, some the present, and some the future.

The fourth dimension is how the *relationship between human beings and nature* is viewed. Some cultures see humans as subjected to nature, others as in harmony with nature, and still others as mastering nature. The last dimension incorporates the culture's views of *human nature*. Some societies view humans as essentially evil, others as a mixture of good and evil, and still others as essentially good.

A few examples will help the interpersonal practitioner to see how an analysis of beliefs and sentiments is useful in practice. Members of Chicano communities can be helped by that culture's characteristic way of seeing relationships among people as lineal; that is, family members have claims upon each other in times of need. Chicanos also come from a culture that has emphasized subjugation to nature and acceptance of the inevitable. These views may affect the types of problems Chicanos choose to work on and the circumstances they may choose to change as well as those they choose to accept.[16] The reader should note, nevertheless, that this form of analysis has been criticized as tending to (1) stereotype cultures and (2) see cultures as static. *Consequently, it should be used with caution.*

Another example comes from Puerto Rican culture. Papajohn and Spiegel see this culture as emphasizing "being" in that the "individual is expressive and feelings are aired, usually with considerable dramatic flair." A new emphasis has been emerging, however, among Puerto Ricans on "doing."[17] The practitioner, therefore, in the Puerto Rican community may have to consider the effects on behavior of conflicts among these values. This will lead to an appreciation of the effects of cultural change on behavior, which should replace an incorrect emphasis on internal factors.

The worker should seek, therefore, to understand the dominant profile of beliefs within a culture, how the individual relates to it, and how it may be changing. The degree to which the individual client perceives and attempts to follow or resist the culture influences, therefore, of his or her group should be assessed. Resistance to cultural influences and subsequent conflicts is often a result of the client's efforts to identify with the larger culture. Such clients experience a social status that social scientists term "marginality" in which individuals identify with aspects of two cultures yet are not fully accepted in either. This is a stressful social position, and the interpersonal practitioner should recognize when a client suffers from his or her marginality and help such clients to develop suitable coping strategies.

Ethnic Analysis and Intervention

A major problem in dealing with something so complex as ethnicity is how to generate ethnically relevant practice principles. We believe one useful way to do this is by identifying information about an ethnic group that can be useful at various stages of the invervention sequence. The following material is illustrative of this approach.

At the first stage of the process, the worker seeks to gain access to a member(s) of the ethnic group. The dimensions we have described that have implications for gaining access are communication, social structure, and economics. Practitioners will have to find ways to avoid acting as, or being seen as, instruments of internal colonial structures. They will also have to learn ways of communicating that are understood by members of the ethnic group, and they will have to possess sufficient knowledge of the communications of members of the ethnic group to initiate a helping process.

One example of these principles occurred in efforts to initiate service in a Puerto Rican community. There were no Puerto Rican staff members in the agency or on its board of directors. The staff recommended to the agency that a citizen's board from the Puerto Rican community be created. This group was to be asked, also, to select members of the board of directors. It was also planned that the citizen's committee would consult with the staff about aspects of Puerto Rican culture that should be considerd in offering services. Some members of the committee were asked to accept paraprofessional positions so that communications with Puerto Rican clients would be enhanced.

After a worker has gained access, the next issue is to examine ethnic factors relevant to defining the worker's role. This is because different ethnic groups have different expectations of the role of the helping person.[18] Some of the variables to consider here are expectations as to how relationships should begin, how informal they should be, how expertise will be demonstrated, and who legitimates the helping person as someone who can help and be trusted. Relevant information is available in studies by Overall and Aronson and Mayer and Timms who note differences in expectations of treatment among people from various social classes.[19]

The next stage of helping is one in which problems for which solutions will be sought through the helping process are identified. Ethnicity is likely to affect how members of the group will define what is and what is not a problem. For example, there are major differences among ethnic groups around whether strong emotions (e.g., anger and depression), interpersonal conflicts, delusions, or not taking responsibility for other family members are likely to be defined as problems that require outside intervention.[20]

After problems are identified, the professional will seek to help the client identify goals and targets for change. In groups such as some Asian-American ones, changes in the individual's situation are not as likely to be sought as is the client's adaptation to the situation. On the other hand, among black clients a change in the situation is likely to be targeted, as well as changes in patterns of individual adaptation. Among some ethnic groups, in addition, changes will be valued that benefit one's peers and family, and individual progress will only be considered as legitimate if obtained as part of group progress. Still other cultures may be more individualist in their orientation.

Ethnicity will also have a strong impact on the means that a culture supports as legitimate to attain goals. The following are a few examples of such means and their ethnic implications:

1. Brown et al. recommend against utilization of group work approaches in the Los Angeles Chinese community. One reason given is a communications one: the variety of distinct Chinese dialects make group discussion difficult. Another is that "the close-knit quality of Chinatown is an even more important reason to avoid group modalities of treatment. Many Chinese wish to keep knowledge of their difficulties within their immediate family."[21]

2. Thomas describes a situational intervention based upon an understanding of one native American's culture.[22] An individual from the Sac and Fox tribe in Tama, Iowa, was part of a small-industry project established by the University of Chicago. His work was essential for the project and had to be completed in a specified time. Unfortunately, his uncle died and he was forced to enter four days of seclusion. The matter was resolved when a member of the same tribe suggested that the individual work in seclusion on the work site and slip his work under the door so that he would see and talk with no one. This is an example of the type of innovative thinking that should color all social work practice and certainly practice with members of minority groups.

3. Attneave[23] describes a "network" approach that was successful with a native American family experiencing severe problems involving a mother and child interaction. The author, who had many insights into the culture because she is native American, was able to involve the person's family successfully to offer help in ways that were appropriate and indigenous to the culture. This approach contrasts sharply to psychologically oriented approaches that are frequently utilized with such problems in the middle-class white culture.

Finally, outcomes must be assessed in terms of satisfactions with outcomes as expressed by the clients. This is certainly a principle with any client, but it is particularly important in work with minorities whose goals and values may be different from those of the worker. We must work to develop outcome measures that are informed by knowledge about ethnic groups rather than approaches proclaimed to be neutral but actually biased by the dominant culture's perceptions of time, meaning, and value.

Gender Conditions

No differences among human beings are more apparent than are those between men and women. Anatomical characteristics clearly distinguish men from women. The issue, however, that has troubled scientists and professionals in all the human disciplines throughout the ages is the relationship of anatomical differences as well as differences in child-bearing functions to social roles, behavior, and temperament. The issue is confounded further by the fact that in our society men occupy positions of greater power than do women. This is true in government, in industry, and in academe. It has been true of the family, also, where women have had to fight for the same rights as men. The fact that in the stereotypical family pattern the man provides financial support and the women performs child-rearing and housekeeping chores also creates many power issues.

Some people have inferred from an analysis of gender issues that men and women live in separate worlds that consist of different values, beliefs, and ways of coping and of perceiving one's self and the environment.[24] Our examination of the relevant research and theory supports this contention. It is ironic and yet understandable that social work literature and theory have treated men and women as if they were the same or, perhaps worse, as if only men existed. This tendency is present in the entire culture and is symbolized by the use of masculine terms to refer to all humanity. This situation is highly undesirable as it has made it likely that male characteristics are assumed to exist in women. When distinctions have been made between the sexes, as often as not cultural conditioning is confused with biological difference and traits are attributed to men and women that are not innate and that often limit the potential for growth of members of both sexes.

With the current evolution of the women's movement, a new awareness of gender issues is emerging in social work. A literature is being created that explores these issues as they affect practice. Sexism in the way in which services are offered and powers allocated is also now being challenged. A full analysis of gender-related issues in practice is beyond the scope of this chapter, although some of the major variables are presented.

One consideration is that of *socialization*. Boys and girls from infancy are taught to express different behaviors. This not only extends to such obvious differences as participation in sports and in play representative of future occupations but also includes how emotions are to be expressed or repressed and whether problems are to be solved independently or with the help of others. As Kagan states, "a capacity to control strong emotion in times of stress and a need to be independent in problem situations . . . are American sex role standards."[25]

The issue of *emotions* is an important one. Men are often deprived of the relief that can come from full emotional expression, particularly feelings of sadness, tenderness, and vulnerability. In addition, this can lead to communication problems between partners as one partner is deprived of an understanding of the authentic reactions of the other. In some marital situations, a split takes place in which the role of the woman is to express the affective side of an issue while the man's is to express the rational and ideational side. This is dysfunctional as it often leads to the man's accusation that the woman is too emotional and the woman's accusation that the man is unfeeling and manipulative.

Another issue is that of *roles*. Tasks that must be fulfilled in all families include securing income, housekeeping, child rearing, maintaining mental health, planning recreation, and promoting linkages to the extended family.[26] In many American families, these are linked to the family member of one sex rather than shared, and this is often a source of dissatisfaction and strain. The situation is changing in all social classes as the wife is now likely to work outside the home. If comparable readjustments are not made in other roles, another source of strain is created.

These considerations are related to the fact that many more women than men are referred to mental health services and that the problems perceived in men are different from those of women.[27] The problems of women have been shown by research to be clearly related to the stresses placed upon women by the contemporary family.[28] In addition, the kinds of behaviors that bring men and women to mental health practitioners tend to be different. For example, men are overrepresented among adolescent delinquents, and this can be seen as a result of the socialization of men into aggressive behavior patterns, competitiveness, and the importance of acquiring goods. Among adults, women are more frequently seen than men for emotional disorders such as depression.[29]

There are many implications for interpersonal practice of a thorough understanding of gender issues. First, we hold to a goal of androgyny, which means that both men and women should have access to a full range of emotions and behaviors. This full range allows the individual to develop the broadest way of coping with life and of becoming a creative person in the process. Social workers, therefore, will have to overcome their own gender biases so as to free men and women to do this. Examples include helping men as well as women to express their emotions and their tenderness and helping women as well as men to behave assertively when they choose to do so.

Another implication is for social workers to recognize barriers to human development that stem from gender constraints. Workers should seek to remove such barriers and to help clients to do the same when relevant to the goals of the helping process. The major constraints with which we deal are likely not only to relate to the occupational and educational spheres but to those of the family, the peer group, and the community as well.

Workers must also challenge the manifestations of sexism that affect their ways of helping. This includes their communication style, assessment, and treatment planning. In a recent social work classroom discussion conducted by one of the authors, male students saw nothing wrong with a client's use of the word "cunt" to refer to a woman, as well as to female genitalia, despite the insistence of the instructor and the women in the class that this word is experienced by women as one that depreciates women and presents women as sexual objects. In a subsequent discussion in the same class, a student described one of her fieldwork cases in which an adolescent stated that she had been raped by the brother of a girlfriend. Several male students immediately asked what the girl had done to provoke the attack. This line of inquiry was taken despite the strong sexist implication—that women provoke attacks upon themselves—of which the students were ignorant. Undoubtedly hundreds of examples can easily be produced that demonstrate how unaware social workers are of gender issues and how they affect their practice.

Another gender issue that merits a full study by social workers is that of homosexuality.[30] It is only recently that the psychiatric profession has acknowledged that homosexuality is not a disease; homosexuals, nevertheless, are subject to some of the worst oppression that our society can provide. They are often excluded from employment, services, educational opportunity, places of recreation, and many other community institutions. Mental health professionals, therefore, will often see homosexuality as the problem rather than society's reaction to it.

Homosexuals wish to avail themselves of interpersonal helping for the same types of problems as heterosexual clients, such as career choices, grief reactions, termination of relationships, interpersonal conflicts, and phobias. It is important for mental health professionals to be able to separate these issues from those of the sexual life-style and partner choice of the homosexual client. Gay male and lesbian clients often perceive (and correctly so) social workers and other helpers as biased against their life-style and unable to see beyond it to other issues. Workers, consequently, should have training in understanding and working with clients who are gay. This will include recognizing some situations when a difference in life-style between a heterosexual worker and a gay client requires a matching of the gay client with a gay worker because the barriers to a relationship may be too great.

The word "homophobia" has been used to refer to an anxious, hostile, or other defensive response to homosexuality. Homophobic responses are not appropriate even when a heterosexual worker is assigned to a heterosexual client, as they may lead the heterosexual client into destructive interactions with homosexuals and may prevent the heterosexual client from fully exploring his or her own sexuality, one that may incorporate homosexual elements. This is yet another prejudice along with others related to ethnicity, age, and gender against which practitioners should struggle.

Age Conditions

Social workers work with people of all ages and must adapt their approaches to the needs and characteristics of each age group. A comprehensive discussion of how a worker differentially assesses and works with people from different age groups is well beyond the scope of this book. It is our purpose, instead, to illustrate some of the issues that arise when workers serve people of different ages. These issues arise out of the following variables:

1. The developmental tasks that people must undertake in each of life's phases. (Social workers must be able to assess the person's development in relationship to these.)
2. The way in which society responds to people of different ages in terms of constraints, statuses, and opportunities.
3. The way in which people of different ages interact with and communicate with others.
4. The meaning that people of different ages attach to the helping process and to the role of the worker.
5. The way in which the agency's service delivery system affects people of different ages.

The worker must remember that stereotyping can occur in reference to age as readily as it can occur to sex and ethnicity. Some workers may assume, for example, that young children or older persons cannot understand what the worker wishes to say when this may be untrue. In addition, as with any other variable, the worker must individualize the client, thus using knowledge about age characteristics flexibly. People develop at different rates. Society also has expectations that are related to chronological age that must be considered. Examples of this are the age for starting school, for being held responsible for various illegal acts, and for reaching legal maturity. An age for compulsary retirement is another example of this.

The worker will take into consideration these issues in relationship to age periods, namely, infancy, young childhood, older childhood, adolescence, young adulthood, adulthood, and senior adulthood. As we have stated, we cannot present a comprehensive analysis of issues affecting each age, but we do offer material that is illustrative of this type of content.

Infancy

Social workers will be involved with infants, for example, when these children are at risk from parental abuse or neglect, when their parents cannot undertake their care, when they fail to thrive, and when they have problems affecting their biological reactions such as eating and sleeping. Social workers generally will not interact with the infant but with the caretaker such as the parent or foster parent. The focus, however, may be upon the interaction between the infant and the caretaker. While workers do not "treat" infants as such, they must understand how to assess infant development and care if their practice involves parents of very young children.

Child protection laws are clear about the responsibility of the state to intervene when infants are at risk. It is only recently that the human service professions have recognized the presence of nonaccidental injuries that have been inflicted by caretakers on children, particularly young children. All social workers must be able to recognize the signs that a child may be at risk of such maltreatment as well as the community resources for following up suspected cases. State laws now require all social workers as well as other professionals to report such cases to the proper authorities, usually protective service agencies, even when a worker is already involved in helping the family.

The methods used, therefore, for help-ing infants requires approaches to the caretakers, usually the parents, as well as to the entire family. At times, it may be necessary for this help to be offered while the child is removed for protection from the family. In extreme cases, social workers will seek to have the rights of the parent terminated so that the child may be placed in a secure environment such as an adoptive home.

Young Childhood

By young childhood, we refer to the period immediately after infancy when the child is first capable of movement, language, and learning but is still primarily the responsibility of the parents rather than of the educational system—roughly from 2 to 5 years of age. These children may come to the attention of social workers because of abuse and neglect but also because of other problems that arise in the child's use of community resources such as preschool programs. The child might be excessively withdrawn or, in contrast, highly aggressive. Parents may also seek help because the child (1) fails to respond to toilet training, (2) has eating problems, or (3) has difficulties in relationships to adults or other children.

At this age, the child is still highly reactive to family circumstances, and social workers work with these problems in the context of the entire family. This will require the social worker to be able to interact with young children, and workers who have this responsibility will learn how to reduce their social (and physical) distance from them through such means as play materials (crayons, clay, dolls).

Many representatives of social organizations react to young children, as well as to older ones, as if they have no opinions and desires of their own apart from their parent's concerns. Social workers should assess the degree to which the young child can express his or her own needs and requests and should be responsive to these.

The worker will be seen by most young children as an extension of the adult world, and often of the parents. Workers must develop the attitude that young children are people in their own right *with rights,* and they will communicate this to the child by words and actions. The shrill "sing-song" speech that some adults, and even teachers, use with children should not be imitated by social workers. Earlier in this century, legal as well as public opinion held that young children were the property of their parents, but this view has been deservedly changing, and this change must be reflected in practice.

Agencies must also communicate to young children an attitude of respect. This applies to the chairs, decorations, play equipment, and inteviewing rooms of the agency. It also has implications for the way in which clients are interviewed. The child who waits anxiously in the waiting room while the adults "conspire" in private is unlikely to be receptive to the worker who participates in this way. It may be an appropriate rather than an inappropriate response for a child to interrupt this private interaction.

Older Childhood

This age group includes children between the ages of the start of public school and adolescence. It coincides roughly with the period referred to in psychoanalytic theory as "latency." Children, during these years, develop basic intellectual skills, learn to relate to peers, and separate themselves for substantial periods of time each day from their families. Problems in all these spheres are brought to social workers. Methods for helping these children are focused on the family because the child's problems frequently are reactive to family interactions. In addition, however, the difficulties that school-age children encounter may also be related to school and peer groups, and social workers focus on these systems as targets also.

School-age children are more able than younger ones to communicate verbally about their situations. Their ability, however, to sustain this type of communication for very long may be limited, and workers will support this interaction with a variety of media such as doll play, games, crafts, and dramatics. An assessment of each child helps the worker to choose forms of communication as it is easy to commit the error of placing too much or too little emphasis on verbal communication.

Children of this age can usually understand the nature of interpersonal helping, and if the worker is clear about the purposes and objectives of the intervention, the child should be able to understand it. Workers, however, should develop such aids to contracting with children as employing anecdotes, diagrams, comic strips, and metaphors.

Adolescence

The tasks that confront adolescents include an emancipation from dependence on the family, a transfer of intimacy from family to individuals of the same age, a resolution of identity issues, and occupational preparation. These are also the areas that can require the help of a social worker. The adolescent's emancipation struggles can take the form of stormy interactions or running away from home. Coupled with identity issues, these can lead to other types of issues, including sexual promiscuity and substance abuse. Occupational and educational problems are also found as adolescents seek to obtain financial resources or to choose routes to future occupations. The struggles of this period can drain energy that is required for educational success. In addition, adolescents may have conflicts regarding their present and future educational situations that can result in a variety of other dysfunctional reactions to schooling.

Social organizations are structured in ways that are problematic for many adolescents. Jobs are scarce, and the adolescent has few opportunties to experience a range of occupations as a way of making occupational choices. The adolescent may also be punished by the legal system for behaviors that are not considred offenses in adults, such as running away from home or school truancy— so-called "status offenses." Educational programs do not meet the needs of adolescents when these youths experience poor instruction, lack of relevant classes, and unresponsive school personnel. These types of problems can add to the psychological and developmental stresses of the period. The social worker must respond to both the adverse circumstances facing the teen-age client as well as the psychological problems the youth has in functioning. Unless both are considered, the adolescent will perceive the worker as another adult who blames the adolescent instead of understanding the problems of the adolescent as the product of interactions between individual and societal circumstances.

Social workers and adolescents must take into consideration a number of facts about adolescent relationships and forms of communication. Adolescents are likely to approach adults with suspicion or even antagonism. This is related to efforts to emancipate themselves from parents and other adults. On the other hand, youths often require support from adults, and this leads, in many cases, to strong emotional attachments to social workers. Workers, therefore, should be prepared to meet either extreme of antagonism or affection with understanding rather than seduction or rejection. The worker should also be aware of the strong bonds that teenagers form with peers; this makes group work an approach that is very suitable to people of this age. The strong attachment to peers is also related to the use of argot that attests to the bonds that exist in the adolescent's subculture. The worker should make efforts to learn about the language as well as the other aspects of the adolescent client's peer culture to understand that person's real world.

The adolescent, in addition, is often caught between social service agencies that are geared either to children or to adults. The child guidance clinic to which an adolescent is referred with a display of toys in the waiting room and in the interviewing room may cause adolescents to feel that they will be treated like children. The adult or family agency, in contrast, may also fail to communicate that it is sensitive to adolescents. This can be best communicated by agencies that have a *visible* adolescent clientele—those with waiting areas that have the ambience of a teenage drop-in center—comfortable chairs, phonograph, teen magazines, a ping-pong table, or similar objects.

Young Adulthood

This period is the one between the completion of secondary school and the assumption of such adult roles as full-time permanent employment and marriage or other long-term commitments. This encompasses the college years for some, while for others this is a period of either apprenticeship to an occupation or a first full-time job. Some of the tasks of adolescence may not yet have been completed as young adults may be dependent on their families and are still struggling to emancipate themselves. For some young adults, adolescence continues as they have not established clear identities or abilities to accept adult responsibilities. The kinds of issues for which people of this age seek help from social workers include completion of such adolescent tasks as determining values, separating from family, or planning for the future. On the other hand, young adults also seek help for the new tasks of this age such as resolving the problems of intimacy that prevent marriage or other long-term relationships or role problems that prevent assumption of work or community roles. The clients' choices can place them in conflict with family or community, and they may wish to help with this.

Society expects young adults to make commitments related to economic independence and the creation of new families. Many young adults wish to explore alternative lifestyles, including sexual and occupational roles that do not meet with the approval of their families. This was the age group most active in the protest movements of the late 1960s, and some of this idealism, we hope, remains even in a more conservative period. Young adults may feel this is the last chance to explore alternative patterns and yet are in conflict about this.

Many young adults are offered excellent services at colleges where counseling programs geared to their needs and interests have been developed. These programs specialize in understanding the family and individual circumstances that hinder the young adult from accomplishing academic, professional, and interpersonal relationship tasks. Young adults who are at work or who are unemployed have far fewer services attuned to their needs.

Adulthood

The adult roles that clients frequently focus on in seeking social work help are those of parent, spouse, and employee. In addition, clients often raise issues as to how they can fulfill their male and female roles. Students of human development have tended to focus on childhood and adolescence, and it is only recently that research has focused on enhancing our understanding of the tasks and phases of adulthood. One phase of development relates to changes in parent roles from the infancy to the adulthood of offspring. Another phase sequence relates to occupational career. Still another occurs as people establish life goals, seek to carry them out, and ultimately come to terms with what they have or have not accomplished.

Social workers are called upon to facilitate adults coping in all of these areas. Typical adult client problems are marital conflict, job dissatisfaction, child-rearing difficulties, and anxious or depressive reactions to life tasks. Social workers increasingly work with adults as part of their family or social networks, as many adult problems represent dysfunctional system functioning as much or more than individual psychopathology. These systemic problems include a lack of social support for family functioning, an inadequate job market, and communities that produce social isolation for their residents.

Social agencies, except for those most geared to children, are typically set up with the needs of adults in mind. One major problem from a service technology point of view, however, is that the rules and procedures are often more supportive of work on a one-to-one than family or group basis. Physical facilities for multiperson interviewing are often lacking. The hours during which the agency is open may not accommodate some clients, particularly those who are employed. Staff with competencies in work with families and groups may not be hired or training offered in these modalities. Psychiatric and other consultants who favor one-to-one frameworks may predominate.

Senior Adulthood

Work with older persons is rapidly expanding as this segment of the society grows rapidly in comparison with other age cohorts. In addition, social workers are becoming more cognizant of the tasks of these individuals and how they may be accomplished. These include a readjustment to unemployed status for those who retire from active employment, a shift of occupations for those forceably retired who wish to continue to work, accommodation to new relationships to children including the grandparent role, adjusting to the loss of loved ones and friends, coping with one's own death and with physical changes or even disability, and learning to use the acquired knowledge of a lifetime in ways that are useful and that serve to maintain a sense of self-respect.

Our society imposes many constraints upon older people: these include forced retirement, reduced income, an assumption of incompetence, and a loss of family roles. A good deal of thought has gone into how a society may be constructed so as to create new opportunities for the aged, but much remains to be implemented. The areas where this is essential and possible relate to employment, community roles, extended family roles, and a more respected position within the society itself. Social workers have a responsibility to help the individual to attain roles he or she seeks as well as to help the society create new opportunities for older persons.

Social workers must overcome their own biases in interacting with older persons. The same tendency to patronize the client that exists in work with younger children may exist in reference to this age group. In addition, the worker may underestimate the ability of older people to understand issues and make rational decisions. There are times, however, when physiological problems do interfere with communication and workers will have to creatively surmount such obstacles. Workers must also handle their own anxieties regarding disability and death, or they may themselves create additional barriers to work with older people.

An issue that often arises in work with the elderly is the assumption that older adults cannot change and that the only role for a social worker is to see that basic needs are met. This is unfortunate because it assumes that a person who is still alive, is dead, which can contribute to the older client's deterioration rather than rehabilitation. An illustration of this occurred when a new worker took over an older persons' group. Unlike the previous worker who had appointed group officers, the new worker held competitive elections. She answered the criticisms of her fellow workers by pointing out that fighting for desired positions and risking a loss is to declare that one is alive. In yet another situation, a group worker with the elderly confronted lengthy discussions in the group about whether fruit or juice should be served at lunch. He suggested that some of this energy should be used for discussions of better pensions for the elderly as well as housing, health care, and transportation. He indicated that he expected the group members to continue to work to improve the quality of their lives rather than pass time primarily on frivolous issues.

Agencies sometimes operate in such a way as to infantilize the elderly. This includes making many decisions for them, inviting other family members to speak for them, and encouraging their passivity so that they do not make "more work" for staff. Workers must examine these tendencies in their agencies as well as in their own personal practices.

Agency Purposes

In the preceding sections of this chapter, we described some of the practice variations that occur with clients of different ethnic backgrounds, sexes, and ages. Another source of variation is the purposes of the agency. In Chapter 1, we divided agency purposes as falling into two broad categories: socialization and resocialization. The socialization purpose was further divided into anomie reduction and role attainment, and the resocialization purpose into social control and alternative role attainment.

The choice of social work methods will differ in settings differentially devoted to anomie reduction, role attainment, social control, and alternative role attainment. Much research will have to be done to demonstrate empirically the best method for accomplishing each purpose. Nevertheless, practitioners can use this typology to generate propositions that conform to current practices and that *can* be tested. To illustrate this, we shall provide a discussion of social work methods when the purpose of a service is primarily *role attainment*. Although a similar analysis could be offered for other purposes and combinations of purposes, the discussion will follow the sequence of the types of decisions confronting workers and clients at different stages of the intervention process.

General Perspectives

Organizations engaged in facilitating role attainment help persons to develop the values, knowledge, and skills they require to attain the roles they have chosen. Examples of these clients are children and teenagers who wish to succeed in school and have trouble doing so, young adults who wish to

form intimate relationships but lack the skills for this, married couples who have young children and who wish to improve their parenting skills, and older persons who anticipate retirement and wish to plan for it. Persons in all these categories seek to perform socially desirable roles and consequently are not viewed as mentally ill or deviant for seeking this type of help. They often do so on a voluntary basis and in a broad sense view themselves as seeking training, a clarification of their tasks, and support to accomplish them. They also may find barriers to accomplishing their tasks in the environment and may wish help in removing or in other ways coping with them. This perspective will have an impact on all the stages of social work helping we have described in this book: assessment, choice of action system, the beginning of work, activities to attain the goals of service, termination, and evaluation. We shall now describe how the tasks of these stages are accomplished when the purpose involves role attainment, either exclusively or as part of a set of purposes relevant to a client system.

Initial Assessment

In assessing persons and their situations relevant to role attainment purposes, the worker will seek to identify the roles that are likely to be targeted. Thus, a social worker who interviewed a person in a program for older retired adults noted that the client expressed concerns about not being employed (occupational role), not having a younger person to care for (parental role), and having lost a spouse through death (spouse role). The client made a determination as to the priority of each of these role concerns and the relevant roles to attain.

The worker will help a client to assess

the skills that he or she already has with reference to the role in question as well as skills that should be acquired. In addition to this skill assessment, the knowledge of the client with reference to roles is assessed. Does the client know the options from which choices can be made? If the client wishes to pursue a new occupational career in retirement, does he or she know the requirements for the career as well as the opportunities? Are there other forms of knowledge that will be required in addition to the skill?

The motivation of the client with reference to the role will also have to be assessed. Motivational issues include the reinforcements the client will secure through performance of the role. Motivation is also derived from the degree to which the role relates to the client's views of his or her identity and purpose. Clients will be more motivated to attain roles that they believe are consistent with their talents, values, and sense of self.

The worker and the client will also assess those aspects of the environment that will support or hinder role attainment. We believe that the existence of *opportunity structures* is an important factor here. The definition of opportunity structures is socially organized access to culturally prescribed goals by legitimate means.[31] This includes opportunities for clients to secure necessary training and resources for role attainment. It also implies that the actual positions are available and that the client is not denied access to them. Examples of deficient opportunity structures are an absence of a remedial reading program needed for a student, of a job training program for an adult, or of a job opening for a skilled worker. Opportunity structures are sometimes unavailable because of discrimination based on the client's gender, age, or ethnicity.

Intervention Context

By intervention context, we mean the choice of one-to-one, family, group, or environmental interventions or even several of these to help the client. Role attainment purposes are often pursued through group work because several clients can often be recruited who face similar role attainment tasks. Successful role attainment groups have been conducted for children who want to succeed in school, or for parents who want to learn improved methods of child rearing, or for older people who want to plan for retirement.

Sometimes, also, barriers to role attainment are found in the family. A talented young adult's family may not provide support for further education when it is within their means to do so, or a spouse may stand in the way of the other spouse's retirement plans because they conflict with his or her own. These are a few examples of occasions when a family approach is essential.

Composition of the Action System

The action system consists of the people with whom the worker interacts on behalf of the client; thus, the action situation can be the client himself or herself. If the action situation is the family or a group, the worker and the client will have to determine who will be included. The compositional issue includes who the worker will be, also.

When a group modality has been chosen, the group members should be similar to each other in their role attainment tasks. There are several reasons for this: role attainment groups are often time limited and short term in nature. This similarity will allow the members to negotiate quickly their shared purposes and begin to work toward their goals. Members will also more quickly be able to assess barriers to role attainment (since they are likely to share these) and to identify sources of support and reinforcement for progress. When barriers are similar, the members may also rapidly generate ideas as to how they can work together to promote environmental change.

An example of this was a group of high school youths who joined a group to help them to remain in school as they wished to complete their schooling despite the difficulties they were having. The school social worker also received a number of referrals of youths who were having peer relationship difficulties, but she decided to form two groups to have homogeneity in regard to role problems. She was an Anglo worker while the members of the group were all Hispanic. Another reason, therefore, for the use of the group was to help the members to receive support from members of their own ethnic group as an Hispanic worker was not available.

Initiating the Action System

The initiation of the action system incorporates the first phase of the helping process in which goals are set, an assessment of the situation is undertaken, a trusting relationship with the social worker is initiated, and mutual expectations are explored. In role attainment circumstances, the client is usually voluntary and highly motivated to assume the role chosen for attention. Because this is a socialization condition, the client may need to be helped to identify intermediate steps to the goal. In a group, for example, to help unemployed people obtain jobs, the following steps were agreed upon: decide upon a type of employment, acquaint one's self with the requirements for the position, secure necessary training, identify sources of information

about jobs, and apply for jobs in the manner most favorable to one's self.

Intervention Targets

By targets, we mean the specific components of one's self or one's situation or both that must be changed to attain goals. In role attainment situations, the personal targets are the motivation, knowledge, and skill of the client relevant to the role. On the other hand, barriers to role attainment also often occur because of deficiencies in the opportunity structures relevant to the role. An example is a Chicano client of a school social worker in a primarily Anglo school. The student wished to succeed in school, but he was hindered by the fact that he was bilingual and had some limitations in his use of English. The school did not have the resources to help him with his language problem. In addition, there were no Hispanic staff members to whom the young man could relate as role models. One of the situational aspects that the social worker targeted was to secure these resources, or substitutes for them, as a means of helping the student to achieve in the student role.

Intervention Strategies

The major client change strategies for role attainment are educational ones such as problem solving, anticipatory socialization, and promoting appropriate reinforcement. Problem solving will focus on helping the client to cope with problems that arise as the client seeks to fulfill role expectations. Anticipatory socialization, usually in the form of role playing, helps the client to practice the behaviors required by the role. The client also requires appropriate reinforcement for role appropriate behaviors. Sometimes this will be supplied by the worker. It is more desirable, however, to promote reinforcement in the natural environment such as that supplied by family members, teachers, employers, or others closely related to the roles in question.

As we pointed out in our discussion of "targets," the environmental opportunity structure is sometimes deficient. The strategies the worker will employ in these circumstances are derived from community organization as well as the interpersonal practice approaches of advocacy and brokerage. The worker will link the client with appropriate resources, will advocate for the client when such resources are denied, and will help to develop resources that are not present in the situation. The last activity we term a community organization component of the work as this may require a needs assessment and community resource allocation process that considers issues not present in the single case but present in a much larger set of people.

Intervention Techniques

By techniques, we mean the actions of the worker during a specific session with the individual, family, or group. The worker will sometimes use value clarification techniques[32] to help the client to make choices of alternative ways of attaining the desired roles. Another technique used in role attainment is "coaching,"[33] which includes the setting of short-term goals, closely observing performances (often through role play) to identify when reinforcement is needed, and offering advice. The worker will also use such behavior modification techniques as establishing a token reinforcement system[34] and group contingencies.[35] Opportunities to observe other persons as models will also be created both within the social work situation as well as beyond it. A helpful technique used in role attainment groups is the creation of a "buddy system" in which pairs of members are created who can work together during parts of the group meeting as well as contact each other for advice and support between meetings. The worker may also make "homework" assignments to clients between sessions that will help them attain their roles.

Termination

Ideally, when clients have attained their goals, their gains are maintained by natural support systems. Thus, once a student has begun to function effectively in the classroom, the teacher and peers should help to maintain this; once a person has been trained for a job and has secured one, the salary obtained through this as well as working conditions should maintain the new position and the associated behaviors. Follow-up activity, however, may be required to help clients in new roles. Sometimes, also, the client selects another role and may also require services to attain that one. The termination process in all these cases should help the client decide how to maintain gains and also take steps toward fulfilling other roles when that is appropriate.

This section of the chapter has suggested how workers can use our typology of types of purposes to develop a service plan when *role attainment* is the focus of work. We intend, when more research has been done, to indicate in a more definitive way how workers should proceed for other purposes (and combinations of purposes).

Summary

This chapter discussed two broad topics: first, how interpersonal practice approaches vary for clients of different ethnic backgrounds, sexes, and ages and, second, how such approaches vary when agency purposes are different. In discussing ethnicity, we presented a framework for analyzing the effect of such variables as the economic factors affecting the culture, the communication pattern present in the culture, the social structure of the ethnic group, the way in which the ethnic group orders its physical environment, and the socialization patterns employed by the ethnic group.

In discussing gender issues, we noted the separate ways in which men and women are socialized in our culture, the different forms of role allocation for each sex, and the manifestations of sexism that exist. We saw this knowledge of ethnic and sex differences as having strong implications for practice.

We then presented a discussion of the kinds of tasks that occur at different stages of the life cycle and the implications this has for accomplishing the purposes of interpersonal practice. The stages that were discussed were infancy, young childhood, older childhood, adolescence, young adulthood, adulthood, and senior adulthood.

The succeeding section of the chapter was devoted to a discussion of how agency purposes affect interpersonal practice procedures. We divided such purposes into socialization and resocialization. Socialization was further subdivided into anomie reduction and role attainment and resocialization into social control and alternative role attainment. These purposes, singly or in some mixture, affect all stages of interpersonal practice from intake to termination. For illustrative purposes, a change process related to the purpose of role attainment was described.

NOTES

1. Milton Gordon, *Assimilation in American Life* (New York: Oxford University Press, 1964), p. 27.

2. Ibid., p. 34.

3. Ibid.

4. Charles Valentine, *Culture and Poverty: Critique and Counter Proposals* (Chicago: University of Chicago Press, 1968), pp. 178–180.

5. Peter Trudgill, *Sociolinguistics: An Introduction* (Baltimore: Penguin Books, 1974), p. 82.

6. "News of the Week in Review." *The New York Times*, December 14, 1980, p. 7.

7. Gerald D. Suttles, *The Social Order of the Slum: Ethnicity and Territory in the Inner City* (Chicago: University of Chicago Press, 1968), pp. 75–76.

8. Ibid., p. 89.

9. Annemarie Brewer, "On Indian Education," *Outrider*, No. 9 (Chicago: Erikson Institute for Early Education, October 1975).

10. Ibid.

11. Ibid.

12. Jules Henry, *Essays on Education* (Baltimore: Penguin Books, 1971), pp. 72–183.

13. Robert Blauner, "Internal Colonialism and Ghetto Revolt," *Social Problems*, Vol. 16. (Spring 1969), pp. 393–408.

14. See, for example, Alan Harwood. *Spiritist as Needed: A Study of a Puerto Rican Community Mental Health Resource* (New York: Wiley-Interscience, 1977); Mircea Eliade, *Shamanism: Archic Techniques of Ectasy* (New York: Pantheon, 1964); and Ari Kiev, *Curanderismo: Mexican-American Folk Psychiatry* (New York: The Free Press, 1968).

15. John Papajohn and John Spiegel, *Transactions in Families* (San Francisco: Jossey-Bass, 1975), p. 21.

16. Ibid., pp. 29–35.

17. Ibid., p. 47.

18. Arnold P. Goldstein, "Evaluating Expectancy Effects in Cross-Cultural Counseling and Psychotherapy," in Anthony Marsella and Paul Pederson, eds., *Cross-Cultural Counseling and Psychotherapy* (Elmsford, N.Y.: Pergamon Press, 1981), pp. 85–101.

19. B. Overall and H. Aronson, "Expectations of Psychotherapy in Patients of Lower Socio-economic Class," *American Journal of Orthopsychiatry*, Vol. 33 (1963), pp. 421–430, and John E. Mayer and Noel Timms, *The Client Speaks: Working Class Impressions of Casework* (New York: Atherton Press, 1970).

20. Martin M. Katz, "Evaluating Drug and Other Therapies Across Cultures," in *Cross-Cultural Counseling*, pp. 159–173.

21. Timothy R. Brown et al., "Mental Illness and the Role of Mental Health Facilities in Chinatown," in Stanley Sue and Nathaniel N. Wagner, eds., *Asian-Americans: Psychological Perspectives* (Palo Alto, Calif.: Science and Behavior Books, 1973), p. 226.

22. Robert K. Thomas, "Colonialism: Domestic and Foreign," in David W. Hartman, ed., *Immigrants and Migrants: The Detroit Ethnic Experience*, published as *Journal of University Studies*, Vol. 10, (Fall 1974), p. 276.

23. Carolyn Attneave, "Therapy in Tribal Settings and Urban Newwork Interventions", *Family Process*, Vol. 8 (September 1969), pp. 192–210.

24. Statement made by Beth Reed in a lecture to a social work class at the University of Michigan in November 1980.

25. Jerome Kagan, "Sex Typing and Sex Role Identity," in Lois Hoffman and Martin Hoffman, eds., *Review of Child Development Research* (New York: Russell Sage, 1964), p. 143.

26. For a report on research findings on allocation of these tasks, see F. Ivan Nye, *Role Structure and Analysis of the Family* (Beverly Hills, Calif.: Sage Publications, 1976).

27. I. Frieze et al., *Women and Sex Roles* (New York: W. W. Norton, 1978).

28. Many of the articles in Vivian Gornick and Barbara K. Moran, eds., *Women in Sexist Society: Studies in Power and Powerlessness* (New York: New American Library, 1971), support this point.

29. Mary C. Schwartz, "Importance of the Sex of Worker and Client," *Social Work*, March 1974, pp. 181–182.

30. See "Policy on Gay Issues," *NASW News*, Vol. 22 (July 1977).

31. Aldred J. Kahn, "From Delinquency Treatment to Community Development" in Paul F. Lazarsfield, William H. Sewell, and Harold L. Wilensky, eds., *The Uses of Sociology* (New York: Basic Books, 1967), p. 483.

32. For example, see Sidney B. Simon, Leland W. Howe, and Howard Kirschenbaum, *Values Clarification: A Handbook of Practical Strategies for Teachers and Students* (New York: Hart, 1972).

33. Anselm Strauss, "Coaching," in Bruce Biddle and Edwin J. Thomas, *Role Theory: Concepts and Research* (New York: John Wiley, 1966), pp. 350–353.

34. T. Allyon and N. H. Azrin, *The Token Economy: A Motivational System for Therapy and Rehabilitation* (Englewood Cliffs, N.J.: Prentice-Hall, 1968).

35. Sheldon Rose, *Group Therapy: A Behavioral Approach* (Englewood Cliffs, N.J.: Prentice-Hall, 1977), p. 91.

Bibliography

Aiken, Michael, and Jerald Hage. "Organizational Alienation: A Comparative Analysis." *American Sociological Review*, Vol. 31 (August 1966), pp. 497–507.

Allyon, T., and N. H. Azrin. *The Token Economy: A Motivational System for Therapy and Rehabilitation*. Englewood Cliffs, N.J.: Prentice-Hall, 1968.

Ardrey, Robert. *African Genesis*. New York: Atheneum, 1961.

Arehart-Treichel, Joan. "The Good Healthy Shining Light." *Human Behavior*, Vol. 4 (January 1975), pp. 16–22.

Atherton, Charles, Sandra Mitchell, and Edna Schein. "Locating Points for Intervention." *Social Casework*, Vol. 52 (March 1971), pp. 131–141.

Attneave, Carolyn. "Therapy in Tribal Settings and Urban Network Interventions." *Family Process*, Vol. 8 (September 1969), pp. 192–210.

Bales, Robert F. *Interaction Process Analysis: A Method for the Study of Small Groups*. Reading, Mass.: Addison-Wesley, 1950.

_____. "Task Roles and Social-Emotional Roles in Problem-Solving Groups." In *Readings in Social Psychology* (3rd ed.), eds. E. E. Maccoby, T. M. Newcomb, and E. T. Hartley, pp. 437–447. New York: Holt, Rinehart and Winston, 1958.

_____, and Fred Strodbeck. "Phases of Group Problem Solving." In *Group Dynamics: Research and Theory*, eds. Dorwin Cartwright and Alvin Zander, pp. 389–400. New York: Harper & Row, 1968.

Bandler, Louise. "Family Functioning: A Psychosocial Perspective." In *The Drifters*, ed. Eleanor Pavenstedt, pp. 225–253. Boston: Little, Brown, 1967.

Bandler, Richard, and John Grinder. *The Structure of Magic*. Palo Alto, Calif.: Science and Behavior Books, 1975.

Baxter, J. C. "Interpersonal Spacing in Natural Settings." *Sociometry*, Vol. 33 (1970), pp. 444–456.

Beal, Lynette. "Corrupt Contract: Problems in Conjoint Therapy with Parents and Children." *American Journal of Orthopsychiatry*, Vol. 42 (January 1972), pp. 77–81.

Beck, A. T. *Cognitive Therapy and the Emotional Disorders*. New York: International Universities Press, 1976.

Becker, Howard, ed. *The Other Side: Perspectives on Deviance*. New York: The Free Press, 1967.

Bednar, Richard L., and Theodore J. Kaul. "Experiential Group Research: Current Perspectives." In *Handbook of Psychotherapy and Behavior Change* (2nd ed.), eds. Sol L. Garfield and A. E. Bergin, pp. 769–816. New York: John Wiley, 1978.

Bell, Norman, and Ezra Vogel. *A Modern Introduction to the Family* (rev. ed.). New York: The Free Press, 1969.

Benjamin, Alfred. *The Helping Interview* (2nd ed.). Boston: Houghton Mifflin, 1974.

Berman, Sanford. *Why Do We Jump to Conclusions?* San Diego, Calif.: International Communications Institute, 1962.

Berne, Eric. *Games People Play*. New York: Grove Press, 1964.

von Bertalanffy, Ludwig. *Robots, Men and Minds: Psychology in the Modern World*. New York: George Braziller, 1967.

——— . *General Systems Theory: Foundations, Development, Application*. New York: George Braziller, 1968.

Bertsche, Ann, and Charles Horejsi. "Coordination of Client Services." *Social Work*, Vol. 25 (March 1980), pp. 94–98.

Bettelheim, Bruno. *A Home for the Heart*. New York: Knopf, 1974.

Biddle, Bruce, and Edwin Thomas, eds. *Role Theory: Concepts and Research*. New York, John Wiley, 1966.

Biestek, Felix. *The Casework Relationship*. Chicago: Loyola University Press, 1957.

Billingsley, Andrew. "Bureaucratic and Professional Orientation Patterns in Social Casework." *Social Service Review*, Vol. 38 (December 1964), pp. 400–407.

Bion, W. R. *Experiences in Groups*. New York: Basic Books. 1969.

Birdwhistell, Ray L. *Kinesics and Context: Essays on Body Motion Communication*. Philadelphia: University of Pennsylvania Press, 1970.

Black, Max. *Models and Metaphors: Studies in Language and Philosophy*. Ithaca, N.Y.: Cornell University Press, 1962.

Blau, Peter. "Orientations Towards Clients in Public Welfare Agency." *Administrative Science Quarterly*, Vol. 5 (1960), pp. 342–346.

——— , and W. Richard Scott. *Formal Organizations*. San Francisco: Chandler, 1962.

Blauner, Robert. "Internal Colonialism and Ghetto Revolt." *Social Problems*, Vol. 16 (Spring 1969), pp. 393–408.

Blenkner, Margaret. *Serving the Aged; An Experiment in Social Work and Public Health*. New York: Community Service Society of New York, 1964.

Blizinsky, Marlin J., and William J. Reid. "Problem Focus and Change in a Brief Treatment Model." *Social Work*, Vol. 25 (March 1980), pp. 89–93.

Bloom, Bernard L. "Focused Single-Session Therapy: Initial Development and Evaluation." In *Forms of Brief Therapy*, ed. Simon Budman, pp. 167–216. New York: Guilford Press, 1981.

Boehm, Werner W. "The Nature of Social Work." *Social Work*, Vol. 3 (April 1958), pp. 10–19.

Boisservain, Jeremy, and Mitchell J. Clyde. *Network Analysis: Studies in Human Interaction*. Paris: Mouton, 1973.

Boulding, Kenneth. *A Primer on Social Dynamics: History as Dialectic and Development*. New York: The Free Press, 1970.

———— . "Economics and General Systems." In *The Relevance of General Systems Theory*, ed. Ervin Laszlo. New York: George Braziller, 1972.

Bowen, Murray. "The Family as the Unit of Study and Treatment." *American Journal of Orthopsychiatry*, Vol. 31 (1961), pp. 40–60.

Brehm, Sharon S. *The Application of Social Psychology to Clinical Practice*. New York: John Wiley, 1976.

Brewer, Annemarie. "On Indian Education," *Outrider*, Vol. 9 (October 1975).

Briar, Scott, "Welfare from Below: Recipients' View of the Public Welfare System." *California Law Review*, Vol. 54 (1966), pp. 370–85.

———— , "Social Casework and Social Group Work: Historical and Social Science Foundations." In *Encyclopedia of Social Work*, Vol. II, pp. 1237–1245. New York: National Association of Social Workers, 1971.

———— , and Henry Miller. *Problems and Issues in Social Casework*. New York: Columbia University Press, 1971.

Brim, Orville, and Stanton Wheeler. *Socialization After Childhood*. New York: John Wiley, 1966.

Brown, Robert A. "Feedback in Family Interviewing." *Social Work*, Vol. 18 (September 1973), pp. 51–56.

Brown, Timothy R., and others. "Mental Illness and the Role of Mental Health Facilities in Chinatown." In *Asian Americans: Psychological Perspectives*, eds. Stanley Sue and Nathaniel N. Wagner, pp. 212–234. Palo Alto, Calif.: Science and Behavior Books, 1975.

Buckley, Walter. *Sociology and Modern Systems Theory*. Englewood Cliffs, N.J.: Prentice-Hall, 1967.

———— , ed. *Modern Systems Research for the Behavioral Scientist*. Chicago: Aldine, 1968.

Budman, Simon, ed. *Forms of Brief Therapy*. New York: Guilford Press, 1981.

Bush, Sherida. "A Family-Help Program That Really Works." *Psychology Today*, May 1977, pp. 48–50, 84–88.

Byers, Paul, and Happie Byers. "Nonverbal Communication and the Education of Children." In *Functions of Language in the Classroom*, ed. Courtney Cazden. New York: Teachers College Press, 1972.

Cadogan, D. A. "Marital Group Therapy in the Treatment of Alcoholism." *Quarterly Journal of Studies in Alcoholism*, Vol. 34 (1973), pp. 1187–1194.

Campbell, Mona. "Extentional and Intentional Levels of Abstraction." In *Teaching General Semantics*, ed. Mary S. Morain, pp. 45–52. San Francisco: International Society for General Semantics, 1969.

Carter, Robert, and Richard Stuart. "Behavior Modification Theory and Practice: A Reply." *Social Work*, Vol. 15 (January 1970), pp. 37–50.

Cartwright, Dorwin. "Influence, Leadership, Control." In *Handbook of Organizations*, ed. J. C. March, pp. 1–47. Chicago: Rand McNally, 1965.

———— , and Alvin Zander, eds. *Group Dynamics: Theory and Research* (3rd ed.) New York: Harper & Row, 1968.

Cattell, R. B., D. R. Saunders, and G. F. Stice. "The Dimensions of Syntality in Small Groups." *Human Relations*, Vol. 6 (1953), pp. 331–356.

Chaiklin, Harris. "Honesty in Casework Treatment." *Social Welfare Forum*, 1973 pp. 266–274. New York: Columbia University Press, 1974.

Cherry, Cholin. *On Human Communication* (2nd ed.). Cambridge, Mass.: M.I.T. Press, 1966.

Cloward, Richard, and Lloyd Ohlin. *Delinquency and Opportunity.* Glencoe, Ill.: The Free Press, 1960.

Cohn, Yona. "Channeling the Probation Interview." *Crime and Delinquency,* Vol. 4 (July 1968), pp. 226–232.

Coll, Blanche D. *Perspectives in Public Welfare: A History.* Washington, D.C.: Government Printing Office, 1969.

Collins, Alice, and Diane Pancoast. *Natural Helping Networks: A Strategy for Prevention.* Washington D.C.: National Association of Social Workers, 1976.

Collins, John. "The Contractual Approach to Social Work Intervention." *Social Work Today,* Vol. 8 (February 1977), pp. 13–15.

Commission on Social Work Practice, National Association of Social Workers. "Working Definition of Social Work Practice." *Social Work,* Vol. 3 (April 1958), pp. 5–8.

Compton, Beaulah, and Burt Gallaway. *Social Work Processes* (2nd ed.). Homewood, Ill.: The Dorsey Press, 1979.

Condon, W. S., and W. D. Ogston. "A Segmentation of Behavior." *Journal of Psychiatric Research,* Vol. 5 (1967), pp. 221–235.

Costin, Lela. *Child Welfare Policies and Procedures.* New York: McGraw-Hill, 1972.

Cox, Fred M., and others, eds. *Tactics and Techniques of Community Practice.* Itasca, Ill.: F. E. Peacock, 1977.

Coyle, Grace. "Group Work and Social Change." *Proceedings of the National Conference of Social Work, 1935,* pp. 393–405. Chicago: University of Chicago Press, 1935.

Croxton, Tom. "The Therapeutic Contract in Social Treatment." In *Individual Change Through Small Groups,* ed. Paul Glasser, Rosemary Sarri, and Robert Vinter, pp. 169–185. New York: The Free Press, 1974.

Devore, Wynetta, and Elfriede G. Schlesinger. *Ethnic-Sensitive Social Work Practice.* St. Louis: C. V. Mosby, 1981.

Delgado, Melvin, and Denise Humm-Delgado. "Natural Support Systems." *Social Work,* Vol. 27 (January 1982), pp. 83–90.

Dewey, John. *How We Think.* Lexington, Mass.: D.C. Heath, 1933.

Diagnostic and Statistical Manual of Mental Disorders (3rd ed.). Washington, D.C.: American Psychiatric Association, 1980.

Dillard, J. L. *Black English.* New York: Random House, 1972.

Dohrenwend, Barbara S., Lawrence Krasnoff, Alexander Askenasy, and Bruce Dohrenwend. "The Psychiatric Epidemiology Research Interview Life Events Scale." In *Handbook of Stress: Theoretical and Clinical Aspects,* pp. 332–363. New York: The Free Press, 1982.

Dubin, Robert. *Theory Building.* New York: The Free Press, 1969.

Efron, D. *Gesture and Environment.* New York: King's Crown Press, 1941.

Eisenberg, Sheldon, and Daniel J. Delaney. *The Counseling Process* (2nd ed.). Chicago: Rand McNally, 1977.

Eisman, Martin. "Social Work's New Role in the Welfare Class Revolution." *Social Work,* Vol. 14 (April 1969), pp. 75–83.

Ekman, Paul, ed. *Darwin and Facial Expression: A Century of Research in Review.* New York: Academic Press, 1973.

———, and Wallace Friesen. "The Repertoire of Nonverbal Behavior: Categories, Origin, Usage, and Coding." *Semiotica,* Vol. 1 (1969), pp. 63–89.

———, and Wallace Friesen. *Unmasking the Face.* Englewood Cliffs, N.J.: Prentice-Hall, 1975.

————— , Wallace Friesen, and Phoebe Ellsworth. *Emotion in the Human Face*. Elmsford, N.Y.: Pergamon Press, 1972.

Eliade, Mircea. *Shamanism: Archaic Technique of Ecstasy*. New York: Pantheon, 1964.

Ellis, Albert, and R. A. Harper. *A New Guide to Rational Living*. North Hollywood, Calif.: Wilshire, 1975.

Epstein, Irwin. "Social Workers and Social Action: Attitudes Towards Social Action." *Social Work*, Vol. 13 (April 1968), pp. 101–108.

————— . "The Politics of Behavior Therapy: The New Cool-out Casework." In *Towards a New Social Work*, ed. Howard Jones, pp. 138–150. London: Routledge and Kegan Paul, 1975.

Epstein, Laura. "Is Autonomous Practice Possible?" *Social Work*, Vol. 18 (March 1973) pp. 5–12.

————— . *Helping People: The Task-Centered Approach*. St. Louis: C. V. Mosby, 1980.

Erikson, Erik H., *Gandhi's Truth: On the Origins of Militant Non-Violence*. New York: W. W. Norton, 1969.

Etzioni, Amitai. *A Comparative Analysis of Complex Organizations*. Glencoe, Ill.: The Free Press, 1961.

————— . *The Active Society: A Theory of Societal and Political Processes*. New York: The Free Press, 1968.

Fabun, Don. *Communications: The Transfer of Meaning*. Beverly Hills, Calif.: Glencoe Press, 1970.

Fanshel, David. *An Overview of One Agency's Casework Operations*. Pittsburgh: Family and Children's Service, 1958.

————— . "The Exit of Children from Foster Care: An Interim Report." *Child Welfare*, Vol. 50 (February 1971), pp. 65–80.

Fisher, Joel. *Effective Casework Practice: An Eclectic Approach*. New York: McGraw-Hill, 1978.

————— , and Harvey Gochros. *Planned Behavior Change: Behavior Modification in Social Work*. New York: The Free Press, 1975.

Folb, Edith. "'Rappin' in the Black Vernacular." *Human Behavior*, Vol. 2 (August 1973), pp. 16–20.

Follett, Mary Parker. *The New State*. New York: Longmans, Green, 1926.

Franks, Virginia. *The Autonomous Social Worker*. Madison: University of Wisconsin School of Social Work, 1967.

Friedson, Eliot. "Dominant Professions, Bureaucracy, and Client Services." In *Human Service Organizations*, eds. Yeheskel Hasenfeld and Richard English, pp. 428–447. Ann Arbor: University of Michigan Press, 1974.

French, J. R., and B. Raven. "The Bases of Social Power." In *Studies in Social Power*, ed. Dorwin Cartwright, pp. 150–167. Ann Arbor, Mich.: Institute for Social Research, 1959.

Freud, Sigmund. "Recommendations for Physicians on the Psychoanalytic Method of Treatment." In *Collected Papers of Sigmund Freud*, Vol. 2, pp. 323–333. New York: Basic Books, 1959.

Frey, Louise, and Golda Edinburg. "Helping, Manipulation, and Magic." *Social Work*, Vol. 23 (March 1978), pp. 88–92.

————— , and Marguerite Meyer. "Explorations and Working Agreement in Two Social Work Methods." In *Explorations in Group Work*, ed. Saul Bernstein, pp. 1–16. Boston: Milford House, 1973.

Frieze, I., and others. *Women and Sex Roles*. New York: W. W. Norton, 1978.

Fusco, Luke J. "Power, Authority, and Influence in Social Work Treatment and the Two Contract Model of Practice." Paper presented at NASW Fifth Biennial Professional Symposium, San Diego, California, November 1977.

Gabriel, Estelle. "Private Practice in Social Work." In *Encyclopedia of Social Work*, Vol. II, pp. 1054–1054. New York: National Association of Social Workers, 1977.

Gallant, Claire. *Mediation in Special Education Disputes*. Washington, D. C.: National Association of Social Workers, 1982.

Galper, Jeffrey. *Social Work Practice: A Radical Perspective*. Englewood Cliffs, N.J.: Prentice-Hall, 1980.

Gans, Herbert. *The Urban Villagers: Group and Class in the Life of Italian-Americans*. New York: The Free Press, 1962.

Garfield, Sol L. *Psychotherapy: An Eclectic Approach*. New York: John Wiley, 1980.

————, and A. E. Bergin eds. *Handbook of Psychotherapy and Behavior Change: An Empirical Analysis* (2nd ed.). New York: John Wiley, 1978.

Garvin, Charles D. *Complementarity of Role Expectations in Groups: Relationship to Worker Performance and Member Problem Solving*, Unpublished doctoral dissertation, University of Chicago, 1968.

————. "Group Process: Usage and Uses in Social Work Practice." In *Individual Change Through Small Groups*, eds. Paul Glasser, Rosemary Sarri, and Robert Vinter, pp. 209–232. New York: The Free Press, 1974.

————. *Contemporary Group Work*. Englewood Cliffs, N.J.: Prentice-Hall, 1981.

————, and Paul Glasser. "The Bases of Social Treatment." In *Individual Change Through Small Groups*, eds. Paul Glasser, Rosemary Sarri, and Robert Vinter, pp. 483–507. New York: The Free Press, 1974.

Geller, Janet A. "Reaching the Battering Husband." *Social Work with Groups*, Vol. 1 (Spring 1978), pp. 27–38.

Gerard, R. W. "Units and Concepts in Biology." In *Modern Systems Research for the Behavioral Scientist*, ed. Walter Buckley, pp. 51–58. Chicago: Aldine, 1968.

Germain, Carel. "Social Study: Past and Future." *Social Casework*, Vol. 49 (July 1968), pp. 406–409.

————. "Casework and Science: An Historical Encounter." In *Theories of Social Casework*, eds. Robert Roberts and Robert Nee, pp. 3–32. Chicago: University of Chicago Press, 1970.

————. *Social Work Practice: People and Environments: An Ecological Perspective*. New York: Columbia University Press, 1979.

————, and Alex Gitterman. *Life Model of Social Work Practice*. New York: Columbia University Press, 1980.

Glasser, Paul, and others. "Group Work Intervention in the Social Environment." In *Individual Change Through Small Groups*, eds. Paul Glasser, Rosemary Sarri, and Robert Vinter, pp. 292–306. New York: The Free Press, 1974.

————, Rosemary Sarri, and Robert Vinter, eds., *Individual Change Through Small Groups*. New York: The Free Press, 1974.

Goffman, Irving. *Asylums: Essays on the Social Situation of Mental Patients and Other Inmates*. Garden City, N.Y.: Doubleday, 1961.

————. *Behavior in Public Places*. New York: The Free Press, 1963.

Golan, Naomi. *Treatment in Crisis Situations*. New York: The Free Press, 1978.

———. "Intervention in Times of Transition: Sources and Forms of Help." *Social Casework*, Vol. 61 (May 1980), pp. 259–266.

———. *Passing Through Life Transitions: A Guide for Practitioners*. New York: The Free Press, 1981.

Goldberger, Leo, and Shlomo Breznitz, ed., *Handbook of Stress: Theoretical and Clinical Aspects*. New York: The Free Press, 1982.

Goldstein, Arnold P. "Evaluating Expectancy Effects in Cross-Cultural Counseling." In *Cross-Cultural Counseling and Psychotherapy*, eds. Anthony Marsella and Paul Pederson, pp. 85–101. Elmsford, N.Y.: Pergamon Press, 1981.

Goldstein, Howard. *Social Work: A Unitary Approach*. Columbia: University of South Carolina, 1973.

Gordon, Milton. *Assimilation in American Life*. New York: Oxford Univesity Press, 1964.

Gordon, Steven B., and Nancy Davidson. "Behavioral Parent Training." In *Handbook of Family Therapy*, eds. Alan S. Gurman and David P. Kniskern, pp. 517–555. New York: Brunner/Mazel, 1981.

Gornick, Vivian, and Barbara K. Moran, eds. *Women in Sexist Society: Studies in Power and Powerlessness*. New York: New American Library, 1971.

Gottlieb, Weiner, and Joe Stanley. "Mutual Goals and Goal Setting in Casework." *Social Casework*, Vol. 48 (October 1967), pp. 471–477.

Gottman, D. M., and S. R. Lieblum. *How to Do Psychotherapy and How to Evaluate It*. New York: Holt, Rinehart and Winston, 1974.

Green, A. D. "The Professional Social Worker in the Bureaucracy." *Social Service Review*, Vol. 40 (March 1966), pp. 71–83.

Green, James. *Cultural Awareness in the Human Services*. Englewood Cliffs, N.J.: Prentice-Hall, 1982.

Griffith, W. "Environmental Effect of Interpersonal Affective Behavior: Ambient Effective Temperature and Attraction." *Journal of Personality and Social Psychology*, Vol. 15 (1970), pp. 240–244.

Grinker, Roy R., and others. *Psychiatric Social Work: A Transactional Casebook*. New York: Basic Books, 1961.

Grinnell, Richard. "Environmental Modification: Casework's Concern or Casework's Neglect?" *Social Service Review*, Vol. 47 (June 1973), pp. 208–220.

Gross, Emma. "Curanderismo, Espiritismo, Shamanism and Social Work." Unpublished paper, School of Social Work, Univeristy of Michigan, December 1979.

Gurman, Alan S., and David P. Kniskern. "Research on Marital and Family Therapy: Progress, Perspective and Prospect. In *Handbook of Psychotherapy and Behavior Change: An Empirical Analysis* (2nd ed.), eds. Sol L. Garfield and A. E. Bergin, pp. 817–902. New York: John Wiley, 1978.

———, and David P. Kniskern, eds. *Handbook of Family Therapy*. New York: Brunner/Mazel, 1981.

Haley, Jay. *Strategies of Psychotherapy*. New York: Grune & Stratton, 1963.

———. *Changing Families: A Family Therapy Reader*. New York: Grune & Stratton, 1971.

———. *Uncommon Therapy: The Psychiatric Techniques of Milton Erickson*. New York: W. W. Norton, 1973.

———. *Problem-Solving Therapy: New Strategies for Effective Family Therapy*. San Francisco: Jossey-Bass, 1976.

Hall, A. D., and R. E. Fagan. "The Definition of a System." In *Modern Systems Research for the Behavioral Scientist*, ed. Walter Buckley, pp. 81–92. Chicago: Aldine, 1968.

Hall, Edward T. *The Silent Language*. Garden City, N.Y.: Doubleday, 1959.

———. *The Hidden Dimension*. Garden City, N.Y.: Doubleday, 1969.

Halleck, Seymour. "The Impact of Professional Dishonesty on Behavior of Disturbed Adolescents." *Social Work*, Vol. 8 (April 1963), pp. 48–55.

Hamilton, Gordon. *Theory and Practice of Social Casework* (2nd ed. rev.). New York: Columbia University Press, 1951.

Haney, William. *Communication and Organization Behavior*. Homewood, Ill.: Richard D. Irwin, 1967.

———. "The Inference-Observation Confusion: The Uncritical Inference Test." In *Teaching General Semantics*. ed. Mary S. Morain, pp. 1–22. San Francisco: International Society for General Semantics, 1969.

Hardman, Dale. "Not With My Daughter You Don't!" *Social Work*, Vol. 20 (July 1975), pp. 278–285.

Harris, Grace E. *Training of Public Welfare Staff in the Use of the Service Contract in Preventing and Reducing Foster Care*. Richmond: School of Social Work, Virginia Commonwealth University, 1978.

Hartford, Margaret E. *Groups in Social Work*. New York: Columbia University Press, 1971.

Hartman, Ann. "To Think About the Unthinkable." *Social Casework*, Vol. 51 (October 1971), pp. 467–474.

———. "Diagrammatic Assessment of Family Relationships" *Social Casework*, Vol. 59 (October 1978), pp. 465–476.

Harwood, Alan. *Rx: Spiritist as Needed: A Study of a Puerto Rican Community Mental Health Resource*. New York: Wiley-Interscience, 1977.

Hasenfeld, Yeheskel. "Organizational Factors in Service to Groups," In *Individuals Change Through Small Groups*, eds. Paul Glasser, Rosemary Sarri, and Robert Vinter, pp. 307–324. New York: The Free Press, 1974.

———, and Richard English. *Human Service Organizations*. Ann Arbor: University of Michigan Press, 1974.

Hayes, F. C. "Should We Have a Dictionary of Gestures?" *Southern Folklore Quarterly*, Vol. 4 (1940), pp. 239–245.

Heap, Ken. *Group Theory for Social Workers: An Introduction*. Oxford: Pergamon Press, 1977.

Hearn, Gordon. *Theory Building in Social Work*. Toronto: University of Toronto Press, 1958.

———. "The General Systems Approach to the Understanding of Groups." *Health Education Monographs*, No. 14, Society of Public Health Educators, 1962.

———. ed. *The General Systems Approach: Contributions Toward an Holistic Conception of Social Work*. New York: Council on Social Work Education, 1969.

———. "General Systems Theory and Social Work" In *Social Work Treatment*, ed. Francis Turner, pp. 343–371. New York: The Free Press, 1974.

Heider, F. "Social Perception and Phenomenal Causality," *Psychological Review*, Vol. 51 (1944), pp. 358–374.

Heiman, Julia R., Leslie LoPiccolo, and Joseph LoPiccolo. "The Treatment of Sexual Dysfunction." In *Handbook of Family Therapy,* eds. Alan S. Gurman and David P. Kniskern, pp. 596–630. New York: Brunner/Mazel, 1981.

Henry, Charlotte. "Motivation of Non-Voluntary Clients," *Social Casework*, Vol. 39 (1958), pp. 130–138.

Henry, Jules. *Essays on Education*. Baltimore: Penguin Books, 1971.

Henry, Sue. *Group Skills in Social Work: A Four-Dimensional Approach*. Itasca, Ill.: F. E. Peacock, 1981.

Hersen, M., and D. H. Barlow. *Single-Case Experimental Designs*. Elmsford, N.Y.: Pergamon Press, 1976.

Hill, William G. "The Family as a Treatment Unit: Differential Techniques and Procedures." *Social Work*, Vol. 11 (April 1966), pp. 62–68.

Hoehn, Saric, et al. "Systematic Preparation of Patients for Psychotherapy." *Journal of Psychiatric Research*, Vol. 2 (1964), pp. 267–281.

Hoffman, Lynn, and Lorence Long. "A Systems Dilemma," *Family Process*, Vol. 8 (September 1969), pp. 211–234.

Hollis, Florence. *Casework: A Psychosocial Therapy*. New York: Random House, 1964.

––––––– , and Mary E. Woods. *Casework: A Psychosocial Therapy* (3rd ed.). New York: Random House, 1981.

Hosch, Dorothea. *Use of the Contract Approach in Public Social Services*. Los Angeles: Regional Research Institute in Social Welfare, University of Southern California, 1973.

Howe, Irving. *World of Our Fathers*. New York: Simon & Schuster, 1976.

Hudson, Walter W. "A Measurement Package for Clinical Workers." Paper presented at the Council on Social Work Education 23rd Annual Program Meeting, Phoenix, Arizona, March 1, 1977.

Izard, Carrol. *The Face of Emotion*. New York: Appleton-Century-Crofts, 1971.

Jackson, Don, ed. *Communication, Family, and Marriage*. Palo Alto, Calif.: Science and Behavior Books, 1967.

––––––– .*Therapy, Communication, and Change*. Palo Alto, Calif.: Science and Behavior Books, 1968.

Janchill, Sister Mary Paul. "Systems Concepts in Casework Theory and Practice." *Social Casework*, Vol. 50 (February 1969), pp. 71–82.

Jayaratne, Srinika. "Analytic Procedures for Single Subject Designs." *Social Work Research and Abstracts*, Vol. 14 (Fall 1978), pp. 30–40.

––––––– , and Rona L. Levy. *Empirical Clinical Practice*. New York: Columbia University Press, 1979.

Jones, Edward E. *Attribution: Perceiving the Causes of Behavior*. Morristown, N.J.: General Learning Press, 1972.

Jones, Russell A. *Self-fulfilling Prophecies*. Hillsdale, N.J.: Lawrence Erlbaum Associates, 1977.

Kadushin, Alfred. "Opposition to Referral for Psychaiatric Treatment," *Social Work*, Vol. 2 (April 1957), pp. 78–84.

Kagan, Jerome. "Sex Typing and Sex Role Identity," In *Review of Child Developmental Research* eds. Lois Hoffman and Martin Hoffman, pp. 137–168. New York: Russell Sage, 1964.

Kahn, Alfred J. "From Delinquency Treatment to Community Development." In *The Uses of Sociology*, eds. Paul F. Lazarsfeld, William H. Sewell, and Harold L. Wilensky, pp. 477–505. New York: Basic Books, 1967.

Katz, Daniel, and R. Kahn. *The Social Psychology of Organizations*. New York: John Wiley, 1966.

Katz, Martin M. "Evaluating Drug and Other Therapies Across Cultures." In *Cross-Cultural Counseling and Psychotherapy*, eds. Anthony Marsella and Paul Pederson, pp. 159–173. Elmsford, N.Y.: Pergamon Press, 1981.

Kazden, Alan E. "The Application of Operant Techniques in Treatment, Rehabilitation, and Education." In *Handbook of Psychotherapy and Behavior Change* (2nd ed.), eds. Sol. L. Garfield and A. E. Bergin, pp. 549–590. New York: John Wiley, 1978.

Kelman, Herbert C., and Donald W. Warwick. "The Ethics of Social Intervention: Goals, Means, and Consequences." In *The Ethics of Social Intervention*, eds. Gordon Bermant, Herbert C. Kelman, and Donald W. Warwick, pp. 3–36. Washington, D.C.: Hemisphere, 1978.

Kiev, Ari. *Curanderismo: Mexican-American Folk Psychiatry*. New York: The Free Press, 1968.

Kiresuk, Thomas, and Geoffrey Garwick. "Basic Goal Attainment Procedures." In *Social Work Processes*, eds. Beulah Roberts and Burt Galaway, pp. 412–421. Homewood, Ill.: The Dorsey Press, 1979.

Kirk, Stuart, and James Greenley. "Denying or Delivering Services," *Social Work*. Vol. 19 (July 1974), pp. 439–447.

Knapp, Carol. *Service Contract Use in Preventing and Reducing Foster Care: Final Evaluation Report*. Washington, D.C.: Administration for Children, Youth and Families, Department of Health, Education and Welfare, December 1, 1980.

Knapp, Mark. *Nonverbal Communication in Human Interaction*. New York: Holt, Rinehart and Winston, 1972.

Knowles, Louis, and Kenneth Prewitt. *Institutional Racism in America*. Englewood Cliffs, N.J.: Prentice-Hall, 1969.

Koestler, Arthur, and J. R. Smythies, eds. *Beyond Reductionism: New Perspectives in the Life Sciences*. New York: Macmillan, 1970.

Kolevzon, Michael S. "Bivariate Analysis: Correlation." In *Social Work Research and Evaluation*, ed. Richard Grinnell, Jr., pp. 481–499. Itasca, Ill.: F. E. Peacock, 1981.

Kravetz, Diane, and Sheldon Rose. *Contracts in Groups: A Behavioral Approach*. Dubuque, Ia.: Kendall/Hunt, 1973.

Kubler-Ross, Elizabeth. *On Death and Dying*. New York: Macmillan, 1969.

Kursh, Charlotte O. "The Benefits of Poor Communication." *The Psychoanalytic Review*, Vol. 58 (Summer 1971), pp. 189–208.

LaBarre, Weston. "The Cultural Basis of Emotions and Gestures." *Journal of Personality*, Vol. 16 (1947), pp. 49–68.

Landy, David. "Problems of the Person Seeking Help in Our Culture," In *The Social Welfare Forum 1960*, pp. 127-145. New York: Columbia University Press, 1960.

Lang, Norma C. "A Broad Range Model of Practice with the Social Work Group." *Social Service Review*, Vol. 46 (March 1972), pp. 76–89.

Lange, Arthur J., and Patricia Jakubowski. *Responsible Assertive Behavior*. Champaign, Ill.: Research Press, 1976.

Langs, R. J. *Resistances and Interventions: The Nature of Therapeutic Work*. New York: Jason Aronson, 1981.

Lantz, James, and Beverly Lenahan. "Referral Fatigue Therapy." *Social Work*, Vol. 21 (May 1976), pp. 239–240.

L'Arate, Luciano. "Skill Training Programs for Couples and Families." In *Handbook of Family Therapy*, eds. Alan S. Gurman and David P. Kniskern, pp. 631–661. New York: Brunner/Mazel, 1981.

Lazlo, Ervin, ed. *The Relevance of General Systems Theory*. New York: George Braziller, 1972.

———— . *The Systems View of the World*. New York: George Braziller, 1972.

Leichter, Hope, and William Mitchell. *Kinship and Casework*. New York: Russell Sage, 1967.

Lerbinger, Otto. *Designs for Persuasive Communication*. Englewood Cliffs, N.J.: Prentice-Hall, 1972.

Lessor, Richard, and Anita Lutkus. "Two Techniques for the Social Work Practitioner." *Social Work*, Vol. 16 (January 1971), pp. 5–6, 9.

Levinger, George. "Continuance in Casework and Other Helping Relationships: A Review of Current Research." *Social Work*, Vol. 5 (July 1960), pp. 40–51.

Levy, L. H. *Psychological Interpretation*. New York: Holt, Rinehart and Winston, 1963.

Lewis, Harold. "Agology, Animation, and Conscientization: Implications for Social Work Education in the U.S.A." *Journal of Education for Social Work*, Vol. 9 (Fall 1973), pp. 31–38.

Liberman, R. P., and V. Smith. "A Multiple Baseline Study of Systematic Desensitization in a Patient with Multiple Phobias." *Behavior Therapy*, Vol. 3 (1972), pp. 597–603.

Lieberman, M., I. Yalom, and M. Miles, *Encounter Groups: First Facts*. New York: Basic Books, 1973.

Lindeman, Eduard, C. *The Community*. New York: Association Press, 1921.

Lippitt, Ronald, Jeanne Watson, and Bruce Westley. *The Dynamics of Planned Change*. New York: Harcourt Brace Jovanovich, 1958.

Little, K. B. "Cultural Variations in Social Schemata." *Journal of Personality and Social Psychology*, Vol. 10 (1968), pp. 1–7.

Lorenz, Konrad. *On Aggression*. New York: Harcourt Brace, 1966.

Lorion, Raymond P. "Research on Psychotherapy and Behavior Change with the Disadvantaged: Past, Present, and Future Directions." In *Handbook of Psychotherapy and Behavior Change* (2nd ed.), eds. Sol L. Garfield and A. E. Bergin, pp. 903–938. New York: John Wiley, 1978.

Lubove, Roy. *The Professional Altruist*. New York: Atheneum, 1969.

Lutz, Werner. *Concepts and Principles Underlying Social Work Practice*, Social Work Practice in Medical and Rehabilitation Settings (Monograph 3). New York: National Association of Social Workers, 1958.

MacGregor, R., A. M. Ritchie, A. C. Serrano, and F. P. Schuster. *Multiple Impact Therapy with Families*. New York: McGraw-Hill, 1964.

Maluccio, Anthony N. "Action as a Tool in Casework Practice." *Social Casework*, Vol. 55 (January 1975), pp. 30–35.

———— . "Promoting Competence Through Life Experiences." In *Social Work Practice: People and Environments*, ed. Carel Germain, pp. 282–302. New York: Columbia University Press, 1979.

———— . *Learning from Clients: Interpersonal Helping as Viewed by Clients and Social Workers*. New York: The Free Press, 1979.

———— , ed. *Promoting Competence in Clients*. New York: The Free Press, 1981.

———— , and Wilma Marlow. "The Case for Contract." *Social Work*, Vol. 19 (January 1974), pp. 28–35.

Mandel, Betty. "Welfare and Totalitarianism." *Social Work*, Vol. 16 (January 1971), pp. 17–26.

Mann, James. *Time Limited Psychotherapy*. Cambridge, Mass.: Harvard University Press, 1973.

Maple, Frank. *Shared Decision Making*. Beverly Hills, Calif.: Sage Publications, 1977.

Margolis, Richard J. "Rural Health and the Politics of Neglect." *Human Services in the Rural Environment*, Vol. 2 (August 1977), pp. 3–6.

Marlatt, G. Alan, and Martha A. Perry. "Modeling Methods." In *Helping People Change: A Textbook of Methods*, eds. Frederick H. Kanfer and Arnold P. Goldstein, pp. 117–128. Elmsford, N.Y.: Pergamon Press, 1975.

Martin, John M. "Social-Cultural Differences: Barriers in Casework with Delinquents." *Social Work*, Vol. 2 (July 1957), pp. 22–25.

Masters, W. H., and V. E. Johnson. *Human Sexual Inadequacy*. Boston: Little, Brown, 1970.

Mayadas, N.S., and W. D. Duehn. "Stimulus Modeling Videotape for Marital Counseling: Method and Application." *Journal of Marriage and Family Counseling*, Vol. 3 (1977), pp. 35–42.

Mayer, John E., and Noel Timms. "Clash in Perspective Between Worker and Client." *Social Casework*, Vol. 50 (January 1969), pp. 32–40.

_____ , and Noel Timms. *The Client Speaks: Working Class Impressions of Casework*. New York: Atherton, 1970.

Mechanic, David. "Sources of Power of Lower Participants in Complex Organizations." *Administrative Science Quarterly*, Vol. 7 (December 1962), pp. 349–364.

Mencher, Samuel. *Poor Law to Poverty Program*. Pittsburgh: University of Pittsburgh Press, 1967.

Mehrabian, Albert. "Communication Without Words." In *Communication: Concepts and Process*, ed. Joseph DeVito, pp. 106–114. Englewood Cliffs, N.J.: Prentice-Hall, 1971.

_____ . *Nonverbal Behavior*. Chicago: Aldine, 1972.

Menninger, Karl. *Theory of Psychoanalytic Technique*. New York: Basic Books, 1958.

Merriam, Ida C. "Financing Social Welfare: Expenditures." In *Encyclopedia of Social Work*, Vol II, pp. 449–456. New York: National Association of Social Workers, 1977.

Meyer, Carol. *Social Work Practice: The Changing Landscape* (2nd ed.). New York: The Free Press, 1976.

Middleman, Ruth, and Gale Goldberg. *Social Service Delivery: A Structural Approach to Social Work Practice*. New York: Columbia University Press, 1974.

Miller, George A. "The Magical Number Seven, Plus or Minus Two: Some Limits on Our Capacity to Process Information." *Psychological Review*, Vol. 63 (1956), pp. 81–97.

Miller, Henry. "Social Work in the Black Ghetto: The New Colonialism." *Social Work*, Vol. 14 (July 1969), pp. 65–76.

Miller, James. "Living Systems: Basic Concepts, Structure, and Process: Cross-Level Hypotheses." *Behavioral Science*, Vol. 10 (1965), pp. 193–237, 337–379, 380–411.

_____ . "The Nature of Living Systems." *Behavioral Science*, Vol. 16 (1971), pp. 277–301.

Miller, Walter L. "Casework and the Medical Metaphor." *Social Work*, Vol. 25 (July 1980), pp. 281–285.

Mills, Theodore. *The Sociology of Small Groups*. Englewood Cliffs, N.J.: Prentice-Hall, 1967.

Milnes, John, and Harvey Bertcher. *Communicating Empathy*. San Diego, Calif.: University Associates, 1980.

Minuchin, Salvador. *Families and Family Therapy*. Cambridge, Mass.: Harvard University Press, 1974.

_____ , and E. Charles Fishman. *Family Therapy Techniques*. Cambridge, Mass.: Harvard University Press, 1981.

Mindel, Charles H., and Robert W. Habenstein. *Ethnic Families in America: Patterns and Variations*. New York: Elsevier, 1976.

Montague, Ashley. *Touching: The Human Significance of the Skin*. New York: Columbia University Press, 1971.

Moos, Rudolf. *Evaluating Treatment Environments: A Social Ecological Approach*. New York: John Wiley, 1974.

Nelsen, Judith. "Dealing with Resistance in Social Work Practice." *Social Casework*, Vol. 56 (December 1979), pp. 587–592.

—————. *Communication Theory and Social Work Practice*. Chicago: University of Chicago Press, 1980.

Newstetter, Wilbur I. "What Is Social Group Work?" *Proceedings of the National Conference of Social Work*. 1935, pp. 291–299. Chicago: University of Chicago Press, 1935.

Nichols, Ralph, and Leonard Stevens. *Are You Listening*. New York: McGraw-Hill, 1957

Nixon, Howard L. *The Small Group*. Englewood Cliffs, N.J.: Prentice-Hall, 1979.

Nye, F. Ivan. *Role Structure and Analysis of the Family*. Beverly Hills, Calif.: Sage Publications, 1976.

Olson, O. H., ed. *Treating Relationships*. Lake Mills, Ia.: Graphic, 1976.

Orcutt, Ben. "A Study of Anchoring Effects in Clinical Judgments." *Social Service Review*, Vol. 38 (December 1964), pp. 408–417.

—————. "Casework Intervention and the Problems of the Poor." *Social Casework*, Vol. 54 (February 1972), pp. 85–95.

Orlinsky, David E., and Kenneth I. Howard. "The Relation of Process to Outcome in Psychotherapy." In *Handbook of Psychotherapy and Behavior Change* (2nd ed.), eds. Sol L. Garfield and A. E. Bergin, pp. 283–330. New York: John Wiley, 1978.

Orne, Martin T., and P. H. Wender. "Anticipatory Socialization for Psychotherapy: Method and Rationale." *American Journal of Psychiatry*, Vol. 124 (1968), pp. 1202–1212.

Ornstein, Robert E., ed. *The Nature of Human Consciousness*. New York: Viking Press, 1973.

Osmond, Humphry. "Function as the Basis of Psychiatric Ward Design." *Mental Hospitals*, April 1957, pp. 23–29.

Overall, Betty, and H. Aronson. "Expectations of Psychotherapy in Patients of Lower Socioeconomic Class." *American Journal of Orthopsychiatry*, Vol. 33 (April 1963), pp. 421–430.

Overton, Alice. "Serving Families Who Don't Want Help." *Social Casework*, Vol. 34 (1953), pp. 304–310.

Palmer, Ted. B. "Matching Worker and Client in Corrections." *Social Work*, Vol. 18 (March 1973), pp. 95–103.

Papajohn, John, and John Spiegal. *Transactions in Families*. San Francisco: Jossey-Bass, 1975.

Papell, Catherine P., and Beulah Rothman. "Social Group Work Models: Possession and Heritage." *Journal of Education for Social Work*, Vol. 2 (Fall 1966), pp. 66–77.

Parloff, Morris B., Irene Elkin Waskow, and Barry E. Wolfe. "Research on Therapist Variables in Relation to Process and Outcome." In *Handbook of Psychotherapy and Behavior Change* (2nd ed.), eds. Sol L. Garfield and A. E. Bergin, pp. 233–282. New York: John Wiley, 1978.

Patti, Rino. "Organizational Resistance and Change: The View from Below." *Social Service Review*, Vol. 48 (September 1974), pp. 367–383.

Perlman, Helen Harris. *Social Casework: A Problem Solving Process*. Chicago: University of Chicago Press, 1957.

———— . "Intake and Some Role Considerations." *Social Casework*, Vol. 41 (1960), pp. 171–177.

———— . *Persona: Social Role and Personality*. Chicago: University of Chicago Press, 1968.

———— . "Putting the 'Social' Back in Social Casework." In *Perspectives on Social Casework*, ed. Helen Harris Perlman, pp. 29–34. Philadelphia: Temple University Press, 1971.

———— . "Social Casework: The Problem Solving Approach." In *Encyclopedia of Social Work*, Vol. II, pp. 1206–1217. New York: National Association of Social Workers, 1971.

———— . *Relationship: The Heart of Helping People*. Chicago: University of Chicago Press, 1979.

Pincus, Allen, and Anne Minahan. *Social Work Practice: Model and Method*. Itasca, Ill.: F. E. Peacock, 1973.

Postner, R., and others. "Process and Outcome in Conjoint Family Therapy." *Family Process*, Vol. 19 (1971), pp. 451–473.

Powell, Thomas. "The Use of Self-Help Groups as Supportive Communities." *American Journal of Orthopsychiatry*, Vol. 45 (October 1975), pp. 756–764.

Rapp, Charles, and John Poertner. "Public Child Welfare in the 1980's: The Emerging Case Management Role." Paper presented at NASW Professional Symposium, San Antonio, Texas, November 1979.

Reding, G. R., L. A. Charles, and M. B. Hoffman. "Treatment of the Couple by a Couple: Conceptual Framework, Case Presentation, and Follow-up Study." *British Journal of Medical Psychology*, Vol. 40 (1967), pp. 243–251.

Redl, Fritz, and David Wineman. *Controls from Within*. New York: The Free Press, 1952.

Reid, William J. "Test of a Task-Centered Approach." *Social Work*, Vol. 20 (January 1975), pp. 3–9.

———— . *The Task-Centered System*. New York: Columbia University Press, 1978.

———— , and Laura Epstein, *Task-Centered Casework*. New York: Columbia University Press, 1972.

———— , and Ann W. Shyne, *Brief and Extended Casework*. New York: Columbia University Press, 1969.

Reissman, Frank. "The 'Helper' Therapy Principle." In *Community Action Against Poverty*, eds. George Brager and Francis Purcell, pp. 217–226. New Haven, Conn.: Yale College and University Press, 1967.

Report of the National Advisory Commission on Civil Disorders. New York: Bantam Books, 1968.

Resnick, Herman, and Rino Patti. "Changing the Organization from Within." *Social Work*, Vol. 17 (July 1972), pp. 48–57.

Reynolds, Bertha C. *Social Work and Social Living*. New York: Citadel, 1951.

Rhodes, Sonya. "Contract Negotiation in the Initial Stage of Casework Service." *Social Service Review*, Vol. 51 (March 1971), pp. 125–140.

Rich, M. E. *A Belief in People: A History of Family Social Work*. New York: Family Service Association of America, 1956.

Richmond, Mary. *Social Diagnosis*. New York: Russell Sage, 1917.

———— . "Some Next Steps in Social Treatment." *Proceedings of the National Conference of Social Work, 1920*, pp. 254–258. New York: Columbia University Press, 1939.

Ripple, Lillian, Ernestina Alexander, and Bernice W. Polemis. *Motivation, Capacity, and Opportunity: Studies in Casework Theory and Practice*. Chicago: School of Social Service Administration, University of Chicago, 1964.

Roberts, Robert W., and Robert Nee, eds. *Theories of Social Casework*. Chicago: University of Chicago Press, 1970.

———, and Helen Northen eds. *Theories of Social Work with Groups*. New York: Columbia University Press, 1976.

Robinson, Virginia. *A Changing Psychology in Social Casework*. Philadelphia: University of Pennsylvania Press, 1930.

Rogers, Carl R. "The Necessary and Sufficient Conditions of Therapeutic Personality Change." *Journal of Consulting Psychology*, Vol. 21 (1957), pp. 95–103.

———. *On Encounter Groups*. New York: Harper & Row, 1970.

Rose, Sheldon, J. Gayner, and J. L. Edleson. "Measuring Interpersonal Competence." *Social Work*, Vol. 22 (1977), pp. 125–129.

Rose, Sheldon. *Treating Children in Groups: A Behavioral Approach*. San Francisco: Jossey-Bass, 1972.

———. *Group Therapy: A Behavioral Approach*. Englewood Cliffs, N.J.: Prentice-Hall, 1977.

Rosenfeld, Jona. "Strangeness Between Helper and Client: A Possible Explanation of Non-Use of Available Professional Help." *Social Service Review*, Vol. 38 (March 1964), pp. 17–25.

Rubenstein, Hiasura, and Mary Bloch. *Things That Matter: Influences on Helping Relationships*. New York: Macmillan, 1982.

Ruesch, Jurgen, and Weldon Kees. *Nonverbal Communication: Notes on the Visual Perception of Human Relations*. Berkeley: University of California Press, 1970.

Ryan, William. *Blaming the Victim*. New York: Pantheon, 1971.

Sager, Clifford J. "Couples Therapy and Marriage Contracts." In *Handbook of Family Therapy*, eds. Alan S. Gurman and David P. Kniskern, pp. 85–132. New York: Brunner/Mazel, 1981.

Salomon, Elizabeth L. "Humanistic Values and Social Casework." *Social Casework*, Vol. 24 (1967), pp. 26–32.

Satir, Virginia. *Conjoint Family Therapy*. Palo Alto, Calif.: Science and Behavior Books, 1967.

Schacter, S., and J. E. Singer. "Cognitive, Social, and Physiological Determinants of Emotional State." *Psychological Review*, Vol. 69 (1962), pp. 379–399.

Scheffler, Israel. *Conditions of Knowledge*. Glenview, Ill.: Scott, Foresman, 1965.

Schein, H. "Organizational Socialization." In *Groups and Organizations*, eds. B. L. Hinton and H. J. Reitz, pp. 210–215. Belmont, Calif.: Wadsworth, 1971.

Schmidt, Juliana T. "The Use of Purpose in Casework Practice." *Social Work*, Vol. 14 (January 1969), pp. 79–84.

Schramm, Wilbur. "How Communication Works," In *Communication: Concepts and Process*, ed. Joseph DeVito, pp. 12–21. Englewood Cliffs, N.J.: Prentice-Hall, 1971.

Schulman, Eveline D. *Intervention in the Human Services: A Guide to Skill and Knowledge* (3rd ed.). St. Louis: C. V. Mosby, 1982.

Schwartz, Arthur and William Goldiamond. *Social Casework: A Behavioral Approach*. New York: Columbia University Press, 1975.

Schwartz, Mary C. "Importance of the Sex of Worker and Client." *Social Work*, Vol. 19 (March 1974), pp. 177–186.

Schwartz, William. "The Social Worker in the Group." In *New Perspectives on Service to Groups*, pp. 7–29. New York: Columbia University Press, 1961.

———. "Private Troubles and Public Issues: One Social Work Job or Two." In *Social Welfare Forum, 1969*, pp. 22–43. New York: Columbia University Press, 1969.

———. "Social Group Work: The Interactionist Approach," *Encyclopedia of Social Work*, Vol. II, pp. 1252–1263. New York: National Association of Social Workers, 1971.

———. "Between Client and System: The Mediating Function." In *Theories of Social Work with Groups*, eds. Robert W. Roberts and Helen Northen, pp. 171–197. New York: Columbia University Press, 1976.

Schwartz, William, and Sarapio Zalba. *The Practice of Group Work*. New York: Columbia University Press, 1971.

Seaburg, James E. "Case Recording by Code." *Social Work*, Vol. 10 (October 1965), pp. 92–98.

Seabury, Brett A. "The Contract: Uses, Abuses, and Limitations." *Social Work*, Vol. 21 (January 1976), pp. 16–21.

———. "Negotiating Sound Contracts with Clients." *Public Welfare*, Vol. 37 (Spring 1979), pp. 33–38.

———, and Madison Foster. "Racism and Sexism in Social Work Agencies: Casing Your Agency from Within." Paper presented at the NASW Minority Affairs Conference, Los Angeles, California, June 1982.

Shaw, Marvin. *Group Dynamics* (2nd ed.). New York: McGraw-Hill, 1976.

Sherman, T. M., and W. H. Cormier. "The Use of Subjective Scales for Measuring Interpersonal Reactions." *Journal of Behavior Therapy and Experimental Psychiatry*, Vol. 3 (1972), pp. 279–280.

Shulman, Lawrence. *The Skills of Helping Individuals and Groups*. Itasca, Ill.: F. E. Peacock, 1979.

Silverman, Phyllis R. "The Client Who Drops Out: A Study of Spoiled Helping Relationships." Unpublished doctoral dissertation, Brandeis University, 1969.

———. "A Reexamination of the Intake Procedure." *Social Casework*, Vol. 51 (December 1970), pp. 625–634.

Simon, Bernice K. "Social Casework Theory: An Overview." In *Theories of Social Casework*, eds. Robert W. Roberts and Robert Nee, pp. 355–395. Chicago: University of Chicago Press, 1970.

Simon, Sidney B., Leland W. Howe, and Howard Kirschenbaum. *Value Clarification: A Handbook of Practical Strategies for Students and Teachers*. New York: Hart, 1972.

Singer, Benjamin. "Assessing Social Errors." *Social Policy*, September–October 1978, pp. 27–34.

Siporin, Max. "Situational Assessment and Intervention." *Social Casework*, Vol. 53 (February 1972), pp. 91–109.

———. *Introduction to Social Work Practice*. New York: Macmillan, 1975.

Smalley, Ruth. *Theory for Social Work Practice*. New York: Columbia University Press, 1967.

———. "Social Casework: The Functional Approach." In *Encyclopedia of Social Work*, Vol. II, pp. 1195–1206. New York: National Association of Social Workers, 1971.

Smith, Arthur L. *Transracial Communication*. Englewood Cliffs, N.J.: Prentice-Hall, 1973.

Sommer, Robert. *Personal Space: The Behavioral Basis of Design*. Englewood Cliffs, N.J.: Spectrum, 1969.

Specht, Harry. "Disruptive Tactics." *Social Work*, Vol. 14 (April 1969), pp. 5–15.

Speck, Ross, and Carolyn Attneave. *Family Networks*. New York: Pantheon, 1973.

Spergel, Irving. *Street Gang Work: Theory and Practice*. Reading, Mass.: Addison-Wesley, 1966.

Spiegel, John. "Some Cultural Aspects of Transference and Countertransference." In *Mental Health of the Poor,* ed. Frank Reissman et. al, pp, 303–320. New York: The Free Press, 1964.

———— . *Transactions*. New York, Basic Books, 1971.

Stanton, Alfred, and Morris Schwartz. *The Mental Hospital: A Study of Institutional Participation in Psychiatric Illness and Treatment*. New York: Basic Books, 1954.

Stein, Herman, and Richard Cloward. *Social Perspectives on Behavior*. New York: The Free Press, 1958.

Stein, Irma. *Systems Theory, Science, and Social Work*. Metuchen, N. J.: Scarecrow Press, 1974.

Stein, Theodore. *Social Work Practice in Child Welfare*. Englewood Cliffs, N.J.: Prentice-Hall, 1981.

———— , and Eileen Gambrill. "Facilitating Decision Making in Foster Care." *Social Service Review*, Vol. 51 (September 1977), pp. 502–513.

———— , Eileen Gambrill, and Kermit Wiltse. "Foster Care: The Use of Contracts." *Public Welfare*, Vol. 32 (Fall 1974), pp. 20–25.

Stotland, E. *The Psychology of Hope*. San Francisco: Jossey-Bass, 1969.

Straus, Murray. *Family Measurement Techniques*. Minneapolis: University of Minnesota Press, 1969.

Strauss, Anselm. "Coaching." In *Role Theory: Concepts and Research*, eds. Bruce Biddle and Edwin Thomas, pp. 350–353. New York: John Wiley, 1966.

Stuart, Richard B. *Trick or Treatment: How and When Psychotherapy Fails*. Champaign, Ill.: Research Press, 1970.

Studt, Eliot. "Fields of Social Work Practice: Organizing Our Resources for More Effective Practice." *Social Work*, Vol. 10 (October 1965), pp. 156–165.

Sundel, Martin, and Sandra Sundel. *Behavior Modification in the Human Services*. New York: John Wiley, 1975.

Suttles, Gerald D. *The Social Order of the Slum: Ethnicity and Territory in the Inner City*. Chicago: University of Chicago Press, 1968.

Taft, Jessie. "The Relation of Function to Process in Social Casework." *Journal of Social Work Process*, Vol. 1 (1937), pp. 1–18.

Thibault, J. W., and H. H. Kelley. *The Social Psychology of Groups*. New York: John Wiley, 1959.

Thomas, Edwin. "Problems of Disability from the Perspective of Role Theory," in *Behavioral Science for Social Workers*, ed. Edwin Thomas, pp. 59–77. New York: The Free Press, 1967.

———— . "Selected Sociobehavioral Techniques and Principles: An Approach to Interpersonal Helping." *Social Work*, Vol. 13 (January 1968), pp. 12–26.

———— . *Marital Communication and Decision Making: Analysis, Assessment and Change*. New York: The Free Press, 1977.

———— , and Ronald Feldman. "Concepts of Role Theory." In *Behavioral Science for Social Workers*, ed. Edwin Thomas. pp. 17–50. New York: The Free Press, 1967.

Thomas, Robert K. "Colonialism: Domestic and Foreign." In *Immigrants and Migrants: The Detroit Ethnic Experience*, ed. David W. Hartman. Published as *Journal of University Studies*, Vol. 10, nos. 2, 3, and 4 (Fall 1974).

Toren, Nina. "The Structure of Social Casework and Behavioral Change." *Journal of Social Policy*, Vol. 3 (1973), pp. 341–352.

Tripodi, Tony, and Irwin Epstein. *Research Techniques for Clinical Social Workers*. New York: Columbia University Press, 1980.

Tropman, John E. *Effective Meetings: Improving Group Decision-Making*. Beverly Hills, Calif.: Sage Publications, 1980.

Tropp, Emanuel. "A Developmental Theory." In *Theories of Social Work with Groups*, eds. Robert W. Roberts and Helen Northen, pp. 198–237. New York: Columbia University Press, 1976.

Trudgill, Peter. *Sociolinguistics: An Introduction*. Baltimore: Penguin Books, 1974.

Turner, Francis J., ed. *Social Work Treatment: Interlocking Theoretical Approaches*. New York: The Free Press, 1974.

Valentine, Charles. *Culture and Poverty: Critique and Counter Proposals*. Chicago: University of Chicago Press, 1978.

Vinter, Robert. "Analysis of Treatment Organizations." *Social Work*, Vol. 8 (1963), pp. 3–15.

Vinter, Robert. "Program Activities: An Analysis of Their Effects on Participant Behavior." In *Individual Change Through Small Groups*, eds. Paul Glasser, Rosemary Sarri, and Robert Vinter, pp. 233–243. New York: The Free Press, 1974.

Wasserman, Harry. "The Professional Social Worker in a Bureaucracy." *Social Work*, Vol. 16 (January 1971), pp. 89–95.

Watson, Goodwin. "Resistance to Change," In *The Planning of Change*, eds. Warren Bennis, Kenneth Benne, and Robert Chin, pp. 489–497. New York: Holt, Rinehart and Winston, 1969.

Watson, O. M., and T. D. Graves. "Quantitative Research on Proxemic Behavior." *American Anthropologist*, Vol. 68 (1966), pp. 971–985.

Watzlawick, Paul. *How Real Is Real?* New York: Random House, 1976.

———. *The Language of Change: Elements of Therapeutic Communication*. New York: Basic Books, 1978.

———, J. H. Beavin, and Don Jackson. *Pragmatics of Human Communication*. New York: W. W. Norton, 1967.

———, John Weakland, and R. Fisch. *Change: Principles of Problem Formation and Problem Resolution*. New York: W. W. Norton, 1974.

Weiner, Myron F. *Therapist Disclosure: The Use of Self in Psychotherapy*. Boston: Butterworth's, 1978.

Weissman, Andrew. "Industrial Social Services: Linkage Technology." *Social Casework*, Vol. 57 (January 1976), pp. 50–54.

Whitaker, James K. "Models of Group Development: Implications for Social Group Work Practice." *Social Service Review*, Vol. 44 (September, 1970), pp. 308–322.

White, Robert W. *The Abnormal Personality*. New York: The Ronald Press, 1956.

Willis, F. N. "Initial Speaking Distance as a Function of the Speaker's Relationship." *Psychonomic Science*, Vol. 5 (1966), pp. 221–222.

Wilson, Gertrude, and Gladys Ryland. *Social Group Work Practice*. Boston: Houghton Mifflin, 1949.

Wilson, Suanna. *Recording: Guidelines for Social Workers*. New York: The Free Press, 1976.
_____ . *Confidentiality in Social Work: Issues and Principles*. New York: The Free Press, 1978.
Yalom, Irving D. *The Theory and Practice of Group Psychotherapy* (2nd ed.). New York: Basic Books, 1975.
_____ . *Existential Psychotherapy*. New York: Basic Books, 1980.
Young, O. R. "A Survey of General Systems Theory." *General Systems*, Vol. 9 (1964), pp. 61–80.

Index